Korea

Simon Richmond

Yu-Mei Balasingamchow, César G Soriano, Rob Whyte

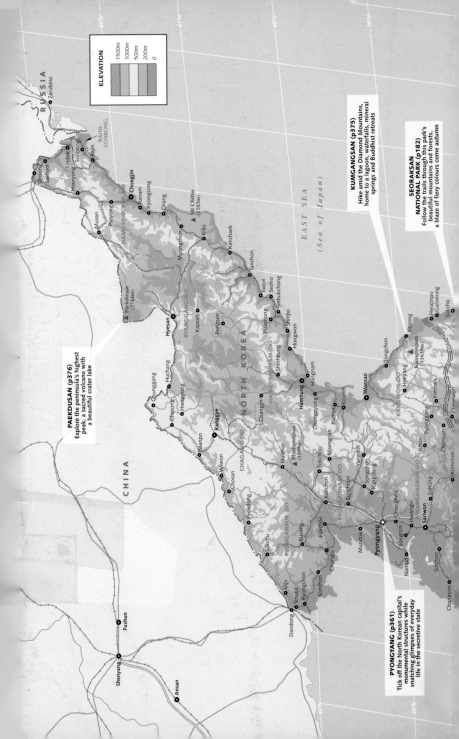

ELEVATION

1500m
1000m
500m
200m
0

RUSSIA

Zarubino

RAJIN-
SONBONG

Onsong
Saebyol
Undok
Hoeryong
Sonbong
Rajin

EAST SEA
(Sea of Japan)

Musan
Puryong
Kyongsong
Ranam
Chongjin

HAMGYONGBUK-DO

Orang

▲ Mt Chilbo
(1103m)

Kilju

PAEKDUSAN (p376)
Explore the peninsula's highest
peak, a sacred volcano with
a beautiful crater lake

▲ Paekdusan
(2744m)

Myongchon

Kimchaek

Hyesan

RYANGGANG-DO

Kapsan

Tanchon

Iwon

Pungsan

Seoho

Sinbukchong

Pukchong

Hongwon

Shinpo

Chunggang

Huchang

Hwapyong

HAMGYONGNAM-DO

Shinheung

Changjin

Hungnam

KUMGANGSAN (p375)
Hike amid the Diamond Mountains,
home to a lagoon, waterfalls, mineral
springs and Buddhist retreats

CHINA

Chasong

Manpo

Kanggye

CHAGANG-DO

Hamhung

Hongpyong

Kumya

Kowon

Wonsan

**SEORAKSAN
NATIONAL PARK (p182)**
Follow the trails through this park's
beautiful mountains and forests,
a blaze of fiery colours come autumn

Wiwon

Chosan

▲ Myohyangsan
(1909m)

Nurhon

Tokchon

Maengsan

Yangdok

Kumgangsan
(1638m)

Tongchon

Kosong

Hwajinpo

Ganseong

Sokcho

Pyoktong

Kuup

Pakchon

Kechon

Songchon

Kangdong

Chungwha

KANGWON-DO

DMZ

KimHwa

Chorwon

Sakchu

PYONGANBUK-DO

PYONGANNAM-DO

Suchon

Hwangju

Pyonggang

Ichon

Cheorwon

Kusong

Pyongyang

Songnim

Ichon

Sariwon

Sohung

Kumchon

PYONGYANG (p361)
Tick off the North Korean capital's
monumental structures while
snatching glimpses of everyday
life in the secretive state

Uiju

Sinuiju

Ryongchon

Sonchon

Chongju

Mundok

Nampo

HWANGHAEBUK-DO

Sinchon

Sariwon

Chaeryon

Shenyang

Fushun

Ansan

Dandong

NORTH KOREA

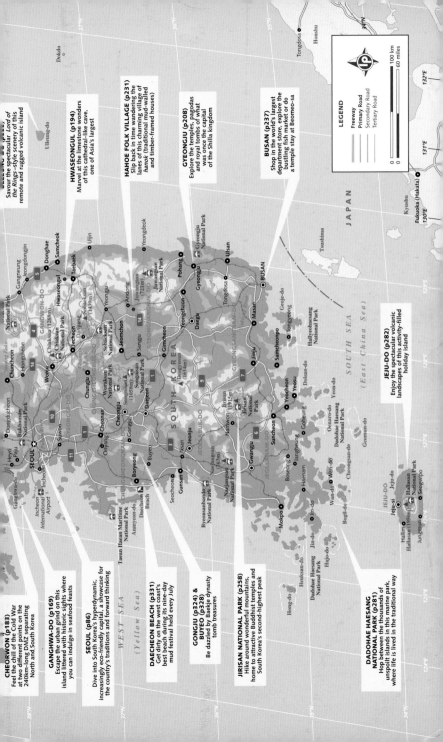

ULLEUNG-DO (p*)**
Savour the spectacular *Lord of the Rings*–style scenery of this remote and rugged volcanic island

HWASEONGUL (p194)
Marvel at the limestone wonders of this cathedral-like cave, one of Asia's largest

HAHOE FOLK VILLAGE (p231)
Slip back in time wandering the lanes of this charming village of *hanok* (traditional mud-walled and timber-framed houses)

GYEONGJU (p208)
Explore the temples, pagodas and royal tombs of what was once the capital of the Shilla kingdom

BUSAN (p237)
Shop in the world's largest department store, explore the bustling fish market or do a temple stay at Beomeo-sa

CHEORWON (p183)
Feel the chill of the Cold War at two different points on the 240km-long DMZ separating North and South Korea

GANGHWA-DO (p169)
Escape the urban grind on this island littered with historic sights where you can indulge in seafood feasts

SEOUL (p86)
Dive into South Korea's hyperdynamic, increasingly eco-friendly capital, a showcase for the country's traditions and forward thinking

DAECHEON BEACH (p331)
Get dirty on the west coast's best beach during its nine-day mud festival held every July

GONGJU (p324) & BUYEO (p328)
Be dazzled by Baekje dynasty tomb treasures

JIRISAN NATIONAL PARK (p258)
Hike around wonderful mountains, home to attractive Buddhist temples and South Korea's second-highest peak

DADOHAE HAESANG NATIONAL PARK (p281)
Hop between the thousands of unspoilt islands in this marine park, where life is lived in the traditional way

JEJU-DO (p282)
Enjoy the spectacular volcanic landscapes of this activity-filled holiday island

LEGEND

Freeway
Primary Road
Secondary Road
Tertiary Road

0   100 km
0   60 miles

On the Road

SIMON RICHMOND Coordinating Author
In the midst of typhoon-strength winds and rain I fronted up at the Boryeong Mud Festival (see boxed text, p332), stripped off and splashed around in the mud pool. Apart from being huge fun it's said to do wonders for your skin.

César G Soriano Baseball, as in America, is South Korea's national pastime. The game is more or less the same, but instead of hot dogs and pretzels vendors sell dried squid and sushi. My seatmates at Gwangju's Mudeung Stadium (p265) plied me with *soju* (the local firewater) and taught me naughty Korean baseball chants. I'm not in Camden Yards anymore!

Yu-Mei Balasingamchow
On the climb up to this enigmatic rock-carved Buddha image in Woraksan National Park (p343), I fell into step with a couple of fashionably dressed hikers. Although they spoke barely any English, our temporary communion was sealed when they offered me the Korean equivalent of trail mix – a raw cucumber, crunchy and sweet.

Rob Whyte I've just finished a 20-minute uphill march to Bongnae Pokpo (p225) on Ulleung-do. It's not a large waterfall, but it's a worthwhile trip because the path weaving through a thick forest leads to a delightful discovery: a cool cave that maintains a year-round temperature of 4°C.

For full author biographies see p420.

Korea Highlights

On these pages travellers and Lonely Planet staff and authors share their top experiences in Korea. Do you agree with their choices, or have we missed your favourites? Go to lonelyplanet.com and tell us your highlights.

KEREN SU

① MASS GAMES, PYONGYANG

There's a loud 'clack' as tens of thousands of schoolchildren flip open tens of thousands of card books, and there he is – smiling across the stadium is the gigantic face of the president for life and beyond, Kim Il-sung. Meanwhile down on the stadium floor more schoolchildren swing tennis racquets, twirl hula hoops or rush around in rubber rings, miming a fun family day on the North Korean beach. They'll soon be followed by the incredible North Korean dancing army, conclusively proving that if wars were decided on the dance floor they could annihilate any foe. It's the Pyongyang Mass Games (p371), the number one attraction for foreign visitors to the reclusive capital. My reaction to the performance was clear cut – I immediately signed up for a repeat visit later the same week.

Tony Wheeler, Lonely Planet Founder, Australia

SIMON RICHMOND

JEJU-DO

Jeju-do (p282) is nice but only go midweek as it gets crowded at other times. Some say overrated, I say awesome. The only way to do it is to have your own wheels – hire a bike of some description and do your own thing. Just hopping on and off buses wouldn't be fun at all, it's best to cruise around the coast and stop when you want. Staying in a *minbak* next to the ocean is great.

lonelyplanet.com Member

JOHN BI

3

2

SSAMBAP, GYEONGJU

Wandering the streets of Gyeongju (p208), marvelling at the grass-covered burial mounds dotting the city, it's time for lunch. The cuisine of choice is *ssambap*. I sit cross-legged and await my feast: up to 20 tiny plates filled with tasty morsels, and a plate of colourful and different shaped vegetable leaves. I wrap and munch away amongst the local South Koreans and the plates keep getting topped up! Different scents and flavours engulf me – this is an experience worth having.

Belinda Wren, Traveller, Australia

SIMON RIC

4

HANGING OUT IN HONGDAE, SEOUL

If you want to get down with the cool kids then Hongdae – the shorthand used for the area around Hongik University, Korea's top art school – is the place to be. Apart from its lively mix of inventive bars, clubs and restaurants there's the weekly Free Market (p144), where you can shop for funky souvenirs and catch live music, and the monthly Club Day event (p141).

Simon Richmond, Lonely Planet Author, USA

GWANGJANG MARKET, SEOUL

Spending time in Seoul's vibrant markets is a must. One of my favourites is Gwangjang (p132), where you can admire the delicate colours and constructions of *hanbok* (traditional Korean clothes) then tuck into a delicious, inexpensive meal at the city's largest food alley, where freshly fried *nokdu binda-etteok* (mung-bean pancakes) are the speciality.

Simon Richmond, Lonely Planet Author, USA

HEYRI, GYEONGGI-DO

It's easy to see why the modern village of Heyri (p154) – with its quirky, eco-friendly architecture, art galleries and laid-back cafes – has become a rural escape for Seoul's artistic, design and literary communities. What's also nice is that kids can be thoroughly entertained, too, in the section devoted to the strawberry-headed cartoon character Dalki.

**Simon Richmond,
Lonely Planet Author, USA**

SUWON'S FORTRESS WALL, GYEONGGI-DO

Spend a leisurely half-day circuiting the intact wall of Suwon's Hwaseong (Brilliant Fortress; p156) – you can pause for views from grand gateways and turrets as well as try your hand at archery.

Simon Richmond, Lonely Planet Author, USA

YU-MEI BALASINGAMCHOW

DEOKSUGUNG, SEOUL

My lasting impressions of Seoul were the amazing colours of the trees with their leaves falling as we went walking around Deoksugung (p108). Everywhere we looked the colours were vibrant. This was in November and it was a lovely time to visit.

Liz Swallow, Traveller, New Zealand

9

8 HAESINDANG PARK, GANGWON-DO

Honourable mention for a quirky sightseeing stop must surely go to this park (p194), dedicated exclusively to showcasing phallic sculptures. What's even more surreal is that it's right next door to a fishing village which has adopted a phallic shape for its little lighthouse as well. You won't see anything like this in the rest of Korea.

Yu-Mei Balasingamchow, Lonely Planet Author, Singapore

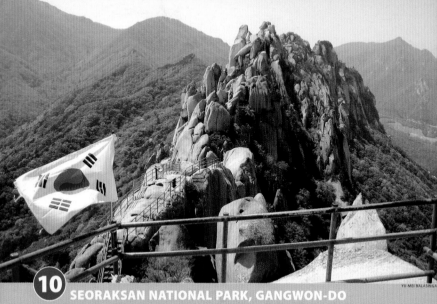

YU-MEI BALASINGA

10 SEORAKSAN NATIONAL PARK, GANGWON-DO

This enormous park (p182) is every bit as magnificent as its reputation suggests. If you have two days, you can make it up to the highest peak, Daecheongbong, and back. If you have only half a day, head up Ulsan Bawi instead – it looks intimidating but there are metal staircases and ropes to help you scale the sections of sheer cliff, and the view at the top is simply stupendous.

Yu-Mei Balasingamchow, Lonely Planet Author, Singapore

Contents

Regional Map Contents

NORTH KOREA p349

SEOUL pp90-1 GANGWON-DO p173

GYEONGGI-DO & INCHEON GWANGYEOK-SI p150

CHUNGCHEONGBUK-DO p336

CHUNGCHEONGNAM-DO p319

GYEONGSANGBUK-DO p199

JEOLLABUK-DO p306

GYEONGSANGNAM-DO p236

JEOLLANAM-DO p262

JEJU-DO p283

Destination Korea

Yin and yang: the blue and red circle at the heart of the South Korean flag neatly symbolises not only the divided Korean peninsula but also the fluid mix of ancient and modern aspects of the country officially called the Republic of Korea (ROK). For the vast majority of visitors a trip to this part of the world means spending time in South Korea. Unfairly overshadowed by the headline-grabbing antics of its bad-boy neighbour, South Korea is a dream destination for the traveller, an engaging, welcoming place where the dazzling benefits of a fully industrialised, high-tech nation are balanced alongside a reverence for tradition and the ways of old Asia.

Academics still quibble over whether the Land of the Morning Calm (a term coined by travel writer Percival Lowell in 1885) is an accurate translation of the old Chinese characters by which all of Korea was once known. Dive into Seoul, powerhouse of Asia's third-largest economy, and calm is likely the last thing you'll feel. This round-the-clock city is constantly on the move, its 'work hard, play hard' population the epitome of the nation's indefatigable, can-do spirit.

Dubbed the world's Design Capital in 2010, Seoul is midway through an ambitious frenzy of reinvention that promises grand architectural statements, greener spaces and cultural rather than industrial targets. Softer 21st-century aspirations aside, the 600-year-old city is founded on a bedrock of tradition that manifests itself in the daily pageantry of the changing of the guard at its meticulously reconstructed palaces and the chants of a shaman on a hillside. You can hardly turn a corner without stumbling across a tourist information booth, a subway station or a taxi that can smooth your way to the next discovery in this multifaceted metropolis.

South Korea's excellent transport infrastructure and compact size mean that within an hour of the urban sprawl more tranquil moments are achievable atop craggy mountain peaks enclosed by densely forested national parks threaded through with picturesque, challenging hiking trails. Get further off the beaten bath than you could believe possible by sailing to remote islands, where farming and fishing folk will welcome you into their homes and simple seafood cafes. Or sample the serenity of a Buddhist temple retreat where the honk of traffic is replaced by meditation and the rhythmic pre-dawn chants of shaven-headed monks.

If all this sounds a little too peaceful for your travelling tastes, rest assured the ROK also knows how to rock. A countrywide itinerary of lively festivals and events means there's almost always a celebration of some sort to attend. If nothing else your tastebuds will be tingling at the discovery of one of Asia's least known, but most delicious cuisines. Friendly Koreans will happily share this and other aspects of their culture with you, regardless of language barriers.

An undercurrent to this bonhomie is the tension rippling out along the 38th parallel separating the two Koreas. The Cold War that has swirled around what is known as the Demilitarized Zone (DMZ) for over half a century got a little hotter during 2009 when North Korea, in the face of international condemnation, went ahead in May with its second ever nuclear test explosion (the first being in 2006). The rogue state followed this up with a short-range missile test. Even though experts believe that North Korea has yet to develop a ballistic missile capable of carrying a nuclear warhead, there was understandable nervousness in Seoul (just 55km south of the border) as well as in Tokyo and Washington.

**FAST FACTS:
SOUTH KOREA**

Population: 49 million

GDP per person:
US$27,646

Life expectancy: 79.1 years

Inflation: 2.16% (August 2009)

Unemployment: 3.8% (July 2009)

Percentage of the population with the surname 'Kim': 21%

Prior to this, relations between the two Koreas had been deteriorating since the election, in December 2007, of Lee Myung-bak as South Korea's president. Heading up the conservative Grand National Party (GNP), Lee had campaigned on a platform of taking a tougher line with the North than had been practised under the previous left-wing government's 'Sunshine Policy' (see p44) – under Lee there would be no more unconditional economic aid. The public were particularly angry about the fatal shooting in 2008 of a South Korean tourist at a resort in North Korea's Kumgang mountains (p375) and the North's refusal to cooperate in a subsequent investigation. Tourist visits from South Korea to the North – a growing source of much-needed foreign income for the dictatorship – were subsequently suspended.

It hasn't helped that all this has been taking place in an environment of uncertainty caused by a physically ailing Kim Jong-il and a lack of clear knowledge of who would take over as the supreme North Korean leader after his demise. The Dear Leader did show up, looking gaunt, for a photo op in August 2009 with former US president Bill Clinton, who had made a surprise visit to gain the release of two female US reporters who had been found guilty in March of entering North Korea illegally. A few weeks later Hyundai Group chairwoman Hyun Jeong-eun prevailed in a similar mission to free a South Korean hostage held by North Korea.

At the August 2009 funeral of Kim Dae-jung, the democracy champion and Nobel Prize winner who was the chief architect of the 'Sunshine Policy', President Lee also met with North Korean envoys. The thaw in frosty North-South relations continued as talks recommenced on allowing brief reunions between Korean families divided by the border, and regular access was restored across the DMZ to the jointly run industrial park in Kaesong. However, the pendulum swung back slightly in September 2009 as the North fessed up to being responsible for a mysterious flash flood on the Imjin River that killed six South Koreans.

While South Korea and Japan remain united in their condemnation of the North's nuclear ambitions, the way some locals rail at their Far East Asian neighbour you'd be forgiven for thinking that WWII had only recently ended. The dispute over ownership of the group of islands and rocks known as Dokdo to the Koreans and Takeshima to the Japanese (p36) looks set to run and run – it's a battle that has as much to do with national pride as it does with the financial implications of Korea surrendering lucrative fishing grounds and the potentially large gas reserves in this part of the Sea of Japan (or East Sea as Koreans would have it). To mark the centenary in 2010 of the start of Japanese colonial rule on the Korean peninsula, President Lee extended an invitation to Japan's Emperor Akihito to visit Seoul, hoping that it would 'put an end to the sense of distance' between the two countries.

President Lee has also been attempting to build better relations with the US, which still has 30,000 troops stationed in the country. However in the summer of 2008, the president and his party were put on the defensive as large, occasionally violent demonstrations against resumed US beef imports brought central Seoul to a standstill. Lee's popularity plummeted and he was forced to apologise for not heeding public concerns over the safety of imported US beef. He also had to backtrack on a long-cherished plan to build a grand canal across the peninsula linking Seoul and Busan.

Hoping to regain his citizens' affection, the man known as 'the Bulldozer' (he was once CEO of Hyundai Engineering and Construction) moderated his tough-guy stance by proposing the kind of eco-friendly, green growth policies (p66) that had stood him in good stead when he was Seoul's mayor.

FAST FACTS: NORTH KOREA

Area: 120,540 sq km

Population: 24 million

Currency: North Korean won (unofficial rate on the black market: 4200KPW = €1; official rate 211KPW = €1)

Minimum military service for men: three years

Unemployment: 0%

Number of internet cafes: none

Getting Started

South Korea is a compact nation, an hour by plane from north to south. Trips can be tailored to suit all budgets and getting around is a breeze thanks to excellent transport infrastructure. North Korea is a whole other story – see p349.

WHEN TO GO

The best time of year to visit is autumn, from September to November, when skies are blue, the weather is usually sunny and warm and the forested mountainsides are ablaze with astonishing fall colours.

Spring, from April to June, is another beautiful season, with generally mild temperatures and cherry blossoms spreading north across the country in April. Camellias, azaleas and other plants and trees flower, but, as with autumn, some days can be cold and wet, so bring warm, rain-proof clothing.

Winter, from December to March, is dry but often bitterly cold, particularly in northern parts. Siberian winds drag January temperatures in most of the country (except Jeju-do) to below zero. This is the time of year when you really appreciate *ondol* (underfloor heating) and *oncheon* (hot-spring spas) as well as the ubiquitous saunas and spicy food. White snow on *hanok* (traditional house) roofs is very picturesque, and winter is the time for skiers, snowboarders or ice-skaters to visit.

View www.kma.go.kr for detailed weather forecasts in English. Also see Climate Charts (p389) for more information.

Try to avoid peak summer, from late June to late August, which starts off with the monsoon season, when the country receives some 60% of its annual rainfall, and is followed by unpleasantly hot and humid weather. Although air-conditioning makes summers much more bearable these days, many locals flee the muggy cities for the mountains, beaches and islands, which become crowded, and accommodation prices double. There is also the chance of a typhoon or two.

COSTS & MONEY

For a developed country, Korea can be a remarkably inexpensive place in which to travel. Transport, simple Korean meals and snacks, alcohol and

---

DON'T LEAVE HOME WITHOUT...

- Checking whether you need to apply for a visa (p395).
- Learning to read the 24 *hangeul* characters (p411) so you can figure out business signs, menus and bus destinations.
- Studying the Food & Drink chapter (p68) so you know the difference between *samgyetang* (ginseng chicken soup) and *samgyeopsal* (barbecued fatty pork).
- Checking your socks have no holes in them as you must remove your shoes to enter Buddhist shrines, traditional restaurants and private homes.
- Packing your hiking boots, as Korea is stuffed with scenic mountains and well-marked trails.
- Improving your skill at charades and gestures as not many Koreans understand English.
- Practising being naked in front of strangers so you can enjoy Korea's many excellent and reasonably priced hot-spring spas (p82).
- Packing a pair of sheets if you're planning to stay in budget accommodation, which often only provide quilts.
- Bringing personal hygiene and brand-name medical items that may be difficult to obtain.

ADVANCE PLANNING

Bballi, bballi! (Quick, quick!) – Korea has built a blockbuster economy on this mantra. The local stereotype is that everything – plans included – can be done hurriedly, at the last possible minute. While this is never the best way to plan a trip, Korea doesn't present a lot to fret about before you touch down.

Think about booking ahead if you wish to stay at a *hanok*, or traditional house, as by design these old structures only house three or four rooms in total. In addition, the top-end international chain hotels can book up when conferences are in town. Hiking on the weekend can be a madhouse. If possible, consider taking a hike on a weekday instead – the same goes for skiing trips in the winter.

Call a few days ahead for the best seats at cultural events, and book the USO tour to the DMZ (p152) as soon as you can, as these fill up. If you're planning on travelling over any of the major holidays (p392), you should book your bus or train travel well ahead of time.

admission prices to many sights are relatively cheap or even – in the case of the country's network of splendid national parks – free.

Budget travellers, staying in backpacker hostels or the cheaper motels or *yeogwan* (p388), avoiding pricey course meals and travelling on buses, can easily get by on around W50,000 a day, probably even less if they are careful spenders. For those who wish to travel in more comfort, a budget of around W100,000 a day is more realistic. If your travel requirements run to four-star or higher accommodation and more lavish cuisine, this jumps to at least W300,000.

HOW MUCH?

Local newspaper W1000

Food-court lunch W5000

Cinema ticket W9000

Steak dinner W40,000

Motel room W40,000

TRAVELLING RESPONSIBLY

Unless you're already based in Asia a journey to Korea not using a flight is most likely off the cards. When the rail link between North and South Korea resumes it will open the way to the development of a Seoul–London train journey. For now though such a trip remains a distant dream.

The most direct rail route for getting to this side of the world from Europe or Asia is to ride the Trans-Siberian Railway: Lonely Planet's *Trans-Siberian Railway* guide provides the low-down on how to get to Vladivostok, from where it's possible to hop on a ferry to Sokcho (p179). There are also regular ferries to Korea from several ports in China (p165) or from Japan (p250).

Once in Korea it's far easier to do your bit for the environment by using the country's excellent public transport system. Seoul's extensive subway and train system is particularly impressive and the city is in the process of moving over to low-polluting natural-gas buses as well as full-hybrid and fuel-cell electric buses. As part of its 'low-carbon, green growth' strategy (p66) the government is promoting cycling and rolling out a raft of other environmentally friendly projects.

For more detail on rail-ferry connections to Korea see www.seat61.com/SouthKorea.htm.

Most garbage is recycled – you can help by putting your rubbish in the appropriate bins for paper, cans and plastic. If you rent an apartment you will need separate rubbish bags for food waste, plastics, metal, paper and so on. The concierge will show you the system. Also try to cut down on waste by refusing unnecessary packaging in shops. A few stores discourage the use of plastic bags by charging for them.

A culture of volunteering is taking root – for options see p396. Organic and vegetarian restaurants are also becoming more popular as part of a boom in general wellbeing or LOHAS (Lifestyles of Health and Sustainability) business and products. The Korean Standards Association has even developed a certification system for them – see http://korealohas.or.kr for some details in English.

TRAVEL LITERATURE

Meeting Mr Kim by Jennifer Barclay (2008) is a recent addition to the limited selection of travel literature on South Korea – a few things are dated since it's based on the author's experiences in 2000 but overall it's an amusing, easy read with some fresh insights into Korean culture.

Brother One Cell by Cullen Thomas (2008; cullenthomas.com) reveals a side of Korea that few visitors ever get (or would want) to see – the inside of a Korean prison. A kind of Korean *Midnight Express,* it's the author's memoir of his 3½-year incarceration for smuggling hashish into the country in 1994.

Korea Bug by J Scott Burgeson (2005; www.kingbaeksu.com) is a Seoul 'zine turned book, featuring interviews with a fascinating set of Seoul characters, including a shaman, a *gisaeng* (similar to a Japanese geisha), artists and directors.

A Peep into Korea by Kevin J Hayes (2006) documents the sporadic adventures of the author and his Korean wife across the country, including to places seldom visited by Western tourists.

Diamond Dilemma by Tariq Hussain (2006) is an outsider's perspective on how Korea is shaping up economically in the early 21st century and how it needs to change to achieve its full potential.

Korea Unmasked by Rhee Won-bok (2002) takes an illuminating and humorous look at contemporary Korean attitudes in a cartoon format by comparing Korea to neighbouring rivals China and Japan.

Korea by Simon Winchester (1988; www.simonwinchester.com) sees this talented writer vividly describing encounters with Korean monks, nuns, artists, marriage arrangers, US generals and, most memorably, a barber during his journey from Jeju-do to Seoul.

Korea and Her Neighbours by Isabella Bird (1898) is an account of the intrepid Victorian author's travels around Korea at a fascinating time in its

---

DECIPHERING KOREAN ADDRESSES & WORDS

In this guidebook we don't use full addresses for places since, in Korea, the actual 'address' is seldom very useful. There are very few signs labelling street names. Indeed, most streets do not have names at all. Every house and building does have an official number, although it's rarely to be found on the outside – and, if it is, it's likely to be in *hangeul*. To complicate matters further, since numbers are assigned to houses when they are built, house No 27 could be next to house No 324. Many larger buildings have names – knowing this may often prove more useful than knowing the address.

A *gu* (구) is an urban district in large cities like Seoul. A *dong* (동) is a neighbourhood inside a *gu.* A single *gu* contains many *dong.* An address like 104 Itaewondong, Yongsan-gu means building No 104 in Itaewon neighbourhood in Yongsan district. However, you could wander around Itaewon for hours without finding this building, even with the help of a Korean friend. It's best to phone the place you're looking for and get directions.

The word for a large street is *ro* (로), which is sometimes spelled as *no.* So, Jongno means Bell St. Large boulevards are divided into sections called *ga* (가). On a Seoul subway map there is a station at Euljiro 3-ga and at Euljiro 4-ga – these are different sections of Eulji St. A *gil* (길) is a street smaller than a *no* or *ro* – Insadong-gil is one such example.

We've provided *hangeul* throughout this book for map references and points of interest, especially where there is no English sign. To transliterate *hangeul* we have gone with the NAKL system used by the Korean government (p411) – you'll still see words when travelling in Korea spelt under a previous system of romanisation, hence the older-style Pusan rather than Busan. Where there are two commonly used transliterations we note that and if a business or organisation sticks with the old method of English spelling or alternative we use that too.

TOP PICKS

KOREAN MOVIES

For more about Korean cinema see p58.

- *Mother* (2009) – director Bong Joon-ho's tense drama about a mum who fights to prove the innocence of her son accused of murder

- *Old Partner* (2008) – this moving documentary – a surprise local hit – follows the twilight years of an aged farmer, his wife and his ox

- *The Host* (2006) – this symbol-laden paean to classic monster movies juggles humour, poignancy and heart-stopping action

- *King and the Clown* (2005) – a surprise Korean blockbuster about two court jesters during the Joseon dynasty, with a homosexual subtext

- *Taegukgi* (2004) – a big-budget (by Korean standards – US$12 million) hit about two brothers caught up in the Korean War

- *Oldboy* (2003) – a disturbing yet brilliant tale of revenge that won the 2004 Cannes Grand Prix

- *Memories of Murder* (2003) – this dramatisation of a real-life serial murder case is a flawless, riveting meditation on Korea's modern history

- *On the Occasion of Remembering the Turning Gate* (2002) – director Hong Sang-soo's trademark ad-libbing brings naturalism to this tale of a man confronting life's disappointments

- *Oasis* (2002) – a difficult, powerfully acted tale of the unexpected love that develops between a sociopath and a severely disabled girl

- *JSA* (2001) – a Park Chan-wook thriller about a friendship between soldiers on opposite sides of the DMZ, and its tragic outcome

ORIGINAL KOREA

- Listen to the ancient chants of shamans on the hills of **Inwangsan** (p109)

- Go inside a **North Korean submarine** (p190)

- Rise pre-dawn to chant sutras with Buddhist monks on a **temple-stay program** (p388)

- March along a North Korean invasion tunnel under the **DMZ** (p152)

- Admire phallic sculptures at **Haesindang Park** (p194)

- Hike in the **world's largest lava tube** (p292)

- Strip off in the luxurious **public bath** (p241) within the world's largest department store

- Sit inside a Buddhist version of paradise in a replica of **King Muryeong's tomb** (p325)

- Go shopping for herbal medicines at Daegu's vast **medicinal herb market** (p204)

- Enjoy a night's stay in a **hanok guesthouse** (p120) in Seoul

FESTIVALS & EVENTS

For more on Korean festivals see p390.

- **Chuncheon International Mime Festival** (May; p174) – Asia's largest mime fest

- **Incheon Bupyeong Pungmul Festival** (May; p164) – Korean folk music and dance

- **Jongmyo Daeje** (May; p119) – stately Confucian rites procession

- **Boryeong Mud Festival** (July; boxed text, p332) – get down and dirty on the beach

- **Chungju World Martial Arts Festival** (September/October; p342) – includes break dancing and music, too

- **Pusan International Film Festival** (September to October; p245) – Asian film jamboree

- **Andong Mask Dance Festival** (September to October; p229) – featuring masks from around the world

- **Gwangju Biennale** (September to November; p266) – top contemporary arts event

- **Baekje Cultural Festival** (October; p325) – huge costumed parades and fireworks

- **Namdo Food Festival** (October; p270) – major foodie celebration

history – when it had only recently emerged from its hermit-like existence and was starting to be colonised by Japan.

INTERNET RESOURCES

Galbijim (http://wiki.galbijim.com) Fun wiki site offering detailed, often quirky information about a whole range of topics and places Korean.

Hermit Hideaways (http://hermithideaways.com) Beautiful inspirational photos of the country by Gregory Curley.

Hi Korea (www.hikorea.go.kr/pt/index.html) A one-stop government website about studying, investing, working and living in Korea.

Korea4Expats (www.korea4expats.com) This comprehensive expat-penned site is a very useful resource on many aspects of Korean life, as well as having details on what to do in Seoul.

Korea.net (www.korea.net) The official website of the Korean Culture and Information Service is a treasure trove of background detail on the ROK.

Korean Tourism Organisation (www.visitkorea.or.kr/intro.html) Tons of useful tourist info in nine different languages.

Learn Korean Language (www.learnkoreanlanguage.com) Get the hang of *hangeul* with some free online help.

Life in Korea (www.lifeinkorea.com) Features an overview of Korea.

Lonely Planet (www.lonelyplanet.com) Book Seoul accommodation and read the latest Thorn Tree traveller's tips on Korea.

The Marmot's Hole (www.rjkoehler.com) Korea in blog form – this round up of Korea-related posts and news by resident expat Robert Koehler is eye-opening, entertaining and addictive.

Itineraries
CLASSIC ROUTES

DISCOVER KOREA
Two Weeks / Seoul to Jeju-do

Set aside four or five days for nonstop **Seoul** (p86), including a day trip north to the **DMZ** (p152). Next head east to **Chuncheon** (p174) where you can cycle around the lake and sample the town's famous chicken dish, *dakgalbi*.

Dine on fresh seafood in **Sokcho** (p178), then hike around the stunning peaks and waterfalls of **Seoraksan National Park** (p182). Follow the coast south to **Gangneung** (p185) to view well-preserved Joseon-era buildings, quirky museums and a tiny North Korean spy submarine at **Jeongdongjin** (p189). Use **Samcheok** (p192) as your base for exploring the huge caves **Hwaseongul** and **Daegeumgul** (p194), as well as **Haesindang Park** (p194), packed with phallic sculptures.

Travel back to feudal times at charming **Hahoe Folk Village** (p231). Continue exploring Korea's past at **Gyeongju** (p208), ancient capital of the Shilla kingdom, where you can spend a couple of days exploring royal tombs, the treasures of its excellent museum and the World Heritage–listed grotto at **Seokguram** (p213).

If you're running short of time, finish up in the bustling port of **Busan** (p237), just three hours by the fastest train to Seoul. It would be a shame, though, to miss the scenic delights and adventure activities of **Jeju-do** (p282), the number one honeymoon destination of newlywed Koreans.

Starting in scintillating Seoul and finishing on the beaches of Jeju-do, connected by frequent and inexpensive flights to Busan and Seoul, this 850km route offers a broad sweep of city delights, historical sights, scenic vistas and unique dining experiences.

North Korea can only be seen as part of a guided tour; for more information see p349.

GOURMET FEAST

Two Weeks / Seoul to Jeju-do

This lip-smacking tour combines sightseeing with the best of Korean cuisine. In **Seoul** (p86), between palace-, museum- and gallery-hopping, feast on everything from royal cuisine to humble street snacks. Be sure not to miss out on the **Noryangjin fish market** (p111).

Fine Chinese food can be found in Incheon's historic **Chinatown** (p164), a subway ride west of Seoul. Another subway ride south of the capital, tuck into *galbi* (beef ribs) after walking the ramparts of **Suwon's fortress wall** (p156).

An hour's bus ride from Daejeon is **Geumsan** (boxed text, p327), centre of Korea's ginseng industry, and packed with shops and restaurants selling all manner of products and dishes using the wonder root. Continue south to **Jeonju** (p306), birthplace of the classic rice dish *bibimbap*.

Learn about Korea's human rights and democracy heroes in **Gwangju** (p262) then sample the area's great selection of *kimchi*. Towards the south coast is the beautiful green-tea plantation **Boseong Daehan Dawon** (p273), where you can enjoy food and drinks made with *nokcha* (green tea).

Nagan Folk Village (p270) is a gorgeous destination at any time of the year, but foodies will want to head here in October for its food festival. *Ureok* (rockfish) is the speciality of **Busan** (p237), which also has a great seafood market – the best place to sample *hoe* (raw fish).

Fly on to **Jeju-do** (p282) where you can dig into the island's unique dishes, such as *jeonbok juk* (abalone rice porridge) and *heukdwaeji* (black pig pork), between touring the sights, such as the world's longest system of lava-tube caves (p292).

Korean cuisine covers such a multitude of flavours and styles that it would take a lifetime to sample everything, but this 1000km itinerary hopping between some of the country's gourmet hotspots is a good start.

ROADS LESS TRAVELLED

WEST TO EAST SEA   *Two Weeks / Incheon Airport to Ulleung-do*

From **Incheon International Airport** (p145) it's a very quick hop to the small, idyllic island of **Muui-do** (p168). Direct buses from Incheon mean there's no need to head into Seoul to reach your next destinations: **Gongju** (p324) and **Buyeo** (p328), the ancient capitals of the Baekje kingdom.

After enjoying the sands and seafood of **Daecheon Beach** (p331) sail to the serene island of **Sapsi-do** (p332), before touring pretty **Anmyeon-do** (p333) and watching the sunset from **Mallipo Beach** (p334).

Travel inland to Daejeon where you can soak at **Yuseong Hot Springs** (p321). From here make your way to Cheongju and on to **Songnisan National Park** (p340), covering central Korea's finest scenic area and home to a 33m-tall gold-plated Buddha statue.

Chungju is the gateway to the equally lovely **Woraksan National Park** (p343) and for a two-hour scenic ferry trip across Chungju Lake to sleepy **Danyang** (p344), small-town Korea at its most charming. From here explore nearby **limestone caves** (p344) and the stately temple complex of **Guin-sa** (p346).

In Taebaeksan Provincial Park visit the mountain-top **Dangun altar** (p196), which honours Korea's mythical half-bear founder. Then board the train in **Taebaek** (p196) bound for Donghae on the coast, from where you can take the ferry to **Ulleung-do** (p222). This sparsely inhabited, ruggedly beautiful volcanic island is a truly off-the-beaten-track experience.

There's a lot to recommend in Seoul, but if you'd prefer to avoid the capital it's possible on this 750km coast-to-coast itinerary starting on the island of Muui-do and finishing 135km out in the East Sea at spectacular Ulleung-do.

THE DEEP SOUTH TRAIL

Two Weeks / Jeonju to Busan

The rural southwest is Korea's greenest region. Start your explorations in **Jeonju** (p306), provincial capital of Jeollabuk-do, which has a fascinating *hanok* village crammed with traditional houses and buildings. See the rock-pinnacle garden and climb a horse's ear at **Maisan Provincial Park** (p311), then go hiking or skiing in beautiful **Deogyusan National Park** (p312).

Scenic splendours and an ancient Buddha carved on a cliff await you at **Seonunsan Provincial Park** (p315). Take a ferry from Gunsan to a slice of island paradise called **Seonyu-do** (p317) or to rarely visited **Eocheong-do**, which attracts bird enthusiasts.

Further south, **Gwangju** (p262), home to several interesting historical sites and museums, will soon be home to a major arts complex. Also don't miss the bamboo town of **Damyang** (p269).

At Mokpo visit the **museums** (p279) before taking a boat to the remote havens of **Heuksan-do** (p281) and **Hong-do** (p281). Admire Korea's centuries-old tradition of pottery at the **Gangjin Celadon Museum** (p274) and taste food and drinks made from healthy green tea at the beautiful **Boseong Daehan Dawon Tea Plantation** (p273).

Go birdspotting in the Ramsar-listed wetlands of **Suncheon Bay** (boxed text, p270), then continue along the coast to Yeosu, where you can hike up to **Hyangiram** (p273), a Buddhist temple perched on a cliff with awesome coastal and island views.

For a final eco experience don't miss the beautiful hike on the unspoiled **Yeonhwa-do** (p253), which is easily reached by ferry from Tongyeong. The trail finishes at the bustling port of **Busan** (p237), Korea's second-largest city.

Fast trains and buses can whisk you from Seoul to Jeonju in less than three hours to start this 850km route around Korea's least-developed region, which offers the opportunity to visit hundreds of unspoilt islands, dine in countless seafood restaurants and dig deep into artistic traditions.

TAILORED TRIPS

KARMA KOREA

Like all journeys, this one around Korea's Buddhist temples begins with a single step. First, learn something about the religion during a temple life program at Seoul's **Jogye-sa** or **Bong-eun-sa** (p113).

Contrast highly modern **Guin-sa** (p346), the headquarters of the Cheontae sect, with **Magok-sa** (p327), an ancient temple in a remote spot with a hall of 1000 pint-sized disciples that are all slightly different.

Daegu can used as base for trips to stunning **Haein-sa** (p207), housing a World Heritage–listed library of over 80,000 14th-century woodblocks, and **Jikji-sa** (p207), a magnificent temple dating back to the 5th century.

Jinan is the access town for **Tap-sa** (p312), a tiny temple surrounded by two 'horse ear' mountains and an extraordinary sculptural garden of 80 stone pinnacles (or towers) that were piled up by a Buddhist mystic, while from Gwangju you can visit **Unju-sa** (p268), with its fine collection of stone pagodas and unusual twin and reclining Buddhas.

Tongdo-sa (p252), said to be Korea's largest and most important Buddhist temple, has an excellent Buddhist art museum containing 30,000 artefacts. Nearby **Seongnam-sa** (p252) is a visual masterpiece set in a provincial park.

Finally, **Bulguk-sa** (p213) is a World Heritage–listed temple that represents the crowning glory of Shilla architecture.

KIDS KOREA

This two-centre itinerary is ideal for parents looking to balance their own travelling needs with those of their toddlers and teens. **Seoul** has an abundant number of kid-friendly attractions (p118) including amusement parks, regular parks, aquariums and, in summer, outdoor swimming pools. Older kids will most likely be happy cruising the capital's vast **shopping malls** and **department stores** (p144) or being part of the audience for the filming of an **e-sports show** (boxed text, p52).

Day trips include the beaches of the **West Sea islands** (p166), Korea's biggest amusement park **Everland Resort** (p158) and the **Korean Folk Village** (p158). These last two can just as easily be visited from **Suwon** (p155), where everyone will have fun hiking around the walls of an 18th-century fortress. North of Seoul the modern village of **Heyri** (p154) is an opportunity to relax and distract small children with some inventive sculptures and art exhibits.

Hop on a flight to **Jeju-do** (p282), an island blessed with a fascinating volcanic landscape and dozens of sandy beaches. Amusement and water parks, circus shows, cycle and skate hire, and a whole raft of adventure activities from quad biking to balloon rides are possible on this fun-packed island with plenty of world-class resorts.

WORLD HERITAGE KOREA

South Korea has eight cultural properties and one natural property inscribed on the Unesco World Heritage list (http://whc.unesco.org/en/statesparties/kr). Several of them can easily be visited in or around Seoul, including the royal ancestral shrine **Jongmyo** (p107), the beautiful palace complex **Changdeokgung** (p105), and sites of the royal tombs of the Joseon dynasty at **Samreung Gongwon** (p112) and **Donggureung** (boxed text, p152).

Within day trip range of the capital is Suwon's impressive fortress **Hwaseong** (p156) and mysterious stone **dolmen sites of Ganghwa-do** (p170). It was on Ganghwa-do that the Tripitaka Koreana, 81,258 wooden printing blocks containing Buddhist scriptures, were originally carved. They now reside at the World Heritage–listed temple **Haein-sa** (p207).

The historic surrounds of **Gyeongju** (p208) – 'the museum without walls' – are sprinkled with outstanding examples of Korean Buddhist art in the form of sculptures, reliefs, pagodas and the remains of temples and palaces. Nearby, in the mountains above the temple Bulguk-sa, is a superb mid-8th-century stone Buddha that resides in the **Seokguram Grotto** (p213).

Lastly, three sites on the volcanic island of Jeju-do – the mountain **Hallasan** (p303), the lava-tube caves at **Manjanggul** (p292) and the crown-like peak of **Seongsan Ilchulbong** (p293) – are testament to Korea's natural beauty.

ACTIVE KOREA

Hiking, skiing, cycling, rafting – name the activity and you'll find battalions of Koreans fully kitted out and crazy for it. Limber up in Seoul by hiring a bike to pedal along the **Han River** (boxed text, p113), or hop on a subway to reach **Bukhansan National Park** (p151), where there are many hiking trails.

Serious hikers will want to tackle **Hallasan** (p303), South Korea's tallest peak, as well as follow 200km of marked trails that make up the **Jeju Olle** (p286). Other favourite hikes includes those in **Wolchusan National Park** (p277), Korea's smallest, which includes a vertigo-inducing 52m bridge spanning two ridges, and **Jirisan National Park** (p258), where 12 peaks over 1000m form a 40km ridge.

Want to get wet? Then join a white-water rafting or kayaking trip on the fast-flowing rivers near **Cheorwon** and **Inje** (boxed text, p176). Or fully submerge yourself off **Seogwipo** (p296), Korea's best scuba-diving destination, with colourful corals, kelp forests and dolphins.

If winter sports are your bag, then the best ski resorts to head to are **Alps** (p185), which has Korea's heaviest snowfall, **Yongpyong** (p190) and **Muju** (p312) in picturesque Deogyusan National Park. Ice climbers can try scaling the frozen waterfall at **Gangchon** (p177).

History

Koreans associate their origins with one of the most beautiful points on the globe, the great mountain on their northern border, Paekdusan (or White-Head Mountain; see p376), with a crystal-pure volcanic lake at its summit. (The North Koreans say that Kim Jong-il was born there, even if most historians think he was born along the Sino-Russian border.)

Koreans remain today a 'mountain people', who identify with hometowns and home regions that, so they argue, differ greatly from other places in Korea. Koreans are also an ancient people: they are one of the few peoples in the world who can trace a continuous history and presence on the same territory going back thousands of years. Since Korea has had next to no ethnic minorities, Koreans have traditionally thought that they are a homogeneous and unique people – and that they always have been.

This chapter, originally written by Korean history expert Dr Bruce Cumings, was updated by Simon Richmond.

THE FIRST KOREAN

The imagined beginning of the Korean nation was the 3rd millennium BC, when a king named Dangun founded old Joseon. Joseon (also spelled Choson) remains the name of the country in North Korea, but South Koreans use the term 'Hanguk', a name dating from the 1890s.

The first Korean – Dangun – was not just a person but a king, and a continuous presence from his time down to the present, a kingly vessel filled by different people at different times, who drew their legitimacy from this eternal lineage. Under its first president, for example, South Korea used a calendar in which Dangun's birth constituted year one – setting the date at 2333 BC. If the two Koreas can't agree on many things, including what to call their country, they can agree on Dangun. In 1993 North Korea announced with great fanfare the discovery of Dangun's tomb at a site close to Pyongyang: 'The founding of Kojoson (old Joseon) by Dangun 5000 years ago marked an epochal occasion in the formation of the Korean nation… The Koreans are a homogeneous nation who inherited the same blood and culture consistently down through history'. All the scribes came forward to proclaim Koreans as the oldest (and therefore finest) people in the world, with one continuous line of history from the 30th-century BC down to the present.

Unfortunately there is no written history of Korea until the centuries just before the birth of Christ, and that history was chronicled by Chinese scribes. But there is archaeological evidence that human beings inhabited this peninsula half a million years ago, and that an advanced people were there seven or eight thousand years ago in the Neolithic period – as revealed by the ground and polished stone tools and pottery they left to posterity. These Neolithic people practised agriculture in a settled communal life, and

Korea's Place in the Sun: A Modern History by Bruce Cumings (2005) offers an overview of Korean history from year one to the 1860s, followed by a close examination of the modern period.

TIMELINE

2333 BC	c 57 BC	372
This is the date given by the *Dongguk Tonggam*, a chronicle of early Korean history compiled in the 15th century, for the founding of the Korean kingdom of Gojoseon by the mythical leader Dangun.	Start of the Three Kingdoms period in which the ancient kingdoms of Goguryeo, Baekje and Shilla ruled over the Korean peninsula and parts of Manchuria.	Buddhism is brought to the kingdom of Goguryeo by the Chinese monk Sundo where it blends with local Shamanism. It takes two centuries for the religion to spread throughout the peninsula.

are widely supposed to have had family clans as their basic social grouping. Nationalist historians also trace many Korean social and cultural traits back to these Neolithic peoples.

THE THREE KINGDOMS

Around the time of Christ three ancient kingdoms emerged that influenced Korean history down to our time. The first state to emerge in the Three Kingdoms era (57 BC–AD 668) was Baekje (Paekche), which was a centralised, aristocratic state melding Chinese and indigenous influence. By the 3rd century AD, Baekje was strong enough to demolish its rivals and occupy what today is the core area of Korea, around Seoul. The common Korean custom of father-to-son royal succession is said to have begun with Baekje king Geun Chugo. His grandson inaugurated another long tradition by adopting Buddhism as the state religion (in 384). The northern kingdom, Goguryeo (Koguryŏ), conquered a large territory by AD 312 and expanded in all directions, especially toward the Taedong River in the south, which runs through Pyongyang. Peninsular geography shaped the political space of Baekje and Goguryeo and a third kingdom called Shilla (Silla), which fills out the trilogy.

Approximately three-quarters of the way down the peninsula, at the 37th parallel, the major mountain range veers to the southwest, dividing the peninsula. This southwest extension of mountains framed Baekje's historic territory, just as it did the Shilla kingdom to the east. Goguryeo, however, ranged over a wild region consisting of northeastern Korea and eastern Manchuria, giving rise to contemporary dreams of a 'greater Korea' in territories that now happen to be part of China and Russia. While South Korea identifies itself with the glories of the Shilla kingdom, which they say unified the peninsula in 668 AD, the North identifies with Goguryeo and says the country wasn't truly unified until the founding of the Goguryeo dynasty. Meanwhile people in the southwestern part of the country felt abused by dictators and left out of the growth of South Korea for decades until one of their own was elected president in 1997 (Kim Dae-jung), and often identified with the Baekje legacy.

BUDDHISM IN KOREA

Buddhism came to Korea from China in the latter part of the Three Kingdoms era, establishing itself first in Goguryeo and Baekje in the late 4th century and then in Shilla in the early 6th century. With royal support the faith spread throughout the peninsula and became the official religion in all three states – and remained so until the end of the 14th century. It wasn't quite the familiar Buddhism of ascetic monks, however – some monasteries became wealthy and owned large estates and thousands of slaves, and some monks dressed in silk robes, rode fine horses and indulged in wine, women and song. Korean

Bronze Age (c 10,000 BC) people on the Korean peninsula built dolmen or stone burial chambers such as those found on the island of Ganghwa-do (p169).

427	668	721
King Jangsu, the 20th monarch of the Goguryeo dynasty, founds Pyongyang by building his capital on the banks of the Taedong River.	Having allied his kingdom with China's Tang dynasty, Munmu of Shilla defeats Goguryeo to become the first ruler of a unified southern Korean peninsula.	King Seongdeok orders the construction of a wall along Shilla's northern border to protect against the forces of Balhae, the successor state to Goguryeo.

Buddhism also incorporated indigenous shamanist beliefs; many of the colourful wooden temples you can still visit in the mountain temples have a small hall dedicated to shamanist deities like the mountain gods and have histories that stretch back over a thousand years.

Far from being pacifists, Korean monks often came to the defence of their country. Many mountain fortresses found throughout the Korean peninsula contained temples and were garrisoned by warrior monks. Toughened by their spartan lifestyle and trained in martial arts, monk warriors played a major part in resisting the Japanese invasions in the 1590s – even though Confucianism had become the state doctrine and the new rulers treated them as lowborn and no better than beggars. Monks were not allowed to enter the gates of Seoul, for example, which is why many temples are hidden away on remote mountains.

Sourcebook of Korean Civilisation (1993) edited by Peter Lee has a wide selection of original historical documents and materials, in translation and with commentary.

Today Buddhist sects in Seoul sometimes come to blows over their disputes, and some monks even marry and have children; the ascetic Seon (Zen) doctrine is the most common one, but has many rivals. If all this sounds heretical, the Korean approach to religion is often eclectic – the same person might be a Christian, a Buddhist and a Confucianist, depending on the day.

SHILLA ASCENDANCY

Shilla emerged victorious on the peninsula in 668, and it is from this famous date that South Korean historians speak for the first time of a unified Korea. This brought an end to the era of the Three Kingdoms, but not before all of them had come under the long-term sway of Chinese civilisation by introducing Chinese statecraft, Buddhist and Confucian philosophy, Confucian practices of educating the young, and the Chinese written language. Artists from Goguryeo and Baekje also perfected a mural art found on the walls of tombs, and took it to Japan where it deeply influenced Japan's temple and burial art. But it is the blossoming of Shilla that still astounds contemporary visitors to Korea, and makes its ancient capital at Gyeongju (Kyŏngju; p208) one of the most fascinating tourist destinations in East Asia.

Shilla had close relations with the great Tang dynasty in China, sent many students to Tang schools, and had a level of civilisation high enough to merit the Chinese designation 'flourishing land in the East'. Shilla culture melded indigenous and Tang influences: in 682 it set up a national Confucian academy to train high officials, and later instituted a civil-service examination system modelled on that of the Tang. But Shilla had a flourishing indigenous civilisation clearly different from the Tang, one that was among the most advanced in the world. Its capital at Gyeongju (p208) was renowned as the 'city of gold', where the aristocracy pursued a high culture and extravagant pleasures. Chinese historians wrote that elite officials possessed thousands of slaves, with like numbers of horses, cattle and pigs. Their wives wore

918	**1231**	**1251**
The Goryeo dynasty is established by King Taejo; it rules Korea until 1392, during which time the territory under its rule expands to the whole Korean peninsula.	As part of a general campaign to conquer China, Mongols invade the Korean peninsula forcing the Goryeo royal court to regroup on the island of Ganghwa-do.	Monks at Jeondeung-sa, Ganghwa-do, complete the 80,000 wooden blocks of the second Tripitaka Koreana, a book of Buddhist scriptures – the first had been destroyed in the 1232 Mongol invasion of the island.

THE INVENTION OF ONDOL

The Balhae people, who lived in a territory where the temperature could dip to -40°C in winter, bequeathed a lasting invention to the Korean people: sleeping on *ondol* floors. This system, that uses flues from a central hearth to heat the floors of each room, is still in wide use in contemporary Korea, with the stone flues covered by waxed and polished rice paper. Ice may form in a water jug on the table while a person sleeps comfortably on a toasty warm *ondol*.

solid-gold tiaras and earrings of delicate and intricate filigree. Scholars studied the Confucian and Buddhist classics and developed advanced methods for astronomy and calendrical science. 'Pure Land' Buddhism, a simple doctrine, united the mass of common people, who like today's Hare Krishnas could become adherents through the repetition of simple chants.

The crowning glory of Gyeongju is the Bulguk-sa (Pulguk-sa) temple, which was rebuilt in the 1970s, and the nearby Seokguram Grotto. Both were built around 750 and are home to some of the finest Buddhist sculpture in the world. Buddhists came on pilgrimages to Gyeongju from as far away as India and Arab sojourners sometimes came to the temple to stay.

In spite of Shilla's military strength, broad territories of the old Goguryeo kingdom were not conquered and a section of the Goguryeo elite established a successor state known as Balhae (Parhae), above and below the Amnok and Tuman boundaries that now form the border between China, Russia and Korea. Balhae's continuing strength forced Shilla to build a northern wall in 721 and kept Shilla forces permanently below a line running from present-day Pyongyang in the east to the west coast. As one prominent South Korean historian wrote, 'Shilla and Balhae confronted each other hostilely much like southern and northern halves of a partitioned nation'.

Like Shilla, Balhae continued to be influenced deeply by the Chinese civilisation of the Tang, sending students to the capital at Ch'angan, on which it modelled its own capital city.

UNIFICATION UNDER GORYEO

A New History of Korea by Lee Ki-baik (1984) takes a cultural and sociological perspective on the country's history.

A formidable military leader named Wang Geon had defeated Shilla as well as some Baekje remnants by 930, and established a flourishing dynasty, Goryeo, from whence came the name Korea. Korea was now fully unified with more or less the boundaries that it retains today. Wang was not just a unifier, however, but a magnanimous one. Regarding himself as the proper lineal king of Goguryeo, he embraced that kingdom's survivors, took a Shilla princess as his wife and treated the Shilla aristocracy with unprecedented generosity. His dynasty ruled for nearly a millennium, and in its heyday was among the most advanced civilisations in the world.

c 1270	1377	1392
Although some military leaders in the south refuse to surrender, Goryeo's rulers agree to a peace treaty with the Mongols. The two empires try to conquer Japan but are thwarted by a heavy sea storm (*kamikaze*).	Monks at Cheongju's Heundeok-sa temple beat Johannes Gutenberg by 78 years by creating the *Jikji*, the world's first book printed using moveable metal type.	Having had King Gongyang and his family murdered, General Yi Seong-gye ascends the throne, naming himself King Taejo and establishing the Joseon dynasty that will rule Korea for the next 500 years.

With its capital at Kaesong (p372), a town 76km north of Seoul, the Goryeo dynasty's composite elite also forged a tradition of aristocratic continuity that lasted down to the modern era. By the 13th century there were two government groupings: civil officials and military officials. At that time the military people were stronger, but thereafter both were known as *yangban* (the two orders), which became the Korean term for aristocracy. Below the hereditary aristocracy were common people like peasants and merchants. Below them were outcaste groups of butchers, tanners and entertainers, who were called *cheonmin* and who lived a castelike existence, often in separated and ostracised villages, and whose status fell upon their children as well. Likewise, slavery was hereditary (matrilineally), with slaves making up as much as 30% of Goryeo society.

The elite fused aristocratic privilege and political power through marriage alliances and control of land and central political office, and fortified this class position to the point of impregnability by making status hereditary. Goryeo established a social pattern in which a landed gentry mixed its control of property with a Confucian- or Buddhist-educated stratum of scholar-officials, usually residing in the capital. Often scholars and landlords were one and the same person, but in any case landed wealth and bureaucratic position became powerfully fused. At the centre, a bureaucracy influenced by Confucian statecraft emerged, which thereafter sought to influence local power and which was a contrast with the Japanese or European feudal pattern of castle towns, landed domains and parcellised sovereignty all backed by a strong military class (although Korea came close to the feudal pattern in the 9th and 10th centuries, when strong walled-town lords and military commanders challenged central power).

The large landed families held their land in perpetuity and could bequeath it to their survivors; its produce was at the service of the owner, after taxes were paid. Worked mostly by peasant tenants who paid rent in kind, this land system often produced vast estates of great wealth worked by hundreds of tenants or slaves, and in its essential form persisted through the subsequent Joseon period and the Japanese colonial period. Family landholding became more important than office-holding in perpetuating aristocratic dominance over time. The wealthy, aristocratic landlord became a beneficence or a plague (depending on your point of view) from early Goryeo down to modern times, and an egalitarian redistribution of the land became a focal point of Confucian reformers, capitalist modernisers and communist agitators alike.

THE RISE OF THE MONGOLS

The Goryeo aristocracy was by no means a class without merit, however. It admired and interacted with the splendid Chinese civilisation that emerged during the contemporaneous Song dynasty (960–1279). Official

1394	1446	1592
King Taejo employs geomancy, or *feng shui* (*pungsu* in Korean), to select Hanyang (Seoul) as Joseon's capital. He starts construction of the Changdeok palace, which is completed in 1412, four years after his death.	Sejong the Great, the fourth king of the Joseon dynasty, oversees the invention of *hangeul*, Korea's unique script, which is announced to the public in the document known as the *Hunminjeongeum*.	Seoul falls to Japan during the Imjin War. Korean forces use metal-covered 'turtle boats' to win several decisive naval battles in the eventually successful quest to expel the invaders.

delegations and ordinary merchants brought Korean gold, silver and ginseng to China in exchange for silks, porcelains and woodblock books. Finely crafted Song porcelains stimulated Korean artisans to produce an even finer type of inlaid celadon pottery – unmatched in the world before or since for the pristine clarity of its blue-green glaze and the delicate art of its inlaid portraits.

Buddhism was the state religion, but it coexisted with Confucianism throughout the Goryeo period. Buddhist priests systematised religious practice by rendering the Korean version of the Buddhist canon into mammoth wood-block print editions, known as the Tripitaka. The first was completed in 1087 after a lifetime of work, but was lost; another, completed in 1251, can still be viewed today at Haein-sa (p207). By 1234, if not earlier, Koreans had also invented movable metal type, two centuries before its inception in Europe.

This high point of Goryeo culture coincided with internal disorder and the rise of the Mongols, whose power swept most of the known world during the 13th century. Korea was no exception, as Kublai Khan's forces invaded and demolished Goryeo's army in 1231, forcing the government to retreat to the island of Ganghwa-do (p169), a ploy that exploited the Mongol horsemen's fear of water. But after a more devastating invasion in 1254, in which countless people died and some 200,000 were made captives, Goryeo succumbed to Mongol domination and its kings came to intermarry with Mongol princesses. The Mongols then enlisted thousands of Koreans in ill-fated invasions of Japan in 1274 and 1281, using craft made by Korea's great shipwrights. The Kamakura Shogunate turned back both invasions with help, as legend has it, from opportune typhoons known as the 'divine wind' or *kamikaze*.

LAST DYNASTY

Korea by Angus Hamilton (1904) is a rare and lively description of life in Korea under the last dynasty.

The overthrow of the Mongols by the Ming dynasty in China (1316–1644) gave an opportunity to rising groups of Korean military men to contest for power. One of them, Yi Seong-gye, grabbed the bull by the horns and overthrew Goryeo leaders, thus becoming the founder of Korea's longest and last dynasty (1392–1910). The new state was named Joseon, harking back to the old Joseon kingdom 15 centuries earlier, and its capital was built at Seoul.

General Yi announced the new dynasty by mobilising some 200,000 labourers to surround the new capital with a great wall; it was completed in six months in 1394, and scattered remnants of it still stand today, especially the Great South Gate (Namdaemun) and the Great East Gate (Dongdaemun).

Yi was generous to his defeated Goryeo antagonists, sending them off to comfortable exile. Such magnanimity encouraged one writer to wax poetic

1666	1767	1776
The Dutchman Hendrick Hamel, held prisoner in the country for 13 years after being shipwrecked off Jeju-do, writes the first Western account of the Joseon dynasty.	Confucianism reaches its height under King Yeongjo, who imprisons his possibly mentally disturbed son Sado in a large rice chest where the Crown Prince starves to death in eight days.	Jeongjo, Sado's son, comes to the throne and emerges as one of Korea's most revered kings by shaking up the social order – the *yangban* elite loses power to a small but growing middle class.

about Yi Seong-gye's virtues – a typical example of how Koreans sing the manifold praises of their leaders, especially dynastic founders:

> His presence is the mighty warrior, firm
> He stands, an eagle on a mountain top;
> In wisdom and resource none can compare,
> The dragon of Namyang is he.
> In judgment on the civil bench,
> Or counsel from the warrior's tent, he rules;
> He halts the waves that roll in from the sea,
> And holds the sun back from its heavenly course.

The deep Buddhist influence on the previous dynasty led the literati to urge the king to uproot Buddhist economic and political influence, which led to exile in the mountains for monks and their disciples. Over many decades the literati thus accomplished a deep Confucianisation of Joseon society, which particularly affected the position of women. Where many women were prominent in Goryeo society, they were now relegated to domestic chores of childrearing and housekeeping, as so-called 'inside people'. Up until recent times the woman's role in Korean society seemed to be as old as the bones in ancestral graves: just as central, just as hidden, and just as unchangeable.

Goryeo society had a relatively strong matrilineal system. It was by no means a matriarchy, but it wasn't the patriarchy of later centuries. A new husband was welcomed into the wife's house, where the children and grandchildren would live. Many men were happy to take this route because women shared rights of inheritance with their male siblings. Women were so valuable that men wanted several; a Chinese envoy in 1123 found a wealthy man in Gaeseong with four. But plural wives weren't dependent on one man; often living apart, they had their own economic underpinnings. Detailed ritual did not surround the marriage act, nor relations between sexes: 'the general free and easy contact between the sexes amazed…Chinese observers.' There were no restrictions on widows remarrying; women took serial husbands, if not several at the same time.

Influential literati in the Joseon dynasty were ideologues who wanted to restore Korean society to its proper path as they saw it, by using the virtues to discipline the passions and the interests. The reforming came in the name of Neo-Confucianism and Chu Hsi, the Chinese progenitor of this doctrine. The result was that much of what we now see as 'Korean culture' or 'tradition' arose from major social reorganisation by self-conscious 15th-century ideologues. Foreign observers declared that Korea was 'more Confucian than China'.

The unquestionable effect of the new reforms and laws was a slow-moving but ultimately radical change in women's social position and an expropriation of women's property, more or less complete by the late 15th century. From then on, the latticework of Korean society was constituted by patrilineal

For books about North Korean history see p351 and for documentaries see the boxed text on p353.

Samurai Invasion by Stephen Turnbull (2002) is a detailed account of the Japanese invasions of Korea in the 1590s.

1796	1800	1834
King Jeongjo moves the royal court to Suwon to be closer to Sado's grave, and builds the Hwaseong fortress (now a World Heritage site) to protect the new palace.	Sunjo succeeds his father as the 23rd king of the Joseon dynasty and reigns for 34 years, during which time Korean Catholics are increasingly persecuted and executed.	The eight-year-old Heonjong, Sunjo's grandson, is named the 24th Joseon king; during his 15-year reign power resides with his mother's family, the Andong Kim clan. He dies without leaving an heir.

DONGHAK DEMANDS

The Donghak Rebellion, which had been building for decades, erupted in 1893 in Jeolla province, attracting large numbers of peasants and lowborn groups of people. The rebels were only armed with primitive, homemade weapons, but they defeated the government army sent against them. The rebellion then spread to neighbouring provinces, and when King Gojong called in Chinese troops, Japanese troops took advantage of the uproar to march into Seoul. The rebels were defeated and their leaders, including Jeon Bong-jun, who was known as the 'Green Pea General' because of his small size, were executed by Japanese firing squads.

The demands of the rebels reveal their many grievances against the Joseon social system:

- Slaves should be freed.
- The low-born should be treated fairly.
- Land should be redistributed.
- Taxes on fish and salt should be scrapped.
- No unauthorised taxes should be levied and any corrupt *yangban* should be severely punished.
- All debts should be cancelled.
- Regional favouritism and factions should be abolished.
- Widows should be allowed to remarry.
- Traitors who support foreign interference should be punished.

descent. The nails in the latticework, the proof of its importance and existence over time, were the written genealogies that positioned families in the hierarchy of property and prestige. In succeeding centuries a person's genealogy would be the best predictor of his or her life chances; it became one of Korea's most lasting characteristics. Since only male offspring could prolong the family and clan lines and were the only names registered in the genealogical tables, the birth of a son was greeted with great fanfare.

Atlas of Korean History by Kim Seong-hwan (2008) is for those who prefer their history text brief and to come illustrated with plenty of cut-out pics and 3D-style maps.

Such historical influences remain strong in both Koreas today, where first sons and their families often live with the male's parents and all stops are pulled out to father a boy. Hereditary aristocratic principles became so ingrained that according to Edward Wagner, who taught Korean Studies at Harvard for 35 years, a relative handful of elite families were responsible for most of the 14,000-odd exam passers of the civil-service examination system in the 500 years of the Joseon, exams being the critical route to official position.

The self-conscious Confucianisation of Korean society had clear negative effects for women and common people, but it also reinforced some of modern Korea's most admirable qualities: the deep concern for family; the broad respect for education (scholars and philosophers were at the pinnacle

1849	1864	1866
The Andong Kims track down the great grandson of King Yeongjo living in poverty on Ganghwa-do. The illiterate and easily manipulated 18-year-old is proclaimed King Cheoljong.	The 11-year-old Gojong, son of the shrewd courtier Yi Ha-eung (later called the Daewongun or 'Prince of the Great Court') is crowned Joseon's 26th ruler, breaking the Andong Kim clan's grip on power.	French forces invade Ganghwa-do, ostensibly in retaliation for the execution of French Catholic priests who had been illicitly proselytising in Korea. They are forced to retreat after six weeks.

of Confucian reform), more or less automatic admiration for elders (and the elderly); and a belief that ultimately human society should be governed by the virtuous, not the powerful or the wealthy.

KOREA & CHINA: A SPECIAL RELATIONSHIP

Smack in the middle of the grand Sejongno boulevard in Seoul is a gigantic statue of Admiral Yi Sun-sin, whose artful naval manoeuvres saved Korea from Japanese conquest in the 1590s (see the boxed text, p38). This statue is a nice symbol of the general idea that for most Koreans most of the time, foreigners might be people intent on invading Korea. Japan is the best case, of course, with the warlord Hideyoshi laying waste to the peninsula only to be turned back by Admiral Yi, and with Japan's victories over China in 1895 and Russia in 1905, establishing Japanese colonial rule in Korea. Mongols, Manchus and others usually grouped as 'barbarians' came charging across Korea's northern borders. But the Mongols and Manchus were also conquerors of China, which made them barbarians, too, and led many Koreans to think that China was not just the centre of an admirable civilisation but also a good neighbour, giving to Korea more than it took away.

General Yi Song-gye founded his dynasty when he refused to send his troops into battle against a Chinese army, and instead turned around and used them to overthrow his own government and make himself king. Not surprisingly, he received the blessing and support of the Chinese emperor, and Korea became a 'tributary' country to China – but more than that, it became the ideal tributary state, modelling itself on Chinese culture and statecraft. Most of the time China left Korea alone to run its own affairs, and Korea was content to look up to China as the centre of the only world civilisation that mattered. This policy was known as *sadae* (serving the great). Because of this special relationship, when Hideyoshi's forces attacked in the 1590s, Chinese troops were sent to help repel them. In just one battle as many as 30,000 Chinese soldiers died.

Sadae was in the background during the Korean War as well, when a huge Chinese army intervened in late 1950 and helped rescue the North from certain defeat. Meanwhile, many South Koreans felt that the behaviour of the Chinese troops during the Korean War was superior to that of any other force, including the American troops. Today China is South Korea's largest trading partner, with thousands of Korean students studying there, while China maintains its long-term alliance with North Korea. So, it can be said that Korea's relationship with China is one of the only foreign entanglements that most Koreans seem happy with, and it's likely to grow ever stronger in the 21st century.

Of course, it isn't clear what the common people thought about China until the modern period, nor were they asked; the vast majority were illiterate in a country that marked its elite according to their literacy – in Chinese.

Hendrick Hamel's fascinating account of his 13 years in Korea, after he and 36 other sailors were shipwrecked on Jeju-do in 1653, is available in Gari Ledyard's *The Dutch Come to Korea*, with full scholarly annotation.

Chihwaseon (2002), which won a prize for director Im Kwon-taek at Cannes, is a visually stunning film based on the true story of a talented, non-conformist painter who lived at the end of the Joseon dynasty.

War Diary of Admiral Yi Sun-sin edited by Sohn Pow-key (1977) is a straightforward and fascinating account by Korea's greatest admiral of the battles, floggings and court intrigues that were his daily preoccupations.

| **1871** | **1876** | **1882** |

| Ganghwa-do witnesses another international tussle as a US diplomatic mission is rebuffed, leading to an armed conflict on the island that leaves 243 Koreans and three Americans dead. | The Japanese prevail in getting Korea to sign the Treaty of Ganghwa, formally opening up three of the nation's ports – Busan, Incheon and Wonsan – to international trade. | A military insurrection in Seoul, supported by the Daewongun, seeks to overthrow King Gojong and his reform-minded Queen Min. The couple escape the city in disguise, but return when support arrives from China. |

KING SEJONG'S GIFT

Hangeul is a phonetic script: concise, elegant and considered one of the most scientific in the world in rendering sounds. It was developed in 1443, during the reign of Korea's greatest king, Sejong, as a way of increasing literacy since it is much simpler and easier to learn than Chinese characters. But the Confucian elite opposed its wide use, hoping to keep the government exams as difficult as possible so that only aristocratic children had the time and money to pass.

Hangeul didn't come into general use until after 1945, and then only in North Korea; South Korea used a Sino-Korean script requiring the mastery of thousands of Chinese characters until the 1990s. Today, though, Chinese characters have mostly disappeared from Korea's public space, to the consternation of Chinese and Japanese travellers who used to be able to read all the street and commercial signs. King Sejong's face, meanwhile, is etched on the W10,000 note.

Everlasting Flower: A History of Korea by Keith Pratt (2007) is a very readable text that takes a cultural approach to Korea's history, focusing partly on the development of its arts.

The aristocrats were enthusiastic Confucianists, as we have seen, adopting Chinese painting, poetry, music, statecraft and philosophy. The complicated Chinese script was used for virtually all government and cultural activities throughout the Joseon period, even though the native alphabet, *hangeul*, was an outstanding cultural achievement.

ROYAL POMP & CEREMONY

Many of the premier cultural attractions in Korea today, such as Seoul's Gyeongbokgung (p106), Namdaemun (p108) and Changdeokgung (p105), are imperial relics of the long-lived Joseon dynasty. They are windows into a time in Korea's history when absolute monarchs ruled. Pomp and ritual also became an essential aspect of royal power, with attention to ritual and protocol developed into an art form. Koreans appeared to break sharply with this royal system in the 20th century; but when we look at the ruling system in North Korea, or the families that run most of South Korea's major corporations, we see the family and hereditary principles of the old system continuing in modern form.

The fascinating *Times Past in Korea: An Illustrated Collection of Encounters, Customs and Daily Life Recorded by Foreign Visitors* (2003) was compiled by Martin Uden, the British ambassador to South Korea – also read his blog at http://blogs.fco.gov.uk/roller/uden/.

It is difficult to imagine the wealth, power and status of Joseon kings in these more democratic times. The main palace, Gyeongbokgung, contained 800 buildings and over 200 gates; in 1900, for example, palace costs accounted for 10% of all government expenditures. In the royal household were 400 eunuchs, 500 ladies-in-waiting, 800 other court ladies and 70 *gisaeng* (female entertainers who were expert singers and dancers). Only women and eunuchs were allowed to live inside the palace – male servants, guards, officials and visitors had to leave at sunset. Most of the women lived like nuns and never left the palace. A *yangban* woman had to be married for years before daring to move in the outer world of society, and then only in a cocoon of clothing inside a cloistered sedan chair, carried by her slaves. In the late 19th century foreigners witnessed these same cloistered upper-class women, clothed and

1884	1894	1895
Progressive forces, backed by Japan, attempt a coup at the royal palace. Again Queen Min calls on the Chinese for help and the revolt is suppressed after three days.	Peasant disillusionment with the corrupt *yangban* upper classes leads to the Donghak Rebellion. The rebels are defeated but the Joseon court responds with the Gabo Reform, abolishing slavery among other sweeping changes.	Queen Min is assassinated at the Gyeongbok palace. Posthumously named Empress Myeongseong, Min is considered a national heroine for her progressive reforms and attempts to maintain Korea's independence.

swaddled from head to toe, wearing a green mantle like the Middle Eastern *chador* (robe) over their heads and bringing the folds across the face, leaving only the eyes exposed. They would come out after the nightly curfew, after the bells rang and the city gates were closed against tigers, and find a bit of freedom in the darkness.

TRIBUTE TO CHINA

Starting from 1637, three official embassies travelled to China every year, at the New Year, the birthday of the emperor and the birthday of the crown prince. Later they were supplemented with another mission at the winter solstice. A new king in Korea or the death of an emperor in China occasioned special missions, since the Korean kings sought approval of the Chinese Son of Heaven. From 1637 until the end of the practice in 1881, Korea sent a total of 435 special embassies and missions to China. The tribute was a tangible symbol of Korea's formal status, which was subordinate to China's, with Korea's kings needing (and wanting) the legitimacy of investiture by the Chinese emperor. The emperor sent gifts in return, even if they did not match what he received, and the lavish hospitality provided to the Chinese emissaries when they came to Seoul was very expensive and could take up 15% of the government's revenue. But the envoys were not allowed to visit the interior of the country, and had to take a single route from the border through Pyongyang and down to Seoul. The Chinese would arrive at Seodaemun, the West Gate of Seoul (demolished by the Japanese in 1915) and be greeted by the king. In 1898 Koreans erected the Independence Gate (located down the road from where the old West Gate stood), when King Gojong declared Korea to be an empire and himself to be Emperor Gwangmu.

The missions were also covers for a lot of Sino-Korean trade. Goods carried to the Forbidden Palace in Beijing varied, but one agreement listed 100 tael of gold and 1000 tael of silver (a tael weighed about 40g, so that meant 4kg of gold and 40kg of silver). The emperor was also to receive 100 tiger skins, 100 deer skins and 400 other animal skins. Also on the gift list were a thousand packs of green tea, rice, ginseng, pine seeds and other Korean delicacies; not to mention horses, swords and buffalo-horn bows; and large quantities of paper, cotton, ramie cloth (an almost transparent textile made from bark) and floral-patterned straw mats from Ganghwa-do. Less publicised were the eunuchs and virgins destined for the emperor's vast harem. In return the Chinese emperor would send the best-quality silk, herbal medicines, porcelain pottery and a library of books, amounting to hundreds of volumes. Tribute trade was thus a cultural and economic exchange between the two countries.

The 300-strong tribute party took one to two months to cover the 1200km route to Beijing, and spent the same amount of time there before beginning the arduous journey home. The embassy included generals, scholars, painters, doctors, interpreters, heralds, secretaries, grooms, umbrella holders and sedan-chair carriers. Jesuit missionaries to Beijing in the 16th century (like foreigners in China today who encounter North Koreans) thought the Koreans they saw in the capital were surly, standoffish and all too self-contained – just as Europeans in the same city three centuries later spoke of 'these strangely-coated people, so proud, so thoroughly uninterested in strangers, so exclusive, so content to go their own way'.

1897	1900	1905
As an independence movement grows in Korea, King Gojong declares the founding of the Korean Empire, formalising the end of the country's ties to China.	The modernisation of Korea's economy and society continues with the opening of a railroad between the port of Incheon and Seoul. In the capital an electricity company provides public lighting and a streetcar system.	The Treaty of Portsmouth formally ends the Russo-Japanese war over Manchuria and Korea. Russia recognises Korea as part of Japan's sphere of influence, further imperilling Korea's attempts to become independent.

LIVES OF THE EUNUCHS

The eunuchs were the most extraordinary people. They could become as powerful as leading government officials because they were around the king and the royal family 24 hours a day. All access to the king was through them, as they were the royal bodyguards and responsible for the safety of their master. This was an easy way to earn money and they usually exploited it to the full. These bodyguard eunuchs, toughened by a harsh training regime of martial arts, were also personal servants to the king and even nursemaids to the royal children. They played so many roles that life must have been very stressful for them, particularly as any mistake could lead to horrific physical punishments.

Although often illiterate and uneducated, a few became important advisors to the king, attaining high government positions and amassing great wealth. Most were from poor families and their greed for money was a national scandal. Eunuchs were supposed to serve the king with total devotion, like monks serving Buddha, never thinking about mundane matters like money or status.

A surprising aspect is that the eunuchs were usually married and adopted young eunuch boys who they brought up as their sons to follow in their footsteps. The eunuch in charge of the king's health would pass on his medical knowledge to his 'son'. Under the Confucian system not only gays but also eunuchs had to get married. The system continued until 1910 when the country's new Japanese rulers summoned all the eunuchs to Deoksugung and dismissed them from government service.

Isabella Bird Bishop visited the newly restored Gyeongbokgung in 1895 and noted in *Korea and Her Neighbours:* 'What with 800 troops, 1500 attendants and officials of all descriptions, courtiers and ministers and their attendants, secretaries, messengers and hangers-on, the vast enclosure of the palace seemed as crowded and populated as the city itself'.

Joseon Royal Court Culture by Shin Myung-ho (2004) details the facts about the unique Confucian royal-court lifestyle. Based on primary sources, the superbly illustrated book gives a human context to the now-empty palaces.

In James Scarth Gale's *History of the Korean People,* Harriet Heron Gale, a missionary, observed the pampered life of the crown prince: 'An army of attendants and maids in long blue silk shirts and yellow jackets hover about his little kingship all day long, powdering his face, painting his lips and finger tips, shaving the top of his head, pulling out his eyebrows, cutting his food into the daintiest of morsels, fanning him with monstrous long-handled fans, never leaving him alone for a moment…even at night guarding and watching by his bedside, singing him to sleep with a queer little lullaby'.

Because the eunuchs were the only 'male' staff allowed to live inside the palaces, they were privy to all the secrets of the state, and had considerable influence because they waited upon the king.

KOREA & JAPAN

In 2005 the South Korean president refused to hold a summit meeting with the Japanese prime minister because the latter insisted on visiting the

1907	**1909**	**1910**
Having angered Japan by trying to drum up international support for his sovereignty over Korea, Gojong is forced to abdicate in favour of his son Sunjong, who becomes the second and last Emperor of Korea.	Independence activist An Jung-geun assassinates Hirobumi Ito, Korea's ex-Resident-General, at the train station in Harbin, Manchuria. It provides the excuse for Japan to move on fully annexing the Korean peninsula.	Although the Emperor refuses to sign the Japan-Korea Annexation Treaty, Japan effectively annexes Korea in August, starting 35 years of colonial rule. Terauchi Masatake is first Japanese Governor General of Korea.

Yasukuni shrine, a memorial to Japan's war dead that happened to include Class A war criminals from WWII, and because all year long both countries squabbled over the ownership of an uninhabited pile of rocks in the East Sea, known as Dok-do (that is, Takeshima). Relations between these two countries have not always been difficult and controversial, but certainly they have been for at least four centuries, since Hideyoshi sought to subdue Korea on the way to conquering China.

In 1592, 150,000 well-armed Japanese troops, divided into nine armies, rampaged throughout Korea looting, raping and killing. Palaces and temples were burnt to the ground and priceless cultural treasures were destroyed or stolen. Entire villages of ceramic potters were shipped back to Japan, along with thousands of ears clipped from dead Koreans, which were piled into a mound in Japan, covered over and retained into modern times as a memorial to this war. A series of brilliant naval victories by Admiral Yi Sun-sin, using iron-clad warships called *geobukseon* (turtle ships), helped to turn the tide against the Japanese. Ming troops also arrived from China, and by 1597 the Japanese were forced to withdraw. A year later Hideyoshi died a broken man. Stout resistance on land and sea thwarted Japanese ambitions to dominate Asia, but only at the cost of massive destruction and economic dislocation in Korea.

Japan's ambitions to seize Korea resurfaced 300 years later, at the end of the 19th century, when Japan suddenly rose up as the first modern great power in Asia. Seizing on the Donghak peasant rebellion in Korea, Japan instigated war with China, defeating it in 1895. After another decade of imperial rivalry over Korea, Japan smashed Russia in lightning naval and land attacks, stunning the world because a 'yellow' country had defeated a 'white' power.

With both China and Russia taken care of Japan was in a secure position to realise its territorial ambitions with regard to Korea, which became a Japanese protectorate in 1905 and a colony in 1910, with the acquiescence of all the great powers. It was a strange colony, coming 'late' in world time, after most of the world had been divided up, and after progressive calls had emerged to dismantle the entire colonial system. Furthermore Korea had most of the prerequisites for nationhood long before most other countries: common ethnicity, language and culture, and well-recognised national boundaries since the 10th century. So the Japanese engaged in substitution after 1910: exchanging a Japanese ruling elite for the Korean *yangban* scholar-officials; instituting central coordination for the old government administration; exchanging Japanese modern education for the Confucian classics; building Japanese capital and expertise in place of the Korean versions – Japanese talent for Korean talent; eventually even replacing the Korean language with Japanese.

Koreans never thanked the Japanese for these substitutions and did not credit Japan with creations. Instead they saw Japan as snatching away the

Wearing a topknot was a traditional male custom that was particularly widespread during Korea's pleasant relations with the Ming dynasty – and then it became a symbol of 'Ming loyalists' in Korea after that dynasty fell. In 1895 King Gojong had his topknot cut off, but conservatives did not follow his example or share his enthusiasm for reforms.

Soup, fish, quail, pheasant, stuffed and rolled beef, vegetables, creams, glacé walnuts, fruits, claret and coffee were on the menu when Isabella Bird Bishop had dinner with King Gojong and Queen Min.

Eunuch (1968), an artistic film directed by Shin Sang-ok, is about a lady who is forced by her father to become the king's concubine although she loves someone else. The film depicts the inner sanctum in those now empty and dusty palaces.

1919	**1926**	**1929**
Following Emperor Gojong's death in January, the March 1st Movement sees millions of Koreans in nonviolent nationwide protests against Japanese rule. A declaration of Independence is read out in Seoul's Tapgol Park.	Emperor Sunjong dies. His half-brother Crown Prince Euimin, who had married into a branch of the Japanese royal family, is proclaimed King Ri of Korea by the Japanese.	A nationwide student uprising in November leads to the strengthening of Japanese military rule in 1931, after which freedom of the press and expression are curbed.

ADMIRAL YI: KOREA'S NAVAL HERO

Admiral Yi Sun-sin is one of Korea's most celebrated historical figures, a 16th-century naval hero who inflicted a series of defeats on the Japanese before he was killed in battle in 1598. Based in Yeosu, Yi perfected the *geobukseon*, or turtle ship, a warship protected with iron sheets and spikes against the Japanese 'grapple and board' naval tactics. Although only a handful were deployed, *geobukseon* replicas can be found on Odong-do (p271) and in museums throughout the country, including Seoul's War Memorial Museum (p111).

The standard Korean warship was the flat-bottomed, double-decked *panokseon*, powered by two sails and hard-working oarsmen. It was stronger and more manoeuvrable than the Japanese warships and had more cannons. With these advantages, clever tactics and an intimate knowledge of the complex patterns of tides and currents around the numerous islands and narrow channels off the southern coast, Admiral Yi was able to defeat the Japanese time and time again. His forces sank hundreds of Japanese ships and thwarted Japan's ambition to seize Korea and use it as a base for the conquest of China.

ancien regime, Korea's sovereignty and independence, its indigenous if incipient modernisation and, above all, its national dignity. Most Koreans never saw Japanese rule as anything but illegitimate and humiliating. Furthermore the very closeness of the two nations – in geography, in common Chinese civilisational influences, and in levels of development until the 19th century – made Japanese dominance all the more galling to Koreans and gave a peculiar intensity to the relationship, a hate/respect dynamic that suggested to Koreans, 'there but for accidents of history go we'.

At the Court of Korea by William Franklin Sands gives a first-hand account of King Gojong and his government between 1890 and 1910.

The result: neither Korea nor Japan has ever gotten over it. In the North countless films and TV programs still focus on atrocities committed by the Japanese during their rule, and for decades the descendants of Koreans deemed by the government to have collaborated with the Japanese occupation authorities were subject to severe discrimination. South Korea, however, punished very few collaborators, partly because the US Occupation (1945–48) reemployed so many of them, and partly because they were needed in the fight against communism.

The Dawn of Modern Korea by Andrei Lankov (2007) is a fascinating, accessible look at early-20th-century Korea and the cultural and social impacts of Westernisation as King Gojong tried to modernise his tradition-bound hermit kingdom.

A certain amount of Korean collaboration with the Japanese was unavoidable given the ruthless nature of the regime under the Japanese colonialists, and then in the last decade of colonial rule when Japan's expansion across Asia caused a shortage of experts and professionals throughout the empire. Ambitious Koreans found new careers opening to them just at the most oppressive point in this colony's history, as Koreans were commanded to change their names and not speak Korean, and millions of Koreans were used as mobile human fodder by the Japanese. Koreans constituted almost half of the hated National Police, and young Korean officers (including Park Chung-hee, who seized power in 1961), and Kim Jae-gyu (who, as

1938	1945	1948
Labour shortages in Japan due to conscription of males to the military result in over 800,000 Koreans emigrating there, either by choice or by force.	With the Allied victory in WWII, Korea is liberated from Japan and divided into two protectorates – the Soviets handling the North and the US the South.	The Republic of Korea is founded in the southern part of the peninsula, with Seoul designated the capital city. The Democratic People's Republic of Korea (DPRK, or North Korea) is also founded.

intelligence chief, assassinated Park in 1979) joined the aggressive Japanese army in Manchuria.

Pro-Japanese *yangban* were rewarded with special titles, and some of Korea's greatest early nationalists, like Yi Gwang-su, were forced into public support of Japan's empire. Although collaboration was an inevitable result of the repression of the Japanese occupation, it was never punished or fully and frankly debated in South Korea, leaving the problem to fester until 2004, when the government finally launched an official investigation of collaboration – along with estimates that upwards of 90% of the pre-1990 South Korea elite had ties to collaborationist families or individuals.

Westernised Japanese and Korean bureaucrats ran the colonial government. They implemented policies that developed industries and modernised the administration, but always in the interests of Japan. Modern textile, steel and chemical industries emerged along with new railroads, highways and ports. Koreans never thanked Japan for any of this, but it left Korea much more developed in 1945 than, say, Vietnam under the French. Still, the main trauma of the occupation was probably psychological rather than political or economic, because Japan tried to destroy the Korean sense of national identity.

The burst of consumerism that came to the world in the 1920s meant that Koreans shopped in Japanese department stores, banked at Japanese banks, drank Japanese beer, travelled on the Japanese-run railway and often dreamed of attending a Tokyo university.

By 1940 the Japanese owned 40% of the land and there were 700,000 Japanese living and working in Korea – an enormous number compared to most other countries. But among large landowners, many were as likely to be Korean as Japanese; most peasants were tenant farmers working their land. Upwards of three million Korean men and women were uprooted from their homes and sent to work as miners, farm labourers, factory workers and soldiers abroad, mainly in Japan and Manchukuo, the Japanese colony in northeast China. Over 130,000 Korean miners in Japan – men and women – worked 12-hour days, were paid wages well under what Japanese miners earned, were poorly fed and were subjected to brutal, club-wielding overseers. The worst aspect of this massive mobilisation, however, came in the form

The Dongnimmun (Independence Gate), built in 1898 in Seoul by the Independence Club, stands where envoys from Chinese emperors used to be officially welcomed to the city.

My Innocent Uncle by Chae Man-shik (2003) is a shocking short story, written in a direct, colloquial style, that portrays a pro-Japanese Korean opportunist who refers to Japan as his home country and wants to marry a Japanese girl. His uncle is innocent of such treacherous views but his opposition to Japanese rule is ineffective.

COMMEMORATING THE INDEPENDENCE MOVEMENT

In South Korea, March 1 is a huge national holiday, honouring the day in 1919 when the death of ex-king Gojong and the unveiling of a Korean declaration of independence sparked massive pro-independence demonstrations throughout the country. The protests were ruthlessly suppressed, but still lasted for months. When it was over the Japanese claimed that 500 were killed, 1400 injured and 12,000 arrested, but Korean estimates put the casualties at 10 times these figures.

1950	**1953**	**1960**
North Korea stages a surprise invasion of the South, triggering the Korean War. North Korean forces occupy Seoul for 90 days before UN forces led by US and South Korean troops mount a counterattack.	The armistice ending the Korean War is signed by the US and North Korea, but not South Korea, leaving the two countries eyeing each other uneasily over the DMZ around the 38th parallel.	Popular protest ousts President Rhee Syngman; attempts at democratic rule fail – a military coup topples the unstable elected government and installs General Park Chung-hee into power in 1961.

THE HOUSE OF SHARING Simon Richmond

An hour's journey south of Seoul, in bucolic countryside, is the **House of Sharing** (www.house ofsharing.org), a very special retirement home. Here live eight women, now in their late 80s or early 90s, who were forced to work in Japanese military brothels across Asia before and during WWII. 'Comfort women' is the euphemism coined by the Japanese military for these women and their existence started to come to international attention in the early 1990s through the courageous testimonies of the victims – 70% of whom were Korean – and their demand for official recognition and compensation from the Japanese government. A study by the UN has put the number of women involved at around 210,000 (the Japanese government claims the figure was only 50,000).

'Violence, starvation, rape, disease, torture and death – these were the common experiences of the so-called "comfort women",' says Heather Evans, one of the volunteer guides leading the monthly English-language tour around the House of Sharing's museum. Most of them were aged between 13 and 16, forced to service between 30 and 40 soldiers a day. At the House of Sharing they prefer the respectful term *halmoni,* which means grandmother. Described as activists, the *halmoni* often take part in the protests held every Wednesday at noon outside Seoul's Japanese embassy (Map pp96–7). The strain of having to do this has taken its toll and so now the old women do not regularly meet visitors to the House of Sharing to share their stories. Instead, video documentaries about them are screened and discussions are held about their plight and the ongoing sexual trafficking of women around the world. The videos and anecdotes from the guides paint these frail, sometimes crotchety women as pillars of strength who after a lifetime of shame and sorrow have chosen to spend their twilight years as campaigners for social justice.

'We must record these things that were forced upon us.' These words by Kim Hak Soon, one of the first Korean *halmoni* to testify about her experiences, introduces the museum exhibition which includes a display of the artworks created by the *halmoni* that reflect their feelings and experiences. It's a heavy-going experience but one not without a sense of hope – both at the resilience of the human spirit and the prospect for reconciliation. The greatest number of visitors to the House of Sharing come from Japan and every year a Peace Road Program brings Korean and Japanese students together to help further understanding of their countries' painfully en-twined history and how they might in future be better neighbours.

of 'comfort women' – the hundreds of thousands of young Korean women who were forced to work as sex slaves for the Japanese armed forces (see the boxed text, above).

It was Korea's darkest hour but Korean guerrilla groups continued to fight Japan in Manchukuo; they were allied with Chinese guerrillas but Koreans still constituted by far the largest ethnic group. This is where we find Kim Il-sung, who began fighting the Japanese around the time they proclaimed the puppet state of Manchukuo in 1932 and continued into the early 1940s. After murderous counter-insurgency campaigns (participated in by many Koreans), the guerrillas numbered only about 200. In 1945 they returned

The Korean Sohn Kee-chung won the gold medal for the marathon at the 1936 Berlin Olympics but he was forced to compete as Kitei Son under the flag of Japan, Korea's occupying power.

1963	**1972**	**1979**
The Democratic Republican Party, a political vehicle for Park, wins the general election, as it does again in 1967. The constitution is amended so Park can run for a third term of office in 1971.	Park dissolves parliament and suspends the constitution. In December he gains approval for a new constitution that turns his presidency into a virtual dictatorship. He's re-elected with no opposition in 1978.	After surviving a couple of assassination attempts (one of which had killed his wife), Park is finally shot dead by the trusted head of his own Central Intelligence Agency.

to northern Korea and constituted the ruling elite from that point down to the present.

Japan's surrender to the Allies in 1945 opened a new chapter in the stormy relationship between the two countries. Thanks to a very soft peace and munificent American support, Japan began growing rapidly in the early 1950s. South Korea got going in the mid-1960s, and today companies and workers in both countries battle each other to produce the best ships, cars, steel products, computer chips, mobile phones, flat-screen TVs and other electronic equipment. The new rivalry is a never-ending competition for world markets, just as sports became another modern-day battleground to decide who is top dog.

THE KOREAN WAR

In the immediate aftermath of the obliteration of Nagasaki, three Americans in the War Department (including Dean Rusk, later Secretary of State) drew a fateful line at the 38th parallel in Korea, dividing this nation that had a unitary integrity going back to antiquity. The line was supposed to demarcate the areas in which American and Soviet forces would receive the Japanese surrender, but Rusk later acknowledged that he did not trust the Russians and wanted to get the nerve centre of the country, Seoul, in the American zone. He consulted no Koreans, no allies and not even the president in making this decision. But it followed on from three years of State Department planning in which an American occupation of part or all of Korea was seen as crucial to the postwar security of Japan and the Pacific. The US then set up a three-year military government in southern Korea that deeply shaped postwar Korean history.

The Soviets came in with fewer concrete plans for Korea and moved more slowly than the Americans in setting up an administration. They thought Kim Il-sung would be good as a defence minister in a new government, but sought to get him and other communists to work together with Christian nationalist figures like Jo Man-sik. Soon, however, the Cold War rivalry overshadowed everything in Korea, as the Americans turned to Rhee Syngman (an elderly patriot who had lived in the US for 35 years) and the Russians to Kim Il-sung.

By 1948 Rhee and Kim had both established separate republics and by the end of the year Soviet troops had withdrawn, never to return again. American combat troops departed in June 1949, leaving behind a 500-man military advisory group. For the only time in its history since 1945, South Korea now had operational control of its own military forces. Within a year war had broken out and the US took back that control and has never relinquished it, illustrating that the US has always had a civil war deterrent in Korea: containing the enemy in the North and constraining the ally in the South.

www.kf.or.kr has video lectures on history (though the sound is not very good) and has a link to *Koreana*, an excellent quarterly magazine with some history articles.

www.twotigers.org has a dozen personal testimonies by Korean 'comfort women' that give a unique insight into their horrifying ordeals.

Under the Black Umbrella: Voices from Colonial Korea by Hildi Kang (2001) is a fascinating and accessible memoir of a Korean woman growing up under Japanese rule.

1980	**1987**	**1988**
The military brutally suppresses a prodemocracy uprising in the southern city of Gwangju, killing at least 154 civilians and wounding or arresting over 4000 others.	Following sweeping national protests, with the strongest concentration in Seoul, Korea's last military dictatorship, under Chun Doo-hwan, steps down to allow democratic elections.	Seoul hosts the Olympic Summer Games, bulldozing and/or concealing slums to build a huge Olympic park and major expressway. Publication of Lonely Planet's first guide to Korea.

In 1949 both sides sought external support to mount a war against the other side, and the North succeeded where the South failed. Its greatest strength came from tens of thousands of Koreans who had been sent to fight in China's civil war, and who returned to North Korea in 1949 and 1950. Kim Il-sung also played Stalin off against Mao Zedong to get military aid and a critical independent space for himself, so that when he invaded he could count on one or both powers to bail him out if things went badly. After years of guerrilla war in the South (fought almost entirely by southerners) and much border fighting in 1949 (with both sides at fault), Kim launched a surprise invasion on 25 June 1950, when he peeled several divisions off in the midst of summer war games; many high officers were unaware of the war plan. Seoul fell in three days, and soon North Korea was at war with the US.

The Korean War by Max Hastings (1988) sees the British historian give a pro-American general overview of the 'forgotten war'.

The Americans responded by getting the UN to condemn the attack and gaining commitments from 16 other countries, although Americans almost always bore the brunt of the fighting, and only British and Turkish combat forces had a substantial role. The war went badly for the UN at first, and its troops were soon pushed far back into a small pocket around Busan (Pusan). But following a daring landing at Incheon (Inchon) under the command of General Douglas MacArthur, North Korean forces were pushed back above the 38th parallel.

The question then became, 'was the war over?' South Korea's sovereignty had been restored and UN leaders wanted to call it a victory. But for the previous year, high officials in the Truman administration had been debating a more 'positive' strategy than containment, namely 'rollback' or liberation, and so Truman decided to march north to overthrow Kim's regime. Kim's long-time relations with Chinese communists bailed his chestnuts out of the fire when Mao committed a huge number of soldiers, but now the US was at war with China.

By New Year's Eve US forces were pushed back below the 38th parallel, and the communists were about to launch an offensive that would soon retake Seoul. This shook America and its allies to the core, Truman declared a national emergency, and WWIII seemed to be at the doorstep. But Mao did not want general war with the US, and did not try to push the UN forces off the peninsula. By spring 1951 the fighting had stabilised roughly along the lines where the war ended. Truce talks began and dragged on for two years, amid massive trench warfare along the lines. These battles created the Demilitarized Zone (DMZ) and the truce talks bequeathed the Quonset huts at Panmunjom (p152), where both sides have met periodically ever since to exchange heated rhetoric and where millions of tourists have visited.

At the end of the war, Korea lay in ruins. Seoul had changed hands no less than four times and was badly damaged, but many prewar buildings remained sufficiently intact to rebuild them much as they were. The US Air

1991	**1992**	**1994**
Following two years of talks, an Agreement of Reconciliation is signed between Seoul and Pyongyang. One of the aims is to make the Korean peninsula nuclear free.	The first civilian to hold the office since 1960, Kim Young-sam is elected president, ushering in a more democratic political era. During his five-year term he presides over a massive anti-corruption campaign.	During negotiations with the Clinton administration over its nuclear program, prior to what would have been a historic summit with Kim Young-sam, North Korea's supreme leader Kim Il-sung dies of a heart attack.

Force pounded the North for three years until all of its cities were destroyed and some were completely demolished, leaving the urban population to live, work and go to school underground, like cavemen. Millions of Koreans died (probably three million, two-thirds of them in the North), millions more were left homeless, industries were destroyed and the entire country was massively demoralised, because the bloodletting had only restored the status quo. Of the UN troops, 37,000 were killed (about 35,000 of them Americans) and 120,000 wounded.

POSTWAR RECOVERY

The 1950s were a time of depressing stagnation for the South but rapid industrial growth for the North. Then, over the next 30 years, both Koreas underwent rapid industrial growth. However, by the 1990s huge economic disparities had emerged. The North experienced depressing stagnation that led finally to famine and massive death, while the South emerged as an economic power ranked 11th in the world, with roughly the GNP of Spain. The North's industrial growth was as fast as any in the world from the mid-1950s into the mid-1970s, and even in the early 1980s its per capita GNP was about the same as the South's. But then the South began to build an enormous lead that soon became insurmountable.

This great triumph came at enormous cost, as South Koreans worked the longest hours in the industrial world for decades and suffered under one military dictatorship after another. Corrupt, autocratic rulers censored the media, imprisoned and tortured political opponents, manipulated elections and continually changed the country's constitution to suit themselves; meanwhile Washington backed them up (except for a brief moment in the 1960s) and never did more than issue tepid protests at their authoritarian rule. Student protests and less-frequent trade-union street protests were often violent, as were the police or military forces sent to suppress them. But slowly a democratisation movement built strength across the society.

When the Korean War ended in 1953, Rhee Syngman continued his dictatorial rule until 1961, when he and his wife fled to Hawaii following widespread demonstrations against him that included university professors demonstrating in the streets of Seoul. Ordinary people were finally free to take revenge against hated policemen who had served the Japanese. Following a military coup later in 1961, Park Chung-hee ruled with an iron fist until the Kennedy administration demanded that he hold elections; he won three of them in 1963, 1967 and 1971 partly by spreading enormous amounts of money around (peasants would get white envelopes full of cash for voting).

In spite of this, the democracy activist Kim Dae-jung nearly beat him in 1971, garnering 46% of the vote. That led Park to declare martial law and make himself president for life. Amid massive demonstrations in 1979 his

Silmido is a 2003 thriller film loosely based on events in the 1960s when South Korean agents were trained on the island of Silmi-do for an operation to assassinate North Korean leader Kim Il-sung.

1996	1997	1998
Korea achieves US$10,000 per capita income and puts two ex-presidents, Chun Doo-hwan and Roh Tae-woo, on trial. Both are jailed on corruption charges but pardoned a year later by President-elect Kim Dae-jung.	Long-time democracy champion Kim Dae-jung is elected president in the midst of a region-wide economic crisis. The International Monetary Fund offers the country a $57 million bailout.	Kim Jong-il takes full power on the 50th anniversary of the founding of North Korea at the same time as his deceased father is proclaimed the country's 'eternal leader'.

own intelligence chief, Kim Jae-gyu, shot him dead over dinner one night, in an episode never fully explained. This was followed by five months of democratic discussion until Chun Doo-hwan, a protégé of Park, moved to take full power. In response the citizens of Gwangju took to the streets in May 1980. The military response was so brutal and wanton (see the boxed text, p265) that it became a touchstone in Korean life, marking an entire generation of young people.

SUNSHINE POLICY

Finally, in 1992, a civilian, Kim Young-sam, won election and began to build a real democracy. Although a charter member of the old ruling groups, Kim had resigned his National Assembly seat in the 1960s when Rhee tried to amend the constitution and had since been a thorn in the side of the military governments along with Kim Dae-jung. Among his first acts as president were to launch an anti-corruption crusade, free thousands of political prisoners and put Chun Doo-hwan on trial. The former president's conviction of treason and monumental corruption was a great victory for the democratic movement. One of the strongest labour movements in the world soon emerged, and when former dissident Kim Dae-jung was elected at the end of 1997, all the protests and suffering and killing seemed finally to have been worthwhile.

Kim was ideally poised to solve the deep economic downturn that hit Korea in 1997, as part of the Asian financial crisis. The IMF demanded reforms of the conglomerates, or *jaebeol* (p50), as the price for its $55 million bailout, and Kim had long called for restructuring the conglomerates and their cronyism with the banks and the government. By 1999 the economy was growing again.

> Read a short biography of Nobel Peace Prize winner Kim Dae-jung at http://nobelprize.org/nobel_prizes/peace/laureates/2000/dae-jung-bio.html.

In 1998 Kim also began to roll out a 'Sunshine Policy' aimed at reconciliation with North Korea, if not reunification. Within a year Pyongyang had responded, various economic and cultural exchanges began, and in June 2000 the two presidents met at a summit for the first time since 1945. Often seen by critics as appeasement of the North, this engagement policy was predicated on the realist principles that the North was not going to collapse and so had to be dealt with as it is, and that the North would not object to the continued presence of US troops in the South during the long process of reconciliation if the US normalised relations with the North – something that Kim Jong-il acknowledged in his historic summit meeting with Kim Dae-jung in June 2000.

Since 2000 tens of thousands of South Koreans have visited the North and big southern firms have established joint ventures using northern labour in a purpose-built industrial complex at Kaesong. There have also been some heartbreakingly brief reunions between family members separated by the conflict 50 years ago.

2000	2002	2003
The June summit between Kim Dae-jung and Kim Jong-il in Pyongyang is the first ever meeting on such a level by the two countries. The same year Kim Dae-jung is awarded the Nobel Peace Prize.	Human rights lawyer Roh Moo-hyun is elected South Korea's 16th president and continues his predecessor's 'Sunshine Policy' of engagement with the North. South Korea and Japan co-host soccer's World Cup.	Following North Korea's withdrawal from the Nuclear Non-Proliferation Treaty, the first round of the so-called 'six-party talks' between North and South Korea, China, Japan, Russia and the US begin in Beijing.

AFTER KIM

When President Kim retired after his five-year term his party selected a virtual unknown, Roh Moo-hyun, a self-taught lawyer who had defended many dissidents in the darkest periods of the 1980s. To the surprise of many, including officials in Washington, he narrowly won the 2002 election and represented the rise to power of a generation that had nothing to do with the political system that emerged in 1945 (even Kim Dae-jung had been active in the 1940s). That generation was mostly middle-aged, having gone to school in the 1980s with indelible images of conflict on their campuses and American backing for Chun Doo-hwan. The result was a growing estrangement between Seoul and Washington, really for the first time in the relationship.

An English version of the Korean President's official website can be found at http://english.president.go.kr/main.php.

Roh continued Kim's sunshine policy of engagement with the North but his mismanagement of the economy and decision to send South Korean troops to Iraq saw his public support plummet. The opposition tried to impeach Roh when, ahead of national parliamentary elections in 2004, he voiced support for the new Uri Party – a technical violation of a constitutional provision for the president to remain impartial. The impeachment failed but Roh's popularity continued to slip and the Uri Party, suffering several defeats by association with the president, chose to distance itself from him by reforming as the Democratic Party.

The end result was a swing to the right that saw Lee Myung-bak of the Grand National Party elected president in 2007, and Roh retire to the village of Bongha, his birthplace in Gyeongsangnam-do. A year and a half later, as a corruption investigation zeroed in on his family and former aides, Roh committed suicide by jumping off a cliff behind the village. The national shock at this sad turn of events rebounded on President Lee who was already suffering public rebuke for opening Korea to imports of US beef (p13).

THE NUCLEAR QUESTION

After a tumultuous 20th century, South Korea is by any measure shaping up to be one of the star performers of the 21st century. Its top companies such as Samsung, LG and Hyundai make products the world wants. Koreans have taken so quickly to the internet that it is now possibly the most wired nation on earth. The talented younger generation has produced such a dynamic pop culture that *hallyu* (the 'Korean Wave') is a huge phenomenon in China, Japan and Southeast Asia, and is gaining popularity in the West.

Go to the Korea Society's website (www. koreasociety.org) to listen to podcasts about Korean current affairs and the country's recent history.

The single anachronism in Korea's progress, however, remains the continuing dispute over the North's nuclear programs. The Clinton and Bush administrations pursued very different policies, with Clinton's people talking directly to the North and getting an eight-year freeze on its plutonium facility, and a near buy-out of its medium and long-range missiles in late 2000. The Bush administration refused bilateral talks with the North and placed it in an 'axis of evil' along with Iraq and Iran. The North responded

2005	2006	2007
The death of King Gojong's grandson Lee Gu in Tokyo at the age of 74 ends the Joseon dynasty's bloodline and any possibility of the return of a monarchy in Korea.	In October North Korea claim to have successfully conducted an underground nuclear test explosion. By the end of the month the country has agreed to rejoin the six-party disarmament talks.	Former South Korean Foreign Minister Ban Ki-moon becomes the eighth UN Secretary-General. Lee Myung-bak, ex-CEO of Hyundai Engineering & Construction and Seoul mayor, becomes South Korea's 17th president.

KOREA'S UNRULY GOVERNMENT

Since 1948 South Korea has had a presidential system of government. The president, who is head of state, head of government and commander-in-chief of the armed forces, is elected every five years and can only sit for one term of office: the current incumbent President Lee Myung-bak was elected in December 2007. He is also the leader of the Grand National Party (GNP), which controls the 299-seat National Assembly. Elections for the assembly are held every four years (the next will be in 2012) and result in 245 directly elected members and 54 appointed through proportional representation. The Democratic Party (DEP) is the main opposition party.

It all sounds pretty orderly and yet *Foreign Policy* magazine in September 2009 cited the National Assembly as one of 'the world's most unruly parliaments' where debates 'are frequently resolved with fists…or whatever heavy object is in the room.' Such were the scenes in 2004 when then President Roh Moo-hyun was being impeached. In 2008 angry opposition lawmakers reached for sledgehammers and electric saws to break into a locked committee room where the governing GNP was attempting to rush though a free trade bill. This was followed up by a 12-day sit-in before the matter was resolved. Fistfights again broke out during the heated debate in July 2009 over media privatisation.

---

by saying it feared a US attack along the lines of the invasion of Iraq and needed a nuclear deterrent to stop it.

Deeply worried about the possibility of conflict, in 2003 China sponsored six-party talks (China, Japan, Russia, the US and both Koreas) to get Washington and Pyongyang talking and negotiating. These intermittent discussions have yet to yield a significant result. On the contrary, the North has successfully tested nuclear bombs, first in October 2006, then again in May 2009. Towards the end of the same year the North began to make gestures that it was willing to re-enter negotiations over its nuclear program.

US President Barack Obama's brief visit to South Korea in November 2009 saw him and President Lee again offer the carrot of economic aid to the North if they returned to international negotiations on nuclear issues. Obama also squeezed a concession from Lee that South Korea would revisit the terms of the proposed free trade agreement with the US so that both countries may move towards ratifying the deal.

2008	2009	2010
President Lee faces his first major domestic challenge as 20,000 people take to the streets of Seoul to protest a government plan to resume US beef imports.	It's a year of mourning as former president Roh Moo-hyun, under investigation for corruption, commits suicide in May, then another former premier, Kim Dae-jung, succumbs to natural causes in August.	Seoul becomes World Design Capital, unveiling its new architectural centrepiece: Dongdaemun Design Plaza & Park, a futuristic complex by architect Zaha Hadid.

The Culture

THE NATIONAL PSYCHE

To understand what makes Koreans tick, you've got to know something about harmony and hierarchy. Harmony – a good feeling or sense of peacefulness – is a highly valued principle that often supersedes logic or truth in shaping social discourse, which can lead to intercultural misunderstandings. For instance, high regard for harmony explains why telling a white lie is rarely considered a social faux pas when the intention is to spare family, friends or colleagues from bad feelings. It also explains why displays of anger are considered the actions of an uneducated person worthy of disdain. Openly direct your wrath at someone – especially someone in authority – and you'll be found at fault regardless of the facts because harmony almost always trumps reason.

Hierarchy is related to harmony. Drawing on Confucian ideals, Koreans believe relationships operate harmoniously when everyone knows their position on the social ladder: the senior sits on the top rung while juniors occupy steps closer to the ground. Position on the hierarchy is largely determined by age or occupation, though other less weighty criteria such as the status of one's university might come into play. People who hold the senior position expect certain privileges including obedience, deep bows and the right to be addressed with honorific language. If you're the junior, well, do what you're told and everybody will get along famously.

Establishing a relationship implies that each person knows who is senior and junior. Once the pecking order has been established, harmony is created by performing the expected behavioural forms, such as using words demonstrating the correct level of respect and familiarity. That's why encounters with new acquaintances are fraught with social landmines: use an inappropriately low level of language and you may insult the other person and make yourself look uneducated.

Tactfully acquiring the information you need to position yourself on the social hierarchy demands social élan. People rarely use direct questions, such as 'How old are you?' Critical data of that nature is often provided by a third party before any meeting, otherwise it's a social two-step with indirect methods of enquiry like, 'I graduated from university in 1986. When did you finish school?'

Indirect questioning about age rarely applies between Koreans and foreign nationals. Often, it's quite blunt so don't be surprised if a new acquaintance asks, 'Excuse me, how old are you?' The intent is rarely malicious. It's just that Koreans can't quite feel comfortable unless they know where you sit on the social ladder.

The country's recovery from the ashes of the Korean War, construction workers on the job seven days a week, or computer-game addicts: they're all strands cut from the same cloth, the country's tenacious, pit-bull spirit. Once Koreans lock onto something, it's difficult to break away. Life is competitive and everything is taken seriously, be it ten-pin bowling, hiking or overseas corporate expansion.

Koreans are also fanatical about health. The millions of hikers who stream into the mountains at weekends are not only enjoying nature but are also keeping fit. Thousands of health foods and drinks are sold in markets and pharmacies, which stock traditional as well as Western medicines. Nearly every food claims to be a 'well-being' product or an aphrodisiac – 'good for stamina' is the local phrase.

The standard Korean greeting – *Anyeong hasseyo?* (안녕하세요) – doesn't mean 'How are you?' The literal translation is 'Are you peaceful?'

Korea has the world's seventh-highest road-fatality rate, 127 deaths per million people.

THE SOCIAL NICETIES

Most locals understand that visitors do not mean disrespect when they commit a minor social faux pas. But you will be even more warmly received when it is obvious that you've gone out of your way to burnish your graces, Korean style.

- Shoes off – In any residence, temple, guesthouse or Korean-style restaurant, leave your shoes at the door. And socks are better than bare feet.

- Artful bow – Though you may see members of the royal court drop to the ground to greet the king on Korean TV dramas, don't get inspired. A quick, short bow – essentially a nod of the head – is most respectful for meetings and departures.

- Use your hands – Give and receive any object using both hands – especially money and gifts.

- Giving gifts – When you visit someone at their home, bring along a little token of your appreciation, such as flowers, chocolates, fruit, a cake from the local bakery or a bottle of wine. It's also a nice gesture to gift-wrap your offering. Your host may at first strongly refuse your gift. Don't worry: this is a gesture of graciousness. Keep insisting, and they will accept it 'reluctantly'. For the same reason, your host will not open the package immediately.

- Get over here – Don't beckon someone using your forefinger. Place your hand out, palm down (palm up is how you call your pet), and flutter all your fingers at once.

- Loss of face – A mishandled remark or potentially awkward scene should be smoothed over as soon as possible, and if you sense someone actively trying to change the subject, go with the flow. An argument or any situation that could lead to embarrassment should be avoided at all costs.

- Smile, you're embarrassed – Often, potential loss of face – say, a moment when someone realises he or she is clearly in the wrong – will result in an unlikely reaction: a wide smile. No, you're not being mocked; you've just been told, 'I'm sorry.' So if a taxi almost mows you down, only to roll down his window and flash you a big grin, he's not off his rocker – he's showing his embarrassment, which is both a form of apology and a gesture of sympathy.

In 2007 total health care spending in Korea was fourth lowest among OECD countries (6.8% of GDP), just ahead of Poland, Mexico and Turkey.

Another aspect of the Korean character is generosity. Fighting to pay the bill is a common phenomenon, though the *quid pro quo* is that one person pays this time and the other fights a little harder to pick up the check next time. If a Korean takes you under their wing it's difficult to pay for anything. When someone comes back from a holiday they often hand out a small souvenir to everyone.

LIFESTYLE

The dream of most people is to buy or rent an apartment in a new complex equipped with the latest gadgetry, like door locks with fingerprint recognition. Although the amenities are modern, many people prefer to sleep the old-fashioned way, which is on a *yo* (a mattress, similar to a futon) on the floor. Most modern homes have tables and chairs but many people sit on the floor when family comes over for a special occasion. Floors are heated from underneath by the *ondol* system.

In 1998 Korea had the highest savings rate as a percentage of household income (25%) among OECD countries. In 2007 that rate dropped to 2.5%.

Renting an apartment can require a substantial cash deposit. In the traditional method of renting, called *jeonse* (전세), the renter makes a deposit roughly equal to 30% to 80% of the market value of the property. At the end of the two-year lease, the cash is returned with no interest paid. Depending on the location and size of property, *jeonse* for a three-bedroom apartment can easily exceed US$150,000. In recent years property owners have started to reduce the *jeonse* and ask for nonrefundable monthly payments, a system called *wolse* (월세).

Except for the important national holidays like Chuseok (Korean Thanksgiving) and Lunar New Year, Koreans rarely entertain at home. Given the preference for a variety of food tastes coupled with the amount of work required to prepare side dishes, it's practical to socialise in restaurants, cafes and bars. It is precisely for this reason that the wife of the first son dreads big holidays: she's expected to prepare and serve a feast for the husband's family.

Parents are typically obsessed with their children's education and spare no expense to push their kids to the top of the class. Going to school is never enough, so middle-income families send their children to after-school private institutes – called *hagwon* – to study science, maths, Korean and English. Families of wealth hire private tutors. Kids from lower-income families are left to fend for themselves as best they can.

High school is a three-year test of endurance to prepare for the university entrance exam. Top students survive on as little as four hours sleep per night while torturing their brains with multiple-choice questions on calculus and the bizarre intricacies of English grammar. It's not all doom and gloom because there's a pot of gold at the end of the rainbow: university. Schools of higher learning are little more than a four-year vacation. With some exceptions, there is little educational value inside the classroom and virtually everyone passes.

> Korea spends more on private education as a percentage of GDP than any other OECD country, but ranks 19th for public spending.

Social pressures to conform to a standard of 'normality' are intense, so perhaps it's not surprising to learn that Koreans are generally intolerant of things such as homosexuality and drug use. In 2009 Korean actress Kim Bu-seon was arrested for smoking marijuana. She spoke out publicly for the legalisation of pot, a battle cry that was met with a barrage of criticism.

Sadly the resulting social pressures to be successful, dutiful and to fit in drive some over the edge. Suicide is a prevalent component of Korean life. Among 28 OECD countries, Korea has the highest suicide rate. In recent years, suicides by high-profile people, including former President Roh Moo-hyun, billionaire Samsung heiress Lee Yoon-hyung and actress Jang Ja-yeon, have shocked the nation.

> OECD suicide rates (deaths per 100,000 people)
>
> Korea 26.1
>
> Canada 11.3
>
> US 11.0
>
> Australia 10.8
>
> UK 6.7

If a single truism could ever capture the essence of life in Korea, it is this: everything is in a constant state of change. As Korea zooms down the highway of modernisation, the basic fabric of life – marriage, family and purity of Korean blood – is undergoing a shift of tectonic proportions. The traditional pattern of arranged marriages at a young age, with the wife forced to stay home and be subservient to her husband and in-laws, is disappearing, fast. A high rate of divorce – now on par with Western countries – coupled with the cost of raising a family has driven down the birth rate.

ECONOMY

Korea is the 11th-largest economy in the world. In 2007 the country reached a national milestone when the per capita GDP surged past US$20,000. The Korean economy is heavily dependent upon on exports with manufacturing representing 40% of GDP. Over the past five years or so, Korean firms have shifted their investment to overseas plants; according to some estimates Korean companies have created one million manufacturing jobs in China alone. Continued interest in offshore low-cost manufacturing environments coupled with 2009's global recession might challenge Korea's ability to sustain historically high annual growth rates.

> In 2008 the country's average urban household income (average family size of 3.3 people) was W3.5 million per month while expenses were W2.8 million.

The government has made announcements about redirecting economic growth in strategic directions. These include high value–added manufacturing sectors such automobiles and LED displays, commercialisation of

---

A BANG LIFESTYLE

In every city and town you can find plenty of *bang* (rooms) that play a large role in the modern Korean lifestyle. They always charge reasonable prices. Some of the different types of *bang*:

DVD bang Small, private rooms with a sofa and a big screen to watch your choice of DVD film in English or with English subtitles. Popular with courting couples.

Jjimjilbang Upmarket dry-sauna complexes to sport loose-fitting uniforms and partake in the Korean art of doing nothing.

Noraebang Rooms full of happy groups of all ages singing their favourite songs. English songs and beverages are available.

PC bang Big rooms full of young, chain-smoking computer-game addicts and the occasional emailer.

---

so-called green growth industries like renewable energy and enhancement of knowledge-based industries.

Jaebeol – huge, family-run corporate conglomerates such as Hyundai, Samsung and LG – continue to dominate Korea's economy although not so much as in previous decades. The links between the *jaebeol* and government remain strong. In 2009 it was Hyundai Group chairwoman Hyun Jeong-eun who, after a visit to North Korea to meet Kim Jong-il, secured the release of a South Korean employee who'd been arrested four months earlier at the industrial park near Kaesong in North Korea that Hyundai operates.

Read about business in Korea at www.softlandingkorea.com.

POPULATION

South Korea's population is 49.1 million, of whom 10.4 million live in the capital Seoul. The greater-Seoul agglomeration, including Incheon-gwangyeok-si and Gyeonggi-do province, has a population of 24.5 million people, making it the second-largest urban area in the world after Greater Tokyo (33.8 million). The country's population density is 480 per sq km, one of the highest in the world, but it actually feels more crowded because 70% of all people live the country's seven major cities (including Gyeonggi province).

Farming and fishing villages are in terminal decline as young people leave for a more alluring life in the cities. Annually, villages are losing an average of 4% of their population. Local governments are powerless to stem the outflow of people who are attracted by educational facilities, health services, entertainment venues and job opportunities that aren't available in regional communities.

In 2006 foreign nationals accounted for 1.4% of the Korean population.

The impact of Korea's internal migration shift is evident in rural areas where many men, often farmers, cannot find a Korean bride. The shortage of local marriageable women has led to the birth of a new industry: imported brides. For a fee, local agencies connect Korean men – mostly from agricultural communities – with brides from poor nations such as Vietnam and the Philippines. In 2007 12% of all marriages in Korea involved a foreign partner. In some areas of the country almost one-quarter of marriages involved a non-Korean bride or groom.

Between 2010 and 2018, about half of the baby-boomer population – 3.1 million people – is expected to retire.

The birth rate of 1.19 babies per woman is one of the lowest in the world. But that's only part of the statistical story. Korean society is getting older. In 2010 11% of the country was 65 years of age or older. By 2050 that percentage is expected to jump to almost 40%.

SPORT

In terms of attendance figures at matches, baseball rules as the most popular spectator sport in Korea, although among the young soccer is seen as the cool sport, particularly with the success of Park Ji-sung, who plays for Manchester United and is captain of the South Korean national team.

Baseball

There are eight professional teams in the Korean Baseball Organization (KBO), all sponsored by major *jaebeol*. Three teams are in Seoul with the other five playing in Korea's largest cities. The season generally runs from April to October and each team plays 133 games. Teams are allowed to sign two foreign players, a strategy initially designed to increase the calibre of play. Recently, some teams have tended to sign fewer than the limit, suggesting that the US$300,000 salary cap per foreign player is no longer sufficient to attract talent that can excel in the KBO.

Korean players have made it to the American Major Leagues. The first was Park Chan Ho, a pitcher who had considerable success with the Los Angeles Dodgers. Another pitcher, Kim Byun-hyun, might be remembered for flipping his middle finger towards the hometown Boston Red Sox fans, but he surely will live forever in the minds of trivia buffs as the man who gave up the home run that moved Barry Bonds past Babe Ruth on the all-time homer list.

Basketball

Ten teams play in the Korean Basketball League (KBL) from November to March. Two foreign players (usually Americans) are allowed on each team. KBL games tend to be a lot of fun for fans, playing in comparatively small centres. Fans have access to low-cost courtside seats and great views of the cheer girls.

During an exciting, come-from-behind finish in 2009, 13,527 fans – the most ever to attend a KBL game – watched the Samsung Thunders beat the KCC Jeonju by sinking a basket with 3.8 seconds on the clock. A rule that prohibited foreign players who exceeded 6ft 8in was repealed in 2009.

Soccer

Soccer is a popular recreational sport played by men and children on the dirt fields at local schools. Outside the World Cup, interest in professional soccer – or the K-League – is lukewarm with average attendance in the 8000 to 12,000 range. There are 15 teams in the K-League. Each team plays 28 matches between March and November.

Korea's greatest soccer player was Cha Bum-keun. During the 1970s and 1980s he played 308 games and scored 98 goals in the German Bundesliga. Later he coached the Korean team during the 1998 World Cup but was fired halfway through the tournament after losing 5-0 to the Netherlands, which at the time was coached by Gus Hiddink. Four years later Hiddink led the Korean national team to its greatest accomplishment, by finishing fourth in the 2002 World Cup.

English website www. rokfootball.com covers all aspects of soccer in Korea.

Taekwondo

Taekwondo is known worldwide as a Korean martial art. By some accounts it is the world's most popular martial art (measured by number of participants) with benefits related to self-defence, physical strength and mental conditioning. Unlike most martial arts that claim to have a history dating back thousands of years, taekwondo has been around for about 50 years. It was cobbled together at the end of WWII by fighters who wanted a sport that, on the surface at least, was unrelated to anything Japanese. Bits were taken from (ahem) karate and blended with lesser-known Korean fighting skills

LET THE E-SPORTS BEGIN   Simon Richmond

With over 15 million people – nearly a third of South Korea's population – registered to play online games, it's easy to believe that e-sports (also known as e-games) are as popular, if not more so, in South Korea than traditional sports such as baseball and soccer. The biggest deal is **StarCraft** (www.blizzard.com/us/starcraft), an 11-year-old military–sci-fi real-time strategy game, that's shifted some five million copies in Korea since its initial release, and is so popular that there are English-teaching books that use StarCraft terms as the basis of their vocabulary and grammar lessons.

'Three of the most famous professional StarCraft players are South Korean,' explains Dan Stemkoski (gamer ID: Artosis), who along with Nick Plott (ID: Tasteless) provides English-language commentary for several of the Korean TV channels devoted to e-sports, including **Ongamenet** (www.ongamenet.com/index.ogn) and **MBC Game** (www.mbcgame.co.kr). Star e-gamers, who play in teams sponsored by major Korean corporations such as Samsung and SK Telecom, are treated like celebrities and can earn six-figure USD salaries. Team-mates live together, are groomed and sent to the gym. They train for 10 hours a day with one day off. Many are burned out by the time they're 25. In one notable case in 2005 a 28-year-old amateur gamer died after playing StarCraft practically nonstop for 50 hours.

The Olympics of e-sports, the **World Cyber Games** (www.wcg.com), started in Korea in 2000 and is run by a Korean company backed by Samsung and Microsoft. It is now often held in other countries but you can still catch big e-game events such as **E-Stars Seoul** (www.estarsseoul.org) in Seoul as well as be in the audience for the regular TV tapings of game tournaments held on the 9th floor of the I Park Mall next to Seoul's Yongsan station (Map pp102–3).

---

such as *taekkyon*, which relies primarily on leg thrusts. By the mid-1950s the name 'taekwondo' was born.

Ssireum, traditional Korean wrestling, involves wrestlers grabbing each other's *satba* (a cloth tied around the waist) and trying to throw their opponent to the ground. Matches typically last a few seconds.

Today, taekwondo thrives as a sport that most boys study as elementary-school students. It is also part of the physical training program that young men must complete as part of their 2.5 years of compulsory military service. Taekwondo in Korea is not a popular spectator sport, however: there are no matches broadcast on TV and there are not many tournaments that draw popular attention outside Olympic contests. Based in Seoul, the **World Taekwondo Federation** (www.wtf.org) plans to build a major Taekwondo park at Muju in the Deogyusan National Park, which will include a spectator stadium.

MULTICULTURALISM

Korea is a monocultural society with marginal hints of multiculturalism. Just over a million foreigners live in Korea. The most populous groups by nationality are Chinese (45%), Vietnamese (20%) and Americans (12%). Foreign residents tend to congregate in pockets, such as Westerners in Seoul's Itaewon or international tradespeople working in the shipbuilding industry on Geoje Island, though none qualify as a distinct cultural community.

According to a 2009 report by *Hankyoreh*, 20% of all foreign nationals in Korea are illegal immigrants.

The Korean monoculture experience distrusts foreign cultures, which occasionally peaks into hypernationalism and rigidity. Despite a generation having passed (and a World Cup tournament having been shared), attitudes to Japan and the Japanese – the former colonial power – remain lukewarm at best and hostile at worst.

Despite the country's attraction, perhaps addiction, to economic and technological change, attitudes about cultural diversity sometimes appear fossilised. A Korean university student with a good command of English was asked if he enjoyed Thai food. His answer was: 'No, I'm Korean. I like Korean food.' This simple exchange encapsulates the Korean conception of multiculturalism: it's un-Korean. It's an age-old idea, a cultural leftover from the 'hermit kingdom' that may be tested in the future as the country's changing demographic comprises a growing multiracial population that could literally transform the face of the nation. It's also a mindset that seems out of place, given the financial and human capital directed towards transforming the country into a regional centre.

It's fashionable in some circles to claim that Korea is becoming a hub of Asia. Many kinds of hubs are bandied about: logistics hub, finance hub, hub of Northeast Asia. Noble ideas, though claims to becoming a regional centre of something sound like hubbub. Korea lacks the social infrastructure (eg international schools, access to English-language medical and governmental services) to support a sizeable international population. Moreover, Korea does not possess the cultural tools to accept or work within a culturally diverse society.

Read in-depth commentary on Korean socioeconomic trends at http://thegrandnarrative.wordpress.com.

At a deep instinctual level, Koreans aren't especially fond of foreigners. They are tolerated for specific and beneficial purposes, like migrant workers doing the dirty, dangerous and difficult work (locally called 3-D work) that Koreans prefer not to do, or expats teaching English to children. But the idea that foreign nationals living in Korea should be treated as equals under the law is, for many people, a difficult idea to accept.

MEDIA
TV
Like in all countries, Korean TV is a wasteland of home-shopping channels, English-language shows, dreadful comedies, singing shows and local programming that fills the void in a lonely person's life. The only local English TV station in the country – excluding the TV arm of the US military, which is available in limited areas – is Arirang, broadcasting a steady stream of cheery news. Korean comedies are popular and usually involve teams of celebrities who shout at each other as they square off in contrived contests

---

KOREAN SOAPS CLEAN UP IN ASIA

Winter Sonata, a soap opera first screened in Korea in 2002, was the first homegrown TV drama to gain a major international following, demonstrating there was an export market for domestic productions.

Most Korean dramas follow a predictable format: melodramatic soundtrack, sappy romance, parental interference, love triangles and memory loss. *Winter Sonata* proved the formula's appeal not just at home but also overseas. It's the story of two high-school sweethearts whose love was quashed by fate. Overcome by the realisation that he might be in love with his half-sister, the hero decides to run away, only to be hit by a car. While he's in hospital, the boy's mother hires a shrink to erase her son's painful memories of growing up as an illegitimate child, gives him a new identity and sends him off to America. Fast-forward 10 years, and the hero with a new identify is back in Korea and, coincidentally, bumps into his old flame.

Bae Yong-joon plays the man with two identities. He's a certified superstar in Japan where middle-aged women fantasise about having a man like Mr Bae: soft, loving and totally into the relationship. So successful was the drama that it's credited with creating a tourism boom to Korea from Japan and has recently been made into an animated version with voices provided by the original actors.

Subsequent dramas that made a big splash in Asia include *Stairway to Heaven, My Lovely Sam Soon, Princess Hours* and the 2009 hit *Boys over Flowers,* which centred on four uber-rich metrosexual high-school boys who form a club called F4. Fate twists the leader's life after a pretty girl from a poor family drops a scoop of ice cream on his shoe and she refuses his command to lick it off. Her defiance piques his interest and, despite his mother, love conquers all.

BUDDHIST BOOT CAMP   Rob Whyte

A Buddhist boot camp – for beginners. That's what I encountered at Beomeo-sa's Temple Stay in Busan (p239). Thought-provoking and educational – though nothing that approached indoctrination – this decidedly experiential program provided an insider's peek into the daily life of a monk. From the monotony of sweeping floors to the beauty of predawn chants, I witnessed a thin slice of temple chores and rituals.

Like any boot camp, there was a physical challenge – the deep bow. Calling this test of endurance a mere 'bow' disguises the dexterity required to perform fluid prostrations with grace and dignity. Unlike a full-on boot camp, the monks didn't get in my face as my prostrations began to falter though I did notice a scornful glance with hints of disgust and disdain. My bowing struggles began while assembling a string of Buddhist beads. The process seemed easy enough: prostrate yourself, squat, thread the string through one bead, stand up. Repeat 108 times. About one-third through, my toes stopped bending and I had to improvise by using my hands for leverage in order to finish the string. I completed the task but it wasn't pretty.

Just before 10pm sack time, the group leader outlined the next day's events. Wake at 3am. Attend a ceremony. Remain silent. I had no way of knowing it then, but the next day would be pure magic.

Rising well before dawn was easy after a well-deserved sleep in the men's quarters, which doubled as a storage room. Outside in the black of night, I admired the crescent moon hanging above the mountains in between gulps of coffee. In the distance I heard two faint drumbeats coming from either side of the Geumjeong mountain ridge. The beats at first were out of sync but slowly came

---

that invariably involve provocative dances, men dressing as women and a man carrying a woman sporting high-heel shoes and hot pants.

TV dramas are a refreshing change for compelling plots and superior production quality. Love triangles, revenge, odd twists of fate involving hospitalisation and memory loss, along with stirring music, are packaged into tender, innocent stories that have captivated women across Asia. Spurred on by soap operas, the growing international demand for Korean pop culture is called *hallyu*, or the Korean Wave.

> Web-based guerrilla news operation www.ohmynews.com is reliant upon reader-journalists for its content.

Newspapers

Korea's print media is dominated by a trio of major conglomerates – the *Chosun, JoongAng,* and *Dong-a* dailies (*ilbo* in Korean) – known locally as *chojungdong,* an amalgam of their names and a testament to their encompassing collective hold. Because of their influence and ties to Korea's *jaebeol,* along with the fact that they thrived under Korea's military dictatorships, some Koreans harbour residual mistrust toward 'the big three'.

Offering a challenge to this media triumvirate is **Hankyoreh** (http://english.hani.co.kr), founded in 1988 by reporters fired for their political beliefs. It focuses on providing a missing left-wing angle to the news. Each side of the media debate is criticised by the other for biased reporting and influence-peddling.

> According to government figures from 2005, 29.3% of the population profess to be Christian, 22.8% are Buddhist while 46.5% express no religious preference.

The country's two English-language newspapers – *Korea Times* and *Korean Herald* – are useful resources for students studying English but receive an 'F' for news coverage. The *International Herald Tribune* is a better read. It's widely available in Seoul but hard to find in other cities (and often a day late even if you can find it).

RELIGION

There are four streams of spiritual influence in Korea: shamanism, which originated in central Asia; Buddhism, which entered Korea from China in the 4th century AD; Confucianism, a system of ethics of Chinese origin; and Christianity, which first made inroads into Korea in the 18th century.

together to form a single tick-tock. That synchronicity was our cue to begin walking in silence to a pavilion where three monks performed a percussion ceremony to awaken the spirits. Deep kettledrum bass tones resonated through my body, energised my spirit and left me in awe at the monks' discipline and strength. After the performance and without fanfare, we entered the hall, where glimmering Buddha statues amid brilliant red and green hues greeted us at the door. A faint hint of incense tickled the air. And, there were the monks. Three dozen or so bald men garbed in loose-fitting cloth all facing south, all moving in unison when the bell chimed.

Our group stood next to the door, where mats and song sheets awaited our arrival. Intuitively, we followed the monks as they bowed and chanted a sublime, hypnotic melody. As I shifted my concentration from being aware of the monks to being in the moment with the monks, I lost track of time. Was I in the hall for 15 minutes or an hour? I never found out. When the last chime had finally sounded, I followed the group back to the study room, where we meditated and worked in silence until well past breakfast. On the way back, I smiled blissfully. Chanting with monks. By far the coolest experience I've had in Korea.

Beomeo-sa's Temple Stay program has a full schedule of activities without feeling rushed. I drank green tea with the temple's head monk, toured the compound and learned how to eat like a monk using the four-bowl system, a contemplative sit-down meal best experienced, not explained, with one exception: you'll never think about food in the same way once you've eaten with a monk. And that is the hallmark of a great boot camp. It changes the way you think.

Shamanism

Historically, shamanism influenced Korean spirituality. It's not a religion but it does involve communication with spirits through intermediaries known as *mudang* (female shamans). Although not widely practised today, shamanist ceremonies are held to cure illness, ward off financial problems or guide a deceased family member safely into the spirit world. A *gut* (ceremony) might be held by a village to ensure the safety of its citizens and a good harvest of rice or fish.

Ceremonies involve contacting spirits who are attracted by lavish offerings of food and drink. Drums beat and the *mudang* dances herself into a frenzied state that allows her to communicate with the spirits and be possessed by them. Resentments felt by the dead can plague the living and cause all sorts of misfortune, so their spirits need placating. For shamanists, death does not end relationships. It simply takes another form.

Few people today profess to believe in shamanism though some of the old ways have become ritualised as superstition. Throwing salt outside the door of a new home or pouring *soju* in front of the tyres of a new car are two ceremonies rooted in shamanism that Koreans perform to drive evil spirits away.

On Inwangsan (p109), a wooded hillside in northwestern Seoul, ceremonies take place in or near the historic Guksadang shrine.

David Mason's book *Spirit of the Mountains* and his website www.san-shin.org/index.html detail the religious significance of mountains in Korea.

Buddhism

When first introduced during the Koguryo dynasty in AD 370, Buddhism coexisted with shamanism. Many Buddhist temples have a *samseionggak* (three-spirit hall) on their grounds, which houses shamanist deities such as the Mountain God. Buddhism flourished through the unified period and contributed important works such as the Tripitaka Korea (81,340 carved woodblocks), which is at Haein-sa (p208). Buddhism was persecuted during the Joseon period, when temples were tolerated only in remote mountains. It suffered another sharp decline after WWII as Koreans pursued worldly goals. But South Korea's success in achieving developed-nation status, coupled with a growing interest in spiritual values, is encouraging a Buddhist revival. Temple visits have increased and large sums of money are flowing into temple reconstruction.

Today, about 90% of Korean Buddhist temples belong to the **Jogye order** (www.koreanbuddhism.net), which claims to have 12,000 ordained monks and nuns. Buddha's birthday is a national holiday, which includes an extravagant parade in Seoul (p106).

Korean Buddhism is also building international attention by operating a Temple Stay program for travellers at facilities across the country – see the boxed text, p54, and p388. Many Koreans take part in these temple stays regardless of whether they are Buddhist or not as a chance to escape societal pressures and clear their minds.

Christianity

Korea's first significant exposure to Christianity was via the Jesuits from the Chinese imperial court in the late 18th century. The Catholic faith spread quickly – so quickly, in fact, that it was perceived as a threat by the Confucian government and was vigorously suppressed, creating thousands of Catholic martyrs (see p110). The Christian ideal of human equality clashed with the Neo-Confucian ethos of a rigidly stratified society. Christianity got a second chance in the 1880s, with the arrival of Western Protestant missionaries who founded schools and hospitals and gained many followers.

Roughly one-third of the nation claims to be Protestant or Catholic. Christian churches in Korea rank globally in terms of size of congregation, weekly attendance and number of active international missionaries. The **Yoido Full Gospel Church** (http://english.fgtv.com) in Seoul claims to have 800,000 members worldwide with weekly services in halls that accommodate 12,000 people.

Confucianism

Confucianism is a system of ethics rather than a religion. Confucius (555–479 BC) lived in China during a time of chaos and feudal rivalry known as the Warring States period. He emphasised devotion to parents, loyalty to friends, justice, peace, education, reform and humanitarianism. He also urged respect and deference for those in authority and believed that men were superior to women and that a woman's place was in the home.

As Confucianism trickled into Korea it evolved into Neo-Confucianism, which blended the sage's original ideas with the quasi-religious practice of ancestral worship and the idea of the eldest male as spiritual head of the family. During its 500-year history as Korea's state philosophy, it became authoritarian and ultraconservative. It continues to shape the way Koreans see the world and how they behave: see the boxed text, opposite.

WOMEN IN KOREA

The traditional role of woman as housewife and mother has changed. In the 1980s only 15% of women in the marrying age bracket – 25 to 29 – were single. Twenty-five years later, more than 40% of women in that cohort are single. Women who marry are discovering that their lives look quite different from that of their mothers. Economic necessity is driving women out of the kitchen and into the workforce. In 2009 40% of all employed people were women; however, with the economic downturn, 80% of all people who lost their jobs in the previous year were women.

Generally, women today are enjoying more financial influence than ever before. Indeed, their newfound disposable income and unique spending patterns spawned a slightly discourteous moniker: the *doenjang* (fermented soybean) woman. This turn-of-phrase label refers to women who prefer

Hyun Jeong-eun, chairperson of the Hyundai Group, grabbed 73rd place on *Forbes* magazine's 2008 list of the world's 100 most powerful women.

THE CONFUCIAN MINDSET

Confucianism is a social philosophy, a prescription for achieving a harmonious society. Not everyone follows the rules but Confucianism does continue to shape the Korean paradigm. It's what makes Koreans different from Westerners. Some of the key principles and practices:

- Obedience and respect towards seniors – parents, teachers, the boss, older brothers and sisters – is crucial. Expect a heavy penalty (including physical punishment) if you step out of line.
- Seniors get obedience, but it's not a free ride. Older sisters help out younger siblings with tuition fees and the boss always pays for lunch.
- Education defines a civilised person. A high-school graduate, despite having built a successful business, still feels shame at the lack of scholastic credentials.
- Men and women have separate roles. A woman's role is service, obedience and management of household affairs. Men don't do housework or look after children.
- Status and dignity are critical. Every action reflects on the family, company and country.
- Everything on and beyond the earth is in a hierarchy. Never forget who is senior and who is junior to you.
- Families are more important than individuals. Everyone's purpose in life is to improve the family's reputation and wealth. No one should choose a career or marry someone against their parents' wishes – a bad choice could bring ruin to a family. Everyone must marry and have a son to continue the family line. For these reasons homosexuality is considered a grossly unnatural act.
- Loyalty is important. A loyal liar is a virtuous person.
- Be modest and don't be extravagant. Only immoral women wear revealing clothes. Be frugal with praise.

expensive brand-name purchases including coffee from an international chain, the price of which costs more than a soybean stew meal.

In the business community, *alpha girls* is a label that highlights the emergence of powerful businesswomen. One of the early trendsetters was Yoon Song-yee who, at the age of 28, was named an executive of KT Telecom. Her career achievements include the distinction of being the youngest woman to graduate with a PhD from the Massachusetts Institute of Technology.

ARTS
Architecture

Buddhist temples, often re-created after the original work was destroyed or had rotted away, hold some of the country's most impressive ancient architecture. The craftsmanship required to mount wooden beams on stone foundations, often built with notches instead of nails, is technically and aesthetically awe-inspiring. The strikingly bold and colourful painted design under the eaves, called *dancheong*, relies on five colours: blue, white, red, black and yellow.

Traditional residential architecture is called *hanok* (see the boxed text, p59), with fine examples being found in Bukchon Hanok Village (p106) in Seoul and Hahoe Folk Village, near Andong in Gyeongsangbuk-do (p231).

Post–Korean War urban architecture invariably reflected a keen interest in budget rather than design. Concrete towers that look like shoeboxes define most urban landscapes. As Korea has become a richer country this uninspiring aesthetic is changing, particularly so in the Seoul–Gyeonggi-do

Seoul's Historic Walks (2008) by Cho In-Souk and Robert Koehler offers eight tours around Seoul, illustrating the transition from traditional to modern architectural styles. Features maps and plenty of photographs.

area, which includes major construction projects such as the Songdo International City in Incheon, which will include the 151 Incheon Tower, a 610m-tall structure that will be world's second-tallest building when completed in 2013.

Hanoak – Traditional Korean Houses (1999) is a fully illustrated book on the exterior and interior design of Korea's traditional one-storey wood-and-tile houses.

Seoul, in particular, is where you'll see the greatest concentration of architectural imagination, with the Zaha Hadid–designed Dongdaemun Design Plaza & Park (p108) and the striking new City Hall (p109) being must-see structures. For more details of how Seoul is changing architecturally see the boxed text, p87. Another worthy architectural project is that at Heyri & Paju Book City (p154), where the small-scale buildings have been purposefully designed to blend in with and complement the environment.

Cinema

After its humble resurrection following liberation and war, Korea's modern film scene is now revered by film buffs worldwide. Key to this climb was the nixing of earlier censorship, coupled with a rise in budgets. A government quota ensuring that Hollywood flicks can't push homegrown releases out of theatres hasn't hurt, either.

An excellent resource for Korean cinema is www.koreanfilm.org, which covers all aspects of the industry and features scads of reviews.

That said, let it be known: like many countries, Korea produces some truly awful mainstream comedies. But excellent major Korean productions don't shy away from major issues, such as the Korean War (*Taegukgi*, 2004) and its turbulent political aftermath (*The President's Last Bang*, 2005). Pervasive social issues in modern Seoul – such as the blistering pace of city life and the shifting notion of family – are tackled in films like *The Way Home* (2002) and *Family Ties* (2006), both quietly touching. *Marathon* (2005) is the inspiring true tale of a devoted Seoul mother struggling to bring up her autistic son amid societal prejudice. Of course, there are films out there for pure entertainment: the horror films *Memento Mori* (1999) and *A Tale of Two Sisters* (2003) provide gruesome shocks for the genre aficionado, and for an action-revenge flick – something Korea excels at – nothing tops the jaw-dropping *Oldboy* (2003).

Filmmaking used to be an old-boys' club. No longer: superb films by female directors are receiving greater recognition. These include Jeong Jae-eun's *Take Care of My Cat* (2001), the pitch-perfect story of five girls coming of age in the suburbs outside Seoul, and Yim Soon-rye's *Waikiki Brothers* (2001), a sobering exploration of those left behind by Korea's economic rise. Yim's *Forever the Moment* (2008) follows the Korean women's handball team into the 2004 Olympics, offering a more reflective take than is the genre standard. Another must-see is Byun Young-joo's *The Murmuring* (1995), a subdued but shattering documentary about the fate of comfort women, Koreans forced into sexual slavery by the Japanese during WWII.

Since being launched in 1996, the Pusan International Film Festival (PIFF; www.piff.org) has grown to become the most respected festival in Asia, and attracts crowds of film enthusiasts.

Korean films are occasionally shown with English subtitles in cinemas, but the best way to see them is on DVD at one of Korea's numerous DVD *bang* (see the boxed text, p50).

Literature

Modern Korean literature is rich, reflective and at times dark. Unfortunately, much of it is inaccessible to the world because of a lack of translations. Slowly, that situation is changing as more Korean works are being translated into English and other international languages.

There are several literary awards in the country, with three prizes considered most prestigious: the Yi Sang Award, the Hwang Sun-won Award and the Dongin Prize. The **Daesan Award** (http://daesan.or.kr/eng/business.html?d_code=1618)

SAVING THE HANOK *Simon Richmond*

'Thirty-five years ago there were around 800,000 *hanok* in South Korea, now there are less than 10,000,' says Peter Bartholomew, a longtime American expat in Korea and chair of the local branch of the Royal Asiatic Society. For over 40 years Bartholomew has been battling the predominant view among Koreans that such traditional houses are an anachronism in their modern country, unworthy of preserving.

Built from wood, stone and plaster, a *hanok* has a tiled or thatched roof depending on whether it was the home of an upper-class *(yangban)* or peasant-class family. There's always an open courtyard providing ventilation and light to the surrounding rooms that are separated by wooden screens often with paper panels. They also use the ingenious underfloor heating system known as *ondol*. Bartholomew has lived in such houses since he first came to Korea in 1968 as a peace-corps volunteer and has owned a *hanok* in the Dongsomun-dong area of northern Seoul since 1974. He bought an adjacent property in 1991.

In 2009 Bartholomew and his neighbours won a two-year legal battle against the city over plans to redevelop the area. 'I deplore the assumption that these old houses are irreparable, dirty and unsanitary,' he says, pointing out that traditional *hanok* are very easy to modernise in just the same way that centuries-old homes across the West have been adapted to contemporary life. The proof of this lies in the success of Seoul's Bukchon area (see p106), where some 900 *hanok* remain. 'But even here the preservation program has only been achieved by the government providing financial incentives to owners for repairs and maintenance,' says Bartholomew.

A small step forward lies in the creation of the **National Trust of Korea** (www.nationaltrust.or.kr), an NGO charged with helping to protect the environment and national relics and of which Bartholomew is a board member. One of the Trust's programs focuses on preservation of *hanok*.

Tourists are also doing their bit by opting to stay in *hanok* guesthouses, the majority of which are clustered in Seoul. Ahn Young-hwan, owner of Rak-Ko-Jae (p129) and Rak-Ko-Jae Andong (p231), was one of the first people to suggest that *hanok* be used in this way. 'People thought I was crazy,' he says, 'but now many more people are doing it.' Ahn plans to start a company that makes prefabricated *hanok* so that a new generation of Koreans can have the experience of living in these traditional homes.

For Ahn, *hanok* are the 'vessels that contain Korean culture' and a way of experiencing the joys of an analogue life in an increasingly digital society. It's a view that Bartholomew underlines when he says that living in his *hanok* has 'filled my life with peace and beauty'.

provides some of the richest prizes – W30 million – in five categories including poetry, fictional work and translations.

Works translated into English that provide a sample of Korean literature include *Toji (1969–1994)*. This serialised novel took Park Kyung-ni 25 years to complete and is considered to be one of the finest literary works in modern Korea. Set in Hadong, South Gyeongsang province, the story follows an aristocratic family during Japanese colonial rule. It's a collection of 16 volumes, some of which have been translated into English.

Land of Exile: Contemporary Korean Fiction (2007) is recognised as the standard collection for post–Korean War short stories. Originally published in 1997, the updated edition has four new pieces including 'From Powder to Powder', a story about an advertising executive who markets cosmetics to keep women looking young while his wife dies from cancer.

The Prophet and Other Stories (1999) is a novella by Lee Cheong-jun documenting the life of a social outcast who is the target of group-think mentality. Written by one of Korea's most respected authors, it's an allegory for life under a dictatorship.

The Dwarf (2006) by Cho Sae-hee recounts the daunting social costs of rapid industrialisation on the working poor during the 1970s through the eyes of a midget.

Still Life with Rice by Helie Lee (1997) is a novel recounting one family's struggle during the Korean War.

The Gingko Bed (1996) is a movie that blends dreams, time travel and two pieces of wood into a love story.

EXPAT KOREAN LITERATURE

A body of modern English-language literature deals with Koreans living abroad and their struggles with identity.

■ *War Trash* by Ha Jin (2004) – A gritty novel about the life of a POW during the Korean War from the perspective of an English-speaking Chinese soldier.

■ *Native Speaker* by Lee Chang-rae (1996) – A political thriller about a second-generation Korean-American man on the outside looking in. Also take a look at Lee's *A Gesture Life* (1999), the story of an older Japanese gentleman who uses grace to mask past mistakes as a soldier in Burma while overseeing Korean comfort women.

■ *Appointment With My Brother* by Yi Mun-yol (2002) – A brilliant novella about a man from the South who meets his half-brother from the North. It's an emotional and stressful meeting for both of them, a collision of two worlds.

■ *The Descendants of Cain* by Hwang Sun-won (1997) – One of Korea's most celebrated authors writes about life in a North Korean village between the end of WWII and the beginning of the Korean War.

Music

Gugak (traditional music) is played on stringed instruments, most notably the *gayageum* (12-stringed zither) and *haegeum* (two-stringed fiddle), and on chimes, gongs, cymbals, drums, horns and flutes. Traditional music can be subdivided into three categories: *jeongak* is a slow court music often combined with elegant dances; *bulgyo eumak* is played and chanted in Buddhist temples; and *samulnori* is a lively style originally played by travelling entertainers. It died out during Japanese colonial rule but was reinvented in the 1970s by musicians playing four traditional percussion instruments.

Korea's traditional music is unlikely to catch on overseas, but that certainly hasn't been the case with the country's pop music, called K-pop – and another aspect of the *hallyu* (Korean Wave). Korean artists have attracted international attention though few have attained the level of commercial success of **BoA** (www.boaamerica.com), a woman with considerable talents and the ability to find new markets, or **Rain** (www.rain-jihoon.com), one of Korea's most versatile entertainers, who can sing, dance, act and run a company. His 2005 album *It's Raining* sold over a million copies.

Other successful artists include cute boy band **Big Bang** (http://ygbigbang.com), the 13-member group **Super Junior** (http://superjunior.smtown.com), which launched its smash hit 'U' via a free online download (400,000 downloads in five hours) and **Wonder Girls** (http://wondergirlsworld.com), five trim and bubbly young women. Their catchy tune 'Nobody but You' garnered some attention in the US in 2009 with an English release and an appearance on a TV talk show.

Painting & Sculpture

Chinese influence is paramount in traditional Korean painting. The brush line, which varies in thickness and tone, is the most important feature. The painting is meant to surround the viewer and there is no fixed viewpoint. Zen-style Buddhist art can be seen inside and on the outside walls of hundreds of temples around the country. Murals usually depict scenes from Buddha's life.

Stone Buddhist statues and pagodas are the most common examples of ancient sculpture. Cast bronze was also common for Buddhas and some marvellous examples can be seen in the National Museum of Korea (p110).

Stone and wooden shamanist guardian posts are common and Jeju-do has its own unique *harubang* or 'grandfather stones' (see boxed text, p288).

Many towns have sculpture gardens and parks – good ones include Olympic Park (p112) and Anyang Art Park (p159).

Korea's best-known modern sculptor is Baek Nam-june, who died in 2006. He was a Korean-American artist who used video monitors to create inspired, sometimes bizarre, work. One of his larger creations, 'The More the Better', is an 18m tower with 1000 monitors on display at the National Museum of Contemporary Art inside Seoul Grand Park (p159). Log on to www.paikstudio.com to learn more about this pioneering artist.

Other modern artists include painter Kim Whanki, mixed-media artist Min Yong-soon, and Kim Tschang-yeul, a painter noted for his dedication to water drops; one of the latter's paintings is at the Leeum Samsung Museum of Art in Seoul (p110).

Read English essays about the Korean arts scene at www.clickkorea.org.

Pottery

Pottery on the Korean peninsula dates back 10,000 years, but the 12th century is regarded as a special time when skilled artisans turned out celadon earthenware with a green tinge. Nowadays Korean celadon earns thousands of dollars at auction. Pottery fans shouldn't miss out on a visit to Icheon Ceramic Village (p160) near Seoul and two pottery villages in Jeollanam-do: the Pottery Culture Centre (p277) and the Gangjin Celadon Museum (p274).

TRADITIONAL COSTUMES

The striking traditional clothing that used to be worn all the time by Koreans is known as *hanbok*. It was as much a part of the local culture as *hangeul* and *kimchi*. Traditionally, women wore a loose-fitting short blouse with long sleeves and a voluminous long skirt, while men wore a jacket and baggy trousers. Both sexes wore socks. Cotton replaced hemp as the main clothing material during the Joseon dynasty. In winter, overcoats were worn over padded clothes and people piled on lots of undergarments to keep out the freezing cold. Designs have varied over the centuries, especially female *hanbok*, but the clothes have maintained their basic pattern of simple lines without any pockets.

Hanbok style followed the Confucian principle of unadorned modesty. Natural dyes were used to create plain colours, although some parts of clothing could be embroidered, and the very rich could afford silk. In the Joseon period clothing was strictly regulated and you could tell a person's occupation and status from the *hanbok* they wore. For instance, poorer people generally had to wear white. Only *yangban* (aristocrats) could wear the black horsehair hats that were a badge of their rank, while a fancy *binyeo* (hairpin) in a big wig was a female status symbol. Scholars (invariably male in those days) wore a plain white gown with wide sleeves. At court, government officials wore special black hats and *heungbae* – embroidered insignia on the back and front of their gowns.

In the summer, lightweight, almost transparent ramie – a cloth made from pounded bark – provides cool and comfortable clothing. You'll often see older men wearing clothes made of ramie during the hot summer months.

Hanbok today is usually only worn at weddings, festivals or other special occasions, and by waitresses in some traditional restaurants. Men prefer Western suits or casual wear, and most women find *hanbok* uncomfortable and unflattering: it restricts their movements, has no pockets and is difficult to clean. In markets and shops you can buy modern or traditional *hanbok*. The everyday *hanbok* is reasonably priced, but the formal styles, made of silk and intricately embroidered, are objects of wonder and cost a fortune.

Hanbok: The Art of Korean Clothing by Sunny Yang (1997) gives a comprehensive history of traditional clothing, with masses of pictures.

Theatre & Dance

DANCE

Popular folk dances include *samulnori* (drum dance), *talchum* (mask dance) and solo improvisational *salpuri* (shamanist dance). *Samulnori* dancers perform in brightly coloured clothing, twirling a long tassel from a special cap on their heads. Good coordination is required to dance, twirl and play a drum at the same time.

Talchum dance-dramas were performed by low-class travelling showmen on market days and usually satirised the *yangban* class. Masks indicated the status of the character – a *yangban*, monk, shaman, grandmother, concubine or servant – and hid the identity of the performer. Mask dance-dramas involved vigorous leaping, comedy and big gestures, together with shouting, singing and reciting. The performers mingled with the audience once their part was over. Today, masks are usually made of wood and every souvenir shop sells them.

There are two major modern-dance festivals held in Seoul. The **MODAFE festival** (www.modafe.org) usually holds performances in the spring. The **Seoul International Dance Festival** (www.sidance.org) has local and international performers taking the stage at venues across the city including the Seoul Arts Centre. During the festival, which usually runs in October, there are discussion forums with choreographers, critics and journalists.

THEATRE

Korea's small, modern theatrical experience is primarily based in Seoul. Commercially safe, nonverbal shows like *Nanta* and *Jump* appeal to an international audience (p143). There's an experimental scene in Daehangno but it's almost entirely in Korean.

KOREAN OPERA

Changgeuk is an opera that can involve a large cast of characters. Another type of opera is *pansori*, which features a solo storyteller (usually female) singing to the beat of a male drummer. The performer flicks her fan to emphasise dramatic moments. For details on Seoul's traditional theatres that stage these shows, see p141.

Environment

THE LAND

South Korea's land area is 96,920 sq km, making it a similar size to Portugal. Bordered only by North Korea, the country has 2413km of coastline along three seas – the West Sea (also known as the Yellow Sea), the East Sea (Sea of Japan) and the South Sea (East China Sea). Its overall length from north to south (including Jeju-do) is 500km, while the narrowest point is 220km wide.

The largest of some 3400 islands is 1847 sq m Jeju-do (p282), a volcanic landmass with spectacular craters and lava tubes. Off the east coast is another scenic volcanic island, Ulleung-do (p222). Korea is not in an earthquake zone, but there are dozens of mineral-laden *oncheon* (hot springs) that bubble up through the ground, some of which have been developed into health spas.

Caves by Kyung Sik Woo (2005) is a lavishly illustrated book on Korean caves by a geological expert and cave enthusiast.

Forested mountains cover 70% of the land, although they are not very high – Hallasan (1950m) on Jeju-do is the highest peak. Many mountains are granite with dramatic cliffs and pinnacles, but there are also impressive limestone caves to visit. The 521km Nakdong and 514km Han rivers are the country's longest. They, like most other larger rivers, have been dammed, creating scenic artificial lakes.

The plains and shallow valleys are still dominated by irrigated rice fields that are interspersed with small orchards, greenhouses growing vegetables, and barns housing cows, pigs and chickens. In the south are green-tea plantations; on frost-free Jeju-do citrus fruit is grown.

Living History of the DMZ by Hahm Kwang Bok (2004) covers the unique ecological zone that separates the two Koreas.

The hundreds of sparsely populated islands scattered off the western and southern coasts of the peninsula have relaxed atmospheres, unspoiled by second-home owners, and a few have attractive sandy beaches. Here you can go way off the beaten track to islands where the inhabitants have never seen a foreigner.

ANIMALS

Korea's forested mountains used to be crowded with Siberian tigers, Amur leopards, bears, deer, goral antelopes, grey wolves and red foxes. Unfortunately these wild animals are now extinct or extremely rare in Korea.

THE SAD PLIGHT OF A NATIONAL TREASURE

According to legend the Korean nation was born from a bear – one of the reasons why Asiatic black bears (also called moon bears because of the crescent moon of white fur on their chests) are accorded the status of a national treasure and a protected species. However, by the late 20th century, the hunting of bears for their meat and use in traditional medicine had contributed to them being thought extinct in the wild in South Korea.

Then in 2001 video-camera footage proved that up to six wild bears were living in a remote part of Jirisan National Park. Soon after the park established a project with the aim of building up a self-sustaining group of 50 bears in Jirisan by 2012. According to **Moonbears.org** (http://moonbears.org), the main Korean campaign group for protection of the animal, in 2009 there were only 11 wild bears in the park and they are threatened by poaching. This is despite the fact that well over 1000 bears are bred at 110 farms across the country for the lucrative bear-meat and gall-bladder trade. The conditions that the bears are kept in are often horrific.

Moonbears.org, Green Korea and other pressure groups want the government to ban such farms, or at the very least actively monitor and police the guidelines introduced to ensure the proper handling of bears in captivity. According to a 2009 report in the *Korea Times* the government is leaning towards promoting the bears' welfare at the same time as considering applications by the bear breeders association to sell bear meat in Korea.

Field Guide to the Birds of Korea by Lee, Koo & Park (2000) is the standard bird guide, but doesn't include all feathered visitors.

International Aid for Korean Animals (www.koreananimals.org/index.htm) promotes animal protection in Korea.

Small efforts are being made to build up the number of wild animals in the country – goral antelopes have been released into Woraksan National Park and there's an ongoing project to protect the tiny population of Asiatic black bears (known in Korea as moon bears) in Jirisan National Park (see the boxed text, p63). Small populations of roe deer and elk live on Bukaksan (see the boxed text, p108) and in Seoul Forest Park (p118).

Magpies, pigeons and sparrows account for most of the birds in the towns and cities, but egrets, herons and swallows are common in the countryside, and raptors, woodpeckers and pheasants can also be seen. Although many are visiting migrants, over 500 bird species have been sighted, and Korea has a growing reputation among birders keen to see Steller's sea eagles, red-crowned cranes, black-faced spoonbills and other rarities.

PLANTS

Northern parts of South Korea are the coldest and the flora is alpine: beech, birch, fir, larch and pine. Further south, deciduous trees are more common. The south coast and Jeju-do are the warmest and wettest areas, so the vegetation is lush. Cherry trees blossom in early spring followed by azaleas and camellias.

Korea's mountainsides are a pharmacy and salad bar of health-giving edible leaves, ferns, roots, nuts and fungi. Many of these wild mountain vegetables end up in restaurant side dishes and *sanchae bibimbap* (a meal of rice, egg, meat and mountain vegetables). Wild ginseng is the most expensive and sought-after plant.

NATIONAL & PROVINCIAL PARKS

With an abundance of river valleys, waterfalls and rocky outcrops, plus brightly painted wooden Buddhist temples and hermitages gracing many mountains, it's not surprising that many visitors rate Korea's national and provincial parks as its top attractions.

Since the first national park, Jirisan, was established in 1967 it has been joined by 19 others covering 38,240 sq km of land (6.5% of the country). With an average of five million visitors a year Bukhansan National Park, located on Seoul's doorstep, has qualified for a Guinness World Record as the national park with the highest number of visitors per square foot in the world.

There are also 22 smaller provincial parks (covering 747 sq km) and 29 county parks (covering 307 sq km) that are just as worthy of a visit as the national parks. All the parks have well-marked hiking trails that can be so popular that trails have to be closed to protect them from serious erosion.

The parks can be enjoyed in every season. In spring cherry blossoms, azaleas and other flowers are a delight; in summer the hillsides and river valleys provide a cool escape from the heat and humidity of the cities; during the summer monsoon, the waterfalls are particularly impressive; in autumn red-coloured leaves and clear blue skies provide a fantastic sight; and in winter

---

JIN-DO DOGS

Jin-do (p276) is home to a special breed of Korean hunting dog, Jindogae, which is as brave, intelligent, loyal and cute as any canine on the planet. They can be a challenge to train and control, but they possess an uncanny sense of direction – one dog was taken to Daejeon but somehow made its way back to the island, a journey of hundreds of kilometres. Being hunting dogs, they are an active, outdoor breed that is not suited to an urban environment. Any other breed of dog found on Jin-do is immediately deported to the mainland in order to maintain the breed's purity. View www.jindos.com and www.kang.org/Jindo.html for photos and more information.

snow and ice turn the parks into a white wonderland, although crampons and proper clothing are needed for any serious hikes at this time of year. Korean winters can be arctic, especially if you're high up in the mountains.

All the parks have tourist villages near the main entrances with restaurants, market stalls, souvenir and food shops, and budget accommodation where big groups can squeeze into a small room. Camping grounds (W3000 for a three-person tent) and mountain shelters (W3000 to W5000 for a bunk) are cheap, but provide only very basic facilities. For more details see **Korea National Parks** (http://english.knps.or.kr).

Top national parks:

Park	Area	Features & Activities
Bukhansan	78 sq km	Great hiking, and subway access from Seoul (p151)
Dadohae Haesang	2344 sq km (2004 sq km marine)	A marine park of scattered, unspoilt islands (p281)
Deogyusan	219 sq km	A top ski resort, a fortress and a magical valley walk (p312)
Gyeongju	138 sq km	A historic park strewn with ancient Shilla and Buddhist relics (p208)
Hallasan	149 sq km	This extinct volcano on Jeju-do is Korea's highest peak (p303)
Jirisan	440 sq km	Straddling two provinces, this giant park's high peaks are popular with serious hikers (East p258 and West p270)
Seoraksan	373 sq km	Korea's most beautiful and second-most-frequented park (p182)
Sobaeksan	320 sq km	Limestone caves and Guin-sa, an impressive temple complex (p346)

Top provincial parks:

Park	Area	Features & Activities
Daedunsan	38 sq km	Granite cliffs, great views and a hot-spring bath (p311)
Gajisan	104 sq km	Scenic views and a famous temple, Tongdo-sa (p252)
Mudeungsan	30 sq km	Near Gwangju with an art gallery and a green-tea plantation (p265)
Namhan Sanseong	36 sq km	Take the subway from Seoul and hike round the fortress wall (p160)
Taebaeksan	17 sq km	Visit the Coal Museum and hike up to Dangun's altar (p196)

ENVIRONMENTAL ISSUES

South Korea's economic growth since 1960 has transformed the country from an agricultural to an industrial society. Sprawling apartment-block cities and huge industrial complexes have been constructed, rivers have been dammed and freeways have been bulldozed through the countryside. Authoritarian governments stamped on any opposition to development projects and the environmental impacts were ignored.

Fortunately the 70% of Korea that is mountainous and forested is still largely undeveloped, and the hundreds of offshore islands are also unspoilt. For a developed country Korea is surprisingly green, as 90% of the population is packed into high-rise city apartments.

Nowadays politics is more democratic, politicians win votes by promising green policies and environmental groups are no longer ignored by the media. Unpopular construction projects can face fierce opposition, as President Lee Myung-bak discovered in 2008 when he was forced to abandon his plan to

Korea's largest environmental nongovernmental organisation is Korea Federation for Environmental Movements (KFEM; www.kfem.or.kr) which has around 80,000 members and 50 branch offices across the country.

create a grand canal between Seoul and Busan by linking up four of Korea's major rivers.

Among the country's most contentious environmental flashpoints are what to do with nuclear waste and land reclamation.

Nuclear Power & Waste Disposal

South Korea relies on 20 nuclear power plants concentrated in four locations (Gori, Ulchin, Wolseong, Yonggwang) to generate around 40% of its electricity – this compares a 15.7% average worldwide. As part of its 'low-carbon, green-growth' plan (below) there are plans to add up to 19 more nuclear facilities by 2030 to boost the level of electricity generation to 60%. However, for over two decades Korea's nuclear-power industry has struggled to find a permanent storage site for the radioactive waste that is being produced – it's a pressing problem as by 2016 the current storage sites at each of the plants will be full.

In November 2005 Gyeongju was chosen as the site of the country's first permanent nuclear-waste dump, with the Korea Hydro & Nuclear Power Corporation set to move its headquarters to the region. Protests naturally followed, despite the fact that in a poll close on 90% of voters had endorsed the plan – a result probably not unconnected to the annual W300 billion (US$323 million) in economic subsidies that central government had promised the region. However in 2009 construction of the storage facility was put on hold under pressure from lawmakers and environmental campaign groups who had uncovered evidence of the site's geological instability.

Land Reclamation

Reclaiming the mud flats off Korea's west coast for farming and construction has become a highly emotive and divisive issue. According to KFEM, since 1990 over 140,000 hectares of coastal wetlands have been reclaimed or are in the process of being reclaimed.

The environmental impact that such projects can have is seen at Saemangeum in Jeollabuk-do where in 2006 a 33km sea wall was built to reclaim 40,000 hectares of mud flats. Opponents, who battled hard against the project during its construction, stressed the importance of the mud flats as a fish and shellfish breeding area and as a vital feeding ground for more than 100,000 migrant birds, including black-faced spoonbills and 12 other threatened species.

In response to the Saemangeum protests, the government declared 60 sq km of wetlands at the Han River estuary in Gyeonggi-do a protected area. Ten smaller wetland areas (covering a total of 45 sq km) had already been protected. In 2008 Korea's Ministry of Environment announced plans to increase the number of protected wetland areas to 30 by 2012 and to increase the nation's list of Ramsar Wetlands from 11 to 16. In one of these wetlands – Suncheon-man (see the boxed text, p270), the winter nesting ground of five endangered crane species – the cancellation of a land-reclamation project in favour of the area's promotion as an ecotourism destination is a positive sign for the future.

View www.greenkorea.org for a pressure group with practical ideas such as Buy Nothing Day, Car Free Day (22 September in Seoul) and Save Paper Day.

Green Korea?

In August 2008 President Lee announced the nation's 'low-carbon, green growth' strategy to reduce greenhouse gas emissions and environmental pollution and to create jobs using green technology and clean energy. While he was the capital's mayor Lee had pushed through the restoration of Seoul's Cheong-gye stream (p106), a project that is generally viewed as an environmental success story.

ENVIRONMENTAL CRUSADER: LEE SUNGJO

At the eco-friendly HQ of the Korea Federation for Environmental Movements (KFEM) in Seoul (Map pp96–7) we talked with coordinator Lee Sungjo, a specialist in energy policy and climate change, about the state of Korea's environment.

How is climate change affecting Korea? We are experiencing much stronger typhoons compared to the 1990s. Farmers who used to grow, say, apples are changing their crops to more tropical fruits as temperatures increase. The biggest problem has been for fishermen – the warming of waters is killing off fish stocks but increasing the population of jellyfish. Other indications of change are 2127 deaths from heatwaves in the last 10 years and 2227 malaria patients in 2007 alone.

What is Korea doing about this issue? Compared to Western countries climate change is not a very popular issue in South Korea. Even though over 90% of Koreans have noticed climate change, we have a relatively small action index of 30% among the population. President Lee has announced a 'low carbon, green growth' policy but the main plank of that policy is to build more nuclear power plants, even though nuclear energy is not 'green'. We'd prefer to see government set targets for energy saving, increase energy efficiency and make much greater use of renewable energy sources. For example Korea could achieve 11% of its energy needs from renewable sources by 2030. Now there's only 1% from that source, and it's unlikely to be more than 5% by 2011.

What are KFEM's main campaigns? We're against the large-scale reclamation of land on the west coast particularly around the mud flats of the West Sea. Projects such as Songdo International City near Incheon (p161) mean we are losing more of these natural areas and the species that live in them every year. We're also fighting the government's so-called 'four-river restoration' project because it will potentially prevent fish from laying eggs in the river shallows, eliminate river and wetlands inhabited by wild animals and plants, and pollute drinking-water sources used by much of the population. Such large construction projects are not a model for sustainable development in the 21st century. According to a poll conducted on 30 June 2009, 66.6% of the Koreans oppose this project.

Do you get any support from government? We stopped accepting donations and contracts from the government and major corporations to fund our projects in October 2008. This loss of funding has affected what we can do… However, recently, our supporting membership has been slightly increasing. This is a difficult period for not only the environmental movement but also the democratic movement in Korea, but we have to work harder to get our messages across to the public. We are trying to move our campaigns in a variety ways not only off-line, but also on the web using online portals and blogs.

Among the 'eco-friendly' projects on the government's national green agenda are the clean-up of four major rivers (the Han, Nakdong, Geum and Yeongsan) and their surroundings to reduce flooding by building dams, banks and water-treatment facilities; the construction of more high-speed railway lines and of hundreds of kilometres of bicycle tracks; the provision of energy-saving 'green homes' and energy-recycling projects including the production of gas from garbage; and the development of hybrid vehicle technologies.

Many of these policies have got the thumbs up from the UN Environment Program but local environmental groups have been less enthusiastic, particularly about the four-river project, which they suspect is a way for the president to revive his failed grand-canal plan. Despite commitments to preserve wetland and coast areas, Seoul is also pushing ahead with a plan to build four tidal power plants along the west coast. The first Korean tidal power plant at Sihwa Lake in Gyeonggi-do south of Yeongjong-do is scheduled for completion in 2010.

Food & Drink

Korean food is robust, gutsy and unapologetic, an enthusiastic assault on the senses that marshals many flavours at once. At times it can be a baffling conflation of flavours from across the spectrum – sweetly spicy with one mouthful, salty with a dash of sour the next. Often it is simply spicy – potent enough to trigger off sweat or tears. At no time will it be bland, unless you forgot the *kimchi* or dipping sauce (both are served on the side, but fundamental to the meal).

Most people associate Korean food with *kimchi* and barbecue, which exhibit some certain quintessentially Korean flavours – the ripe tartness of fermented leaves, the delicate marinade of grilled meat. But that's just the starting point. While the basic building blocks of the cuisine are recognisably Asian (garlic, ginger, green onion, black pepper, vinegar and sesame oil), Korean food strikes out on its own in combining them with three essential sauces: *ganjang* (soy sauce), *doenjang* (fermented soybean paste) and *gochujang* (hot red pepper paste). The other distinctive feature is that the main course is always served not only with *bap* (steamed rice), soup and *kimchi*, but also a procession of *banchan* (side dishes) trooping out of the kitchen. Above all, Koreans see mealtimes as an occasion to feed both the body and the spirit, by eating with family, friends or colleagues – always convivial, with the group; rarely, if ever, alone.

All told, a Korean meal is an embarrassment of flavours, full and unrepentant. There's some talk of watering down the more feisty recipes to make them more palatable to foreigners, but that would be a real pity when it's precisely those aggressive flavours that make Korean food so memorable – and addictive – in the first place.

STAPLES & SPECIALITIES

Rice & Noodles

One way to ease into Korean food is with rice, porridge and noodle dishes. *Bibimbap* is a tasty mixture of vegetables, meat and an egg on top of rice. The

---

SAY KIMCHI

You'll see it at every meal (including breakfast) and often as an ingredient in the main course as well. What began as a pickling method to preserve vegetables through Korea's harsh winters, has become a cornerstone of its cuisine.

With its lurid reddish hues and limp texture, *kimchi* doesn't look like that appealing, but just one bite packs a wallop of flavours: sour, spicy, with a sharp tang that often lingers through the meal. The most common type is *baechu kimchi*, made from Chinese cabbage, but there are over 180 varieties, made with radish, cucumber, eggplant, leek, mustard leaf and pumpkin flower, among others. Some are meant to be eaten in tiny morsels or wrapped around rice. Others, such as *bossam kimchi*, are flavour-packed packages containing vegetables, pork or seafood. One that belies its fiery reputation is *mul kimchi*, a fairly bland cold soup, similar to gazpacho.

To make *kimchi*, vegetables are salted to lock in the original flavour, then seasoned with garlic, red pepper powder, green onions, ginger, fish sauce and other spices, and left in earthenware jars to ferment for hours, days or even years. *Kimchi* can be made all year round using seasonal vegetables, but traditionally it is made in November. Many regions, restaurants and families have their own recipes, which are jealously guarded and handed down through the generations.

Today *kimchi* is usually bought in stores and families have a medium-sized refrigerator specially for it (also to keep the smell contained). Health-wise it is high in fibre and low in calories. If you believe the hype, it can also lower cholesterol, fight cancer and prevent SARS and H1N1 swine flu.

ingredients are laid out in a deep bowl according to the five primary colours of Korean food – white, yellow, green, red and black – which represent the five elements. To eat it, just stir everything up (go easy on the red *gochujang* if you don't want it too spicy). A common variant is *dolsot bibimbap,* served in a stone hotpot; for Koreans, the highlight of this is *nurungji,* the crusty rice at the bottom. In national parks you'll come across *sanchae bibimbap,* made with local vegetables. Vegetarians can usually order *bibimbap* without meat or egg, while more adventurous eaters can try it with raw fish *(hoedeopbap)* or raw beef *(yukhoe bibimbap).*

Milder than *bibimbap* is *juk* (rice porridge), which comes in savoury versions mixed with ginseng chicken, mushroom or seafood, or sweet incarnations with pumpkin and red bean. The thick, black rice porridge is sesame. *Juk* is considered a healthy meal, good for older people, babies or anyone who's ill. It's usually served in restaurants that specialise in it.

Noodle *(myeon)* dishes are the other staple. A common dish is *naengmyeon,* buckwheat noodles served in an icy beef broth, garnished with vegetables, Korean pear, cucumber and half a boiled egg. You can add *gochujang, sikcho* (vinegar) or *gyeoja* (mustard) to taste. *Naengmyeon* is especially popular in summer, or eaten after *galbi* (beef ribs) or other meat-heavy meals. Sometimes it's served with a small bowl of meat broth, piping hot, that you can drink with your meal (but it's not for pouring onto the noodles). *Bibim naengmyeon* pairs the cold noodles with *bibimbap* ingredients.

Japchae are clear 'glass' noodles stir-fried in sesame oil with strips of egg, meat and vegetables. It's popular at parties and used to be served to Joseon monarchs. *Gimbap* joints (see p71) often serve *ramyeon* (instant noodles) in spicy soup. A Koreanised Chinese dish is *jajangmyeon,* wheat noodles in a black-bean sauce with meat and vegetables, which is adored by children (and nostalgic adults).

The Korea Tourism Organisation website has an extensive food section (http://english.visitkorea.or.kr/enu/1051_Food.jsp).

Meat

Beef is highly prized because it is expensive; pork is more affordable. *Bulgogi* describes thin slices of meat, marinated in sweetened soy sauce, while *galbi* are short ribs, similarly flavoured. These terms usually refer to beef but can also be used for pork *(dwaeji).* Another popular cut is *samgyeopsal* (streaky pork belly).

At barbecue restaurants, every table has its own small grill and diners take their time to savour different cuts of freshly grilled meat. The server places the raw meat on the grill, after which diners are responsible for cooking, though restaurants often assist foreign customers. Grilled meats are usually eaten wrapped in *ssam* (vegetable leaves) with slices of fresh garlic, green pepper, *kimchi* and a daub of spicy *ssamjang* (soybean and red pepper sauce). The usual vegetables used for *ssam* are lettuce, perilla (which Koreans call wild sesame), crown daisy and seaweed. Other dishes eaten *ssam*-style are *bossam* (steamed pork and *kimchi), modeumhoe* (assorted raw fish) and the surprisingly meaty *jokbal* (pigs' feet steamed in *ganjang).*

Dog meat is still eaten, although it's less popular with the younger generation. *Bosintang* (dog-meat soup) is said to make men more virile and is eaten on the hottest days of the year.

Fish & Seafood

Hoe (raw fish) is extremely popular in coastal towns, despite the comparatively high prices. *Saengseonhoe* (sliced raw fish) is served with *ssam* or *ganjang* with wasabi, and there's usually a steaming pot of spicy *maeuntang* (fish soup) to complete the meal. *Chobap* is raw fish served over vinegared rice. Restaurants near the coast also serve squid, barbecued shellfish, octopus and crab. More gung-ho eaters can have a go at *sannakji* (raw octopus, not live but wriggling from post-mortem spasms) or *hongeo* (ray, served raw and fermented, or steamed in *jjim* – neither of which masks its pungent ammonia smell).

WE DARE YOU

Beondegi Silkworm larvae
Bosintang Dog-meat soup
Doganitang Ox kneecaps soup
Ganjang gejang Raw crab marinated in soy sauce
Hongeo Fermented raw ray
Mettugi Fried grasshoppers
Sannakji Raw baby octopus
Yukhoe Seasoned raw minced meat

Soups, Stews, Hotpots & *Jjim*

Many Korean dishes are served as boiling or sizzling hot off the stove or grill as they can get it. Besides the soup that accompanies every meal, there are many hearty and piquant main-course soups called *tang* or *guk*: the former is simmered longer and has softer ingredients. Soups may be served hot or cold, even icy. They range from bland broths such as *galbitang* or *seolleongtang*, to spicy soups such as *maeuntang* and *haemultang*. If you find a soup too spicy, tip in some rice.

Gamjatang is a rich, spicy peasant soup with meaty bones and potatoes. *Haejangguk* or 'hangover soup' (to help dispel the night's excesses) is made from a *doenjang* base, with bean sprouts, vegetables and sometimes cow's blood. *Samgyetang* is a ginseng chicken soup, infused with jujube, ginger and other herbs. It's not at all spicy and very easy on the palate – the idea is to be able to taste the hint of ginseng and the quality of the chicken. Though it originated as court cuisine, it is now seen as a summer tonic, meant to be eaten on the hottest days of the year.

Jjigae are more like stews, often orangey, spicy and served in a stone hotpot. The name of the *jjigae* – usually *dubu* (tofu), *doenjang* and *kimchi* – refers to the main, but not the only, ingredient; they all have vegetables and meat or fish. *Budae jjigae* ('army stew') was concocted during the Korean War using leftover hot dogs, Spam and macaroni scrounged from American bases.

A step up from *jjigae* in richness and variety of ingredients is *jeongol*, often translated as a casserole or hotpot. Raw ingredients are arranged in a shallow pan at the table, then topped off with a spicy broth and brought to a boil. Also unlike *jjigae*, *jeongol* is rarely served in individual portions. Common *jeongol* dishes are *dubu*, mushroom or seafood.

Jjim are dishes where the main ingredient is marinated in sauce, then simmered in a broth until the liquid is reduced. It's a popular serving style for prawns, crab and fish, and Andong has its *jjimdak* (prepared with chicken). Novices beware: *jjim* is *extremely* spicy.

Fried Food

Stir-fried dishes are called *bokkeum*, whipped up with sesame oil, green onion, *ganjang*, garlic, black pepper, salt, ginger and fish sauce. The main ingredient may be octopus, chicken or pork.

Savoury pancakes are very popular side dishes. *Bindaetteok* are made with mung-bean flour while *jeon* are made with wheat flour; *bindaetteok* tend to be heavier on the batter. Common fillings are *kimchi*, spring onion (*pajeon*) and seafood (*haemul pajeon*).

Jeongsik

Often translated as a set menu or table d'hôte, this is a spread of banquet dishes all served at once: fish, meat, soup, *dubu jjigae*, rice, noodles, steamed

Cooking at home? Try *Korean Cooking Made Easy* by Kim Young-hee (2006), *Growing Up in a Korean Kitchen* by Hi Soo Shin Hepinstall (2001) or *Quick & Easy Korean Cooking* by Cecilia Hae-Jin Lee (2009).

egg, shellfish and a flock of *banchan*. It's a good way to sample a wide range of Korean food at one sitting. *Hanjeongsik* (Korean *jeongsik*) may denote a traditional royal banquet spread of 12 dishes, served on *bangjja* (bronze) tableware.

Light Eats

For some inexpensive respite from *banchan*-laden meals, pop into a *gimbap* or *mandu* joint. *Gimbap* are colourful rolls of *bap* (rice) flavoured with sesame oil and rolled in *gim* (dried seaweed). Circular *gimbap* contains strips of vegetables, egg and meat. *Samgak* (triangular) *gimbap* is only available in convenience stores and is topped with a savoury fish, meat or vegetable mixture. If you refer to it as sushi, you run the risk of offending some Koreans (unlike sushi, the rice is not vinegared and not topped with raw fish).

Mandu are dumplings filled with meat, vegetables and herbs. Fried, steamed or served in soup, they make a tasty snack or light meal.

Breakfasts

Traditional breakfasts are lighter versions of lunch or dinner: soup, rice, some *banchan* and the inevitable *kimchi*. Modern breakfasts tend towards Western-style pairings of coffee and a pastry or sandwich, procured from a cafe, convenience store or bakery.

Useful online resources are My Korean Kitchen (www.mykoreankitchen.com) and Hannaone's Korean Recipes (www.hannaone.com).

Desserts

While desserts are not traditional in Korean dining, sometimes at the end of a meal you'll be served fruit as well as tea or *sujeonggwa*, a cold refreshing drink made from cinnamon and ginger. Many restaurants have self-serve coffee machines.

Western-style bakeries and ice-cream parlours abound, although cakes are generally saved for special occasions such as weddings and milestone birthdays. Bakeries and street vendors sell a mind-boggling array of bite-sized sweets: *hangwa* and *dasik* (traditional sweets and cookies, the latter made in a mould), and *tteok* (rice cakes) flavoured with nuts, seeds and dried fruit.

The classic summer dessert is *patbingsu*, a bowl heaped with shaved ice, some *tteok* and sweet red-bean topping with a splash of condensed milk. Modern toppings include strawberries, green-tea powder, and fresh or canned fruit.

DRINKS

Every restaurant serves *mul* (water) or tea. If there isn't a bottle on your table, look for the self-serve water dispenser.

SAUCY SIDE DISHES

It's not a Korean meal unless there's *kimchi* and *banchan* (side dishes) on the table. *Banchan* is meant to create balance in the meal in terms of saltiness, spiciness, temperature and colour. The number of *banchan* (which excludes soup, *kimchi*, stew and sauces) varies with how elaborate the meal it is, ranging from three in an ordinary meal, to 12 in traditional royal cuisine, to a perhaps anxiety-inducing 20 or more in a full-scale *jeongsik* (set menu or table d'hôte).

Banchan consists mostly of vegetables but may include fish, meat or *jeon* (savoury pancake). Every region has its own specialities. Besides the usual cabbage *kimchi*, it's common to see radish or cucumber *kimchi*, and dishes with spinach, seaweed, other green vegetables, garlic, bean sprouts, tofu, *bindaetteok* (mung-bean pancake), quail eggs, small clams, anchovies – just about anything the chefs can dream up. Some are spicy, but many are not. You most certainly don't have to eat it all, though if you like a particular dish and finish it, you can ask for refills (within reason).

LOCAL SPECIALITIES

- *ureok* (rockfish) – Busan (p237)
- *dakgalbi* (spicy chicken grilled with vegetables and rice cakes) – Chuncheon (p174)
- *maneul* (garlic) – Danyang (p344)
- *sundubu* (soft or uncurdled tofu) – Gangneung (p185)
- *oritang* (duck soup); *tteokgalbi* (grilled patties of ground beef) – Gwangju (p262)
- *okdomgui* (grilled, semi-dried fish); *jeonbok-juk* (abalone rice porridge); *heukdwaeji* (black-pig pork) – Jeju-do (p282)
- *bibimbap* (rice with vegetables, meat and egg) – Jeonju (p306)
- *ojing-eo* (squid) served *sundae* (sausage) style – Sokcho (p178)
- *galbi* (beef ribs) – Suwon (p155)
- *chungmu gimbap* (rice, dried seaweed and *kimchi*) – Tongyeong (p253)
- *gatkimchi* (leafy mustard *kimchi*) – Yeosu (p271)

Tea is a staple and the term is also used to describe drinks brewed without tea leaves. The most common leaf tea is *nokcha* (green tea), grown on plantations in Jeju-do (p302) and Jeollanam-do (p273). Black tea is harder to find. Non-leaf teas include the ubiquitous *boricha* (barley tea), *daechucha* (red-date tea), *omijacha* (five-flavour berry tea), *yujacha* (citron tea) and *insamcha* (ginseng tea). They may be served hot or cold.

In recent decades, Koreans have taken to coffee in a big way, drinking about 300 cups a year per person. Most of it is instant coffee, the overly sweet 3-in-1 (coffee, cream and sugar) mix churned out by vending machines (W300). Brewed coffee costs quite a bit more and is abundantly available (though the quality varies greatly) at Western-style cafes, from foreign imports like Starbucks to Korean chains like Angel-in-us Coffee, Caffe Pascucci, Holly's and Terarosa.

Bottled and canned soft drinks are everywhere. Some uniquely Korean choices are grape juice with whole grapes inside, and *sikhye*, rice punch with rice grains inside. Health tonics, made with fibre, vitamins, ginseng and other medicinal herbs, are available in shops and pharmacies.

Alcoholic Drinks

Drinking, and drinking heavily, is very much a part of Korean socialising, and an evening out can quickly turn into a blur of bar-hopping. The most common poison of choice is *soju*, the mere mention of which tends to elicit looks of dismay from foreigners. The stuff is, to put it bluntly, ethanol mixed with water and flavouring. Cheaper varieties (sold in convenience stores for as little as W1000) have all the subtlety of really awful moonshine, while those distilled from grain (W7000 and up) offer a far more delicate flavour. The cheap stuff has an alcohol content of 20% to 35%, while the good stuff goes up to 45%. The latter includes Andong *soju* and 'white *soju*' – look for them in Gyeongsangbuk-do and Gyeongsangnamdo respectively.

Koreans drink enough *soju* that the brand Jinro Soju (you'll see the green bottles everywhere) is the top-selling brand of spirits *worldwide*. The size of the *soju* bottle is calculated to fill only seven glasses, so that drinkers have to order two or more bottles to make sure everyone's glass is filled on each round. Always pour for your elders, never pour for yourself, and use both hands to hold your glass when it's being filled. Most importantly, remember that the stuff might go down easy, but can induce a killer hangover the next day.

Fortunately, *soju* isn't the only homegrown option. *Makgeolli* is a traditional farmer's brew made from unrefined, fermented rice wine. Much lower in alcohol content than *soju*, it has a cloudy appearance and a sweetish yoghurty flavour. It is traditionally served in a kettle and poured into small bowls. *Dongdongju* is similar, with rice grains floating in it. Both are popular tipplers in national parks, where it's practically ritual to swig down a bowl or two after (or during) an arduous hike.

A host of sweetish traditional spirits are brewed or distilled from grains, fruits and roots. Many are regional or seasonal, and easier on the oesophagus than *soju*. *Bokbunjaju* is made from wild raspberries, *meoruju* from wild fruit, *maesilju* from green plums and *insamju* from ginseng.

Finally: beer or *maekju*, possibly the least exciting of all Korean alcohol. Local brands, all lagers, are the rather bland Cass, Hite and O.B. Guinness and other imported beers are increasingly available, and a few microbreweries have started up, mainly in Seoul. Wine is much more common than it used to be, although choices are limited.

When Koreans go out to drink, they'll order *anju* (bar snacks) as well. Forget what you know about piddling bowls of peanuts or crisps. While traditionally *anju* meant *kimchi*, *dotorimuk* (acorn jelly) or *dubu kimchi*, these days you'll get heaped plates of oil-soaked food – fried chicken, French fries or vegetable *twigim* – that can be a meal in itself.

> Want to learn how to make Korean dishes such as *kimchi*? Seoul is the best place to take cookery courses in English (p117).

CELEBRATIONS WITH FOOD

Tteok (rice cakes) are associated with many traditional festive occasions, and small, family-run *tteok* shops are a common sight. The Lunar New Year is celebrated with *tteokguk* (rice-cake soup), Chuseok (Thanksgiving) with *songpyeon* (crescent-shaped rice cakes with red-bean filling), and the winter solstice with *patjuk* (red-bean porridge with rice-cake balls).

WHERE TO EAT & DRINK

Options for eating out range from casual bites at a market stall to an elaborate *jeongsik* meal at a lavish restaurant. Larger establishments often call themselves *sikdang* (restaurant) or *jib* (house). Many places serve a small menu of less than 10 specialities; only those at national parks and tourist villages tend to have a wider range. Restaurants outside major cities are unlikely to have menus in English.

Most meals cost under W7000 and dishes that cost W15,000 and up are usually meant for sharing, such as *jeongol*, *jjim*, whole fish or servings of *galbi* or *samgyeopsal*. Menu prices usually include *banchan* and rice; if the latter is not included, it's about W1000. Most restaurants serve water, tea and a few types of alcohol, and may have a self-serve instant coffee machine but not soft drinks. Tipping is not expected, though high-end restaurants often add a 10% service charge.

It's worth reiterating that eating out is a social activity, so solo travellers may encounter a quizzical '*Honja?*' ('Alone?'). The odd restaurant may turn away solo diners because they only serve meals in portions for two (especially for *jeongsik* and barbecue). You can promise to order (and eat) a two-person portion, but if they're adamant about not serving you, don't take it personally.

Street food consists more of snacks than meals, though as they're frequently drenched in sauce and oil, a few bites can be quite filling. They cost W500 to W4000 and include *tteokbokki* (rice cakes in a spicy and rather overwhelming orange sauce), *dakkochi* (grilled chicken skewers), *sundae*

> Not sure what to order? Take a look over Seoul Eats' Dictionary of Popular Korean Dishes (www.seouleats.com/2008/01/dictionary-of-popular-korean-dishes.html) and 'English Name of Korean Food' (www.dynamic-korea.com/cuisine/english_name/eng_name.php?menugubun=4), maintained by the Embassy of the Republic of Korea in the US.

(sausages containing vegetables and noodles) and *odeng* (processed seafood). In warm weather look for *pojangmacha*, the tarp-covered food stalls that sell street snacks, sit-down meals and *soju*. They stay open well into the wee hours of the night.

Like any good developed country, South Korea has plenty of modern convenience food. Except for small towns, there's no shortage of American fast food or the local McDonald's-like chain Lotteria. Department stores and malls usually have food courts, and 24-hour convenience stores are everywhere. The latter sell quick eats such as instant noodles (boiling water is available), *gimbap* and sandwiches.

Most restaurants and convenience stores sell alcohol, but for categorically alcohol-fuelled outings, look for bars and *hof*. The latter term, inspired by German beer halls, has come to mean any watering hole that serves primarily Korean beer, with the requisite plate of fried chicken and other *anju*.

VEGETARIANS & VEGANS

South Koreans eat 1.6 million tons of *kimchi* every year and when the country's first astronaut went into space in 2008, he took a specially engineered 'space *kimchi*' with him.

Although Korean cuisine uses lots of vegetables, much of it is pickled or cooked with meat or seafood. *Dubu jjigae* may be made from beef or seafood stock, and *beoseot deopbap* (mushrooms on rice) may contain a few slices of pork. Even *kimchi* is often made with fish sauce. The only assuredly meat-free meals are those served at Buddhist temples or restaurants.

The safest bet is to ask about the ingredients or order something like *bibimbap* without the ingredients you don't eat. Be as specific as you can – for instance, saying 'no meat' may not suffice to omit seafood.

EATING WITH KIDS

Despite the dominant spicy and sour flavours, there's plenty of Korean food that children can enjoy. *Bulgogi* and *galbi* are flavourful but not spicy if you skip the dipping sauces, and kids might get a kick out of cooking dinner at the table or wrapping their own *ssam*. *Gimbap* is colourful and mild-flavoured, while *bibimbap*, *japchae* and *pajeon* contain identifiable (and again, colourful) ingredients. Many *banchan* go down easy and are fun to sample. Some restaurants have play areas and soft-serve ice-cream machines.

Street vendors sell child-friendly snacks such as *hotteok* (wheat pancake with honey, sugar, peanuts and cinammon), *bungeoppang* and *gukhwappang* (respectively, fish-shaped and flower-shaped waffles containing red-bean paste). *Tteokbokki* is very popular with Korean children and teenagers, but the spicy sauce smothering it can be a bit much.

HABITS & CUSTOMS

In traditional restaurants, remove your shoes at the door, putting them on shoe racks if provided. Diners sit on thin cushions on the floor and you can stack a few cushions for more comfort. The menu is often simply hanging on the wall. You can order a main course, which will come with rice, soup,

WHY METAL BOWLS & CHOPSTICKS?

One of the most striking things about Korean tableware is the preponderance of stainless steel – bowls, cups, dishes and utensils – even though Korea has one of the world's great ceramic-making traditions and neighbouring countries use ceramic bowls and chopsticks made of plastic or wood. The most common explanation for this is that the Joseon kings insisted on silver chopsticks and bowls because silver would tarnish in the presence of poison. The custom was passed down to the common people, although they could only afford baser metals. Metal is also easy to clean and hard to break.

DINING DOS & DON'TS

Dos

■ Do take off your shoes in traditional restaurants where everyone sits on floor cushions. Sit with your legs crossed or to the side.

■ Do pour drinks for others if you notice that their glasses are empty. It's polite to use both hands when pouring or receiving a drink.

■ Do ask for *gawi* (scissors) if you're trying to cut something and your spoon won't do it.

■ Do place the chopsticks and spoon back in their original position at the end of the meal.

Don'ts

■ Don't start or finish your meal before your seniors and elders.

■ Don't touch food with your fingers, except when handling *ssam*.

■ Don't eat rice with chopsticks – always use a spoon.

■ Don't pick up bowls and plates from the table to eat from them.

■ Don't leave your chopsticks or spoon sticking up from your rice bowl. This is taboo, only done with food that is offered to deceased ancestors.

■ Don't pour drinks for yourself (unless you're alone).

■ Don't blow your nose at the table.

■ Don't tip.

kimchi and *banchan*. Don't feel guilty about leaving *banchan* as no one is expected to finish everything.

If the table is not set, there will be an oblong box containing metal chopsticks and long-handled spoons, as well as metal cups and a bottle of water or tea. You can hand out the utensils and cups once you've ordered. Meals are eaten communally, so most dishes (except for individual portions of rice) are placed in the centre. The spoon is meant for rice, soup and any dish with liquids; chopsticks are for everything else. Avoid using the chopsticks and spoon together in one hand at the same time.

Korean eat out – a *lot* – and love to sit and sup on a main course for several hours (and over several bottles of *soju*). Diners eat a bit from one dish, a bite from another, a little rice, a sip of soup, mixing spicy and bland any way they want. The main point, always: just enjoy the food.

FOOD GLOSSARY
Food
FISH & SEAFOOD

chobap	초밥	raw fish on rice
ganjang gejang	간장게장	raw crab marinated in soy sauce
garibi	가리비	scallops
gwang-eohoe	광어회	raw halibut
hongeo	홍어	ray, usually served raw
jangeogui	장어구이	grilled eel
kijogae	키조개	razor clam
kkotgejjim	꽃게찜	steamed blue crab
modeumhoe	모듬회	mixed raw-fish platter
nakji	낙지	octopus
odeng	오뎅	processed seafood cakes in broth
ojingeo	오징어	squid

ojingeo sundae	오징어순대	stuffed squid 'sausage'
saengseongui	생선구이	grilled fish
saeugui	새우구이	grilled prawns
samchigui	삼치구이	grilled mackerel
ureok	우럭	rockfish

GIMBAP 김밥

chamchi gimbap	참치김밥	tuna gimbap
chijeu gimbap	치즈김밥	cheese gimbap
modeum gimbap	모듬김밥	assorted gimbap
samgak gimbap	삼각김밥	triangular gimbap

KIMCHI 김치

baechu kimchi	배추김치	cabbage kimchi; the classic spicy version
kkakdugi	깍두기	cubed radish kimchi
mul kimchi	물김치	cold kimchi soup
oisobagi	오이소박이	stuffed cucumber kimchi

MEAT DISHES

bossam	보쌈	steamed pork with kimchi, cabbage and lettuce wrap
bulgogi	불고기	barbecued beef slices and lettuce wrap
dakgalbi	닭갈비	spicy chicken pieces grilled with vegetables and rice cakes
dwaeji galbi	돼지갈비	pork ribs
galbi	갈비	beef ribs
heukdwaeji	흑돼지	black pig
jjimdak	찜닭	spicy chicken pieces with noodles
jokbal	족발	steamed pigs' feet
kkwong	꿩	pheasant
metdwaejigogi	멧돼지고기	wild pig
neobiani/tteokgalbi	너비아니/떡갈비	large minced meat patty
ogolgye	오골계	black chicken
samgyeopsal	삼겹살	barbecued (bacon-like) streaky pork belly
tangsuyuk	탕수육	Chinese-style sweet-and-sour pork
tongdakgui	통닭구이	roasted chicken
yukhoe	육회	seasoned raw beef

NOODLES

bibim naengmyeon	비빔냉면	cold buckwheat noodles with vegetables, meat and sauce
bibimguksu	비빔국수	noodles with vegetables, meat and sauce
jajangmyeon	자장면	noodles in Chinese-style black-bean sauce
japchae	잡채	stir-fried 'glass' noodles and vegetables
kalguksu	칼국수	wheat noodles in clam-and-vegetable broth
kongguksu	콩국수	wheat noodles in cold soybean soup
makguksu	막국수	buckwheat noodles with vegetables
naengmyeon	냉면	buckwheat noodles in cold broth
ramyeon	라면	instant noodles in soup
udong	우동	thick white noodle broth

RICE DISHES

| *bap* | 밥 | boiled rice |
| *bibimbap* | 비빔밥 | rice topped with egg, meat, vegetables and sauce |

bokkeumbap	볶음밥	Chinese-style fried rice
boribap	보리밥	boiled rice with steamed barley
daetongbap	대통밥	rice cooked in bamboo stem
dolsot bibimbap	돌솥비빔밥	bibimbap in stone hotpot
dolsotbap	돌솥밥	hotpot rice
dolssambap	돌쌈밥	hotpot rice and lettuce wraps
gonggibap	공기밥	steamed rice
gulbap	굴밥	oyster rice
hoedeopbap	회덮밥	bibimbap with raw fish
honghapbap	홍합밥	mussel rice
jeonbokjuk	전복죽	rice porridge with abalone
juk	죽	rice porridge
kimchi bokkeumbap	김치볶음밥	fried kimchi rice
kongnamul gukbap	콩나물국밥	spicy rice bean-sprout porridge
ojingeo deopbap	오징어덮밥	squid rice
pyogo deopbap	표고덮밥	mushroom rice
sanchae bibimbap	산채비빔밥	bibimbap with mountain vegetables
sinseollo	신선로	meat, fish and vegetables cooked in broth
ssambap	쌈밥	assorted ingredients with rice and wraps

SNACKS

beondegi	번데기	boiled silkworm larvae
bungeoppang	붕어빵	fish-shaped waffle with red-bean paste
dakkochi	닭꼬치	spicy grilled chicken on skewers
delimanju	데리만주	custard-filled minicakes
gukhwappang	국화빵	flower-shaped waffle with red-bean paste
hotteok	호떡	wheat pancake with sweet filling
jjinppang	찐빵	giant steamed bun with sweet-bean paste
mettugi	메뚜기	fried grasshoppers
norang goguma	노랑고구마	sweet potato strips
nurungji	누룽지	crunchy burnt-rice cracker
odeng	오뎅	processed seafood
patbingsu	팥빙수	shaved-iced dessert with tteok and red-bean topping
tteok	떡	rice cake
tteokbokki	떡볶이	pressed rice cakes and vegetables in a spicy sauce

SOUPS

bosintang	보신탕	dog-meat soup
chueotang	추어탕	minced loach-fish soup
dakbaeksuk	닭백숙	chicken in medicinal herb soup
dakdoritang	닭도리탕	spicy chicken and potato soup
doganitang	도가니탕	ox kneecaps soup
galbitang	갈비탕	beef-rib soup
gamjatang	감자탕	meaty bones and potato soup
haejangguk	해장국	bean-sprout soup ('hangover soup')
haemultang	해물탕	spicy assorted seafood soup
hanbang oribaeksuk	한방 오리백숙	duck in medicinal soup
heukyeomsotang	흑염소탕	goat soup
kkorigomtang	꼬리곰탕	ox tail soup
maeuntang	매운탕	spicy fish soup
manduguk	만두국	soup with meat-filled dumplings
oritang	오리탕	duck soup
ppyeohaejangguk	뼈해장국	meaty bones hotpot

samgyetang	삼계탕	ginseng chicken soup
seolleongtang	설렁탕	beef and rice soup
tokkitang	토끼탕	spicy rabbit soup

STEWS

budae jjigae	부대찌개	'army stew' with hot dogs, Spam and vegetables
dakjjim	닭찜	braised chicken
doenjang jjigae	된장찌개	soybean paste stew
dubu jjigae	두부찌개	tofu stew
galbijjim	갈비찜	braised beef ribs
gopchang jeongol	곱창전골	tripe hotpot
kimchi jjigae	김치찌개	kimchi stew
nakji jeongol	낙지전골	octopus hotpot
sundubu jjigae/jeongol	순두부찌개/전골	spicy uncurdled tofu stew/hotpot

OTHER

bindaetteok	빈대떡	mung-bean pancake
dongchimi	동치미	pickled radish
donkkaseu	돈까스	pork cutlet with rice and salad
dotorimuk	도토리묵	acorn jelly
gujeolpan	구절판	eight snacks and wraps
hanjeongsik	한정식	Korean-style banquet
jeongsik	정식	set menu or table d'hôte, with lots of side dishes
mandu	만두	filled dumplings
omeuraiseu	오므라이스	omelette with rice
pajeon	파전	green-onion pancake
sangcharim	상차림	banquet of meat, seafood and vegetables
shabu shabu	샤브샤브	DIY beef and vegetable casserole
sigol bapsang	시골밥상	countryside-style meal
siksa	식사	budget-priced banquet
sujebi	수제비	dough flakes in shellfish broth
sundae	순대	noodle and vegetable sausage
sundubu	순두부	uncurdled tofu
twigim	튀김	seafood or vegetables fried in batter
wangmandu	왕만두	large steamed dumplings

Drinks
NONALCOHOLIC

boricha	보리차	barley tea
cha	차	tea
daechucha	대추차	red-date tea
hongcha	홍차	black tea
juseu	주스	juice
keopi	커피	coffee
mukapein keopi	무카페인 커피	decaffeinated coffee
mul	물	water
nokcha	녹차	green tea
omijacha	오미자차	five-flavour berry tea
saenggangcha	생강차	ginger tea
saengsu	생수	mineral spring water
seoltang neo-eoseo/ppaego	설탕 넣어서/빼고	with/without sugar
sikhye	식혜	rice punch
ssanghwacha	쌍화차	herb tonic tea

sujeonggwa	수정과	cinnamon and ginger punch
sungnyung	숭늉	burnt-rice tea
uyu	우유	milk
uyu neo-eoseo/ppaego	우유 넣어서/빼고	with/without milk
yujacha	유자차	citron tea

ALCOHOLIC

bokbunjaju	복분자주	wild berry liquor
dongdongju/makgeolli	동동주/막걸리	fermented rice wine
insamju	인삼주	ginseng liquor
maekju	맥주	beer
maesilju	매실주	green plum liquor
Sansachun	산사춘	rice wine with Chinese hawthorn
soju	소주	vodka-like drink

Active Korea

For travellers who enjoy a little more physical activity than simply eating and shopping on their holiday, Korea will not disappoint. From hiking and mountain biking to skiing and scuba diving, Korea is a year-round, outdoor lovers' paradise. Less extreme but equally enjoyable activities include birdwatching, cycling and walking. And after a hard day of activity, relax in one of Korea's hot springs or saunas, health-and-beauty bargains that are popular 24 hours a day, 365 days a year. You can simmer in ginseng, green-tea and mud baths as well as bake in mugwort and jade saunas.

BIRDWATCHING

Birds Korea (www. birdskorea.org) has wonderful photos of Korean birds and loads of info for bird lovers.

With some of the widest and most extensive tidal flats in the world, the Korean peninsula is a natural magnet for our feathered friends. More than 500 species of birds (p64) have been spotted in Korea including 34 threatened species; most are just visiting on their migratory route between Siberia and Manchuria in the north and Southeast Asia and Australia in the south. One of Korea's most famous visitors is the hooded crane, which winters in **Suncheon Bay** (p270), a wetland park on Jeollanam-do's south coast that is a popular birding spot.

The best areas for birdwatching in Korea are on the west coast and islands, but birds can often be found in the most unlikely places. The **DMZ** (p152) is a paradise pit stop for migrating birds because it's been uninhabited for 50 years. In the midst of Seoul, on a pair of islets in the Han River, is the **Bamseom Island Bird Sanctuary** (Map p93); it's off-limits to humans but birds – including mandarins, mallards, spotbills and great egrets – can be spotted with binoculars from an observation platform in the Han River Park in Yeouido.

CYCLING & MOUNTAIN BIKING

Mountain bikers should check out www.mtbk -adventure.com, a useful online resource run by Korea-based expats that details a selection of possible trails.

Almost every city with a waterfront and hordes of tourists has a stand where bikes can be hired. Most are geared towards leisure riders with couples and families in mind, so expect well-marked, paved, flat trails designed for pleasure rather than intense cross-country exhilaration. To hire a bike, some form of ID is usually required; a helmet or lock is almost never included.

People who value full mobility in their limbs rarely venture onto Seoul's streets with a bike between their legs, but the bicycle trails along the **Han River** (p113) are ideal for a comfortable, car-free family outing. Bikes can be hired on Yeouido, which is a good starting point for a 90-minute, 7km sprint to the World Cup Stadium or a more ambitious 38km ride to Olympic Park. The paved paths are dotted with parks, sports fields, gardens and the occasional snack bar. Further east and north of the river, bikes of similar quality and price can be hired at Ttukseom Resort.

Travellers in good shape can circumvent **Jeju-do** (p289; bicycle hire W5000 to W8000 per day). The 200km pedal trek around the oval island takes about three to five days depending on the condition of the road and your legs. Hwy 1132 runs around the entire island and has bicycle lanes on either side. Shore roads also have bike lanes but it's a less developed system and not always bike-friendly. The inland scenery is greener and the roads are less busy but they lack bicycle lanes.

Off Jeju-do's eastern coast, **U-do** (p294) offers a comparatively short but testing 17km island spin past a lighthouse perched on a 132m-high cliff. Hire your bicycle (W5000 per two hours) near the ferry docks.

Located in the centre of the Gogunsan Archipelago, 50km off the coast of North Jeolla province, **Seonyu-do** (p317; bicycle hire W3000 per hour) is a pretty, undeveloped island, ideal for travellers looking for a day-trip escape to a picture-postcard setting. Pedal around laid-back fishing villages, cross bridges over to neighbouring islands or follow the paved trail alongside a 2km white sandy beach and aqua ocean. Bring a picnic or enjoy a fresh seafood meal by the ocean.

Pretty and relaxing **Chuncheon** (p174) is the antithesis of most busy Korean cities. During the day, ferry your bicycle over to Jung-do for a short island ride amid horse-drawn carriages, while looking out for waterbirds nesting in the reeds. In the late afternoon, cruise on two wheels along the shores of Uiam Lake for a pedal-stopping sunset view. Bikes can be hired outside the lakeside **tourist information centre** (per hr/day W3000/5000; ⊙ 9am-7pm).

DIVING

Korea has a surprisingly active scuba-diving scene. The top dive site is just off Seogwipo on Jeju-do's southern coast, and has good visibility, colourful coral, kelp forests inhabited by schools of fish and the occasional visiting dolphin. The subterranean ecology around Jeju-do is a unique mixture of the tropical and temperate.

For the low down on scuba-diving courses, dive clubs and dive sites in Korea, visit www.scubainkorea.com.

The best diving operation in Seogwipo is **Big Blue 33** (p298), run by Ralf Deutsch, an experienced diving enthusiast who speaks English, German and Korean (see below).

For a unique underwater experience, go scuba diving with the sharks, turtles, rays and giant groupers in **Busan Aquarium** (☎ 051-740 1700; www.scubainkorea.com/Shark_Diving/Shark_Diving.htm; certified/noncertified divers W75,000/W95,000). Even nondivers can do it after a two-hour training session with an English-speaking instructor. The 30-minute dives take place on Saturdays and Sundays.

Besides Seogwipo on Jeju-do; Hong-do off the south coast; Pohang, Ulleung-do and Dragon Head off Sokcho; and a wreck dive off Gangneung are all underwater sites on the east coast worth exploring. Even the west coast has some dive operators, for instance at Daecheon beach, but visibility can be poor. Much of the country's coastal waters are unexplored, so who knows what you might discover.

GOLF

In 1998, Se Ri Pak put South Korea on the map by winning the US Women's Open. Today, Korean women dominate the American LPGA Tour and golf has become a national pastime. There are about 260 golf courses in South Korea. The most popular golfing destination is Jeju-do, particularly the scenic oceanfront course at **Jungmun Resort** (p301).

RALF DEUTSCH: OWNER, BIG BLUE 33 DIVE SHOP

I'm originally from Osnabruck, Germany. In 2001, after six years of teaching at Jeju University, I decided to start a dive shop to cater to the growing number of non-Korean-speaking visitors. When I opened Big Blue 33, I only had 300 dives under my belt; now I've done more than 2400. The underwater world of Jeju is a unique combination of cold and warm water. So you will see cold-water-loving kelp forests and flounder right next to warm-water marine life such as soft coral and lionfish. This is due to the *kuroshio,* or black current, that brings warm water from the tropics and mixes with the cold waters here, creating an interesting mix that creates good diving conditions. September and October offer the best conditions, when the water is 27°C and visibility is 40m. Jeju-do is a good island. It's beautiful, it has a nice climate, the people are nice and I have a job I enjoy.

Unfortunately, golf here is not cheap. An average 18-hole round of golf will set you back W300,000, that is, if you can even find a tee time. That's where virtual golf, at **golf cafes**, comes into play. There are now 3000 golf cafes around the country, so you'll find one in just about any city. A round of virtual golf at chains like **Golfzon** (http://company.golfzon.com) costs about W30,000. There are also regular golf practice ranges (see p113).

HIKING

View www.adventureko
rea.com for hiking adven-
tures and activity tours
from Seoul organised by
enterprising Seok-jin.

Taekwondo might be the country's national sport, but hiking is the number-one leisure activity in mountainous Korea. There are thousands of trails, with everything from easy half-day walks to strenuous mountain-ridge treks. Maybe it's the intoxicatingly fresh air, or the occasional *soju* (local vodka) pick-me-up, but Korea's hiking trails are frequented by some of the country's most hospitable people.

Most of the exhilarating mountain trails, like those on Jirisan (p258) and Seoraksan (p182), are located in the country's outstanding national parks. Basic shelters are available but expect a full house during holidays, summer months and autumn weekends. If you're planning a major overnight mountain trek, shelter reservations two weeks in advance are recommended. About one quarter of the trails may be closed at any one time to allow the mountain to regenerate itself. Visit the **National Park Authority** (www.knps.or.kr) website for contact numbers, trail closure information and online reservations.

The country's 20 national parks are as beautiful in winter as they are in summer, and snow on temple roofs provide wonderful photo opportunities. Keep in mind though that appropriate clothes and exposure precautions are a must as temperatures can reach Siberian levels and whiteout blizzards are possible up in the mountains.

Three of our favourite hikes are:

Hallasan (☎ visitors centre 064-713 9950; www.hallasan.go.kr) Hiking up this ancient volcano to the crater lake at the summit (1950m) is a highlight of any Jeju-do trip. There are four separate trails, each with its unique characteristics and ability levels (p303). The nearest towns are Seogwipo or Jeju-si.

Mudeungsan Provincial Park (eng.gjcity.net) This popular urban park (p265) is easy to reach from Gwangju and fills up with cheery hikers every weekend. The challenging trails take you past Buddhist temples, odd rock formations, colourful fields of azalea, the Chunseolheon green-tea plantation and numerous hilltop restaurants.

Visit www.jejuolle.
org and koreaclimbs.
blogspot.com, two great
resources for hiking in
Korea.

Yeonhwa-do (eng.tongyeong.go.kr) Located off the picturesque Tongyeong coast in Gyeong-sangnam-do, this undeveloped and largely undiscovered island is a splendid escape for travellers looking for a leisurely three-hour hike to breathtaking ocean vistas. The nearest town is Tongyeong (p253).

HOT-SPRING SPAS

Koreans love hot food, hot baths and hot saunas – the hotter the better. Korea has many *oncheon* (hot-spring spas) where the therapeutic mineral-laden water that wells up from the depths of the earth is piped into communal baths. Equally popular are all kinds of saunas. Some saunas are fairly spartan but modern, luxurious ones called *jjimjilbang* have a gym, hairdresser, cafe, TV, internet access and more. In Korean spas you can bathe like Cleopatra in just about anything: hot and cold mineral water, green tea, ginseng, mud, mugwort, coffee, seawater and pine needles. Prices vary with the luxurious-ness of the facilities and most are open 24 hours.

The water in the big public baths varies from hot to extremely hot, but there may also be a cold bath, including a 'waterfall' shower. Relaxing in a

---

RESPONSIBLE HIKING

■ Pay any fees required by local authorities.

■ Be sure you are healthy and feel comfortable walking for a sustained period.

■ Obtain reliable information about route conditions.

■ Be aware of local laws, regulations and etiquette about wildlife and the environment. Do not hike closed trails.

■ Walk only on trails within your realm of experience.

■ Be aware that weather conditions can change quickly and seasonal changes alter trails. These differences will influence how you dress and the equipment to carry.

---

hot bath is good therapy as the heat soaks into weary bodies, soothing tired muscles and minds.

Most spas also have sauna rooms, usually made of wood or stone, but all are as hot as a pizza oven. If you want to suffer more, you can be pummelled by a masseur, which costs extra. Many bathers take a nap lying down on the dormitory floor with a block of wood for a pillow. Stay all day, or all night, if you want to; nobody will hassle you to leave.

Among our favourite spas:

Boryeong Mud Skincare Center Daecheon Beach (p331)
Deokgu Hot Springs Hotel Uljin (p234)
Hurshimchung Busan (p242)
Miranda Spa Plus Icheon (p161)
Silloam Fomentation Sauna Seoul (p114)
Yousung Spa Daejeon (p321)
Yulpo Haesu Nokchatang Boseong (p273)

The website www.koreaontherocks.com is a great resource for those wanting to go rock and ice climbing across the country.

ICE SKATING

Indoor ice skating is available all year at Seoul's **Lotte World** (p112). In winter a giant outdoor rink is set up in Seoul Plaza outside **City Hall** (Map pp100-1; admission W1000; ☺ 10am-10pm Mon-Thu, until 11pm Fri & Sat, mid-Dec-mid-Feb) and there are also temporary outdoor rinks at the Grand Hyatt and Sheraton Walkerhill hotels.

KAYAKING, CANOEING & RAFTING

Gangwon-do's northwest is the hot spot for kayaking, canoeing and rafting trips from mid-April to October. See the boxed text on p176 for details. Adventure Korea and the United Service Organizations (p118) also offer white-water rafting trips.

MARTIAL ARTS

Korean martial arts attract worldwide interest. Of the many forms of Korean martial arts, **taekwondo** is the most well known and is an official Olympic sport.

Millions of Korean children learn taekwondo in private academies, and you can often see them in local neighbourhoods heading to evening classes in their taekwondo outfits. All trainee soldiers in Korea also learn taekwondo. It is based on *taekkyon,* a martial art that is thousands of years old and is featured on ancient Goryeo tomb murals. *Taekkyon* is a defensive art that teaches movement, while taekwondo is known for its high kicks.

The Seoul-based **World Taekwondo Federation** (www.kukkiwon.co.kr) has regular competitions and demonstrations as well as training programs for beginners –

see p114. The **Taekwondo Park** is a massive theme park and museum currently under construction near Jeollabuk-do's Muju Ski resort. (p312).

Lesser-known Korean martial arts include **gicheon** (www.gicheon.org), an indigenous and ancient martial art. The mind/body discipline is based on six body postures and special exercises are designed to promote joint flexibility and free up the gi energy paths. **Hapkido** is a gentle martial art that uses deep breathing to achieve focus, and practitioners are taught to make use of their opponent's aggression and weak points to achieve victory. The Zen Buddhist practice of **sunmudo** focuses on breathing as an aid to attaining enlightenment. To watch demonstrations or take part in sunmudo training, head to the mountain temple at Golgul-sa (p214).

English-speaking martial art groups advertise in the Korea Herald on Thursdays. The World Martial Arts Festival, held every October in Chungju (see the boxed text, p342), includes obscure martial arts from many countries.

SKIING & SNOWBOARDING

With soaring mountains and a reliable snow record, Korea is a natural for winter sports. Skiing and snowboarding are relatively new phenomena in Korea, but today there are 14 ski resorts and more in the works. The epicentre of Korea's ski scene is Gangwon-do province; after narrowly losing the bidding for the 2010 and 2014 Winter Olympics, Gangwon-do's Pyeongchang county is now the leading contender to host the 2018 games.

With its Olympic aspirations, Korea has invested US$1.8 billion to build **Alpensia** (p190) a world-class ski resort that partially opened in 2009. When completed, Alpensia (a portmanteau of 'Alps' and 'Asia') will include a ski jump, a stadium, cross-country and biathlon courses, an ice-ridge climbing centre, golf course, water park and an Olympic village with five-star hotels.

STRIPING DOWN THE PUBLIC BATH

The public bath is more than a place to clean up. It's a social event. Families come here for quality time, businesspeople cultivate commercial relationships and mothers gather to discuss their children's education. Bathhouses in the West may be associated with seedy behaviour, but this most definitely is not the case in Korea.

A public bath (목욕탕), sometimes called a spa or sauna, is a room with warm, hot and cold-water tubs, saunas and a massage area (for a fee). Bathhouses have separate facilities for men and women, and everybody walks around naked (no swimwear or underwear!).

Most bathhouses have a jjimjilbang (찜질방), a co-ed room where people watch TV, read or do nothing. There are also specialty rooms like the Cold Room (it's like the inside of your freezer) or the Oxygen Room (O_2 made from thin air!). Everybody wears a loose-fitting uniform. Most jjimjilbang are open 24 hours and allow guests to sleep overnight on the floor or in a bunk bed.

Enter the public bath and place your footwear in a locker near the front desk, remove the key and give it to the person at the counter, which is where you pay. The basic fee gets you into the bath. A separate charge gets you a uniform and access to the jjimjilbang. After paying you'll receive a locker key. Go to the locker, strip down, place your belongings inside and put the key around your wrist or ankle. Next, shower in the bathing area before jumping into the tubs.

Rotating between the hot and cold tubs is the secret to an enjoyable experience. It stimulates blood circulation, creates a tingling sensation on the skin and produces a feeling of euphoria. Many Koreans prefer to sit on the ledge and dangle their feet in the hot water for 20 minutes or more. This bathing technique slowly warms the body and stimulates a body-cleansing sweat. When you're ready to do nothing, return to your locker, put on the uniform and follow the signs to the jjimjilbang. Stay as long as you like. When you're done, return to the bath for another round or get changed, return the locker key and retrieve your shoes. After a few hours, the feeling of euphoria begins to dissipate. That's OK, because you can do the whole thing again tomorrow.

POOL & FOUR BALL

There are pool halls all over the country that cost around W7000 an hour per table. Look for the obvious 'billiard cues and balls' signs outside. They often have pool (called 'pocketball' in Korea) and tables for games of 'four ball', which is similar to billiards, but there are no pockets and players must make cannon shots. Two red balls and two white ones are used. The players (any number) hit the white balls in turn. The object of the game is to hit both of the red balls in one shot without hitting the other white ball. It sounds easy but it isn't.

You score minus one if you are successful, and you also get to take another turn. You score nothing if you hit just one red, and you score plus one if you hit the other white ball or miss everything. Beginners start with a score of three points and when you improve you start with five points, then eight and so on. When your score reaches zero, to finish you must do a more difficult shot – hit one red and two side-cushions or two reds and one side-cushion without hitting the other white ball.

Gangwon-do's most famous current slopes are at **Yongpyong Ski Resort** (p190). It's Korea's oldest and biggest ski resort, with sweet slopes ranging from bunny options to black-diamond runs. It also has cross-country courses and the usual comforts of a ski resort town.

In north Gangwon-do, **Alps Ski Resort** (p185) is much smaller but gets the heaviest powder in the province and is spectacularly set near the North Korean border.

Nearby, **Gangchon Ski Resort** (p177) has 10 slopes and six lifts, but offers a unique off-slope activity: ice climbing on the nearby frozen waterfall, Gugok Pokpo. This 50m waterfall is spectacular at any time of the year but provides ice-climbers with an exciting challenge when it freezes between December and February. Ask for information about *bingbyeok deungban* (ice climbing).

Further southwest in Jeollabuk-do, **Muju Ski Resort** (p312) has the only slopes located within a Korean national park, the picturesque Deogyu-San National Park. Opened in 1990 Muju has become one of the country's top winter playgrounds – its 26 slopes have something for everyone, from bunny beginner to mogul-hardened monster. It's après-ski facilities set in an alpine-themed village are the best.

Less than 2km from the spa hotels of Suanbo Hot Springs in Chungcheongbuk-do, **Sajo Ski Resort** (p342) is modest, but has seven slopes and three lifts, and the hot springs make for an oh-so-relaxing return after you're done conquering the slopes.

For details of ski resorts within day trip range of Seoul see the boxed text on p160.

The ski season runs December to March. Lift tickets cost about W40,000 to W60,000 and equipment rentals about W30,000 per day, but your best bet is to buy a package deal. Packages can be bought in travel agents and include bus transport to and from Seoul, lift tickets, ski and clothing rental, and, if required, lessons and accommodation. An overnight package varies from W50,000 for a night in a *minbak* (private home with rooms for rent) or youth hostel, to over W250,000 for flashy condos and stylish hotels. Avoid the overcrowded weekends, especially at resorts near Seoul, as Koreans ski like they drive.

Beautiful Wildflowers in Korea (2002), published by the Korea Plant Conservation Society, has photos of 200 native flowers and will encourage you to stop and ID flowers on your travels.

Seoul 서울

Having been revived, phoenix-like, from the rubble of the Korean War, locals like to call their 600-year-old capital the 'miracle on the Han'. But as Seoul sets out with typical national zeal to reshape itself from a hardened concrete and steel economic powerhouse into a softer-edged 21st-century urban ideal of parks, culture and design, the signs are that the real miracle is currently unfolding. No stranger to cosmetic surgery, Seoul has signed up for the full face lift and lipo deal. Following on from the highly successful disinterring and landscaping of the central Cheong-gye stream comes the refashioning of the Han River parks, part of a plan to draw citizens towards the broad waterway splitting this immense metropolis into two distinct halves. As the city adopts the mantle of World Design Capital, other projects (see the boxed text opposite) are in the works, not least of which are the Dongdaemun Design Plaza & Park, the futuristic vision of star-architect Zaha Hadid, and the eco-friendly new City Hall.

In the rush for the new, Seoul's illustrious history hasn't been entirely jettisoned. Restoration of palaces and Namdaemun gate is ongoing and there's a plan to reconnect the fortress wall remains, parts of which snake over the forested mountains encircling the city that provide such wonderful refuge from the pressures of urban life. The joys of eating, drinking, shopping and general merrymaking are all in abundant evidence – from Apgujeong's chic boutiques to Hongdae's bars and restaurants. An old Korean proverb goes 'even if you have to crawl on your knees, get yourself to Seoul!' With so much going on, never has this been more sound advice.

HIGHLIGHTS

- Lose yourself in the picturesque, atmospheric streets of **Bukchon Hanok Village** (p106)

- Listen to shamans' chants on the hills of **Inwangsan** (p109)

- Stroll beside the **Cheong-gye-cheon** (p106) and return at night to see spectacular laser light shows

- Soak up the serenity of the Secret Garden at World Heritage–listed **Changdeokgung** (p105)

- Hike the ancient fortress walls to the summit of **Bukaksan** (p108) for panoramic views of the city

- Test your bargaining skills at the all-night **Namdaemun** (p108) or **Dongdaemun** (p108) markets

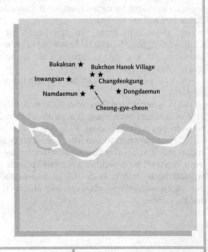

Bukaksan ★ Bukchon Hanok Village
Inwangsan ★ ★ ★
Namdaemun ★ ★ Changdeokgung
★ Dongdaemun
Cheong-gye-cheon

| ■ TELEPHONE CODE: 02 | ■ POPULATION: 10.4 MILLION | ■ AREA: 605 SQ KM |

REDESIGNING SEOUL: CHUNG KYUNG-WON

From 2010 Seoul is the World Design Capital, an accolade it is living up to with a series of ambitious projects covering everything from the typography of signage, creating symbols such as the official mascot Haechi (a mythical lion-like creature), deciding on the city's official colours and constructing complexes such as the Dongdaemun Design Plaza & Park (p108) and the new City Hall (p109). To find out more about how the city is changing we talked with the head of Design Seoul Headquarters and Deputy Mayor Chung Kyung-won, the man holding the purse strings of a US$100 million annual budget.

Why does Seoul need redesigning? After the Korean War totally destroyed everything in the city we had to rebuild quickly. There wasn't the energy or the resources to do this properly until the 1990s. There were urban plans but they were not so successful, especially in the older part of the city north of the Han River. The last mayor Lee Myung-bak started to change Seoul with the restoration of the Cheong-gye-cheon (p106). The current mayor Oh Se-hoon fully understands the importance of good design and wants to revitalise Seoul based on this. He set up the Design Seoul Headquarters in April 2007.

What projects have you been working on? We created the **Seoul Design Olympiad** (http://sdo. seoul.go.kr/eng/) as an annual event to promote design to Seoul's citizens – some two million people visited the first event in 2008. There is also a variety of missions to improve the quality of public design in the city, for example, the drawing up of guidelines on both public and commercial signs. There are several major 'renaissance' projects: along the Han River where major public facilities are being developed and improved; on Namsan where we want to improve access, the quality of facilities and use sustainable approaches by employing more natural materials in this central green area; and giving a facelift to the city's major streets creating historical, digital media, green and creative arts corridors.

HISTORY

When Seoul became the capital of Korea following the establishment of the Joseon dynasty in 1392 (p30) its population was around 100,000. Just over 600 years later this has ballooned to 10.42 million (or 24.5 million if you consider the wider metro area), making Seoul one of the world's largest cities.

During the 20th century Seoul suffered first under Japanese colonial rule and then during the Korean War when it was almost entirely destroyed. Rebuilt from the 1960s, Seoul is the country's centre of cultural, economic and political power. Past mayors have gone on to become South Korea's president, including the present incumbent Lee Myung-bak. The current mayor is Oh Se-hoon, who comes up for re-election in June 2010.

ORIENTATION

You'll spend the bulk of your time north of the meandering Han River that splits Seoul into two distinct regions, that are themselves split into 25 *gu* (administrative districts). This is home to historic Seoul, a relatively compact, walkable area once defined by fortress walls (p108).

Most tourist sights are clustered around the palaces in Gwanghwamun and Jongno-gu, while Seoul Station – eventual terminus for the A'rex train from Incheon International Airport – is just south of here in central Jung-gu.

Namsan, crowned by N Seoul Tower, the green hill at the heart of the old city, is sandwiched between Myeong-dong shopping district to the north and the foreigner-friendly zone of Itaewon to the south. Not far off to the west are the youthful party districts of Sinchon and Hongdae (short for Hongik University).

The largest mid-river island of Yeoui-do is like a mini-Manhattan with high rises and Korea's parliament.

South of the river, modern Gangnam and Apgujeong are the city's hubs of ostentation with expensive housing, shops and entertainment. Here you'll also find giant complexes such as COEX Mall and Olympic Park.

Maps

The Korea Tourism Organisation (KTO) office (Map pp96–7) and other tourist offices around town have an extensive selection of free maps.

INFORMATION
Bookshops
Bandi & Luni's (Map pp90-1; ☎ 6002 6002; COEX Mall; ⏰ 10am-10pm; ⊙ Line 2 to Samseong, COEX Exit)
There's also a branch in the Jongno Tower basement (Map pp96-7; ☎ 2198 3000; ⊙ Line 1 to Jongno, Exit 3).
Kyobo Bookshop (Map pp96-7; ☎ 3973 5100; ⊙ Line 5 to Gwanghwamun, Exit 4) Head to section F to find English-language books.
Seoul Selection (Map pp96-7; ☎ 734 9565; www. seoulselection.com; ⏰ 9.30am-6.30pm Mon-Sat; ⊙ Line 3 to Anguk, Exit 1) Best place for books, CDs and DVDs about Korea in English. Also has internet access.
What The Book? (Map p104; ☎ 797 2342; www.what thebook.com; Sobangseo-gil, Itaewon; ⏰ 10am-8pm Mon-Sat, from noon Sun; ⊙ Line 6 to Itaewon, Exit 3) New and second-hand English-language books as well as a wide range of American magazines.

Emergency
For general emergency numbers see the inside front cover. Phone ☎ 1330 for the 24 hour English-language tourist information and help line.

Internet Access
Internet rooms are on almost every street – look for the 'PC 방' sign. Most are open 24 hours and charge W1000 to W2000 per hour. Many backpacker guesthouses, hotels, cafes, tourists offices and government buildings offer free broadband internet access and wi-fi coverage is also widespread.

Laundry
Backpacker guesthouses and motels usually provide free use of a washing machine although you'll usually have to pay for drying. Dry-cleaning shops are fairly common, but they're not cheap.

Left Luggage
Most subway stations and bus terminals have lockers. Small lockers cost W1000 a day and the ones large enough for a backpack are W2000.

Media & Internet Resources
The glossy monthly magazine **Seoul** (http://travel. seoulselection.com) is well worth picking up; go to the website to also register for their useful weekly newsletter about what's going on in the city. Other free monthly magazines with plenty of Seoul-related content include **Groove Korea** (www.groovekorea.com) and **10 Magazine**

(www.10magazine.asia). Also tune into the English-language radio station **TBS eFM** (http://tbsefm.seoul. kr/) on 101.3 MHz for lots of info on what's happening in the city.
For information on the web go to:
Discovering Korea (www.discoveringkorea.com) Matt Kelly's blog is a goldmine of info on the city and other aspects of Korean culture.
Korea4Expats (www.korea4expats) Comprehensive expat-penned site with lots of useful info.
Seoul Metropolitan Government (http://english. seoul.go.kr) City's official site.
Seoulstyle.com (www.seoulstyle.com) The low-down on what's stylish in Seoul.
Visit Seoul (www.visitseoul.net) Official city tourism-devoted site.

Medical Services
Most facilities don't accept international insurance so bring cash or credit cards.
Daewon Dental Clinic (Map p104; ☎ 794 0551; Itaewon; ⏰ 10am-1pm & 2-6.30pm Mon-Fri, 10am-2pm Sat; ⊙ Line 6 to Itaewon, Exit 4) Gentle Dr Park can take care of your dental problems.
International Clinic (Map p104; ☎ 790 0857; www. internationalclinic.co.kr; Hannam Bldg, Itaewonno, Itaewon; ⏰ 9am-6pm Mon-Fri, 9am-3pm Sat, closed noon-2pm; ⊙ Line 6 to Itaewon, Exit 2)
Samsung Medical Center (Map pp90-1; ☎ 3410 0200; www.samsunghospital.com; 50 Ilwondong, Gangnam-gu; ⏰ 8.30am-noon, 1-5pm Mon-Fri; ⊙ Line 3 to Irwon, Exit 1)
Severance Hospital (Map p93; ☎ 2228 5810, emergencies 012 263 6556; http://sev.iseverance.com; ⏰ 9am-12.30pm, 1.30-4.30pm Mon-Fri, 9.30-11am Sat; ⊙ Line 2 to Sinchon, Exit 3) The International Health Care Centre is on the 3rd floor of the large building beside Yonsei University.

Money
Credit cards are readily accepted and more ATMs in Seoul accept foreign credit cards these days – look for one that has a 'Global' sign or the logo of your credit card company. Many banks offer a foreign-exchange service. There are also licensed moneychangers, particularly in Itaewon, that keep longer hours than the banks and provide a faster service, but may only exchange US dollars cash.

Post
Post offices are common and offer free internet access.
Anguk Post Office (Map pp96-7; ☎ 735 2005; Insa-dong; ⏰ 9am-6pm Mon-Fri; ⊙ Line 3 to Anguk, Exit 1)

SEOUL IN...

Four Days

Take an early morning stroll around **Bukchon Hanok Village** (p106), pausing for refreshments in one of Insa-dong or Samcheong-dong's cafes and teahouses in between browsing a few of the area's equally ubiquitous **art galleries** (p115). Admire the pageantry of the changing of the palace guard at **Gyeongbokgung** (p106) at noon, then lunch at **Tobang** (p133) or the fancier **Min's Club** (p134). Join the day's last tour of beautiful **Changdeokgung** (p105), then grab an early dinner at one of the *bindaetteok* stalls in **Gwangjang Market** (p132) before taking your seat at a fun non-verbal show such as **Nanta** or **Jump** (p143).

Start day two enjoying the art and architecture at the splendid **Leeum Samsung Museum of Art** (p110); afterwards take lunch at one of the many international restaurants of Itaewon (p135). If you've not had your fill of museums opt for either the **National Museum of Korea** (p110) or the **War Memorial Museum** (p111), but don't try to do both! Freshen up with a soak in the tubs at **Silloam Fomentation Sauna** or **Dragon Hill Spa** (p114) then follow the **night walking tour** (p114), which includes the cable car up to **N Seoul Tower** (p107) atop Namsan.

On day three look back at Namsan from the peak of Bukaksan (p108) having hiked along part of the city's old fortress walls. Reflect on Korea's recent tragic history at **Seodaemun Prison** (p109), then get some more exercise by exploring the temples and shrines of **Inwangsan** (p109) where you might come across a shaman uttering sounds that do not seem of this world. Treat yourself in the evening to the traditional performing-arts show and royal-cuisine meal at **Korea House** (p135).

A stroll along the **Cheong-gye-cheon** (p106) to **Dongdaemun** (p108) is a good way to begin day four; shop in the markets for cheap fashion and see how the Dongdaemun Design Plaza & Park are shaping up. Head south to the fascinating **Noryangjin Fish Market** (p111) for lunch then hire a bike in Yeoui-do and cycle along the Han River to the World Cup Stadium and back (see the boxed text, p113). Soak up the youthful vibe of Hongdae at night enjoying great restaurants and bars such as **Chin Chin** (p138) and **Vinyl** (p139).

Seven Days

On day five explore more sights south of the river including **Olympic Park** (p112), scattered with interesting sculptures, the atmospheric Buddhist temple **Bong-eun-sa** (p111) and the mammoth **COEX Mall** (p144). More shopping can be done in the chic boutiques of Apgujeong and along tree-lined Garosu-gil (p145). Dip into Gangnam nightlife with a meal and traditional rice wines at **Baekseju ma-eul** (p139).

Round out the week with a couple of day trips, the best being to the **DMZ** (p152) and to **Suwon** (p155).

Central Post Office (Map pp100-1; ☎ 6450 1114; Sogongno, Myeong-dong; ☺ 9am-8pm Mon-Fri, to 1pm Sat & Sun; ⊕ Line 4 to Myeong-dong, Exit 6) This basement office also sells train tickets.

Toilets

A huge effort has gone into improving standards, so Seoul nowadays has plenty of clean, modern and well-signed public toilets. Virtually all toilets are free of charge. As always, it's wise to carry a stash of toilet tissue around with you just in case there's none available.

Tourist Information

There are over 20 tourist information booths around the city.

The main ones are:

Cheong-gye-cheon Tourist Information Centre (Map pp96-7; Sejongno, Gwanghwamun; ☺ 9am-10pm; ⊕ Line 5 to Gwanhwamun, Exit 6)

Gyeongbokgung Tourist Information Centre (Map pp96-7; ☎ 720 7465; Gwanghwamun; ☺ 9am-6pm; ⊕ Line 3 to Gyeongbokgung, Exit 5)

Insa-dong Tourist Information Centre (Map pp96-7; ☎ 734 0222; Insadong-gil, Insa-dong; ☺ 10am-10pm; ⊕ Line 3 to Anguk, Exit 6) Free internet. Two more centres are at the south and north entrances to Insadong-gil.

Itaewon Subway Tourist Information Centre (Map p104; ☎ 3785 2514; Itaewon; ☺ 9am-10pm; ⊕ Line 6 to Itaewon) Free internet, but may close earlier in winter.

(Continued on page 105)

GREATER SEOUL

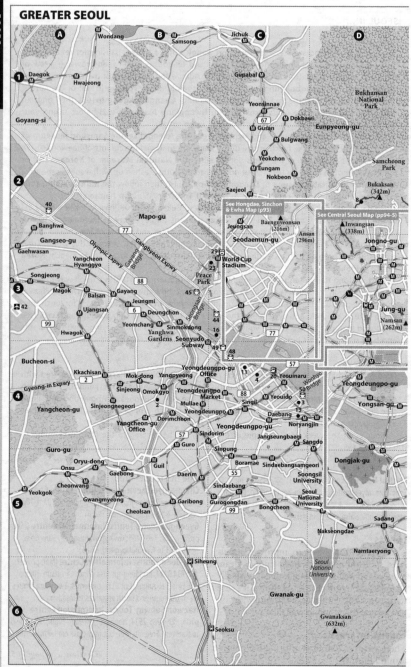

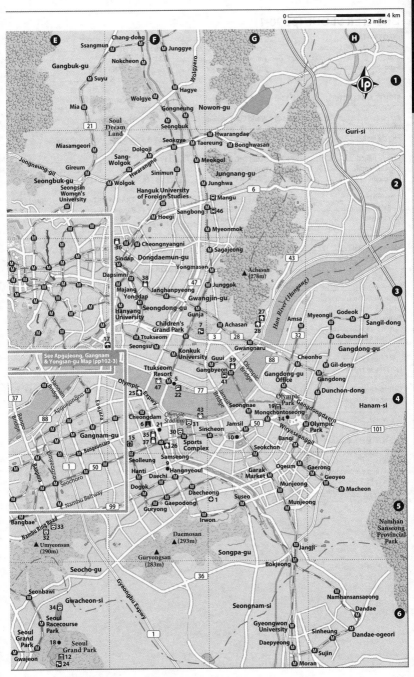

GREATER SEOUL (pp90-1)

HONGDAE, SINCHON & EWHA

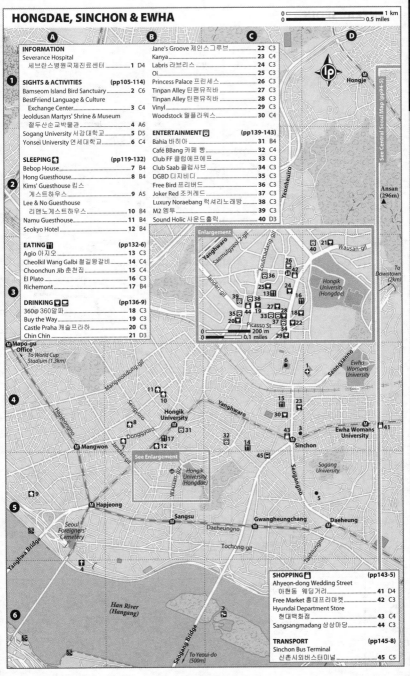

0 ────── 1 km
0 ────── 0.5 miles

SEOUL

CENTRAL SEOUL

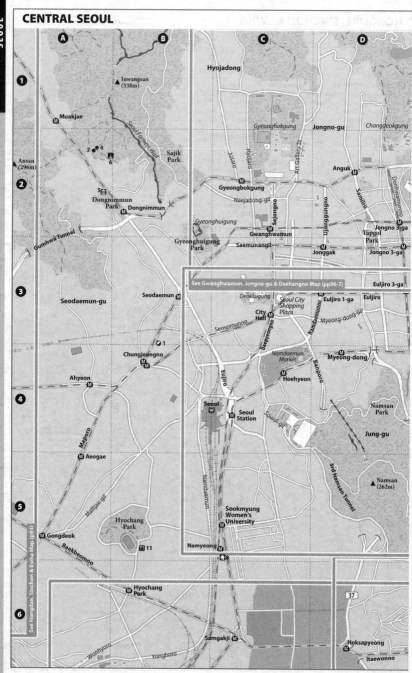

A B C D

1

▲ Inwangsan (338m)

Hyojadong

M Muakjae

Gyeongbokgung Jongno-gu Changdeokgung

Juiro

Hyoja-ro

Art Gallery St

2

▲ Ansan (296m)

7 ● 4
6

Sajik Park

Anguk M

Donhwamunno

5 🏛
Dongnimmun Park

M Dongnimmun

M Gyeongbokgung

Naejadong-gil

Sejongno

Samilro

Yulgongno

Jongno 3-ga M

Gumhwa Tunnel

Gyeonghuigung

Gwanghwamun M

Tapgol Park

Jongno 3-ga

Gyeonghuigung Park

Saemunangil

Jonggak

3

See Gwanghwamun, Jongno-gu & Daehangno Map (pp96-7)

Euljiro 3-ga

Seodaemun-gu

Seodaemun M

Deoksugung

Seoul City Shopping Plaza

Euljiro 1-ga Euljiro

Namdaemunno

Myeong-dong-gil

City Hall M

Seosomunno

Daepyeongno

Banpo-ro

Myeong-dong M

Namdaemunno

● 1

Chungjeongno M

Euljiro

Namdaemun Market

Hoehyeon M

4

M Ahyeon

Maporo

Seoul 🏛

Seoul Station

Sowol-gil

Namsan Park

Jung-gu

M Aeogae

5

Maltijae-gil

Hyochang Park

Namdaemun

Sookmyung Women's University

▲ Namsan (262m)

3rd Namsan Tunnel

M Gongdeok

Baekbeomno

🍴 11

Namyeong M

🏨 8

6

See Hongdae, Sinchon & Ewha Map (p93)

M Hyochang Park

37

Wonhyoro

Yonghoro

Samgakji M

Noksapyeong M

Itaewonno

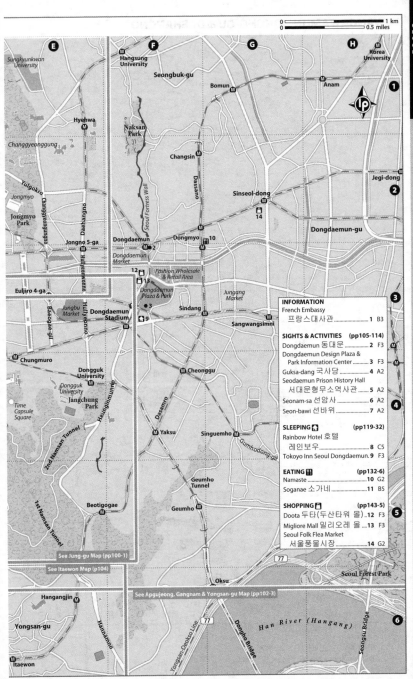

INFORMATION
French Embassy
  프랑스대사관 1 B3

SIGHTS & ACTIVITIES (pp105-114)
Dongdaemun 동대문 2 F3
Dongdaemun Design Plaza &
  Park Information Center 3 F3
Guksa-dang 국사당 4 A2
Seodaemun Prison History Hall
  서대문형무소역사관 5 A2
Seonam-sa 선암사 6 A2
Seon-bawi 선바위 7 A2

SLEEPING (pp119-32)
Rainbow Hotel 호텔
  레인보우 8 C5
Tokoyo Inn Seoul Dongdaemun. 9 F3

EATING (pp132-6)
Namaste 10 G2
Soganae 소가네 11 B5

SHOPPING (pp143-5)
Doota 두타(두산타워 몰) ..12 F3
Migliore Mall 밀리오레 몰 ..13 F3
Seoul Folk Flea Market
  서울풍물시장 14 G2

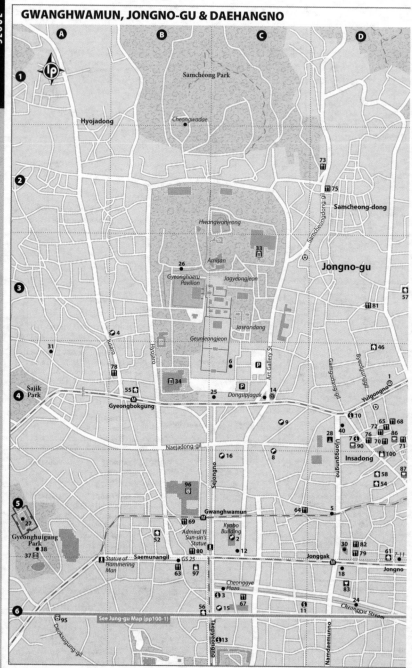

GWANGHWAMUN, JONGNO-GU & DAEHANGNO

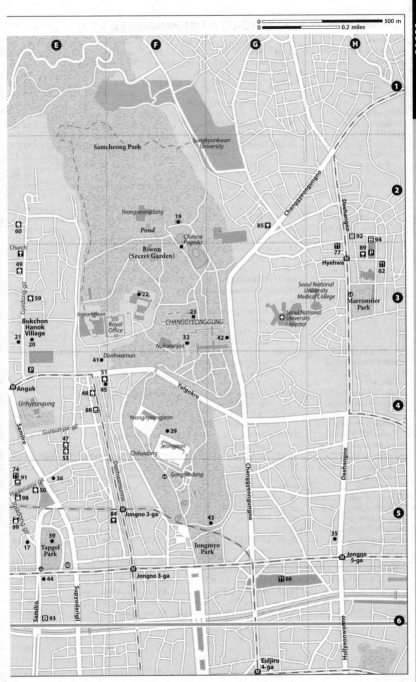

GWANGHWAMUN, JONGNO-GU & DAEHANGNO (pp96–7)

JUNG-GU (pp100-1)

INFORMATION
Canadian Embassy
캐나다대사관 **1** A1
Central Post Office **2** C2
Namdaemun Market
Tourist Information
Centre **3** C3
Namdaemun Market
Tourist Information
Centre **4** C2
Namsangol Office 남산골
한옥마을 입구 **5** F3
Russian Embassy
러시아대사관 **6** B1
Seoul Center for Culture &
Tourism **7** D2
Seoul Global Center **8** C1
UK Embassy 영국대사관 **9** B1

SIGHTS & ACTIVITIES   (pp105-114)
Anglican Church 대한
성공회 대성당 **10** B1
Bank of Korea Museum
한국은행화폐금융박물관
.... **11** C2
City Hall.. **12** C1
Deoksugung Ticket Office
덕수궁매표소 **13** B1
Hwangudan **14** C1
Kyungdong Presbyterian
Chruch 경동 교회 **15** H2
Myeong-dong Catholic
Cathedral 명동성당 **16** D2
N Seoul Tower 엔서울타워 **17** E5
Namdaemun 남대문 **18** B2
Namsangol Hanok Village
남산골 한옥마을 **19** F3
National Museum of
Contemporary Art,
Deoksugung
덕수궁미술관 ....(see 20)
Seokjojeon 석조전 **20** B1

Seoul Animation Center.............. **21** D3
Seoul Museum of Art
서울시립미술관 **22** B1
Signal Beacons
남산봉수대지 **23** E4
Silloam Fomentation
Sauna
실로암사우나찜질방............... **24** A3
Tour DMZ.......................................(see 28)

SLEEPING   (pp119-132)
Hotel Prince 프린스호텔 **25** D2
Hotel Shilla 신라호텔 **26** H3
International Seoul
Youth Hostel........................ **27** E3
Lotte Hotel 롯데호텔
서울.................................... **28** C1
Metro Hotel 메트로호텔 **29** D1
Millennium Seoul Hilton
서울힐튼호텔 **30** B4
Namsan Guesthouse
남산게스트하우스 **31** D3
Pacific Hotel 퍼시픽호텔............ **32** D3
Seoul Backpackers 서울
백팩커스 **33** B3
Westin Chosun
웨스틴조선호텔 **34** C1

EATING   (pp132-6)
Andong Jjimdak
안동찜닭 **35** D2
Baekje Samgyetang
백제삼계탕 **36** D2
Food Court ....(see 17)
Gogung 고궁............................... **37** E2
Korea House 한국의집 **38** F2
Lotte Mart 롯데마트 **39** A3
Myeong-dong Gyoja
명동교자 **40** D2
Myeong-dong Gyoja
명동교자 **41** D2
n. Grill ....(see 17)

Samarkand 사마리칸트.............. **42** H1
Sinsun Seolnongtang
신선설농탕 **43** D2
Yoogane 유가네 **44** D2

DRINKING   (pp136-9)
O'Sulloc 오설록티하우스 **45** D2
Pierre's Bar....................................(see 28)

ENTERTAINMENT   (pp139-143)
Chungdong Theatre..................... **46** B1
Cinus... **47** D2
Korea House Restaurant
& Theatre .... (see 38)
Myeong-dong Nanta
Theatre **48** D2
National Theatre
국립극장 **49** G4
Seoul Namsan
Gugakdang **50** F3
Seven Luck Casino .... (see 30)

SHOPPING   (pp143-5)
Lotte Avenuel
롯데에비뉴엘 **51** C1
Lotte Department Store
롯데백화점............................ **52** C1
Lotte Duty Free Shop.................. (see 52)
Lotte Young Plaza
롯데영플라자 **53** C2
Migliore Mall 밀리오레 **54** D2
Namdaemun Market.................... **55** C2
Shinsegae 신세계백화점 **56** C2

TRANSPORT   (pp145-8)
Bus Stop for N Seoul
Tower **57** E5
Funicular to Namsan
Cable Car............................. **58** D3
Namsan Cable Car
Station
남산케이블카매표소................. **59** D3

SEOUL

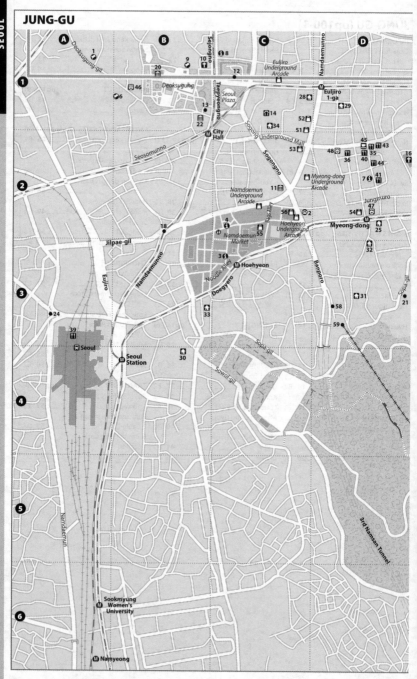

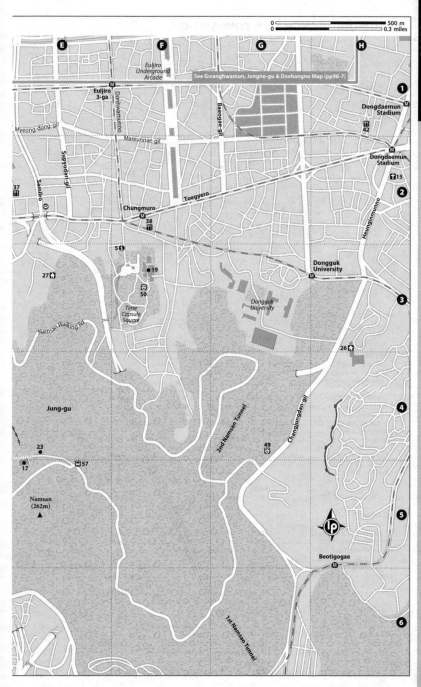

See Gwanghwamun, Jongno-gu & Daehangno Map (pp96-7)

APGUJEONG, GANGNAM & YONGSAN-GU

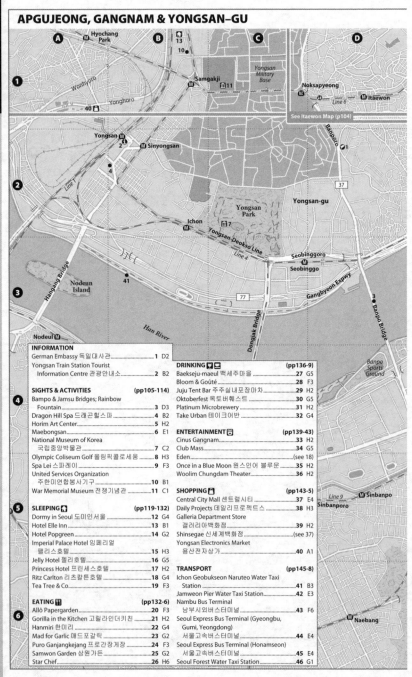

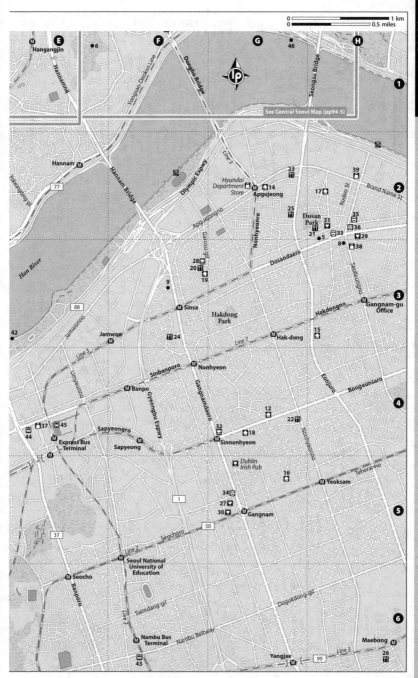

ITAEWON

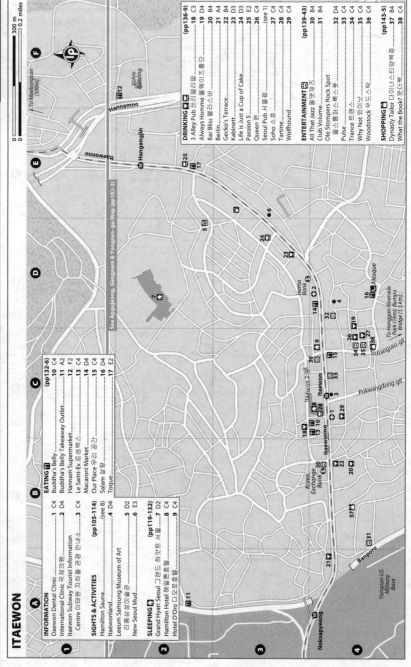

(Continued from page 89)

KTO Tourist Information Centre (Map pp96-7; ☎ 1330; www.visitkorea.or.kr; Gwanghwamun; ✆ 9am-8pm; ⊕ Line 1 to Jonggak, Exit 5) The best information centre; knowledgeable staff, free internet and many brochures and maps.

Namdaemun Market Tourist Information Centre (Map pp100-1; ☎ 752 1913; Namdaemun Market; ✆ 9am-6pm; ⊕ Line 4 to Hoehyeon, Exit 5) You'll find two info kiosks within the market.

Seoul Center for Culture & Tourism (pp100-1; ☎ 3789 7961; 5th fl, M Plaza Bldg, Myeong-dong; ⊕ Line 4 to Myeong-dong, Exit 6) Offers guide services, free internet, culture and language programs.

Yongsan Train Station Tourist Information Centre (Map pp102-3; ☎ 1330; Yongsan-gu; ✆ 5am-10pm; ⊕ Line 1 to Yongsan)

Visas

Seoul Immigration Head Office (Map pp90-1; ☎ 2650 6212; http://seoul.immigration.go.kr; Mok-dong; ✆ 9am-6pm Mon-Fri; ⊕ Line 5 to Omokgyo, Exit 7) Always busy, so take something to read.

Seoul Global Center (Map pp100-1; ☎ 1688 0120; http://global.seoul.go.kr; 3rd fl, Seoul Press Centre, 25 Taepyeongno 1-ga, Jung-gu; ✆ 9am-6pm Mon-Fri; ⊕ Line 1 or 2 to City Hall, Exit 4) Can help with re-entry permits and some visa issues. They also offer plenty of other free information to foreigners living in Seoul as well as language classes and programs on Korean culture.

DANGERS & ANNOYANCES
Demonstrations & Riots

A common sight on central Seoul's streets – particularly around Gwanghwamun and Seoul Plaza – are squadrons of fully armed riot police. Student, trade-union, anti-American, environmental and other protests occasionally turn violent. Keep well out of the way of any confrontations that may occur.

Environmental Hazards

In April Seoul is plagued by periodic yellow dust storms that reduce visibility and hamper breathing. Sand, combined with airborne particulates of industrial pollution – including heavy-metal concentrations of lead and copper largely emanating from China's booming manufacturing sector – form a potent witch's brew that on occasion requires pedestrians to wear face masks to minimise health risks. Check the situation at www.seoul.amedd.army.mil/sites/yellowsand/default.asp.

Road Safety

Drivers tend to be impatient, with *kimchi*-hot tempers, and most of them, including bus drivers, routinely go through red lights. Don't be the first or last person to cross over any pedestrian crossing. Also keep two eyes out for cars parking on pavements and motorcyclists who routinely speed along pavements and across pedestrian crossings. A high proportion of road deaths (38%) are pedestrians, so take extra care.

SIGHTS
Gwanghwamun & Jongno-gu
광화문, 종로구

Seoul's fascinating feudal past can be glimpsed in the palaces around Gwanghwamun (the name of the main gate to Gyeongbokgung), and within **Jongno-gu** (www.jongno.go.kr), the southern boundary of which is defined by the revitalised Cheong-gye-cheon. Here you'll also find Insa-dong (인사동), Samcheong-dong (삼청동) and Bukchon Hanok Village, all areas that should be high on your visit list for their plethora of attractive souvenir shops, teahouses, restaurants and small museums, often in converted *hanok* (traditional mansions). Note that the narrow streets in these areas can get jammed on weekends and holidays, particularly so Insadong-gil (인사동길).

CHANGDEOKGUNG 창덕궁

If you only have time to visit one of Seoul's five major palace complexes, make it this one. **Changdeokgung** (Map pp96-7; ☎ 762 8261; www.cha.go.kr; entry by guided tour in English adult/child W3000/1500; ✆ English tours 11.30am, 1.30pm, 3.30pm Tue-Sun Dec-Mar, Tue & Wed & Fri-Sun Apr-Nov; ⊕ Line 3 to Anguk, Exit 3) generally can only be visited on a guided tour lasting around 90 minutes (check the website for times of tours in Korean, Chinese and Japanese). However, on Thursdays between April and November, you can go on **unescorted tours** (adult/child W15,000/7500; ✆ 9.15am-6.30pm Apr-Nov, last entry 4.30pm). It's possible that unescorted tours will be offered more regularly in the future. Changdeokgung was originally built in 1405 as a secondary palace, but when Gyeongbokgung (Seoul's principal palace) was destroyed during the Japanese invasion in the 1590s, it became the primary palace until 1896. The compound's highlight is the **Biwon** (비원), aka the Secret Garden, a serene glade among large, ancient trees. Pavilions hang over the edge of a square lily pond, with other halls and a two-storey library.

GYEONGBOKGUNG 경복궁

Although **Gyeongbokgung** (Map pp96-7; ☎ 3700 3900; www.royalpalace.go.kr; adult/youth/child W3000/1500/free; ☼ 9am-5pm Wed-Mon Mar-Oct, to 4pm Nov-Feb, to 7pm Sat & Sun May-Aug; ❺ Line 3 to Gyeongbokgung, Exit 5) translates as 'Palace Greatly Blessed By Heaven' it has been anything but during its turbulent 600 year history. Burned down in 1592 by invading Japanese the palace lay in ruins for nearly 300 years until it was rebuilt in 1865, a project that virtually bankrupted the government. In 1895 Empress Myeongseong (Queen Min), was murdered in her bedroom here by Japanese assassins. During early-20th-century Japanese colonial rule, most of the palace was again destroyed. Work on restoring the complex to its former glory will take decades more; during our research trip **Gwanghwamun** was under reconstruction set for completion in 2010.

The main palace building, and an impressive sight, is the ornate two-storey **Geunjeongjeon**, where kings were crowned, met foreign envoys and conducted affairs of state. North of here and to the west is **Gyeonghoeru**, a large raised pavilion resting on 48 stone pillars and overlooking an artificial lake with two small islands. State banquets were held inside and kings went boating on the pond.

An audio commentary and a free guided tour (at 11am, 1.30pm and 3.30pm) are available to learn more about the palace. Soldiers in Joseon-era uniforms stand guard and there are regular **changing of the guard ceremonies** (on the hour from 10am to 4pm).

In the palace compound's northeast corner, the fascinating **National Folk Museum** (☎ 3704 3114; www.nfm.go.kr; admission free with palace entry) is divided into three large sections and uses models, varied film techniques, photos of Korea now and a century ago, and apartment mockups to illustrate social life down the ages. A highlight is an amazingly colourful funeral bier (it looks like a fantasy Noah's ark). See the website for details of free music and dance performances on weekend afternoons.

At the palace's southwest corner the **National Palace Museum** (☎ 3701 7500; www.gogung.go.kr; admission free with palace entry; ☼ 9am-5pm Tue-Fri, to 6pm Sat & Sun) has royal artefacts that highlight the wonderful artistic skills of the Joseon era – royal seals, illustrations of court ceremonies, and the gold-embroidered *hanbok* (traditional clothing) and exquisite hairpins worn by the queens and princesses. Note this museum

closes on a different day to the palace and that an admission charge of W2000 may be reintroduced. The restaurant here is worth trying.

BUKCHON HANOK VILLAGE 북촌한옥마을

Meaning 'North Village', Bukchon, between Gyeongbokgung and Changdeokgung, is home to around 900 *hanok,* Seoul's largest concentration of these traditional Korean homes (see the boxed text, p59). Although an increasingly touristy area, it's a pleasure to get lost in the streets here admiring the buildings' patterned walls and tiled roofs contrasting with the modern city in the distance.

To find out more about the area head first to the **Bukchon Traditional Culture Centre** (Map pp96-7; ☎ 3707 8270; http://hanok.seoul.go.kr; admission free; ☼ 9am-6pm Mon-Fri; ❺ Line 3 to Anguk, Exit 3), which has a small exhibition about *hanok* and is housed, appropriately enough, in a Bukchon *hanok*. There are English-speaking volunteers here and you can pick up a free walking map and booklet.

CHEONG-GYE-CHEON 청계천

A raised highway was torn down and cement roads removed in this US$384-million urban-renewal project to 'daylight' the **Cheong-gye-cheon** (Map pp96-7; www.cheonggyecheon. or.kr; ❺ Line 5 to Gwanghwamun, Exit 5), a stream running through the centre of northern Seoul and out to the Han River. The result is a beautifully landscaped oasis flowing past footbridges, waterfalls and a variety of artworks where citizens flock to dangle their feet in the water and escape the urban hubbub. Highlights include a free video and e-postcard facility at Cheonggye Plaza, the western end of the stream spiked by the giant pink-and-blue spiral sculpture entitled *Spring;* and the mesmerising *Digital Garden* and *Digitial Canvas* **laser light shows** (free; ☼ 7-9pm Feb, Mar & Sep, 8-10pm Apr-Aug, 6-8pm Oct-Jan).

JOGYE-SA 조계사

This busy Buddhist **temple** (Map pp96-7; ☎ 732 2115; www.jogyesa.org; ☼ 4am-9pm; ❺ Line 3 to Anguk, Exit 6) is the headquarters of the Jogye sect which emphasises Zen meditation. Its focal point is the shrine **Daeungjeon**, decorated with murals of scenes from Buddha's life, carved floral latticework doors and three giant Buddha statues.

You'll also find here the **Central Buddhist Museum** (☎ 2011 1960; adult/child W2000/1000; ☼ 9am-

6pm Tue-Sun) where you can look at antique woodblocks, symbol-filled paintings and other Buddhist artefacts. Temple Life and Templestay programs (p113) can also be arranged; the main Templestay office is opposite Jogye-sa on Ujonggungno.

Seoul's annual **Lotus Lantern Festival** (www.llf. or.kr/eng) is centred here, the highlight being an evening parade from Dongdaemun to Jogye-sa with 100,000 lanterns, usually held on the Sunday preceding Buddha's birthday. Check the website for details.

JONGMYO 종묘

Surrounded by dense woodland, the impressive buildings of World Heritage–listed **Jongmyo** (Map pp96-7; ☎ 765 0195; http://jm.cha.go.kr; adult/child W1000/500; ☷ 9am-5pm Wed-Mon Mar-Oct, to 4.30pm Wed-Mon Nov-Feb; ◉ Line 1, 3 or 5 to Jongno 3-ga, Exit 11) house the spirit tablets of the Joseon kings and queens and some of their most loyal government officials. Their spirits are believed to reside in a special hole bored into the wooden tablets.

In the small park at the entrance of the royal shrine, male pensioners gather to play *baduk* (go) and *janggi* (a variation of Chinese chess), and to picnic, nap and even dance to *trot* music. A tranquil city centre walk can be had from Jongmyo's grounds through to those of Changgyeonggung via a connecting bridge over Yulgongno – if you do this you'll only need to pay entrance to one of the properties.

CHANGGYEONGGUNG 창경궁

Meaning 'Palace of Flourishing Gladness', **Changgyeonggung** (Map pp96-7; ☎ 762 4868; http:// cgg.cha.go.kr; adult/youth W1000/500; ☷ 9am-5pm Wed-Mon Mar-Oct, to 4.30pm Wed-Mon Nov-Feb; ◉ Line 4 to Hyehwa, Exit 4) suffered the indignity of being turned into a zoo during the colonial period. The oldest surviving structure is the 15th-century stone bridge over the stream by the main gate, while the main hall, **Myeongjeongjeon**, with its latticework and ornately carved and decorated ceiling, dates back to 1616. Stroll to the northern corner of the extensive grounds to discover an impressive **botanical glasshouse**, built in 1909 and recently restored. At 7.30am on Saturdays in July and August **traditional music concerts** (☎ 580 3300; www.ncktpa.go.kr; admission free) are staged here and are well worth attending.

GYEONGHUIGUNG 경희궁

This lonely **palace** (Map pp96-7; ☎ 724 0274; admission free; ☷ 9am-6pm Tue-Sat, 10am-6pm Sun & holidays;

◉ Line 5 to Gwanghwamun, Exit 7) once served as a villa for Joseon royalty. The quiet compound blends nature with attractive architectural sightlines, created by black-tiled roofs climbing step-wise up the back-side of a hill. The best reason for visiting is to view spectacular hour-long displays of **taekwondo** (☎ 567 4988; www.taekwonseoul.org; www.kukkiwon.or.kr; admission free; ☷ 2pm Wed-Sat, Mar-early Dec). There are also taekwondo lessons offered (p114).

Jung-gu 중구

Branding itself the city's belly button the district of **Jung-gu** (www.junggu.seoul.kr) stretches from the old southern city gate of Namdeamun to the eastern gate of Dongdeamun, both surrounded by markets. To the south is Namsan, downtown Seoul's green lung and focus of one of the city's 'renaissance' projects (see the boxed text, p87).

N SEOUL TOWER & NAMSAN
서울 타워, 남산

The iconic **N Seoul Tower** (Map pp100-1; ☎ 3455 9277; www.nseoultower.com; Namsan; adult/youth/child W7000/5000/3000; ☷ observatory 10am-11pm; ◉ Line 4 to Myeong-dong, Exit 3) offers panoramic, if often hazy, views of the immense metropolis. Come at sunset and you can watch the city morph into a galaxy of twinkling stars and view the video art presentation *Electronic Fire* bathing the tower in projected flames and laser lights.

The tower has become a hot date spot with the railings around it festooned with locks inscribed with lovers' names. There are plenty of dining options from a budget **food court** (meals W7000; ☷ 10am-10pm) at the tower's base to the **n.Grill** (meals W40,000; ☷ 11am-11pm) revolving restaurant on the highest viewing level.

There are many walking routes up Namsan. Alternatively from the Namsan station, take the **cable car** (Map pp100-1; ☎ 753 2403; one-way/return W6000/7500; ☷ 10am-11pm), or yellow bus 2 from outside Exit 4 of Chungmuro subway station (Line 3 or 4) or bus 3 from outside the Hamilton Hotel in Itaewon.

NAMSANGOL HANOK VILLAGE
남산골한옥마을

Five upper-class Joseon-era traditional homes moved here from different parts of Seoul make up this attractive **tourist village** (Map pp100-1; ☎ 2266 6923; Namsan; admission free; ☷ 9am-8pm Wed-Mon May-Sep, to 6pm Wed-Mon Oct-Apr; ◉ Line 3

SEOUL

CLIMBING BUKAKSAN

By the late 14th century a 18.2km wall defined the historic city of Seoul linking up the peaks of Bukaksan (342m), Naksan (125m), Namsan (262m) and Inwangsan (338m). As Seoul modernised parts of the wall were demolished and today only 10.5km of it remains; one of the city's many plans is to rebuild the missing sections – such as the stretch that is part of the new Dongdaemun Design Plaza & Park.

In 2007, the section of the wall around **Bukaksan** (Map pp90-1; www.bukak.or.kr; admission free; ☻ 9am-3pm Apr-Oct, 10am-3pm Nov-Mar), which had been off-limits to civilians for 40 years because of its proximity to the presidential compound of Cheongwadae (aka the Blue House), was opened up to the public. Hiking this stretch provides a strenuous two-hour workout, a chance to view wild deer, and – weather permitting – amazing views of the city. The wall is in excellent condition and with the high security (plenty of soldiers, CCTV cameras every 20 paces, no photos allowed except for at designated spots) you get a vivid sense of its original purpose as the city's last line of defence. Check the website for details of where you can start and finish the walk – there's no need to register in advance but be sure to bring along your passport to gain access.

---

or 4 to Chungmuro, Exit 4). The austere architecture and furniture conjure up the lost world of Confucian gentlemen scholars.

Weavers, cooks, calligraphers and kite-makers can be spotted at the weekend, while traditional music takes place some evenings at the **Seoul Namsan Gugakdang** (☎ 2261 0513; www.sngad.or.kr). On the right of the entrance gate is an **office** (☎ 2264 4412; 10.30am-3.30pm) that provides free tour guides around the village.

DONGDAEMUN & DONGDAEMUN DESIGN PLAZA & PARK 동대문

Constructed in the 14th century, **Dongdaemun** (Map pp94-5; ◉ Lines 4 & 1 to Dongdaemun; Exit 9) served as the Great Eastern Gate of the Seoul fortress and, like similar structures in the city, looks stunning when illuminated at night. The existing stone gate was built in 1869 and repaired after the Korean War. Nearby, the sprawling Dongdaemun market – an area of separate, mainly indoor markets – is fun to explore, especially late at night since most stalls stay open until the very early hours.

On the site of the demolished Dongdaemun Stadium, the new **Dongdaemun Design Plaza & Park** (http://ddp.seoul.go.kr) is taking shape. Part of the park should be open by the time of this guide's publication, with architect Zaha Hadid's innovative, low-rise 'Metonymic Landscape' – a complex looking like something out of *Star Trek* – set for completion at the end of 2010. To see how the whole thing will look on completion, and to get an idea of how other parts of Seoul are being revamped, visit the **Dongdaemun Design Plaza & Park Information Center** (Map pp94-5; ☻ 10am-9pm; ◉ Line 2, 4 & 5 to Dongdaemun Stadium, Exit 2).

NAMDAEMUN 남대문

Since its debut in 1398 Namdaemun (Map pp100-1), the Great South Gate, has been reconstructed many times – a disastrous fire in 2008 being the latest occasion for this impressive structure to again rise for the ashes. The gate's position amid a traffic island, however, is not ideal.

Immediately east of the gate is vibrant **Namdaemun market** (www.namdaemunmarket.co.kr; ☻ 24hr; ◉ Line 4 to Hoehyun, Exit 5) where day and night over 10,000 stores deal in everything from seaweed to spectacles. Pick up an English map outlining the market's different areas from one of two **tourist information booths** (☻ 8.30am-6pm). If you're hungry, there are plenty of places to eat, including **noodle alley** near gate 6.

DEOKSUGUNG 덕수궁

This downtown **palace** (Map pp100-1; ☎ 771 9955; http://english.cha.go.kr; adult/youth/child W1000/500/free; ☻ 9am-9pm Tue-Sun; ◉ Line 1 or 2 to City Hall, Exit 2) used to be three times as big as it is now. It's worth visiting for its pretty gardens and ponds surrounding an extraordinary potpourri of contrasting architectural styles.

Towards the rear of the grounds, there are two neoclassical buildings. **Seokjojeon** (Map pp100-1; admission free) was completed in 1909 and holds a collection of crafts, while next door is the **National Museum of Contemporary Art, Deoksugung** (Map pp100-1; ☎ 2022 0600; adult/youth W3000/2000; ☻ 9am-5.30pm Tue & Wed, 9am-8.30pm Thu & Fri, 9am-6.30pm weekends & holidays Mar-Oct, 9am-5pm Tue, Wed, Sat, Sun, 9am-8.30pm Thu & Fri Nov-Feb), an annex of the main gallery out at Seoul Grand Park (p159).

The **changing of the guards** (10.30am, 2pm & 3pm Tue-Sun mid-Feb–Dec) is an impressive ceremony that involves 50 participants dressed up as Joseon-era soldiers and bandsmen. Free guided tours of the palace in English take place at 10.30am on weekdays and at 1.40pm at the weekend.

CITY HALL & SEOUL PLAZA
Built using eco-friendly principles the new **City Hall** (Map pp100–1), set for completion in February 2011, is a modern re-interpretation of traditional Korean design, with its cresting wave facade of glass providing shade like eaves found on palaces and temple roofs. It will include a library, performance hall and eco plaza, and incorporate the facade of the old City Hall, an imposing stone building dating from 1926.

From mid-May to the end of August grassy **Seoul Plaza** fronting the City Hall is the scene for free performances most nights; see www.casp.or.kr for details. In summer there's also a water fountain that kids love to splash in.

SEOUL MUSEUM OF ART 서울시립미술관
Housed in the old Supreme Court this three-floor **art gallery** (Map pp100–1; 120; www.seoulmoa.org; adult/child W700/free; 10am-9pm Tue-Fri, 10am-7pm weekends & holidays Mar-Oct, closes 1hr earlier Nov-Feb; Line 1 to City Hall, Exit 1) is usually worth visiting for its blockbuster international exhibitions which will cost extra.

West Seoul
INWANGSAN & GUKSA-DANG
인왕산, 극사당
It's well worth slogging up the slopes of **Inwangsan** (White Tiger Mountain; Map pp94–5; Line 3 to Dongnimmun station, Exit 2) to see Seoul's most famous shamanist shrine. Respect is essential during your time on the mountain. Taking photographs could interfere with the performance of important ceremonies.

From the subway exit turn left at the first alley. At the five-alley crossroads, fork right up the steps and you'll soon reach the colourful gateway to the shamanist village. **Guksa-dang**, behind the Buddhist-Shaminist temple **Seonam-sa** was originally built on Namsan peak in the 1390s. The Japanese demolished it in 1925, but it was secretly rebuilt on Inwangsan. Inside the shrine are paintings of shamanist gods, and the altar is often loaded with rice cakes, fruit and even a pig's head – food offerings for the spirits.

From the shrine walk left and up some steps to the extraordinary **Seon-bawi**, another sacred Shaminist site. This Dali-esque outcrop of rock provides spectacular views of the city. To the east is part of Seoul's old **fortress wall**, which you can follow back down to the main road and subway. For more about Inwangsan see www.san-shin.net/Inwangsan.html.

SEODAEMUN PRISON HISTORY HALL 독립공원 서대문형무소 역사관
Chilling tableaux display the various torture techniques employed by the colonial Japanese on Korean patriots at this former **prison** (Map pp94–5; 303 9750; www.sscmc.or.kr; adult/youth/child W1500/1000/500; 9.30am-6pm Tue-Sun Mar-Oct, to 5pm Tue-Sun Nov-Feb; Line 3 to Dongnimmun, Exit 5) turned history museum. In the brick buildings you can walk through nightmarish punishment chambers and claustrophobic cellblocks that

---

CHURCHES IN SEOUL
Many neon-lit crosses punctuate the Seoul skyline at night. Among the central churches of historic note are:

- **Anglican Church** (대한 성공회 성당; Map pp100–1; 738 8952; www.skh.or.kr; Line 1 or 2 to City Hall, Exit 3) An imposing Renaissance-style church built in the shape of a cross with Korean-style tiles on the roof – it's a fine example of architectural fusion.

- **Myeong-dong Catholic Cathedral** (명동 성당; Map pp100–1; 774 1784; Line 4 to Myeong-dong, Exit 6) Elegant, red-and-grey-brick Gothic-style cathedral completed in 1898 by Chinese bricklayers. It gained notoriety by providing protestors with sanctuary during Korea's post-war period of military rule. English-language worship occurs at 9am on Sunday.

- **Kyungdong Presbyterian Church** (경동교회; Map pp100–1; 2274 0161; www.kdchurch.or.kr; Lines 2, 4 & 5 to Dongdaemun Stadium, Exit 4) Designed by Kim Swoo-geun, one of Korea's foremost post-WWII architects, this ivy-clad red-brick building was inspired by hands in prayer. Open for services on Wednesday at 7.30pm and 10am and 11.30am on Sunday.

VIEWS FROM (AND OF) A BRIDGE

A couple of different perspectives on Seoul can be had within short walking distance of Itaewon. For a panoramic view of the Han River looking towards Gangnam take a short hike up to the pavilion atop **Maebongsan** (매봉산; Map pp100–1), part of Eunbong Neighbourhood Park northeast of the junction of Itaewonno and Hannamno: you reach the park by crossing the pedestrian bridge over Hannamno near Hangangjin subway station and walking north.

For a closer look at the river head south down Pokwangdong-gil from Itaewon (which, incidentally, is one of the fast-disappearing areas of central Seoul to retain an old Asian shopping atmosphere) to the pedestrian tunnel that leads to a section of the Hanggan Riverside Park. Walk west towards the double-decker **Banpo Bridge** (Map pp102–3). On weekends at intervals between 12.30pm and 9.20pm, the world's longest fountain rains down in graceful arcs from the upper level. At night, coloured lights turn the water sprays into a rainbow which can also be viewed from the lower level of **Jamsu Bridge** which has a couple of cycle lanes and footpaths.

---

were also used by the Korean authorities after independence. Excavations, building renovations and landscaping of the grounds was in progress during our research visit.

WORLD CUP STADIUM & PARK
월드컵주경기장

Apart from still hosting soccer matches the **World Cup Stadium** (Map pp90–1; www.sisul.or.kr/index.jsp; ⊖ Line 6 to World Cup Stadium station, Exit 1) has partly morphed into a mall with a giant hypermarket, food court, multiplex cinema, members'-only gym and a 24-hour public bath (see p114). Soccer fans can relive the highs and lows of the 2002 tournament at the stadium's **museum** (adult/child W1000/500; ☻ 9am-6pm).

JEOLDUSAN MARTYRS' SHRINE &
MUSEUM 절두산 순교 성지

Commemorating the hideous torture and murder of thousands of Catholics in 1866, **Jeoldusan** (Map p93; ☎ 2126 2200; www.jeoldusan.or.kr; admission by donation; ☻ museum 9.30am-5pm Tue-Sun; ⊖ Line 2 or 6 to Hapjeong station, Exit 7), meaning 'beheading hill', includes a church, a small museum (under renovation at the time of research) and a sculpture park. It's a 10-minute walk from the subway exit.

Yongsan-gu 용산구

Dominated by the Yongsan US military base, **Yongsan-gu** (http://english.yongsan.go.kr), south of Namsan is home to the foreigner enclave of Itaewon (이태원), an increasingly upscale dining and partying destination with intriguing contrasts, such as the infamous 'hooker hill' slap up against Seoul's main mosque. The area is also home to a triad of top museums.

LEEUM SAMSUNG MUSEUM OF ART

If you have time to visit just one art gallery in Seoul, the **Leeum** (Map p104; ☎ 2014 6901; www.leeum.org; admission permanent collection adult/youth W10,000/6000, special collection W15,000/11,000; ☻ 10.30am-6pm Tue-Sun; ⊖ Line 6 to Hangangjin, Exit 1) – a masterful combination of contemporary architecture and exquisite art – should be your first choice.

The complex is made up of three contrasting buildings designed by leading international architects. **Museum 1**, the work of Mario Botta, houses refined traditional works – beautiful ceramics, metal work and Buddhist paintings. Modern art, both Korean and international, is the focus of **Museum 2**, in a building designed by Jean Nouvel. Museum 3, the **Samsung Child Education & Culture Center**, is the vision of Rem Koolhaas, and is used for special exhibitions. Outdoor works include a couple of Louise Bourgeois' giant spider sculptures.

NATIONAL MUSEUM OF KOREA
국립중앙박물관

Housed in a grand, marble-lined, modernist building this **museum** (Map pp102-3; ☎ 2077 9000; www.museum.go.kr; admission free; ☻ 9am-6pm Tue, Thu & Fri, 9am-9pm Wed & Sat, 9am-7pm Sun; ⊖ Line 1 or 4 to Ichon, Exit 2) cleverly channels natural light to show off Korea's ancient treasures. Fronting it are picturesque gardens with a reflecting pond, ancient stone pagodas, the original Bosingak bell and Dragon Falls.

Inside you'll find galleries devoted to the various ruling dynasties, from simple comb-design pots and dolmens to the skilful and imaginative Baekje-era incense holder and the intricate gold work of the Silla dynasty crowns and necklaces. If your time and stamina is limited head straight to the wonderful ancient ceramics that Korea is famous for (3rd floor). Note that an admission charge of W2000 may be reintroduced in 2010.

WAR MEMORIAL MUSEUM 전쟁 기념관
This huge **museum** (Map pp102-3; ☎ 709 3139; www.warmemo.co.kr; adult/student/child W3000/2000/1000; ⏱ 9.30am-6pm Tue-Sun; ⊚ Line 4 or 6 to Samgakji, Exit 12) documents the history of warfare in Korea and has an especially good section on the Korean War (1950–53).

On the 1st floor are paintings and panoramic displays illustrating many fierce battles fought against invading Mongol, Japanese and Chinese armies. There is a replica of one of the famous iron-clad turtle warships (*geobukseon*) used to defeat the Japanese navy in the 1590s. Upstairs visitors can view heaps of black-and-white documentary footage (with English commentary) of the main battles and events of the Korean War, and subject themselves to the Combat Experience Room (every 30 minutes from 9.30am to 4.30pm).

Every Friday at 2pm from April to June and in October and November a military band performs, and a marching parade culminates in an awesome display of military precision and weapon twirling by the honour guard.

South of the Han River
Gangnam (강남), Apgujeong (압구정), Jamsil (잠실) and the island of Yeoui-do (여의도) are all located south of the river. Pretty much undeveloped until the 1960s this section of Seoul tends to be much more modern than districts north of the Han. Built on a grand scale, the wide, long boulevards are lined with buildings that are often architectural statements. Sights are more diffuse, so you'll find yourself using the subway or taxis to get around rather than walking.

BONG-EUN-SA 봉은사
Just north of the COEX Mall and Convention Centre, this Buddhist **temple** (Map pp90-1; ☎ 3218 4801; www.bongeunsa.org; Jamsil; ⊚ Line 2 to Samseong, Exit 6) is spread among a forested hillside and has a quieter, more secluded atmosphere than Jogye-sa (p106). Founded in AD 794, the buildings have been rebuilt many times over the centuries.

Entry to the temple is through **Jinyeomun** (Gate of Truth), protected by four fierce guardians. On the left is a small hut where an English-speaking volunteer guide is usually available. Try to visit on Thursday at 2pm for the interesting two-hour long Temple Life program (see p113).

NORYANGJIN FISH MARKET
고랑진수산시장
Every kind of marine life is swimming around in tanks, buckets and bowls at Seoul's fascinating **fish market** (Map pp90-1; ☎ 814 2211;

ARCHITECTURE AS ART

While the northern half of Seoul has some notable pieces of contemporary architecture, it's south of the Han River that ambitious modern buildings benefit from showcase spots along super-wide boulevards. Among our favourites are:

■ **Horim Art Center** (Map pp102-3; ☎ 541 3525; www.horimartcenter.org; adult/child W8000/5000; ⏱ 10.30pm-6pm Tue, Thu-Sun, to 8pm on Wed; ⊚ Line 3 to Apgujeong, Exit 6) Designed by Tehje Architecture Office this is exactly the sort of stylish complex you'd expect to find in chic Apgujeong (but so often don't). The building's design was inspired by pottery and inside the lustrous walls is a museum devoted to this Korean art form.

■ **Kring Gumho Culture Complex** (www.kring.co.kr; Map pp90-1; ⊚ Line 2 to Samseong, Exit 1) Looking like a giant music speaker crossed with a slab of Swiss cheese this incredible steel-clad building was designed by Unsangdong Architects (www.usdspace.com). Inside are offices, exhibitions spaces, a cinema and a cafe.

■ **Tangent** (Map pp90-1; www.daniel-libeskind.com/projects/show-all/tangent; ⊚ Line 2 to Apgujeong, Exit 2) Hyundai Development Company commissioned Daniel Libeskind to work with Seoul-based firm Himma on their headquarters – the result is one of Seoul's boldest architectural statements, an enormous sculpture in glass, concrete and steel, reminiscent of a painting by Kandinsky.

■ Apgujeong's **Galleria mall** (see p144) is worth visiting at night to admire the lighting effects playing across its luminous shell facade.

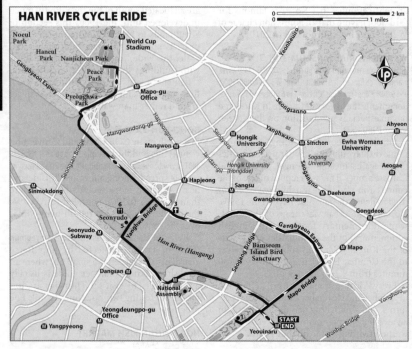

HAN RIVER CYCLE RIDE

www.susansijang.co.kr; ⊗ 24hr; ⊕ Line 1 or 9 to Noryangjin, Exit 1). Giant octopuses, stingray and lobsters are just some of the vast number of sea creatures on sale from close on 800 merchants. Auctions kick off around 1am and vendors are open all day. You can buy your fish, have it filleted and then retire to one of several restaurants on the upper floor to eat it; see p136 for a recommendation. The market, first established here back in 1927, is planning to modernise by constructing a building with a rooftop garden.

OLYMPIC PARK 올림픽 공원
Over 130 delightfully quirky sculptures, some of them the size of a house, are scattered across this **park** (Map pp90-1; www.sosfo.or.kr; ⊗ 5.30am-10.30pm; ⊕ Line 8 to Mongchontoseong, Exit 1) built for the 1988 games. Also here is the **Seoul Olympic Museum** (☎ 410 1354; www.88olympic. or.kr; admission free; ⊗ 10am-5.30pm Tue-Sun).

SAMREUNG GONGWON 삼릉공원
The World Heritage–listed tombs of the Joseon dynasty are scattered around Seoul and Gyeonggi-do (see the boxed text, p152).

Meaning 'Three Tomb Park', **Samreung Gongwon** (Map pp90-1; ☎ 568 1291; Jamsil; adult/youth W1000/500; ⊗ 6am-5.30pm Tue-Sun Mar-Oct, 6.30am-8pm Tue-Sun Nov-Feb; ⊕ Line 2 or Bundang Line to Seolleung, Exit 8) is a tranquil compound in the heart of Gangnam-gu that's home to the burial mounds and attendant statuary of King Seongjong (r 1469–94), King Jeongjong (r 1506–44) and King Seongjong's second wife, Queen Jeonghyeon Wanghu.

LOTTE WORLD AMUSEMENT PARK
롯데월드
Kids and adults alike love the massive entertainment hub of **Lotte World** (Map pp90-1; ☎ 411 4921; www.lotteworld.com; Jamsil; ⊗ 9.30am-11pm; ⊕ Line 2 or 8 to Jamsil, Exit 3; &), which includes an amusement park, an **ice-skating rink** (B3 fl; per session adult/child W13,000/12,000, skate rental W4500; ⊗ 10am-10pm), a theatre, multiplex cinema, department store, folk museum, shopping mall, hotel *and* restaurants.

The main attraction is **Lotte World Adventure & Magic Island** (day pass adult/youth/child W35,000/30,000/26,000; ⊗ 9.30am-11pm), a mainly indoor Korean version of Disneyland. Outdoor

HAN RIVER CYCLE RIDE

Dedicated cycle paths run along much of both sides of the Han River. This 16km route loops from Yeoui-do across the river to the World Cup Stadium and back, providing great views along the way. Take subway Line 5 to Yeouinaru station and leave by Exit 2. Walk west a block to **Yeoui-do Park (1)** and locate exit 8 to find the **bicycle rental stall** (Map pp90–1; ☎ 011-9143 6413; www.rollingstars.co.kr; per hr W3000; ☼ 9am-11pm; ♿).

Cycle out of the park and across the **Mapo Bridge (2)**, taking the blue ramp down to the north bank of the river. Head west for about 4km until you reach a steep cliff at the top of which is **Jeoldusan Martyr's Shrine (3**; p110). Continue west under the Yanghwa and Seongsan bridges until you reach a small bridge across a stream. Turn right after crossing this bridge and then left (at the sign) to pedal uphill to reach the **World Cup Stadium (4**; p110).

Retrace your route back to the Yanghwa bridge and carry your bike up the stairs to the pathway on the west side. On an island about halfway along the bridge is the beautifully landscaped **Seonyu-do Park (5**; admission free; ☼ 6am-midnight), an award-winning space created from an old water-filtration plant. Chain up your bike outside before entering to explore lily-covered ponds, plant nurseries and exhibitions halls, as well as getting some refreshments at the fast-food cafe-bar **Naru (6**; ☎ 2675 2112; meals W4000-8000; ☼ 10am-11pm) which has wonderful river views.

Continue from the park back to the south bank of the Han River and pedal back towards Yeoui-do, passing the green-domed **National Assembly (7)** building on the way.

Magic Island is in the middle of Seokchon Lake and is closed in bad weather.

The **Folk Museum** (3rd fl; adult/youth/child W5000/3000/2000; ☼ 9.30am-8pm) uses imaginative techniques like dioramas, scale models and moving waxworks to bring scenes from Korean history to life. The price is included in the day-pass ticket for Lotte World Adventure & Magic Island.

63 CITY

At the Yeoui-do's eastern tip, the gold-tinted glass **63 City** (Map pp90–1; ☎ 789 5663; www.63.co.kr; ☼ 10am-9pm; ☺ Line 5 to Yeouinaru, Exit 4; ♿), one of Seoul's tallest and most stylish skyscrapers, offers three child-pleasing attractions: the aquarium **Sea World** (adult/youth/child W15,000/13,000/11,000; ☼ 10am-10pm), with penguin, seal and sea lion shows; **Art Hall** (adult/youth/child W8000/7500/6500; ☼ movies 10am-9pm), an IMAX theatre showing hourly movies with English-language commentary in an earphone; and **Sky Art** (adult/youth/child W9000/8000/7000; ☼ 10am-midnight), which combines a 60th-floor observation deck with changing art exhibitions. A **triple ticket** (adult/youth/child W26,000/23,000/20,000) makes for a big day out.

ACTIVITIES
Buddhist Temple Programs

The two-hour Temple Life program at **Bongeun-sa** (W10,000; ☼ 2pm Thu) includes lotus-lantern making, *dado* (tea ceremony), a temple tour and *Seon* (Zen) meditation (see p111). No reservation is required for this, but if you want to take part in their overnight Templestay program you'll need to book in advance.

A similar Temple Life program is offered at **Jogye-sa** (Map pp96–7; ☎ 732 5292; by donation) and you can also enquire about having meditation lessons and a four-bowl Buddhist monk meal (W30,000).

Opposite Jogye-sa, on the third floor of the Templestay office, the **Dharma Group** (Map pp96–7; ☎ 722 2206; www.idia.or.kr; admisson free; ☼ 4pm Sat) includes meditation, a Buddhist service, a talk and tea.

Cycling

Bicycles can be rented at several parks along the Han River including on Yeoui-do (see the boxed text, above), Ttukseom Resort (Map pp90–1), Seoul Forest Park (Map pp90–1) and Olympic Park (Map pp90–1). Rental is W3000 per hour and you'll need to leave some form of ID as a deposit.

Golf & Baseball Practice

Take aim at an indoor driving or batting range of which Seoul has plenty.

Baseball Hitting Practice (Map pp96–7; Insadong-gil, Insa-dong; 11 balls W1000; ☼ 9am-1am; ☺ Line 1 to Jonggak, Exit 3) Whack baseballs pitched to you by machine.

Olympic Coliseum Golf (Map pp102–3; ☎ 514 7979; www.olympicgolf.co.kr; Seolleungno, Gangnam;

🕑 6am-11pm; 🚇 Line 3 to Apgujeong, Exit 2) Hit golf balls, use the gym and spa, all for W35,000 (70 minutes).

Saunas, Spas & Gyms

The top hotels have attractive facilities that nonguests can sometimes use for a hefty price. Instead, join locals sweating it out at *jjimjil-bang* (traditional sauna) complexes, some of which have great spa baths, as well as internet, DVD rooms, cafes and sleeping areas. Open round the clock, these places can double up as bargain crash pads. If you use the *jjimjil-bang* as well as the sauna you'll pay a higher entrance charge.

Dragon Hill Spa (Map pp102-3; ☎ 792-0001; www.dragonhillspa.co.kr; day/night W10,000/12,000, Sat & Sun W12,000 all day; 🕑 24hr; 🚇 Line 1 to Yongsan, Exit 1 or 2) This luxe complex, a beguiling mix of gaudy Las Vegas bling and Asian chic, offers outdoor baths, charcoal saunas, crystal salt rooms and ginseng and cedar baths, a golf driving range, cinema and rooftop garden with an Indian Barbeque Village.

Hamilton Sauna (Map p104; ☎ 6393 1370; day/night/overnight W6000/8000/10,000; 🕑 24hr; 🚇 Line 6 to Itaewon, Exit 1) A small but well-equipped facility with gym, great tubs and scorching saunas.

Itaewonland (Map p104; ☎ 749 4122; www.itaewonland.com; Hannam-dong, Yongsan-gu; admission W5000, after 8pm W6000; 🕑 24hr; 🚇 Line 6 to Itaewon, Exit 2) This popular bathhouse and *jjimjilbang* complex is up a flight of steep steps from the Itaewon strip.

New Seoul Mud (뉴서울 머드; Map p104; ☎ 749 8802; sauna W10,000; 🕑 9am-midnight; 🚇 Line 6 to Hangangjin, Exit 1) Beauty treatments (from W60,000) include foot massages, ginseng baths, special soft mud packs and skin scrapes as well as body oil, milk, mugwort and steam treatments.

Silloam Fomentation Sauna (실로암사우나찜질방; Map pp100-1; ☎ 364 3944; www.silloam sauna.com; sauna adult/child W6000/4500; sauna & jjimjilbang adult/child before 8pm W8000/6000, after 8pm W12,000/8000; 🕑 24hr; 🚇 Line 1 or 4 to Seoul Station, Exit 1) Across the street from Seoul Station, this spick-and-span foreigner-friendly operation (lots of signs in English), with a wide range of baths and sauna rooms, is great if you need to freshen up before or after a trip out to the airport, or get into town late and need a temporary place to stay.

Spa Lei (Map pp102-3; ☎ 545 4113; www.spalei.co.kr; day/night W12,000/14,000; 🕑 24hr; 🚇 Line 3 to Sinsa, Exit 5) Luxurious women-only spa providing excellent services in an immaculate, stylish environment. Staff is helpful and are used to dealing with foreigners. From the subway exit go straight and take the second turning on the left. Spa Lei is in the basement to your left.

World Cup Spaland (Map pp90-1; ☎ 302 7002; www.sponspa.co.kr; day/night W6000/7000; 🕑 24hr; 🚇 Line 6 to World Cup Stadium, Exit 1; 🚻) Inside the World Cup stadium. Facilities include a kid's play area.

Swimming

Most top-end hotels have pools, but are generally only open to hotel guests. An exception is the **Hamilton Hotel** (p130; Mon-Thu W12,000; Fri-Sun W15,000; 🕑 10am-6pm) – the summer weekend pool parties here see the body beautiful crowd out in force, blinged to the max!

In July and August outdoor swimming pools in the parks along the Han River get super packed. You'll need to follow the rules – swimming is allowed only at specified times and wearing a swimming cap is essential. On Yeoui-do parasols surround separate **swimming pools** (Map pp90-1; adult/youth/child W4000/3000/2000; 🕑 9am-7pm Jul & Aug; 🚇 Line 5 to Yeouinaru, Exit 2; 🚻) for children, teenagers and adults. The **Ttukseom pools** (Map pp90-1; 🚇 Line 7 to Ttukseom Resort, Exit 2 or 3; 🚻) have similar prices and hours.

Taekwondo

To get a quick taste of what's involved in this traditional Korean martial art sign up for the **Taekwondo Experience Program** (☎ 567 4988; www.taekwonseoul.org; www.kukkiwon.or.kr; W20,000; 🕑 11am, 1pm & 3pm Tue-Sun) held at Gyeonghuigung (p107).

WALKING TOURS
Seoul By Night

While you can do this circular walk to the top of Namsan and back during the day, it's best to start it around dusk. Seoul takes on a special quality at night – the neon and floodlights spark into action, people come out to shop and play and there's plenty of free entertainment.

Take Line 1 to Jonggak station, Exit 4. At street level turn 180 degrees and you'll see the traditional bell pavilion **Bosingak** (**1**; 보신각) contrasting with the contemporary **Jongno Tower** (**2**). Now only rung at New Year when crowds gather to celebrate, during the Joseon dynasty the bell was struck 33 times at dawn (for the 33 heavens in Buddhism) and 28 times at sunset (for the 28 stars that determine human destiny) to signal the opening and closing of the city gates.

Turn right onto Gwanggyo and head a block south towards the Cheong-gye-cheon (see p106) to join the crowds enjoying this restored stream. You'll be returning here at

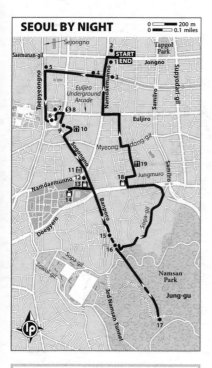

SEOUL BY NIGHT

WALK FACTS

Start/Finish Jonggak station
Distance 7km
Duration 3 hours

the end of the walk to see the computer-and-laser-generated artworks **Fractal Flowers (3)** and **Digital Canvas (4)**, the latter best viewed from the small arched wooded bridge across the stream.

Head west along the stream to its terminus at a waterfall and emerge at Cheong-gye Plaza and the giant candy-pink-and-sky-blue spiral-shell sculpture **Spring (5)** by Coosje Van Bruggen and Claes Oldenburg. Turn left onto tree-lined Taepyeongno, walking past the Seoul Finance Center on the left towards the grassy park **Seoul Plaza (6)** fronting the building site of the new **City Hall (7)**. On the right-hand side pop into the **exhibition centre** (admission free; ⏰ 10am-7pm) to see how Seoul's governmental nerve centre will rise like a glass and steel wave to the side of the old City Hall.

Cross the streets at the intersection beside the **Busan Bank (8)** to emerge on the southeast side of the plaza to find an elaborate **Chinese gateway (9**; under restoration at the time of research) beyond which, tucked beside the Westin Chosun Hotel, is **Hwangudan (10)**, one of the city's hidden treasures. This is all that remains of an elaborate complex dating from 1899 at which King Gojong performed the Rite of Heaven.

Swing around the hotel and continue southeast along Sogongno, past a strip of upmarket tailors (Seoul's equivalent of Saville Row), to reach the colonial architectural ensemble with socialist-realist-style bronze statues. On the north side is the **Bank of Korea (11**; admission free; ⏰ 10am-5pm Tue-Sun) now a currency museum; the architecture ensemble is surrounded by a **fountain (12)**; and to the south is **Shinsegae department store (13**; p144). If you're in the mood for shopping, **Namdaemun market (14**; p108) is immediately to the west.

Drop down into the underground shopping arcade and emerge at gate 6 to head up towards the free **funicular (15)**, that saves some legwork to reach the **cable car (16**; p107) leading to the base of the **N Seoul Tower (17**; p107). Alternatively you could climb up the mountain in around 20 minutes.

Try to time your arrival at the summit to coincide with the **Soul of Light** (⏰ first 10 mins of hr, 7-11pm Mar-Oct, 6-10pm Nov-Feb) show which sees the tower engulfed in projected flames and strafed by laser lights. Afterwards, either walk back down Namsan or hop on yellow bus 5 which will drop you at Myeong-dong station near **Migliore department store (18)**. Negotiate your way through the shopping crowds to slurp noodles at **Myeong-dong Gyoja (19**; p134) before returning to the Cheong-gye-cheon for the laser light shows.

Art Galleries Walk

Photographs highlighting climate change; dreamy modern renditions of traditional Korean landscape paintings; quirky public art sculptures; and a portrait of Hitler with 2m-long moustache: a sample of what you might encounter on this stroll through Seoul's eclectic contemporary art scene, starting in up-and-coming Tongui-dong west of Gyeongbokgung and progressing to Samcheong-dong and Insa-dong to the east. Set aside the better part of a day to see everything, especially if you want to tour the

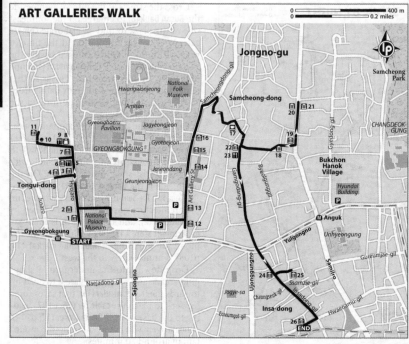

ART GALLERIES WALK

0 — 400 m
0 — 0.2 miles

WALK FACTS

Start Gyeongbokgung station
Finish Anguk station
Distance 3.5km
Duration 2 to 3 hours

palace and linger in one or more of the area's multitude of restaurants and cafes. Unless otherwise mentioned the galleries are free. Don't do this walk on Sunday or Monday when many of the galleries will be closed.

'Visitors to Seoul are often quite surprised by the diversity of art and number of galleries here,' says Monica Cha, owner of **Gallery Cha (1**; ☎ 730 1700; ⊗ 11am-7pm Mon-Fri, noon-6pm Sat), specialising in emerging Korean artists. Cha is our guide on the walk – she starts by recommending the nearby **Daelim Contemporary Art Museum (2**; ☎ 720 0667; www.daelimmuseum.org; charge varies with exhibition; ⊗ 10am-6pm) in a building with a lovely garden to the rear.

Back on the main road at the next corner is **Jean Art Gallery (3**; ☎ 738 7570; www.jeanart.net), one of the pioneers of the Tongui-dong gallery

scene. Look for the metallic butterfly sculpture between the gallery's two red-brick buildings; art inside includes a 2m-tall dotted pumpkin sculpture by Japanese artist Yayoi Kusama. Further down the street peek into the **packing crate (4)**, turned into a one-room gallery, one of several projects in the area by **Kunstdoc** (☎ 722 8897; www.kunstdoc.com).

Return to the main street and perhaps pause for a bowl of buckwheat noodles at the simple eatery **Memilgguj Pilmuryep (5**; 메밀 꽃 필 무렵; ☎ 734 0367; meal W6000; ⊗ noon-8pm): 'It's very popular at lunch time,' says Cha. Turn left here to find a row of *hanok*; on the left down an alley is the gallery and studio **Ryugahon (6**; 류가헌) in one of the *hanok*.

Return to the main road, pass the non-profit gallery **Brain Factory (7**; ☎ 725 9520; www. brainfactory.org; ⊗ 11am-6pm Tue-Sun) then turn left again into a street lined with appealing places to eat and shop including the second-hand book shop **Gagarin (8**; ☎ 736 9005; ⊗ 12.30-7.30pm Tue-Sun) and the mid-century modern design cafe **mk2 (9**; ☎ 730 6420; ⊗ 11am-11pm). Around the corner to the right you won't miss **Zein Xeno (10)**, a red-painted building with a pair of green legs sticking out of its facade. Nearby is another appealing cafe-bakery, **Goghi** (**11**; 카페 고희; ☎ 734 4907; www.goghi.kr; ✆ 11am-10pm), with changing exhibitions on its walls.

Retrace your steps back to the palace entrance, passing through the grounds to the east side to locate some of Seoul's most established gallery spaces. **Gallery Hyundai** (**12**; ☎ 287 3500; www.galleryhyundai.com; ✆ 10am-6pm) has two outlets close by each other here; their main gallery is now south of the river in Gangnam. Pause to see what's showing at **Kumho Museum of Art** (**13**; ☎ 720 5114; www. kumhomuseum.com; W1000; ✆ 10am-6pm Tue-Sun). Next along is an old military building being converted to house the new annex of the **National Museum of Contemporary Art** (**14**; p159), and the galleries **Hakogojae** (**15**; ☎ 720 1524; www.hakgojae. com; 10am-7pm Tue-Sat, to 6pm Sun), in a converted *hanok*, and **Kukje** (**16**; ☎ 735 8449; www.kukje.org; ✆ 10am-6pm); be sure to search out Kukje's second gallery space tucked away off the main strip and look up to the roof of the main building to spot the running woman sculpture by Jonathan Borofsky, the American artist who created the giant *Hammering Man* statue near Gyeonghuigung (p107).

Follow the main road to the right, then take a sharp turn right to head into the heart of Samcheong-dong packed with gift shops, boutiques and more galleries; 'I think this area has become too commercial' says Monica, who does favour the funkily decorated cafe **Kopi Bangasgan** (**17**; 커피 방앗간; ☎ 732 7656; ✆ 8.30am-11pm). Turn right at Coffee Factory and head downhill to the junction. Turn left at the tourist information office and follow the road over the hill, passing tiny **Void Gallery** (**18**) at the sharp end of the block on which you'll find a branch of the Wood & Brick cafe-bakery (see p132); its few art works are always on display through the glass windows.

Turn left at the junction and look for the sculpture 'Eating a Biscuit Together' that doubles as a bench in front of the **Bukchon Art Museum** (**19**; ☎ 741 2296; ✆ 11am-6pm Mon-Sat). Monica's pick of another couple of galleries worth seeing in the area are **Gallery Skape** (**20**; ☎ 011 9700 8130; www.skape.co.kr; ✆ 10am-7pm Tue-Fri, 10am-6pm Sat & Sun) and, across the road, **One and J. Gallery** (**21**; ☎ 745 1644; www.oneandj.com; ✆ 11am-6pm Tue-Sun).

Return to the tourist information centre – across the road is the long-established **Artsonje Center** (**22**; ☎ 733 8945; www.artsonje.org/ asc; adult/student/child W3000/1500/1000; ✆ 11am-7pm Tue-Sun) – there's invariably an interesting exhibition here, as well as an appealing book cafe and art-house cinema. Heading south towards Insa-dong, is one of Monica's favourite eateries: **Cheonjinpoja** (**23**; 전진포자; meal W5000), a simple place serving meat, seafood or vegetable-stuffed dumplings.

At the end of the street turn left to find Anguk station; alternatively, if you're still in search of more art, there are scores more galleries across the road along and around Insadong-gil, including **Artside** (**24**; ☎ 725 1020; www.artside.org; ✆ 10am-6.30pm), **Insa Gallery** (**25**; ☎ 735 2655; www.insagallery.net; ✆ 10am-6pm) and the venerable **Sun Art Center** (**26**; ☎ 734 0458; www. sungallery.co.kr; ✆ 10am-6pm).

COURSES
Cooking & Korean Culture
Yoo's Family (Map pp96-7; ☎ 3673 0323; www.yoos family.com; ✆ Mon-Sat; W20,000-60,000; ⊕ Line 3 to Anguk, Exit 4), housed in a *hanok*, offers practical demonstrations of Korean culture. Lessons include the traditional tea ceremony (*dado*), print-making from carved wooden blocks, Korean cooking (making *kimchi* and *bulgogi*) and dressing up in *hanbok* (traditional clothing). A minimum of two persons is required. There are lots of photo opportunities and the teaching style is informal and relaxed.

Korean cooking courses in English start at 10am and 2pm on weekdays at **Seoul Culinary College** (Map pp96-7; ☎ 742 3567; www.hancooking.co.kr; ✆ office 9am-10pm Mon-Fri; ⊕ Line 1, 3 or 5 to Jongno 3-ga, Exit 5), also known as Han's Cooking Class. Book one week ahead, no minimum number. The one-hour *kimchi* course costs W60,000, while the two-hour courses cost W80,000 to W100,000. The price includes a lavishly illustrated Korean cookbook.

Language
BestFriend Language & Culture Exchange Center (Map p93; ☎ 365 9875; www.bestfriendcenter.com; ✆ classes 1pm-10pm; ⊕ Line 6 to Sinchon, Exit 4) Unconventional language centre that offers Korean language classes based on a coupon system. Pay for a number of sessions and come when you can.

Sogang University (Map p93; ☎ 705 8088; www. sogang.ac.kr; ⊕ Line 6 to Sinchon, Exit 6) Gets good reviews for its student-centred, communicative approach to language learning. New programs commence four times during the academic year with one-month sessions during the summer and winter vacations.

YBM Sisa (Map pp96-7; ☎ 2278 0509; http://kli.ybmedu. com; office ☺ 6.30am-9pm Mon-Fri, 9am-4pm Sat & Sun; ◎ Line 1, 3 or 5 to Jongno 3-ga, Exit 15) Korean classes (maximum size 10) for all ability levels cover grammar, writing and conversation. Ten-day courses (W115,000) are held in the evening, 20-day courses are held during the day. Lessons last just under two hours, and courses start at the beginning of each month.

Yonsei University (Map p93; ☎ 2123 3465; www.yskli. com; Sinchon; ◎ Line 6 to Sinchon, Exit 6) Runs highly recommended part- and full-time Korean language and culture classes for serious students.

SEOUL FOR CHILDREN

There are many ways to entertain the little ones in and around Seoul. Apart from the big amusement park Lotte World (p112) try the following:

Children's Grand Park (Map pp90-1; ☎ 2290 6114; www.childrenpark.or.kr; admission free; ☺ 5am-10pm; ◎ Line 7 to Children's Grand Park, Exit 1; ♿) An enormous playground including a zoo (open 10am to 6pm) with pony and camel rides (adult/child W5000/4000), botanical garden and amusement park.

COEX Aquarium (Map pp90-1; ☎ 6002 6200; www. coexaqua.com; adult/youth/child W15,500/13,000/10,000; ☺ 10am-8pm; ◎ Line 2 to Samseong, Exit 6; ♿) An amazing collection of sea creatures including piranhas, sharks, turtles and jellyfish. You could also try 63 City's Sea World aquarium (p113).

Seoul Animation Center (Map pp100-1; ☎ 3455 8341; www.ani.seoul.kr; admission free; ☺ 9am-5.50pm Tue-Sun; ◎ Line 4 to Myeong-dong, Exit 1 or 3; ♿) Up the hill on the way to the cable car you'll find this museum and cinema devoted to cartoons and animation – not just from Korea. There's an extensive DVD/video library from which you can choose your favourite animation.

Seoul Forest Park (Map pp90-1; ☎ 462 0253; www. seoulforest.or.kr; admission free; ☺ 24hr; ◎ Line 2 to Ttukseom, Exit 8; ♿) A 10-minute walk from Ttukseom station is a very pleasant area to enjoy some time in natural surroundings. Hire a bicycle (W3000 per hour) or a pair of rollerblades (W4000 per hour) from the rental stall (open 9am to 10pm) located by Gate 1. Among the trees and lakes are deer enclosures, eco areas, an insect exhibition, a plant nursery and fountains in which kids love playing.

The non-verbal shows *Nanta, Jump* and the *Drawing Show* (p143) are all great family entertainment. Other options, all easy day trips out of the city, include Seoul Grand Park (p159) where you'll find the country's best zoo; and the thrill rides and funfairs of Everland Resort (p158).

TOURS

If you join a tour, ensure it has an English-speaking guide if you want to get anything out of it. Tours usually include lunch and shopping stops. Go to www.startravel.co.kr or www.seoulcitytour.net for examples of tours and prices, and visit the KTO tourist information office (p105) for tour leaflets and advice.

Adventure Korea (☎ 018-242 5536; www.adventure korea.com) offers a variety of multi-day tours all around Korea to destinations as varied as Jeju-do and even Kaesong in North Korea (relations between the two Koreas permitting). Paintball, bungee-jumping and white-water rafting adventures are also on their busy itinerary.

The **Royal Asiatic Society Korea Branch** (Map pp96-7; ☎ 763 9483; www.raskb.com; Room 611, Korean Christian Bldg; ☺ 10am-noon & 2-5pm Mon-Fri; ◎ Line 1 Jongno 5-ga, Exit 2) organises brilliant tours to all parts of South Korea, usually at weekends. Check their website for the schedule. Non-members are welcome to join, and all tours are led by English speakers who are experts in their field. The tours are reasonably priced, usually W30,000 to W50,000. The Society also organises lectures twice a month.

Seoul City Tour Bus (☎ 777 6090; www.seoulcitybus. com; ☺ Tue-Sun) has comfortable and colourful tour buses that run between Seoul's top tourist attractions north of the Han River – they're a good option if you want to see as much as possible in a short time. You can hop on and hop off anywhere along the two routes – downtown (adult/child W10,000/8000; 9am to 7pm Tuesday to Sunday, half-hourly) and around the palaces (adult/child W12,000/8000; 10am to 5pm Tuesday to Sunday, hourly). Ticket holders receive considerable discounts on tourist attractions. Buy tickets on the bus, which starts from in front of Dongwha Duty Free Shop in Gwanghwamun (Map pp96-7). A night tour (adult/child downtown W5000/3000, palaces W10,000/6000) also operates.

The **United Service Organization** (USO; Map pp102-3; ☎ 795 3028; www.uso.org/korea; Yongsan-gu; ☺ 8am-5pm Mon-Sat; ◎ Line 4 & 6 to Samgakji, Exit 10), the US military's entertainment wing, organises tours for American troops and civilians, including the best tour to the DMZ (p152). Other all-day tours include the historical and unspoilt island of Ganghwa-do (US$38) and white-water rafting excursions (US$55) out in the wilds of Gangwon-do. In winter, skiing trips are organised.

FESTIVALS & EVENTS

Seoul has a busy calendar of festivals worth watching out for. Visit www.knto.or.kr for locations and dates that vary from year to year.

April

Yeoui-do Cherry Blossom Festival When the cherry blossoms bloom and the air is clear, the streets of Yeoui-do look great. Take Line 5 to Yeoui-do, Exit 2, and walk towards the National Assembly.

May

Jongmyo Daeje On the first Sunday in May this ceremony honours Korea's royal ancestors, and involves a parade of the royal carriage from Gyeongbokgung (p106) through downtown Seoul to the royal shrine at Jongmyo (p107), where spectators can enjoy traditional music and an elaborate, all-day ritual.

Buddha's Birthday On the Sunday before Buddha's birthday, a huge parade is held from Dongdaemun to Jogye-sa (p106) starting at 7pm.

Hi Seoul Festival (www.hiseoulfest.org) The first half of what is now a twice-yearly major festival of arts and performances around the city organised around different themes.

July

Puchon International Fantastic Film Festival (www.pifan.com) Bringing together films and filmgoers from across Asia and the world to Bucheon (Puchon), just outside of Seoul, to feast on the best in sci-fi, fantasy and horror. Theatres are within walking distance from Songnae Station, Line 1, toward Incheon.

Seoul International Cartoon & Animation Festival (www.sicaf.org) Half a million animation fans pack auditoriums in Seoul each year to see why the city is an epicentre of animated craftsmanship.

August

Seoul Fringe Festival (www.seoulfringe.net in Korean only) Mime, punk and art take over the streets, clubs and galleries around Hongik University (Map p93) during the last two weeks in August.

September

Korea International Art Fair (www.kiaf.org) COEX's convention centre is the location for this fair in which over 200 local and international galleries participate.

Seoul Medicinal Herb Market Festival Held at Seoul's biggest herbal medicine market at Gyeong-dong (p145), this festival offers free medicinal consultation and shamanist ceremonies, affording attendees a rare glimpse into this fascinating tradition.

Seoul Drum Festival (www.drumfestival.org) Focusing on Korea's fantastic percussive legacy, this decade-old event brings together from around the world all kinds of ways to make a lot of noise.

October

Seoul Performing Arts Festival (www.spaf21.com) Held for a month from mid-October, this is the city's most prestigious performing arts fest with works by Korean and a wide range of international companies and artists in venues from Daehangno to Gangnam.

Sajik Daeje A re-enactment of a royal thanksgiving ceremony at the altar in Sajik Park (Map pp94-5).

SLEEPING

Seoul has a good selection of budget accommodation including several backpackers, some even in *hanok*. There's also no shortage of top-end places, with a few promising new options in the works during our research trip. In the midrange, if you're looking for somewhere memorable rather than ubiquitously bland, your options will be narrowed to Bukchon's *hanok* guesthouses and the handful of design-conscious operations scattered around the city.

For Seoul, budget places are those that offer double rooms with en-suite facilities for under W50,000, midrange places are between W51,000 and W200,000 and the top end is over W200,000. Prices don't normally change with the seasons although some hotels and guesthouses may offer special deals online or at quiet times.

Gwanghwamun & Jongno-gu
BUDGET

Inn Daewon (대원여관; Map pp96-7; ☎ 738 4308; dm/s/d from W19,000/25,000/35,000; ◎ Line 3 to Gyeongbokgung, Exit 4; 🔀 🖳) Run by the kindly Mr Kim and his wife, this well-maintained inn has the cheapest *hanok*-style accommodation. Everything is cramped, and guests sleep on floor mattresses, except in the dorm. Toilets and showers are shared, and the steep stairs up to the dorm could be tricky after a night of clubbing.

Gwanghwa Hotel (광화모텔; Map pp96-7; ☎ 738 0751; r from W40,000; ◎ Line 5 to Gwanghwamun, Exit 7; 🔀 🖳) The helpful owner speaks a little English and she takes great pride in her motel. The rooms and bathrooms are immaculate, and larger than most in this price range. They're all a bit different, so look at a few before settling in. Huge TVs and ornate, faux-Regency furniture combined with the central downtown location make this an excellent budget option.

MIDRANGE & TOP END

YMCA Tourist Hotel (Map pp96-7; ☎ 734 6884; www.ymca.or.kr/hotel; s/d/tw/r 55,000/70,000/80,000/110,000; ✗ ▣) We can't guarantee whether its fun to stay at the YMCA, but this 8th-floor hotel in a very central location offers a decent range of clean, simply furnished rooms and friendly service. No breakfast, but there's a coffee shop on the ground floor and a multitude of fast-food options nearby.

Koreana Hotel (코리아나호텔; Map pp96-7; ☎ 2171 7000; www.koreanahotel.com; r from W191,000; ◉ Line 1 or 2 to City Hall, Exit 3; ✗ ▣) A marble lobby and welcoming staff are a promising start, but the standard rooms fail to thrill. The executive queen rooms (W322,000) are an improvement and include the usual executive-floor extras. A handful of restaurants offer global grazing but Koreana's three big advantages are location, location, location.

Bukchon, Insa-dong and Around

The neighbourhood between Gyeongbokgung and Changdeokgung used to be home for high court officials – with tons of atmosphere and close to many sites it's the best place to be based, especially if you stay in one of the many restored *hanok*. Bare in mind that *hanok* rooms are small, bathrooms are cramped (but modern), and you sleep on a thin *yo* mattress on an *ondol*-heated floor.

BUDGET

Holiday in Korea (홀리데이인코리아호스텔; Map pp96-7; ☎ 3672 3113; www.holidayinkorea.com; Iksun-dong; dm/s/d & tw W17,000/39,000/44,000; ◉ Line 3 to Anguk, Exit 4; ✗ ▣) With 30 rooms, this is Seoul's largest backpacker guesthouse. The motel-style rooms are plain but have all you need. There's a kitchen and a lounge packed with PCs where DVDs are shown on a big screen. A simple breakfast is included in the rates and there's even an elevator.

Beewon Guesthouse (비원장; Map pp96-7; ☎ 765 0670; www.beewonguesthouse.com; Iksun-dong; dm/tr from W19,000/58,000, d & ondol from W40,000; ◉ Line 3 to Anguk, Exit 4; ✗ ▣) Combining facility-filled motel-style rooms with free, guesthouse-style communal facilities, this guesthouse is clean and

tidy and appeals to an older clientele. Look for an orange-tiled building, behind the main road Donhwamunno.

Guesthouse Korea (게스트하우스 코리아; Map pp96-7; ☎ 3675 2205; www.guesthouseinkorea.com; Sumun 2-gil; dm/s W18,000/32,000, d & tw W39,000; ◉ Line 3 to Anguk, Exit 4; ✗ ▣) Fussy types might say this backpackers is a bit messy, but it's also a friendly place to park your pack. All rooms have private bathroom and there's breakfast thrown in for the price.

Banana Backpackers (바나나 백패커스; Map pp96-7; ☎ 3672 1973; www.bananabackpackers.com; Iksun-dong; dm/s/d/f W20,000/35,000/45,000/65,000; ◉ Line 3 to Anguk, Exit 4; ✗ ▣) Multicoloured and mural-covered walls, plus plenty of banana motifs, lift this place above run-of-the-mill backpackers. The usual washing machine, computer and kitchen facilities are here, and the rooms are reasonable for a budget place; however you couldn't swing a banana in their tiny en suite bathrooms.

Saerim Hotel (세림 호텔; Map pp96-7; ☎ 739 3377; Eorumgol-gil, Insa-dong; r W50,000; ◉ Line 3 to Anguk, Exit 6; ✗ ▣) Flatscreen TVs as large as the double beds feature in this excellent-value, quiet and clean hotel in the heart of Insa-dong. The rooms are as good as they get in Seoul at this price, and everything works. The new wallpaper designs are quite flash. Some rooms have computers at no extra cost.

MIDRANGE

Seoul Guesthouse (서울게스트하우스; Map pp96-7; ☎ 745 0057; off Gyedong-gil; www.seoul110.com; s/d/f W35,000/50,000/100,000; ◉ Line 3 to Anguk, Exit 3; ✗ ▣) This wooden *hanok* has a rambling garden, and helpful English-speaking hosts (who have two lovely big dogs). It's a delightful place to stay. Except in the more expensive rooms, the computers, TV lounge, washing machine and kitchen facilities are all shared. They also have a separate *hanok* sleeping up to six that can be rented for W200,000.

Bukchon Guesthouse (북촌 게스트하우스; Map pp96-7; ☎ 743 8530; www.bukchon72.com; Gyedong-gil, Bukchon; s/tw/d/tr W40,000/60,000/70,000/90,000; ◉ Line 3 to Anguk, Exit 3; ✗ ▣) The five rooms are small and bathrooms are shared, but the historical ambience at this *hanok* is priceless. Breakfast is included.

(Continued on page 129)

ENTER THE HERMIT KINGDOM

Nurturing traditions and a history stretching back millennia, yet also striding confidently into a fully wired future, Korea offers ancient temples and palaces, striking pieces of contemporary architecture and the latest electronic gizmos. It has one of the world's most delicious yet relatively undiscovered food cultures, and as the hordes of hikers tramping through the mountainous country's spectacular array of national parks will attest, it's a wonderful place to savour the beauty of nature.

ANTHONY PLUMMER

A Sense of History

Fragments of Korea's tumultuous past litter the peninsula, from the megalithic stone tombs of Ganghwa-do to the invasion tunnels dug under the Demilitarized Zone (DMZ) by North Korean troops. Glimpses of how Koreans once lived can be had in Seoul's reconstructed palaces and well-preserved villages, where the elegant homes of the *yangban* (aristocrats) nestle beside the thatched cottages of the peasantry.

① Changdeokgung

Tucked away at the rear of this World Heritage–listed Seoul palace (p105) is Biwon, a serene secret garden where pretty pavilions and the royal library overlook a placid lotus pond.

② Panmunjom & the DMZ

Few places can provide such a frisson as Panmunjom (p152), the Korean War truce village straddling the line that splits North from South Korea, surrounded by one of the world's most heavily fortified borders.

③ Bulguk-sa & Seokguram Grotto

The Unesco stamp of approval also goes to this magnificent temple (p213) set on a series of stone terraces, and the nearby grotto, a feat of mid-8th-century engineering and home to a beatific image of Buddha.

④ Hahoe Folk Village

Korea's ancient pastoral and Confucian traditions survive into the 21st century in Hahoe (p231), a charming village of thatched- and tiled-roofed *hanok* (traditional mud-walled and timber-framed houses) snuggled into a bend of the Nakdong River.

⑤ Haein-sa

Imagine the lives of the 13th-century monks who carved the Tripitaka Koreana into over 80,000 blocks of birch wood as you view the sacred Buddhist texts housed at this beautiful temple (p207), another World Heritage site.

124

Pop-Cultural Powerhouse

After the destruction of a bloody civil war South Korea has bloomed into an economic wonder and pop-cultural powerhouse. Seoul is known as the 'miracle on the Han' – a capital studded with ambitious buildings, stacked with eclectic art galleries and pulsing to a digital beat. Also don't miss out on the chance to enjoy Korea's cinematic arts, part of the *hallyu* (Korean Wave) sweeping across Asia.

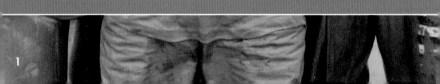

1

❶ Boryeong Mud Festival

What started as a way for the resort of Dae-cheon Beach to promote the health and beauty benefits of its mineral-laden mud has boomed into one of Korea's most ebullient events, a week-long wallow in the grey stuff (see boxed text, p332).

❷ Korean Movies

Catch up on the latest Korean movies by dropping by one of the cinemas in Seoul (p140) that screen films with English sub-titles, or do what many courting Korean couples do and check into a private DVD *bang* (DVD screening room).

❸ Modern Architecture

Seoul is in the midst of a grand makeover, throwing up amazing structures, such as its new City Hall (p109), the Dongdaemun Design Plaza & Park (p108) and the Kring Gumho Culture Complex (p111), that strad-dle the line between architecture and mam-moth sculptural art.

❹ Jeju-do

This scenic volcanic island (p282), home to Korea's highest peak, is also where you'll find the beachside resort of Jungmun, the spot to see honeymooning couples – many dressed identically – riding horses or visiting the kitsch Teddy Bear Museum.

❺ Heyri

Packed with interesting small-scale architec-ture, the village of Heyri (p154) is a haven for contemporary Korean creativity where artists and craftspeople live and work in a leafy environment of quirky galleries and relaxed cafes.

A Movable Feast

Ask most people what they know about Korean cuisine and they'll tell you that they eat dog and have a passion for *kimchi*. But that's just the tip of a very tasty feast. Every day in Korea is an edible adventure with a sensational array of unusual dishes and drinks to fall instantly in love with. Different parts of the country have their own specialities, making a culinary tour one of the most delicious ways to see Korea.

❶ Royal Food Banquets
Leave plenty of room in your stomach and money in your wallet to splash out at a Seoul restaurant, such as Korea House (p135), which specialises in a feast of delicately prepared, beautifully presented dishes fit for royalty.

❷ Seoul or Busan Fish Markets
Stroll the fish markets of Seoul (p111) or Busan (p244) – where stalls display all manner of weird and wonderful seafood – then retire to one of the restaurants within the complexes to enjoy a delicious, super-fresh meal.

❸ Jeonju *Bibimbap*
Legend has it that the quintessential Korean dish of *bibimbap* (rice topped with vegies, meat, an egg and spicy sauce) was invented in the historic southern Korean town of Jeonju (p306), home also to a traditional wine museum.

❹ Sokcho Squid *Sundae*
Every day fishing boats return to the north-east-coast city of Sokcho (p178) with the main ingredient for the unusual seafood sausage of squid *sundae* – a hearty mix of squid with noodles, tofu, seaweed and vegies in a pork casing.

❺ Chuncheon *Dakgalbi*
Chuncheon (p174), the picturesque 'City of Lakes', is home to *dakgalbi,* one of Korea's best food inventions – chicken, pressed rice cakes and vegies stir-fried at the table in a spicy chilli sauce, the dregs of which are used to make scrumptious fried rice.

Green Korea

For all its rapid industrialisation South Korea remains a relatively green place – and, following a barrage of environmentally friendly government policies, will hopefully become greener in the future. Even in the megalopolis of Seoul nature bursts through the concrete, glass and steel thanks to the proximity of mountainous national parks, nature reserves and major river-revival projects.

1 SIMON RICHMOND; 2 JOSE FUSTE RAGA/PHOTO

1 Seoraksan National Park

The spectacular autumn colours of the foliage in this national park (p182) attract coachloads of crowds – avoid them by visiting at other times of the year when you can enjoy hiking through dense forests past intriguing rock formations.

2 Cheong-gye-cheon

The disinterring of this long-buried stream (p106) and the landscaping of its banks has created a natural oasis in the heart of the Seoul metropolis; it's a glowing example of how to both green and revitalise a city.

3 Yeonhwa-do Hiking

One of the hundreds of islands scattered off Korea's southern coasts, unspoiled Yeonhwa-do (p253) is criss-crossed with trails, one leading to Yongmeori – pinnacles of rock cascading into the sea, said to resemble a dragon's head.

4 Boseong Daehan Dawon Tea Plantation

After taking in the attractive ranks of green-tea bushes at this southern plantation (p273) you'll be more than ready for a cuppa. Not only is the brew refreshing, it also has health benefits.

5 Maisan Provincial Park

No excuses! Old-aged pensioners easily make it to the peak of Ammaisan (685m) in this lovely provincial park (p311), so lace up your hiking boots and hit the trail.

(Continued from page 120)

Anguk Guesthouse (안국게스트하우스; Map pp96-7; ☎ 736 8304; www.anguk-house.com; Hakdang-gil, Bukchon; s W50,000, d & tw W70,000; ◉ Line 3 to Anguk, Exit 1; ✕ ▣) Down a quiet alley, the four varnished wood guest rooms at this *hanok* are spread around a courtyard. All have en suite as well as a computer, and beds rather than *yo* mattresses. The kitchen can be used to make a DIY breakfast. Owner Mr Kim speaks English.

our pick Tea Guesthouse (티 게스트하우스; Map pp96-7; ☎ 3675 9877; www.teaguesthouse.com; Gyedong-gil, Bukchon; s/f W50,000/150,000, d & tw W80,000; ◉ Line 3 to Anguk, Exit 3; ✕ ▣) An enchanting *hanok* in a lovely garden setting that has a traditional-style room where breakfast, included in the rates, is served. The bedrooms have ultra-modern computers/TVs, and the shared bathrooms are of a high quality.

Hotel Sunbee (썬비호텔; Map pp96-7; ☎ 730 3451; www.hotelsunbee.com; d/tw/ondol W84,000/96,000/121,000; ◉ Line 3 to Anguk, Exit 6; ✕ ▣) This hotel has a great location close to Insadong-gil. Their double beds are huge and the rooms are decorated tastefully. Many rooms come with a wide-screen TV and computer. Breakfast is toast and orange juice in your room.

TOP END

Rak-Ko-Jae (락구재; Map pp96-7; ☎ 742 3410; www.rkj.co.kr; Bukchon; s/d/f W180,000/250,000/400,000; ◉ Line 3 to Anguk, Exit 2; ✕ ▣) This beautifully restored *hanok*, with an enchanting garden, comes closest to providing a luxury traditional experience, modelled after Japan's *ryokan*. The guesthouse's mud-walled sauna is included in the prices as well as breakfast, traditional tea ceremony and copious amounts of housemade spirits. It's worth ordering their excellent dinner (W50,000). En-suite bathrooms are tiny though.

Fraser Suites (프레이저스위츠; Map pp96-7; ☎ 6262 8888; www.frasershospitality.com; Nakwon-dong; 1/2/3-bedroom apt W330,000/440,000/550,000; ◉ Line 3 to Anguk, Exit 5; ✕ ▣ ♨) These fully equipped serviced apartments are modern, light and spacious, great for a long-term stay for which major discounts are available. Staff tries hard to make this a home-away-from-home and its location, steps away from Insadong-gil can't be beat. A buffet breakfast is included in the rates.

Dongdaemun, Myeong-dong & Namsan

BUDGET

Seoul Backpackers (서울백팩커스; Map pp100-1; ☎ 3672 1972; www.seoulbackpackers.com; Hoehyeon; s/d W40,000/50,000; ◉ Line 4 to Hoehyeon, Exit 4; ✕ ▣) Offering well-decorated but small rooms (all en suite), with feature walls covered in funky print wallpaper. A lack of communal areas means the usual guesthouse sociability is limited. From the subway exit take the first alley on the left and walk uphill.

Namsan Guesthouse (남산게스트하우스; Map pp100-1; ☎ 752 6363; www.namsanguesthouse.com; Myeong-dong; d & tw W45,000, ondol W55,000-80,000; ◉ Line 4 to Myeong-dong, Exit 2; ✕ ▣) The friendly, guitar-playing manager Mr Kim tries hard to please his guests with the usual freebies plus free bicycles and even cheap mobile-phone hire. When the weather's fine the outdoor garden patio is a big plus. A group could negotiate to share an *ondol* room.

International Seoul Youth Hostel (Map pp100-1; ☎ 319 1318; www.seoulyh.go.kr; tw/ondol/q W60,000/100,000/120,000; ◉ Line 4 to Chungmuro, Exit 4; ✕ ▣) The slightly isolated position, 10 minutes' walk up Namsan from the subway exit, is compensated for at this modern hostel by huge rooms, a large kitchen for self-catering and a delightful roof-top garden. There's also a climbing wall and a restaurant.

MIDRANGE

Tokoyo Inn Seoul Dongdaemun (Map pp94-5; ☎ 2267 1045; www.toyoko-inn.com; Dongdaemun; s/d/tw W60,000/70,000/80,000; Lines 2, 4 & 5 to Dongdaemun Stadium, Exit 4; ✕ ▣ ✕) You've got to hand it to this Japanese business hotel group for bagging a prime spot close to the future Dongdaemun Design Plaza & Park. Small, clean and well-equipped rooms (with plenty of single ones) are great value with rates including a simple breakfast.

our pick Metro Hotel (메트로호텔; Map pp100-1; ☎ 752 1112; www.metrohotel.co.kr; Myeong-dong; s/d/tw W74,000/88,000/122,000; ◉ Line 2 to Euljiro 1-ga, Exit 6; ✕ ▣) North of fashionable Myeong-dong is this appealing, professionally run hotel with boutique aspirations. Splashes of style abound, beginning with the flashy, metallic-style lobby and its laptops. Room size and design vary – ask for one of the larger ones with big windows (room numbers which end in '07'). Prices cover a Western breakfast.

Hotel Prince (프린스호텔; Map pp100-1; ☎ 752 7111; www.hotelprinceseoul.co.kr; Toegyero, Myeong-dong;

d/tw/ondol W130,000/155,000/200,000; Line 4 to Myeong-dong, Exit 2;) Rooms are smallish but sparkling, with some bright primary colours to alleviate an otherwise all-white regime. Online booking discounts can make the Prince an excellent deal and rates include a buffet breakfast.

Pacific Hotel (퍼시픽호텔; Map pp100–1; 777 7811; www.thepacifichotel.co.kr; Myeong-dong; d & tw from W176,000; Line 4 to Myeong-dong, Exit 3;) Bell boys in caps greet you at this hotel that exudes old-fashioned elegance. Light neutral colours, greenery and a natural-wood effect are the design style. Bathrooms are a tad cramped, but there's a big sauna and spa bath in the building as well as a roof-top garden.

TOP END

Lotte Hotel (롯데호텔서울; Map pp100–1; 771 1000; www.lottehotelseoul.com; Myeong-dong; r/ste from W385,000/528,000; Line 2 to Euljiro 1-ga, Exit 8;) Ask for a recently renovated room in the older building, if you want modern style with everything up to date. Other rooms, even in the new block, can be businesslike and surprisingly plain. There's a women-only floor with a book-lined lounge. Renowned French chef Pierre Gagnaire's restaurant and bar is on the 35th floor.

Westin Chosun (웨스틴조선호텔; Map pp100–1; 317 0404; www.westin.com/seoul; Myeong-dong; r from W428,000; Line 2 to Euljiro 1-ga, Exit 4;) Not Seoul's most spectacular hotel, but the relaxing atmosphere and the conscientious staff keep it a cut above the rest. Each stylish room comes with a rent-free mobile phone and choice of 10 types of pillows.

Also recommended:

Hotel Shilla (신라호텔; Map pp100–1; 2233 3131; www.shilla.net/en/; r W420,000; Line 3 to Dongguk University, Exit 5;) A dependable level of luxury but not the most convenient location stuck part way up Namsan.

Itaewon & Yongsan-gu

MIDRANGE

Hotel D'Oro (디오로호텔; Map p104; 749 6525; fax 749 0033; Itaewonno, Itaewon; d/ste from W66,000/110,000; Line 6 to Itaewon, Exit 2;) This reasonably chic hotel offers sparkling modern equipment and furnishing, and free soft drinks rather than an expensive minibar. It's really an up-market motel, so there's no restaurant.

Hotel Elle Inn (Map pp102–3; 792 8700; www.hotelelleinn.com; r/ste W99,000/176,000; Line 1 to Namyeong, Exit 1;) The day rates are the give-away that this is a love hotel, but it's a very respectable one with facility filled, elegantly designed rooms. Check in after 10pm and the room rate drops to W70,000. It's also one of the closest hotels to the USO if you have to join their early morning DMZ tour (see p118).

Hamilton Hotel (해밀튼호텔; Map p104; 794 0171; www.hamilton.co.kr; Itaewonno, Itaewon; s W100,000; d & tw W132,000; Line 6 to Itaewon, Exit 1;) This workhorse of the Itaewon strip is no stunner, with old-fashioned, although pretty spacious, rooms. In its favour is its location, and facilities such as a sauna, gym and outdoor pool (all available to in-house guests for 50% off the regular rates).

Other recommendations:

Rainbow Hotel (호텔레인보우; Map pp94–5; 792 9993; www.rainbowinseoul.com; d/tw/ondol/tr W55,000/63,000/65,000/73,000; Line 1 to Namyeong station, Exit 1;) No frills place that's convenient for the USO.

TOP END

Grand Hyatt Seoul (그랜드하얏트서울; Map p104; 797 1234; www.seoul.grand.hyatt.com; Itaewon; r/ste from W336,000/464,000; Line 6 to Itaewon, Exit 2;) Making the most of its hilltop views the Grand Hyatt oozes class. Rooms are a bit smaller than at rivals but all have been freshly renovated and sport a contemporary look. Pamper yourself in their spa, dance the night away at popular club JJ Mahoney's or swim in their excellent outdoor pool which, come winter, is turned into an ice rink.

Hongdae

BUDGET

Kims' Guesthouse (킴스게스트하우스; Map p93; 337 9894; www.kimsguesthouse.com; Hapjeong-dong; dm/s/d W18,000/32,000/42,000; Line 2 or 6 Hapjeong, Exit 8;) Run by a friendly English-speaking brother and sister this is a pleasant modern suburban house with a balcony and a patio in a quiet residential area not far from Hongdae and the Han River. Kims' has all the usual communal guesthouse facilities including shared bathrooms. It's a challenge to find, so download the map from their website.

our pick **Bebop House** (Map p93; 8261 4835; http://bepob-guesthouse.com; Seogyo-dong; dm W20,000–23,000, s/d/tr W50,000/60,000/75,000; Line 2 Hongik University, Exit 1;) A little tricky to find (check their website for directions) but a real gem that captures the youthful, arty buzz of Hongik. The white-washed house used to be an architect's office and is decorated with very funky wallpapered walls and tons of posters. Food is provided in the kitchen for you to make breakfast.

Lee & No Guesthouse (리앤노게스트하우스; Map p93; ☎ 070-8291 4878; www.lnguesthouse.com; Yunnam-dong; dm/s W22,000/40,000, d & tw W50,000; ❷ Line 2 to Hongik University, Exit 2; ✖ ▣) Down a quiet cul-de-sac is this four-room guesthouse run by laid-back Mr Lee and his wife. Bathrooms are shared but there's a patio and a bigger-than-usual free breakfast. From Exit 2, take the second left, then cross over the road to Hana Bank and walk straight for five minutes. Turn right at Grazie Espresso, and it's on your left. They also run the nearby Namu Guesthouse (www.namugh.co.kr) occupying a spacious, modern unit in an apartment block.

Also recommended:

Hong Guesthouse (Map p93; ☎ 010-6315 6696; www.hostelseoulkorea.com; Seogyo-don; dm/s/d with shared bathrooms W18,000/38,000/48,000, en-suite room W80,000; ❷ Line 2 to Hongik University, Exit 1; ✖ ▣) The garden could do with some weeding but this backpacker house is otherwise clean and well set up with a friendly young English-speaking manager.

MIDRANGE

Seokyo Hotel (Map p93; ☎ 330 7777; www.hotelseokyo.co.kr; d or tw from R120,000; Line 2 to Hongik University, Exit 1; ✖ ▣) Next to the airport bus stop this business hotel is patronised by airline cabin crews, and super convenient for partying in the Hongik area. Not all rooms have been upgraded so ask to see a few. The gym and spa/sauna are a plus and you can grab breakfast in their lobby cafe.

Walker Hill
TOP END

W Seoul Walkerhill (서울워커힐; Map pp90-1; ☎ 465 2222; www.wseoul.com; r from W390,000; ❷ Line 5 to Gwangnaru, Exit 2; ✖ ▣ ▣) One of the city's best designed hotels with spectacular public areas and generally fab-licious rooms. However – call us picky – but in Wonderful (ie standard) rooms, boxy cathode ray TVs strike a bum note; when even budget motels have giant flat plasma screens, such electronics are retro in a bad way. Also problematic is its distant location from most sights, although there's a free shuttle bus to Gwangnaru station every 10 to 20 minutes.

Apgujeong, Gangnam & Jamsil
MIDRANGE

Tea Tree & Co (Map pp102-3; ☎ 542 9954, fax 512 9959; Garosu-gil; r from W70,000; ❷ Line 3 to Sinsa, Exit 7; ✖ ▣) Right on fashionable Garosu-gil, this sparkling new upmarket motel doesn't need to offer food with so many good places to eat nearby. Rooms are decorated all in white with stylish big bathrooms; ask for the terrace rooms with outdoor jacuzzi bath.

Princess Hotel (프린세스호텔; Map pp102-3; ☎ 544 0366; Apgujeong; r/ste W80,000/120,000; ❷ Line 3 to Apgujeong, Exit 2; ✖ ▣) If you need to be close to Apgujeong's shopping action this love motel with a headily scented lobby is a possibility. Suite options include a spiffy hot-pink number with circular bed.

Jelly Hotel (젤리호텔; Map pp102-3; ☎ 553 4737; www.jellyhotel.com; Gangnam; r from W90,000; ❷ Line 2 to Gangnam, Exit 8; ✖ ▣) The more expensive rooms of this upscale love motel are spacious, exotic and classy. Every room is different – check them out on the lobby screen – the most spectacular (and expensive) has a full-size pool table and a heart-shaped spa!

Dormy In Seoul (도미인서울; Map pp102-3; ☎ 6474 1515; www.dormy.co.kr; Gangnam; studio from W110,000; ❷ Line 2 to Gangnam, Exit 7; ✖ ▣) These light, modern studio apartments have all the conveniences of home. Toilets are cramped but there is a walk-in shower. Don't expect anything special and you won't be disappointed. The price is reasonable and includes a buffet breakfast and internet access.

Hotel Popgreen (Map pp102-3; ☎ 544 6623; www.popgreenhotel.com; Apgujeong; r/ste W110,440/177,600; ❷ Line 3 to Apgujeong, Exit 2; ✖ ▣) Light, modern and reasonably sized rooms and bathrooms are on offer, with touches of style here and there. Rooms vary so check out more than one – suites are just bigger rooms. Rates include breakfast in their pleasant cafe.

Hotel Blue Pearl (블루펄호텔; Map pp90-1; ☎ 3015 7777; Jamsil; d & ondol W130,000, tw W180,000; ❷ Line 7 to Cheongdam, Exit 14) There's a modern Zen-like simplicity to this hotel, contrasting sharply with the raging traffic outside. A corner room like Room 601 has great views, but rooms on the other side away from the road are quieter. Rooms sport computers.

TOP END

our pick Park Hyatt Seoul (Map pp90-1; ☎ 2016 1234; www.seoul.park.hyatt.com; Daechi 3-dong, Gangnam-gu; r/ste from W300,000/450,000; ❷ Line 2 to Samseong, Exit 1;

⊠ ⌨ ⓢ) A discreet entrance – look for the rock sticking out of the wall – sets the Zen minimalist tone for this gorgeous property. Each floor only has 10 rooms with spot-lit antiquities lining the hallways. Spacious rooms ingeniously combine the high tech with the traditional, and come with luxurious bathrooms that have quite rightly been classed among the best in Asia.

Imperial Palace Hotel (임페리얼팰리스호텔; Map pp102-3; ☎ 3440 8000; www.imperialpalace.co.kr; Eonjuro, Gangnam; r from W330,000; ⓔ Line 7 to Hak-dong, Exit 1; ⊠ ⌨ ⓢ) Opulence and no-expense-spared are the twin themes at this luxurious hotel. The antiques and wood panelling create a stately, genuinely European ambience, from the magnificent lobby to the well-appointed rooms and immaculate spa.

Also recommended:

Lotte World Hotel (롯데월드호텔; Map pp90-1; ☎ 419 7000; www.lottehotelworld.com; Jamsil; r/ste from W375,000/432,000; ⓔ Line 2 or 8 to Jamsil, Exit 4; ⊠ ♿ ⌨ ⓢ) Book ahead for a room on one of the two fun floors decorated with Lotte World's colourful cartoon characters as well as PlayStations.

Ritz Carlton (리츠칼튼호텔; Map pp102-3; ☎ 3451 8000; www.ritzcarltonseoul.com; Gangnam; r/ste from W385,000/451,000; ⓔ Line 9 to Sinnonhyeon, Exit 4; ⊠ ⌨ ⓢ) A gracious note is struck immediately by the violist and soprano providing recitals in the lobby of this top-class hotel.

EATING

Dining out is one of the great pleasures of Seoul with literally tens of thousands of options, from cheap street stalls proffering deep fried snacks and *tteokbokki* (thick bullets of pressed rice cake in a spicy red sauce with tons of other ingredients) to fancy restaurants serving royal Korean cuisine and seafood so fresh it's still wriggling on the plate.

The following picks only skim the surface of what's on offer. Seoul's many food blogs, such as www.seouleats.com and www.zenkimchi.com, provide additional reasons to salivate. Also note that some cafes (p136) and bars (p137) are good places to dine.

Gwanghwamun & Jongno-gu

ourpick Gwangjang Market (관장시장; Map pp96-7; meals R4000-7000; ⏱ 9am-10pm Mon-Sat; ⓔ Line 1 to Jongno 5-ga, Exit 7) Also spelled 'Kwangjang', this market feels like it's been frozen in time: everything is still traditional and unmodernised. At its heart is Seoul's largest food alley

(or *meokjagolmok*), with some 200 stalls specialising in dishes such as crispy, thick *nokdu bindaetteok* (mung-bean pancake; W4000) that are big enough to be shared by two. Pair them up with healthy bowls of *bibimbap* or *boribap* (mixed rice and barley topped with a selection of vegies).

Jongno Bindaeddeok (종로빈대떡; Map pp96-7; ☎ 737 1857; meals W5,000-14,000; ⏱ noon-2am; ⓔ Line 5 to Gwanghwamun, Exit 1) A sterling example of a dumpy-looking restaurant that serves great food. Most people come for the *bindaetteok* with beef (고기빈대떡) or seafood (해물빈대떡). The *sogogigukbap* (소고기국밥; spicy beef soup) is also delicious. Turn right out of the exit, walk straight and turn left at the first street.

Namaste (나마스테; Map pp96-7; ☎ 2198 3301; www.namasterestaurant.co.kr; World Food Court, basement Jongno Tower; meals W6,000-20,000; ⏱ 11am-10pm; ⓔ Line 1 to Jonggak, Exit 3) This genuine Indian-Nepalese restaurant tempts downtown office workers with its large menu of thalis, lassis, naan breads and all the usual Indian favourites like tandoori and masala tea. Lunch times, with W10,000 thalis on offer, can be hectic. The original branch is a subway stop east of Dongdaemun (Map pp94–5; ☎ 2232 2286; 2nd fl Kumkang Bldg; Sungin-dong; ⓔ Line 1 & 6 to Dongmyo, Exit 1).

Tosok-maeul (토속 마을; Map pp96-7; meals W7000-10,000; ⏱ 24hr; ⓔ Line 1 to Jonggak, Exit 3) Super spicy *gamjatang* (a soup of beef bones and potato) is served up in this rustic diner that also specialises in *sundae* (blood sausage). The uncompromising side dishes are salty-and-fishy-as-hell shrimps, radish and cabbage *kimchi*, raw onions and raw chillies. Thankfully the rice is plain, and there are plenty of paper tissues to deal with runny noses and sweaty brows.

Yukmi (육미; Map pp96-7; ☎ 738 0122; meals W8000-10,000; ⏱ 24hr; ⓔ Line 1 to Jonggak, Exit 3) Classic no-frills seafood-and-alcohol joint. Expect it to be full of smoking salarymen, talking loudly. Order the *hoideopbap* (회덮밥; chunks of tuna and roe on rice; W4500) and *Samjigui* (삼지구이; baked mackerel) and enjoy with draught beer, *soju* (local vodka) or rice wine.

Wood & Brick (Map pp96-7; ☎ 735 1157; www.woodnbrick.com; meals W8000-20,000; ⏱ 8am-10pm; ⓔ Line 5 to Gwanghwamun, Exit 7) If you're tired of Korean, this Italian restaurant, wine bar and gourmet deli and bakery will fill the spot nicely. Their sandwiches and baked goods are excellent and they also do pretty good pizza and pasta. There's another branch in Bukchon (☎ 747 1592; open 10.30am to 3pm, and 6pm to 10pm; ⊕ Line 3 to Anguk, Exit 2).

Café Sobahn (카페소반; Map pp96-7; ☎ 730 7423; www.sobahn.co.kr; meals W10,000-15,000; ⊗ 8am-10pm; ⊕ Line 5 to Gwanghwamun, Exit 6) Check out the mini greenhouse where this slick operation grows its own multicoloured sprouts, one of several great toppings for their contemporary takes on *bibimbap*. They also do a variety of *juk* (rice porridge) dishes for breakfast. Presentation is great and service super friendly.

Tosokchon Samgyetang (토속촌 삼계탕; Map pp96-7; ☎ 737 7444; meals W13,000-19,000; ⊗ 10am-10pm; ⊕ Line 3 to Gyeongbokgung, Exit 2) This 30-year-old icon is housed in a sprawling *hanok*, and for many locals – and even ex-presidents who order take-out – it's the best in Seoul. Despite the crowds, the *samgyetang* (chicken stewed with ginseng) arrives fast and still bubbling. Tip some salt and pepper together into a small saucer and use it as a dip. From the subway station's Exit 2, walk straight for 100m, turn left at the GS25 convenience store and it's on your left.

Nanxiang (Map pp96-7; ☎ 3789 0874; www.nanxiang.co.kr; B2 fl, Seoul Finance Center; meals W20,000-30,000; ⊗ 11am-11pm; ⊕ Line 5 to Gwanghwamun, Exit 5) One of the better choices among the many restaurants and cafes that are clustered beneath the Seoul Finance Center. Heavenly Chinese dumplings are Nanxiang's forte – you can see them being freshly made in the open kitchen.

Hanmiri (한미리; Map pp96-7; ☎ 757 5707; www.hanmiri.co.kr; lunch/dinner from W25,000/50,000; ⊗ 11.30am-3pm & 6-10pm; ⊕ Line 5 to Gwanghwamun, Exit 5) Try a modern take on royal cuisine at this elegant contemporary-styled restaurant with windows overlooking the Cheong-gyecheon. It's unique, gourmet and foreigner-friendly. There's a second branch in Gangnam (Map pp102–3; ☎ 569 7165; 2nd fl, Human Starville, Nonhyeonno; ⊕ Line 2 to Yeoksam, Exit 6).

Bukchon, Insa-dong & Samcheong-dong

Tobang (토방; Map pp96-7; Insadong-gil; meals W4000; ⊗ 10am-7pm; ⊕ Line 3 to Anguk, Exit 6) A white sign with two Chinese characters above a doorway leads the way to this small traditional restaurant, where you sit on floor cushions under paper lanterns and enjoy authentic home cooking for bargain prices. Excellent side dishes include raw crab in red-pepper sauce, a minimalist soup, rice and lettuce wraps.

Samcheong-dong Sujebi (삼청동수제비전문; Map pp96-7; ☎ 735 2965; meals W6000; ⊗ 11am-9pm; ⊕ Line 3 to Anguk, Exit 1) The outstanding *sujebi* (수제비; dough flakes in shellfish broth) is probably the city's best. It's not spicy, but if you need a little zip, add green pepper-flavoured sauce from the tabletop container.

Koong (궁; Map pp96-7; ☎ 733 9240; www.koong.co.kr; off Seokjeongol-gil, Insa-dong; meals W7000; ⊗ 11.30am-9.30pm; ⊕ Line 3 to Anguk, Exit 6) Koong's traditional Kaeseong dumplings, prepared from the recipe of a 94-year-old grandmother, are legendary. Enjoy them in a flavourful soup along with chewy balls of rice cake.

Osegyehang (오세계향; Map pp96-7; ☎ 735 7171; www.go5.co.kr; Insadong 4-gil, Insa-dong; meals W7000-14,000; ⊗ noon-3pm & 4-9pm; ⊕ Line 3 to Anguk, Exit 6) This modern vegetarian restaurant is run by members of a Taiwanese religious sect. The fusion-style food combines all sorts of mixtures and flavours. The barbecue-meat-substitute dish is particularly flavoursome. Non-alcoholic beer and wine is served.

Dimibang (디미방; Map pp96-7; ☎ 720 2417; Insadong 3-gil, Insa-dong; meals W8000; ⊗ noon-10pm Mon-Sat; ⊕ Line 3 to Anguk, Exit 6) This owner has written books about medicinal herbs and the meals and drinks are full of them. *Sanyakjuk* (herbal rice porridge) and *yakbap* (medicinal hotpot rice) are both subtly flavoursome. The herbal tea and alcoholic herbal brews are special too. Two people is the minimum to try the set meals starting at W13,000.

Gogung (고궁; Map pp96-7; ☎ 736 3211; www.gogung.co.kr; basement, Ssamzie-gil, Insa-dong; mains W8000-20,000; ⊗ 11am-9pm; ⊕ Line 3 to Anguk, Exit 6) Try traditional *Joenju bibimbap* (W11,000), a dish of rice boiled with cow bones and covered in a colourful assortment of toppings including raw beef and egg, as well as *moju*, a sweet cinnamon homebrew. There's also a branch in Myeong-dong (Map pp100–1; open 11am to 10pm).

Jirisan (지리산; Map pp96-7; ☎ 723 4696; Insadong 3-gil, Insa-dong; meals from W10,000; ⊗ noon-10pm; ⊕ Line 3 to Anguk, Exit 6) Justly popular, authentic restaurant and a great place to try *dolsotbap* (hotpot rice, W10,000).

Solmoe-maeul (솔뫼마을; Map pp96-7; ☎ 720 0995; Samcheongdong-gil; meals W10,000-22,000; set courses W20,000 & 26,000; ⊗ noon-10pm; ⊕ Line 3 to Anguk, Exit 1)

Warning! Do not order the enormous set course here unless you are starving – the excellent multicourse meals includes *bulgogi*, and a special *gujeolpan* using pink radish wraps. It's upstairs from the street and has a balcony.

Chilgapsan (칠갑산; Map pp96-7; ☎ 730 7754; Sambong-gil; meals W14,000; ☼ 11.30am-10pm; ◉ Line 1 to Jonggak, Exit 2) The speciality in this convivial, sit-on-floor-cushions restaurant is the excellent *neobiani* (너비아니), a beef patty the size of a small plate. Meant for sharing, it comes with a dressed green salad. The barley and rice *bibimbap* is original – you mix in *doenjang jjigae* (spicy tofu soup). Look for a building with a white frontage covered with ivy.

Sanchon (산촌; Map pp96-7; ☎ 735 0312; www.sanchon.com; lunch/dinner W22,000/39,600; ☼ 11.30am-10pm; ◉ Line 3 to Anguk, Exit 6) Come more for the appealing atmosphere than the all-vegetarian temple food, a meal of 20 small courses that's exactly the same at lunch and dinner (the premium at night is for the traditional dance and music show at 8pm).

Baru (바루; Map pp96-7; ☎ 2031 2081; 5th fl, Templestay Bldg, Insa-dong; meals W25,000-53,000; ☼ noon-3pm & 6-9pm; ◉ Line 3 to Anguk, Exit 6) Gathering rave reviews for its exquisite take on temple-style cuisine is this new restaurant, although it's difficult to believe that monks ever eat food this elegantly presented.

Min's Club (민가다헌; Map pp96-7; ☎ 733 2966; lunch W19,000-45,000, dinner W58,000-75,000; ☼ noon-11.30pm, last serving 9.30pm; ◉ Line 3 to Anguk, Exit 6) Old-world architecture meets new-world cuisine in this attractive restaurant in a restored 1930s *hanok*. The Euro-Korean cuisine is more European than Korean, but it's all beautifully presented and delicious. You can also drop by for just tea between 2.30pm and 6pm.

Daehangno

Tonjangyesul (톤장예술; Map pp96-7; ☎ 745 4516; meals W7000; ☼ 9am-11pm; ◉ Line 4 to Hyehwa, Exit 3) Serves a tasty fermented bean paste and tofu stew with a variety of rustic side dishes at bargain prices – no wonder it's well patronised by the area's student population.

Bongchu Jjimdak (봉추찜닭; Map pp96-7; ☎ 3676 6981; Maronie-gil; meals W20,000; ☼ 11am-midnight; ◉ Line 4 to Hyehwa, Exit 1 or 2) A popular restaurant serving *jjimdak* (chicken, vegies and noodles cooked in a spicy sauce with the kick of a horse), with paper lanterns and

Zen-style decor. You need two people for this party food.

Myeong-dong & Dongdaemun

Sinsun Seolnongtang (신선설농탕; Map pp100-1; ☎ 777 4531; Myeong-dong-gil, Myeong-dong; meals W6000-15,000; ☼ 24hr; ◉ Line 4 to Myeong-dong, Exit 7) The decor is neat and simple, and everyone receives free *boricha* (barley tea). *Mandu* (dumplings), tofu or ginseng can be added to the beef broth, but purists will want to stick to the traditional version.

Myeongdong Gyoja (명동교자; Map pp100-1; ☎ 776 5348; www.mdkj.co.kr; Myeong-ryebang-gil, Myeong-dong; meals W7000; ☼ 10.30am-9.30pm; ◉ Line 4 to Myeong-dong, Exit 8) Their special *kalguksu* (noodles in a meat, dumpling and vegetable broth) is famous, so it's busy busy busy and eating here is a matter of 'queue, pay, eat, leave!' If the place is full, there's a second branch further down the street opposite Andong Jjimdak.

Samarkand (사마리칸트; Map pp100-1; ☎ 2277 4261; www.samarikant.com; off Beorumul-gil, Dongdaemun; meals W10,000; ☼ 9am-midnight; ◉ Line 2, 4 or 5 to Dongdaemun station, Exit 12) Try Central Asia favourites such as *shurpa* (meat, vegetables and chickpeas in a tasty broth) and *shashlik* (minced meat on a huge skewer) at this laid-back family-run Uzbeki restaurant. Sitting in the armchairs with Uzbeki pop DVDs on the TV is like eating in someone's living room. They also serve the good Russian beer Baltika.

Yoogane (유가네; Map pp100-1; ☎ 3789 3392; www.yoogane.co.kr; Myeong-ryebang-gil, Myeong-dong; meal W10,000-15,000; ☼ 11am-11pm; ◉ Line 4 to Myeong-dong, Exit 8) You've got to try *dakgalbi* (spicy pan-fried chicken prepared at the table) while you're in Korea and this inexpensive chain is a good place to do it. Make sure you ask for fried rice after – it's cooked in the same pan and is wonderfully delicious.

Baekje Samgyetang (백제삼계탕; Map pp100-1; ☎ 776 3267; Myeong-dong 2-gil, Myeong-dong; meals W13,000-20,000; ☼ 9am-10pm; ◉ Line 4 to Myeong-dong, Exit 6) No-frills place famous for its brisk service and reliable *samgyetang*, served with a thimbleful of *insamju* (ginseng wine). The 2nd-floor restaurant has a sign with red Chinese characters.

Andong Jjimdak (안동찜닭; Map pp100-1; ☎ 310 9174; off Myeong-dong-gil, Myeong-dong; meals W15,000-25,000; ☼ 11am-11pm; ◉ Line 4 to Myeong-dong, Exit 7) A convivial young crowd comes to this popular chain for the *jjimdak* experience, a very spicy concoction of chicken, noodles, potatoes and vegetables that comes on a platter meant for sharing. The signboard has white Chinese characters.

ourpick Korea House (한국의집; Map pp100-1; ☎ 2266 9101; www.koreahouse.or.kr; Namsan; set course W57,200-99,000; ☯ noon-2pm & 5.30-7.20pm Mon-Sat, 6.30-8pm Sun; ◉ Line 3 or 4 to Chungmuro, Exit 3) A dozen courses make up the delicious royal banquet at this top-class restaurant with attached theatre (p141). The subtle, fresh flavours are quite different from the strong flavours usually associated with Korean food. The *hanok*, the *hanbok*-clad waitresses, the *gayageum* (zither) music and the platters and boxes the food is served in are all part of the experience.

Itaewon & Yongsan-gu

Soganae (소가네; Map pp94-5; ☎ 719 0077; meals W5500; ☯ 7.30am-10pm; ◉ Line 5 to Hyochang Park, Exit 2) Opposite Hyochang Stadium and close by a pleasant park, this simple restaurant is one of several along this strip patronised by Seoul's taxi drivers. The fried fish meals, with serve yourself *banchan* (side dishes), are a bargain and very tasty.

Buddha's Belly (Map p104; ☎ 796 9330; www.buddhasbelly.co.kr; Itaewon 2-gil; meals W9000-13,000; ☯ 11.30am-2am; ◉ Line 6 to Itaewon, Exit 1) It's not difficult to understand why this restaurant and lounge bar, on the main dining strip behind the Hamilton Hotel, is a much-recommended locals' favourite. The cooking is authentic and the ambience relaxed. Their original tiny takeaway outlet (☎ 793 2173) is down the hill past Noksapyeong, with a few seats for dine-in customers.

Toque (Map p104; ☎ 794 3834; Hannam-dong; meals W15,000-20,000; ☯ 11.30am-11pm; ◉ Line 6 to Hangangjin, Exit 2) A US-trained chef runs this casual diner that always attracts a crowd from the International School opposite; W13,000 gets you a choice of two mini-burgers with a range of toppings.

Our Place (우리공간; Map p104; ☎ 792 7884; Itaewanno; meals R15,000-30,000; ☯ 4pm-3am; ◉ Line 6 to Itaewon, Exit 3) Hong Suk-chun, one of the very few openly gay celebs in Seoul, is the driving force behind this lovely Italian bistro occupying the top floors of a tower overlooking Itaewon – ask for a table on the terrace. The same company also runs the My Thai, My China and My Chelsea restaurants in the area.

Salam (살람; Map p104; ☎ 793 4323; www.turkeysalam.com; meals W20,000; ☯ noon-10pm, closed 1st & 3rd Mon of month; ◉ Line 6 to Itaewon, Exit 3) Uphill from the subway and next to the mosque, this classy Turkish restaurant and bakery is great for a meal of hummus, kebabs and pide (Turkish pizza).

Macaroni Market (Map p104; ☎ 749 9181; 2nd fl Hannam Bldg, Itaewonno; meals W20,000-30,000; ☯ 11am-2am; ◉ Line 6 to Itaewon, Exit 2) This upscale, spacious deli, cafe, restaurant and bar is an indication of how fancy Itaewon is becoming these days. The food is pleasant enough and the big balcony windows provide a ringside seat on all the street action.

Le Saint-Ex (르생떼스; Map p104; ☎ 795 2465; Itaewon 2-gil, Itaewon; meals W28,000-50,000; ☯ 6pm-midnight; ◉ Line 6 to Itaewon, Exit 1) The blackboard menu at this very French bistro with consistently good food and service is always tempting. The W17,600 lunch sets are excellent.

Hongdae & Sinchon

Richemont (Map p93; ☎ 332 7778; Seogyoro, Hongdae; snacks W500-7000; ☯ 8am-11pm; ◉ Line 2 to Hongik University, Exit 5) For when rice and *kimchi* just won't cut it, this above-average bakery sells real bread, specialist chocolates and their own ice lollies as well as offering a good-value European breakfast for W4500.

Choonchun Jip (춘천집; Map p93; ☎ 323 5597; meals W10,000; ☯ 24hr; ◉ Line 2 to Sinchon, Exit 2) The specialty is *dakgalbi*, a boneless chicken dish with chunks of cabbage, leek and carrot smothered in a spicy sauce. The staff cook the food at your table, so there's nothing to do except wait and put on the apron. To find it turn left at the lane between Starbucks and the SK Telecom store.

Cheolkil Wang Galbi (철길왕갈비; Map p93; ☎ 332 9543; meal W25,000; ☯ 24hr; ◉ Line 2 to Sinchon, Exit 8) Mr Oh did so well with his original humble *galbi* joints either side of the now-disbanded railway tracks (hence the name meaning 'train track *galbi*') that he was able to build this sprawling palace of grilled meats. Platters of beef and pork sizzle invitingly at every table.

Agio (아지오; Map p93; ☎ 334 7311; Eoulmadang 2-gil, Hongdae; meals W10,000-20,000; ☯ noon-midnight; ◉ Line 2 to Hongik University, Exit 5) Sit outside under the spacious courtyard under shady trees or inside this charming Italian restaurant that serves mainly organic salads and pastas, but specialises in large, thin-crust pizzas (W18,000).

El Plato (Map p93; ☎ 325 3515; Hongdae; meals W20,000; ☻ 5pm-1am Mon-Fri, noon-1am Sat & Sun; ☻ Line 6 to Sangsu, Exit 2) Tasty tapas and paella are the specialities of this relaxed Spanish restaurant, which also serves a refreshing glass of sangria.

Apgujeong, Gangnam & Around

Allô Papergarden (Map pp102-3; ☎ 541 6933; www. papergarden.co.kr; meals W10,000-15,000; ☻ 11am-1am; ☻ Line 3 to Sinsa, Exit 8) Back a street from trendy tree-lined Garosu-gil you'll find this combined boutique, cafe and restaurant with an open courtyard and two levels. Apart from the usual salads, pasta and brunch items they do a refreshing *moca bingsoo*, a nice twist on the traditional Korean shaved-ice-and-red-bean dessert, spiced up with a shot of coffee.

Mad for Garlic (매드포갈릭; Map pp102-3; ☎ 546 8117; www.madforgarlic.com; Apgujeongno; meals W15,000-30,000; ☻ 11.30am-midnight; ☻ Line 3 to Apgujeong, Exit 2) With dishes like 'Dracula Killer', you know what to expect at this popular Italian bistro chain. Garlic is everywhere including in the air, thanks to the open-concept kitchen that unleashes an appetising aroma in this brick-and-mortar basement restaurant.

Gorilla in the Kitchen (고릴라인더키친; Map pp102-3; ☎ 3442 1688; www.gorillakitchen.co.kr; Dosan Park; meals W20,000-30,000; ☻ 11am-1am; ☻ Line 3 to Apgujeong, Exit 2) Owned by Korean actor Bae Yong-jun, this chic restaurant-bar (last food orders are at 10pm) has a handle on fine Euro dining, and most meals come up trumps. It's a great place to chill out over a lazy brunch at weekends.

Busan Ilbeonji (부산일번지; Map pp90-1; ☎ 813 7799; meals W20,000-60,000; ☻ 10.30am-10.30pm; ☻ Line 1 to Noryangjin, Exit 1) Generous super fresh fish and crab meals are a bargain at Mrs Moon's restaurant up on the 2nd floor of the Noryangjin fish market (p111). If you're not up for the full raw fish platter try *kkotge* (a crab in a spicy or mild soup) for W10,000 per person, which includes great side dishes such as garnished tofu, sweet red beans, pumpkin, raw fish salad and shredded jellyfish.

Samwon Garden (삼원가든; Map pp102-3; ☎ 548 3030; www.samwongarden.com; Dosan Park; meals W35,000; ☻ 11.45am-10pm; ☻ Line 3 to Apgujeong, Exit 2) Serving top-class *galbi* for over 30 years, Samwon is surrounded by beautiful traditional gardens including several waterfalls.

Puro Ganjangkejang (프로간장게장; Map pp102-3; ☎ 543 4126; www.prosoycrab.co.kr; Sinsa; meals W50,000-70,000; ☻ 24hr; ☻ Line 3 to Sinsa, Exit 4) Around since 1980, this is *the* place in Sinsa to try delicious soy marinated raw crab (간장게장). The W50,000 small crab is big enough for two to share, but if there's just one of you the lovely ladies here are likely to let you have half for W25,000 and even cut up the crab to make it easier for you to eat.

Star Chef (Map pp102-3; ☎ 529 8248; Maebong; meals W50,000-70,000; ☻ Line 3 to Maebong, Exit 4) Young chef Kim Hu-nam's modern Korean bistro gets rave reviews from Seoul's foodie community. It's worth coming here to try dishes such as a melt-in-the-mouth octopus salad, *bulgogi* and grilled mushroom organic salad, and crisply fried whole mullet that's aptly described as The Amazing Fish.

Self-Catering

You can pick up snacks, drinks etc at the zillions of 24-hour convenience stores dotted around the city, while fresh food is available at Namdaemun Market (p108). Also don't pass up a chance to browse the splendid basement food halls of the major department stores such as Shinsegae (p144) – picnicking on all the free samples is Seoul's cheapest meal deal!

If a big or specialised grocery shop is called for, head to the following:

Hannam Supermarket (Map p104; ☎ 702 3313; ☻ 9am-8pm; ☻ Line 6 to Hangangjin, Exit 2) Not cheap but stocks hard-to-find Western food items. From the subway exit, take the overhead crosswalk, then walk right – it's in the basement of the Volvo building.

Lotte Mart (롯데마트; Map pp100-1; ☎ 390 2500; Seoul Station; ☻ 10am-midnight; ☻ Line 4 & 5 to Seoul Station, Exit 1) Giant discount store that's part of the Seoul Station complex.

DRINKING
Cafes & Teashops

Seoul's cafes and teashops make a big effort to create memorable decor with, for example, birdsong, books, running water and ethereal music adding to the atmosphere – all of which compensates for a drink that can cost more than a meal. Insa-dong in particular is packed with appealing places to rest up over a beverage.

INSA-DONG

ourpick Dawon (다원; Map pp96-7; ☎ 730 6305; off Seokjeongol-gil; teas W6000-7000; ☻ 11am-11pm; ☻ Line 3 to Anguk, Exit 6) The perfect place to unwind on a warm summer evening is under the shady fruit trees in this secret courtyard enjoying a refreshing *omijacha hwachae* (fruit and five-flavour berry punch). In winter sit indoors in *hanok* rooms decorated with scribbles or in the garden pavilion. Small exhibition spaces surround the courtyard.

Jilsiru Tteok Café (질시루 떡 카페; Map pp96-7; ☎ 741 0258; Donhwamunno; www.kfr.or.kr; teas W6000; ❤ 9am-9pm; ◉ Line 1, 3 or 5 to Jongno 3-ga, Exit 6) *Tteok* – soft, delicately flavoured gourmet rice cakes – are made by hand here with all sorts of flavours such as lemon, coffee, even *kimchi*. There's another branch on Insadonggil (☎ 733 5477; open 10am to 9pm; ◉ Line 3 to Anguk, Exit 6)

Sinyetchatjip (신 옛찻집; Map pp96-7; ☎ 732 5257; Insadong-gil; teas W6000; ❤ 10am-10pm; ◉ Line 3 to Anguk, Exit 6) Red and blue parrots in a cage, fish tanks and a green courtyard are part of the decor of this atmospheric teashop which also offers alcoholic drinks such as wild-strawberry wine and quince wine.

Yetchatjip (옛찻집; Map pp96-7; ☎ 722 5019; teas W6000; ❤ 10am-11pm; ◉ Line 3 to Anguk, Exit 6) Half a dozen little songbirds fly around inside Seoul's most famous teashop. Antique bric-a-brac so clutters this hobbit-sized teashop that it's hard to squeeze past and find somewhere to sit. Try the hot *mogwacha* (quince tea) with a subtle fruity flavour or the tangy, vitamin-filled *yujacha* (citron tea).

DAEHANGNO

Mindeulleyeongto (민들레영토; Map pp96-7; ☎ 745 5234; www.minto.co.kr; Maronie 2-gil, Daehangno; drinks W7000; meals from W10,000; ❤ 10am-midnight; ◉ Line 4 to Hyehwa, Exit 2; 👶) Spread over five floors, this place offers masses of different zones and hideaway spots, each with its own decor and furniture. A friendly dog guards the doorway and workers dressed like Heidi have their own special wave. The name, which has something to do with dandelions, is usually shortened to Minto.

MYEONG-DONG

O'Sulloc (오설록티하우스; Map pp100-1; ☎ 774 5460; Myeong-dong-gil, Myeong-dong; cakes & teas W6000; ❤ 9am-11pm; ◉ Line 4 to Myeong-dong, Exit 6) Impeccably presented green-tea drinks and cakes are created here in this smart, green-themed teahouse. All the green tea comes from Jeju-do, Korea's southerly, semi-tropical island, where the best tea is reputed to grow.

ITAEWON

Life is Just a Cup of Cake (Map p104; ☎ 794 2908; www.cupcake.co.kr; cupcakes W4800; ❤ noon-9pm; ◉ Line 6 to Itaewon, Exit 2) Super cute cafe specialising in iced cup cakes which come in many different flavours – chocolate is a favourite. Ask the English-speaking owner/baker Saem Lee about her special orders of mini cupcakes.

Passion 5 (Map p104; ☎ 2071 9505; Hannan-dong; snacks W5000-10,000; ◉ Line 6 to Hangangjin, Exit 2) Housed in a building that looks like the HQ of a trendy design firm, this might just be Seoul's best bakery, with a cafe if you can't wait to get home to try their sweet and savoury delights, including handmade chocolates.

Tartine (Map p104; ☎ 3785 3400; pies W6600; ❤ 10am-10.30pm; ◉ Line 6 to Itaewon, Exit 1) Looking for dessert? You won't go wrong with the scrumptious fruit pies and other confections at this charming bakery-cafe run by an American baker. It's down the first alley after the Hamilton Hotel.

HONGDAE

Princess Palace (프린세스; Map p93; ☎ 335 6703; drinks W7000; ❤ 10am-4am; ◉ Line 2 to Hongik University, Exit 5) Candles and chandeliers light the steps down to this winter palace of a cafe. White curtains around the tables give privacy to your little white princess world. Ballads, a glittery decor and dainty cakes add to the princess effect.

APGUJEONG & GANGNAM

Bloom & Goûté (Map pp102-3; ☎ 545 6659; Garosu-gil, Sinsa; drinks W5000, food W5000-10,000; ❤ 10.30am-midnight Mon-Sat, 11am-midnight Sun; ◉ Line 3 to Sinsa, Exit 8) Typical of the Euro-chic vibe of Garosul-gil is this cafe combined with a florist. It serves a good range of desserts and baked treats in a relaxing atmosphere with streetside tables.

Take Urban (테이크어반; Map pp102-3; ☎ 519 0001; Bongeunsaro, Gangnam; drinks W2800-5000, food W6000-11,000; ❤ 8am-midnight; ◉ Line 9 to Sinnonhyeon, Exit 3) On the ground floor of a building that looks like a giant concrete cheese grater is this sophisticated and spacious cafe, with indoor and outdoor options, heaps of designer-style fresh bakery items and organic coffee.

Bars

Apart from the following, drop by one of the many *hof* – the cheaper drinking joints serving local draught beer, *soju* and, invariably, fried chicken, or one of the tent bars and food carts that line streets around Jongno-gu. Craving expat company? Then Itaewon is your drinking destination, although Hongdae is increasingly taking on an international vibe and is generally one of the most fun nightspots in the city (see the boxed text, p141).

GWANGHWAMUN & JONGNO-GU

Gaeul (가을; ☎ 730 7537; Map pp96-7; ⏰ 11am-1am Mon-Sat; ⦿ Line 5 to Gwanghwamun, Exit 8) Since 1984 this 2nd-floor live-music bar has been a favourite among office workers for a night of alcohol-fuelled dancing and singing to old Korean pop songs and the odd Neil Diamond number. You have to order at least one food dish (the fruit plate is big enough to feed a small army).

Top Cloud Bar (Map pp96-7; ☎ 2230 3000; www.top cloud.co.kr; 33rd fl, Jongno Tower; ⏰ 8.30pm-1am; ⦿ Line 1 to Jonggak, Exit 3) This classy candlelit bar and restaurant offers a magical night view of Seoul along with live jazz music – for which you'll have the pleasure of paying W15,400 a beer.

DAEHANGNO

Comfort Zone (Map pp96-7; ☎ 762 4793; comfortzone. cyworld.com; ⦿ Line 4 to Hyehwa, Exit 4) Spacious cafe-bar that lives up to its title with comfy sofas on two colourfully decorated levels and a spacious outdoor area. Happy hour with half-price draught beers runs from 5pm to 8pm.

MYEONG-DONG

Pierre's Bar (Map pp100-1; ☎ 317 7183; www.pierre gagnaire.co.kr; Lotte Hotel; ⦿ Line 2 to Euljiro 1-ga, Exit 8) Specialising in vodka and champagne this glam-to-the-max bar attached to Pierre Gagnaire's restaurant offers boudoir-like booths for intimate liaisons. Cocktails kick off at W15,000 or you can sample three vodkas for W36,000.

ITAEWON

Hostess bars are concentrated on the first road off to the left up the hill opposite the Hamilton Hotel, known locally as Hooker Hill (not to be confused with Homo Hill, the strip of gay bars and clubs on the next parallel street; see the boxed text, p141).

3 Alley Pub (쓰리앨리펍; Map p104; ☎ 749 3336; Itaewon 2-gil, Itaewon; ⏰ noon-1am Sun-Thu, noon-2am Fri & Sat; ⦿ Line 6 to Itaewon, Exit 1) Mixing together a friendly pub atmosphere with top-notch European-style pub grub (mains W15,000) and nine draught beers is a formula that makes this place an expat magnet, especially with the older crowd.

Bar Bliss (블리스바; Map p104; ☎ 749 7738; www. winebarbliss.com; Beodeunamu-gil, Itaewon; ⏰ 7pm-3am;

⦿ Line 6 to Itaewon, Exit 4) Away from the main gay strip, this is a gay-friendly but not exclusively gay bar. It features a chill-out, relax-on-cushions, shisha-pipe zone and a reclining Buddha – bliss indeed!

Berlin (Map p104; ☎ 749 0903; ⏰ 11.30am-2am; ⦿ Line 6 to Itaewon, Exit 1) This sophisticated cafe, lounge and restaurant, set away from the main Itaewon drag, has an airy terrace with a view across to the Yongsan US military base; later in the evening a DJ plays.

Gecko's Terrace (Map p104; ☎ 749 9425; cnr Itaewonno & Bogwangdong-gil; ⏰ 11am-2am; ⦿ Line 6 to Itaewon, Exit 4) Comfortable and popular 2nd-floor bar and restaurant with a global menu (meals W11,000), lunch specials and draught beers, plus the obligatory-in-Itaewon darts and pool.

Kabinett (Map p104; ☎ 790 7034; www.kabinett.co.kr; Itaewon; ⏰ 5.30pm-1.30am; ⦿ Line 6 to Itaewon, Exit 2) This boutique wine bar and restaurant reflects Itaewon's evolution into one of Seoul's hip party destinations.

Other recommendations:

Seoul Pub (서울펍; Map p104; ☎ 793 6666; Itaewonno; ⏰ noon-3am Sun-Thu, noon-6am Fri & Sat; ⦿ Line 6 to Itaewon, Exit 4) With a real pub atmosphere, lubricated by plenty of pitchers and the Guinness and Kilkenny on tap.

Wolfhound (Map p104; ☎ 749 7971; http://wolfhound pub.com; ⏰ 3pm-2am Mon-Fri, 11am-2am Sat & Sun; ⦿ Line 6 to Itaewon, Exit 4) If you're looking for an Irish pub this is a good one, with great grub to boot.

HONGDAE & SINCHON

Hang out with the cool kids sipping canned beer outside Hongdae's Buy The Way (Map p93) convenience store or try the following:

360@ (360 알파; Map p93; ☎ 323 2360; Hongik-gil, Hongdae; ⏰ 2pm-5am; ⦿ Line 2 to Hongik University, Exit 5) Dip your feet in the pool, sit in a shady garden swing seat or recline on a bed indoors at this eccentric bar, full of places to relax as you listen to their tunes.

Castle Praha (캐슬프라하; Map p93; ☎ 334 2181; Solnae 6-gil, Hongdae; ⏰ noon-3pm & 5pm-2am; ⦿ Line 2 to Hongik University, Exit 5) Hidden away down an alley is the most extraordinary facade in Seoul, with an equally bizarre dungeon-cum-cellar interior for the vintage restaurant, the home-brew bar, the bakery and cafe.

ourpick Chin Chin (Map p93; ☎ 334 1476; Hongdae; ⏰ 11-2am; ⦿ Line 2 to Hongik University, Exit 2) Zhang Ki Chul is a man on a mission: to get people to take *makgeolli* (a Korean style of rice wine) seriously. Once you've tried the various artisan brands at this chic resto-bar you'll find your opinions shifting Zhang's way. The modern Korean food is delicious and beautifully presented. Among one of Zhang's great discoveries is how good a cocktail of *makgeolli* and beer tastes. Also on the menu *makgeolli* ice cream and *makgeolli* expresso!

Jane's Groove (제인스그루브; Map p93; ☎ 3143 5375; Wausan-gil, Hongdae; ✆ 7pm-4am; ✪ Line 6 to Sangsu, Exit 2) This chameleon-like bar has computer games, darts and screens, plus dance and chill-out zones. It sometimes morphs into a karaoke, open-mic, fancy-dress or live-music joint (admission up to W15,000).

Kanya (가야; Map p93; ☎ 312 5618; Myeongmul-geori, Sinchon; ✆ 4pm-5am; ✪ Line 2 to Sinchon, Exit 3) This basement *hof* has stone statues and dramatic down lighting, giving it a more upmarket feel. The menu is the usual assortment of shared dishes – spicy seafood noodles and Cajun chicken (not in the least Cajun) are OK – but really it's about the *soju* and beer. Try their strawberry yoghurt *soju* cocktail.

Oi (Map p93; ☎ 334 5484; Hongdae; ✆ 1pm-3am Sun-Thu, 1-5pm Fri & Sat; ✪ Line 2 to Hongik University, Exit 5) Imagine an all-white Hobbit-land interior of caves, platforms, ponds and small bridges: that's the dreamy atmosphere of this quirky cafe-club where you can chill out over a hookah pipe and cocktails. There's an outdoor terrace and over the summer they host crazy water-pistol parties (cover charge W5000 to W10,000). Take the elevator up to the 4th floor of the building opposite the Adidas shop to find it.

Tinpan Alley (틴팬뮤직바; Map p93; ☎ 322 6949; Hongdae; ✆ 7pm-4am Sun-Thu, to 6am Fri & Sat; ✪ Line 6 to Sangsu, Exit 1) Blame it on the B52s (Baileys, Kahlúa, Bacardi 151 and Cointreau), but there's usually dancing on the tables in the early hours – the railings on the ceiling are to hang on to! There's a cover charge (W10,000 including a drink) after 10pm on Friday and Saturdays and if it's full (it usually is) then there's a second one across the street.

Vinyl (Map p93; Wausan-gil, Hongdae; ✆ 4pm-2am, to 3.30am Fri & Sat; ✪ Line 6 to Sangsu, Exit 1) Here's a neat idea – all drinks sold in plastic, IV-style bags with straws. Either drink your Midori Sour cocktail in this cute little bar or take it with you as you wander around Hongdae.

Woodstock (월플라워스; Map p93; ☎ 334 1310; Sinchon; ✆ 7pm-4am; ✪ Line 2 to Sinchon, Exit 2) Years of scribbles have built up all over the walls,

tables and chairs in this popular bar where the big attraction is the loud rock music selected from their huge collection.

APGUJEONG & GANGNAM

Baekseju ma-eul (백세주마을; Map pp102-3; ☎ 595 1003; www.ksdb.co.kr; Gangnam; ✆ 11am-1am; ✪ Line 2 to Gangnam, Exit 5) See the website's English pages to learn more about the excellent range of traditional rice wines available at this basement drinking and dining outlet for brewer Kooksoondang. There's also a branch in Jongno-gu (Map pp96–7; ☎ 720 0055; ✪ Line 2 to Jonggak, Exit 4) overlooking Bosingak.

Juju Tent Bar (주주실내포장마차; Map pp102-3; ☎ 512 3333; Dosandaero, Gangnam; ✆ 6pm-6am; ✪ Line 3 to Apgujeong, Exit 6) Particularly popular in summer, this outdoor bar near Apgujeong has a retractable roof. Beer and *soju* is W4000 while the menu has trad food, chicken gizzards, chicken feet, grilled eel, stews and fish (meals W12,000 to W20,000).

Oktoberfest (옥토버훼스트; Map pp102-3; ☎ 3481 8881; off Seomyeong-gil, Gangnam; ✆ 4pm-1am; ✪ Line 2 to Gangnam, Exit 6) It's much quieter than Oktoberfest at this microbrewery in a large bare-brick and natural-wood cellar. Four freshly produced beers along with German-style meats are served by frock-clad lasses (platters W11,000 to W50,000).

Platinum Microbrewery (Map pp102-3; ☎ 466 6604; www.platinumbeer.com; ✆ 4pm-4am Mon-Sat, to 2am Sun; ✪ Line 3 to Apgujeong, Exit 6) This basement-level microbrew bar, offering seven types of brews, has a battleship-grey interior that creates the impression you're inside a submarine. Quaff back a couple pints of the Morphine brew with 8.4% alcohol and you might imagine you're in most any place.

ENTERTAINMENT

Tickets for all kinds of entertainment, from theatrical shows and concerts to movies and sporting events can bought online at www.ticketlink.co.kr.

Casinos & Betting

Korean nationals cannot enter casinos, but if you dress smartly you should gain entry to any of the following high-class gambling dens:
Seven Luck (www.7luck.com) Millennium Seoul Hilton (Map pp100-1; ☎ 2021 6000; ✪ Line 1 to Seoul station, Exit 8) COEX Mall (Map pp90-1; ☎ 3466 6000; ✪ Line to Samseong station, Exit 5 or 6)

GAY & LESBIAN SEOUL

For most visitors, queer Seoul amounts to Itaewon's 'Homo Hill' (🔘 Line 6 to Itaewon, Exit 3). By 1am every Friday and Saturday this slope is thick with foreigners and English-speaking Koreans. People congregate on the street and drift between **Queen** (퀸; Map p104; ☎ 793 1290; 🕙 8pm-3am, to 6am Fri, closed Mon), **Always Homme** (올웨이즈홈므; Map p104; ☎ 798 0578; 🕙 8pm-4am, to 6am Fri & Sat) and **Soho** (소호; Map p104; ☎ 797 2280; 🕙 8pm-4am Tue-Thu, 6pm-4am Fri-Sun), all fun bars where dancing is encouraged.

The same strip has a couple of tiny meet-market dance clubs which host late-night drag shows – **Trance** (트랜스; Map p104; ☎ 797 3410; W10,000; 🕙 10pm-5am) and **Why Not** (와이낫; Map p104; ☎ 795 8193; W10,000; 🕙 8pm-6am). If you require a bit more space to shake your booty then there's **Pulse** (Map p104; W15,000) down on the main Itaewon strip. Elsewhere in Itaewon, **Bar Bliss** and **Berlin** (p138) are also gay-friendly places for a relaxed drink.

The real queer area of the city, however, is Nagwon-dong between Tapgol Park and Jongno 3-ga subway station, supporting around 100 gay bars and small clubs. Not all are welcoming of foreigners, but the English-speaking owner of **Barcode** (Map pp96-7; ☎ 03672 0940; 🕙 7pm-3am; 🔘 Jongno 3-ga, Exit 3) is very friendly and will happily provide you with a map (in Korean) detailing venues in the area and beyond. This stylish, spacious cocktail bar is found on the second floor – look for the English sign as you come out of the subway. Alternatively you could hang out at the open-air food stalls around Jongno 3-ga.

Lesbians tend to congregate over in Sinchon and Hongdae where you'll find **Labris** (라브리스; Map p93; ☎ 333 5276; Wausan-gil, Hongdae; 🕙 7pm-2am Mon-Thu, to 5am Fri-Sun; 🔘 Line 2 to Hongik University, Exit 5), an 8th-floor women-only social-cum–dance club which attracts locals and foreigners. DJ nights are Fridays to Sundays when the minimum charge for a drink and compulsory *anju* is W12,000.

At the end of May Seoul pins up its rainbow colours for the **Korean Queer Cultural Festival** (www.kqcf.org), culminating in a parade through downtown, and is usually held in conjunction with the **Seoul LGBT Film Festival** (www.selff.com). For a good blog posting on gay Seoul see http://discoveringkorea.wordpress.com/2009/06/19/video-queer-seoul/.

Sheraton Grande Walkerhill (쉐라톤그랜드워커힐호텔; Map pp90-1; ☎ 450 4826; www.walkerhill.co.kr; 🕙 24hr; 🔘 Line 5 to Gwangnaru, Exit 2)

Seoul Racecourse (서울경마장; Map pp90-1; ☎ 509 1221; www.kra.co.kr; admission W800; 🕙 races 11.30am-5pm Sat & Sun Sep-Jun, 1-9pm late Jul-late Aug; 🔘 Line 4 to Seoul Racecourse Park, Exit 2) If cards aren't your calling, try the pony races at this well-organised facility. International guests use the lounge on the 4th floor of the Lucky Ville Grandstand, where interpreters help visitors place a wager.

Cinemas & DVD Rooms

You will find multiplex cinemas in most malls and busy commercial districts. Tickets cost about W7000 and films are usually screened from 10am to 11pm, though some theatres screen films after midnight. English-language films are usually shown in their original language with Korean subtitles. Most cinemas sell tickets with assigned seating.

Under a program sponsored by the Seoul Metropolitan Government, **Cinus** (www.cinus.

co.kr) occasionally screens new Korean movies with English subtitles at its **Gangnan** (Map pp102-3; 🔘 Line 3 to Apgujeong, Exit 6) and **Myeong-dong** (Map pp100-1; 🔘 Line 4 to Myeong-dong, Exit 6) multiplexes.

Cinemateque KOFA (한국 영상 자료원; Map pp90-1; ☎ 3153 2001; www.koreafilm.org; admission free; 🔘 Line 6 to Susaek, Exit 2) It costs nothing to see the classic Korean films at one of the three cinemas in this new home of the Korean Film Archive. See the website for directions from the subway exit.

DVD *bang* (DVD screening rooms) are another opportunity to watch Korean movies with English subtitles. The cost is generally W7000 per person. Busy commercial districts around universities have heaps of DVD *bangs*; try **Cine Castle DVD** (씨네캐슬; Map pp96-7; Maronie-gil; 🕙 noon-2am; 🔘 Line 4 to Hyehwa, Exit 2).

Clubs
ITAEWON

Apart from the gay-friendly clubs (see the boxed text, above), check out **Club Volume** (Map

SEOUL •• Entertainment 141

p104; ☎ 1544 2635; www.clubvolume.com; ⊙ noon-3am
Sun-Thu, to 6am Fri & Sat; ⊙ Line 6 to Itaewon, Exit 4), one of
the biggest, slickest players in this busy nightlife
district with a top-line sound system and lighting. See the website for its DJ schedule.

HONGDAE

Bahia (바히아; Map p93; ☎ 335 1512; Saemulgyeol
2-gil, Hongdae; admission W5000; ⊙ 6pm-midnight Tue-
Thu, to 1am Fri-Sun; ⊙ Line 2 to Hongik University, Exit 5)
Seoul's best Latin American dance club with
a friendly atmosphere has mirrors down one
side so you can check out your moves.

Club Saab (클럽사브; Map p93; ☎ 324 6929;
Wausan-gil, Hongdae; admission W10,000; ⊙ 8pm-5am
Wed-Mon; ⊙ Line 2 to Hongik University, Exit 5) Five DJs
a night with a hard hip-hop attitude play here.
It's the nearest thing to gangsta rap in Seoul.

Joker Red (조커레드; Map p93; ☎ 016-706 7545;
www.jokerred.co.kr; Hongdae; admission W5,000; ⊙ 9pm-
5am Fri & Sat; ⊙ Line 2 to Hongik University, Exit 5) Up to
seven DJs, including Sunshine and Shai, spin
the tables at this 'we love techno' club. It's
larger and smarter than many others, with
enough red lights to justify its name.

M2 (엠투; Map p93; ☎ 3143 7573; www.ohoo.
net/m2; Hongdae; admission Sun-Thu W10,000, Fri & Sat
W20,000; ⊙ 9.30pm-4.30am Sun-Thu, 8.30pm-6.30am
Fri & Sat; ⊙ Line 2 to Hongik University, Exit 5) Deep
underground is M2, one of the largest and
best Hongdae clubs. It has a high ceiling and
plenty of lights and visuals. Top local and international DJs spin mainly progressive house
music. Wednesday is ladies' night.

GANGNAM

Eden (Map pp102-3; ☎ 6447 0042; www.eden-club.
co.kr; admission Sun, Tue-Thu W20,000, Fri & Sat W30,000;
⊙ 8.30pm-4am Sun, Tue-Thu, to 6am Fri & Sat; ⊙ Line 9
to Sinnonhyeon, Exit 3) Lavish laser shows, leggy
models, stratospheric drink prices and tons
of security mark out Eden as the late-night
haunt of Seoul's smart set.

Club Mass (Map pp102-3; ☎ 599 3165; www.clubmass.
net; admission W20,000; ⊙ 8.30pm-6am Tue-Sun; ⊙ Line
2 to Gangnam, Exit 5) A young, friendly crowd bop
to electronic and house music in this spacious
basement strafed by a dazzling lightshow.

Karaoke

Seoul has thousands of *noraebang* (karaoke
rooms), where friends and work colleagues
sing along to well-known songs, including
plenty with English lyrics. Most *noraebang*
open from 2pm to 2am, and prices start at
around W12,000 an hour, although luxury
ones or large rooms cost more.

Luxury Noraebang (럭셔리노래방; Map p93;
☎ 322 3111; Eoulmadang-gil; room per hr W10,000-36,000;
⊙ 24hr; ⊙ Line 2 to Hongik University, Exit 5) Act out
your rock star fantasies at this top-flight karaoke hall; the front rooms with floor-to-ceiling
windows overlooking Hongdae's main drag,
are for exhibitionists.

Live Music
TRADITIONAL & CLASSICAL
One of the best places to get a taste of a range
of traditional Korean music, including *pansori* singing and drumming, is Korea House
(p135). The one-hour performances begin at
7pm and 8.50pm except Sunday (one show at
8pm) and cost W35,000.

Seoul Arts Centre (서울예술의전당; Map pp90-1;
☎ 580 1300; www.sac.or.kr; ⊙ Line 3 to Nambu Bus
Terminal, Exit 5) The national ballet and opera
companies are based at this sprawling arts
complex which sports a circular opera house
with a roof shaped like a Korean nobleman's
hat. It also houses a large concert hall and a
smaller recital hall in which the national choir,
the Korea and Seoul symphony orchestras
and the **Seoul Performing Arts Company** (www.spac.
co.kr) stage shows. A couple more theatres and
three art galleries complete the package. To
reach it, walk straight on from the subway exit
and turn left at the end of the bus terminal,
or else hop on bus 12 (W800) or grab a taxi
(W2000).

**National Centre for Korean Traditional Performing
Arts** (국립국악원; Map pp90-1; ☎ 580 3300;

CLUB DAY

Hongdae has become synonymous with all
that's indie and underground in Seoul's (and
thus Korea's) music scene. The area around
Korea's top art school is packed with small
venues and clubs, 21 of which on the last
Friday of each month collaborate in **Club
Day** (www.clubculture.or.kr; W15,000; ⊙ 8pm-
6am). Tickets for the event, sold at the participating venues and around Hongdae,
allow you to roam freely between earlier
evening live performances and late night/
early morning DJ sets. The area becomes
a sea of people (over 15,000 attended the
100th event in August 2009) but the atmosphere is infectious.

www.gugak.go.kr; tickets W8000-10,000; ⓖ Line 3 to Nambu Bus Terminal, Exit 5) Holds weekly performances Tuesday (7.30pm March to December except mid-July to mid-August), Thursday (7.30pm March to July, September to December) and Saturday (5pm weekly). It's down the road from the Seoul Arts Centre.

Sejong Centre for the Performing Arts (세종문화회관; Map pp96-7; ☎ 399 1111; www.sejongpac.or.kr; Sejongno, Gwanghwamun; ⓖ Line 5 to Gwanghwamun, Exit 1) Centrally located, this leading arts complex puts on major music, drama and art shows – everything from large-scale musicals to fusion *gugak* (traditional Korean music) and gypsy violinists. It has a grand hall, a small theatre and three art galleries.

ROCK AND POP

Concerts by visiting superstars are often held in Olympic Park or Jamsil sports complex. Also check out www.koreagigguide.com.

Café BBang (카페 빵; Map p93; ☎ 011-9910 1089; cafebbang.cyworld.com; Hongdae; ⏰ 7pm-6am; ⓖ Line 2 to Hongik University, Exit 4) Basement venue where you're sure of catching something interesting – apart from music they also host film screenings, art exhibitions and parties.

Club FF (클럽에프에프; Map p93; ☎ 011-9025 3407; Hongdae; admission W10,000; ⏰ 7pm-6am; ⓖ Line 2 to Hongik University, Exit 6) A top live venue with up to eight bands playing at the weekend until midnight. Afterwards it becomes a dance club with DJs. The youthful groups let rip with attitude and style.

DGBD (디지비디; Map p93; ☎ 322 3792; Hongdae; admission W10,000; ⏰ 8-11pm; ⓖ Line 2 to Hongik University, Exit 5) A legendary live-music venue (previously called Drug) where all the top Hongdae bands have played over the years. It's standing-room only, although there are a few chairs and a balcony. The menu is mainly rock but not always.

Free Bird (프리버드; Map p93; ☎ 335 4576; 2fl; Eoulmadang 2-gil, Hongdae; admission Mon-Thu free, Fri-Sun W13,000; ⏰ 6pm-midnight; ⓖ Line 2 to Hongik University, Exit 5) Offering a range of live music from death rock to *Sound of Music* outtakes, the long-running Free Bird generally puts on solid shows. A handful of acts play every evening. Wednesday is audition night.

Ole Stompers Rock Spot (올스톰퍼스록스폿; Map p104; ☎ 795 9155; Solmanaru-gil, Itaewon; ⏰ 7pm-2am Sun-Thu, to 4am Fri & Sat; ⓖ Line 6 to Itaewon, Exit 3) This muso-owned Itaewon pub offers classic live rock most Fridays and Saturdays around 10pm. Look out for their Battle of the Bands shows, which have big prize money and attract top local talent, both Korean and expat.

Sound Holic (사운드홀릭; Map p93; ☎ 3142 4203; www.soundholic.co.kr; Hongdae; admission W10,000-20,000; ⏰ 8pm-6am Tue-Sun; ⓖ Line 2 to Hongik University, Exit 5) New, larger venue for this reliable club/bar hosting mainly rock bands.

Woodstock (우드스탁; Map p104; ☎ 749 6034; Itaewonno, Itaewon; admission free; ⏰ 6pm-late; ⓖ Line 6 to Itaewon, Exit 2) Up on the 3rd floor, expat bands blast out rock music every Friday and Saturday, starting around 9pm. Bars named Woodstock are usually deliberately scruffy dens, and this one is no exception.

JAZZ

All That Jazz (올댓재즈; Map p104; ☎ 795 5701; www.allthatjazz.kr; admission W5000; ⏰ 7pm-1am; ⓖ Line 6 to Itaewon, Exit 1) A fixture on the Seoul jazz scene and one of the classier joints in Itaewon, with an interior reminiscent of the Rat Pack days. Sets kick off from 9pm, except Friday when they start at 8.30pm and weekends from 7pm.

Live Jazz Club (라이브재즈; Map pp96-7; ☎ 743 5555; admission W7000; ⏰ 5pm-3am; ⓖ Line 4 to Hyehwa, Exit 2) This large but intimate venue, with black decor subtly blended with blue neon, attracts top Korean jazz stars such as saxophonist Lee Jeong-suk and his quartet. Enjoy two or three sessions every evening.

Once in a Blue Moon (원스인어블루문; Map pp102-3; ☎ 549 5490; www.onceinabluemoon.co.kr; 85-1 Gungdam-dong; admission free; ⏰ 5pm-2am; ⓖ Line 3 to Apgujeong, Exit 6) An intimate and famous live jazz club where two groups of performers each play two sets between 7.30pm and 12.40am. Free admission is balanced out by W15,000 cocktails and beers.

Sport

Apart from attending one of the more traditional sports listed below, consider being in the audience for the taping of a computer game tournament at the e-Sports Stadium on the 9th floor of the I Park Mall above Yongsan Station. It's a free, eye-opening experience into the glitzy, high-stakes world of Korean online gaming (see p52 for more details).

BASEBALL

Watch South Korea's best players slug it out in **Jamsil Baseball Stadium** (잠실야구장; Map pp90-1; admission W8000-30,000; ⓖ Line 2 to Sports Complex,

Exits 5 or 6). There are three Seoul teams in the eight-team Korean League and two of them – the Doosan Bears and the LG Twins – play at Jamsil, so games are held there nearly every evening during the March to October season, except for the summer break. Matches are well attended and have a good family atmosphere. They usually start at 6.30pm.

BASKETBALL

Seoul has two teams, **Samsung Thunders** (www. thunders.co.kr) and **SK Knights**, in the 10-team **Korean Basketball League** (www.kbl.or.kr). Matches are played from November to March at **Jamsil Gymnasium** (잠실실내체육관; Map pp90-1; admission W15,000-25,000; ⊕ Line 2 to Sports Complex, Exits 7 or 8), with play-offs continuing until May.

SOCCER

FC Seoul (www.fcseoul.com; tickets W8000-12,000) plays its home K-league matches between March and November at either 3pm or 7pm in the World Cup Stadium (p110). Also don't pass up an opportunity to see the national team playing at this giant stadium, the atmosphere is electric as local supporters cheer them on.

Theatre

Drama and big musical shows – including all the usual Broadway/London hits – are massively popular in Seoul. The city has also developed several home-grown non-verbal performance shows that have gone on to international acclaim and are well worth seeing.

Nanta (난타전용관; Map pp96-7; ☎ 739 8288; nanta.i-pmc.co.kr/en/index.asp; tickets W50,000-60,000; ♥ 2pm, 5pm & 8pm Mon-Sat, 3pm & 6pm Sun; ⊕ Line 1 to City Hall, Exit 1; ♿) Set in a restaurant kitchen this brilliantly entertaining show blends drumming, audience participation and slapstick comedy. From the subway exit turn onto the lane close to Deoksugung's gate and follow the road along the stonewall. There's a second troupe performing the show south of the Han River at the Woolim Chungdam Theater (Map pp102–3; ☎ 739 8288; ⊕ Line 3 to Apgujeong, Exit 6).

Jump (Map pp96-7; ☎ 722 3995; www.hijump.co.kr; seats W40,000 & 50,000; ⊕ Line 1 to Jonggak, Exit 4; ♿) Meet the wackiest Korean family ever, all crazy about martial arts. This fun-filled high-energy show packed with impressive acrobatics, slapstick humour and audience participation is

guaranteed fun entertainment. See the website for the performance schedule.

Drawing Show (Map pp96-7; ☎ 766 7848; www.drawing show.com; Hyehwha; adult/child W30,000/20,000; ⊕ Line 4 to Hyehwha, Exit 1; ♿) Funny characterisation, the use of different art techniques, impressive special effects and pantomime frolics all ensure this show's appeal – kids in particular will love it.

Chongdong Theatre (Map pp100-1; ☎ 751 1500; www.mct.or.kr; tickets W30,000-40,000; ♥ 8pm Tue-Sun; ⊕ Line 1 or 2 to City Hall, Exit 2) Centrally located theatre where you can catch the musical show *Miso*, which blends traditional Korean music, *pansori* singing, *samulnori* (traditional percussion music) and fan-dancing. English subtitles on a screen explain the songs.

National Theatre (국립극장; Map pp100-1; ☎ 2274 3507; www.ntok.go.kr; Namsan; ⊕ Line 3 to Dongguk University, Exit 6) Drama, dance, opera and classical Korean music performances are offered at this complex on the eastern slope of Namsan. It's a 15-minute walk from the subway exit or take the yellow bus 2 from the bus stop just behind Exit 6.

SHOPPING

Antiques

Insadong-gil sports plenty of antique shops but serious buyers should head to **Janganpyeong Antiques Market** (Map pp90-1; ♥ 10am-4.30pm Mon-Sat; ⊕ Line 5 to Dapsimni, Exit 2) to explore hundred of small shops housed in three separate buildings. Browse old furniture, paintings, pottery, *yangban* (aristocrat) pipes, horsehair hats, wooden shoes, fish-shaped locks, embroidered status insignia and masses of stone statues.

At the subway exit walk over to the orange-tiled **Samhee 6** building behind the car park. A similar arcade on the left is **Samhee 5**. After visiting them, walk back to Exit 2 and go left along the main road for 10 minutes to reach a brown-tiled arcade, **Janganpyeong**, with another section behind it. You can't miss them with all the stonework stored permanently outside.

Arts, Crafts & Souvenirs

Insa-dong and Samcheong-dong's many small art galleries display paintings (see Art Galleries Walk, p115, for some recommendations), while art-and-craft shops sell handmade papers, cards and calligraphy brushes.

Eco Party Mearry (Map pp96-7; ☎ 720 9005; www.mearry.com; ❤ 10am-8pm; Insadong-gil; Line 3 to Anguk, Exit 6) On the 2nd floor of Dukwon Gallery is this emporium of quirky gifts made from recycled materials – old street banners turned into shopping bags, kids T-shirts made into cute gorilla plushy toys and scraps of leather fashioned into wallets and purses.

Free Market (Map p93; ☎ 325 8553; cnr Wausan-gil & Eoulmadang 2-gil, Hongdae; ❤ 1-6pm Sat in summer; Line 2 to Hongik University, Exit 6) The creative kids of Hongdae lay out their funky wares at this outdoor market, with live music. The similar Hope Market runs here on Sunday afternoons, but has no live music.

Kukjae Embroidery (Map pp96-7; ☎ 732 0830; Insadong-gil; ❤ 10am-8pm; Line 3 to Anguk, Exit 6) This shop (and other branches nearby) has some of the most exquisite embroidery you will ever see. The owner, Mrs Kim Chang-O, is a legend who has exhibited all over the place, and examples of her designs have been official gifts given by Korean presidents to foreign leaders.

Sangsangmadang (Map p93; ☎ 330 6205; www.sangsangmadang.com; Eoulmadang-gil, Hongdae; ❤ noon-10pm; Line 2 to Hongik University, Exit 5) The ground floor of this arts building, in which you'll also find galleries, an indie cinema, concert hall and cafe, sells tons of creative stuff from top Korean designers – much of it small enough to bring home as gifts.

Ssamzie-gil (Map pp96-7; Insadong-gil; ❤ 10.30am-9pm Sun-Thu, to 10pm Fri & Sat; Line 3 to Anguk, Exit 6) This stylish four-storey complex that spirals around a courtyard is a popular stop for one-off clothing, accessories or gifts. Check out the Ssamzie brand shop to the rear for their fun cartoon-theme items.

Department Stores & Malls

Feeling overwhelmed by Seoul's sheer volume of shopping possibilities? Try narrowing your focus to one of the following big department stores or mega malls.

Central City Mall (Map pp102-3; ☎ 6282 0114; www.centralcityseoul.co.kr; Gangnam; ❤ 10am-10pm; Line 3 or 7 to Express Bus Terminal, Exit 7) A popular mall next to the express bus terminal that includes a branch of the department store Shinsegae (☎ 3479 1234; open 10.30am to 8pm), a food court and a six-cinema multiplex.

COEX Mall (Map pp90-1; ☎ 6002 5312; www.coexmall.com; ❤ 10am-10pm; Line 2 to Samseong, Exit 6) It would be easy to spend several days browsing, eating and playing in this massive underground mall reputed to be the largest in Asia. Apart from the numerous shops, including a branch of Hyundai Department Store, you'll also find a multiplex cinema, aquarium, theatre and a missable *kimchi* museum here.

Lotte Department Store (Map pp100-1; ☎ 771 2500; Namdaemunno, Myeong-dong; ❤ 10.30am-8pm; Line 2 to Euljiro 1-ga, Exit 8) Four classy Lotte stores are linked together – the main department store, Lotte Young Plaza, Lotte Avenuel and a duty-free shop. It's impossible not to get lost inside this busy retail beehive of brands but it's an experience not to be missed. There's also a large branch of the department store at Lotte World Amusement Park (see p112).

Galleria (Map pp102-3; ☎ 344 9414; Apgujeongno; ❤ 10.30am-8.30pm; Line 3 to Apgujeong, Exit 1) If you want to play Audrey Hepburn staring wistfully into Tiffany's, don a Helen Kaminski hat, try on a Stella McCartney dress or slip into a pair of Jimmy Choos, the east wing of fashion icon Galleria is the place to be. Dozens of top fashion-designer stores are packed into the two Galleria buildings, the west wing of which is covered in plastic discs that turn psychedelic at night.

Shinsegae (Map pp100-1; ☎ 310 1602; www.shinsegae.com; ❤ 10.30am-8pm Mon-Fri, closed 1 Mon a month, to 8.30pm Sat & Sun; Line 4 to Hoehyeon, Exit 7) The flagship of this department store chain is the Seoul equivalent of Harrods, occupying a handsome colonial-era building (with a sculpture garden on the roof). The spiffy New Annex building has a fantastic food market in the basement.

Electronics

Yongsan Electronics Market (Map pp102-3; ❤ 10am-7.30pm, partly closed 1st & 3rd Sun; Line 1 to Yongsan, Exit 3) If it plugs in you can find it at this geeky universe of high-tech marvels. Bargaining is the order of the day as marked prices are typically lacking, so do what the locals do – check out the prices on the web before arriving. Leave the train station plaza via Exit 3, turn right, then right again and walk through the pedestrian overpass to enter the first building of Yongsan Electronics Town on the 3rd floor. Go down a floor to the popular Mac store, and near there another pedestrian overpass goes to the countless shops that line both sides of the main street.

Techno Mart (Map pp90-1; ☎ 3424 0114; ❤ 10am-8pm, closed 2nd & 4th Tue; Line 2 to Gangbyeon, Exit 1) It's less overwhelming than Yongsan Electronics Market but you still have to check prices before you go, as many items have no price stickers. Mobile phones and computers are towards the top of the building.

Fashion

No luck finding a party outfit in the department stores and malls? Shimmy on over to the district of Myeong-dong (Map pp100–1), home to all the major global fast-fashion labels, including Asian faves Uniqlo, Basic House and Bean Pole. The streets fill up every evening with shoppers, hawkers and people shouting out the latest sale into a megaphone. It can be an overwhelming experience that borders on sensory overload. South of the river well-heeled fashionistas can taxi hop between outposts of Armani and Louis Vuitton along Apgujeong's Brand Name Street (Map pp102–3).

Ahyeon-dong Wedding Street (Map p93; Sinchon; 10am-8pm Mon-Fri; Line 2 to Ewha Womans University, Exit 4) The one-off designer dresses in the shop windows provide an amazing fashion show with plenty of revealing insights into Korean ideas of glamour.

Doota (Map pp94-5; 3398 3114; www.doota.com; 7pm-5am Mon, 10.30am-5am Tue-Sat, 10.30am-11pm Sun; Line 2 & 4 to Dongdaemun Stadium, Exit 14) Dongdaemun is all about fast fashion and this eight-floor complex in the Doosan Tower races to keep ahead of the game; it's packed with interesting local designers' wares, all at bargainable prices.

Daily Projects (Map pp102-3; 3218 4072; www.dailyprojectsseoul.blogspot.com; Seolleungno, Gangnam; 11am-8.30pm; Line 3 to Apgujeong, Exit 2) Come here for trendsetting fashions from young local designers bursting with ideas and talent. The complex also hosts a flea market on the first and third Sundays of the month.

Dynasty Tailor (Map p104; 3785 3035; dynastybruce@gmail.com; off Itaewonno; 10am-8pm; Line 6 to Itaewon, Exit 4) Dynasty has a good reputation – their suits are all handmade in the traditional way by expert tailors just a few doors down from the shop. Pure wool suits cost W250,000 to W300,000 and take about three days to make.

Migliore Mall (Map pp100-1; 2124 0005; www.migliore.co.kr; Myeong-dong; 11am-11.30pm Tue-Sun; Line 4 to Myeong-dong, Exit 6) Always teeming with young trendsetters, this iconic, high-rise Myeong-dong mall is packed with small

fashion shops. There's also a huge branch (Map pp94–5) in Dongdaemun.

Markets

Apart from Dongdaemun (p108), Namdaemun (p108) and Noryangjin Fish Market (p111) there are a couple more markets that are worth exploring.

Gyeong-dong Medicinal Herb Market (Map pp90-1; 8am-6.30pm; Line 1 to Jegi-dong, Exit 2) You could spend hours exploring the biggest and best Asian medicine market in Korea. All the leaves, herbs, roots, flowers and mushrooms piled up in the shops and stalls are medicinal.

Seoul Folk Flea Market (Map pp94-5; 2232 3367; www.pungmul.seoul.go.kr; Sinseol-dong; 10am-6pm, closed 2nd & 4th Tue of month; Line 1 or 2 to Sinseol-dong, Exit 6 or 10) Spilling out of a two-storey building into the surrounding area, here you'll find a fascinating collection of artworks, collectables and general bric-a-brac from wooden masks and ink drawings to Beatles LPs and valve radios.

GETTING THERE & AWAY
Air

For details of airline companies and flights in and out of Seoul, see p398.

INCHEON INTERNATIONAL AIRPORT

Award-winning **Incheon International Airport** (Map p150; 032-741 0114; www.airport.kr), 52km west of Seoul, handles most of Korea's international flights with limited domestic connections to Jeju-do, Busan and Daegu.

International arrivals are on the 1st floor, where you'll find **tourist information centres** (032-743 2660, 032-741 7560; 7am-10pm), ATMs, foreign currency exchange booths, and mobile phone rental desks. Outside the airport doors, buses depart for destinations in Seoul and elsewhere. The A'rex train to Gyeyang station (for connections to Incheon) and Gimpo Airport (for connections to Seoul) leaves from the B1 level.

The 3rd-floor departures area has places to eat and drink. To obtain a tax refund on goods purchased at shops participating in the tax-refund scheme, show the goods and receipts to a customs officer at the check-in counter. Once past immigration control, take the stamped receipt to a **Global Refund counter** (7am-9pm) to get your money.

Inside the terminal opposite gates 11 and 43 transit passengers can grab some rest at

Incheon Airport Transit Hotel (☎ 032-743 3000; www. airgardenhotel.com; 6hr r/deluxe/ste W60,000/72,000/108,000; ❌ ▭ ❌). Add W12,000 for double occupancy. For other accommodation close to the airport see p168.

GIMPO INTERNATIONAL AIRPORT

Direct flights link **Gimpo International Airport** (김포국제공항; Map pp90-1; ☎ 2660 2114; www. airport.co.kr/doc/gimpo_eng/index.jsp; ❸ Line 5 or 9 to Gimpo International Airport), 18km west of the city centre, with 14 cities in Korea and 25 international destinations (mostly in China and Japan). The 1st floor is for arrivals, the 2nd floor is for checking in and the 3rd floor is for departures. The **tourist information centre** (☎ 3707 9465; ☽ 9am-9pm) is beside gate 2 on the 1st floor. Airport services include banks, car-hire counters and restaurants.

CALT

If you're flying on Asiana, Korean Air, Qantas or Delta you might be able to check your luggage and go through customs and immigration procedures at the **CALT** (City Airport, Logis & Travel; Map pp90-1; ☎ 551 0077; www.calt.co.kr; COEX Mall, Jamsil; ☽ approx 5.20am-6.30pm; ❸ Line 2 to Samseong, Exit 5) – call them to check first. Passengers with goods to declare at customs that are stored inside checked bags may use this terminal: anyone with goods to declare in a carry-on bag must check in at the airport. Nonstop buses run every 10 minutes to Incheon (W14,000) or Gimpo (W6500) airports. Allow 90 minutes to get from CALT to Incheon and 60 minutes to Gimpo airport.

Bus

Seoul is well served by very frequent intercity buses – outside of busy holidays you can turn up, get your ticket and go. The prices quoted below are for regular services – you'll pay more for deluxe and night buses; see p403 for details of different types of buses.

The **Seoul express bus terminal** (Map pp102-3; ☎ 536 6460; www.kobus.co.kr; www.easyticket.co.kr; ❸ Line 3, 7 or 9 to Express Bus Terminal) connects with major cities and has two buildings: the Gyeongbu-Gumi-Yeongdong terminal and Honamseon terminal. The former connects with cities like Busan (W29,900, 4½ hours), Daegu (W15,500, three hours 40 minutes) and Daejeon (W9600, two hours). The latter, connected to the Central City complex, has routes to the Jeolla provinces and southern coastal area. Destinations in-clude Mokpo (W18,700, 4½ hours) and Jeonju (W11,500, three hours).

Seoul's other bus terminals include the following:

Dong-Seoul Bus Terminal (Map pp90-1; ☎ 455 3161; www.ti21.co.kr; ❸ Line 2 to Gangbyeon, Exit 4) Service to Icheon, Incheon, Gongju, Boryeong, Cheonan, Suncheon, Sokcho, Andong and Jirisan National Park.

Nambu Bus Terminal (Map pp102-3; ☎ 521 8550; www.nambuterminal.co.kr; ❸ Line 3 to Nambu Bus Terminal, Exit 5) Services towns south of Seoul, including Gongju, Cheonan and Cheongju.

Sangbong Bus Terminal (Map pp90-1; ☎ 435-2129; ❸ Line 7 to Sangbong, Exit 2) Services to cities north and east of Seoul including Chuncheon.

Sinchon Bus Terminal (Map p93; ☎ 324 0611; ❸ Line 2 to Sinchon, Exit 7) Services to Ganghwa-do (see p169; W4200; every 15 minutes).

Train

Most trains leave **Seoul Station** (Map pp100-1; ❸ Line 1 & 4 to Seoul Station), which has high-speed Korea Train Express (KTX), *Saemaul* (express) and *Mugunghwa* (semi-express) services to many parts of the country. KTX destinations and one-way fares from Seoul station include Busan (W44,800, two hours 40 minutes) and Daejeon (W19,500, 55 minutes).

Yongsan Station (Map pp102-3; ❸ Line 1 & Jungang Line) handles KTX and train connections with South Chungcheong and the Jeolla provinces; KTX fares include Gwangju (W38,400) and Mokpo (W43,000). There is no KTX service from Cheongnyangni station (Map pp90-1; ❸ Line 1 to Cheongnyangni), but there are *Saemaul* and *Mugunghwa* connections. Services include Wonju (*Mugunghwa* W6600, two hours) and Andong (W21,000, four hours 20 minutes). For current fares and detailed schedules visit the website of the **Korea National Railroad** (www.korail.go.kr).

East of the centre, long-distance services to destinations in eastern Gyeonggi-do and Gangwon-do leave from **Cheongnyangni Station** (Map pp90-1; ❸ Line 1 to Cheongnyangni), while south of the Han River, **Yeongdeungpo Station** (영등포역; Map pp90-1; ❸ Line 1 to Yeongdeungpo) is a major *Saemaul/Mugunghwa* station.

GETTING AROUND
To/From Incheon International Airport
BUS

Airport limousine buses run every 10 to 30 minutes from around 5.30am to 10pm and the trip to downtown Seoul takes around 80 minutes depending on traffic conditions. Regular limousine buses cost W9000 and run along a dozen routes, while **KAL deluxe limousine buses** (www.kallimousine.com; W14,000) run along four routes and drop passengers off at most major hotels around Seoul as well as Seoul Station.

Limousine buses also run every 10 minutes to Gimpo airport along a special airport road, which takes about 30 minutes and costs W5000 on the City limousine buses or W6500 on the KAL ones.

TAXI
Regular taxis charge W65,000 for the 70-minute journey to downtown Seoul and a deluxe or jumbo taxi costs W95,000. From midnight to 4am regular taxis charge 20% extra.

TRAIN
At the time of research the new **A'rex train** (www.arex.or.kr) ran only as far as Gimpo International Airport (W3200, 33 minutes), where it's possible to transfer to either subway Line 5 or 9. By December 2010 it's expected that this express train line will be completed through to Seoul Station with stops at Digital Media City (subway Line 6), Hongik University (Line 2), Gongdeok (Lines 5 and 6) and Seoul Station (Lines 1 and 4).

To/From Gimpo International Airport
The A'rex train should be connected directly to Seoul Station from here in 2010. Otherwise subway Lines 5 and 9 run from Gimpo International Airport (W1300, 35 minutes to downtown), as do limousine buses (W3000) and taxis (regular W25,000, deluxe W35,000). Between the Gimpo and Incheon airports, take the A'rex train (W3200), a limousine bus (standard W5000, deluxe W6500), or taxi (W45,000).

Public Transport
Bus, subway, taxi and train fares can all be paid using the rechargeable, touch-and-go **T-Money card** (http://eng.t-money.co.kr). The basic card can be bought for W2500 at any subway station booth, bus kiosks and convenience stores displaying the T-Money logo; reload it with credit at any of the aforementioned places and get money refunded that hasn't been used (up to W20,000) at a participating convenience store before you leave Seoul. It not only saves you time buying tickets, but also gives you a W100 discount per trip.

BUS
It is easier and usually quicker to travel around Seoul by subway, but the city has a comprehensive and reasonably priced **bus system** (☎ 414 5005; www.bus.go.kr), which operates from 5.30am to midnight. Some buses run on a few routes until 2am. Some bus stops have some bus route maps in English, and most buses have their major destinations written in English on the outside and a taped announcement of the names of each stop in English, but hardly any bus drivers understand English.

Long-distance express red buses run to the outer suburbs, green buses link subways within a district, blue buses run to outer suburbs and yellow short-haul buses circle small districts. The useful yellow bus 2 does a loop around Namsan from N Seoul Tower to Namsangol Hanok Village and the National Theatre. Pay with a T-money prepaid card and bus tickets cost W100 less and transfers between bus and subway are either free or discounted. Put your T-money card to the screen as you exit as well as when you get on a bus, just as you do on the subway.

SUBWAY
Seoul's excellent, user-friendly **subway system** (www.smrt.co.kr; 5.30am-midnight) is a bargain and will take you just about everywhere you need to go save for the top of Namsan. The minimum fare is W1000 (W900 with a T-money card) which takes you up to 12km. The one-hour trip to Suwon (p155) costs only W1200 and trains run as far as Incheon (p161) to the west, Cheonan to the south and Bukhansan National Park (p151) to the north.

Apart from escalators, most subway stations have lifts or stair lifts for wheelchairs, clean toilets and plenty of English signage. Neighbourhood maps inside the stations help you decide which of the subway exits to take (we provide the Exit number for all listings).

Taxi
Regular taxis are a good deal for short trips. The basic fare for 2km is W2400 and rises W100 for every 144m or 35 seconds after that if the taxi is travelling below 15 km/h. A 20% surcharge is levied between midnight and 4am. Deluxe taxis are black with a yellow stripe and cost W4500 for the first 3km and

W200 for every 164m or 39 seconds, but they don't have a late-night surcharge. Few taxi drivers speak English, but most taxis have a free interpretation service whereby an interpreter talks to the taxi driver and to you by phone; if you want to be sure of getting an English-speaking driver flag down an orange **International Taxi** (☎ 1644 2255; www.internationaltaxi.co.kr); these can be reserved in advance for 20% extra on the regular fare and can be chartered on an hourly or daily basis for longer journeys. All taxis are metered and tipping is not required.

Water Taxis

As part of the Han River renaissance project there is an expanded service of **water taxis** (☎ 1588 3960; www.pleasantseoul.com; 10am-10.30pm Apr-Oct, to 8pm Nov-Mar) along three routes linking

up 13 stations around the city: Jamsil Pier (Map pp90–1), Ttukseom Resort (Map pp90–1), Seoul Forest (Map pp102–3), Jamweon Pier (Map pp102–3), Ichon Geobukseon Naruteo (Map pp102–3), Yeoui 119 (Map pp90–1), Yeouinaru Station (Map pp90–1), Yanghwa Dangsan Station (Map pp90–1), Yanghwa Ferry (Map pp90–1), Seonyu-do (Map pp90–1), Mangwon (Map pp90–1), Nanji (Map pp90–1) and Banghwa (Map pp90–1).

Check the website for booking details and rates which range from W2300 to W60,000 (for the hire of a taxi boat seating up to seven passengers) depending on the distance covered; Monday to Friday between 7am and 8.30am and between 6.30pm and 8pm there are cheaper commuter boat services offered as well.

Gyeonggi-do & Incheon-gwangyeok-si
경기도 & 인천광역시

Encircling Seoul are the province of Gyeonggi-do and the metropolitan area of Incheon-gwangyeok-si, which includes the expanding city of Incheon and the nearby islands flaking into the muddy West Sea like crumbs from a doughnut. Here lie illustrious historical sites – several of them World Heritage listed – timeless temples, cultural villages, sandy beaches and tree-covered mountains that are crying out to be climbed in summer and skied in winter.

All the region's destinations are within easy day-trip range of Seoul, although to get the most from some places it's best to stay overnight or even longer. Incheon International Airport's excellent transport connections and location on the island of Yeongjong-do means that you needn't even go into Seoul first to visit many places.

The ancient dolmen (simple stone tombs) scattered across the island of Ganghwa-do are proof of the area's long and fascinating history. It was here that the 'hermit kingdom' started to be forced out of its self-imposed isolation in the mid-19th century. The resulting mingling of cultures several decades later in nearby Incheon can still be viewed in the port's colourful Chinatown.

For a chilling reminder of cold-war animosities, hop on a DMZ-bound tour bus and catch glimpses of North Korea from the Joint Security Area. Impressive fortifications (minus the barbed wire and landmines) are the principal draw of Suwon, while in Icheon the lures are a chance to buy beautiful Korean pottery or wallow in hot-spring baths. Travellers with children can enjoy Seoul Grand Park, Anyang Art Park and Everland Resort – Korea's answer to Disneyland.

HIGHLIGHTS

- Hike to the granite peaks and mountainside temples in **Bukhansan National Park** (p151)

- Discover Korea's colonial past and **China-town** (p163) on a walk through Incheon

- Fathom the bizarre terror-meets-tourism experience of a trip to the **DMZ** (p152)

- Stride along the World Heritage–listed **fortress wall** (p156) of Suwon then enjoy a meal of **beef-bone soup** (p157)

- Chill out in **Heyri** (p154), a quirky contemporary village devoted to art and low-key architecture

- Escape to one of the lovely islands of the West Sea such as **Muui-do** (p168)

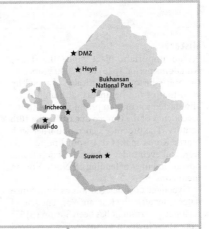

TELEPHONE CODE: 031/032 · POPULATION: 13.04 MILLION · AREA: 11,085 SQ KM

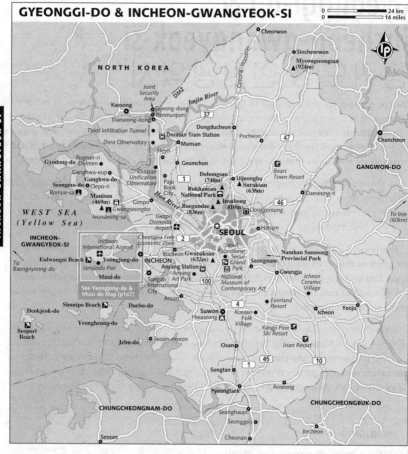

GYEONGGI-DO & INCHEON-GWANGYEOK-SI

0 — 24 km
0 — 14 miles

History

As an important place since the Three Kingdoms period (p26) over 2000 years ago, the area's history is practically wrapped up with that of the peninsula, although it really started to come to prominence with the ascendency of the Goryeo dynasty in the 10th century. The province's current border with North Korea makes it a front line for this war, and even today tunnel-detection teams operate in hopes of fending off North Korean incursions.

Gyeonggi-do's designation as a province dates from after the Korean War. The seat of regional government has been Suwon (p155) since 1967. Incheon-gwangyeok-si was hived off from Gyeonggi-do in 1981 and continues to grow with giant areas of landfill in the West Sea having been converted recently into the new urban centres of Songdo International City and Cheongna.

National & Provincial Parks

The proximity of beautiful **Bukhansan National Park** (opposite) to Seoul means that the splendid views from its multiple peaks often have to be shared with hundreds of other hikers; minimise the crowds by starting early or visiting during the week.

Namhan Sanseong Provincial Park (p160) is also an easy day trip from Seoul that offers hiking, wildflower and bird viewing, and interesting meandering along ancient fortress walls.

Getting There & Around

All the key sights are within day-trip distance of Seoul by the full range of public transport. Taxis are economical, even for longer jaunts, but are especially useful for quick trips once you've reached your destination.

GYEONGGI-DO

Apart from the key places and sights listed following you can find out more about what this province offers the visitor at http://english.gg.go.kr.

BUKHANSAN NATIONAL PARK
북한산 국립공원

This granite peak–studded **national park** (☎ 031-873 2791; http://bukhan.knps.or.kr) is so close to Seoul that it's possible to visit by subway – which partly accounts for why it sees over 10 million visitors a year. It offers sweeping mountaintop vistas, maple leaves, rushing streams and remote temples. Even though it covers nearly 80 sq km, the park's proximity to the city means it gets crowded, especially on weekends.

The park's highest peak is **Baegundae** (836m), while rock climbers particularly enjoy **Insubong** (810m), a free-climber's dream with some of the best multipitch climbing in Asia and routes of all grades. Tree-shaded valleys with cooling streams also provide a chance to wallow in nature for those who'd rather not hike so far or so high. Camping (from W3000 per night) is possible in summer or you can stay in basic mountain huts (W5000).

Dobongsan Hike 도봉산

For this hike, largely through tree-shaded ravines, add time for a picnic lunch. Moderate fitness is required.

Take subway Line 1 north from Seoul to Dobongsan station. It takes 45 minutes from City Hall if your train goes all the way (not all do).

Exit the station and follow the other hikers across the road, past food stalls and hiking-gear shops (don't get distracted by all the great deals!). After about 15 minutes you should reach the **Dobong Park information Center** (1; ☎ 909 0497; ⏲ 7.30am-6pm), which has a basic hiking map in English. A path left goes to Uiam, but walk straight on for the 3km, 1¼-hour hike up to Jaunbong (자운봉, 739m). Almost immediately on the right

is **Gwangnyun-sa (2)**, a typical Buddhist temple and monastery, many of which are scattered around the green hillsides.

Continue along the river and the crowds start to thin out as you ascend past another temple on the left, and, later, **Dobongdaepiso** (3; shelter; ☎ 954 5209), housing a rustic coffee shop and large, multiperson wooden bunk beds (W3000 per person). The shelter is a 40-minute hike from the information office.

Follow the signs to Jaunbong, still 1km away. The rock-strewn path is generally easy to follow, and there tend to be other hikers around if you have any difficulty. Keep on plodding upwards for half an hour and then stop at the big rock. This is where the real adventure begins as you go left for a short, sharp climb up the rock face to the top of **Jaunbong (4)**, with its exhilarating, top-of-the-world 360-degree views.

Back down at the big rock (no sign), go down the gully and then up along the top of the ridgeline. This section is not for the faint-hearted – you have to use ropes and railings to go up and over and down the big rocks. The **Podaeneugsan (5**; ridge) section of the hike takes around one hour, but longer at weekends and holidays due to the crowds of

GYEONGGI-DO & INCHEON-GWANGYEOK-SI

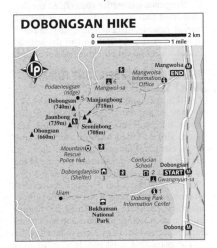

DOBONGSAN HIKE

Mangwolsa **END**
Mangwolsa Information Office
Podaeneugsan (ridge)
Mangwol-sa
Dobongsan (740m) ▲ 5 Manjangbong (718m)
Jaunbong (739m) ▲ 4
Seoninbong (708m)
Obongsan (660m)
Mountain Rescue Police Hut
Confucian School   Dobongsan **START**
Dobongdaepiso (Shelter) 3
Gwangnyun-sa
Uiam
Dobong Park Information Center 1
Bukhansan National Park
Dobong

HIKE FACTS

Start Dobongsan station
Finish Mangwolsa station
Distance 10km
Duration Five hours plus lunch

THE ROYAL TOMBS OF THE JOSEON DYNASTY

Inscribed on Unesco's World Heritage list in June 2009 were the 40-odd **royal tombs of the Joseon dynasty** (http://whc.unesco.org/en/list/1319) scattered across Gyeonggi-do with a couple also in the North Korean city of Kaesong. In these tombs, each similarly arranged on hillsides according to the rules of Confucianism and feng shui, are buried every Joseon ruler right up to the last, Emperor Sunjong (r 1907–10). Tomb entrances are marked by a simple red-painted wooden gate, stone pathway and hall for conducting rites in front of the humped burial mounds decorated with stone statuary – typically a pair of civil officers and generals, plus horses and protecting animals such as tigers and rams.

The largest and most attractive tomb complex is **Donggureung** (동구릉; ☎ 031-563 2909; adult/child W1000/500; ☷ 6am-6.30pm Mar-Oct, to 5.30pm Nov-Feb) in Guri, around 20km northeast of central Seoul. Here lie seven kings and 10 queens, including the dynasty's founder King Taejo: in contrast to the other neatly clipped plots in this leafy park, his mound sprouts rushes from his hometown of Hamhung (now in North Korea) that – in accordance with the king's predeath instructions – have never been cut. To reach the complex take subway Line 2 to Gangbyeon to connect with bus 1-1 or 9-2, around a 40-minute trip from central Seoul.

A more centrally located tomb complex is that of Samreung Gongwon (p112).

---

hikers. There are alternative, easier routes if this one should prove too daunting.

At the sign for **Mangwol-sa** (6; 망월사) turn right for the 15-minute descent to this isolated and beautiful mountainside temple dating back to the 7th century. From here it's a 40-minute walk along a boulder-filled stream to the **Mangwolsa information office (7)**. At the first restaurant bear right, and at the *jokbal* (pork hocks) restaurant bear left, and you reach Mangwolsa subway station (on the left) 30 minutes after leaving the information office.

THE DEMILITARIZED ZONE (DMZ) & JOINT SECURITY AREA (JSA)

The 4km-wide and 240km-long buffer known as the Demilitarized Zone (DMZ) slashes across the peninsula, separating North and South Korea. Lined on both sides by tank traps, electrical fences, landmines and two armies in full battle readiness, it is one of the scariest places on earth. It is also one of the most surreal since it has become a major tourist attraction with several observatories allowing you to peek into North Korea. For history buffs and collectors of weird and unsettling experiences, a visit here is not to be missed.

The place that most people want to go is the Joint Security Area (JSA), 55km north of Seoul, inside of which is the truce village of Panmunjom (see right) – there's nowhere else in South Korea where you can get so close to North Korea and North Korean soldiers without being arrested or shot, and the tension is palpable. The only way in this heavily

restricted area is on an organised tour – note citizens of certain countries, including South Korea, are not allowed on these tours. There are also strict dress and behavioural codes.

Though your tour will likely be a quiet one, the soldier 'tour guides' will remind you that this frontier is no stranger to violent incidents, one of the most notorious being in 1976 when two US soldiers were hacked to death with axes by North Korean soldiers after the former had tried to chop down a tree obstructing the view from a watch tower. Camp Bonifas, the joint US-ROK army camp just outside the DMZ, is named after one of the slain soldiers.

The following describes the major stops on the USO tour (see opposite), one of the most popular; other tours may not follow this exact itinerary.

Panmunjom 판문점

Tours kick off with a rapid-fire briefing by the soldier guides at Camp Bonifas before you board specially designated buses to travel into the JSA towards the collection of blue-painted UN buildings that constitute Panmunjom. Official meetings are still sometimes held here and in the main conference room, mikes on the tables constantly record everything said. Straddling the ceasefire line, this is the only place where you can safely walk into North Korea. South Korean soldiers stand guard inside and out in a modified taekwondo stance – an essential photo op – and their North Korean counterparts keep a steady watch, usually, but not always, from a distance.

Back on the bus you'll be taken to one of Panmunjom's lookout posts from where you can see the two villages within the DMZ (see the boxed text, below). Before leaving the camp you'll drop by the **Monastery Visitors Centre** selling DMZ baseball caps, T-shirts and other souvenirs. Nearby is the world's most dangerous golf course, with just one 192yd, par three hole surrounded by barbed wire and landmines. The bunkers here are made of concrete rather than sand.

Dora Observatory

Next on the tour itinerary is a visit to this **observatory** (use of binoculars W500; 10am-5pm Tue-Sun) where you can peer through binoculars for a closer look at North Korea, including Kaesong city and Kaesong Industrial Complex, where cheap North Korean labourers are employed by South Korean conglomerates. At the foot of the mountain stands Dorasan train station, currently the northern terminus of South Korea's rail line – a symbol of the hope for the eventual reunification of the two Koreas and a chance to ride through to Pyongyang (p361).

Third Infiltration Tunnel 제3땅굴

After lunch the tour highlight is walking along 265m of the 73m-deep **Third Infiltration Tunnel** (031-940 8341; 9am-5pm Tue-Sun) discovered in 1978. Since 1974 four tunnels have been found running under the DMZ, dug by the North Koreans so that their army could launch a surprise attack. A walk down here is not for the claustrophobic or the tall: creeping hunched over to reach the coiled barbed wire at the triple concrete wall–blocked end of the tunnel, you'll realise why they issue hard hats to protect heads from knocking the low ceiling. The guide will point out how the North Koreans painted the rocks black so they might claim it was a coal mine!

Tour Companies

It's worth booking ahead for the popular tours offered by the US army's social and entertainment organisation, the **United Service Organizations** (USO; Map pp102-3; 02-724 7003; www.uso.org/korea; tours US$70; office 8am-5pm Mon-Sat, tours 7.30am-3pm Tue, Thu, Sat; Line 1 to Namyeong, Exit 2). They include Panmunjon, Dora Observatory and the Third Tunnel. If you don't bring a packed lunch, it's an extra W6000 for *bibimbap* (rice, egg, meat and vegies with chilli sauce) or W10,000 for *bulgogi* (thin slices of meat, marinated in sweetened soy sauce). You'll have to get yourself to the USO to check in for the tour at 7am and it likes payment four days in advance at the same office although it will accept credit-card bookings over the phone if you're not based in Seoul.

If you're just looking to visit the JSA and Panmunjon, then **Tour DMZ** (Map pp100-1; 02-755 0073; www.tourdmz.com; 6th fl, Lotte Hotel, Myeongdong, Seoul; Mon-Fri/Sat W77,000/78,000; Line 2 to Euljiro 1-ga, Exit 8), which runs tours twice daily Monday to Saturday and has a more central departure point than the USO one, is worth considering.

LIVING INSIDE THE DMZ

The DMZ is far from devoid of life. On the south side is Daeseong-dong (대성동), a government-subsidised village where the resident families live in modern houses with high-speed internet connections and earn a tax-free annual income of over US$80,000 from their 7-hectare farms. There's an 11pm curfew, and soldiers stand guard while the villagers work in the rice fields or tend their ginseng plants.

On the North Korean side of the line Gijeong-dong (기정동) is known by the South as Propaganda Village because virtually all the buildings are empty or just facades – the lights all come on and go off here at the same time at night. The village's primary feature is a 160m-high tower flying a flag that weighs nearly 300kg, markedly larger than the one on the South Korean side. It's believed that some workers from the nearby Kaesong Industrial Complex may now be living in Gijeong-dong.

Ironically, the dearth of human intervention in the DMZ for over 50 years has made it an environmental haven. No other place in the world with a temperate-zone climate has been so well preserved. This has been a great boon to wildlife: for example, the DMZ is home to large flocks of Manchurian cranes. Environmentalists hope that the day the two Koreas cease hostilities, the DMZ will be preserved as a nature reserve.

Plenty of other tour companies offer DMZ tours (Seoul's main KTO office, p105, can offer advice on these) but they tend to be more expensive. Also check before putting money down what's on the itinerary and whether time will be filled out with shopping stops. Also be sure to check the refund-rescheduling options if a tour is cancelled, which they can be.

HEYRI & PAJU BOOK CITY
헤이리 & 파주출판도시

Less than 10km south of the DMZ, Heyri is a charming village of small-scale contemporary buildings that couldn't be more of a contrast to the heavily fortified, doom-laden border. Originally it was conceived as a 'book village' (something like Hay-on-Wye in the UK) connected to the nearby publishing centre of Paju Book City. Many of the 370 or so people who now live here are artists, writers, architects and other creative souls; with its scores of small art galleries, cafes, boutique shops and quirky private collections turned into minimuseums it has been dubbed an 'art valley'.

Get your bearings by heading first to the **Tourist Information Office** (☎ 031-946 8551; www. heyri.net; ☺ 9am-6pm Mon-Sat) where you can pick up a good English guidebook (W3000) detailing the many places to see in Heyri, including the primary-coloured playground area devoted to the cartoon character **Dalki** (www. ilikedalki.com) created by the Ssamzie accessories brand – kids will adore this. Also worth a look is **Cine Palace** (☎ 031-957 7763; adult/child W3000/2000; ☺ 11am-7pm), the amazing movie-related memorabilia collection of Mr Son, including many film posters and models of cinema and cartoon characters.

Just wandering around the village is a pleasure. Interesting pieces of architecture and sculpture abound, most created with materials that reflect and fit in with the natural environment. No building is over three storeys, roads twist naturally and everywhere is beautifully landscaped with lots of greenery: one building even has plants growing off its side!

If you enjoy this kind of contemporary architecture, it's also worth visiting **Paju Book City** (www.pajubookcity.org), 10km south of Heyri towards Seoul. This hub of Korea's publishing industry is a very futuristic-looking place with more original building concepts. The Asia Publication Culture & Information Centre is a particularly good example: it's partly clad in rusting steel that picks up the colours of the environment and is juxtaposed with a beautiful example of a *hanok* (traditional mansion), dating from 1834 and transposed here from the province of Jeollabuk-do.

In between Heyri and Paju, the **Odusan Unification Observatory** (오두산 통일 공원; ☎ 031-945 3171; www.jmd.co.kr; adult/youth W2500/1300; ☺ 9am-6pm Apr-Sep, to 5.30pm Oct, Nov & Mar, to 5pm Dec-Feb) provides another chance to gaze across the DMZ into North Korea. If you want to see anything at all in detail, you have to use the pay telescopes for viewing.

Sleeping & Eating

Rates for accommodation, much of which is in private residences, rise for Friday and Saturday nights when many people visit from Seoul.

ourpick Motif £1 (☎ 031-949 0901; www.motif1. co.kr; d from W120,000; ✖ ▣) The bohemian-chic home of traveller and writer Lee An-soo is typical of Heyri – packed with art, beautifully designed rooms that are worthy of a boutique hotel and a library of 10,000 books to browse. All the four doubles and one family room have bathrooms and guests can use the kitchen.

Step (☎ 031-946 4870; r from W120,000; ✖ ▣) These simple modern apartments with self-catering facilities and traditional mattress-on-floor beds are good for families or groups. Rates don't change for weekends or holidays.

House in the Forest (☎ 031-8071 0127, 018-363 2660; kamigo@hanmail.net; d from W150,000; ✖ ▣) English-speaking Mr Kim retired from the Korea Tourism Organisation and had this award-winning home that climbs up the hillside built. He and his wife allow guests to share part of it, with rooms that are very comfortable and come with TV, DVD, fridge and (for some) a balcony.

Lachem (☎ 031-946 3478; meals from W10,000; ☺ 11am-9.30pm) Beside the gallery Jin Art is this stylish restaurant serving tasty and nicely presented modern takes on Korean dishes.

Foresta (☎ 031-949 9303; www.heyribookhouse.co.kr; meals W25,000; ☺ noon-9pm) Inside the Hangil Book House and overlooking a leafy glade in the midst of Heyri is this appealing Italian restaurant offering a variety of pasta (from W18,000) and steaks (W40,000) dishes. It also has a kids menu (W11,000).

Chocolate Design Gallery (☎ 031-948 5199; www. chocolategallery.co.kr; drinks W6000; ☺ 11am-6pm Mon-

Fri, 10am-8pm Sat & Sun) In Heyri practically every gallery (and there are a lot of them) has an attached cafe. Chocoholics will appreciate this one offering handmade confections using the cocoa bean. It also hosts chocolate-making and bakery classes.

Getting There & Away

Bus 200 (W1800, 45 minutes, every 20 minutes) leaves from outside Hapjeong station on subway Lines 2 and 6 in Seoul and passes by Odusan on its way to Heyri. For Heyri get off at Community House (커뮤니티하우스) where you'll find the tourist information office. Staff can advise on the buses from Heyri to Paju Book City.

SUWON 수원

pop 1.08 million

It was King Jeongjo, the 22nd Joseon dynasty ruler, who had the idea of moving the national capital from Seoul to Suwon, 48km south, in 1794. The fortress walls that surrounded the original city were constructed but the king died and power stayed in Seoul. Named Hwaseong, Suwon's impressive World Heritage–listed fortifications remain the best reason for visiting the city, where you'll also find the faithfully restored palace Hwaseong Haenggung. Suwon is also close to the Korean Folk Village (p158) and Everland Resort (p158) and can be used as a base to visit both.

GYEONGGI-DO & INCHEON-GWANGYEOK-SI

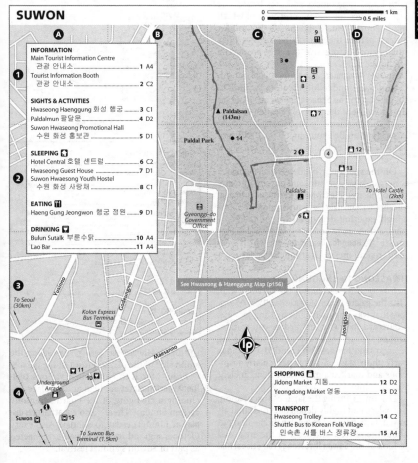

SUWON

0		1 km
0		0.5 miles

INFORMATION
Main Tourist Information Centre
관광 안내소 **1** A4
Tourist Information Booth
관광 안내소 **2** C2

SIGHTS & ACTIVITIES
Hwaseong Haenggung 화성 행궁 **3** C1
Paldalmun 팔달문 **4** D2
Suwon Hwaseong Promotional Hall
수원 화성 홍보관 **5** D1

SLEEPING
Hotel Central 호텔 센트럴 **6** C2
Hwaseong Guest House **7** D1
Suwon Hwaseong Youth Hostel
수원 화성 사랑채 **8** C1

EATING
Haeng Gung Jeongwon 행궁 정원 **9** D1

DRINKING
Bulun Sutalk 부룬수닭 **10** A4
Lao Bar **11** A4

SHOPPING
Jidong Market 지동 **12** D2
Yeongdong Market 영동 **13** D2

TRANSPORT
Hwaseong Trolley **14** C2
Shuttle Bus to Korean Folk Village
민속촌 셔틀 버스 정류장 **15** A4

See Hwaseong & Haenggung Map (p196)

▲ Paldalsan
(143m)

Paldal Park

Paldalsa

Gyeonggi-do Government Office

To Hotel Castle (2km)

To Seoul (30km)

Kolon Express Bus Terminal

Yusinno

Godeungno

Maesanno

Jeongjoro

Underground Arcade

Suwon

To Suwon Bus Terminal (1.5km)

Information

The **main tourist information centre** (Map p155; ☎ 031-228 4672; www.suwon.ne.kr; ☺ 9am-6pm Mar-Oct, to 5pm Nov-Feb) is on the left outside the railway station. There's a **tourist information booth** (Map p155; ☺ 9am-6pm) near Paldalmun at the start of the fortress walk, as well at several other points around the walls.

Sights & Activities

HWASEONG 화성

Suwon's **fortress wall** (Map p156; http://ehs.suwon.ne.kr; admission W1000; ☺ 24hr), with its command posts, observation towers, entrance gates and fire-beacon platform, was innovative for its time and makes for a fascinating two-hour historical walk. Constructed of earth and faced with large stone blocks and grey bricks, the wall stretches for 5.7km, nearly all of which has been restored. Walk outside the wall for at least part of the way, as the fortress looks much more impressive the way an enemy would see it.

Start at **Paldalmun**, also known as Nammun (South Gate), and follow the steep steps off to the left up to the **Seonam Gangu**, an observation point near the peak of **Paldalsan** (143m). Near the command post, **Seojangdae**, is the large Hyowon Bell you can toll (W1000), and **Seonodae**, a tower that was used by crossbow archers.

On the wall's north side is **Hwahongmun**, a watergate over a stream, and the **archery centre** (see opposite). Nearby is **Dongbukgongsimdon**, another watchtower but with a unique design – a high, tapering structure with rounded corners, a stone base and a brick tower. Further on are the **Bongdon beacon towers**, which were used to send messages around the country.

HWASEONG HAENGGUNG 화성행궁

Before or after circuiting the fortress wall, visit the **palace** (Map p155; admission W1500; ☺ 9am-5pm) that was originally built by King Jeongjo. Courtyard follows courtyard as you wander around the large walled complex where King Jeongjo's mother held her grand 61st-birthday party (the 61st is considered particularly auspicious and marked a major date in an ancient Korean's life).

Destroyed during the Japanese occupation, the palace had highly detailed records that allowed its meticulous reconstruction – find out about the process and see how the area used to look at the **Suwon Hwaseong Promotional Hall**

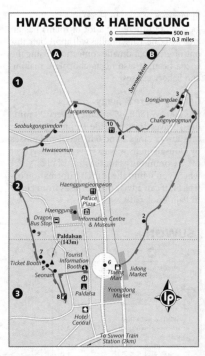

HWASEONG & HAENGGUNG

SIGHTS & ACTIVITIES	
Archery Centre	**1** B1
Bongdon Beacon Towers 봉돈 봉수대	**2** B2
Dongbukgongsimdon 동북공심돈	**3** B1
Hwahongmun 화홍문	**4** B2
Hyowon Bell	**5** A3
Paldalmun	**6** B3
Seojangdae 서장대	**7** A3
Seonam Gangu	**8** A3
Seonodae 서노대	**9** A2

EATING 🍴	
Yeonpo Galbi 연포 갈비	**10** B1

DRINKING 🍸	
Yeonmucheong 연무정	(see 1)

(☎ 031-228 4410; admission free; ☺ 9am-6pm) on the south side of the plaza in front of the palace.

From March to November, various **traditional performances** are held at the palace, including a changing of the guard ceremony at 2pm Sunday. There's also a **martial arts display** at 11am Tuesday to Sunday. Also every October a grand **royal procession** is reenacted as part of Suwon's annual festival.

ARCHERY

At Yeonmudae in the northeast corner of the fortress is the **archery centre** (Map p156; ☎ 031-225 8910; admission W2000; ☺ 9.30am-5.30pm, every 30min) where you can practise firing 10 arrows. This traditional sport is one for which Koreans often win Olympic medals.

Sleeping

Although Suwon is an easy day trip from Seoul, there are several good places to stay should you choose to make it a base for seeing other sights in the region. Prices are also cheaper than in Seoul.

Hwaseong Guest House (Map p155; ☎ 031-245 6226; www.hsguesthouse.com; dm/r W15,000/25,000; ☒ ▢) This new backpackers, decorated with a variety of flowery wallpapers, is run by friendly English-speaking folk. The four-bed dorms have two bunk beds and share a bathroom. There's a kitchen for self-catering and several good restaurants nearby including a Japanese place downstairs. Groups of 10 or more can organise Korean cooking and culture classes. To find it turn left at Compador Bakery on Paldalro north of Paldamun.

Suwon Hwaseong Youth Hostel (수원화성 사랑채; Map p155; ☎ 031-245 5555; http://hs.suwon.ne.kr; d, tw or ondol from W30,000; ☒ ▢) Tucked behind the Suwon Hwaseong Promotional Hall is this professionally run place, more of a hotel than a hostel (you need be a party of four to take advantage of its four-bed dorm rooms). Their spacious *ondol* rooms, with repro antique furnishings and private bathrooms, are particularly nice and good value.

Hotel Central (호텔 센트럴; Map p155; ☎ 031-246 0011; www.suwoncentral.com; d/tw/ste incl breakfast W60,000/75,000/180,000; ☒ ▢) This standard business hotel set back from the main road, south of Paldamun, with a funky restaurant-bar with retro-style purple and red couches, is worth a look.

Hotel Castle (호텔 캐슬; off Map p155; ☎ 031-211 6666; www.hcastle.co.kr; d/tw/ste from W250,000/275,000 /350,000; ☒ ▢) Suwon's top-end option is a little distant from the fortress but provides all the creature comforts you'll need, including a choice of three restaurants, a men-only sauna and gym.

Eating & Drinking

Suwon is renowned for its *galbi* (beef) dishes, including *galbitang,* meaty bones in a broth. There are plenty of restaurants near the fortress walls, but the main place to meet carousing locals is close by Suwon station: lively bars cluster along and around the pedestrian street that starts between Face Shop and Paris Baguette.

Haeng Gung Jeongwon (행궁정원; Map p155; ☎ 031-244 2021; palace plaza; meals W7000-39,000; ☺ 10am-10pm) A good spot to sample *galbitang.* The restaurant is easy to spot – three storeys high with large balconies, opposite the Suwon Hwaseong Promotional Hall.

Yeonpo Galbi (연포갈비; Map p156; ☎ 031-255 1337; meals W7000-35,000; ☺ 11.30am-10pm) Down the steps from Hwahongmun, this famous restaurant serves up its special Suwon version of *galbitang* – chunks of meat and a big rib in a seasoned broth with noodles and leeks. Look for the building with a facade of logs.

Yeonmucheong (연무정; Map p156; ☎ 031-257 0099; teas from W5000; ☺ 10am-10pm) Rest your feet, sip local teas and nibble sweet rice cakes in this antique-style teashop above the archery centre.

Bulun Sutalk (부룬수닭; Map p155; ☎ 031-274 0608; ☺ 5pm-3am) Look for the iron rooster and low wooden shutter doors for the entrance to this bohemian fantasy bar with rose petals scattered on the stairs, mammoth melted candles, crystal chandeliers and plenty of scatter cushions. Order nibbles (the Cajun chicken platter for W17,000 is good), a flagon of beer or cocktails and enjoy a chilled evening with Suwon's hipsters. It's five minutes' walk northeast of the station along Maesanno on the corner where you'll find SK Telekom.

Lao Bar (Map p155; ☎ 031-244 2446; ☺ 5pm-5pm) This spacious bar sports a pool table and electronic darts. Stick around until midnight and you'll catch the barman's famous fire show. It's at the first turning to the left along the pedestrian street, on the corner where you'll see the English sign Luxury.

Shopping

At the end of the walk around the wall, the Jidong (지동) and Yeongdong (영동) markets (Map p155) make for a fascinating wander with lower prices than Seoul.

Getting There & Away
BUS

Catch bus 5, 5-1 or 7-1 (W1000, 15 minutes) outside Suwon train station to go to the city's bus terminal. Buses depart from there for the following:

Destination	Price (W)	Duration	Frequency
Busan	23,100	5hr	12 daily
Daegu	14,500	3½hr	14 daily
Gwangju	13,700	4hr	every 30min
Gyeongju	19,400	4hr	12 daily
Incheon	4100	1½hr	every 15min

TRAIN
Subway Line 1 runs from Seoul to Suwon (W1500, one hour) but make sure you're on a train that heads to the city after the line splits at Guro otherwise you'll end up on an Incheon-bound service. Regular KTO train services from Seoul are speedier (30 minutes) but not as frequent.

From Suwon, trains depart frequently to cities all over Korea:

Destination	Price S/M class (W)	Duration
Busan	35,600/24,000	5hr
Daegu	25,000/16,900	3hr 10min
Daejeon	11,100/7400	1hr 10min
Jeonju	20,800/14,000	3hr
Mokpo	33,200/22,300	5hr

Getting Around
Outside the train station on the left, buses 11, 13, 36 and 39 go to Paldalmun (10 minutes, W1000). A taxi is W3000.

Walk through the car park and up the hill at the rear of the palace to the find the 54-seat **Hwaseong Trolley** (Map p155; adult/youth/child W1500/1100/700; 🕙 10am-5.10pm). This trolley bus, pulled by an engine car fashioned as a Chinese dragon, winds around in and out of the fortress wall to the archery field at Yeonmudae.

KOREAN FOLK VILLAGE 한국 민속촌
Around 250 thatched and tiled Korean traditional houses and buildings make up this attractive **folk village** (☎ 031-288 0000; www.koreanfolk.co.kr; adult/youth/child W12,000/9000/8000; 🕙 9am-6.30pm Mar-Oct, to 5pm Nov-Feb) that takes at least half a day to look around. Set around a river are a temple, a Confucian school and shrine, a market, a magistrate's house with examples of punishments, storehouses, a bullock pulling a cart, and all sorts of household furnishings and tools. Artisans wearing *hanbok* (traditional Korean clothing) create pots, make paper and weave bamboo, while other workers tend to vegetable plots, pigs and chickens.

Throughout the day traditional musicians, dancers, acrobats and tightrope walkers perform, and you can watch a wedding ceremony. A string of other attractions – folk museums, exhibitions, an amusement park, a haunted house and horse riding – cost a little extra. The village also has a variety of inexpensive rustic restaurants as well as a folksy food court.

Getting There & Away
At Suwon's main Tourist Information Centre (p156) you can buy tickets for the Korean Folk Village and catch the free shuttle bus (30 minutes, every hour from 10.30am to 2.30pm). The last shuttle bus leaves the folk village at 5pm (5.30pm on weekends). After that time, walk to the far end of the car park and catch city bus 37 (W1000, one hour, every 20 minutes) back to Suwon station.

EVERLAND RESORT 에버랜드
The fourth-largest amusement park in the world, **Everland Resort** (☎ 822-759 1940; www.everland.com) offers more than just thrill rides and fairy floss. Set in lush hillsides, 40km south of Seoul, the resort is split into several parts, each of which can be visited separately.

The main Disneyland-style **theme park** (day pass adult/child W35,000/26,000; 🕙 9.30am-10pm Sep-Jun, to 11pm Jul & Aug) is a huge area filled with fantasy buildings, fairground attractions, impressive seasonal gardens and live music and parades. Highlights include the world's biggest wooden roller-coaster and a 15-minute African Safari bus ride offers close-up views of several live beasts including tigers, lions, giraffes, zebras and elephants. Lit up at night, the park takes on a magical atmosphere and there are always fireworks.

Next door is **Caribbean Bay** (adult/child Sep-Jun W30,000/23,000, Jul & Aug W65,000/50,000; 🕙 10am-5pm Sep-Jun, 9.30am-11pm Jul & Aug), a superb water park. The outdoor section is usually open from June to September and features a huge wave pool that produces a mini-tsunami every few minutes and water-based thrill rides. The indoor section includes a small wave pool, water slide, spa and sauna. As with the main theme park, at peak times you'll be waiting anything up to two hours for the most popular rides here.

A free shuttle bus runs from Everland's main entrance to the **Hoam Art Museum** (☎ 031-320 1801; www.hoammuseum.org; adult/child W4000/3000; 🕙 10am-6pm Tue-Sun) and you are well advised to take it. The serenely beautiful **Hee Won** traditional Korean gardens induce a calm frame of mind so that visitors can fully appreciate the art treasures inside the museum. Each one of the paintings, screens, celadon and other exhibits, part of the original collection of the Samsung Group's founder Lee Byung-chui, reveals stunning skill and craftsmanship.

Sleeping & Eating

There's so much to see here that staying over is worth considering. There are two accommodation options: **Home Bridge Hillside Hostel** (☎ 031-320 8849; r & ondol from W50,000; ⚄ 💻) is the older but quite acceptable property, while **Home Bridge Cabin Hostel** (☎ 320 9740; r from W130,000; ⚄ 💻) offers Heidi-esque log cabins and hotel rooms, the most expensive with balconies overlooking the park. Rates at both places are higher on Saturday nights and during July and August. The best deal is to stay over on Sunday when rates are slashed in half. Bookings can be made via the Everland website and guests can use their one-day park passes over two days.

Throughout the resort you can eat simple Korean- or Western-style meals for around W10,000.

Getting There & Away

The fastest way from Seoul is to take subway Line 2 to Gangnam station, leave by Exit 6 and find the bus stop for service 5002 (W1800, 50 minutes, every 15 minutes). Alternatively, from outside Suwon's train station, hop on bus 66 (W1400, one hour, every 30 minutes).

SEOUL GRAND PARK 서울대공원

Indeed grand in scale, this park includes Korea's top zoo and an excellent contemporary art museum. There are hiking trails and a river beside which people picnic.

The **zoo** (☎ 02-500 7114; http://grandpark.seoul.go.kr; adult/youth/child W3000/2000/1000; ⏰ 9am-7pm Apr-Sep, to 6pm Oct-Mar), one of the largest in the world, is home to a long list of exotic creatures including the popular African ones, and has a successful history of breeding, including tigers and pandas. It includes an indoor botanic garden housing a forest of cacti, numerous orchids and carnivorous pitcher plants.

The large and striking **National Museum of Contemporary Art** (☎ 02-2188 6114; www.moca.go.kr; admission free, special exhibitions adult/child W3000/1500; ⏰ 10am-6pm Tue-Sun, to 5pm Nov-Feb) is spread over three floors and is surrounded by a sculpture garden. The dazzling highlight is Nam June Paik's *The More the Better*, an 18m-tall pagoda-shaped video installation that uses 1000 flickering screens to make a comment on our increasingly electronic universe. There are plans to open an annexe of the museum in Seoul's Samcheon-dong district (see Art Galleries Walk, p115).

Getting There & Away

Take subway Line 4 to Seoul Grand Park station (W1000), which is 45 minutes from City Hall. Leave by Exit 2 and then either walk (10 minutes) or take an elephant-inspired **tram** (adult/youth/child W800/600/500) to the park entrance. Another option is to take the **cable car** (adult/youth/child one-time ticket W5000/3500/3000). A free shuttle bus also runs every 20 minutes from the subway station (outside Exit 4) to the National Museum of Contemporary Art.

ANYANG ART PARK 안양예술공원

A short bus ride north of Anyang, 20km south of Seoul, is the **Anyang Art Park** (http://en.anyang. go.kr/new/D040000.jsp; admission free) – 52 quirky pieces of sculpture by both Korean and international artists dotted along the rocky river bank and among the trees of a wooded valley. Pieces include the spinning *Dancing Buddha*, the *3-D Mirror Labyrinth*, the *Anyang Crate House Dedicated to the Lost (Pagoda)*, made of mulitcoloured plastic German beer crates, and the freaky *Boy + Girl* that messes with perspective. Climb up to the spiral observatory for a fantastic view across the valley, or go outside the park to explore several of the Buddhist temples that cling to the hillsides.

Back by the river is all the commercial activity typically associated with a resort area – it can get very busy here with family outings and picnics on the weekend. You could check out what's showing in the **Anyang Art Center** (☎ 031-389 5391; www.ayac.or.kr; ⏰ noon-7pm) in a sleek minimalist building designed by Portuguese architect Álvaro Siza (admission varies) or go splash around in **Anyang Waterland** (안양워터랜드; ☎ 031-474 3673; www.anyang waterland.com; adult/child W32,000/27,000; ⏰ 10am-10pm). Alternatively, enjoy *mechuri* (메추리), quail roasted over charcoal, available at several stalls such as **Sunolaepang** (수 노래방) with the blue awning next to the art centre.

Getting There & Away

Anyang is on Line 1 of the subway. Take Exit 1 from the station and find the stop for bus 2, which runs a regular loop route to the park

---

SKIING IN GYEONGGI-DO

Come the snow season, usually from December to February, there is a handful of ski resorts within easy reach of Seoul (an hour or less by bus). Usually there are free shuttle buses from Seoul – see the websites for details, but you might also want to look into travel-agency package deals that include transport, accommodation, ski-equipment hire and lift passes. The main resorts to head to are:

Bears Town Resort (☎ 031-540 5000; www.bearstown.com) Located 50 minutes northeast of Seoul, this resort has 11 slopes, two sledding hills and nine lifts all named after bears. Accommodation includes a youth hostel and condominium; facilities include a supermarket, heated pool, sauna, bowling alley and tennis courts. English-speaking instructors, snowboarding and night skiing are available. USO, the American troops' activities organisation (see p118), runs ski tours to this resort and anyone is welcome to join.

Jisan Resort (☎ 02-3442 0322, 031-638 8460; www.jisanresort.co.kr) It can get busy at this popular resort, 56km south of Seoul and a 40-minute bus ride from Gangnam. Jisan has five lifts, a variety of slopes including some for snowboarding, English-speaking instructors, night skiing and condo accommodation. In 2009 a big outdoor rock festival was held here in July; it may become an annual event.

Yangji Pine Resort (☎ 02-744 2001, 031-338 2001; www.pineresort.com) Around 40 minutes' drive southeast of Seoul, this resort has six slopes, one sledding hill, six lifts and great views from the top. Accommodation is in a youth hostel or condo-style hotel, the latter having a heated pool and bowling alley.

(W800, 10 minutes), on the left outside Lotte Department Store.

NAMHAN SANSEONG PROVINCIAL PARK 남한산성 도립공원

Completed in 1626, **Namhan Sanseong** (☎ 031-742 7856), a temple-fortress complex and wall 20km southeast of downtown Seoul, is famous for its beautiful pine forests, wildflowers and oaks. It once guarded the city's southern entrance, while Bukhan Sanseong guarded the northern approaches. Buddhist monks – soldiers rather than pacifists in those days – lived here and kept watch. Numerous hiking options wind through the forests, some of them paralleling the old fortress walls.

To get here take subway Line 8 to Namhan Sanseong. Leave by Exit 1 and take a bus or taxi to Namhan Sanseong-ipgu, the park entrance.

ICHEON 이천
pop 198,619

Famous for its numerous potters and ceramic vendors, Icheon is 60km southeast of Seoul and surrounded by mountains. Shoppers and ceramics lovers may want to stay here overnight to have time to look around or dabble in making something at a hands-on workshop, but otherwise the place can easily be visited in a day from Seoul.

Sights & Activities
SEOLBONG PARK 설봉공원
Head here first to not only pick up a good local area map and other tourist information at the visitors centre (☎ 031-644 2020; http://tour.icheon.go.kr; ☼ 9am-5pm) but also to enjoy the parklands and variety of ceramic sculptures that surround the small lake. The park's **World Ceramic Centre** (☎ 031-631 6501; www.wocef.com; admission free; ☼ 9am-6pm Tue-Sun) is one of three local venues for the **World Ceramics Biennale** (www.wocef.com) held usually from late April through mid-May in odd-numbered years. This massive event brings together potters, vendors and viewers from around the world.

If you have the energy, it's a steep 30-minute walk uphill from the visitors centre to the 1000-year-old **Yeongworam Hermitage** (영월암) founded by the Jogye Buddhist sect. Ancient ginkgo trees shade the brightly painted buildings, reconstructions of the originals damaged by fire. Moss, a giant bell and a carved cliff-face Buddha overlooking the city all make this a picturesque place to visit.

ICHEON CERAMIC VILLAGE 이천 도예촌
Don't come here expecting picturesque riverside huts or wispy-bearded characters labouring over kick wheels: the Icheon Ceramic Village (Icheon Doyechon) is a busy town with a main street full of traffic, and the many potteries are spread out over a wide urban area. The lack of rural aesthetics is compensated for by the huge selection of wares, making it a fascinating destination for ceramics lovers.

Catch a taxi (W5000) or local bus 114 (W1300) from outside the bus terminal and get off after 15 minutes near **Songpa Pottery** (송파 도예; ☎ 031-633 6587; www.songpadoye.com;

9.30am-7.30pm), the large traditional building with blue-green roof tiles. Around here are several large pottery shops. Across the road and set back from the main strip in a lovely wooden building is **Hanguk Pottery** (한국 도예; ☎ 031-638-7037; 9.30am-5.30pm), where you can find the classy celadon glazed wares of a master potter and view a traditional-style kiln.

You can also view a large collection of celadon pottery at the **Haegang Ceramics Museum** (해 강 도자 미술관; ☎ 031-634 2266; www.haegang.org; adult/child W2000/500; 9.30am-5.30pm Tue-Sun) – it's located back towards downtown Icheon.

To make your own cup or bowl visit **Namyang** (남양; ☎ 031-632 7142; per class W15,000; 10am-5pm), where you can don a smock and sit down at a slippery mass of spinning clay, or hand-build something under the tutorage of the kindly Mr Lee and his English-speaking son. To have your efforts fired and posted home (even overseas) will cost around W30,000 per kilogram extra.

MIRANDA SPA PLUS 미란다 온천

Attached to the Miranda Hotel Icheon (see Sleeping, following), and just a five-minute walk from Icheon bus terminal, the splendid **Spa Plus** (스파 플러스; ☎ 031-639 5000; www.miranda hotel.com; adult/child spa only W14,000/9000; all facilities W37,000/27,000; 6am-10pm) is a large complex that has ultramodern facilities. Treat yourself to hot, warm and cold baths, a waterfall bath, and rice-wine, herbal, pinewood and fruit baths.

Sleeping

If you do need to stay over, there are numerous options to choose from, including plenty of inexpensive motels.

Now It's the Moon Time (☎ 031-633 7373; r from W45,000;) Gets points for the crazy name (it's also known as the IMT Hotel), but this love hotel is spotlessly clean and very tastefully done, with heated toilet seats, jacuzzi-style baths, a DVD collection (not only racy titles, but normal ones too) and popcorn! Add W10,000 to the rates on Friday and Saturday.

Miranda Hotel (미란다호텔; ☎ 031-633 2001; www.mirandahotel.com; r/ste W173,000/300,000;) Icheon's snazziest hotel is located next to Spa Plus (above), where guests receive a 30% discount, and overlooks a small lake with a pavilion on an island. There's also a bowling alley (per game/shoe hire W3000/1000,

open from 10am to 2am). The lobby has fine examples of locally made ceramics.

Eating

Icheon is also famous for its rice, which some claim is so good that 'it needs no side dishes'. The good news is that it is indeed pretty tasty and that it's always dished up with plenty of side dishes at the following recommended places.

Donggang (동강; ☎ 031-631 8833; meals from W10,000; 9.30am-10pm) On the main road near the entrance to Seolbong Park, this restaurant looks modern from the outside but inside is decorated with traditional *giwa* (tiled) roof details and paper and wood screens. The set menus are reasonably priced.

Gomijeong (고미정; ☎ 031-634 4811; meals W10,000-30,000; 10.30am-9.30pm) On a hillside outside town, Gomijeong serves a wonderful assortment of preset courses that vary by price. The paper screens, floor seating and flower-pattern wallpapered walls all make this a treat worth taking a taxi for.

Getting There & Away

Buses run from Seoul Express Bus Terminal (Map pp102–3) and Dong-Seoul Bus Terminal (Map pp90–1) to Icheon (W4000, one hour, every 15 to 40 minutes). Once in Icheon most places are no more than a W4000 taxi ride away.

INCHEON-GWANGYEOK-SI

You can find out more about this metropolitan area covering the coastal city and many islands in the West Sea at http://english .incheon.go.kr.

INCHEON 인천

☎ 032 / pop 2.63 million

Made internationally famous in 1950 during the Korean War when the American General Douglas MacArthur led UN forces in a daring landing behind enemy lines, Incheon is a bustling, industrial port 36km west of Seoul. It is also the place where Korea opened up to the world in 1883, ending centuries of self-imposed isolation. Fragments of the hybrid urban culture that developed can still be viewed in the city today, particularly in the colourful Chinatown area, Korea's largest

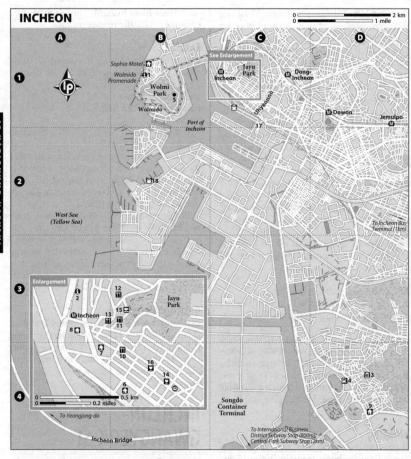

and most prominent such community. Come here to sample some different foods, stroll along the Wolmido waterfront, or use Incheon as a skipping stone to the West Sea islands.

A thriving metropolis with its own subway system (connected to Seoul's) and a new monorail around the seaside Wolmido area, Incheon is expanding exponentially by building a trio of free economic zones on landfill in the bay, two of which – Songdo International City and Yeongjeong-do – will be connected by the 12.34km Incheon Bridge, the fifth-longest such structure in the world. In particular Songdo International City is billed as a model urban development designed around high-tech buildings and networks, using best-practice eco-friendly principles, with a business district, the Songdo ConvensiA convention centre and a large central park. At its heart will be the soaring **151 Incheon Tower**, a 610m building set to be the second tallest in the world when completed in 2013.

Information

Tourist information centre (http://english.incheon. go.kr) Incheon subway station (☎ 032-777 1330; ⏰ 9am-6pm); Wolmido promenade (☎ 032-765 4169; ⏰ 9am-6pm Sep-Jun, 10am-8pm Jul & Aug)The staff is very helpful at the principal office outside the subway station, with lots of excellent maps, tourist info and suggestions not only for the city, but for the surrounding islands as well. Smaller information centres are in the bus terminal and at Wolmido.

Sights

Incheon is a sprawling city – its notional centre is around the Incheon Bus Terminal but there's little of major interest here for visitors. The most interesting area to explore is Chinatown (see right). Songdo to the south is also worth making time for, if only to witness the rising from the sea of the massive new Songdo International City and Incheon Bridge out to Yeongjong-do.

SONGDO 송도

Some 70,000 UN and South Korean troops took part in the surprise landing in Incheon in 1950, supported by 260 warships. Find out about this daring attack at the sombre yet strikingly designed **Incheon Landing Memorial Monument Hall** (인천 상륙 작전 기념관; ☎ 032-832 0915; www.landing915.com; admission free; ☿ 9am-6.30pm Mar-Oct, to 5pm Nov-Feb, closed Mon) through recently renovated displays and old newsreel films of the Korean War.

Next door is **Incheon Metropolitan City Museum** (인전광역시립박물관; ☎ 032-440 6130; adult/child W400/free; ☿ 9am-6pm Tue-Sun), which has an excellent collection of celadon pottery and some interesting historical displays.

Kids will enjoy the large **Songdo Resort** (☎ 032-832 0011; www.songdoresort.co.kr; admission W3000; ☿ 9.30am-8pm May-Oct, 9am-6pm Nov-Apr), which combines a fairground with thrill rides, paddle boats, a water slide and swimming in a large saltwater lake. It's open 24 hours from mid-July to late August and individual rides cost extra.

WOLMIDO 월미도

Although this oceanfront entertainment area, facing the island of Yeongjong-do, is marketed as 'romantic', we found it shabby and tacky. However, its boardwalk is set for an upgrade and there's a new monorail system connecting it to the city so things could be looking

up. Otherwise try a hike up to the free **Wolmi Observatory** in **Wolmi Park** where you'll find some traditional Korean architecture and will have good views across the port and towards Yeongjong-do. There are also plans to build a cable car up to this vantage point.

Chinatown Walking Tour

The walk around Chinatown and the old colonial area of Incheon can take longer if you linger.

From the station pass through the **First Paeru (1)**, the ornate traditional gate that marks one of the entrances to Chinatown. Head uphill, then veer left at the junction to find the steps leading up to the **Third Paeru (2)** and **Café Castle** (p165). Uphill is Jayu Park (Jayu means freedom), Korea's first modern-style park designed by a Russian civil engineer in 1888, containing the **monument for the centenary of Korea-USA relations (3)** and, further on, a statue of **General MacArthur (4)**.

From the statue follow the steps downhill and the road that leads you to **Jung-gu District Hall (5)**, a building that has been renovated and expanded since it was first built in 1883. Turn left and walk two blocks to admire the bottle-cap mosaic facade of **Bboya (6**; p165) then retrace your steps a block, taking a left then right turn. Along this street are three former **Japanese bank buildings (7, 8, 9)**, which date back to the 1890s when Korea was opened up to foreign companies. One has been turned into an interesting **museum (8**; 인천개항장근대건축전; ☎ 032-760 7549; admission free; ☿ 9am-6pm) outlining the history of the area. Opposite is the **Fog City International Café (10**; p165).

At the junction, turn right and climb the **stone lantern–lined steps (11)** that once split Chinatown from the Japanese Settlement – at the top is a statue of **Confucius (12)**. To the left a **mural (13)** decorates both sides of the street

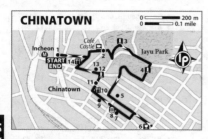

CHINATOWN

WALK FACTS

Start Incheon subway station
Finish Incheon subway station
Distance 2km
Duration one hour

illustrating historical scenes from the classic Chinese novel *The Three Kingdoms*. Turn right when you reach the main Chinatown 1st street – the profusion of red paper lanterns will clue you into whether you're in the right place. Grab refreshments at one of the many eateries along here such as the **Wonbo** (**14**; right), before returning to where you started the walk.

Tours

You can pick up two tours outside Incheon subway station. Contact the tourist information centre there (p162) for airport-tour departure times, which vary depending on the season, and to find out about the Gangwha-do theme tour (adult/child W10,000/5000), which runs twice a day on weekends from April to October.

Downtown tour (☎ 032-772 4000; 2hr 40min tours adult/child W1500/750) Runs eight times daily.

Incheon International Airport tour (3hr tours adult/child W10,000/5000) Runs six times daily.

Festivals & Events

Incheon Bupyeong Pungmul Festival (www.bpf. or.kr) Dance along to traditional folk music performances *(pungmul)* and experience other aspects of Korean culture. Held in May.

Pentaport Rock Festival (www.pentaportrock.com) This three-day music fest at the end of July, featuring a mix of top international and Korean acts, is Korea's equivalent of Glastonbury.

Chinese Day Cultural Festival (www.inchinaday. com) This September event is held in Jayu Park and around Chinatown.

Sleeping

With the exception of the Ramada Songdo, all the following are located within walking distance of Incheon subway station. There are plenty more hotels and motels scattered around Incheon including some rundown motels out at Wolmido.

Hong Kong Motel (☎ 032-777 9001; r W30,000; ☒) One of the best budget options, this love hotel is clean, with crisp sheets, linoleum floors and even small sofas in the rooms. It faces the Paradise Hotel on the opposite side of the street.

Paradise Hotel (☎ 032-762 5181; www.paradise incheon.co.kr; d/tw/ste from W130,000/130,000/200,000; ☒ ☐) On a hill overlooking the port, this long-established upmarket hotel has a few hip boutique-style renovated rooms (although they have no windows). Use of the sauna (W7500) is 50% cheaper for in-house guests.

Ramada Songdo (☎ 032-830 2200; www.ramada -songdo.co.kr/eng/default.asp; ondol/r from W132,000/146,520; ☒ ☒ ☐) Offers posh furnishings, several restaurants, and views of Songdo International City. You'll need to pay extra to use its gym.

our pick **Harbor Park Hotel** (☎ 032-770 9500; www. harborparkhotel.com; r from W242,000; ☒ ☐) Incheon's best hotel sports a sleek contemporary design both inside and out, with floor-to-ceiling windows providing great views of the harbour and hillsides from every wood tone–decorated room. There's a good gym (free for guests) and tempting top-floor buffet restaurant (adult/child W35,000/23,000).

Eating

The best place to eat is Chinatown where you can feast at some 40 different places on a wide range of reasonably authentic dishes. Wolmido's promenade also offers plenty of touristy seafood restaurants.

Wonbo (원보; ☎ 032-773 7888; meals W4000; 9am-9pm) Big pork-filled dumplings steamed or fried are the speciality of this no-frills place.

Jageumseong (자금성; ☎ 032-761 1688; meals W5000-10,000; 11am-9.30pm) Lots of red-and-gold lanterns and dragon decorations mark out this Beijing-style Chinese restaurant, which also serves spicier Szechuan dishes.

Gonghwachun (공화춘; ☎ 032-765 0571; meals W3000-50,000; 11am-10pm) The set meals are the best deal at this quite posh and formal restaurant. A W25,000 set meal offers eight courses, not large portions but well presented and with contrasting seafood flavours. Also included is the invented-in-Incheon-Chinatown *jajangmyeon* (noodles with black bean sauce).

Mandabok (만다복; ☎ 032-773 3838; meals W10,000-20,000; ⏰ 11am-10pm) Guarded by a pair of terracotta warriors, this is one of Chinatown's fanciest restaurants with a refined interior and top-notch cuisine. Try the sweet-and-sour pork (W15,000). There are 10 different types of tea on the menu.

Fog City International Café (☎ 032-766 9024; www.wtcwine.com; meals W10,000-22,000; ⏰ 8.30am-midnight) If you're tired of Korean or Chinese food, drop by this appealing modern all-day cafe serving a mix of sandwiches, salads, pizza and pasta. Outdoor tables provide a view out to the docks.

Drinking

Café Castle (☎ 032-773 2116; www.cafecastle.co.kr; ⏰ 11.30am-midnight) Enjoy coffee, tea and snacks at this intimate, homely cafe festooned with greenery. There's a fantastic view from its rooftop garden.

Bboya (뽀야; ☎ 032-762 8800; ⏰ 4pm-1am) This unique cafe-bar is entirely covered both inside and out by colourful mosaics created from plastic and metal caps from beer bottles, health drinks and fruit juices.

Min (민; ☎ 032-764 0384; ⏰ 7pm-1am) With a painting of smiling Chinese on its outside wall this cosy bar, part of a row of colonial-era shophouses, is a hangout for students from the local art college who sip beers and *soju* and tuck into cheap savoury pancakes.

Getting There & Away

For details about Incheon International Airport see p145.

BOAT

Yeonan Pier (☎ 032-880 3150; www.icferry.or.kr) and **International Ferry Terminal 2** (☎ 032-764 1820; www.icferry.or.kr) are the departure points for regular international ferries to a number of Chinese cities (see p401) as well as the islands of the West Sea.

To/From China

Ferries link 10 Chinese ports with Incheon. Some are crowded with petty traders, but they provide a cheaper option than flying. The cheapest fares offer a thin mattress on a dormitory floor, while the more expensive

fares give you a small cabin with a bunk bed and TV. Child fares are usually half the adult fare, and some ferry companies offer students a 20% discount. Prices listed on p166 are for one-way tickets and sailing times are subject to variation. Most ferries leave Incheon from Yeonan Pier, but the larger boats depart from International Ferry Terminal 2.

To/From West Sea Islands

Yeonan Pier also has a domestic ferry terminal where boats leave for Jeju-do (from W65,000, 13 hours) and 14 of the larger inhabited islands in the West Sea. More frequent services are provided in summer, when many holidaymakers head out to the beaches and seafood restaurants on these attractive and relaxing islands.

Ferries (adult/child W3000/1000, 15 minutes, every 30 minutes) shuttle between Wolmido promenade and Yeongjong-do from 7am to 9pm.

BUS

Incheon's **bus terminal** (☎ 032-430 7114; ⓔ Incheon Line 1 to Incheon Bus Terminal) is attached to a branch of Shinsegae department store, and has a pharmacy, post office, cinema and tourist info centre. From here you can take direct long-distance buses all over South Korea. For Seoul it's faster, cheaper and easier to connect via subway.

Destination	Price (W)	Duration	Frequency
Busan	32,700	4½hr	hourly
Cheonan	7100	1½hr	every 30min
Cheongju	8600	2hr	every 30min
Chuncheon	11,300	3hr	six daily
Gongju	10,400	2½hr	five daily
Incheon Int'l Airport	8000	1hr 10min	every 30min
Jeonju	18,600	3hr	hourly
Suwon	4200	1hr	every 20min

TRAIN

Subway Line 1 from Seoul (W1500) takes around 70 minutes, though it branches at Guro so make sure you're on an Incheon-bound train. Line 1 connects with Incheon's subway Line 1 at Bupyeong (부평).

Getting Around
BUS & TAXI

Buses (W1000) and taxis leave from outside Dong-Incheon and Incheon subway stations. **International Ferry Terminal 2** Take bus 23 from Incheon subway station or a taxi (W2500).

KOREA–CHINA FERRIES FROM INCHEON

Ferries Leaving from Incheon's Yeonan Pier

Destination	Phone; Website	Price (W)	Duration	Departures
Dalian	032-891 7100; www.dainferry.co.kr	115,000-231,000	17hr	5pm Tue, Thu & Sat
Dandong	032-891 3322; www.dandongferry.co.kr	115,000-210,000	16hr	5pm Mon, Wed & Fri
Qinhuangdao	032-891 9600; www.qininferry.com	115,000-180,000	23hr	7pm Mon, 1pm Thu
Shidao	032-891 8877; www.huadong.co.kr	110,000-170,000	15hr	6pm Mon, Wed & Fri
Yantai	032-891 8880; www.hanjoongferry.co.kr	120,000-140,000	15hr	8pm Tue, Thu & Sat
Yingkou	032-891 5858; www.yingkouferry.com	115,000-130,000	24hr	9pm Tue, 1pm Sat

Ferries Leaving from Incheon's International Ferry Terminal 2

Destination	Phone; Website	Price (W)	Duration	Departures
Lianyungang	032-770 3700; www.lygferry.com	115,000-140,000	24hr	7pm Tue, 3pm Sat
Qingdao	032-777 0490; www.weidong.com	110,000-140,000	13hr	7pm Tue, Wed & Sat
Tianjin	032-777 8260; www.jinchon.co.kr	115,000-160,000	24hr	1pm Tue, 7pm Fri
Weihai	032-777 0490; www.weidong.com	110,000-140,000	16hr	5pm Tue, Thu & Sat

GYEONGGI-DO & INCHEON-GWANGYEOK-SI

Songdo Hop on bus 6, 6-1 or 16 from Dong-Incheon or take a taxi (W7000).

Wolmido It's a 20-minute walk from Incheon subway station or a W3000 taxi ride.

Yeonan Pier Take bus 12 or 24 from Dong-Incheon, or hail a taxi (W8000).

Yeongjong-do Bus 306 from Incheon subway station goes to the airport island (see right; W4100, every 10 minutes).

SUBWAY & MONORAIL

Incheon's Line 1 runs in a north–south direction and intersects with Seoul's Line 1 subway at Bupyeong. At its northern terminus the line connects with the A'rex express to Incheon International Airport at Gyeyang (개양) while in the south it terminates at the International Business District of Songdo International City. The basic fare is W1000 and T Money (p147) cards can be used.

The monorail that runs around Wolmido from next to Incheon subway station should be operating by the time you read this.

WEST SEA ISLANDS

Sandy beaches, sea views, rural scenery, vineyards, fresh air and fresh seafood – the islands of the West Sea (also known as the Yellow Sea) are a perfect escape from urban Korea. Dozens of islands are technically part of the Incheon municipality, even though it can take hours to reach them by boat or bridges. Some islands have rare smooth-stone beaches. The stones are called *mongdol* and it takes centuries of tidal ac-

tion to produce them. It is illegal to collect these stones, so don't take any home with you.

Other than to relax on the beaches, the major reason Koreans visit the islands is to indulge in a *saengseon hoe* (raw fish) culinary safari. Island restaurant menus typically include *saengseon chobap* (vinegared rice with raw fish), *saengseongui* (grilled fish) and *maeuntang* (spicy fish soup). Always be sure to check the price before ordering – the species of fish as well as the season and the cooking (or noncooking) method greatly influence the cost, which can vary from so-so reasonable to 'Oh-my-god-it-costs-*that*-much?' outrageous.

Before embarking for the islands, stock up with cash – moneychanging facilities and ATMs are next to nonexistent in these far-flung corners of Korea.

Minbak (private homes with rooms for rent) and *yeogwan* cost W30,000 to W40,000, but prices double in July and August when the island beaches are crowded. However, at other times (even warm weekends in June and September) you may well have the beach to yourself.

Yeongjong-do 영종도

Although Yeongjong-do is home to Korea's busiest international airport, its (best) western beaches aren't disturbed by air traffic. **Eulwangni Beach** (을왕리 해수욕장) is the most popular – even when the tide goes out, there's more sand than mud. Many motels and a resort have been built here, as well as restaurants and stores.

From Eulwangni, it's a 20-minute walk north along the road to **Wangsan Beach** (왕산 해수욕장), which has a less developed beachfront – just some fishing boats, a few restaurant shacks and watersports equipment for hire during the summer season.

At the time of research the popular seafood market at **Yeongjong-do Wharf** (where you'll alight if you take the ferry from Wolmido) was closed for reconstruction. From behind the market, bus 222 (W1000, 20 minutes, hourly) will drop you near the islet of **Jamjin-do** (잠진도), connected by causeway to Yeongjong-do, if you want to visit Muui-do (p168). The A'rex train line has also been extended to terminate at Yongyuimsiyeok station, which is a much shorter bus ride to Jamjin-do.

SLEEPING
Eulwangi Beach

A wide range of accommodation is available at Eulwangni Beach, including beachside camping near the pine groves.

Carib Beach Motel (카리브 모텔; ☎ 032-751 5455; s/d W40,000/80,000; ⊠) Shaped like a ship, but this love motel offers appealing views from the 'porthole' windows and it's just steps away from the water. There's a karaoke bar in the basement. Prices are up to 50% higher on Saturdays and during summer.

Golden Sky International Resort (☎ 032-745 5000; www.goldensky.co.kr; apt from W200,000; ⊠) Brand-new resort hotel where the rooms are actually apartments with self-catering facilities. There's sufficient space in the studios to

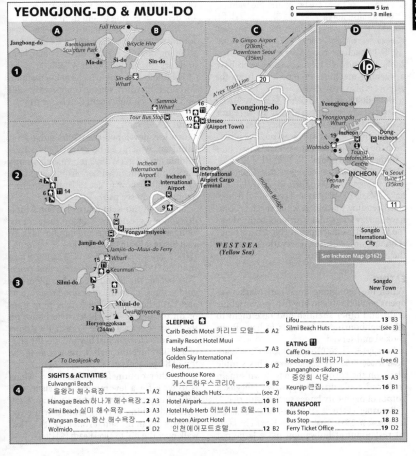

YEONGJONG-DO & MUUI-DO

cram in four people (two in the bed and two on mattresses on the *ondol* floor). Sweeping views across the beach and an attached spa and pool complex are among the pluses, as well as a free shuttle bus to the airport.

Airport Business District & Airport Town Square

Just outside Incheon International Airport is the Airport Business District, not to be confused with Airport Town Square, two stops away on the A'rex train at Unseo – this latter area has lots of small hotels if ones at the former are full. Although neither area is ideal for the beach, they are good places to crash if you have an early departure or late arrival from Incheon Airport. Rates are typically higher on the weekend. Some hotels provide a free pick-up or drop-off service, otherwise there are buses and the train.

Guesthouse Korea (게스트하우스코리아; ☎ 032-747 1872; Airport Business District; www.guest houseinkorea.com; dm/s/d or tw W20,000/38,000/48,000; ✖ 🖳) Spacious rooms have kitchenettes, cable TV and free internet; some even have a washing machine. Free pick-up from the airport is also provided.

Hotel Hub Herb (허브허브 호텔; ☎ 032-752 1991; Airport Town Square; r from W70,000; ✖ 🖳) Lamé bedspreads seem more Versailles than Korea. Rooms are cramped but clean but like others here the price goes up at weekends.

Incheon Airport Hotel (인천에어포트호텔; ☎ 752 2066; www.incheonairporthotel.co.kr; Airport Town Square; s/d & ondol W115,000/135,000; ✖ 🖳) All rooms have TVs, DVD players and (yes, ugly) fridge-sized vending machines, while special rooms have snazzy triangular whirlpool baths, desktop PCs and fax machines. A golf driving range is on the roof. Advance reservations can drop the price by W20,000 or so.

EATING

When the Yeongjong-do Wharf Market re-opens you'll be able to buy fish, prawns, blue crabs and other shellfish and take them to the neighbouring restaurants to have them cooked and served.

Keunjip (큰집; ☎ 032-752 1442; Airport Town Square; meals W5000-10,000; ✖ 5.30am-10pm) This simple place, on the corner of the new town's main crossroad, cooks up a tasty *ppyeohaejangguk*, a hotpot of big meaty bones served with rice.

Hoebaragi (회바라기; ☎ 032-746 3611; Eulwangni Beach; meals W30,000-70,000; ✖ 11am-11pm) The largest restaurant at Eulwangni has a large red sign. Apart from *hoe* (raw fish), you can try barbecue prawns, crab or shellfish here.

Caffe Ora (☎ 032-752 0888; Eulwangni Beach; ✖ 10am-11pm) Overlooking both Eulwangni and Wangsan beaches, this modernist piece of architecture could be mistaken for the villain's headquarters in a James Bond movie. It's actually nothing more sinister than a high-class coffee shop and bakery with an eye to snagging the smart Seoul. Its beverages and cakes aren't cheap, but the views, supercool ambience and polished service all make it well worthwhile.

GETTING THERE & AWAY

The **International Airport Course Tour Bus** (adult/child W6000/3000; ✖ tours depart 9.45am-4.45pm) runs six times daily around Yeongjong-do from outside Incheon subway station. You can hop-on/hop-off the tour bus whenever you want. See p165 for details of getting to and from Incheon.

On Wolmido promenade is the ticket office for the **car ferry** (adult/child W3000/1000; ✖ 7am-9pm) to Yeongjong-do. Ferries run every half-hour and cars cost an additional W7500.

For details of getting to Incheon International Airport, from where you can connect to bus 301 or 316 to reach Eulwangni Beach, see p146.

Muui-do 무의도

Much less developed than Yeongjong-do is Muui-do, which can be reached via a five-minute ferry trip (W3000 return, half-hourly until 7pm, 6pm in winter) from Jamjin-do. For details of how to get to Jamjin-do from Yeongjong-do see p167.

Stepping onto Keunmuri wharf on Muui-do, you are greeted by seafood restaurants, along with the island bus and minibus taxi. To visit **Hanagae Beach** (하나개 해수욕장; ☎ 032-751 8833; www.hanagae.co.kr; adult/child W2000/1000) take the bus (W1000) or negotiate a taxi price. This beach, the island's best, has plenty of golden sand, a handful of seafood restaurants and basic beach huts under the pine trees or on the beach. The chalet-style house on the beach was used in the Korean TV drama *Stairway to Heaven*. Just beyond it is the start of a 2.5km hike through dense woods to the top of **Horyonggoksan** (호룡곡산; 244m).

Another option from Keunmuri wharf is to walk for a few minutes to **Keunmuri**, a delightfully traditional fishing village. Crab pots and fishing nets lie around while red peppers dry in the sun. From here it's a 1km walk over the hill to **Silmi Beach** (실미 해수욕

장; ☎ 032-752 4466; adult/child W2000/1000), which has a freshwater swimming pool, campsites and huts under the pine trees. At low tide you can walk to **Silmi-do** (실미도), an uninhabited island where the Korean movie of that name was filmed.

SLEEPING & EATING

Both Hanagae and Silmi beaches offer camping (W5000 per night) and basic accommodation in beach huts (from W30,000).

Family Resort Hotel Muui Island (☎ 1566 4466; http://muuiland.co.kr; 4-/8-person unit from W80,000/15,000; ☒) This attractive complex of self-catering units is set amid landscaped gardens with a lovely view across Keunmuri to the ocean. All rooms have double beds with more people able to sleep on the *ondol* floors.

Lifou (☎ 032-747 0053, 011-269 4224; www.lifou.kr; d W150,000; ☒) Offering wonderful sea views, this small self-catering complex has both *ondol* and Western-style rooms that are sparkling clean and well equipped. White wicker furniture gives it a casual feel.

Junganghoe-sikdang (중앙회식당; Keunmuri; meals to share W30,000; ☺ vary) Buy a heap of shellfish which is enough for three or four people and includes scallops, mussels and trumpet shells. Cook it up at a barbecue set in your table, but watch out for popping shells! This simple restaurant is just before the right turn to Silmi Beach.

GANGHWA-DO 강화도
pop 57,700

For a brief period in the mid-13th century when the Mongols were rampaging through the mainland, the island of Ganghwa-do became the location of Korea's capital. Situated at the mouth of the Han River, South Korea's fifth-largest island continued to have strategic importance and was the scene of bloody skirmishes with French and US forces in the 19th century as colonial powers tried to muscle in on the 'hermit kingdom'. Going even further back, Bronze Age people built many dolmen here: 70 of them have been inscribed on Unesco's World Heritage list.

It's not just Ganghwa-do's fascinating history that makes it worth visiting. Given over to small-scale agriculture (it's famous for its 'stamina-producing' ginseng), the island provides a welcome rural respite from the sometimes craziness of Seoul. Here egrets stalk through verdant rice fields and gulls swarm around the ferries that connect over to the neighbouring island of Seongmo-do, home to one of the country's most important temples, Bomunsa, with a cliff-carved Buddha and beautiful old pines. Numerous seafood restaurants also make dining on Ganghwa-do a pleasure.

The **Dolmen Cultural Festival** (celebrating this unique ancient burial ground with festivities that include a dolmen construction re-enactment)

ISLAND HOPPING IN THE WEST SEA

There are many more West Sea islands that it's possible to visit. One of the easiest to reach, just 3km north of Wolmido, is tiny, uninhabited **Jagyak-do** (작약도), which is decked out with *jagyak* (peonies) in summer, thus the island's name. Ferries (adult/child W7000/4000, 15 minutes, hourly from 10.40am to 5.40pm) depart from Incheon's Yeonan Pier.

Deokjeok-do (덕적도), 77km southwest of Incheon, is one of the most scenic islands. Along its southern shore is the spectacular 2km-long **Seopori Beach** backed by a thick grove of 200-year-old pine trees through which runs a hiking trail. The island also has many unusual rock formations and it's worth climbing the highest peak, Bijobong (292m), for the grand view. There are plenty of *yeogwan* and *minbak* as well as a camping ground at Seopori Beach if you decide you'd like to stay over. Get here on the high-speed ferry (☎ 032-887 2891; W18,600, 50 minutes, twice daily) from Incheon's Yeonan Pier.

If you really want to get off the beaten track head to **Baengnyeong-do** (백령도), South Korea's westernmost point, around 120km northwest of Icheon and only 12km from North Korea. Take a tour around this scenic yet heavily militarised island by boat to view the dramatic coastal rock formations for which it's best known. **Sagot Beach** is 3km long and consists of sand packed so hard that people can (and do) drive cars on it. In contrast, some of the other beaches in the area are pebble. The Koreans like to walk barefoot on the pebbles or even lie down on them, because they believe that the resulting acupressure is good for their health. The island is served by a high-speed ferry (W57,400, four hours, three daily) from Incheon's Yeonan Pier.

and the **Ganghwa-do Azalea Festival** are both held in October.

Ganghwa-eup 강화읍

The island's main town, Ganghwa-eup, is not particularly scenic, but is just 2km beyond the northern bridge and acts as a base for visiting all attractions. The **tourist information centre** (☎ 032-30 3515; www.ganghwa.incheon.kr; ☽ 9am-6pm Mar-Oct, to 5pm Nov-Feb) in the bus terminal has helpful staff who can provide you with English maps and leaflets.

In the town you'll find the serenely quiet remains of the small **Goryeongungji Palace** (고려궁지; adult/child W900/600; ☽ 8.30am-6pm), built in 1231 when it was surrounded by an 18km **fortress wall**. The fortress was destroyed in 1866 by French troops, who invaded Korea in response to the execution of nine French Catholic missionaries. Some 2km of walls and three major gates have since been renovated. The French army burnt many priceless books and took 300 back to France where they still remain, though recently the French government has been less opposed to returning this part of Korean heritage.

The **market** near the bus terminal sells locally grown ginseng and *hwamunseok* (화문석) – reed mats with floral designs that are beautiful but expensive. Woven baskets are cheaper, easier to transport and have similar designs.

Around Ganghwa-eup

The small but modern **Ganghwa History Hall** (강화 역사관; ☎ 032-932 5464; adult/child W1300/700; ☽ 9am-7pm) reveals the island's interesting history and is located near the fortification Gapgot Dondae (갑곶돈데) close to the northern bridge. Inside you'll see the original big bronze bell that once rang at the island's palace, as well as a gory diorama of Korean soldiers defending the island against attacking US forces in 1871.

Frequent buses (W100, five minutes) connect the museum to Ganghwa-eup bus terminal 2km away. If you're coming from Seoul on the bus, ask the driver to drop you off at the turn-off, rather than in Ganghwa-eup bus terminal.

Jeondeung-sa 전등사

The Tripitaka Koreana (see the boxed text, p208), 80,000 wooden blocks of Buddhist scriptures, was carved between 1235 and 1251 at this attractive **temple** (☎ 032-937 0125; www.jeondeungsa .org; adult/youth/child W1800/1300/1000; ☽ 6am-sunset), in the island's southeast. You can do a temple stay here (p388) and sip traditional teas at the

charming teahouse **Chunrimdawan** (tea W5000; ☽ 8.30am-7.30pm May-Oct, 9.30am-4.30pm Nov-Apr).

Manisan 마니산

This **park** (☎ 032-937 1624; adult/youth/child W1500/800/500; ☽ 6am-6pm) is in the island's southwest, 14km from Ganghwa-eup. On the 469m summit is **Chamseongdan** (참성단), a large stone altar said to have been originally built and used by Dangun, the mythical first Korean, who was born in 2333 BC. Every 3 October on National Foundation Day (a public holiday), a colourful shamanist ceremony is held here. The 3km walk to the top from the bus stop includes over 900 steps, takes an hour and on a fine day the views are splendid.

Hourly buses from Ganghwa-eup run to Manisan (W1000, 30 minutes).

Bugeun-ni Dolmen 부근리 고인돌

The biggest **dolmen** (admission free; ☽ 24hr) on Ganghwa-do is an impressive sight and has a top stone weighing more than 50 tonnes. Cheesy small-scale replicas of other ancient relics such as Stonehenge and Easter Island statues can be seen at the parklike site too, where a new interpretation centre was being built during our visit. Take a bus (W100, 15 minutes) or taxi (W2500, 10 minutes) here from Ganghwa-eup.

Oepo-ri 외포리

If you have been yearning for a close look at seagulls, come to Oepo-ri, a picturesque fishing village on the west coast about 13km from Ganghwa-eup. Flocks of the birds swoop around the ferries between Oepo-ri to

---

CYCLING ON GANGHWA-DO

The perfect way of exploring part of Ganghwa-do is to rent a bike from the **souvenir stall** (☎ 032-933 3692; mountain bike/tandem per hr W2000/4000, per day W8000/12,000; ☽ 9am-5pm) beside the Ganghwa History Hall. From here, a 15km cycle path runs alongside the seaside highway towards the Gangwha Choji Bridge. It's a scenic, mainly flat jaunt, though the summer sun can be scorching. Eel restaurants, rice fields, flowers and seagulls will greet you along the way. You'll also have a chance to explore several of the stone fortifications that line the coast including those at Gwangseoungbo (광성 보) and Chojijin (초지진).

Seongmo-do happily snatching snacks proffered by the delighted passengers.

Even if you stay on land, there's a quiet beauty here. The views of the harbour and mud flats seem to be cut from a Korean painting. Fishing trawlers, either sun dappled or mist cloaked, chug in and out of the port, through a backdrop of lavender-coloured islands; it's not hard to imagine that life here has been little changed for decades.

The seafood market (turn right after you get to the water) has good prices and there are decent restaurants and *yeogwan* (motels with small en suites). It's also the terminal for the ferry to **Seongmo-do** (성모도), where the main attraction is the temple Bomunsa.

Buses from Ganghwa-eup (W1000, 30 minutes) take a scenic cross-island route to reach Oepo-ri. Ferries depart for Seongmo-do (below), as well as other islands.

Bomun-sa 보문사

Situated high (steep walk, many stairs, catch your breath at the top) in the pine-forested hills of Seongmo-do, this **temple** (☎ 032-933 8271; adult/child W2000/1000; ⏰ 8am-7pm) is a highlight of a visit to this area. It has some superbly ornate painting on the eaves of its buildings. The grotto and 10m-tall Buddha rock carving are standouts. Korean women come here in hopes of conceiving sons, and the Korean grandmothers you see aren't praying for sons for themselves but for their daughters. *Minbak* and restaurants are dotted around the island's coastline, but you can make this a day trip from Seoul if you don't mind getting up early and returning late.

Ferries (☎ 932 6007) depart Oepo-ri for Seongmo-do (adult/child W2000/1000, 10 minutes, every 30 minutes) between 7am and 9pm. The ferry transports cars too (W14,000 return). On Seongmo-do a bus (W1000, hourly on weekdays, every 30 minutes on weekends) takes you near the temple but it's a *steep* climb up.

Sleeping

Apart from the options mentioned following, consider bedding down at one of the several *minbak* on Seongmo-do, or doing a temple stay at Jeondeung-sa (opposite).

Ganghwa Youth Hostel (강화 유스호스텔; ☎ 032-933 8891; www.gh-yh.co.kr; Oepo-ri; dm/f W12,000/70,000; 🖭) *Ondol* rooms are the deal at this typical youth hostel, which is a kilometre or so north of Oepo-ri, set up on a hill past some ramshackle motel buildings.

Heart Motel (하트모텔; ☎ 032-933 0710; Ganghwa-eup; r W35,000, Sat & Sun W50,000; ❄ 🖭) The accommodation nearest Ganghwa-eup's bus terminal has large, comfortable rooms, dark hallways and a friendly owner. Rooms with internet access cost W5000 more. Turn left outside the bus terminal and it's a five-minute walk along the main road.

Penthouse Motel (펜트하우스모텔; ☎ 032-934 9967; Oepo-ri; r W40,000; ❄ 🖭) This love hotel in Oepo-ri will do the trick if you're looking for clean and reasonably comfortable accommodation. Rooms sport big jacuzzi baths.

Royal Hotel (☎ 032-937 8767; www.royalspa.co.kr; r from W90,000; ❄ 🖭) Ganghwa-do's only real hotel is within walking distance of Jeondeung-sa in the south of the island. It offers both *ondol* and Western-style rooms with prices shooting up by 30% at weekends. Beneath the hotel there's a waterpark (adult/child W34,000/27,000) that hotel guests can use for a 40% discount.

Eating

Gourmands flock to Ganghwa-do to sample seafood, with different fishing villages on the island renowned for certain types. In Deurih-mi (더리미), on the east coast between the Ganghwa and Choji bridges, a dozen restaurants specialise in eel (장어), which can be served raw, salted, marinated in a special sauce and – tastiest of all – grilled over charcoal. Seonsu (선수) on the southeast coast is the place to head for herring served raw sashimi style.

Ganghwa-eup Bus Station restaurants (☎ 032-934-1239; meals W2000-6000; ⏰ 10am-9pm) On the 2nd floor of the terminal several places offer various inexpensive Korean meals. There's a coffee shop as well (open 8.30am to 8pm).

Oepo Hweojjib (외포횟집; ☎ 032-932 6662; meals W30,000-40,000; ⏰ 10am-9pm) Next to where the ferry docks from Seongmo-do is this seafood restaurant where you can sit and gaze at the ocean. The set-course menus (from W65,000) aren't cheap but come with a feast of side dishes.

Getting There & Away

There are frequent buses from Seoul's Sinchon Bus Terminal (Map p93) to Ganghwa-eup (W4200, 1½ hours, every 10 minutes from 5.40am to 11pm). The island is big so, if time is tight, consider taking a tour: several leave from Seoul (check with the KTO Tourist Information Centre, p105) and there's also one from Incheon (p164). Also consider hiring a car or chartering a taxi to get around.

Gangwon-do 강원도

From the soaring peaks of Seoraksan National Park to the tranquil beaches abutting the East Sea, Gangwon-do has all the elements for a postcard-perfect vacation. This is where many Seoulites escape – to get lost in the mountains, chow down on Chuncheon's fiery chicken dish *dakgalbi* or the coastal towns' raw fish, or leap into a frenzy of adventure sports.

While the province may not have that much by way of cultural antiquities, what it does have – Gangneung's 400-year-old Dano Festival, for instance – it celebrates with zest. And Gangwon-do can be quirky too. Near Samcheok you'll find a park full of unabashed phallic sculptures standing cheek by jowl with a humble fishing village, while Gangneung has a museum dedicated to its founder's lifelong obsession with all things Edison.

Politics turned Gangwon-do into a border province with North Korea, with the Demilitarised Zone (DMZ) lining its northern boundary. Along the coast you'll see sobering reminders of the division: barbed wire, military lookout posts and, at Jeongdongjin, a captured North Korean submarine. Not far from the border, you can wander through bullet-ridden buildings near Cheorwon, crumbling but not forgotten, or at Goseong Unification Observatory train your binoculars on the legendary mountain Kumgangsan in the North.

In July and August, a surge of domestic tourists arrives on the beaches and mountains to get their fill of summer. Beaches are swarmed on New Year's Day too, for catching the first sunrise of the year over the East Sea. At other times Gangwon-do can be a restful change from Seoul, close by yet empty and foreigner-scarce enough to give a taste of Korean life beyond the capital.

GANGWON-DO

HIGHLIGHTS

- Hike the breathtaking peaks of **Seoraksan National Park** (p182)
- Marvel at the limestone wonders of cathedral-like cave **Hwaseongul** (p194)
- Get your fill of quirky Korea – gramophones galore at the **Chamsori Gramophone & Edison Museum** (p187) in Gangneung and phallic sculptures at **Haesindang Park** (p194) in Sinnam
- Make a pilgrimage to the mountaintop altar to Dangun in **Taebaeksan Provincial Park** (p196)
- Squint at North Korea from the war ruins at **Cheorwon** (boxed text, p183)

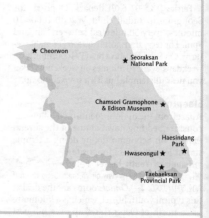

★ Cheorwon

★ Seoraksan National Park

Chamsori Gramophone ★ & Edison Museum

Haesindang Park

Hwaseongul ★

★ Taebaeksan Provincial Park

■ TELEPHONE CODE: 033	■ POPULATION: 1.5 MILLION	■ AREA: 16,874 SQ KM

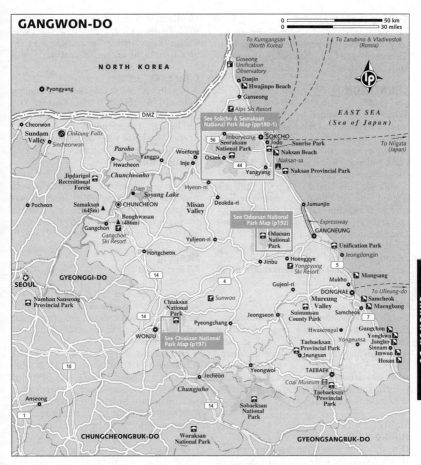

GANGWON-DO

History

Gangwon-do is the southern half of a province that once straddled the border (the Northern half is romanised as Kangwon-do). Some areas north of the 38th Parallel belonged to the North from 1945 till the end of the Korean War, and it's not uncommon to come across families with relatives in the North.

During the war this province saw many fierce battles for strategic mountaintops. Subsequently its rich natural resources, including coal and timber, were industrialised, spurring the development of road and rail links. When many coal mines closed in the 1990s, the province had to create alternative employment opportunities, such as tourism.

National & Provincial Parks

Of the province's three national parks, **Seoraksan** (p182) is the most well-loved and well-hiked, with stunning peaks that have attained legendary status.

Odaesan (p191) and **Chiaksan** (p197) offer incredible views and challenging hikes, the latter boasting some of the highest temples and peaks in the country.

Taebaeksan Provincial Park (p196) occupies a special place in the hearts of the Korean people for its mist-shrouded associations with the mythical founding father of the country, Dangun. Meanwhile, at **Naksan Provincial Park** (p182), a demure Goddess of Mercy statue can be found basking in a glorious location by the seaside.

Getting There & Around

Bus routes are excellent, while train lines cover only the south of the province and, in the west, Chuncheon and Gangchon. Sokcho has regular ferry services to Russia and Japan.

CHUNCHEON 춘천
pop 265,000

While it's surrounded by gorgeous mountains, the charms of **Chuncheon** (www.chuncheon. go.kr) are mostly artificial: shimmering lakes created by dams, the fiery chicken dish *dakgalbi*, and well-loved if schmaltzy settings for the enormously popular TV drama *Winter Sonata* (see the boxed text, p53). Still, it's a good base for outdoor activities and its proximity to Seoul makes it a popular weekend getaway. With several universities here, Chuncheon is also shaking off some of that small-town feel with a burgeoning shopping and nightlife scene. Every May it hosts the very popular **Chuncheon International Mime Festival** (www.mimefestival.com).

Information

Not far from downtown, a large **tourist information centre** (☎ 244 0088; http://en.gangwon.to) inside a blockish brown brick building is well-stocked with information for the whole province. There is English-, Chinese- and Japanese-speaking staff, and free internet access. There is also a smaller **tourist information office** (☎ 250 3896) at the bus terminal.

Sights
JUNG-DO 중도

Directly across from Chuncheon on Uiamho (Uiam Lake), the little island of Jung-do is packed in true Korean style with enough recreational options to occupy a school-full of children. Take your pick from cycling (per hour W4000), jetskiing (W50,000 for 15 minutes) and motorboat rides (W40,000 to W80,000), or opt for rowing or waterskiing. There's also an outdoor swimming pool (open in July and August), sports fields and picnic areas.

There are a couple of restaurants and a general store, but most visitors bring their own picnic. Camping (W3000) and simple **self-catering pension accommodation** (☎ 242 4881; www.gangwondotour.com; r W22,000-55,000, weekends ⁻ 000-66,000; 🗯) are available.

⸱ get to Jung-do, take bus 74 heading ⸳ m downtown Chuncheon (W1100,

10 minutes). The ferry pier is off the main road. **Ferries** (adult/child return W5300/3400, bicycles W1000 extra; every 30 min; ☺ 9am-6pm) take five minutes to make the uneventful crossing.

UIAM LAKE 의암호

A bicycle path skirts the lake from Ethiopia Café (p176) round to the Korean War Memorial, the Soyang River Maiden statue and beyond. The memorial is dedicated to a Korean War battle when outnumbered South Korean defenders at Chuncheon held back the invading North.

The route makes a particularly attractive ride just before sunset. Grab a **bicycle** (per hr/day W3000/5000, ID required; ☺ 9am-7pm) from the stall opposite the Ethiopia Café. You can also hire rowing boats (per hour W6000) and swan paddle boats (per hour W8000 to W10,000).

Sleeping

Hill House Motel (힐 하우스 모텔; ☎ 241 0331; Okcheondong 42-6; r W30,000; 🗯) The English signs say 'Hill House' and 'Good Time' – the latter suggesting, not inaccurately, that this is the kind of place with condom machines in the hallways. Rooms are on the small side but have decent fittings.

Grand Motel (그랜드모텔; ☎ 243 5021; Okcheondong 39-6; r W35,000, Sat W40,000; 🗯 💻) Run by a kind and helpful family, this motel has comfortable, good-sized rooms. There's a free pick-up service from the bus terminal and train station, and the family can also provide information for sightseeing in Chuncheon and nearby.

IMT Hotel (IMT호텔; ☎ 257 6111; www.imthotel.co.kr; r W55,000; 🗯 💻) For those who like their love hotels with sleek, black hallways and large bold prints on the walls. Rooms are plush and ultramodern, with high-tech showers, enormous TVs and snazzy-looking desktop computers.

Sejong Hotel Chuncheon (춘천 세종 호텔; ☎ 252 1191; www.chunchonsejong.co.kr; r & ondol W84,700, summer W96,800; 🗯 ✕ 💻 🗯) Nestled on the slope of Bong-uisan, this hotel offers unrivalled views of Chuncheon and the surrounding countryside. Rooms are nice, with all the mod cons, and some ground-floor rooms have a patio.

Eating

Chuncheon's gastronomical pride and joy is *dakgalbi* (닭갈비) – chicken pieces, *tteok*

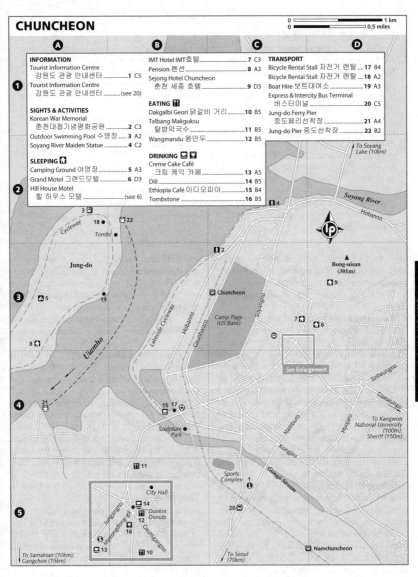

CHUNCHEON

0	1 km
0	0.5 miles

INFORMATION
Tourist Information Centre
강원도 관광 안내센터 1 C5
Tourist Information Centre
강원도 관광 안내센터 .... (see 20)

SIGHTS & ACTIVITIES
Korean War Memorial
춘천대첩기념평화공원 2 C3
Outdoor Swimming Pool 수영장 .. 3 A2
Soyang River Maiden Statue 4 C2

SLEEPING
Camping Ground 야영장 5 A3
Grand Motel 그랜드모텔 6 D3
Hill House Motel
힐 하우스 모텔 .... (see 6)

IMT Hotel IMT호텔 7 C3
Pension 펜션 8 A3
Sejong Hotel Chuncheon
춘천 세종 호텔 9 D3

EATING
Dakgalbi Geori 닭갈비 거리 10 B5
Talbang Makguksu
탈방막국수 11 B5
Wangmandu 왕만두 12 B5

DRINKING
Creme Cake Café
크림 케익 카페 13 A5
Dill 14 B5
Ethiopia Café 이디오피아 15 B4
Tombstone 16 B5

TRANSPORT
Bicycle Rental Stall 자전거 렌탈 17 B4
Bicycle Rental Stall 자전거 렌탈 18 A2
Boat Hire 보트대여소 19 A3
Express & Intercity Bus Terminal
버스터미널 20 C5
Jung-do Ferry Pier
중도페리선착장 21 A4
Jung-do Pier 중도선착장 22 B2

GANGWON-DO

(rice cakes) and vegetables cooked with spicy chilli paste on a sizzling hot iron plate in the middle of the table. Off the downtown Myeongdong shopping area, Dakgalbi Geori (닭갈비 거리; Dakgalbi Street) is a lively street with more than 20 such restaurants (meals W8000 to W10,000). Most places will only serve *dakgalbi* to at least two diners,

and a serving for two is often enough to feed three.

Restaurant staff usually help foreign customers with the cooking. They'll also offer aprons or plastic bags for stashing your jackets (tip: don't wear white). When the food is ready, wrap it in *ssam* (vegetable leaves), with a daub of *ssamjang* (bean paste) and some garlic

GANGWON-DO *(vertical sidebar)*

GET YOUR ADRENALIN ON

With rushing rivers, rugged mountains and fairly unspoiled scenery, Gangwon-do's northwest has become a hotbed for kayaking, canoeing and rafting trips from mid-April to October. Trips from **Cheorwon** (철원; www.cwg.go.kr) make forays onto the Hantangang (*gang* means river) in the Sundam Valley, while those from **Inje** (인제; www.inje.go.kr) head to the Naerincheon (*cheon* is usually translated as 'stream' – clearly a misnomer in this case). Neither course is extremely difficult unless monsoon rains whip them up to Class IV intensity.

Kayaking and rafting trips cost W30,000 (three hours) to W55,000 (seven hours), including instruction, and most companies offer pick-up from Seoul. Companies based in Cheorwon include **Hanleisure** (☎ 455 0557; www.hanleisure.com) and **Sundam Leisure** (☎ 452 3034; www.leports114.com). In Inje, try **X-Game** (☎ 462 5217; www.injejump.co.kr) or **Paddler** (☎ 461 1659; www.paddler.co.kr). Adrenalin junkies can top off their visit with a bungee jump with Sundam Leisure in Cheorwon (W30,000) or X-Game in Inje (W35,000).

Intercity buses serve Cheorwon from Dong-Seoul (W8800, 2½ hours, every 20 minutes) and Chuncheon (W12,400, 2½ hours, hourly). Inje can be reached from Dong-Seoul (W15,000, three hours, every 30 minutes), Chuncheon (W7900, 1½ hours, every three hours) or Sokcho (W8200, two hours, hourly).

---

for extra kick. If you have room at the end of the meal, order rice or *makguksu* (buckwheat noodles) to mop up the leftover sauce.

There are alternatives to all that spicy chicken.

Wangmandu (왕만두; ☎ 241 5480; meals W3000-5000) This hole-in-the-wall eatery is a good place to fill up on its namesake dish (large steamed dumplings), as well as *mandu* (dumplings) served fried (군만두), in soup (만두국) or in soup with rice cakes (떡만두국). There's also *gimbap* (sesame-oil flavoured rice wrapped in seaweed), *naengmyeon* (buckwheat noodles in cold broth) and *bibimbap* (rice topped with egg, meat, vegetables and sauce). Go up the lane beside Dunkin' Donuts and it's on the right at the first intersection – look for the sign with a cartoon character holding a plate of dumplings.

Talbang Makguksu (탈방막국수; ☎ 254 2518; meals W5000-8500) Decorated with masks and pots, this cheery restaurant is famous for *makguksu*, a Gangwon-do speciality. The buckwheat noodles are served cold, garnished with vegies, pork slices and half a hard-boiled egg. You can have it dry or add broth from a kettle, as well as mustard, sugar and vinegar to taste; go easy on the *gochujang* (red pepper paste) if you don't want it too spicy. The restaurant is on the ground floor of a grey two-storey building with a red sign.

Drinking

Smack in the middle of Myeongdong, **Tombstone** draws a mix made up of expat teachers and young Koreans. Look for the red sign at ground level and head up to the bar proper on the 3rd floor. More avid party-goers can head to the back gate of **Kangwon National University** (Gangwondae humun; 강원대 후문). There are plenty of bars and cafes, or try **Sheriff**, another cowboy Western-inspired joint.

Coffee-wise, **Ethiopia Café** (이디오피아) is the main establishment at the lakefront, near the Memorial Hall for Ethiopian Veterans of the Korean War with its triple-pointed roof. Myeongdong shopping street has plenty of cafes that fill up with young people; **Creme Cake Café** (크림 케익 카페; ☎ 244 8795) above KFC has better cakes than most, while tucked away off the main strip, the seemingly Laura Ashley–inspired **Dill** (☎ 254 9978) has cosy couches and dainty tea sets.

Shopping

Chuncheon's main shopping district is Myeongdong (yes, the same name as the one in Seoul), and includes a sprawling underground mall. A glitzy new four-storey mall, Myungdong 1st Str., was being built at the time of research.

Getting There & Away

Buses and trains take about the same time from Seoul if there aren't any traffic jams. On weekends, seats on both can be sold out. The train station (Namchuncheon) and bus terminals are about 3km south of the town centre.

BUS

The express and intercity bus terminals are located beside each other. Departures from the **express bus terminal** (☎ 256 1571) include Daegu (W16,300, four hours, 11 daily) and Gwangju (W21,700, 4½ hours, four daily).

From the intercity bus terminal:

Destination	Price (W)	Duration	Frequency
Cheongju	15,400	3½hr	hrly
Cheorwon	12,400	2½hr	hrly
Dong-Seoul	8500	1¾hr	every 20min
Gangneung	10,600	3½hr	every 30min
Sokcho	13,500	2hr	hrly

TRAIN

Trains to Chuncheon's Namchuncheon station depart from Seoul's Cheongnyangni (W5400, two hours, hourly). From Namchuncheon it's a quick taxi ride to downtown Chuncheon.

Maps may show two train stations, Namchuncheon and Chuncheon; the latter is scheduled to open only in late 2010 (note: it's been delayed before).

GETTING AROUND

Taxis are inexpensive and good for shuttling between downtown, the lakefront and the bus terminal or train station.

AROUND CHUNCHEON
Samaksan 삼악산

The highest mountain near Chuncheon, **Samaksan** (☎ 262 2215; adult/youth/child W1600/1000/600; ☼ sunrise-sunset) offers incredible views of the town and surrounding lakes. The hike up to the peak (645m) can be strenuous and takes at least two hours, passing pretty waterfalls near the base and several temples.

To get to the ticket office, take bus 3, 5, 50 or 50-1 (W1100, 15 minutes, 10km) heading south along Jungangno in Chuncheon. Get off after about 15 minutes, when you see the green road sign saying 'Seoul 79km'.

Gangchon 강촌

A resort village to the hilt, this place has *pension* (upmarket rural retreats) and motels, *dakgalbi* restaurants, scooter and bike rental places, *noraebang* (karaoke rooms) and DVD rooms – all packed along one narrow street. It's ridiculously popular with university students for MT or 'Membership Training', a rite-of-passage overnight orientation session

packed with group 'bonding' activities and, more often than not, excuses to get drunk. In other words, despite its idyllic setting, this town may not always be the place for a peaceful getaway, though it's an agreeable day trip from Chuncheon. On weekends, expect bumper-to-bumper traffic.

Most visitors come to see **Gugok Pokpo** (구곡 폭포; ☎ 261 0088; adult/youth/child W1600/1000/600; ☼ 8am-sunset), a 50m-high waterfall that's a 15-minute walk from the park entrance. Another path from the entrance leads up **Bonghwasan** (봉화산; 486m; closed in April), which takes about an hour.

From Gangchon's main street, you can take bus 50 or 50-1 to the waterfall entrance, or hire a bicycle (per hour/day W3000/5000; ID required). Cycle away from the train station and, immediately after you cross the bridge, look for the yellow sign on the right for the cycleway at Gugok 1-gil (not to be confused with the road Gugok-gil).

In winter, Gugok Pokpo is a popular spot for *bingbyeok* (ice climbing). **Gangchon Ski Resort** (☎ 02-449 6660, 033-260 2000) has 10 slopes of varying difficulty and six lifts. The resort operates a shuttle bus from Gangchon train station during ski season. It's 6km back towards Seoul – follow the river.

GETTING THERE & AWAY

From along Jungangno in Chuncheon, take bus 3, 5, 50 or 50-1 (W1100) heading south. Bus 50 and 50-1 turn into the town and terminate at the entrance to Gugok Pokpo. The others don't turn into Gangchon but stop along the highway, across the bridge from Gangchon.

Trains heading to Chuncheon stop at Gangchon (W4500) about 15 minutes before they reach Chuncheon.

Soyang Lake 소양호

Created by one of Korea's largest dams, this lake is 64km long, with serene waters lapping lazily at the edge of rolling green hills. Ferries ply only two routes across the water, leaving the picturesque scene largely undisturbed. The **one-hour ferry route** (adult/child W10,000/5000; ☼ 9.30am-5.30pm) is a 20km loop around the entire lake, with somewhat repetitive scenery. More popular is the **15-minute route** (adult/child W5000/3000, ☼ every 30min, 9.30am-5.30pm). The 4km run across the bay discharges passengers at a pier, from where it's a gentle 30-minute walk up to the temple **Cheongpyeong-sa** (청평사;

GANGWON-DO

adult/youth/child W1300/800/500). This small temple is snuggled against the mountainside and built in Joseon style; tradition has it that the first temple on this site was built in AD 973.

To get to Soyang Dam from Chuncheon, catch bus 11 (W1100, 40 minutes) heading north along Jungangno. The service ends at the top of the dam, after which it's a 1km stroll past the market stalls to the ferry pier. Near the Cheongpyeong-sa pier are **restaurants** selling *gamja jeon* (potato pancake) and *sanchae bibimbap* (*bibimbap* with mountain vegetables).

SOKCHO 속초
pop 85,000

Despite its proximity to Seoraksan National Park (p182), **Sokcho** (http://sokcho.gangwon.kr/foreign/eng) is more of a fishing town than a tourist town. The main commercial activity – and its attendant aromas – are clustered along the waterfront. For most domestic tourists, the main draw is the chance to sup on fresh raw fish with the tang of salt in the air. The beaches also get crowded on New Year's Eve when people gather to watch the first sunrise of the year.

Sokcho is only about 60km from the border and was part of the North from 1945 to the end of the Korean War. Most of the coastline is lined with barbed wire. At night, remember that lights in the water are to attract squid; lights on the beaches are to detect infiltrators.

There are small **tourist information booths** (☎ 639 2689; ☒ closed Jan) outside the express and intercity bus terminals. For more comprehensive information, stop by the tourist information centre (p183) at Sunrise Park.

Sleeping

Motels are clustered around the town's two bus terminals; those around the express bus terminal are within walking distance of the beach. In July and August room rates can double or triple. You can also camp on the beach then (W4000 to W8000 per night, shower W1300).

ourpick The House Hostel (더하우스 호스텔; ☎ 633 3477; www.thehouse-hostel.com; s/d W20,000/30,000, Jul & Aug W40,000/50,000; ☒ ☐) Within five minutes' walk of the intercity bus terminal, this is everything good backpacker accommodation should be. It combines the niceties of Korean motel rooms – water dispenser, mini-fridge and basic toiletries – with amenities such as bike rentals, free laundry and free breakfast (cereal, bread, coffee and tea). The quirky common lounge and charming, light-filled breakfast room are great for meeting travellers, and the English-speaking young owner is helpful with travel advice.

Motel Big Star (큰별 모텔; ☎ 637 4477; Yeongnanghaean-gil; r W30,000, Sat W50,000) Sitting snugly beside the Sokcho Lighthouse, this motel has very nice rooms with a brand-new feeling. Expect to pay about W10,000 more for a sea view.

Dongkyeong Motel (동경모텔; ☎ 631 6444; r W40,000; ☒) Located right beside the intercity bus terminal, this hotel has decent rooms with the usual dashes of frumpy decor.

Samsung Motel (삼성모텔; ☎ 636 0069; r W30,000, Sat W40,000; ☒ ☐) On the outside it looks like a fairyland castle knock-off; inside, rooms are bright and in good shape, though it's odd to see such decorative wood furniture parked on linoleum floors. Four rooms have internet-enabled computers.

Hotel Good Morning (굿모닝가족호텔; ☎ 637 9900; www.goodmorninghotel.net; Haeoreum-gil; r W60,000, Sat W80,000; ☒ ☐) This spiffy nine-storey hotel is one of the nicest near the beach. Rooms have contemporary dark-wood floors, tasteful decor and floor-to-ceiling windows to take advantage of the view.

Eating

The mainstay of the local cuisine is *modeumhoe* (모듬회; assorted raw fish), served with *banchan* (side dishes), *ssam* (vegetable leaves) *ganjang* (soy sauce) with wasabi, and spicy soup. The best place to soak up the atmosphere and flavours is on the waterfront. At the southern harbour of **Daepohang**, you can poke around the market stalls or bump elbows with the locals at casual eateries where the proprietor will kill, slice and serve your meal within minutes of scooping it live out of the tank. Alternatively partake of a more civilised (though not necessarily quiet) meal at a seafood restaurant.

The northern harbour of **Dongmyeonghang** offers a similar but tamer experience, as the stalls have been moved into a proper building, with a communal eating hall upstairs. You can also take away your meal to eat on the breakwater.

A large platter of *modeumhoe* costs W30,000 to W100,000. Order from the tanks, or tell your hosts your budget and let them assemble a meal for you. Don't forget the *soju* (local vodka).

Another local speciality is squid *sundae* (sausage). *Sundae* is usually made with a pork casing, but here squid is used, stuffed with minced noodles, tofu, onion, carrot, seaweed and seasoning, and then sliced and fried in egg.

Daepohang is south of Sokcho, on the way to Naksan (p182). Take bus 1, 1-1, 7, 7-1, 9 or 9-1 (W1240, 10 minutes) heading south and get off at the giant parking lot for the harbour. Dongmyeonghang is near the intercity bus terminal.

Hanyanggol (한양골; ☎ 635 7588; meals W5000) Opposite the express bus terminal is this two-storey building, topped with a green sign with a cutesy cartoon character floating on a cloud. Try the *wangmandu* (large steamed dumplings) or *kalguksu* (wheat noodles in clam-and-vegetable broth).

Tongnamuchon (통나무촌; ☎ 631 2918; meals W5500-8000) This cosy restaurant specialises in *makguksu* (buckwheat noodles with vegetables) and *galbitang* (beef-rib soup), or you can splurge on duck *bulgogi* (오리 불고기; marinated duck; W35,000). The restaurant is in the middle of a residential neighbourhood – look for the bright red signboards pointing the way.

Wangsibri (왕십리; ☎ 636 7849; meals W7000; ⏰ 5pm-midnight) If seafood isn't your thing, fill up at this no-frills all-you-can-eat barbecue joint, where locals perch on stools and feast till closing time.

Jinyang Hoetjip (진양횟집; ☎ 635 9999; meals W10,000-120,000) A modest establishment celebrated for its squid *sundae*. It also serves raw fish platters, including *mulhoe* (seasoned raw fish in water). The restaurant has fish tanks interspersed with greenery out front.

Shopping
Sokcho's main shopping area is along Jungangno, around the central market. Buses 1, 1-1, 7, 7-1, 9 and 9-1 ply this road. There is an E-Mart about 250m from the express bus terminal.

Getting There & Away
BOAT
From the Sokcho International Ferry Terminal (속초항 국제 여객 터미널) **Dong Chun Ferry Co** (☎ 02-720 0101; www.dongchunferry.co.kr) operates a twice-weekly service (three times a week

in summer) to Zarubino (one-way from W232,800; 16 hours) in Russia. The ferry anchors at Zarubino for five to six hours, then continues for a further four hours on to Vladivostok (W244,800). For the cheapest fare you sleep on the floor and share facilities. The more expensive fares entitle you to a cabin for two or four people with your own bed, TV and bathroom. In Vladivostok you can connect to the Trans-Siberian railway.

The ferry company also provide a bus from Zarubino to Hunchun in China which takes about two hours. Koreans use this for package tours to Paekdusan (p376) on the China–North Korea border. For more details see www.visitkorea.or.kr/enu/GK/GK_EN_2_3_5.jsp.

Since August 2009, a new weekly ferry service also connects Sokcho with Niigata on the island of Honshu, Japan. It leaves on Mondays at noon, reaches Niigata the next day, then continues to Zarubino (another 22 hours from Niigata).

BUS
Buses leave Sokcho express bus terminal for Seoul Gangnam (W15,800, 4½ hours, every 30 minutes).

Departures from Sokcho intercity bus terminal include the following:

Destination	Price (W)	Duration	Frequency
Busan	39,200	7½hr	11 daily
Chuncheon	13,600	2hr	hrly
Daegu	23,800	3½hr	1 daily
Dong-Seoul	13,900	4hr	hrly
Gangneung	7100	1hr	every 20min

Getting Around
Many buses (1, 1-1, 7, 7-1, 9 and 9-1) connect the intercity bus terminal, via the town's main street Jungangno, to the express bus terminal and Daepohang.

AROUND SOKCHO
Goseong Unification Observatory
고성 통일 전망대
elev 700m
While this area was part of the North from 1945 to 1953, today this **building** (☎ 682 0088; www.tongiltour.co.kr; adult/child W3000/1500; ⏰ 9am-4.30pm Mar-Jun & Sep-Oct, 9am-5.30pm Jul-Aug, 9am-3.50pm Nov-Feb) is the closest most South Koreans can get to glimpsing that world. There are binoculars (W500 for five minutes) installed on the viewing deck, and inside the observatory is a large map (Korean

lonelyplanet.com

GANGWON-DO

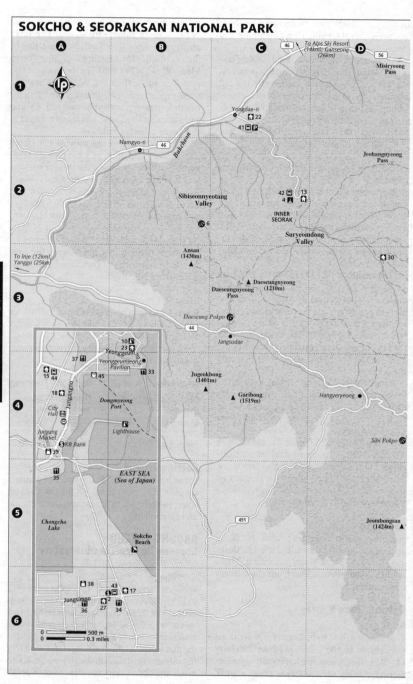

SOKCHO & SEORAKSAN NATIONAL PARK

To Alps Ski Resort
(14km); Ganseong
(26km)

Misiryeong
Pass

Yongdae-ri

Namgyo-ri

Jeohangnyeong
Pass

Sibiseonnyeotang
Valley

INNER
SEORAK

Suryeomdong
Valley

Ansan
(1430m)

Daeseungnyeong
(1210m)

Daeseungnyeong
Pass

Daeseung Pokpo

Jangsudae

Jugeokbong
(1401m)

Garibong
(1519m)

Hangyeryeong

Sibi Pokpo

To Inje (12km);
Yanggu (25km)

Yeonggeum
Yeonggeumjeong
Pavilion

City
Hall

Jungang
Market

KB Bank

Dongmyeong
Port

Lighthouse

EAST SEA
(Sea of Japan)

Chongcho
Lake

Sokcho
Beach

Jeombongsan
(1424m)

Jungsimno

Jungangno

0   500 m
0   0.3 miles

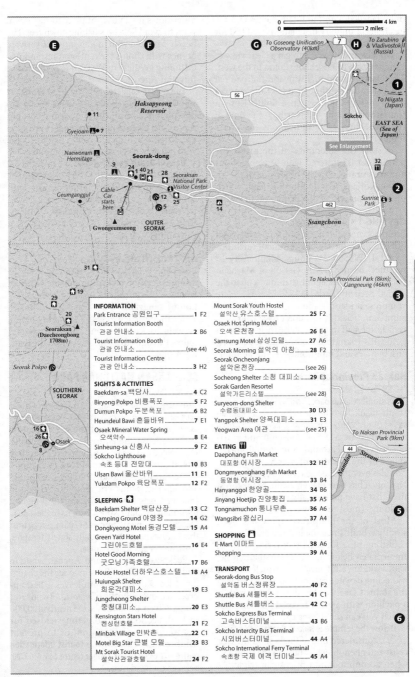

GANGWON-DO

INFORMATION

Park Entrance 공원입구 **1** F2
Tourist Information Booth
  관광 안내소 **2** B6
Tourist Information Booth
  관광 안내소 ....(see 44)
Tourist Information Centre
  관광 안내소 **3** H2

SIGHTS & ACTIVITIES

Baekdam-sa 백담사 **4** C2
Biryong Pokpo 비룡폭포 **5** F2
Dumun Pokpo 두문폭포 **6** B2
Heundeul Bawi 흔들바위 **7** E1
Osaek Mineral Water Spring
  오색약수 **8** E4
Sinheung-sa 신흥사 **9** F2
Sokcho Lighthouse
  속초 등대 전망대 **10** B3
Ulsan Bawi 울산바위 **11** E1
Yukdam Pokpo 육담폭포 **12** F2

SLEEPING

Baekdam Shelter 백담산장 **13** C2
Camping Ground 야영장 **14** G2
Dongkyeong Motel 동경모텔 **15** A4
Green Yard Hotel
  그린야드호텔 **16** E4
Hotel Good Morning
  굿모닝가족호텔 **17** B6
House Hostel 더하우스호스텔 **18** A4
Huiungak Shelter
  희운각대피소 **19** E3
Jungcheong Shelter
  중청대피소 **20** E3
Kensington Stars Hotel
  켄싱턴호텔 **21** F2
Minbak Village 민박촌 **22** C1
Motel Big Star 큰별 모텔 **23** B3
Mt Sorak Tourist Hotel
  설악산관광호텔 **24** F2

Mount Sorak Youth Hostel
  설악산 유스호스텔 **25** F2
Osaek Hot Spring Motel
  오색 온천장 **26** E4
Samsung Motel 삼성모텔 **27** A6
Seorak Morning 설악의 아침 **28** F2
Seorak Oncheonjang
  설악온천장 ....(see 26)
Socheong Shelter 소청 대피소 **29** E3
Sorak Garden Resortel
  설악가든리소텔 ....(see 28)
Suryeom-dong Shelter
  수렴동대피소 **30** D3
Yangpok Shelter 양폭대피소 **31** E3
Yeogwan Area 여관 ....(see 25)

EATING

Daepohang Fish Market
  대포항 어시장 **32** H2
Dongmyeonghang Fish Market
  동명항 어시장 **33** B4
Hanyanggol 한양골 **34** B6
Jinyang Hoetjip 진양횟집 **35** A5
Tongnamuchon 통나무촌 **36** A6
Wangsibri 왕십리 **37** A4

SHOPPING

E-Mart 이마트 **38** A6
Shopping **39** A4

TRANSPORT

Seorak-dong Bus Stop
  설악동 버스정류장 **40** F2
Shuttle Bus 셔틀버스 **41** C1
Shuttle Bus 셔틀버스 **42** C2
Sokcho Express Bus Terminal
  고속버스터미널 **43** B6
Sokcho Intercity Bus Terminal
  시외버스터미널 **44** A4
Sokcho International Ferry Terminal
  속초항 국제 여객 터미널 **45** A4

only) labelled with mountain names and the locations of military installations (red text for the North, white text for the South).

On a clear day, you can get a clear view of Kumgangsan (p375), about 20km to the west. The North-bound highway and railroad fell quiet after the South suspended Kumgangsan tours in July 2008, when a South Korean tourist was shot by the North; at the time of research, there were indications that tours might resume.

Despite the solemnity of the place, the parking lot is cluttered with souvenir shops and restaurants. On the other side of the lot is the Korean War Exhibition Hall, which provides something of a primer on the war.

GETTING THERE & AWAY

From downtown Sokcho or the bus stop right outside the intercity bus terminal, catch bus 1 or 1-1 (W4560, 1½ hours, 44km, every 15 minutes) headed north. Get off at Machajin (마차진) and walk about 10 minutes up to the Tongil Security Park (통일안보공원). Here you present identification and purchase your admission ticket. If you don't have your own vehicle, the staff might be able to help you hitch a ride. It's 10km to the observatory; pedestrians, bicycles and motorbikes are not allowed.

Naksan Provincial Park
낙산 도립공원

This small coastal **park** (☎ 670 2518; admission free) south of Sokcho is home to the temple **Naksan-sa** (낙산사; ☎ 672 2448; admission free; ☼ 5am-7pm), established in AD 671 and enjoying glorious sea views all around. A majestic 15m-tall statue of the Goddess of Mercy, Gwaneum, presides over the East Sea from a promontory. Notably it has never fallen victim to the forest fires that have periodically razed the temple buildings (most recently in 2005).

Most of the temple complex has been stoutly rebuilt since the last fire and the surrounding pine forest is recovering as well. Immediately below the statue is a small shrine, with a window strategically constructed so that a kneeling devotee can look up and gaze upon the statue's face. Farther down a side path is a pavilion with a glass-covered hole through which you can see the sea cave below.

Below the temple is **Naksan Beach** (낙산해수욕장), considered one of the best on the east coast and phenomenally busy in the summer, when accommodation prices can triple. At other times it's a pleasant place to stay if you want to avoid Sokcho's fishing-town feel. The beach is packed with motels, *minbak* (private homes with rooms for rent) and restaurants. Camping (W2000 to W4000) is permitted in July and August.

Euisangdae Condotel (의상대콘도텔; ☎ 672 3201; www.euisangdae.tc.to; r W40,000, Sat W60,000; ✖ 💻) doesn't look like much from the outside, but rooms are clean and sharp, and enjoy great views right on the beachfront. They also come with kitchenettes and desktop computers.

Naksan Beach Hotel (낙산비치호텔; ☎ 672 4000; www.naksanbeach.co.kr; r W80,000, Sat W130,000; ✖ 💻) is the most upmarket option, with comfortable rooms, restaurants and a seawater **sauna** (nonguests/guests W7000/5000; ☼ 5.30am-8pm). Ask for a room at the front to get a great view of the sunrise.

GETTING THERE & AWAY

Bus 9 and 9-1 (W1240, 15 minutes, every 15 minutes) can be picked up outside either of Sokcho's bus terminals, heading in the direction of Yangyang. Get off at Naksan Beach. You can approach Naksan-sa via the beach, or walk backwards along the highway and follow the signs to approach it from the landward side.

SEORAKSAN NATIONAL PARK
설악산 국립공원

This **park** (☎ 636 7700; http://seorak.knps.or.kr/Seoraksan _eng; adult/youth/child W2500/1000/600; ☼ 2hr before sunrise-2hr after sunset) is one of the most beautiful and iconic on the entire Korean peninsula. Designated by Unesco as a Biosphere Protection Site, it boasts oddly shaped rock formations, dense forests, abundant wildlife, hot springs and ancient Shilla-era temples. Seoraksan (Snowy Crags Mountain) is the third highest mountain in South Korea, with its highest peak Daecheongbong standing at 1708m. Set against this landscape are two equally stately temples, Sinheungsa and Baekdamsa.

Peak season is July and August, while in mid-October visitors flock in to see the changing colours of the autumn leaves – best appreciated over a bottle of *meoruju* (wild fruit wine). Given the park's size (nearly 400,000 sq km), sections are sometimes closed for restoration or preservation, or to prevent wildfires. Check with the **tourist information centre** (☎ 635 2003) or **ranger centre** (☎ 636 7700) before you head out.

A DIFFERENT SIDE TO THE DMZ

Say 'DMZ' (Demilitarised Zone) and most people think of Panmunjom (see p152). But the little-touristed town of **Cheorwon** (철원; www.cwg.go.kr) presents a more haunting version. Under the North's control from 1945, it saw fierce fighting during the Korean War and was built anew after the war, as part of the South. But even today it feels dusty and untended, with more scarecrows than farmers, more army trucks than family pick-ups and more military checkpoints than farmhouses.

Most of the war sites lie within the Civilian Control Zone that spans 20km from the border, so visitors must present identification and register with the **Hantangang Tourism Office** (한탄강 관광지 관리사무소; ☎ 450 5558) at the Iron Triangle Memorial Hall (철의 삼각 전적관) for an official two-hour **tour** (adult/child W2000/1000; ◷ 9.30am, 10.30am, 1pm & 2.30pm, closed Tue & holidays). You must have your own vehicle or hitch a ride. The first stop is the **Second Tunnel**, dug by the North in 1975. About 1km of it lies in the South and it's large enough for purportedly 16,000 soldiers to stream through per hour. A 150m staircase leads down to the tunnel, then it's a well-lit albeit damp 500m stretch to where the tunnel was discovered, just 300m from the border.

The next stop is the **Cheorwon Peace Observatory**, 1km from the DMZ. There are coin-operated binoculars for gazing at the North and its 'propaganda village' Seonjeon. A short drive down the road is the petite **Woljeong-ri Station**, left as a memorial to the railway line between Seoul and Wonsan, and housing the battered, twisted remains of a bombed train. Beside the station is the outsized Cheorwon Crane Park building, for viewing migratory birds in winter (the DMZ has inadvertently become a wildlife refuge for endangered cranes and herons).

After passing a few battle-scarred buildings, the tour ends at the former Labor Party (that is, Communist Party) **headquarters**. The surviving facade is very evocative, but its associations are less than pleasant: when Cheorwon was part of the North, many civilians were imprisoned and tortured here.

A tourism official tags along on the tour but as a chaperone, not a guide, so don't expect any commentary. Brochures in English are available at the tourism office. Except for school groups, the tour is not very popular, so for travellers hoping to hitch a ride it's a hit-or-miss situation. Still, this is one way to see the DMZ without paying an exorbitant fee and being hustled onto coaches, and it can be a more solemn and reflective visit at that.

Orientation

The park is divided into three sections, unconnected by road. Outer Seorak is the most accessible and popular area, nearest to Sokcho and the sea. Seorak-dong has hotels, motels, *minbak*, restaurants, bars, *noraebang* and general stores. Inner Seorak covers the western end of the park and is the least commercialised. Southern Seorak is the name given to the Osaek (Five Colours) area, which is famous for its mineral springs.

Information

A helpful **tourist information centre** (☎ 635 2003; ◷ 9am-6pm Mar-Oct, 9am-5pm Nov-Feb) is rather inconveniently located at Sunrise Park, where the Seorak-dong access road joins the main coast road (Hwy 7). Free internet access is available. The **ranger centre** (☎ 636 7700; ◷ 9am-5pm) at the entrance to Outer Seorak has some information in English and a left-luggage facility (W1000 to W3000).

Outer Seorak 외설악

Within 20 minutes' walk of the park entrance is Sinheung-sa, a temple complex that has stood on this site since AD 652. From here, paths diverge for Daecheongbong and the rocky face of Ulsan Bawi.

The ascent to **Daecheongbong** is a solid tramp of five to seven hours and 10km to 14km, depending on the route. It can also be approached from Osaek in Southern Seorak. Many Korean hikers time their arrival at the peak to catch the sunrise. There are mountain shelters of varying quality en route (see Sleeping, p184).

A shorter but still strenuous hike is the two-hour, 4.3km route to **Ulsan Bawi**, a spectacular granite cliff that stands at 873m. The trail passes **Heundeul Bawi**, a massive 16-tonne boulder balanced on the edge of a rocky ledge, which can be rocked to and fro by a small group of people. It's a popular spot for photos. From here, it's a hard-going but rewarding climb (including an 808-step metal staircase) to Ulsan Bawi. There are stupendous views all the way to Sokcho on a clear day – well worth the effort.

An easier option is the hour-long hike to a couple of **waterfalls**: Yukdam Pokpo, a series of six small falls, and the 40m-high Biryong Pokpo. The 2km hike starts at the stone bridge beyond the cable-car station.

The least taxing and quickest way to get some good views is to ride the **cable car** (☎ 636 7362; adult/child return W8500/5500; 🕙 7am-6pm summer, 8.30am-5pm other months), which drops you a 10-minute walk from the remains of the fortress **Gwongeunseong**, believed to date back to the 13th century. The cable car runs every 20 minutes, more frequently during peak season.

Inner Seorak 내설악

The relatively uncrowded river valleys in the northwestern section of the park are well worth exploring. From the park entrance near Yongdae-ri, take a shuttle bus (see Getting There & Away, opposite) or hike 6.5km to the serene temple of **Baekdam-sa** (☎ 462 2554; 🕙 sunrise-sunset), which faces east and is best appreciated in the morning. From there, you can ramble along the **Suryeomdong Valley** for an hour or two, and even connect to Outer Seorak (seven hours, 14km).

Alternatively, from Namgyo-ri there's a splendid 2½-hour hike in the Sibiseonnyeotang Valley to Dumun Pokpo. After another two hours uphill you can turn right for a 30-minute hike up **Ansan** (1430m) or turn left for Daeseungnyeong (1210m), which takes the same amount of time. You can also approach Ansan from the south, via a hiking trail from Jangsudae.

Southern Seorak 남설악

It's easier to hike up Daecheongbong from **Osaek Hot Springs** in the south, though the climb is still steep and difficult. Budget four hours up and three hours down, then soak away the strain in the **hot-spring pools**. You can also descend on the other side to Seorak-dong (six hours).

Sleeping

The widest range of accommodation is at Seorak-dong. Accommodation rates can double in July and August, and also tend to inflate in October. At other times, the upmarket ho-

tels offer significant discounts. Basic camping (W3500 to W7000) facilities are available in Seorak-dong, Jangsudae and Osaek.

Mountain shelters cost W5000 to W8000. There are four along the Outer Seorak routes to Daecheongbong – at Jungcheong, Yangpok, Huiungak and Socheong. Reservations are accepted only for **Jungcheong** (☎ 672 1708; http://english.knps.or.kr/knps_eng/parks/reservation_01.asp), which is just 100m below the peak. **Suryeomdong** (☎ 462 2576) shelter is located on the trail from Baekdam-sa.

SEORAK-DONG 설악동

There is a cluster of accommodation, shops and restaurants about 2km from the park entrance. If you're on the bus from Sokcho, get off after you see the Seoraksan National Park Visitor Center on your left. Most of the *yeogwan* (motels with small en suite) are along the lanes behind the restaurants.

Seorak Morning (설악의 아침; ☎ 632 6677; www.seorakmorning.com; r W30,000; 🍴) The former Meorujang has been transformed into a sharp-looking *pension*, with bright and cosy rooms. The owners speak a little English.

Sorak Garden Resortel (설악가든리소텔; ☎ 636 7474; r & ondol W30,000; 🍴 💻) Simple, clean rooms with sufficient comforts and no pretensions. The 3rd-floor rooms at the front offer the cheapest mountain views in the area.

Mt Sorak Tourist Hotel (설악산관광호텔; ☎ 636 7101; r W121,000; 🍴 💻) The only hotel inside the park has its own private access road and restaurant. Rooms are clean and nice, though with the food and souvenir stores out front, it can get noisy sometimes.

Kensington Stars Hotel (켄싱턴호텔; ☎ 635 4001; www.kensington.co.kr; d & ondol W169,000; tw W199,000; 🍴 💻) Just 400m from the park entrance, tucked into the crook of a majestic Korean mountain, is this unexpected English oasis – with traditional teddy bears and Edwardian armchairs in the lobby, and red double-decker buses parked outside. Rooms are suitably plush and those at the front have great views.

About 2km further from the park is a second cluster of tourist facilities, including **Mount Sorak Youth Hostel** (설악산 유스호스텔; ☎ 636 7116; www.sorakyhostel.com; dm/f W25,000/50,000, Fri & Sat W30,000/75,000; 🍴 💻). It's the cheapest option for solo travellers but you'll have to bus it to the park entrance (W1000, five minutes, every 10 minutes).

INNER SEORAK

The 1km road from Yongdae-ri to the park entrance is flanked by farmhouses, *minbak* (W20,000) and restaurants. It's a good place to spend the night if you'd like to wake up to your own slice of rural Korean idyll.

SOUTHERN SEORAK

All the accommodation is bunched around the Osaek hot-spring pools.

Osaek Hot Spring Motel (오색 온천장; ☎ 672 3635; www.osaek.co.kr; r W25,000; 🍴 💻) Simple rooms in a cosy-looking red-brick building. The bear-like owner speaks a little English and guests can use the *oncheon* (hot-spring spa) downstairs.

Seorak Oncheonjang (설악온천장; ☎ 672 2645; www.sorakjang.com; r W30,000, Fri & Sat W40,000; 🍴 💻) This motel has pleasant rooms spread over two neat white buildings, with the lobby in the rear one. The *oncheon* is free for guests, as is internet use. Rooms go up to W70,000 during peak periods.

Green Yard Hotel (그린야드호텔; ☎ 672 8500; r & ondol W75,000; 🍴 💻) The only high-end hotel, this mountain chalet–inspired complex has smart rooms with all the creature comforts. The *oncheon* (W8000) looks a little industrial from the entrance, but has lovely outdoor bath areas.

Eating

As in many national parks, the restaurants around Seoraksan serve popular fare such as *sanchae bibimbap* (W5000) and *sanchae jeongsik* (banquet dishes; W8000), both of which feature local vegetables.

Getting There & Away

The access road to Outer Seorak branches off the main coast road at Sunrise Park, halfway between Sokcho and Naksan. From outside Sokcho's intercity bus terminal or opposite its express bus terminal, catch bus 7 or 7-1 (W1000, 20 minutes, every 10 minutes), which terminates at Seorak-dong.

Buses from Sokcho's intercity bus terminal run every hour to Osaek (W4000) and Jangsudae (W5400). From Dong-Seoul, there are also eight buses daily to Osaek (W18,800). At Osaek, buy your bus ticket at the general store that's about 10m from the bus stop.

Also from Sokcho's intercity bus terminal, buses bound for Jinburyeong (six daily from 6.30am to 5.50pm) make stops at Yondae-ri (W6600) and Namgyo-ri (W7000). From Yongdae-ri, it's a 1km walk to the park entrance. There, you can hike or take a shuttle bus (adult/child one way W1800/1000, 15 minutes, every 20 minutes) to Baekdam-sa; it runs from 7am to 5.30pm.

ALPS SKI RESORT
알프스 스키 리조트

Opened in 1984 on the site of an old army base, this **resort** (☎ 681 5030; www.alpsresort.co.kr) is nowhere as large as the nearby Yongpyong Ski Resort (p190), but it receives the heaviest snowfalls of any resort in Korea. Thanks to its proximity to Seoraksan National Park, it also has spectacular scenery. There are eight slopes and five lifts, but business operations were uncertain at the time of research.

GANGNEUNG 강릉
pop 220,097

Gangneung (www.gangneung.go.kr) is the largest city on the Gangwon-do coast and looks it too, with wide roads often crowded with traffic. Its pockets of attractiveness lie towards the sea, particularly near Gyeongpo, while its cultural hotspots – well-preserved Joseon-era buildings and the 400-year-old shamanist Dano Festival (see the boxed text, p189) – are matched by quirky modern attractions, such as a museum lovingly dedicated to Thomas Edison and a North Korean submarine on display in nearby Jeongdongjin (p190). With natty motels and a decent bar scene as well, the town is a good place to linger for a few days if you're looking for an experience that's off the beaten track without being too small-town.

The **tourist information centre** (☎ 640 4414; www.gntour.go.kr) is beside the bus terminal, with English-, Mandarin- and Japanese-speaking staff. There is also a small booth in front of the train station, and another at Gyeongpo Beach. The main shopping area is downtown, in the warren of lanes near Jungang Market.

Sights
OJUKHEON 오죽헌

Revered as the birthplace of the paragon of Korean womanhood Sin Saimdang (1504–51) and her son the philosopher and government official Yi Yulgok (1536–84), this **complex** (☎ 648 4271; adult/youth/child W3000/2000/1000; 🕙 9am-6pm Mar-Oct, 9am-5.30pm Nov-Feb) contains one of the oldest surviving Joseon-dynasty

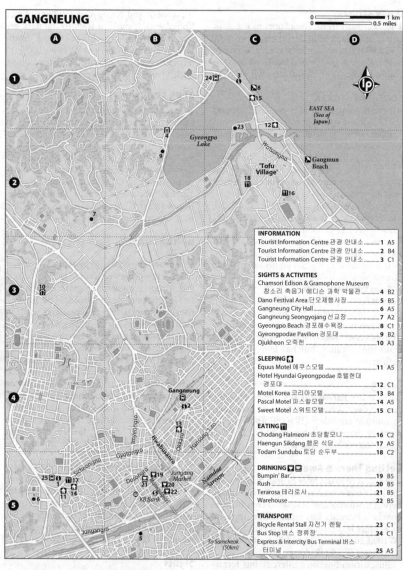

homes. The sprawling space has the feel of an elegant park, with buildings nestled amid punctiliously maintained gardens, lotus pools and the black-stemmed bamboo groves for which the property is named.

Sin Saimdang was an accomplished poet and artist, and is traditionally regarded in Korea as a model daughter, wife and mother.

Her visage graces the new W50,000 note – a move that has irked some women's groups, who say it reinforces the idea that women should devote themselves to their children at home as Sin did, teaching her son the Confucian classics.

Yi Yulgok, also known by his pen name Yiyi, appears on the W5000 note, with Ojukheon on its front and back. Yi won first prize in the state examination for prospective government officials and went on to serve the king. Unfortunately his advice to prepare against a possible invasion by Japan was ignored – to the kingdom's peril after Yi's death, when the Japanese invaded in 1592.

Many of Sim's paintings are on display at Ojukheon, including a delicate folding screen with eight studies of flowers and insects. The building Eojegak preserves a children's textbook which Yi authored and hand-wrote, *Gyeokmongyogyeol.*

Ojukheon is 4km from downtown Gangneung. From right outside the bus terminal, take bus 202 (W1100, 10 minutes, every 30 minutes) and make sure it's the one heading to Gyeongpo (경포). The bus stop outside Ojukheon is well signposted.

GANGNEUNG SEONGYOJANG 강릉선교장
Dating back to the late Joseon dynasty, this national cultural **property** (☎ 640 4799; adult/youth/child W3000/2000/1000; 🕙 9am-6.30pm) was for 300 years the home of a *yangban* (aristocratic) family. It was built for a descendant of the brother of King Sejong (the monarch who invented *hangeul*, the Korean phonetic alphabet), and has been restored in keeping with the original floor plan and architectural style.

The complex includes residential quarters, a library and a pavilion overlooking a lotus pond. It's very pretty but somewhat lifeless, like a movie set; in fact, a number of Korean films and TV shows have been shot here. The servants' quarters has unfortunately been turned into a gift shop, but you can try your hand at some traditional games outside.

To get here, take bus 202 and get off about five minutes after Ojukheon.

CHAMSORI GRAMOPHONE & EDISON MUSEUM
참소리 축음기 에디슨 과학 박물관
This whimsical **museum** (☎ 655 1130; www.edison.kr; adult/youth/child W7000/6000/5000; 🕙 9am-5pm; 👶) combines the two loves of private collector Son Sung-Mok (see the boxed text, p188): gramophones and Thomas Edison. There are hundreds of antique gramophones (or phonographs, as Edison termed them) and music boxes, as well as a colourful collection of Edison's other inventions and related devices, from cameras and kinetoscopes to toys and typewriters. Some of these items are the only one of their kind. Though the tour is in Korean only, the guide demonstrates the use of some antique music boxes and other contraptions – good fun for children and anyone interested in 'retro' technology.

Take bus 202 for Gyeongpo and get off at the Gyeongpo Beach stop (five minutes after Seongyojang).

GYEONGPO BEACH 경포해수욕장
The largest beach on the east coast has 1.8km of flat, white-sand beach running down to moody, steel-grey waters. It's besieged by visitors during the official season (10 July to 20 August). At other times, the noisy strip of beachside restaurants and motels doesn't detract too much from the charm of the wind-twisted pine trees.

There is a small **tourist information booth** (☎ 640 4537; 🕙 9am-5pm). Camping is possible during the official season but only at a **private site** (☎ 010-2058 9469; W35,000).

GYEONGPO LAKE & GYEONGPODAE PAVILION 경포호, 경포대
Immediately behind Gyeongpo Beach is **Gyeongpoho**, which attracts local residents looking for a little peace and quiet. It hosts a Cherry Blossom Festival in early April.

There's a 4km bicycle path along the lakeshore, passing some traditional pavilions. The most prominent of these is **Gyeongpodae**, from which it is said – most poetically – that you can 'see' five moons: the moon itself and its four reflections – in the sea (now obscured by pine trees), in the lake, in your obligatory glass of alcohol, and in your own mind.

Bicycles (per hour W3000) can be rented from stalls at the northern end of the lake. Gyeongpodae is a short walk from the Chamsori Gramophone & Edison Museum.

Sleeping
The motels around the bus terminal are set back on a little lane parallel to the main road Sicheongno. They're more attractive than the skeevy ones around the train station. The better hotels are at Gyeongpo Beach. Prices go up in July and August, particularly for beach accommodation, which can easily double.

Motel Korea (코리아모텔; ☎ 646 3876; r W30,000; 🞬) This love motel has low-ceilinged rooms, pink walls, tiny Juliet balconies and a DVD library unabashedly displayed in the hallway. It'll do for a night if you're arriving late on the train.

GRAMOPHONES & GIZMOS GALORE

Ask Mr Son Sung-Mok about any item in his Chamsori Gramophone & Edison Museum (p187), and he'll tell you a story about it. He has amassed over 10,000 gramophones, Edison inventions and their technological descendants from around the world, only a fraction of which are on public display.

Mr Son's best story just might be the one about his very first gramophone, a Columbia G241 made in the 1920s and given to him by his parents when he was a boy in Wonsan (in what is today North Korea). When the family fled south during the Korean War, the 12kg phonograph was the only possession he lugged along. It now takes pride of place beside the entrance to the museum shop.

As for Mr Son's favourite story, he'll point at the American coin-slot phonograph on the museum's ground floor, beside the staircase. Dating from the 1900s, it's the only one of its kind left, so when it came up for auction in Argentina, Mr Son was determined to get it. Even falling victim to an armed robbery en route didn't stop him from making it to the auction and putting in a successful bid.

Mr Son's fascination with gramophones extends to the man who invented and patented the phonograph, Thomas Edison. Mr Son notes that Edison didn't do well in school yet was curious enough to learn on his own. Through this museum, Mr Son hopes to inspire Korean children to be likewise curious and interested in many things. He also has plans for a children's museum, a movie museum and perhaps a school to train curators.

Gramophones are still his first love, though, whether he's tinkering with one, savouring its music or looking for new acquisitions. A consummate collector for over 40 years, he avers, 'I will keep collecting till I die'.

Equus Motel (에쿠스모텔; ☎ 643 0114; r without/with computer W30,000/40,000, Sat W40,000/50,000; ✗ ▢) This love motel has sleek rooms that are the best value for money around the bus terminal. Rooms have neat black decor and enormous TVs, and better rooms come with treadmills and whirlpool baths.

Pascal Motel (파스칼모텔; ☎ 646 9933; r W40,000, Sat W55,000; ✗ ▢) Though not as swish as Equus Motel, this set-up has nice, clean rooms and there's no extra charge for internet access (just ask for a room with a computer). Look for the faded cream building with semi-circular red-framed windows.

Sweet Motel (스위트모텔; ☎ 644 2437; r W40,000; ✗) Sweet views indeed at this beachfront love motel. There's some odd blue ultraviolet lighting, but rooms are generally clean and nice.

Hotel Hyundai Gyeongpodae (호텔현대경포대; ☎ 651 2233; www.hyundaihotel.com/gyeongpodae; r W140,000, ste 300,000; ✗) Perched on a hill overlooking Gyeongpo Beach, this hotel has comfortable if unexciting rooms, a private beach area and tennis courts. Expect to pay about W30,000 more for a sea view.

Eating & Drinking

There are heaps of raw fish and seafood restaurants along the beach, but Gangneung's prized speciality is sundubu (순두부), soft or uncurdled tofu made with sea water in Chodang, the 'tofu village'. At its plainest, sundubu is served warm in a bowl, with ganjang (soy sauce) on the side. It can also be prepared in jjigae (순두부찌개; stew) or jeongol (순두부전골; casserole).

In Chodang, there are about 20 restaurants, one of the most well-known of which is **Chodang Halmeoni** (초당할모니; ☎ 652 2058; meals from W8000). For a more rustic experience, try **Todam Sundubu** (토담순두부; ☎ 652 0336; meals W5000-6000), which has floor seating inside a quaint wooden house beside Heogyun-Heonanseolheon Park (허균 허난설헌 유적공원). To get to Chodang, take bus 206, 207 or 230 (W1100, 30 minutes) from outside the bus terminal.

Cheap eats can be found at the upper level of the bus terminal or downtown near Jungang Market. Also near the bus terminal is the family-run **Haengun Sikdang** (행운식당; ☎ 643 3334; meals W5000-8000), with good, simple fare like kimchi jjigae (kimchi stew) or doenjang jjigae (soybean paste stew); if you like squid or octopus, try the stir-fried ojing-eo bokkeum (오징어볶음) or nakji bokkeum (낙지볶음).

If it's good coffee or bread-packed breakfasts you're craving, check out **Terarosa** (테라로사; ☎ 648 2710; www.terarosa.com; meals W5000-10,000), a cosy cafe that roasts and brews about 20 varieties of coffee, bakes its own bread and serves sandwiches and pasta.

While hardly eclectic, Gangneung's night-life is one of the livelier scenes in Gangwon-do. If you like nursing a beer at the bar, try **Bumpin' Bar**, down an alley opposite Terarosa; inside the ramshackle wooden house is a narrow low-ceilinged bar that grooves to the owner's vinyl collection of classic rock. On the other side of Jungangno are **Rush**, a basement club with live music every weekend, and **Warehouse** (☎ 646 6379), a roomy 2nd-floor nightspot with a pool table and, on weekends, a busy dance floor.

Getting There & Away
BUS
Gangneung's express and intercity **bus terminals** (☎ 643 6093) share the same building, near the entrance to Hwy 7. Express buses to Seoul (W13,300, 2½hr) from Gangneung head to Dong-Seoul (every 40 minutes) and Gangnam (every 20 minutes).

Intercity departures include the following:

Destination	Price (W)	Duration	Frequency
Chuncheon	10,600	3½hr	every 40min
Daejeon	15,000	3½hr	7 daily
Samcheok	4800	1hr	every 10min
Sokcho	7100	1hr	every 20min
Wonju	7200	1½hr	hrly

TRAIN
Seven *Mugunghwa* (semi-express) trains connect Gangneung (W22,200, 6½ hours) daily with Seoul's Cheongnyangni station via Wonju. There's also a special 'seaside train' to Samcheok (p193).

Getting Around
Buses 202 and 303 (every 25 minutes) connect the bus terminal with the train station. For bus 202, check that it's heading downtown (시내); otherwise it goes to Gyeongpo (경포). Figuring out bus routes is a piece of cake – a quick-reference sheet in English, Chinese or Japanese is available at the tourist information centres.

AROUND GANGNEUNG
Jeongdongjin 정동진
This small coastal town (www.jeongdongjin. co.kr) has an unlikely hotchpotch of offbeat tourist attractions, while Koreans know it for its beachside train station, which appeared in a popular TV drama *Hourglass* (hence the hourglass-inspired tourist souvenirs). Another landmark is the ship-shaped Sun Cruise Resort that sits atop a headland at the southern end of town.

While Jeongdongjin gets busy (and more expensive) in summer, the rest of the time it's every bit the dozy seaside village. Motels and restaurants are clustered around the train station and Hourglass Park (모래시계공원); the restaurants serve mostly *sundubu* (opposite), raw fish and seafood.

There are small **tourist information booths** at Unification Park and Hourglass Park.

GETTING INTO THE SPIRIT

The highlight of Gangneung's calendar is the shamanist Dano Festival (Danoje; 단오제), celebrated for one week on the fifth day of the fifth lunar month (around the last week of May). It's one of the biggest holidays in Korea and has been recognised by Unesco as a 'Masterpiece of the Oral and Intangible Heritage of Humanity'. For foreigners, it's a great opportunity to revel it up Korean-style, while learning about some of the country's oldest spiritual beliefs.

Danoje is the climax of a month-long series of shamanist and Confucian ceremonies for peace, prosperity and bountiful harvests. On the first day there's a lantern parade to welcome a mountain spirit, who unites with his 'wife', another spirit dwelling in Gangneung. During the festival people present their wishes to both, while female shamans perform the *dano gut* ritual. On the final day the people send off the male spirit back to the mountain.

Other activities include a Gwanno mask pantomime performance and traditional games such as *ssireum* (wrestling, for men) and swing competitions (for women, ostensibly). Visitors can paint masks, sample the festival tipple *sinju* and wash their hair in iris water (to cleanse the body of evil spirits – glossy hair is a nice bonus). It has all the ruckus and colour of a medieval fair, with modern-day carnival acts and a massive festival market thrown in.

The centre of activity is the Dano Cultural Center. Gangneung City Hall provides multilingual festival guides, as well as special tours in English to explain the Danoje traditions.

SIGHTS
Unification Park 통일 공원

The **park** (☎ 640 4469; adult/youth/child W2000/1500/1000; ◷ 9am-5.30pm Mar-Oct, 9am-4.30pm Nov-Feb) consists of two areas: a seafront display of a warship and a North Korean submarine, and a hillside 'security exhibition hall' (통일 안보전시관) with military planes parked outside. The former is undoubtedly more popular – when else are you going to get to poke around the insides of a North Korean sub?

The 35m-long **submarine** was spying on military facilities near Gangneung in 1996 when it ran aground off Jeongdongjin. The commander burnt important documents (the fire-blackened compartment is still visible) and the 26 soldiers made a break for shore, hoping to return to the North. It took the South 49 days to capture or kill them (except one, who went missing); during the manhunt 17 South Korean civilians and soldiers were killed and 22 injured.

The **warship**, while considerably larger than the submarine, has a less dramatic story: built in America in 1945, it saw action in WWII and the Vietnam War, and was donated to South Korea in 1972. Its interior has been refurbished for an exhibition on Korean naval history.

The security exhibition **hall** is on the hill behind the submarine and warship display, a 30-minute walk along a road with no pavement or shade. The hall has a detailed exhibition on the 1996 incident, but with little English text, it might only be military buffs who find it interesting.

Unification Park is 4km north of the train station along the coastal road. As you exit the train station, turn left and look for the bus stop along the row of restaurants. Take bus 111, 112 or 113 (W1100, 10 minutes, hourly).

Haslla Art World 하슬라아트월드

Sitting atop a hill, this **park** (☎ 644 9411; www.haslla.kr; adult/child W5000/4000; ◷ 7am-10pm Mar-Nov, 8am-5pm Dec-Feb; ⬤) has contemporary Korean sculptures set amid a pleasant 25-hectare garden with winding paths and boardwalks. On a clear day, there are incredible sea views. It's a nice ramble for an hour or so; round it up with some traditional Korean tea at the cafe.

The park is 1.5km north of the train station. Take bus 11, 112, 113, or 114 (W1100, five

minutes, hourly), and walk up a steep slope to the park entrance.

GETTING THERE & AWAY
Bus

Bus 109 (W1450, 45 minutes, every one to two hours) leaves from the bus stop outside Gangneung's bus terminal for Jeongdongjin, 20km south. Buses 111, 112 and 113 (W1100, 35 minutes, hourly) leave from downtown Gangneung.

Train

Eleven trains daily connect Jeongdongjin to Gangneung (W2500, 15 minutes) and Donghae (W2500, 25 minutes). Jeongdongjin is also a stop on the 'seaside train' that runs between Gangneung and Samcheok (p193).

GETTING AROUND

Local buses are infrequent; taxis are a better option. A trip between any of the sights costs W5000 to W8000.

Yongpyong Ski Resort
용평스키 리조트

With world-class facilities and lots of trees, **Yongpyong** (☎ 335 5757; www.yongpyong.co.kr; ⬤) is one of Asia's best ski resorts. The buildings manage to be charming without being kitschy, and on a clear day it's possible to glimpse the East Sea from the slopes. It has twice been part of Pyeongchang County's bid to host the Winter Olympics, missing out on the 2010 and 2014 Games by a few votes each time (Pyeongchang is trying again for the 2018 Games).

The season runs from November to March and there are 31 slopes for skiers and snowboarders, plus mogul bumps, cross-country trails and two half-pipes. It also hosts an International Ski Festival in February. A lifts-and-gondola day pass costs W68,000/53,000 (adult/child), while a day's ski equipment rental is W26,000/20,000 (adult/child). Snowboards cost W34,000 for daytime hire. Day-long ski classes (in English) for a group of 10 are W50,000/40,000 (adult/child).

Package deals including transport and accommodation are offered with discounts outside the peak season. Yongpyong is also a draw for fans of the TV drama *Winter Sonata* – many key scenes were filmed here. Nearby, the **Alpensia** (알펜시아; www.alpensia.com) resort debuted in late 2009 with ski and winter sports facilities, but details were not fully available at the time of research.

SLEEPING

Although there's a range of **sleeping options** (☎ 335 5757), most are pretty pricey for what you get. It's possible to snag 50% discounts from March to October.

Yongpyong Hostel (용평호스텔; up to 5 people W70,000; 🖵) Hidden among the pines like a Swiss chalet, this is a good option for friends on a budget who don't mind sharing a room. It's closed from March to October, except for group bookings.

Dragon Valley Hotel (드래곤밸리호텔; r W250,000, ste W500,000; 🖵 🖥) The nicest hotel in the resort, this is close to the slopes and has attentive staff and good rooms.

Condominiums (콘도미니움; up to 4 people from W240,000; 🖵) Some rooms come with kitchenettes. Condominiums closer to the slopes cost quite a bit more (from W330,000).

GETTING THERE & AWAY

From Gangneung's intercity bus terminal, take a bus to Hoenggye (W2200, 30 minutes, every 20 minutes), where you can catch a free **shuttle bus** (10 minutes, 15 daily, operates 5.30am to 11.30pm) for Yongpyong. The latter are puce-coloured and marked with the resort name. They wait across the street, to the left as you exit from the bus terminal at Hoenggye. A taxi from Hoenggye to Yongpyong costs W7000.

The resort also has a **private shuttle bus** (☎ 02-2201 7710, round-trip adult/child W28,000/22,000) operating twice daily from Seoul (2½ hours).

ODAESAN NATIONAL PARK
오대산 국립공원

This **park** (☎ 332 6417; http://odae.knps.or.kr/Odaesan _eng; admission free; ⏰ 9am-7pm) has great hiking possibilities, superb views and two prominent Buddhist temples: Woljeong-sa and Sangwon-sa. Like Seoraksan, Odaesan (Five Peaks Mountain) is a high-altitude massif and the best times to visit are late spring and early to mid-autumn, when the foliage colours are richest.

There are two main entrances to the park: from the south at Dongsan-ri and from the northwest at Sogeumgang. The former leads to the temples and the main hiking trail to the highest peak **Birobong** (1563m). The trail begins at Sangwon-sa and is a fairly steep 6.5km climb, about three hours round-trip. Gung-ho

hikers can continue from Birobong along a ridge to **Sangwangbong** (1493m), then back down to the road and to the temple (12.5km, five hours).

A separate trail runs 13.3km from Sogeumgang to Jingogae, passing several waterfalls and **Noinbong** (1338m). The route takes about seven hours one way. The trail linking Jingogae to the western half of Odaesan is currently closed for restoration.

Woljeong-sa 월정사

The Shilla-era **temple** (☎ 334 6606; www.woljeongsa. org) was founded in AD 645 by the Zen Master Jajang to enshrine relics of the historical Buddha. Although it fell victim to fires and was even flattened during the Korean War, one treasured structure that has survived from the Goryeo dynasty is the octagonal nine-storey pagoda in the main courtyard, with the figure of a kneeling bodhisattva before it. The younger buildings around it are decorated with intricate religious art. There is a **museum** (adult/child W1000/500; ⏰ 9.30am-11am, 12.30-4.30pm, closed Tue) of Joseon-era Buddhist art and you can arrange a temple stay (p388) here.

Sangwon-sa 상원사

Ten kilometres beyond Woljeong-sa is Sangwon-sa, where the hiking trail begins. The temple's intricately decorated bronze bell was cast in AD 725 and is the oldest bell in Korea (and one of the largest as well). Another prized object is the wooden statue of the bodhisattva of wisdom Munsu (in Sanskrit, Manjusri) – made in the 15th century, it is said, on the order of King Sejo after the bodhisattva cured his skin disease.

The temple is a 300m walk from where the bus drops you. It also has a **teashop** (per mug W4000-6000) with many healthful brews. An unusual concoction is *kkamang miseut garu* (까망미숫가루), made from a mixture of barley, black sesame, rye and other grains.

Sleeping & Eating

A small village of *minbak* and restaurants is on the left side of the access road, about 1km from the turnoff from Hwy 6. It's a 40-minute walk south of Woljeong-sa, or you can take the bus. Halfway between the temples is Dongpigol campground (W3000 to W6000) and Odaesan Shelter (W5000 to W10,000).

Sogeumgang also has a *minbak* village and campground.

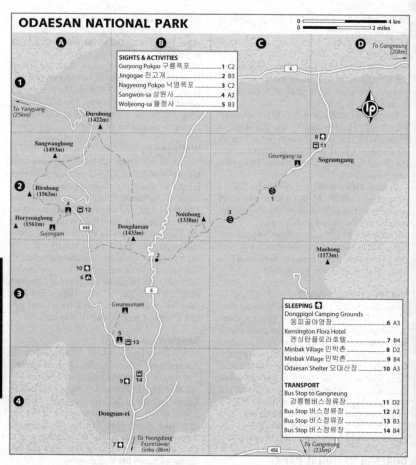

ODAESAN NATIONAL PARK

SIGHTS & ACTIVITIES		
Guryong Pokpo 구룡폭포	1	C2
Jingogae 진고개	2	B3
Nagyeong Pokpo 낙영폭포	3	C2
Sangwon-sa 상원사	4	A2
Woljeong-sa 월정사	5	B3

SLEEPING 🏠		
Dongpigol Camping Grounds 동피골야영장	6	A3
Kensington Flora Hotel 켄싱턴플로라호텔	7	B4
Minbak Village 민박촌	8	D2
Minbak Village 민박촌	9	B4
Odaesan Shelter 오대산장	10	A3

TRANSPORT		
Bus Stop to Gangneung 강릉행버스정류장	11	D2
Bus Stop 버스정류장	12	A2
Bus Stop 버스정류장	13	B3
Bus Stop 버스정류장	14	B4

Kensington Flora Hotel (켄싱턴플로라호텔; ☎ 330 5000; www.kensingtonflorahotel.co.kr; r W180,000, ste W280,000; ✄ 🖥) Formerly known as the Odaesan Hotel, this tall deluxe hotel is about 2.5km from the southern park entrance, with sweeping views all around. Rooms are suitably plush and during low season discounts of up to 50% are possible.

Getting There & Away

To get to the southern park entrance near Dongsan-ri, take an intercity bus from Gangneung (W3500, 50 minutes, every 10 minutes) to Jinbu. At Jinbu, local buses (W1100, 12 per day) run from the **bus terminal** (☎ 335 6307) to Woljeong-sa (20 minutes) and Sangwon-sa (another 20 minutes). Look for

the white buses towards the rear of the terminal lot. Bus schedules are helpfully posted at all these stops, or you can get them from Gangneung's tourist information centres.

To get to Sogeumgang, take local bus 303 (W1100, 50 minutes, hourly) from right outside the Gangneung bus terminal. It drops you at the *minbak* village; it's 500m to the park ranger station and the hiking trail begins another 500m beyond.

SAMCHEOK 삼척
pop 71,000

Sedate little **Samcheok** (www.samcheok.go.kr) is the gateway to an unusual mix of sightseeing spots. Within an hour's bus ride are spectacular limestone caves, an inimitable 'penis park' (phallic sculptures, not body parts) and pretty beaches tucked away in quiet coves. The town used to host a Penis Sculpture Festival, but that was shut down by Christian protesters. It still has a rousing Full Moon Festival in February, with tug-of-war competitions.

The only sightseeing spot in town is the **Mystery of Caves Exhibition** (동굴신비관; ☎ 574 6828; adult/youth/child W3000/2000/1500; ☽ 9am-6pm Mar-Oct, 9am-5pm Nov-Feb; ♿), in a building that resembles a wedding cake dripping with brown icing. The exhibits (some in English) contain elaborate detail on cave formation and there's a 20-minute IMAX film at 10.30am, 2pm and 3pm.

The **tourist information centre** (☎ 575 1330; ☽ 9am-6pm) is outside the express bus terminal and has English-speaking staff. Detailed bus schedules are available in English for buses to Hwaseongul, Daegeumgul and Haesindang Park (p194).

Sleeping & Eating

International Motel (국제 모텔; ☎ 575 5577; yjmb7878@korea.com; r without/with computer W30,000/35,000; ✉ 🖳) The spiffiest motel in the area, if you don't mind having your room number in bordello-like red lights over the door. Rooms are a little small, but with smart dark-wood decor and ultramodern bathrooms.

Hanil Motel (한일장; ☎ 574 8277; r without/with computer W30,000/40,000; ✉ 🖳) Run by a kindly *ajeossi* (middle-aged man), this motel is starting to look worn out but still has clean, decent rooms.

Eunmi Gamjatang (은미 감자탕; ☎ 574 5333; meals W5000-7000) This friendly eatery specialises in a hearty *gamjatang* (meaty bones and potato soup) served in a *jeongol* (hotpot) or *ttukbaegi* (뚝배기; earthenware dish); you'll need at least two people to order. Solo diners can try the *galbitang* or *yukgaejang* (spicy beef soup with vegetables).

Yeongbin (영빈; meals W5000-13,000) The seafood offerings here tend to be spicy, like *haemuljjim* or *agwijjim* (아귀찜; seafood or angler fish steamed in a spicy sauce). Milder options are the robust *haemultang* (spicy assorted seafood soup) or *haemul kalguksu*.

Getting There & Away

BUS

The express and intercity bus terminals sit beside each other. Express buses to Seoul

(W15,900, 3½ hours) run to Gangnam (every 35 minutes) and Dong-Seoul (hourly).

Intercity bus destinations include the following:

Destination	Price (W)	Duration	Frequency
Busan	27,400	5hr	9 daily
Daegu	27,500	6½hr	17 daily
Donghae	1500	20min	every 10min
Gangneung	4800	1hr	every 10min
Sokcho	11,800	2½hr	3 daily
Taebaek	5600	2hr	hrly
Wonju	10,300	3hr	3 daily

TRAIN

In 2007 Korail introduced a special **'seaside train'** (☎ 573 5473; www.seatrain.co.kr) between Samcheok and Gangneung. Train carriages have been remodelled so that passengers

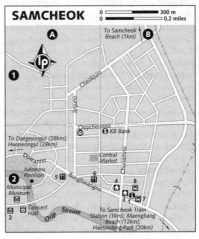

GANGWON-DO

face the extra-large windows looking out to sea (instead of the conventional front-back arrangement). From Samcheok, the train makes stops at Donghae, Jeongdongjin and several beach stations before terminating at Gangneung (W10,000 to W15,000, one hour 20 minutes). The sea views are lovely, but the route also passes some unattractive stretches of industrial landscape.

Trains depart Samcheok at 8.40am, 12pm and 4.10pm, and return from Gangneung at 10.30am, 2.15pm and 5.40pm.

AROUND SAMCHEOK
Hwaseongul & Daegeumgul
환선굴, 대금굴

Up in the mountains, just 28km from Samcheok, lie two immense limestone caves, each with its own charms. The majestic **Hwaseongul** (☎ 570 3255; adult/youth/child W4000/2800/2000; ☺ 8am-6pm Mar-Oct, 8.30am-5pm Nov-Feb) is one of the largest in Asia, with almost 2km of steel stairways that take visitors through cathedral-sized caverns – up, down and around its varied formations. As with many caves in Korea, while Hwaseongul's natural beauty is breathtaking, garish lighting and kitschy names have been added to 'enhance' the experience. Some nifty formations to look out for are the heart-shaped hole over the correspondingly named Bridge of Love, the rimstone that resembles a fried egg, and a difficult-to-spot calcite growth that resembles a tiny statue of the Virgin Mary.

Daegeumgul (adult/youth/child W12000/8500/6000; ☺ 8am-6pm Mar-Oct, 8.30am-5pm Nov-Feb) was opened to visitors in 2007 and can only be visited on a guided tour (one hour, every 30 minutes, Korean only), which starts with a 10-minute monorail ride up to the cave. The cave is much narrower than Hwaseongul, so it feels more intimate and some visitors wind up pawing every outcrop of limestone within reach (resist the urge to do so, as the oils and acids from human skin will discolour the elegant white rock). There's a fair bit of stair-climbing as you're taken to see an underground river and a 20m-high underground waterfall.

Between the two caves, Hwaseongul is the more impressive but Daegeumgul is easier if you don't relish the idea of hoofing up to the cave on your own. Both are cool inside (10°C to 14°C) and well-lit; a torch (flashlight) is not required.

Tickets for Hwaseongul can be purchased at the main **ticket booth** (☎ 570 3255), then it's a 30-minute climb to the cave entrance – gentle at first, steep-going for the last 500m. Tickets for Daegeumgul include the monorail ride and same-day admission to Hwaseongul. They can only be purchased online (http://samcheok.mainticket.co.kr) and the website accepts only credit cards issued by a Korean bank. Print your confirmation slip and present it at the ticket booth. The monorail station is 250m from the ticket booth.

GETTING THERE & AWAY
Bus 60 (W2700, 50 minutes, six daily from 6.10am to 6.50pm) heads from Samcheok's intercity bus terminal for the cave. The last bus leaves the caves at 7.30pm.

Haesindang Park 해신당 공원
Of all the things you'd expect to find in a fishing village like Sinnam (신남), odds are a **'penis park'** (☎ 570 3568; adult/youth/child W3000/2000/1500; ☺ 9am-6pm Mar-Oct, 9am-5pm Nov-Feb, closed Mon) is not one of them. There are over 50 phallic sculptures, some taking the form of park benches or drums. These carvings were entered for a contest in Samcheok's now-defunct Penis Sculpture Festival; today they attract joshing *ajumma* and *ajeossi* (middle-aged women and men). There's an elaborate series representing the 12 animals of the Chinese zodiac and outside the park stands a red lighthouse with the same, uh, peculiarities.

The phallic obsession originates with a local legend about a drowned virgin whose restless spirit was affecting the village's catch. A fisherman discovered that she could be appeased if he answered the call of nature while facing the ocean, so the village put up phalluses to placate her. A small shrine to this spirit stands at the seaward end of the park.

The park also contains the **Fishing Village Folk Museum** (어촌 민속 전시관), focusing on the history of fishing and shamanist rituals in the region, and sexual iconography in other cultures.

From Samcheok's intercity bus terminal, take bus 24 (W1600, 45 minutes, 20km, hourly) from the platform on the right. You can enter Haesindang Park from the top of the headland (where there's a huge parking lot) or from the entrance in Sinnam. The easier walk is to start at the top, work your way down and exit at the village.

Beaches

The closest beaches are **Samcheok Beach** (삼척 해수욕장), found immediately to the north of town, and **Maengbang Beach** (맹방 해수욕장), about 12km south. The former has shallow waters, making it popular with families, and the usual assortment of motels and restaurants. Maengbang Beach has no buildings, although tented stalls spring up during beach season (10 July to 20 August). It's less frantic than Samcheok Beach, but the downside is that it's about a 2km walk from the bus stop.

Bus 10 (W1100, 30 minutes, five daily) runs from Samcheok's intercity bus terminal to Samcheok Beach. Maengbang Beach is on the route for bus 24 (W1100, 25 minutes).

Donghae 동해
pop 96,000

The only reason to come to **Donghae** (www.dh.go.kr) is to catch the ferry service to the island of Ulleung-do (p222). If you have time to kill, there's a small cave, **Cheongok Donggul** (천곡동굴; ☎ 532 7303; adult/youth/child W4000/1100/700; ⏱ 8am-6pm), but it's paltry compared to those near Samcheok (opposite).

The ticket office for Cheongok Donggul doubles up as a **tourist information centre**.

SLEEPING & EATING

The better motels are near the defunct express bus terminal, near the intersection of Taepyeongno and Cheongongno. It costs less than W3000 for a taxi to the combined intercity-express bus terminal; motels near the latter look decidedly seedier.

Ritz Carlton Motel (리츠칼튼모텔; ☎ 533 2272; r without/with computer W30,000/35,000; 🅿 💻) Despite its dusty-looking exterior, this motel right beside the bus terminal vehicle entrance has clean and simple rooms.

Sam Motel (샘모텔; ☎ 532 1212; r W30,000; 🅿 💻) This pleasant-looking establishment has cosy rooms, some with faux Victorian fixings, others looking like they belong in an IKEA catalogue. Internet access is available in the lobby only. Look for the sand-coloured building with the sign 'Motel'.

Donghae Hilton Hotel (동해힐튼관광호텔; ☎ 533 7722; www.dhhilton.com; r W80,000; 🅿 💻) No relation to the Hilton chain, this stern-looking hotel has nice rooms, though not as nice as you'd expect for the price. Ask about discounts (up to 50%) in low season.

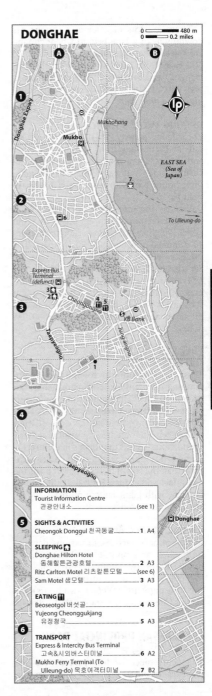

There are lots of cafes and restaurants downtown. In a lane behind Cheongongno are **Yujeong Cheonggukjang** (유정청국; ☎ 533 7222; meals W6500-13000), which specialises in *jeongsik*, and **Beoseotgol** (버섯골; ☎ 532 2632; meals W5000-15,000), which serves mushroom *jjigae* and *bibimbap*.

GETTING THERE & AWAY
The Ulleung-do **ferry** (☎ 531 5891; one way W49,000) sails at 10am daily from March to October and departs from the island at 5.30pm; departure times may vary. The crossing takes three hours. Non-Korean citizens must have their passport.

Express and intercity buses operate from the same terminal. Express buses to Seoul (W15,300, three hours) go to Gangnam (every 40 minutes) and Dong-Seoul (hourly). The intercity bus schedule almost mirrors the Samcheok schedule (p193).

Trains run to Gangneung (W2900, 45 minutes, 10 daily) and Seoul's Cheongnyangni station (W18,500, six hours, seven daily); the latter also stop at Taebaek (W3800, 1½ hours).

TAEBAEK 태백
pop 51,000 / elev 650m
This dinky mountain town is the main jumping-off point for visitors to Taebaeksan Provincial Park. The train station, bus terminal, **tourist information centre** (☎ 550 2828; http:// tour.taebaek.go.kr; 9am-5pm), accommodation and motels are bunched up around a small roundabout just off the town's main street. Taebaek has longer winters and cooler summers than the rest of the country. It hosts the lively **Taebaeksan Snow Festival** at the end of January, with giant ice sculptures, sledding and igloo restaurants.

Getting There & Away
Buses connect Taebaek to various destinations such as Dong-Seoul (W23,500, 5½ hours, every two hours) and Samcheok (W5600, 1¼ hours, hourly). Seven trains run to Gangneung (W6600, two hours) and Seoul's Cheongnyangni station (W14,700, 4½ hours) daily.

TAEBAEKSAN PROVINCIAL PARK 태백산 도립공원
The centrepiece of this **park** (☎ 550 2740; adult/youth/child W2000/1500/700; sunrise-sunset) is

Taebaeksan (Big White Mountain) – for shamanists, one of the most sacred mountains in Korea. Near its summit of Janggunbong (1568m) is **Cheonjedan** (천제단), an altar connected with Korea's mythical founder Dangun. The stark stone structure stands 3m high and is believed to have been used since the Shilla dynasty. Ceremonies are performed here on New Year's Day and during the Taebaek Festival (Taebaekje; 태백제) from 3 to 5 October. There is a shrine to Dangun (단군성전), with a rare outdoor statue of its namesake, about 800m from the park entrance.

Cheonjedan is a 4.5km hike northwest from the park entrance; allow 2½ hours to get there. The other peak, **Munsubong** (1546m), is 4km from the park entrance and 3km from Cheonjedan. The park is especially crowded during Taebaekje and when the royal azaleas bloom in June. Most of the hiking signs are in Korean only.

Near the park entrance is a shrine of a different sort: **Taebaek Coal Museum** (태백 석탄 박물관; ☎ 550 2743; admission included with park entrance fee; 9am-5pm), with a mine-head contraption at one end. The extensive exhibits document the history of coal mining in Korea and this region, which used to be the country's main coal-mining area.

If you're spending the night, the prefab-looking tourist village beside the park entrance is a nicer option than the town.

Getting There & Away
Bus 33 leaves from Taebaek's bus terminal (W1000, 25 minutes, every 30 minutes).

WONJU 원주
pop 306,000
The closest major town to Chiaksan National Park, **Wonju** (http://english.wonju.go.kr/) is home to several universities and military bases, so it has lots of young people hanging around and a rather chaotic intercity bus terminal. If you must spend the night, avoid the dingy area around the latter; there are nicer restaurants and (love) motels around the smart-looking express bus terminal.

There is no tourist information centre in Wonju.

Getting There & Away
From the **express bus terminal** (☎ 747 4181), buses run to Seoul Gangnam (W6500, 1½ hours,

every 20 minutes), Gangneung (W7200, 1½ hours, hourly) and Gwangju (W18,100, four hours, eight daily).

Buses from the **intercity bus terminal** (☎ 746 5223; www.wonjuterminal.co.kr) head to Cheongju (W8000, 1½ hours, hourly), Gangneung (W7200, 1½ hours, hourly) and Samcheok (W10,300, three hours, three daily).

Trains (W6300, 1¾ hours, hourly) run between Wonju and Seoul's Cheongnyangni station.

CHIAKSAN NATIONAL PARK
치악산 국립공원

This **park** (☎ 732 5231; http://chiak.knps.or.kr/Chiaksan _eng/; adult/youth/child W1600/600/300; ☺ sunrise-sunset) may be the smallest of the national parks in Gangwon-do, but it offers challenging hikes and is a very do-able weekend trip from Seoul. A popular but strenuous route starts from **Guryong-sa** (구룡사; Nine Dragon Temple) up to 1288m-high **Birobong** (three hours, 5.6km); it's possible to continue another 5.4km down to **Hwanggol** (황골; two hours). There are also hiking trails from Geumdae-ri and Seongnam-ri, running about 6km to the peak Namdaebong (1181m).

The main *minbak* and restaurant village is outside the Guryong-sa entrance. Camping is available at **Daegok** near Guryong-sa and **Geumdae-ri** (☎ 731-1289; small/large tent W3000/ W6000). There are no mountain shelters.

Getting There & Away
The park is 20km northeast of Wonju. To get to Guryong-sa, turn left as you exit Wonju's intercity bus terminal and walk to the T-junction. Use the underpass to cross the main road. From the bus stop on the other side, take buses 41 or 41-1 (W1100, 40 minutes, every 25 minutes), which drop you at the car park near the park entrance. Guryong-sa is 800m in.

To get to Hwanggol, go to the same underpass but don't cross the main road. Follow it to

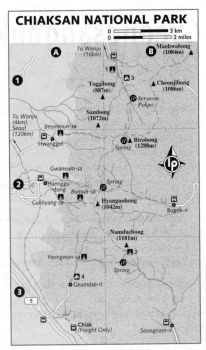

SIGHTS & ACTIVITIES
Guryong-sa 구룡사 1 B1
Sangwon-sa 상원사 2 B3

SLEEPING ☐
Daegok Camping Ground 대곡야영장 3 B1
Geumdae-ri Camping Ground 금대리야영장 4 A3

the right, which puts you at the bus stop. Bus 82 runs a loop service to Hwanggol (W1100, 30 minutes, hourly), while buses 21 to 25 run to Geumdae-ri and Seongnam-ri (W1100). At Hwanggol, the bus can be picked up at the stop opposite the Italian restaurant Pino.

All these buses also pass the Wonju train station.

Gyeongsangbuk-do
경상북도

Gyeongsangbuk-do's natural beauty is seconded only by its profusion of spectacular temples, ancient pagodas, rock-carved Buddhas and tombs. Gyeongju, once the capital of the Shilla dynasty (57 BC–AD 935), is often called 'the museum without walls' for its historical treasures, many of which are outdoors. The oddly symmetrical 'hills' in the centre of town are serene pyramids – stately reminders of the dead they still honour. Thankfully, this beautiful city was spared the ravages of bombings in the Korean War; even today it retains a 19th-century feel.

Come here and find treasures in all directions. Andong, in the north, offers mouth-watering mackerel, a fascinating folk village, strong *soju* (locally brewed vodka) and many temples. To the south, check out Daegu's medicinal herb market or walk through the crowds in the Yasigolmok to experience a wall-to-wall-people feel.

While technically in Gyeongsangbuk-do's southern sister (Gyeongsangnam-do), Haein-sa is a must-see temple-library most easily accessed via Daegu: check out the 1000-year-old wooden tablets, preserved in a building so ahead of its time that modern science hasn't improved it.

In the 'Sea of Korea', as Koreans call it, is the rugged island of Ulleung-do with seemingly endless opportunities to enjoy spectacular coastal landscapes. Even further east lies Dok-do (aka Takeshima), a fishing ground still disputed today.

GYEONGSANGBUK-DO

HIGHLIGHTS

- See and smell the fascinating **medicinal herb market** (p204) in Daegu
- Marvel at the 80,000-plus wooden tablets of the Buddhist sutras at the temple **Haein-sa** (p207)
- Slip back into the Shilla era in **Gyeongju** (p208)
- Walk along the rocky coast line of **Ulleung-do** (p222)
- Admire centuries-old architecture in **Hahoe** (p231) and **Andong** (p228)

Ulleung-do ★

Hahoe ★ ★ Andong

Daegu ★
★ Haein-sa
★ Gyeongju

■ TELEPHONE CODE: 054 (DAEGU: 053) ■ POPULATION: 5.1 MILLION ■ AREA: 20,023 SQ KM

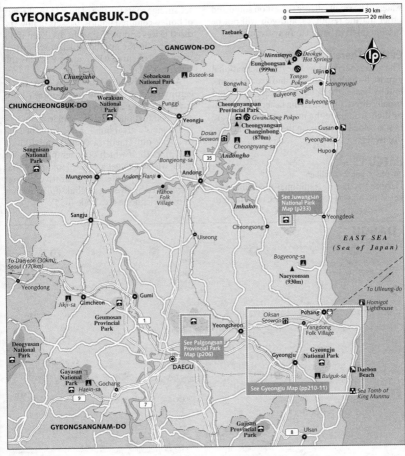

GYEONGSANGBUK-DO

History

This beautiful province holds many of South Korea's oldest treasures. Whether you plan on meandering through central Gyeongju or want to create your own elixir of eternal life in Daegu's herbal medicine market, you will find that the area's historical events are more tangible here, less a part of the distant past and more a part of the present. At the centre of South Korea, this area was once the capital of the Shilla empire (57 BC–AD 935), and as such was a central part of Korean government and trade. During this almost 1000-year-long empire, the Shilla rulers created alliances with China to defeat Japanese threats, as well as to repel other Korean invaders. During this time Confucian laws were widely adopted and informed all aspects of Korean life including who, where, and when a person could marry.

National Parks

Gyeongsangbuk-do's national parks provide wonderful hiking and photographic opportunities and are surprisingly close (thanks to KTX high-speed trains) to Seoul. Weekend trips to **Gyeongju National Park** (p214), **Palgongsan Provincial Park** (p206) or **Juwangsan National Park** (p232) will bring you face to face with stunning scenery and temples, and will be less peopled (even in the peak seasons) than some of the parks closer to Seoul.

The remote island of **Ulleung-do** (p222), although not a park proper, might just as well be one: its jagged cliffs plunge down into steel-blue waters. The small villages subsist on squid and other marine resources, and you will not be disappointed to be so far away from Seoul.

Getting There & Around

The area is serviced by Daegu's international airport, by high-speed KTX and express trains, and by buses (the latter are cheap, quick and usually direct, often arriving faster than a train or flight). Some of the more remote areas are best accessed by car or (in the case of Ulleung-do) by ferry.

DAEGU 대구
☎ 053 / pop 2.46 million

Daegu's fascinating traditional-medicine market is its biggest tourist draw. Come here to see strange roots the size of human thighs, jars of honey-coloured liquids, baskets of flowers, dried leaves and medicinal herbs. Even if it's pouring rain the avenues smell fragrantly of these ancient cures, which many Koreans still swear by today.

A simple, two-line subway system makes getting around easy, and the country's third largest city has great restaurants, good nightlife and neon that put parts of Seoul to shame.

Daegu is a great hub for day trips: be sure to check out Haein-sa (p207) and Jikji-sa (p207), both of which offer temple stays for those wishing to get a closer look. Note that Daegu is a separate administrative district surrounded by Gyeongsangbuk-do, which has its own telephone area code (054).

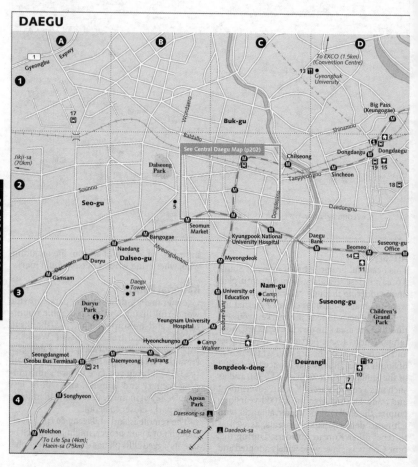

DAEGU

Orientation

At 885 sq km Daegu covers a larger area than Seoul. Most of the city's attractions are within easy walking distance from a subway station. Taxis are easy to find and most city sites can be reached with a W5000 fare. The airport is a 30-minute drive from the city, to the northeast.

Information

Daegu has a **tourist information centre** (☎ 053 1330, 627 8900; 🕑 9am-5pm) at all major transit points and destinations including the airport, outside Dongdaegu station, at Duryu Park (all Map pp200–1), in the central shopping district and by the herbal medicine market (both Map p202). All have comprehensive

local maps in English and reams of pamphlets. If you need online information, Dongdaegu station has internet terminals (W500 for 15 minutes).

Kyobo Books (Map p202; ☎ 425 3501; 2nd fl, Kyobo Bldg; 🕑 9.30am-5pm; 🔘 Line 1, Jungangno, Exit 2) is a good place for English-language books.

Sights & Activities
MARKETS & SHOPPING STREETS

Daegu is a shopper's dream. In addition to good prices on brand-name goods (clothes, shoes, bags etc) at the various department stores, Daegu has numerous speciality markets that make for a fascinating stroll even if you're not going to part with any won.

Start at the **Seomun Market** (서문시장; Map pp200–1; 🕑 9am-6pm Mar-Oct, 9am-5pm Nov-Feb, closed 2nd & 4th Sun; 🔘 Line 2, Seomun Market, Exit 1), a hulking, multistorey complex with over 4000 shops in six sections. Bustling yet orderly, it's

GYEONGSANGBUK-DO

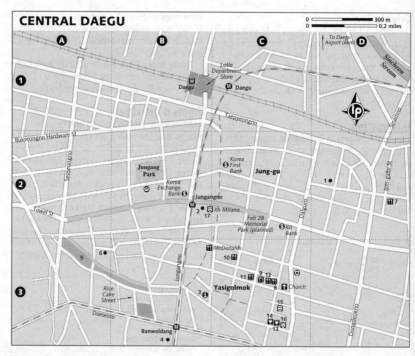

CENTRAL DAEGU

been one of Korea's big-three markets since 1669, even if the current buildings have little of that historic character. Outside the subway exit, turn 180 degrees and walk around the corner.

Yasigolmok (야시골목; Map p202; Ⓜ Line 1, Jungangno, Exit 2) is the heart of Daegu's shopping district, with clothing and fashion outlets, bustling day and night.

DAEGU NATIONAL MUSEUM
국립 대구 박물관

Maybe the best feature of this **museum** (Map pp200-1; ☎ 768 6051; http://daegu.museum.go.kr; admission free; ⏰ 9am-6pm Tue-Fri, 9am-7pm Sat, Sun & holidays, closed Mon) is the opportunity to see and understand the inside workings of an ancient burial tomb. The English-language signage is lacking so consider taking a free English tour (10am to 6pm Tuesday). From central Daegu take bus 242 or 427 to Daegu National Museum, or from Dongdaegu station take bus 814 or 514.

C & WOOBANG LAND C&우방 랜드

Got kids? Spend the day playing at this **amusement park** (Map pp200-1; ☎ 620 0100; day pass adult/youth/child W24,000/22,000/19,000; ⏰ 9.30am-10pm; Ⓜ Line 2, Duryu, Exit 12; 🚹) in the huge Duryu Park west of the city centre.

BULLO-DONG TUMULI PARK
불로동 고분 공원

If you're already in the north end of the city, stop by **Bullo-Dong Tumuli Park** (off Map pp200-1; ☎ 940 1224; admission free; ⏰ 9am-6pm), an enormous open space covering some 330,000 sq metres. The grassy hillocks rising like bumps across the valley are tumuli (burial mounds, similar to those in Gyeongju). Dating from the 2nd to the 6th century AD, the tumuli are for both nobles and commoners – the higher the location on the hill, the higher the status of the person.

PUBLIC BATHS

Greenvill (그린빌 찜질방 사우나; Map p202; ☎ 427 6665; admission W7000; ⏰ 24hr; Ⓜ Line 1 or 2, Banwoldang, Exit 1) is not large, but this modern and centrally located bath and *jjimjilbang* has a soothing mixure of hot, warm and cold tubs. The spacious *jjimjilbang* has a scorching-hot room (81°C) and an ice-cold room. It's a 24-hour facility, so guests can sleep overnight.

Life Spa (수목원 생월 온천; off Map pp200-1; ☎ 641 0100; www.lifespa.kr; admission W9000; ⏰ 24hr; 🚇 Line 1, Jincheon), in western Daegu, is a beautiful facility with 1100 sq metres of tubs and sweat rooms, a fitness centre and rooftop pools. Take the subway to Jincheon station, Exit 3. Walk to the intersection and turn right. From here, it's a quick taxi ride; ask for 'sumokwon saengwol oncheon' (수목원 생월 온천).

Tours

The city **tourist information centre** (☎ 627 8900; www.daegucitytour.com; adult/youth/child W5000/4000/3000) offers six themed tours to local attractions; prices do not include admissions, meals etc. Tour programs change weekly and reservations are required 24 hours in advance. To enquire or book a seat, go online or call the tour centre. Tour buses depart the tourist centres in Duryu Park and outside Dongdaegu train station.

Travellers with limited time might consider the **Palgongsan** tour (six daily departures starting at 10am; adult/youth W5000/3000; reservations not required). Jump on and off the bus at some of the area's best sites. Buy a ticket and get on the bus at the Dongdaegu station tourist information booth.

Sleeping

BUDGET & MIDRANGE

Rojan Motel (로잔 모텔; Map pp200-1; ☎ 766 0336; r W25,000; 🚇 Line 2, Beomeo, Exit 4) By far the best deal in Gyeongsangbuk-do, this spotless, no-frills motel offers clean, crisp sheets and a private bathroom. Credit cards accepted.

Hera Motel (헤라모텔; Map pp200-1; ☎ 958 2200; d/tw W50,000/70,000, add W10,000 weekends; 🚇 Line 1, Dongdaegu, Exit 1; ❄) If walking distance to Dongdaegu station is important, this nice-looking motel is one of the better choices in an area dominated by downtrodden inns with W30,000 rooms. Queen-sized beds, wide-screen TVs and modern bathrooms look great though some of the banged-up furnishings suggest this love motel sees a lot of in-out action. Turn right out of Dongdaegu station, walk to the pedestrian bridge, but do not cross. Walk right down the steps to the street. It's straight ahead on the right.

Hotel the Palace (Map pp200-1; ☎ 471 9911; www.gardenhotel.co.kr; d/tw/ste W60,000/65,000/120,000; 🚇 Line 1, Yeongnam University Hospital, Exit 2; ❄) The recent name change from the Garden Hotel to something more regal can't disguise the remarkably simple, at times drab, rooms and halls that could use a serious cleaning. It's near the US military camps and is used to catering to English-speaking guests.

Hotel Ariana (호텔 아리아나; Map pp200-1; ☎ 765 7776; www.ariana.co.kr; d/tw from W130,000/150,000; 🚇 Line 2, Beomeo, Exit 4; ❄ 💻) Nicely updated property with clean, sometimes characterless rooms, and baths equipped with plexiglass walls and oversized showerheads. It's near the Deurangil restaurant district.

TOP END

Hotel Inter-Burgo (인터불고 호텔; Map pp200-1; ☎ 6027-114; http://hotel.inter-burgo.com; r W126,000-319,000; 🚇 Line 1, Haean, Exit 3; ❄ 🅿 🏊) It's really two hotels in one. The older annex, with a hint of Spanish influences, has dated furnishings and lower prices compared with the newer, larger next-door property. Spend the afternoon in the beer garden beside the outdoor pool and waterfall.

Taegu Grand Hotel (대구 그랜드 호텔; Map pp200-1; ☎ 742 0001; www.taegugrand.co.kr; d/tw/ste from W214,000/214,000/300,000; 🚇 Line 2, Beomeo, Exit 3; ❄ 💻) This immaculate property blends minimalism with style and touches like king-sized beds and widescreen TVs. Room sizes vary, so ask for the Family Twin if you need more space.

Eating

Around the Yasigolmok district (Map p202) are literally hundreds of cafes, bars and nightclubs. For an impressive selection of restaurants, Deurangil (Map pp200–1) has close to 200 choices that include Korean *Hanu* beef as well as a variety of other Asian cuisines.

Gimbapjjang (김밥짱; Map p202; ☎ 425 0343; dishes W2000-4000; ☺ 10am-2am; ⊕ Line 1, Jungangno, Exit 2) Nearly across the street from Gaejeong, *naengmyeon* (냉면; buckwheat noodles in an icy broth) and *mandu* (만두; dumplings) are on the menu at rock-bottom prices.

Woo-hoo Sutbul Galbi (우후 숯불갈비; Map pp200–1; ☎ 958 2060; servings from W5000; ☺ noon-10pm) Fresh and economical *samgyupsal* (삼겹살; fatty pork) draws boisterous students from nearby Gyeongbuk University (note: sometimes spelled as Kyungpook University). The side dishes are minimal, the interiour is plain, but the meat quality is superb. After eating, spend the night exploring the nearby bars, coffee shops, singing rooms and pool halls. Take a taxi to Gyeongbuk University (경북대북문앞) and ask a student on the street for directions.

Gaejeong (개정; Map p202; ☎ 424 7051; dishes from W5500; ☺ 11am-10pm; ⊕ Line 1, Jungangno, Exit 2) A popular place specialising in chewy and tasty *naengmyeon* and soft tofu.

Bongsan Jjim-galbi (봉산 찜갈비; Map p202; ☎ 425 4203; dishes from W6000; ☺ 10am-10pm; ⊕ Line 1, Jungangno, Exit 2) Located on Daegu's famous *jjim-galbi* street, this quaint restaurant has been serving spicy steamed beef for 40 years. The friendly owner, Mr Choi, speaks English and is happy to accommodate customers who prefer less spice in their food.

Into (인투; Map p202; ☎ 421 3965; dishes from W8000; ☺ noon-11pm; ⊕ Line 1, Jungangno, Exit 2) A European cafe that serves fine pastas and tasty salads. With just four dining tables, it looks and smells like someone's home kitchen. French and Italian dishes are the specialities with a menu that changes regularly.

Seokryujip (석류집; Map pp200-1; ☎ 764 6100; meals from W8000; ☺ 10am-10pm; ⊕ Line 2, Beomeo, Exit 3) Dog or goat, which do you prefer? Try both at this slightly hidden shop and see for yourself if Korea's fabled stamina-producing food really works. From the main street, it's behind a petrol station.

Geumgok Samgyetang (금곡 삼계탕; Map p202; ☎ 424 4449; meals W10,000; ☺ 11am-10pm; ⊕ Line 1, Jungangno, Exit 2) A local favourite in easy walking distance of the downtown markets. Order one of the three menu items: ginseng-infused chicken, barbecue chicken, or a half-order of the latter (W5000).

Dijon (디존; Map p202; ☎ 422 2426; mains from W27,000; ☺ 11am-10pm, last order 9.30pm; ⊕ Line 1, Jungangno, Exit 2) Here's that romantic restaurant you were looking for. Come here for French and Mediterranean dishes like seared duck breast or roast pork with apple-cider sauce. And, first impressions inside the door are tasteful: a dimly lit ambiance, a hint of garlic in the air and a rose on every table.

Drinking

The central shopping district is teeming with *hof* (local pubs), singing rooms, bars and cafes. Daegu has a gay district with a few bars near the express bus terminal (Map pp200–1).

Dior is (Map pp200-1; ☎ 741 3655; drinks W3000; ☺ 10am-midnight Mon-Sat, 10am-10pm Sun; ⊕ Line 2, Beomeo, Exit 3) Superb coffee house with comfy sofas and a small outdoor patio. Outside Beomeo station, Exit 3. For java lovers, the late opening is irksome.

Tombo (톰보; Map pp200-1; ☎ 745 5425; drinks W3000-10,000; ☺ 8pm-3am; ⊕ Line 1, Dongdaegu, Exit 4.) Foreign visitors might start at this tiny shot

---

DAEGU'S HERBAL MEDICINE MARKET 한약 시장

This **market** (Map p202; ⊕ Line 1 or 2, Banwoldang, Exit 4), west of the central shopping district, has a history as vast as its scope. It dates from 1658, making it Korea's oldest and still one of its largest. Begin at the **Yangnyeong Exhibition Hall** (☎ 257 4729; admission free; ☺ 9am-5pm, closed Sun) for an introduction to *insam* (ginseng), reindeer horns and the people who popularised them – there's usually someone who speaks English at the tourist booth outside who'll show you around. Then head out to the street to stock up on everything from lizards' tails to magic mushrooms (the latter with a prescription, of course); you might also catch a glimpse of someone receiving acupuncture. On the days ending with 1 or 6 (except the 31st), *yangnyeong sijang* (a wholesale market) takes place downstairs in the exhibition hall.

bar near the express bus terminal for a mix of 20- to 40-somethings, both local and foreign.

Budha (부다; Map p202; ☎ 252 6835; side dishes W8000; ☻ 5pm-5am; ☻ Line 1 or 2, Banwoldang, Exit 3) One of the city's funkiest bars-restaurants. Wine bottles and candles line the entrance, there's a hint of incense in the air and private rooms are created by sheer drapes. Remove your shoes at the entrance. It's between the Bus pub and G2 club (below).

Bus (버스; Map p202; ☎ 427 3312; side dishes W10,000, drinks W3500-5000; ☻ 5pm-10am; ☻ Line 1 or 2, Banwoldang, Exit 3) This bus-turned-pub is on a side street right near G2 club. It's a popular hang-out for people in their 20s; if you're over 30, the staff won't let you in.

Entertainment

There is a huge Xn Milano complex that houses the Hanil Gukjang cinema (Map p202), where there are often English-language movies.

G2 (Map p202; ☎ 246 1623; admission before 11pm W6000, after 11pm W15,000; ☻ 8pm-9am; ☻ Line 1 or 2, Banwoldang, Exit 3) Bump around in trance-inducing, blacklit darkness. The funk, hip-hop and reggae are ear-splitting – just the way most of the crowd wants it.

Frog (Map p202; admission W12,000, US soldiers W5000; ☻ 9pm-6am; ☻ Line 1 or 2, Banwoldang, Exit 3) Five floors of hip-hop and electronic music for you and a few thousand of your closet friends.

Getting There & Away
AIR
Asiana and Korean Air connect Daegu with Seoul and Jeju. International destinations include Shanghai, Bangkok and Beijing.

BUS
There are five bus terminals (Map pp200–1): an **express bus terminal** (☎ 743 3701; ☻ Line 1, Dongdaegu, Exit 4), by Dongdaegu train station, plus Dongbu, Seobu, Nambu and Bukbu (east, west, south and north) intercity terminals. This list is not meant to be comprehensive, and note that buses to some destinations leave from multiple terminals, so it's best to inquire which is most convenient. Some bus terminals are connected by Daegu's subway system.

From the express bus terminal, which is three separate buildings each housing different companies:

Destination	Price (W)	Duration	Frequency
Andong	7300	1½hr	every 30min
Busan	6100	1¾hr	every 1-2hr
Daejeon	8400	2hr	every 3hr
Dongseoul	23,100	4hr	every 30min
Gyeongju	3900	50min	every 30-60min
Jinju	8900	2¼hr	hrly
Seoul	22,900	4hr	every 10min

From **Dongbu intercity bus terminal** (☎ 756 0017; ☻ Line 1, Dongdaegu, Exit 4):

Destination	Price (W)	Duration	Frequency
Gyeongju	3900	1hr	every 15min
Pohang	7400	1½hr	every 10min

From **Seobu intercity bus terminal** (☎ 656 2825; ☻ Line 1, Seongdangmot, Exit 3):

Destination	Price (W)	Duration	Frequency
Busan	8700	2hr	8 daily
Haein-sa	6200	1½hr	every 40min
Jinju	8100	2hr	every 30-60min
Tongyeong	12,000	2½hr	every 30-50min

From **Bukbu intercity bus terminal** (☎ 357 1851; ☻ Line 2, Duryu, Exit 1):

Destination	Price (W)	Duration	Frequency
Andong	6500	1½	every 30min
Chuncheon	16,600	5½hr	5 daily

TRAIN
Dongdaegu station (Map pp200–1), on the eastern side of the city, is the main station for long-distance trains. It's also near the express bus terminal. Daegu station, closer to downtown, is used mostly for *Tonggeun* (commuter-class) and *Mugunghwa* (semi-express) trains.

You'll find good connections to Seoul and Busan. KTX (high-speed) trains run every 10 to 30 minutes to Seoul (W34,200, two hours). Frequent KTX service to Busan is available (W10,800, one hour), though consider *Saemaul* (express; W10,300, 1¼ hours) or *Mugunghwa* (W7000, 1½ hours) services to increase your departure options without adding a significant amount of travel time. KTX service has frequent trains to Daejeon (W16,900, 45 minutes). Check www.korail.go.kr for schedules and fares.

Getting Around
TO/FROM THE AIRPORT
Daegu's airport is northeast of the city, about 2km from the express bus terminal. From

downtown, take Line 1 to Ayanggyo station, Exit 3, and catch bus 401, 101 or Express 1. A taxi from the airport to the centre will cost around W8000 and takes about 20 minutes.

BUS & SUBWAY

Local bus fares are W1100, but can vary with routes. To get to Deurangil from central Daegu or Dongdaegu station, take bus 401. From Dongdaegu train station, exit the building and walk right to the pedestrian bridge. Do not cross the bridge, instead walk right down the stairs. The bus stop is down the road.

Two subway lines crisscross the city centre. Tokens cost W1100.

AROUND DAEGU
Palgongsan Provincial Park
팔공산 도립공원

Just 20km north of Daegu, this park is sprawling, mountainous and well-visited. Its highest peak, **Palgongsan** ('Mountain of the Eight Meritorious Officers'; 1192m) received its name around the end of the Shilla period after

eight generals saved Wang-Geon, the founding king of the Goryeo kingdom.

The park's most popular destination is **Donghwa-sa** (동화사; ☎ 982 0101; admission W2500; ❧ 9am-6pm), the province's leading temple, with a history stretching back to AD 493.

Gatbawi (갓바위; ☎ 983 8586; www.seonbonsa. org; admission free) is a medicinal Buddha and national treasure, some 850m above sea level and said to date back to 638. This Buddha is famed for the flat stone 'hat' hovering over its head, 15cm thick. Incense wafts and mountain mist make it quite a spiritual experience. Plan on a challenging though enjoyable two-hour return trip from the bus stop. About 20 minutes into the hike, the trail leads to a small temple. For a longer though less-steep hike, pick up the dirt trail behind the temple. For a shorter though steeper walk up stone steps, turn left at the small pagoda in the temple compound. Note: the trails are often packed on weekends.

The **Palgongsan Skyline Cable Car** (☎ 982 8801; return W6000; ❧ 9.45am-sunset) is the quickest way to ascend Palgongsan. The 1.2km-long ride

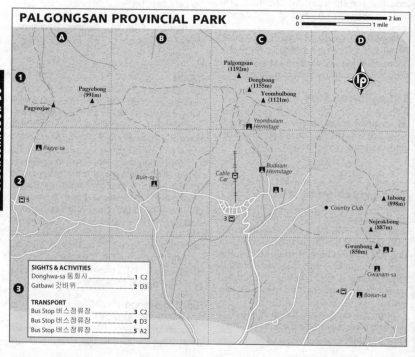

PALGONGSAN PROVINCIAL PARK

drops you at the observatory (820m), which affords a panoramic view of Daegu.

Bus 401 (W1100) runs between Dongdaegu station and the tourist village below Gatbawi. Bus 급행 (Geuphaeng; W1300) connects Donghwa-sa and the bus stop near Dongdaegu station, running at least once every 12 minutes and taking 50 minutes to complete the journey.

Haein-sa 해인사

This Unesco World Heritage **temple** (☎ 055-931 1001; admission W3500; ✆ 8-11am & noon-5pm Wed-Mon) should be on every visitor's not-to-be-missed list.

Haein-sa holds 81,258 woodblock scriptures, making it one of the largest Buddhist libraries of its kind. Known as the **Tripitaka Koreana** (see the boxed text, p208), the blocks are housed in four buildings at the temple's upper reaches, complete with simple but effective ventilation to prevent deterioration. Although the buildings are normally locked, the blocks are easily visible through slatted windows.

As well as being one of Korea's most significant temples, Haein-sa is also one of the most beautiful. Part of its beauty lies in the natural setting of mixed deciduous and coniferous forest. At prayer times (3.30am, 10am and 6.30pm), the place can feel otherworldly.

The main hall, **Daegwangjeon**, was burnt down during the Japanese invasion of 1592 and again (accidentally) in 1817, though miraculously the Tripitaka escaped destruction. It escaped a third time, during the Korean War, when a South Korean pilot working for the Allied forces refused to allow them to bomb it.

The **Haein-sa museum** (☎ 055-934 3150; admission W2000; ✆ 10am-5.30pm, closed Tue) showcases temple treasures and has a reverie on Haein-sa in contemporary art upstairs. It is a short walk from the main road, and the temple is a further 15-minute walk. At the time of research the museum was closed for remodelling.

Hikers will want to challenge **Gayasan** (1430m), the main peak in the national park, and a pretty one, though the 1100m stretch up from Haein-sa is known to be tough.

SLEEPING & EATING

Haein-sa is a popular day trip from Daegu, but there are options to spend the night. Probably the most interesting is Haein-sa itself,

which participates in the **temple stay program** (http://80000.or.kr; weekdays/weekends W30,000/50,000). Don't expect luxury – men and women sleep in separate *ondol* (underfloor-heated) dorms, but it's a worthwhile option to experience the 3.30am prayer service.

Gobau (고바우; ☎ 932 5599; r W30,000; meals W9000) A beautiful place to stay with kind owners. Rooms are simple, comfy, clean and floor-heated, with yellow linoleum. Try the restaurant (open 7am to midnight) where *sanchae jongsik* (산채 정식; rice with vegetables) is the main dish.

Haeinsa Hotel (해인관광 호텔; ☎ 933 2000; www.haeinhotel.co.kr; d/tw/ste W87,000/94,000/200,000; ✖) Comfort at the top of the hill, with fountains, a polished lobby, coffee shop, restaurant and sauna. The hotel offers a weekday discount.

Jeonju (전주; ☎ 931 2323; www.jjbab.com; dishes W5000-10,000; ✆ 7am-9pm) Who would have thought bus-terminal food could be this good? On the 2nd floor, this shop serves tasty *bibimbap* (비빔밥; vegetables, meat and rice). For a uniquely Korean countryside experience, check out the toilet.

GETTING THERE & AWAY

Although it's in Gyeongsangnam-do, Haein-sa is most easily accessed by bus (W6200, 1½ hours, every 40 minutes) from Daegu's Seobu (south) intercity bus terminal.

Jikji-sa 직지사

Jikji-sa (☎ 436 6084; adult/youth/child W2500/1500/1000; ✆ 7am-6.30pm Mar-Oct, 7am-5.30pm Nov-Feb) is a postcard-pretty temple in a quiet forest. The delicate paintings on the temple buildings have a refinement and grace that is very appealing, as are the giant timbers that support the structures, and the faded, cracked wood.

Of the 40 original buildings, about 20 still exist, the oldest dating from the 1602 reconstruction. Highlights include the **Daeungjong**, with stunning Buddhist triad paintings on silk (1774) that are national treasures, and the rotating collection in the temple's **Buddhist art museum** (☎ 436 6009; admission W1000; ✆ 9am-5.30pm Mar-Oct, 9am-4.30pm Nov-Feb, closed Mon).

SLEEPING & EATING

Many visitors day trip to Jikji-sa, while some join the **temple stay program** (☎ 436 6084; http://eng.templestay.com; per night W50,000). There's a well-established tourist village by the bus stop with

---

TRIPITAKA KOREANA

The **Tripitaka Koreana**, also known as the Goryeo Buddhist canon, is one of the world's most significant Buddhist sacred texts. Tripitaka literally means 'three baskets', representing the three divisions of Buddhism: the Sutra (scriptures), Vinaya (laws) and the Abhidharma (treatises).

The Tripitaka Koreana has been preserved on more than 80,000 beautifully carved woodblocks, which took 16 years to complete. The first set of blocks, completed in 1087, was destroyed by Mongolian invaders in 1232. A reconstructed set, the one on display today, was completed in 1251. From carefully selecting appropriate birch wood, then soaking it in brine and boiling it in salt before drying it, to locating and constructing a sophisticated repository, the techniques involved were so complex and the artwork so intricate that they remain an inspiration today. The woodblocks are housed and preserved in the 15th-century hall, **Janggyong Pango**, a masterpiece of ingenuity in its own right; its techniques include charcoal beneath the clay floor and different-sized windows to minimise variations in humidity. Despite the ravages of Japanese invasion and fires that destroyed the rest of the temple complex, the repository remained standing with the woodblocks preserved intact.

During the 1970s, President Park Chung-hee ordered the construction of a modern storage facility for the woodblocks. The facility was equipped with advanced ventilation, temperature and humidity control. However, after some test woodblocks began to grow mildew the whole scheme was scrapped. Today the four storage halls and woodblocks are inscribed on the Unesco World Heritage list to ensure their continued preservation. In a bold attempt to ensure accessibility to more people, Haein-sa's monks have completely transcribed the works onto a single CD-ROM and translated the classical Chinese text into modern-day Korean.

---

minbak (private homes with rooms for rent), *yeogwan* (budget motels) and restaurants.

GETTING THERE & AWAY

Jikji-sa is reached via Gimcheon (population 152,000), about 20 minutes by bus. Local buses 11, 111, and 112 (W1300) depart every 10 minutes from Gimcheon's **intercity bus terminal** (☎ 432 7600). The temple complex is a pleasant 15-minute walk from the bus stop.

Gimcheon can be reached by train on the line connecting Daegu (50 minutes) and Seoul. If you're using KTX from Seoul, transfer at Daejeon and take a local line to Gimcheon.

By bus:

Destination	Price (W)	Duration	Distance
Andong	10,200	2hr	125km
Daegu	4600	1¼hr	88km
Daejeon	5400	1¼hr	88km
Gochang*	5700	1¼hr	65km

*for Haein-sa & Gayasan National Park

GYEONGJU 경주
pop 280,000

Known as 'the museum without walls', Gyeongju holds more tombs, temples, rock carvings, pagodas, Buddhist statuary and palace ruins than any other place in South Korea. And like most museums, not everything is worth seeing. Most visitors touring the city centre are taken aback by the distinctive urban landscape created by round grassy tombs – called tumuli – and traditional architecture with colourful hip roofs set against a canvas of green rolling mountains.

Two of Gyeongju's not-to-be-missed sites – Bulguk-sa and Seokguram – are in the outlying districts and within reach via public transport. Gyeongju covers a vast area – some 1323 sq km – so plan on several days of travel if you want to visit some of the lesser-known places. Bus transport to these areas is satisfactory though personal transport is a better option if you value speed and flexibility.

In 57 BC, around when Julius Caesar was subduing Gaul, Gyeongju became the capital of the Shilla dynasty, and it remained so for nearly 1000 years. In the 7th century AD, under King Munmu, Shilla conquered the neighbouring kingdoms of Goguryeo and Baekje, and Gyeongju became capital of the whole peninsula. The city's population eventually peaked at around one million, but as empires do, Shilla eventually fell victim to division from within and invasion from without.

The city began a cultural revival in the late 20th century – with much preservation and restoration work thanks to President Park Chung-hee in the 1970s.

Orientation & Information

Central Gyeongju is compact, encompassing the bus and train terminals (20 minutes' walk apart) and, between them, sights, lodgings and dining.

About 5km east of the centre is Bomunho, a lakeside resort with a golf course, luxury hotels and posh restaurants. A 16km drive southeast brings you to Bulguk-sa, one of Korea's most famous temples. From here it's a quick ride to Seokguram, a mountain grotto with a historic Buddha.

There are central **tourist information kiosks** (Map p212; express bus terminal ☎ 772 9289; train station ☎ 772 3842) and in the car park near Bulguk-sa (Map pp210–11), all with English-speaking staff and comprehensive English-language maps.

Sights

CENTRAL GYEONGJU

Tumuli Park

The huge, walled **Tumuli Park** (Map p212; ☎ 746 6317; admission W1500; 9am-10pm) has 23 tombs of Shilla monarchs and family members. From the outside, they look like grassy hillocks – much more subtle than the Egyptian pyramids, but they served the same purpose; many of the tumuli have yielded fabulous treasures, on display at the Gyeongju National Museum (right). On colder days, the park closes at sunset.

One of the tombs, **Cheonmachong** (Heavenly Horse Tomb), is open to visitors. A cross-section display shows its construction. The tomb is 13m high and 47m in diameter and was built around the end of the 5th century. Facsimiles of the golden crown, bracelets, jade ornaments, weapons and pottery found here are displayed in glass cases around the inside of the tomb.

Noseo-dong Tombs

Across the street and closer to the main shopping area is the Noseo-dong district (Map p212), where there are other Shilla tombs for which there is no entry fee. **Seobongchong** and **Geumgwanchong** are adjacent tombs built between the 4th and 5th centuries. They were excavated between 1921 and 1946, the finds including two gold crowns. Across the road is **Bonghwadae**, the largest extant Shilla tomb at 22m high and with a circumference of 250m; adjoining is **Geumnyeongchong**. Houses covered much of this area until 1984, when they were removed.

Respect these places – do not climb or picnic on them.

Wolseong Park

Southeast of Tumuli Park, this park has the Far East's oldest astrological observatory, **Cheomseongdae** (Map p212; ☎ 772 5134; admission W500; 8am-6pm Apr-Oct, 9am-6pm Nov-Mar), constructed between AD 632 and 646. Its apparently simple design conceals amazing sophistication: the 12 stones of its base symbolise the months of the year. From top to bottom there are 30 layers – one for each day of the month – and a total of 366 stones were used in its construction, corresponding to the days of the year (OK, maybe it was a leap year). Numerous other technical details relate, for example, to the tower's position in relation to certain stars.

A few minutes' walk south from Cheomseongdae is the site of **Banwolseong** (Castle of the Crescent Moon; Map pp210-11; admission free), once a fabled fortress. Now it's attractive parkland, with some walls and ruins. The only intact building is **Seokbinggo** or 'Stone Ice House' (early 18th century, restored 1973), which was once used as a food store.

Anapji Pond

Today, **Anapji Pond** (Map pp210-11; ☎ 772 4041; admission W1000; 8am-sunset Sep-May, 7.30am-7pm Jun-Aug) is a popular spot for couples to take prewedding photos. From June to early August, magnificent lotus blossoms seem to fill the horizon.

In the past, it was a pleasure garden to commemorate the unification of the Korean peninsula under Shilla. The buildings here burned in 935 and many relics ended up in the pond itself, to be rediscovered only when it was drained for repair in 1975. Thousands of well-preserved relics were found including wooden objects, a die used in drinking games, scissors and a royal barge – you can see them in the Gyeongju National Museum (below).

Gyeongju National Museum

국립경주박물관

Arguably the best history museum in Korea, the **Gyeongju National Museum** (Map pp210-11; ☎ 740 7518; http://gyeongju.museum.go.kr; admission free; 9am-6pm, until 9pm Sat & holidays Mar-Dec) is where you can appreciate the significance of this ancient city in one fell swoop. In addition to the main hall, you'll find an entire building devoted to the findings at Anapji Pond and an art hall focusing on Buddhist works.

GYEONGJU

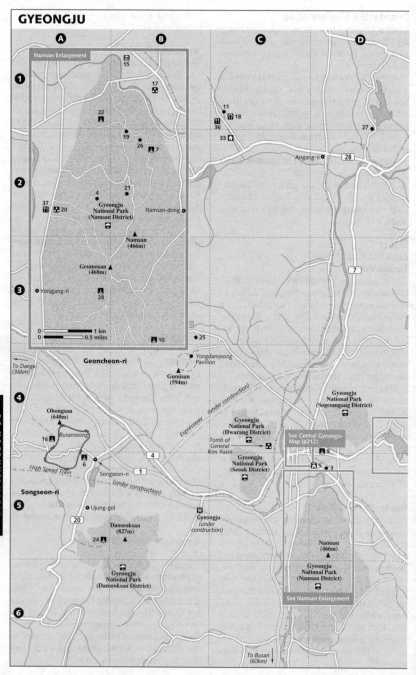

Namsan Enlargement

15

17

11
18

36

33

Angang-ri

28

19
26
7

22

27

4
21

37
20

Gyeongju National Park
(Namsan District)

Namsan-dong

Namsan
(466m)

Geumosan
(468m)

Yongjang-ri

28

0   1 km
0   0.5 miles

10

25

Geoncheon-ri

Yongdamjeong
Pavilion

Gumisan
(594m)

To Daegu
(36km)

Expressway (under construction)

Gyeongju
National Park
(Sogeumgang District)

Obongsan
(640m)

Busanseong

16

Gyeongju
National Park
(Hwarang District)

Tomb of
General
Kim Yusin

See Central Gyeongju
Map (p212)

9

6

High Speed Train

Songseon-ri

(under construction)

Gyeongju
National Park
(Seoak District)

5
3

Songseon-ri

Ujung-gol

20

Danseoksan
(827m)

24

Gyeongju
(under
construction)

Namsan
(466m)

Gyeongju
National Park
(Danseoksan District)

Gyeongju
National Park
(Namsan District)

See Namsan Enlargement

To Busan
(60km)

GYEONGSANGBUK-DO

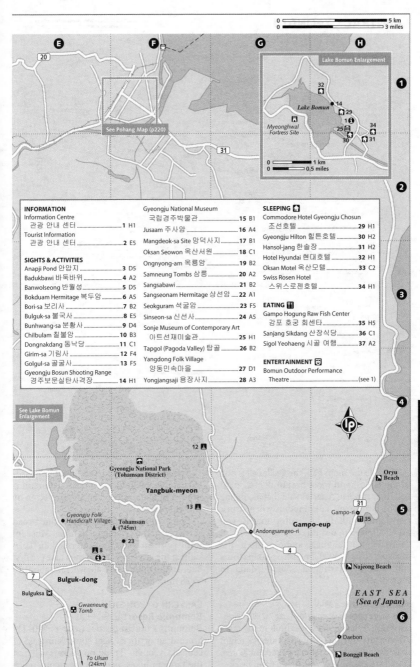

GYEONGSANGBUK-DO

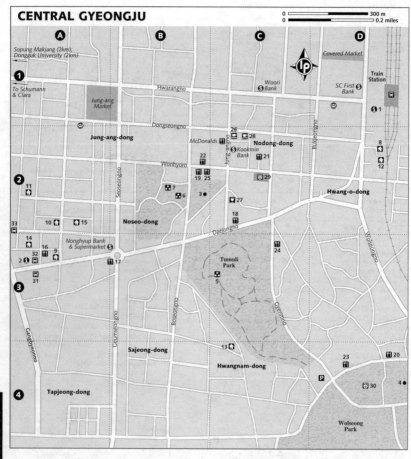

CENTRAL GYEONGJU

Outside the main hall, the **Emille Bell** is one of the largest and most beautifully resonant bells ever made in Asia. It's said that its ringing can be heard over a 3km radius when struck only lightly with the fist. Unfortunately, you aren't allowed to test this claim.

An English-language audio guide to the museum costs W3000. English-speaking tours run Saturdays starting at 1.30pm (March to November).

Bunhwang-sa 분황사
This large **pagoda** (Map pp210-11; ☎ 742 9922; admission W1300; ☽ sunrise-sunset) was built in the mid-7th century during Queen Seondeok's reign, making it the oldest datable pagoda in Korea. It's a rare example of one made from brick.

The magnificently carved Buddhist guardians and stone lions are a main feature; it is unique in that each entrance is protected by two guardians.

To get here, follow the willow-lined road across from the Gyeongju National Museum until you reach the first intersection. Turn right at the intersection and then take the first lane on the right. The walk will take about 20 to 25 minutes.

EASTERN GYEONGJU
Bomunho Resort 보문 단지
Bomun is a tourist district (Map pp210–11) around an artificial lake some 5km east of central Gyeongju. Tradition-seekers will find the tandem bikes, paddle boats, conference

centres and such less appealing, but it is home to Gyeongju's top-end lodgings. The lake and extensive parklands are great for strolling or bike riding, though the area doesn't have the character of the town centre.

The **Sonje Museum of Contemporary Art** (Map pp210-11; ☎ 745 7075; www.artsonje.org; admission W3000; ☒ 10am-6pm, closed Mon), behind the Hilton Hotel, holds three exhibition spaces with seasonal exhibitions plus a permanent collection containing paintings, sculpture and mixed media. Hardly a must-see for art enthusiasts, it's a worthwhile stop if you're already in the area.

Traditional dancing and musical performances are held on a regular basis from April to October at **Bomun Outdoor Performance Theatre**, located below the information centre by the lake.

If history and hiking are wearing thin, the **Gyeongju Bosun Shooting Range** (Map pp210-11; ☎ 741 7007; www.kjshooting.com; 10 bullets from W20,000; ☒ 11am-9pm Mon-Fri, 10am-9pm Sat & Sun) is something different. Choose a pistol from the menu, put on the goggles and earphones and take 10 shots at a paper target. It's in a small plaza next to the Daemyung Resort hotel.

Bulguk-sa 불국사

On a series of stone terraces about 16km southeast of Gyeongju, set among gnarled pines and iris gardens that would make Van Gogh swoon, this **temple** (Map pp210-11; ☎ 746 9913; adult/youth/child W4000/3000/2500; ☒ 6.30am-6pm Apr-Oct, 7am-5pm Nov-Mar) is the crowning glory of Shilla architecture and is on the Unesco World Cultural Heritage list. The excellence

of its carpentry, the skill of its painters (particularly the interior woodwork and the eaves of the roofs) and the subtlety of its landscapes all contribute to its magnificence.

The approach to the temple leads you to two national-treasure '**bridges**' (now closed for preservation). One of these bridges has 33 steps, representing the 33 stages to enlightenment. Two more national treasures are the pagodas standing in the courtyard of the first set of buildings that somehow survived Japanese vandalism. The first, **Dabotap**, is of plain design and typical of Shilla artistry, while the other, **Seokgatap**, is much more ornate and typical of the neighbouring Baekje kingdom. The pagodas are so revered that replicas appear in the grounds of the Gyeongju National Museum (p209).

You can reach Bulguk-sa from central Gyeongju via buses 10 or 11 (W1500). There's a **tourist information booth** (☎ 746 4747) in the car park, near the bus stop.

Seokguram Grotto 석굴암

In the mountains above Bulguk-sa is the famous grotto of **Seokguram** (Map pp210-11; ☎ 746 9933; adult/child/youth W4000/3000/2500; ☒ 6.30am-6pm Apr-Oct, 7am-5.30pm Nov-Mar), also on the Unesco World Cultural Heritage list. Chipmunks dance in the thick woods leading up to the rotunda, where sits an image of the Sakyamuni Buddha surrounded by over three dozen guardians and lesser deities. This Buddha's position looking out over the East Sea (visible in clear weather) has long made him regarded as a protector of his country.

Seokguram was quite a feat of engineering when it was constructed in the mid-8th century. Huge blocks of granite were quarried far to the north at a time when the only access to the Seokguram site (740m above sea level) was a narrow mountain path. Seokguram can be a magical place, especially when it is raining and the mists cloak the mountaintops.

Buses run hourly between the car parks for Bulguk-sa and Seokguram (W1500, 15 minutes). From the Seokguram car park, it is a 400m walk along a shaded gravel track and up the stairs to the grotto. Alternatively, there is a hiking trail between the Seokguram ticket office and Bulguk-sa (about 3.2km).

Golgul-sa 골굴사

Finally, a **temple** (Map pp210-11; ☎ 744 1689; www.sunmudo.com; admission free) where you can do more than just look around. The Buddha carved out of solid rock by Indian monks in the 6th century is kind of interesting but the real draw here, attracting 2000 international visitors every year, is *sunmudo,* a Korean martial art that blends fighting skills with meditation. Short 20-minute demonstrations take place at 3pm Sundays at **Sunmudo University** on the temple grounds and *sunmudo* training is available through the **temple stay program** (per night incl meals W40,000). Reservations are recommended though not always necessary. Most of the program is taught in English.

From Gyeongju intercity bus terminal, take a bus towards Gampo-ri or Yangbuk-myeon (bus 100 or 150) and ask the driver to drop you off at Andongsamgeo-ri, where the turn-off to the temple goes off to the left. Golgul-sa is a 20-minute walk down the road.

Girim-sa 기림사

About 3.5km down the road from Golgul-sa, **Girim-sa** (Map pp210-11; ☎ 744 2922; admission W3000; ⏲ 8am-8pm) is one of the largest complexes in the vicinity of the Shilla capital. Its size (14 buildings and growing) compares with that of Bulguk-sa, but the compound lacks a 'wow' factor, which might explain why it receives comparably fewer visitors.

From Golgul-sa, there is no public transport to Girim-sa. If you're without personal transport, the choices are walking 3.5km down the road alongside rice paddies, or asking for a lift.

Gampo-ri 감포

About 44km east of Gyeongju City, **Gampo-ri** (Map pp210–11) is a tiny coastal village famous for raw fish and king crab. It's also a convenient pit stop for road trips along the rugged eastern shoreline.

Driving your personal transport to Gampo-ri from Gyeongju is the most attractive travel option. The road twists and turns through the rolling green mountains of Gyeongju National Park. Buses depart Gyeongju intercity bus terminal every 20 to 30 minutes (W1500).

SOUTHERN GYEONGJU (NAMSAN) 남산

This mountain, south of the city centre, is one of the region's most rewarding areas to explore, a place where you can easily combine the athletic with the spiritual. It's beautiful, and strewn with relics, active temples, monasteries and sites for impromptu religious observance. Among the relics found (so far) are 122 temple sites, 64 stone pagodas, 57 stone Buddhas, and many royal tombs, rock-cut figures, pavilions and the remains of fortresses, temples and palaces.

You can choose from hundreds of paths, many of which run alongside streams that tumble down the mountain. The paths and tracks are well trodden, though at times you will need to head off the main trails to scout for relics that are not immediately visible, since only a few of them are signposted. See the boxed text, opposite, for some day-hike suggestions.

You can also check with tourist offices at Gyeongju or Bomunho for additional maps and information about trail conditions.

Buses 11, 500, 501, 503, 505, 506, 507 and 591 all pass by Namsan.

Samneung 삼릉

The only reason to come to this **pine grove** (Map pp210-11; admission free; ⏲ 24hr) is to start a hike up Namsan; see the boxed text, opposite. On your way up, you may pass the tumuli of three Shilla kings. Another tomb, located away from the others, is said to contain King Gyeongae, who was killed when robbers raided Poseokjeongji during an elaborate banquet, setting the stage for the dynasty's collapse.

Tours

Korean-language **tour buses** (☎ 743 6001; 6-9hr tours excl lunch & admissions; W7000-12,000) access all the sights and depart from the intercity bus terminal (Map p212) at 8.30am and 10am.

NAMSAN DAY HIKING ROUTES

Central Namsan

There are numerous trails through Namsan; the most convenient starting at Samneung (Map pp210-11). Whichever route you take, be sure to include detours – necessary to hunt for relics off-track. There's virtually no English signage, but with some *hangeul* (Korean phonetic alphabet) skill you should do fine. If the weather's clear, you can be assured of fine views and reasonable trails.

Three-hour course Head up from Samneung, breaking to take in several relief carvings and statues along the way, to the hermitage **Sangseonam** (상선암), where you'll find lovely views across the valley and maybe a monk chanting. Continue up past the rock formation **Badukbawi** (바둑바위) and along the ridge to **Sangsabawi** (상사바위), then walk back the way you came.

Five-hour course Instead of doubling back from Sangsabawi, continue on to the summit of **Geumosan** (금오산, 468m) to **Yongjangsaji** (용장사지, Yongjang temple site), where you can view the seated Buddha image carved in stone and the three-storey stone pagoda. Descend to **Yongjang-ri** (용장리, Yongjang village), from where you can catch a bus back to central Gyeongju.

Eight-hour course Follow the route as far as Yongjangsaji, but instead of heading down towards Yongjang-ri head across the ridge to **Chilbulam** (칠불암, hermitage of seven Buddhas), Namsan's largest relic with images carved in natural rocks and stone pillars. From here it's mostly downhill towards the road and about another 1km to **Namsan-dong** (남산리, Namsan village) on the eastern side of the park, from where it's an easy bus ride back to town.

Northeastern Namsan

Take local bus 11 from Gyeongju and get off as soon as the bus crosses the river, about 2.5km past the Gyeongju National Museum. Off the main road is a fork – take the left branch and you can wind your way to **Bori-sa** (보리사), a beautifully reconstructed nunnery set amid old-growth trees and ancient images. It is possible to head over the hill behind Bori-sa to **Tapgol** (탑골, Pagoda Valley), but it's a rough climb. It's easier to backtrack down to the fork and take the other branch. Follow the river for several hundred metres until you come to a small village. Turn left here and head up the road through Tapgol and you'll reach the secluded hermitage **Ongnyong-am** (옥룡암). In the upper corner are ponderous boulders covered with Korea's greatest collection of **relief carvings**.

Returning to the bridge and looking towards the main road, you will see two **stone pillars** standing in a thicket of trees amid rice paddies. These pillars are all that remain standing of **Mangdeok-sa**, a huge Shilla-era temple complex. From there it's an easy trip back towards the National Museum, about 20 minutes. Depending on your route, this itinerary might take you a half-day.

Sleeping

Lodgings are everywhere, so finding a room in and around the bus terminals and train station to match your budget won't be a problem. Higher-end lodgings and restaurants are at Bomunho, with some less expensive options just east from the lake.

Other motels are sprinkled around the western area of Central Gyeongju and offer a similar price and quality to those listed.

BUDGET

Hanjin Hostel (한진 여관; Map p212; ☎ 771 4097; http://hanjinkorea.wo.to; dm/s/tw W15,000/30,000/40,000;

💻) You'll either love it here or it will freak you out. The rooms are dingy, but the walls are covered with paintings by the owner's daughter. The kitchen, courtyard and roof deck are great places to commune with other travellers. The owner speaks English and Japanese and hands out free maps.

Nakwon-jang Yeoinsuk (낙원장 여인숙; Map p212; ☎ 742 4977; s/d W15,000/20,000) Clean, simple, fan-cooled *ondol*-style rooms steps away from the train station. Many have no shower, just a hose with which to splash yourself.

Arirang-jang Yeoinsuk (아리랑장 여인숙; Map p212; ☎ 772 2460; r W20,000) Shabby but inexpensive, this place has tiny, odd-shaped *ondol* rooms. It's close to the train station, right behind the bakery.

Sarangchae (사랑채; Map p212; ☎ 773 4868; www.kjstay.com; s/d & tw incl breakfast from W20,000/30,000; ▢) This place has lots of character and a hostel-type atmosphere in a traditional Korean house offering rooms with *ondol* or beds. It's well decorated, has a courtyard, kitchen, internet, laundry machines and friendly owners who speak English. It is centrally located, right behind the south wall of Tumuli Park. Booking ahead is essential.

Taeyang-jang Yeogwan (태양장 여관; Map p212; ☎ 773 6889; r Sun-Fri/Sat W25,000/30,000; ✖) Right near the Hanjin Hostel, this spotless motel has a rock garden in the lobby and a friendly owner. Thick velour curtains give the otherwise plain rooms a Victorian feel.

MIDRANGE

Two nice choices are in Bomunho. There are lots of options near the bus terminals.

Hansol-jang (한솔장; Map pp210-11; ☎ 748 3800; fax 748 3799; r from W40,000; ✖) Simple rooms, both *ondol* and beds, each with a tiny balcony and decor that draws extensively on orange. It's located on a small road opposite the Hilton hotel; the main feature here is quiet surroundings off the beaten path, though Bomunho is just a 15-minute walk away. Rates jump on weekends and during the summer.

Hotel Cherbourg (쉘브르 모텔; Map p212; ☎ 777 1930; r from W40,000, Sat W70,000; ✖ ▢) Swanky rooms with cool amenities like wide flatscreen TVs, cosy faux-wood floors and open concept bathrooms. One of many new motels behind the intercity bus terminal, this one is almost as good as the others and a little cheaper.

Show Motel (쇼모텔; Map p212; ☎ 771 7878; r from W50,000, Sat W80,000; ✖ ▢) One of the snazziest motels behind the bus terminal. There's lots of attention to detail in the rooms, like LAN connections, up-to-date desktop computers, a spacious interior, saunas in the bathroom, and a complimentary bottle of (Korean) port. If you want quality, this is it – but you pay for the perks.

Swiss Rosen Hotel (스위스로젠 호텔; Map pp210-11; ☎ 748 4848; www.swissrosen.co.kr; r weekdays/weekends from W60,000/120,000; ✖) Across from Hansol-jang, the Swiss Rosen is a nice deal even if the rooms are not enormous. Ask about package deals with free breakfast and bike rentals.

Gyeongju Park Tourist Hotel (경주 파크 관광호텔; Map p212; ☎ 777 7744; www.gjpark.com; d/tw W78,000/92,000; ✖ ▢) One of the few places in Korea to offer nonsmoking options. Some rooms on the 2nd floor are above a nightclub, but these have in-room internet terminals to compensate. There's a 30% discount in the off-peak season.

TOP END

Gyeongju's top lodgings sit along the lake at Bomunho.

Commodore Hotel Gyeongju Chosun (조선호텔; Map pp210-11; ☎ 745 7701; www.chosunhotel.net; r from W143,000; ✖ ▢) The slightly stodgy exterior belies the rich interior of this thoroughly modern property. There's nice woodwork in the rooms, Gyeongju green and terracotta-coloured motifs downstairs, and one of the city's favourite spas.

Hotel Hyundai (현대 호텔; Map pp210-11; ☎ 748 2233; www.hyundaihotel.com; r from W230,000; ✖ ▢ ▣) Marble everywhere, gardens by the lake, a fitness club and balconies in each room. Disabled travellers will appreciate the care given to accessibility.

Gyeongju Hilton (힐튼 호텔; Map pp210-11; ☎ 745 7788, toll free 00798-651 1818; www.hilton.com; r from W254,100; ✖ ▣) A real Miró hangs in the lobby of this Gyeongju chain. It has a sauna, squash courts, pool and gym. The Hilton owns the nearby museum, so a night's stay includes free admission should you care to see more art than is in the lobby.

Eating

Gyeongju's greatest concentration of choices is in the city centre. Southeast of Tumuli Park is a street full of *ssambap* restaurants (쌈밥; lots of side dishes, which you wrap up in lettuce and other leaves).

Sigol Yeohaeng (시골 여행; Map pp210-11; ☎ 771 4089; meals W3500-10,000; ◷ 9am-9pm) Opposite the entrance to Samneung, this 20-year-old restaurant specialises in *mukun kimchi* (묵은 김치), a spicy noodle-and-broth dish made with *kimchi* aged at least three years.

Bukang Sikdang (부강 식당; Map p212; ☎ 743 9337; meals from W5000; ◷ 6am-10pm) A five-minute walk from the intercity bus terminal, it's one of the few downtown restaurants to open early in the morning. Don't be put off by the staid interior. The *gomtang* (곰탕; beef soup) is a delicious and welcome alternative to spicy food for breakfast.

Sopung Makjang (Off Map p212; 소풍 막장; servings from W5000; 🕑 5.30pm-5.30am) This boisterous meat restaurant caters to Dongguk University students with budget cuts like *samgyupsal* (삼겹살, fatty pork) and a local favourite called *makchang* (막창) – grilled cow or pig intestines – which tastes much better when the outside is grilled to a crisp. A W10,000 taxi ride from downtown is the best way here. It's a short walk from the main intersection near the university main gate. Ask the taxi driver for '*Dongguk dae sageori*' (동국대 사거리).

Pyeongyang (평양; Map p212; ☎ 772 2448; meals W6000-18,000; 🕑 11am-9pm) Don't be put off by the sign out front reading 'tourist restaurant'; plenty of locals love it too for *bulgogi* (불고기; marinated beef), *naengmyeon* (냉면; spicy cold noodles) and other Korean faves.

Silla Buffet (신라 부페; Map p212; ☎ 741 7600; adult/child W6500/4000; 🕑 lunch noon-3pm, dinner 6-9pm) Arguably Gyeongju's most economical place to load up on buffet standards like *bulgogi*, *tangsuyuk* (탕수육; sweet and sour pork), soup, vegies, rice and *kimchi*. It's on the 2nd floor opposite the Terrace and Kisoya.

Kisoya (기소야; Map p212; ☎ 746 6020; meals W7000-23,000) Next door to Terrace (see below) with a similar setting and decent menu of Japanese standards with Korean touches. Vegie options are available. As with Terrace, the tumulus adds excitement to the meal.

Terrace (테라스; Map p212; ☎ 773 8084; meals W8300-27,000; 🕑 10.30am-midnight) Clean and contemporary, offering steak and pasta.

Kuro Ssambap (구로쌈밥; Map p212; ☎ 749 0600; per person W9000; 🕑 11am-9pm) Eclectic collection of birds, rocks, figurines, pottery and other folk arts make this a unique place to dine. Orders include 28 refillable side dishes.

Sukyeong Sikdang (숙영 식당; Map p212; ☎ 772 3369; meals from W15,000; 🕑 11am-8.30pm) Since 1979, this cosy restaurant with a delightfully cluttered and rustic interior has been serving tasty *pajeon* (파전; green onion pancake) made from organic ingredients and homemade *dongdongju* (동동주; rice wine). It's near the east wall of Tumuli Park.

Gampo Hogung Raw Fish Center (감포 호궁 회 센타; Map pp210-11; ☎ 744 3550; crab meals W30,000 person; 🕑 7am-midnight) King crab and raw fish are the specialities of this bustling restaurant near the Gampo harbour. Crab dinners start with a small selection of side dishes and finish with a pot of spicy fish soup that tastes better

after adding a splash of soy sauce. It's customary to negotiate the price of a crab meal before going inside.

For dessert, try Gyeongju *bang* (baked barley pancakes with red-bean paste sandwiched inside). **Danseongmyeongga** (단석명 가; Map p212; ☎ 741 7520; 🕑 8am-11pm) claims to have originated the trend. **Hwangnam Bread** (황남빵; Map p212; ☎ 749 7000; 🕑 8am-11pm), which serves a thicker, heavier version of this Gyeongju icon, is on the north side of Tumuli Park.

Drinking

There are numerous clubs, bars and pubs near Dongguk University. Bars change names frequently, but chances are university students walking around speak enough English to recommend a place or two.

Cheon Tak (촌닭; Map p212; drinks from W2000; 🕑 4pm-2am) On a downtown side street, this minimally decorated bar is ideal for a nightcap or an evening of cheap boozing. *Dongdongju* (동동주; rice wine) is served on wood tables with traditional side dishes like *bindaetteok* (빈대떡; mungbean pancake) and *pajeon* (파전).

About Coffee (Map p212; ☎ 777 3863; drinks W3500; 🕑 11am-11pm) Certified baristas, a free chessboard and splendid espresso served with a complimentary sweet treat make this one of the city's best coffee houses. It's near a clock on a narrow lane opposite McDonald's.

Esmeralda (Map p212; ☎ 749 9449; drinks W2500; 🕑 10am-11pm) A decent espresso bar down the lane from About Coffee with a modern interior better suited to amorous couples than hard-core coffee drinkers.

Entertainment

There are outdoor traditional dance and music performances every Saturday during April, May, September and October (3pm to 5pm) on the stage (Map p212) in Wolseong Park. More regular traditional performances are held at Bomunho (Map pp210–11) between April and October. Weekend performances of Korean dance and music at Bomunho start at 7.30pm or 8.30pm with additional Thursday and Friday shows in May, July and August. Check with KTO (☎ 1330) for more details.

For more contemporary fare, there's a cluster of cinemas (Map p212) in central Gyeongju.

Getting There & Away

AIR

There is no airport at Gyeongju itself, but the airports at Busan (Gimhae) and Ulsan are readily accessible. Ulsan's airport is closer, but Gimhae has more flights.

BUS

Gyeongju's **express bus terminal** (Map p212; ☎ 741 4000) and **intercity bus terminal** (p212; ☎ 743 5599) are adjacent to one other. Buses from the express bus terminal:

Destination	Price (W)	Duration
Busan	4000	1hr
Daegu	3900	1hr
Daejeon	17,700	3hr
Seoul	27,600	4½hr

Buses from the intercity bus terminal:

Destination	Price (W)	Duration
Busan	4000	1hr
Daegu	3900	1hr
Pohang	2900	1hr
Ulsan	3800	1hr

TRAIN

Gyeongju–Seoul *Saemaul* (luxury express) services run up to six times daily (W37,700) from the **train station** (Map p212; ☎ 743 4114). There is also one overnight *Mugungwha* train (W25,300). Trains connect Busan via Dongdaegu, so it's usually faster to take a bus. At the time of writing, construction of KTX service to Gyeongju was underway with an expected completion date of 2011.

Getting Around

TO/FROM THE AIRPORT

Several direct buses link Gyeongju with both the Ulsan airport (W4500, four daily) and Busan's Gimhae airport (W9000, 12 daily). Buses leave from Gyeongju's main intercity bus terminal.

BICYCLE

Hiring a bicycle for a day is a great way of reaching the sites in Gyeongju. There are some bike trails around Namsan (but it's rather hilly) and Bomunho.

There are bicycle-rental shops everywhere, and the rates are standard: a bike costs W3000 hourly or W10,000 to W12,000 daily. Tandem bikes are plentiful around Bomunho and usually cost W6000 per hour. Outside the intercity bus terminal, a six-hour scooter rental costs W40,000.

BUS

Many local buses (regular/deluxe W1000/1500) terminate just outside the intercity bus terminal, alongside the river. For shorter routes (eg to Bulguk-sa), buses can be picked up along Sosongno and Daejeongno.

Buses 10 (which runs clockwise) and 11 (counterclockwise) run a circuit of most of the major sights including Bulguk-sa, Namsan and Bomunho, as well as the bus terminals and Gyeongju train station (every 15 minutes). Bus 150 departs from the train station to the eastern sights, via the Bomunho Expo arena (every 30 minutes). Bus 100 makes a similar initial route.

TAXI

If your time is limited and you want to cover a lot of ground in a short time, taxis are often available for day hire outside the train and bus stations. Rates are negotiable but hover around W125,000/175,000 for five/seven hours. Do not expect the driver to speak much English.

AROUND GYEONGJU

Many tourists do this area as a day trip out of Gyeongju – and wish they'd budgeted time to stay overnight. It's hard to improve on the outstanding examples of traditional Korean architecture in sublime settings.

Yangdong Folk Village
양동 민속 마을

Getting here is not easy, but your journey to this Joseon-dynasty village (Map pp210–11) will be rewarded with an up-close, intimate look at superb traditional architecture in a decidedly uncommercial setting. Designated as a cultural preservation area, the entire village replete with stone walls, straw-thatched roofs and green gardens is a photographer's dream.

Set aside a half-day to admire the 180 or so houses typical of the *yangban* class – a largely hereditary class based on scholarship and official position. Most of the homes here are still lived in, so you need to observe the usual courtesies when looking around; some of the larger mansions stand empty and are open to the public. There are descriptive plaques with English explanations outside some of the more important structures. If buildings are locked, you may be able to ask for a key nearby. There are no entry fees to any of the buildings.

When it's time for a break, try one of the area teashops, like **Uhyangdaok** (우향다옥; dishes W4000-13,000; ⏰ noon-10pm). It's in a rustic building with simple treats like green tea, wine and light meals. No English is spoken here but the owner is quite helpful. From the large signboard near the bus stop, walk towards the village and look for the sign that reads '762 8096'. If you want to stay the night, there are two small *ondol* rooms (W30,000) for rent. Early breakfast is possible but you need to ask ahead of time.

From Gyeongju, buses 200, 201, 202, 203 and 206 will get you to within 1.5km of Yangdong. From the bus stop, follow the train line and then go under it. There's only one road into the village, about a 30-minute walk.

Oksan Seowon & Around 옥산 서원

Traditional Confucian academies – *seowon* – like this one, aren't much to look at but they do hold considerable historical importance. Established in 1572 in honour of Yi Eon-jeok (1491–1553), Oksan Seowon (Map pp210–11) was one of the most important. It was enlarged in 1772 and was one of the few *seowon* to escape destruction in the 1860s. However, an early-20th-century fire destroyed some of the buildings here; today only 14 structures remain.

SIGHTS
Dongnakdang 독락당
A 10-minute walk beyond Oksan Seowon up the valley road will bring you to **Dongnakdang** (Map pp210-11; admission free; ⏰ by appointment), a beautiful collection of well-preserved buildings, constructed in 1515 and expanded in 1532 as the residence of Yi Eon-jeok after he left government service. The walled compound is partly occupied by descendants of Master Yi himself.

Due to past vandalism, the family requests visitors to book appointments in advance (ask at tourist offices). They will open up the inner rooms and answer any questions (in Korean).

SLEEPING & EATING
Oksan Motel (옥산 모텔; Map pp210-11; ☎ 762 9500; d W30,000; ❄) About 500m from Dongnakdang,

the Oksan has modern *ondol* or bedrooms with a shower and a patio in front of the property.

Sanjang Sikdang (산장식당; Map pp210-11; ☎ 762 3716; chicken/duck stew for 2-4 people W30,000/35,000) This place specialises in free-range duck and chicken. *Tojongdak baeksuk* (토종닭 백숙) and *orihanbang baeksuk* (오리한방 백숙) are chicken and duck stews served with rice porridge. Note: stews take up to 50 minutes to prepare, so you can relax in the outdoor seating area or have a Korean speaker call before you arrive. It's between Dongnakdang and the Oksan Motel.

GETTING THERE & AWAY
Bus 203 (W1500, six daily departures) to Angang-ri connects Gyeongju train station and Oksan Seowon.

Songseon-ri 송선리
Close to the summit of the thickly forested Obongsan (640m), **Bokduam hermitage** (Map pp210–11) features a huge rock face out of which 19 niches have been carved. The three central niches hold a figure of the historical Buddha flanked by two bodhisattva (Munsu and Bohyeon); the remainder house the 16 arhat monks who have attained Nirvana. The carving is recent and although there's an unoccupied house up here, the actual hermitage was burned down in 1988 after an electrical fault started a blaze. There is also a statue of Gwanseeum, the Goddess of Mercy, just beyond the rock face. Just below the hermitage is a stunning viewpoint from the top of a couple of massive boulders. It's a great place for a picnic lunch.

The trail is easy to follow, but bring water as there are no springs along the way. The walk up will take around an hour. From the bus stop in Songseon-ri, follow the creek up along the narrow road about 500m to a small temple (Seongam-sa). The trail starts just to the left of this temple and is well marked with *hangeul*.

A further 3.8km up the road from the bus stop for Bokduam and Jusaam, remote **Sinseon-sa** near the top of Danseoksan (827m) was used as a base by General Kim Yu-shin in the 7th century. It has seen a bit of renovation work since then. About 50m to the right as you face the temple are some ancient rock carvings in a small grotto – it's believed to be one of the oldest cave temples in Korea. It's about a two-hour circuit walk from the bus stop. There's a little village along the way, about 2.5km from the bus stop.

Bus 300 (W1500, every 25 minutes) travels to Obongsan and stops near Jusaam. If you're looking for a more direct route to Sinseon-sa, take bus 350 (W1500, every one to two hours) and get off at Ujung-gol (우중골). From the

intercity bus terminal tourist information booth, catch either bus at the stop near Paris Baguette.

POHANG 포항
pop 508,000

Pohang is a surprisingly enjoyable city if you're looking for great food and quiet beach

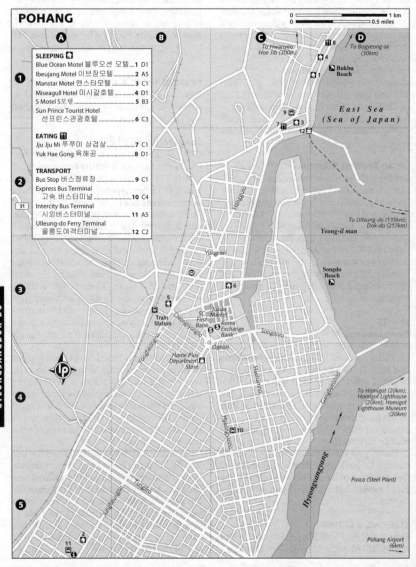

POHANG

SLEEPING 🏠		
Blue Ocean Motel 블루오션 모텔....**1** D1		
Ibeujang Motel 이브장모텔................**2** A5		
Manstar Motel 맨스타모텔................**3** C1		
Miseagull Hotel 미시갈호텔............**4** D1		
S Motel S모텔................................**5** B3		
Sun Prince Tourist Hotel		
선프린스관광호텔........................**6** C3		
EATING 🍴		
Jju Jju Mi 쭈쭈미 삼겹살..................**7** C1		
Yuk Hae Gong 육해공 **8** D1		
TRANSPORT		
Bus Stop 버스정류장.......................**9** C1		
Express Bus Terminal		
고속 버스터미널..........................**10** C4		
Intercity Bus Terminal		
시외버스터미널..........................**11** A5		
Ulleung-do Ferry Terminal		
울릉도여객터미널........................**12** C2		

To Hwanyeo Hoe Jib (300m)

To Bogyeong-sa (30km)

Bukbu Beach

East Sea (Sea of Japan)

To Ulleung-do (135km); Dok-do (217km)

Yeong-il man

Yukgeori

Songdo Beach

Jukdo Market

SC First Bank

Korea Exchange Bank

Ogeori

Train Station

Home Plus Department Store

To Homigot (20km); Homigot Lighthouse (20km); Homigot Lighthouse Museum (20km)

Posco (Steel Plant)

Hyeongsangang

Pohang Airport (6km)

strolls. Better known as home for **Posco** (Pohang Iron & Steel Company, the world's second-largest steel maker), it's also the main springboard to the island of Ulleung-do. The city is somewhat staid, though Bukbu Beach on the north side of town is a lively place with a pretty boardwalk, outdoor restaurants overlooking the beach and a slightly surreal nightscape when the colossal Posco plant emits a soft orange glow. Unlike some of the country's more famous beaches, Bukbu has a relaxed, *bon vivant* atmosphere, mostly quiet beach-road traffic and restaurants open until sunrise. The two city intersections, Ogeori (오거리; five-road intersection) and Yukgeori (유거리; six-road intersection) brim with cafes, clothing stores, *hof* (local pubs), restaurants and game parlours.

Orientation & Information

Bukbu Beach, adjacent to the ferry terminal, is 1.7km long, making it one of the longest sandy beaches on Korea's east coast. There's no English spoken at the **information booth** (☎ 245 6761; ⏰ 9am-6pm Mon-Sat Jul & Aug, until 5pm Sep-Jun) outside the intercity bus terminal but there are plenty of bilingual brochures and a detailed bus-route map (Korean only); a booth outside the ferry terminal is not regularly staffed. Buses 105 and 200 go to Bukbu Beach from the intercity bus terminal.

Sights

BOGYEONG-SA 보경사

You'll need a full day to explore the offerings in and around this **temple** (☎ 262 1117; admission W2000; ⏰ 7am-7pm). About 30km north of Pohang, Bogyeong-sa is a gateway to a beautiful valley boasting 12 waterfalls, gorges spanned by bridges, hermitages, stupas and the temple itself. There are good hikes including **Naeyeonsan** (930m). The 20km return trip to the summit – **Hyangnobong** – from Bogyeong-sa takes about six hours.

The well-maintained trail to the gorge and waterfalls branches off from the tourist village. It's about 1.5km to the first waterfall, 5m-high **Ssangsaeng Pokpo**. The sixth waterfall, **Gwaneum Pokpo**, is an impressive 72m and has two columns of water with a cave behind it. The seventh waterfall, about 30m high, is called **Yeonsan Pokpo**.

Further up the trail, the going gets difficult; the ascent of Hyangnobong should only be attempted if the day is young.

The temple is 15 minutes' walk from where the buses from Pohang terminate, and there's a tourist village with souvenir shops, restaurants, *minbak* and *yeogwan*.

Bus 500 (W1500, 45 minutes, every 30 to 90 minutes) runs between Pohang's intercity bus terminal and the temple, though some require a transfer at Cheongha. The easiest route is to catch one of three buses that travel directly to the temple (7.35am, 11.20am and 4.20pm). Otherwise, take 500 to Cheongha, get off at the tiny terminal and wait for a connecting bus (W1000, 15 minutes, every 10 to 90 minutes). A taxi from Cheongha to the temple costs W12,000.

HOMIGOT 호미곶

This district, on a natural cape that protects Pohang's harbour, is a popular spot at sunrise, especially 1 January. The **lighthouse museum** (☎ 284 4857; admission W700; ⏰ 10am-6pm Tue-Sun) has a large collection of national and international lighthouse memorabilia.

Catch bus 200 in front of the intercity bus terminal. Hop off at Guryeongpo (구룡포), the final stop (W1500, every 12 minutes), then catch a bus going to Daebo (W1000, 20 minutes, every 40 minutes).

Sleeping

There are about two dozen *yeogwan* around the intercity bus terminal with rooms from W25,000. For better scenery and quality, head up to Bukbu Beach where there is a growing number of snazzy beachfront motels.

Ibeujang Motel (이브장 모텔; ☎ 283 2253; d from W30,000; ☒) Fancy mirrors seem tragically out of place in these otherwise stark, linoleum-floored rooms. The red lamp is the only hint that this is a love motel.

S Motel (S 모텔; ☎ 247 0073; r from W35,000; ☒ 🖳) The yellow linoleum is off-putting and the rooms are smallish (but not stuffy) and have PCs and TVs. It's near the train station opposite a small waterfall.

Sun Prince Tourist Hotel (선프린스관광호텔; ☎ 242 2800; r from W35,000; ☒) Both *ondol* and Western-style rooms are available at the Sun Prince, a nice option for those not wanting a love motel. Red-tile floors, sculpted bathtubs and flowered quilts are just a few of the nice touches. Rates double on the weekend.

Manstar Motel (맨스타 모텔; ☎ /fax 244 0225; r W35,000, Sat add W5000; ☒ 🖳) Down a street off the main drag, the Manstar has decent rooms for budget travellers, seashell-design baths and the kind owner speaks English. Some rooms have a computer.

Blue Ocean Motel (블루오션 모텔; ☎ 232 2100; r regular/special/VIP W50,000/70,000/80,000, add W20,000 weekends & summer season; 🍴 🖵) Stylish by design, it's hard to find fault with this Bukbu Beach property. Tasteful decor and spacious layout plus steam saunas, flatscreen TVs and computers in every room.

Miseagull Hotel (미시갈 호텔; ☎ 254 8400; d/tw from W50,000/70,000; 🍴) Looking out over Bukbu Beach, some of the modestly furnished rooms have sea views, but this is a second choice if the newer properties are full.

Eating

For fresh seafood head to Bukbu Beach, where there's a string of restaurants with your meal waiting in tanks along with some good barbecue options. Pohang's unique dish is *mulhoe* (물회), a spicy soup with raw fish.

Jju Jju Mi (쭈쭈미; ☎ 232 6363; servings from W6000; ⏲ 5-10pm) Come here for unique *samgyupsal* (삼겹살): tangy pork on a skewer cooked at your table on a rotisserie. It's behind the Manstar Motel.

Hwanyeo Hoe Jib (환여횟집; ☎ 246 1225; dishes from W10,000; ⏲ 10am-10pm) About 1km from the Pohang ferry terminal, this restaurant is well-known on the Bukbu Beach strip for *mulhoe*.

Yuk Hae Gong (육해공; ☎ 256 0605; dishes from W25,000; ⏲ 5pm-5am) Take a seat in the outdoor patio overlooking the beach and enjoy barbecued shellfish, called *jogae gu-e* (조개 구이). Shells filled with seafood, cheese and onion look, smell and taste wonderful. It's often brimming with a boisterous late night crowd – look for the restaurant with a gravel patio floor. If full, many nearby shops have a similar menu.

Getting There & Away

AIR

Asiana and Korean Air both have Seoul–Pohang services. For more information call the **airport** (☎ 289 7309).

BOAT

See p227 for details of ferries travelling to Ulleung-do.

BUS

Departing from Pohang's **intercity bus terminal** (☎ 272 3194):

Destination	Price (W)	Duration	Frequency
Andong	14,800	2hr	9 daily
Busan	7300	1½hr	every 10min
Daegu	7400	2hr	30 daily
Seoul	22,400	4½hr	every 40min
Uljin	12,900	2hr	every 10-25min

The express bus terminal (a five-minute taxi ride from the intercity bus terminal) has connections to four cities.

Destination	Price (W)	Duration	Frequency
Daejeon	19,500	3¼hr	hrly
Masan	11,000	2¼hr	5 daily
Gwangju	25,000	4hr	4 daily
Seoul	29,000	4½hr	every 40min

TRAIN

There are a couple of trains from **Pohang station** (☎ 275 2394) to Seoul (*Saemaul*; W38,300, five hours, 8.40am and 5.25pm).

Getting Around

Local buses cost W1000/1500 (regular/deluxe). Bus 200 runs between the airport and the intercity bus terminal.

ULLEUNG-DO 울릉도
pop 10,200

Come to Ulleung-do to get away from it all, in the truest sense. The scenery is spectacular, offering vistas of spun-cotton clouds over volcanic cliffsides, seabirds and fishing boats, quiet harbours and a breathtaking jagged coastline.

In the rainy season the green hues are even more vivid, saturating the hills like an overtoned colour photograph. In autumn, the hills are a patchwork of reds, greens and yellows from the turning leaves.

An extinct volcano some 135km east of the Korean peninsula, Ulleung-do today is mainly a fishing community that sees enough tourism to warrant a sprinkle of hotels and restaurants. Other industries include the production of taffy made from pumpkin and woodcarvings made from native Chinese juniper – all offered for sale at the island's many tourist shops.

Orientation & Information

Most visitors arrive from the mainland to the port of Dodong-ri, on the island's southeastern side. A new port in nearby Sadong-ri has been under way for years, but its completion date is unknown. On the coast north of Dodong-ri is the busy village of Jeodong-ri,

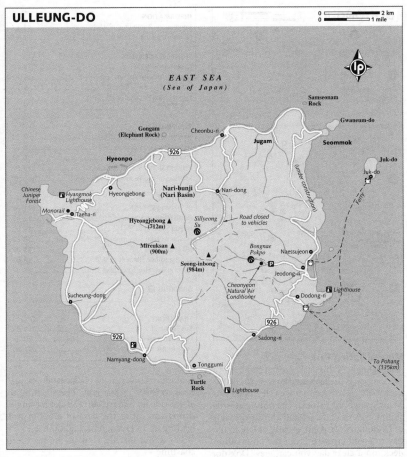

ULLEUNG-DO

EAST SEA
(Sea of Japan)

Samseonam Rock

Gwaneum-do

Gongam
(Elephant Rock)   Cheonbu-ri

Jugam   Seommok

Juk-do

Hyeonpo

926

Juk-do

Chinese
Juniper
Forest

Hyangmok
Lighthouse   Hyeongjebong

**Nari-bunji
(Nari Basin)**   Nari-dong

(under construction)   Ferry

Monorail   Taeha-ri

Hyeongjebong ▲
(712m)

Sillyeong
Su

Road closed
to vehicles

Mireuksan ▲
(900m)

Bongnae
Pokpo   Naessujeon

▲   Jeodong-ri

Seong-inbong
(984m)   Lighthouse

Cheonyeon
Natural Air
Conditioner   Dodong-ri

Sucheung-dong

926

926

Sadong-ri

To Pohang
(135km)

Namyang-dong   Tonggumi

**Turtle
Rock**   Lighthouse

which retains a traditional fishing-village feel. The other main points of interest to tourists are the monorail in Taeha-ri leading to a mountaintop view of the sea, and Nari-bunji, a basin on the north side of the island.

There's no English spoken at the **information booth** (Map p224; ☎ 790 6454; ◷ 9am-6pm) by the Dodong-ri ferry terminal; however, there are bilingual maps and bus schedules in Korean. You can change money or withdraw cash from the 24-hour bank machine at Nonghyup Bank in Dodong-ri.

Sights

DODONG-RI 도동리
Dodong-ri is the island's administrative centre and largest town. Like a pirate outpost,

its harbour is almost hidden away in a narrow valley between two forested mountains, making it visible only when approached directly. It's also the island's main tourist hub, meaning the greatest selection of lodging and dining options.

Behind the ferry terminal, a spiral staircase leads to a seaside **walking trail** offering spectacular views of the sea crashing into jagged rocks. About 1.5km down the path, you'll find a **lighthouse** and, if you choose, a trail leading to Jeodong-ri (it's a two-hour return trip). The one-hour return walk to the lighthouse should be on every traveller's must-do list, but you'll need a flexible schedule as the path is closed when ocean tides are too strong.

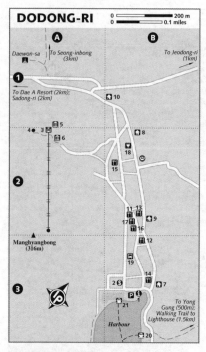

Mineral Spring Park 약수 공원

The highlight of this park, a 350m climb above Dodong-ri, is the **cable car** (Map p224; ☎ 791 7160; return W7500; ⏱ 6am-8pm) across a steep valley to Manghyangbong (316m). The ride up affords stunning views of the sea and a bird's-eye view of Dodong-ri. Visit either early or late in the day to avoid crowds. From the observation deck, on a clear day you can view Dok-do, some 92km away.

The park's namesake *yaksu gwangjang* (mineral-water spring) is near the top. The water has a distinctive flavour (think diet citrus soda-meets-quartz) and some claim drinking it has all sorts of medicinal benefits, though there are always risks with drinking untreated water. Nearby, you'll find a rock-climbing wall and a small temple.

Also in the park are two **museums** (Map p224; ☎ 790 6421; admission free; ⏱ 7am-6pm), the Dok-do Museum and Ulleung-do's simple historical museum; the exhibits are mostly in Korean.

TAEHA-RI 태하리

In the northwest corner of the island about 20km from Dodong-ri, Ulleung-do's most re-

cent tourist investment is a **monorail** (Map p223; admission W4000; ⏱ 8am-5pm). The six-minute, 304m ride up a sharp cliff (39-degree angle) drops you off at the base of a 500m trail leading up to Hyangmok Lighthouse (향목 등대) and a terrific view of the northern coastline.

Buses to Taeha-ri leave the Dodong-ri terminal (W1500, 40 minutes, every 40 minutes).

NAMYANG-DONG 남양

The coastal road from Dodong-ri to Taeha-ri leads through Namyang (Map p223), a tiny seaside community with spectacular cliffs covered with Chinese juniper and odd **rock formations**.

Sunset Point Pavilion (Ilmoljeon Mangdae) is a steep 15-minute walk above the town, commanding great views of the ocean and, yes, of the sunset. To get there, follow the western creek out of town and cross the bridge after the school. A small trail continues up to the pavilion.

JEODONG-RI 저동리

Jeodong-ri (Map p223) is a fishing village with picturesque sea walls, fishing nets, and seagulls. The boats with the lamps strung around like oversize holiday lights are for catching squid. If you prefer a quieter alternative to Dodong-ri, try staying here instead – but we mean quiet.

A steep 1.5km walk from Jeodong-ri is the car park to **Bongnae Pokpo** (Map p223; ☎ 790 6422; admission W1200; ⏰ 6am-7pm Apr-Oct, 8am-5pm Nov-Mar). Source of the island's drinking water, the waterfall is quite spectacular during the summer.

On the return trip, cool down in **Cheonyeon Natural Air Conditioner** (천연 에어콘), a cave that maintains a year-round temperature of 4°C.

Buses serve the car park from Dodong-ri via Jeodong-ri (W1500, 15 minutes, every 40 minutes).

NARI-BUNJI 나리 분지

Nari Basin (Map p223) is on the northern slope of **Seong-inbong** (984m), the island's highest peak and the summit of a dormant volcano. Nari is the only place on the island that's reasonably flat, so there are several farms here.

It's also a popular place to start or conclude a hiking expedition (right).

Minbak, camping and restaurants are available. At the restaurants by the campground, you might try *hanjeongsik* (Korean banquet; W8000) or *sanchae deodeokjeon* (산채 더덕전; mountain vegetable and *deodeok* pancake; W7000) accompanied by *dondongju* (동동주; rice wine; W6000).

Activities

BOAT TRIPS

A **round-island tour** (W23,000; ⏰ departs 9am & 3pm) is a great way to admire Ulleung-do's dramatic landscape. Tours depart from Dodong-ri ferry terminal (Map p224) and last around two hours. In nonpeak seasons they may be cancelled.

Other sightseeing boats run to **Juk-do** (Map p223; W15,000; ⏰ 10am & 3pm), a nature preserve 4km from Ulleung-do. Visitors are welcome to take a picnic to eat on the island. It takes about 1½ hours including walk or picnic time.

With a reservation and sufficient demand, speedy boats (W45,000, 3¼ hours) run out to **Dok-do**, but you can't go onto the island. See the boxed text, p226, for more information about Dok-do.

During the annual squid festival (three days in mid-August), you may be able to board boats and even ride a vessel out to sea. The rest of the year it's interesting to watch the boats in the evening when they head out to sea with their lanterns glaring.

HIKING

Various pathways lead to the summit of **Seong-inbong**, but the two main routes run from Dodong-ri (about five hours return) or Nari-bunji (four to five hours return).

From Dodong-ri, take the main road towards **Daewon-sa**. Just before you reach the temple, there is a fork in the trail and a sign (in Korean) pointing the way to Seong-inbong (a steep 4.1km).

From Nari-bunji, enter the thick forest, adhering to the right-hand path, and you'll arrive at fields of chrysanthemum. Further on you'll pass a traditional home. Finally, at the entrance to the virgin forest area and picnic ground, the steep ascent of Seong-inbong takes you (one hour) through a forest of Korean beech, hemlock and lime.

Just below the peak, as you descend to Dodong-ri, is a trail off to the right, down to Namyang-dong (1½ hours).

If you're not up for a major hike, try the 5km return trip from the Nari basin bus stop to **Sillyeong Su** (신령수), a mountain spring. The walk cuts through a thick forest and is an easy one-hour stroll while waiting for the van to take you back to Cheonbu for a connection back to Dodong-ri.

Sleeping

Ulleung-do has loads of choices starting at W30,000, though luxury travellers will be disappointed – even shocked. Room rates rise steeply in peak season (from W50,000 to W100,000 in July, August and holidays) – coinciding with a flood of boisterous Korean travellers on package tours – so book ahead.

Camping is available on the beach at Namyang-dong, Naessujeon and Sadong-ri. Toilets and showers are available at the latter two during summer. Camping (free) and *minbak* (W30,000) are also available at Nari-bunji. Most everything in Jeodong-ri, including sleep options, is near the police station.

DODONG-RI

Haniljang Motel (한일장 여관; Map p224; ☎ 791 5515; d W30,000; ❄) Nicer than some surrounding options; *ondol* rooms are fairly large. It's close to the port, right across from the supermarket.

Sanchang-jang Yeogwan (신창장여관; Map p224; ☎ 791 0552; d W30,000; ✗) Orchids brighten up an otherwise grim stairway, but this aging *yeogwan* has good, clean *ondol* rooms and is in the centre of town. If no one is at the reception desk, inquire in the restaurant below.

Khan Motel (칸 모 텔; Map p224; ☎ 791 8500; www.motelkhan.com; d W70,000; ✗ 🖳) One of the nicest properties on the island with both *ondol* and Western-style rooms. The rooms are smallish though the large TVs, computers and night-club (open 5pm to 1am) are all pluses. The owner is a great resource for guests looking for hard-to-find ferry tickets during the busy travel season. Prices jump to W100,000 in July and August.

Hotel Ulleung-do (울릉도 호텔; Map p224; ☎ 791 6611; ondol/r W50,000/80,000; ✗) Calling this place a hotel might raise your expectations about quality. It's more like a large *yeogwan* with lots of *ondol* rooms and a popular choice for groups who want to economise by sharing a room and don't mind the minimal furnishings.

Pension Skyhill (스카이힐; Map p224; ☎ 791 1040; d/ondol W60,000/50,000; ✗) Near the top of town, it's a popular destination for groups of university students, so some of the facilities – like a shared kitchen and rooftop barbecue facilities – look a little worn out.

Dae A Resort (대아 리조트; ☎ 791 8500; www.daearesort.com; r/ste from W90,000/220,000; ✗ 🖳) Arguably the island's most expensive property, but come here for the mountaintop view of the sea, not the boxy rooms with small TVs and simple bathrooms. From the middle of July to August, there's an outdoor swimming pool, which is when room rates double in price. The hotel is in Sadong-ri, a W4000 taxi ride from Dodong-ri.

JEODONG-RI
Many lodgings in town offer free pick-up from Dodong-ri ferry terminal with advance notice.

Jeil Minbak (제일 민박; ☎ 791 5170; ondol W30,000; ✗) All *ondol* rooms, one with a kitchenette (same price). Yellow linoleum is off-putting, but the rooms air out well and the owner is extremely kind. Some rooms have port views. Don't confuse this with the Jeil Motel nearby.

Nakwon-jang Yeogwan (낙원장 여관; ☎ 791 0580; r from W30,000; ✗) Simple, no-nonsense rooms, some without windows, with a choice of *ondol* or Western-style. It's central and close to the bus stop.

Kaiser Motel (카이저 모텔; ☎ 791 8900; r W40,000; ✗) Basic rooms are stuffy but clean. It's a good non-*yeogwan* option for those wanting Western style.

Jeil Motel (제일 모텔; ☎ 791 2637; r from W40,000, VIP W50,000; ✗ 🖳) Lions greet you at the top of the stairs. The regular rooms are smallish with faux-wood floors and not much of a view, but they are spotless. VIP rooms are enormous and have couches, computers, internet, sculptures and snazz. Guests get a small discount at the next-door sauna (W5000, open 5am to 8pm).

Eating & Drinking
Outdoor seafood stalls are ubiquitous in Ulleung-do. There are a few scattered *mandu/naengmyeon/gimbap* shops where you can eat for as little as W3000, and some casual outdoor restaurants by the harbour with outdoor seating. Nari-dong has restaurants, too.

DODONG-RI
Yong Gung (용궁; Map p224; dishes from W15,000; ☺ 8am-10pm) It's not much to look at, just a few plastic chairs and tables and a canteen-style kitchen, but this is where you'll find serenity by the sea: sit near the coast with a bottle of *soju*, a platter of raw fish and watch the ocean crash onto the rocky shoreline. Mr Jeong (who speaks passable English) and his brother run the place and personally catch the seafood on

offer by diving for sea creatures each morning. It's about 500m from the ferry terminal on the seaside walking trail.

99 Sikdang (99 식당; Map p224; ☎ 791 2287; dishes W5000-20,000; ⊗ 6.30am-10pm) Potted plants outside the doorway mark the door of this friendly place that's received press throughout Korea for its *ojing-eo bulgogi* (오징어 불고기; squid grilled at table with vegetables and hot pepper sauce). *Ttaggaebibap* (딱개비밥; shellfish with rice) is also a favourite.

Ulleung Raw Fish Town (울릉횟타운; Map p224; meals W6000-10,000) Serves mainly seafood stews and raw fish.

Sanchang-hoe Sikdang (산창회식당; Map p224; mains W6000-15,000; ⊗ 6.30-midnight) Downstairs from Sanchang-jang Yeogwan, it specialises in *honghapbap* (mussel rice) served with a locally-cultivated mountain plant called *myeong-e* (명이) and a generous bowl of *miyeokguk* (미역국; seaweed soup).

Haeun Sikdang (해운식당; Map p224; ☎ 791 0002; entrees W6000-15,000; ⊗ 6.30am-9pm) Across the street from the 99, offering similar fare that's just as delicious though the interior and service are scruffy. For a unique Ulleung-do dish, try the *oh-sam bulgogi* (오삼불고기), grilled squid mixed with *samgyupsal*.

Amso Hanmari Sikdang (암소한마리 식당; Map p224; ☎ 791 4344; servings W9000-15,000) One of many restaurants serving organic beef from 'medicinal cows' (약수불고기) raised on herbs. The beef's tough texture might make you wonder if the herbs justify the cost (W15,000/150g). The tender *samgyupsal* (삼겹살; fatty pork) is a better deal (W9000/150g).

Tema (테마; Map p224; ☎ 791 3122; drinks from W3000) Across from the Hotel Ulleung-do, it's a quiet place to relax and enjoy a drink. It's also one of the few bars in Dodong-ri that doesn't require customers to purchase side dishes; it's on the 2nd level above a vacant shop.

Koreaned-out? **Jeil Jegwa** is a comfy bakery with a table for you to enjoy sweet treats. Self-caterers will find numerous tiny grocery stores and the larger **Hannam Chain Supermarket** just up from the ferry terminal.

JEODONG-RI

Gyeongju Sigyuk Sikdang (경주식육식당; ☎ 791 3034; dishes W6000-15,000; ⊗ 10am-10pm) Serves *yaksu bulgogi* (약수불고기; medicinal herb-marinated beef; W15,000/serving), but you have to order a minimum of three servings. The mixed-vegetable dishes and *sanchae*

bibimbap (산채 비빔밥; rice mixed with mountain vegetables) are tasty.

Byeoljang Sigyuk Sikdang (별장 식육식당; ☎ 791 0028; dishes W6000-15,000; ⊗ 9am-10pm) Diagonally across the street from Gyeongju Sigyuk Sikdang, this has a similar menu and an attractive interior with bamboo and paper screens. Seating is on the floor.

Nokdu Bindaeddeok (녹두 빈대떡; ☎ 791 5948; dishes from W10,000; ⊗ 9am-8pm) Maybe the island's only funky restaurant, this friendly shop has outdoor floor seating under trees overlooking a landscaped garden filled with statues, pagodas and a crane. The menu is limited but the food is delicious; try the crispy *bindaetteok* (빈대떡; mungbean pancake) and a platter of homemade *muk* (묵; acorn jelly) mixed with spicy onions and carrots. It's on the path leading to Bongnae Pokpo not far from the ticket office. Look for two Korean totems in front of a black gate. It also has *minbak* rooms for W50,000.

Getting There & Away

You should carry your passport – you'll need the number in order to board the ferry and you may need it to register your departure from Pohang.

FERRY

You can get to Ulleung-do by **ferry** (☎ 242 5111; www.daea.com) from Pohang (standard/1st class W57,600/64,400, three hours, one daily) but ferries are subject to cancellation in poor weather. The departure timetable varies month to month. If assigned seats are unavailable you have the option of buying a floor-seating ticket in a common room for a slight discount. Ferries from Mukho (W53,300, 2½ hours) may only run during July and August.

It is best to reserve your tickets to and from the island, especially during summer. Otherwise you can buy your ticket at the terminal first thing in the morning, but you may go on a waiting list. If your ferry is cancelled you need to rebook your ticket. Advance bookings and news about cancelled ferries can be obtained in Ulleung-do (☎ 791 0801), Pohang (☎ 242 5111) and Mukho (☎ 531 5891). Call **KTO** (☎ 1330) for more details. Some travel agents make reservations and sell tickets.

Getting Around

BUS

Buses run between Dodong-ri and Jeodong-ri every 30 minutes (W1000, 10 minutes).

GYEONGSANGBUK-DO

Eighteen daily buses go from Dodong-ri via Namyang-dong (W1500, 25 minutes) to Cheonbu-ri (W1500, 65 minutes), where you can transfer to Nari-bunji via a van (W1000, 10 minutes, eight daily). Timetables are posted at the Dodong-ri bus terminal. Korean-language bus tours (two/four hours W13,000/18,000) starting from the plaza near the ferry terminal are an option but they don't always allow enough time to enjoy the sights.

TAXI

Taxis, usually 4WD, regularly ply between Dodong-ri and Jeodong-ri (W4000). All day trips can be arranged for about W150,000.

ANDONG 안동

pop 184,000

The whole area surrounding Andong, roughly in the middle of Gyeongsangbuk-do, is peaceful, rural and notable for having preserved much of its traditional character. Famous for its mackerel, its strong *soju* and its wooden masks, Andong makes a good base for exploring the numerous sights outside the city.

Orientation & Information

Some sights are a considerable distance away and getting to them requires a series of bus rides, often with inconvenient schedules. Ask at the tourist information booth for help planning your trip.

The **tourist office** (☎ 852 6800; www.andong.go.kr; ☺ 9am-6pm) is outside the train station. The staff are very helpful.

Hiring a taxi (W120,000) for the day is an air-conditioned luxury that's well worth it if you're enduring summer's heat.

Sights & Activities

ANDONG FOLK VILLAGE & FOLKLORE MUSEUM 안동 민속 마을, 박물관

On a hillside 40 minutes' walk from the centre of town, **Andong Folk Village** is a repository for homes moved to prevent them from being submerged by the construction of Andong Dam in 1976. Relocated and partially reconstructed traditional-style buildings range from peasant farmhouses to elaborate mansions of government officials with multiple courtyards. The village looks so authentic that the TV network KBS has used it as sets for historical dramas.

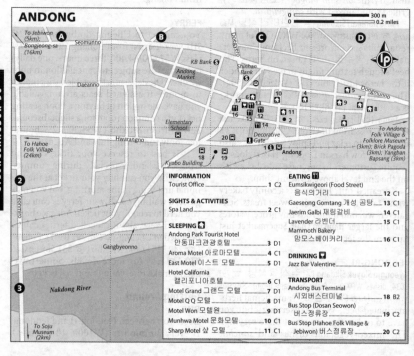

ANDONG

Just next door to the folk village is **Andong Folklore Museum** (☎ 821 0649; admission W1000; ⏲ 9am-6pm Mar-Oct, until 5pm Nov-Feb). It offers clear displays of Korea's folk traditions from birth through to death.

The village is about 4km east of Andong, close to the dam wall on the opposite side of the river from the main road. Catch bus 3 (W1000, every 35 minutes) and hop off at *minsokchon* (folk village). A taxi costs about W4500.

If you're walking (about 40 minutes) or have your own transport, stop off at the seven-storey Shilla-period **brick pagoda**, the largest and oldest brick pagoda in Korea. It looks oddly like someone went wild with oversize Lego and is well worth a peek. If you miss this one, there's another behind the tourist info booth.

SOJU MUSEUM 소주 박물관

This small **museum** (☎ 858 4541; www.andongsoju. net; admission free; ⏲ 9am-5pm Mon-Sat) has decent English explanations and displays of seasonal traditional meals, plus oddities like 'The Birthday Table of Queen Elizabeth Herself' when she visited Andong in 1999. The heady 45% *soju* of Andong may or may not be to your taste, but its significance has been pre-served with its designation as an intangible cultural property.

On the grounds of the Andong Soju Brewery, the museum houses a couple of displays that detail the distilling process, the drinking ceremony and a history of *soju* labels. A (thimble-sized) taste of the liquor is given at the end of your visit.

The museum is in the south of Andong, across the Nakdong River, and best reached by taxi (W4000). By bus, catch 34 or 36 (W1000, 10 minutes) from the stop opposite the bus terminal, near an elementary school.

JEBIWON 제비원

No, it's not a Star Wars character, though this huge rock-carved **Amitaba Buddha** (admission free; ⏲ 24hr) overlooking a park does bear a faint resemblance to Jabba the Hutt. The body and robes of this Buddha are carved on a boulder over 12m high, on top of which are the head and hair – carved out of two separate pieces of rock.

Catch bus 54 (W1000, every 30 minutes) opposite the bus terminal and ask the driver to drop you off at Jebiwon. Getting here by

bus is easy. Moving on to the next destination requires some imaginative travel techniques because there are no obvious bus stops on the street. You could stand on the street and wait for a bus or taxi, or ask anyone nearby for directions to Andong or Yeongju, which is 45km north. Don't be surprised if someone offers you a lift.

PUBLIC BATHS

Spa Land (스파랜드; ☎ 857 8118; admission W6500; ⏲ 24hr) is a comfortable downtown bath-house. It's not large but the tubs are clean and, because it's a 24-hour facility, guests can sleep overnight on the floor. Opposite the train station, it's easy to find: look for the tallest building with a "P" on the top.

Festivals & Events

Andong Mask Dance Festival (held at the end of September to early October) is a great time to visit Andong. It brings together a colour-ful array of national and international mask dance troupes. It is usually held in tandem with Andong's folk festival, showcasing per-formances of traditional music and dance. Check with **KTO** (☎ 1330) for details.

Sleeping

There are plenty of inexpensive *yeoin-suk* (family-run hotels with small rooms) around the bus terminal, though they're not pretty. The area opposite the train station has modern properties with attractive in-room amenities.

Motel Q (Q 모텔; ☎ 857 6878; r W30,000; 🍴 🖵) White walls, pink cushions and leafy trim seems a bit campy, but it's a good deal for the price. All rooms have desktop PCs and real bathtubs.

Motel Grand (그랜드 모텔; ☎ 859 0014; r W30,000; 🍴) Opposite Motel Q, it has red 'mood' lighting, dark faux-wood floors and bamboo patterns.

Aroma Motel (아로마 모텔; ☎ 856 6644; d from W35,000, Sat add W10,000; 🍴 🖵) Large rooms have TVs, coffee, wood-grain linoleum, and the lobby has photos of area attractions. *Ondol* rooms are nicer, but rooms with beds are available.

Motel Won (모텔 원; ☎ 859 0096; s/tw W40,000/50,000; 🍴 🖵) One of the newer prop-erties across the street from the train station, the modern rooms are a little boxy though spacious and clean; most have computers.

ANDONG'S MASKED BALL

In late September/early October, masks and their admirers come from all over the world to join in a host of mask-related festivities. In Hahoe Folk Village (24km from Andong), masked dancers perform traditional dances in the pine forests to the delight of crowds. Andong City has numerous mask-related shows, and a mask-making contest pits artisan against artisan in a delightful 'mask off' to see who can make the best mask. Firework displays are another popular attraction.

Every weekend at 3pm from May to October (as well as Sunday at 3pm in March, April and November), **Byeolsingut Talnori** performances take place in a small stadium near Hahoe's car park. These shows are a must-see; plus, they're free, although donations are demanded by hard-working *halmeoni* (grandmas). If you can't make it to a performance, you can view many masks at the Hahoe Mask Museum (opposite).

According to legend, the Hahoe mask tradition came about when the residents of Hahoe got frustrated with their hoity-toity noble clan. One clever craftsman carved a likeness of one of the most obsequious, much to the delight of his peers. Byeolsingut Talnori is a traditional dance style created by the common folk for the common folk to satirise the establishment. Characters wear masks representing social classes including corrupt monks and the rich, some with bulging eyes and crooked mouths. The conflicts among them are portrayed in amusing combinations of popular entertainment and shamanism. Accompanying the dance are the sounds of *nong-ak*, a traditional farmers' musical percussion quartet. For more information, visit www.maskdance.com or call Andong's tourist office (p228).

Munhwa Motel (문화 모텔; ☎ 857 7001; d W40,000, Sat add W5000; ✕ ▣) Features a lobby devoid of all furniture, and dark hallways. Rooms are clean and there are large TVs and 'mood' lights. Some rooms have closets the size of wine cellars. A coffee shop (open 9.30am to 7pm) is on the 1st floor.

Andong Park Tourist Hotel (안동 파크관광 호텔; ☎ 859 1500; d/tw/VIP W50,000/60,000/70,000; ✕) Andong's establishment choice, though unless you need a business centre or the marbled lobby, there's not much reason to pay a 50% premium for essentially the same thing as budget motels offer. Rooms are so-so clean, comfortable, and charmless.

Other properties include:

Hotel California (캘리포니아 호텔; ☎ 854 0622; d from W40,000; ✕ ▣) A tasteful love motel with a style that won't jar sensibilities.

Sharp Motel (샾 모텔; ☎ 854 0081; s/special/VIP W40,000/50,000/60,000; ✕ ▣) Go for the special room. It's spacious, comes with nifty gadgets and a provocative mural.

East Motel (이스트 모텔; ☎ 852 7755; d/tw/special W40,000/60,000/70,000; ✕ ▣) The pictures on the exterior wall tell the whole story about this place.

Eating & Drinking

You could eat each meal in Andong on Eumsikwigeori, the restaurant row in the town centre, marked by the decorative gate off the main street.

Jaerim Galbi (재림 갈비; ☎ 857 6352; servings W5000-17,000; ☾ 11am-10pm) A meat restaurant with *Hanu* beef and locally raised pork.

Lavender (라벤더; ☎ 855 8550; set meals W5000-16,000; ☾ 11am-10pm Tue-Sun) White and airy, this is a civilised pasta and salad place – pastas come with garlic bread, salad and coffee.

Yangban Bapsang (양반 밥상; ☎ 855 9900; www.yangban.net; meals W6000-15,000; ☾ 10.30am-9pm) Mackerel served golden, skin crispy, flesh tender – melts on the tongue the way mackerel was meant to. Not far from the Andong Folk Village, it's across the street from the entrance to the wooden bridge and the K water building.

Gaeseong Gomtang (개성 곰탕; meals from W6000, ☾ 8am-10pm) For an early breakfast, forget the nearby donut shop and come here for satisfying *hanu gomtang* (한우 곰탕; beef soup made from cow bones). Opposite Hotel California.

Mammoth Bakery (맘모스 베이커리; ☎ 857 6000; coffee W3000, breads W1000-4000; ☾ 8am-11pm) Friendly owner with good espresso and fresh tasty treats. If the weather is nice, enjoy your drink on the outdoor patio.

Jazz Bar Valentine (☎ 843 0069; ☾ 8pm-3am, closed every 2nd Sun) A dimly lit bar with plush chairs, though the 'jazz' is more easy listening.

Getting There & Away

BUS

The **bus terminal** (☎ 857 8296) serves both express and regular buses.

Destination	Price (W)	Duration	Frequency
Busan	14,600	2½hr	every 30-60min
Daegu	7300	1½hr	every 15-30min
Daejeon	13,4600	3hr	every 30min
Dongseoul	17,200	3hr	every 15-30min
Gyeongju	12,000	1¾hr	7 daily
Juwangsan	3500	35min	every 15-60min
Pohang	11,900	2hr	every 2hr
Ulsan	13,500	2¾hr	7 daily
Yeongju*	4600	1hr	every 20-40min

* transfer to Buseok-sa and Uljin

TRAIN

Destination	Price (W)	Duration	Frequency
Daegu	7100	2hr	1 daily
Dongdaegu*	6900	2hr	3 daily
Gyeongju	7400	2hr	4 daily
Seoul	14,300	5½hr	6 daily
Seoul	21,200	4hr	2 daily

* transfer to Busan

Getting Around

The tourist office hands out a helpful local bus timetable with English explanations. The town is small enough to get around on foot, and local buses serve all the sights.

HAHOE FOLK VILLAGE
하회 민속 마을

Arrive early in the morning and the mystical beauty of this **village** (Hahoe Minsok Maeul; ☎ 854 3669; admission W2000; ⏱ 9am-6pm Mar-Oct, 9am-sunset Nov-Feb) creates the illusion that you are in another time.

Walk down the dirt road and you'll pass small garden plots of squash vines, corn and green chilli peppers, all overshadowed by riverbank escarpments. Down the road, farm fields stretch out to the horizon. On your left, a magnificent village of centuries-old homes, so impeccable in design you'd swear you were living in the Joseon dynasty.

While other Korean folk villages can be tourist productions, this one has 230 residents maintaining old ways, and the government helps with preservation and restoration. There is a tourist information booth at the entrance to the village, and a lotus pond that (in season) is filled with beautiful blooms. Remember to respect people's privacy if you step beyond the entrance gates.

Two kilometres back in the direction of Andong, **Hahoe Mask Museum** (☎ 853 2288; www.maskmuseum.com; admission W2000; ⏱ 9.30am-6pm) houses a remarkable collection of traditional

Korean masks, as well as masks from across Asia and countries as diverse as Nigeria, Italy and Mexico. The English signage here is excellent. See the boxed text, opposite, for more on Hahoe's mask traditions and dance performances.

Two daily buses to and from Hahoe follow a bumpy dirt road and make a 10-minute stop at **Byeongsan Seowon** (☎ 853 2172; admission free; ⏱ 9am-6pm Apr-Oct, 9am-5pm Nov-Mar), a former Confucian academy dating from 1572. This spot, boasting some original buildings, is way off the tourist map except during summer – when the riverbank is busy with young people picnicking and enjoying the relaxing atmosphere. There are a couple of places to buy snacks by the river.

Most homes in Hahoe have *minbak* rooms for rent, like **Bunnam** (☎ 852 8550; http://home.invil.org/bunnam; r W50,000-100,000; ⏾), a traditional structure with a courtyard, *yo* (floor mattresses) and a shared bathroom. The friendly owner can't speak English but knows how to cook a meal (W7000).

For more luxury and privacy in a traditional setting, try **RakKoJae Andong** (☎ 054-857 3410, 010-5286 1855; www.rkj.co.kr; Hahoe Folk Village; s/d W100,000/160,000; ⏾ ⏾). Blending seamlessly with the surrounding thatched-roof *hanok* (traditional houses) is this four-room, up-market guesthouse facing the river. Each traditionally designed room comes with modern comforts like satellite TV and a fridge plus an odd *hinoki* (pine) bathtub. There's a mud-walled *jjimjilbang* and rates include a traditional breakfast.

Bus 46 (W1650, 50 minutes, eight daily) runs out to Hahoe from Andong.

ANDONG HANJI 안동한지

About 4km from the folk village, this **paper museum** (☎ 858 7007; ⏱ 9am-6pm Mon-Sat) offers the chance to see modern paper made in the traditional way. Mulberry bark is stripped, soaked, bleached and mashed to make pulp, which is then screened out into giant blocks – the sheets of paper are then removed one by one and dried by hand on a large metal 'iron'. Samples of the paper, plus fascinating exhibits of its uses, are on display in the museum. There are even evening gowns made from it, worn yearly in a fashion show held in Seoul.

Take bus 46 (W1650, 50 minutes, eight daily), which leaves from Andong.

GYEONGSANGBUK-DO

DOSAN SEOWON 도산 서원

If the sloping setting and attractive buildings of **Dosan Seowon** (☎ 856 1073; adult/youth/child W1500/700/600; ⏰ 9am-6pm Mar-Oct, 9am-5pm Nov-Feb) give you a feeling of *déjà vu*, open your wallet – you'll find an image of this revered Confucian academy on the back of the W1000 note.

Some 28km to the north of Andong, Dosan Seowon was founded in 1574 in honour of Yi Hwang (aka Toegye 1501–70), Korea's foremost Confucian scholar – he's on the *front* of the W1000 banknote. For centuries during the mid-Joseon dynasty, this was the most prestigious school for those who aspired to high office, and qualifying examinations for the civil service took place here. It's a beautiful spot, with mountains on one side and farm fields below. On the grounds, small lotus ponds harbour hundreds of frogs, which glisten on their lily leaves like jewels.

Bus 67 (W1100, 40 minutes) runs from Andong along the main road, dropping you off about 2km from the *seowon;* four buses daily continue the last 2km.

CHEONGNYANGSAN PROVINCIAL PARK
청량산 도립공원

Beyond Dosan Seowon, this **park** (☎ 672 1446; admission free; ⏰ 8.30am-6pm) boasts spectacular views and tracks wandering along cliff precipices. In addition to the mountain Cheongnyangsan, the summit of which is **Changinbong** (870m), there are 11 scenic peaks, eight caves and a waterfall, **Gwanchang Pokpo**. A spiderweb of tracks radiates out from Cheongnyang-sa and most are well-marked. The largest temple in the park is **Cheongnyang-sa** and there are a number of small hermitages. Built in AD 663, the temple is quite scenic, sitting in a steep valley below the cliffs. **Ansimdang**, at the base of the temple, is a pleasant teahouse.

It takes about five hours to complete a round trip of the peaks, returning to the bus stops, or about 90 minutes to the temple and back again.

Across the street from the park entrance, there are a dozen *minbak,* shops, restaurants and the **Cheongnyangsan Museum** (admission free; ⏰ 9am-6pm), a modest effort with artefacts related to the area's agricultural history and clean public toilets.

From Andong, bus 67 (W2000, one hour, six daily) continues past Dosan Seowon to the park. If you're travelling from points north of the park, you may need to transfer at Bonghwa (W3500, 40 minutes, four times daily).

BUSEOK-SA 부석사

Is there such a thing as travelling karma? Well, seek out the **Temple of the Floating Stone** (☎ 633 3258; admission W1200; ⏰ 6am-8pm Apr-Sep, 6am-6pm Oct-Mar) and judge for yourself. The determination required to reach this serene, way-out-of-the-way temple 60km north of Andong results in sublime views over a misty valley and a peacefulness that even the non-spiritual will feel.

Though burnt to the ground in the early 14th century by invaders, it was reconstructed in 1358 and escaped destruction during the late-16th-century Japanese invasions. This stroke of good fortune preserved the beautiful main hall, **Muryangsujeon**, making it one of the oldest wooden structures in Korea. It also has what are considered to be Korea's oldest Buddhist wall paintings, as well as a unique, gilded-clay, sitting Buddha. Below the entrance there is a small tourist village with restaurants and *minbak.*

Transport to Buseok-sa is from Yeongju or Punggi (bus number 55/27, W2300/4000, 50 minutes/one hour, every 30-90 minutes). From the temple bus stop it's a steep but pretty climb up a graded hill, past cornfields and peach groves. Not all buses travel to the temple so you might end up in the village of Buseok. From the village bus stop at a four-corner intersection, a taxi ride to the temple costs W5000. The temple bus stop has a time-table for buses back to Yeongju and Punggi.

There's not much to see or do in Yeongju, though spending the night in this quiet town sets you up for a morning departure to Buseok-sa. The street behind the intercity bus terminal has a few sleep options. Try **Swiss Motel** (☎ 631 2300; r W35,000, with computer W40,000).

JUWANGSAN NATIONAL PARK
주왕산 국립공원

Far to the east of Andong and reaching almost to the coast, this 106-sq-km **park** (admission W2000; ⏰ sunrise-1hr before sunset) is dominated by impressive limestone pinnacles that seem to appear from nowhere. Beautiful gorges, waterfalls and cliff walks also feature, and with any luck you'll see an otter or protected Eurasian flying squirrel, among the 900-plus wildlife species here.

Orientation & Information

The main gateway to the park is the town of Cheongsong, about 15km away. At the park entrance, the **information centre** (☎ 873 0014; 2nd fl, bus terminal; ⏰ 9am-5.30pm) has English

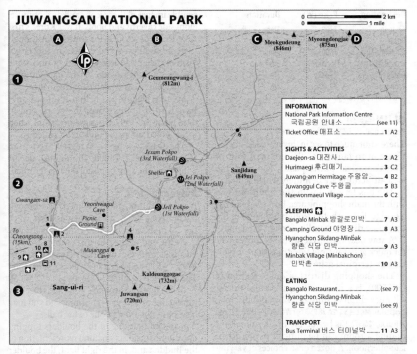

JUWANGSAN NATIONAL PARK

INFORMATION
National Park Information Centre
국립공원 안내소 .... (see 11)
Ticket Office 매표소 **1** A2

SIGHTS & ACTIVITIES
Daejeon-sa 대전사 **2** A2
Hurimaegi 후리매기 **3** C2
Juwang-am Hermitage 주왕암 **4** B2
Juwanggul Cave 주왕굴 **5** B3
Naewonmaeul Village **6** C2

SLEEPING
Bangalo Minbak 방갈로민박 **7** A3
Camping Ground 야영장 **8** A3
Hyangchon Sikdang-Minbak
향촌 식당 민박 **9** A3
Minbak Village (Minbakchon)
민박촌 **10** A3

EATING
Bangalo Restaurant .... (see 7)
Hyangchon Sikdang-Minbak
향촌 식당 민박 .... (see 9)

TRANSPORT
Bus Terminal 버스 터미널박 **11** A3

and Korean maps detailing hiking routes, distances and estimated calories burned. Be sure to check here for local trail conditions.

Sights & Activities

Most visitors to the park are content to see the waterfalls and caves, but for a more rigorous experience try hiking up from Daejeon-sa to **Juwangsan** (720m; once known as **Seokbyeongsan** or 'Stone Screen Mountain'; 1¼ hours), along the ridge to **Kaldeunggogae** (732m, 15 minutes) and then down to **Hurimaegi** (50 minutes), before following the valley back to Daejeon-sa (1¾ hours).

On the way back down take the side trip to **Juwanggul Cave**; the track first passes **Juwang-am Hermitage**, from where a steel walkway takes you through a narrow gorge to the modest cave.

Also within the park is **Naewonmaeul**, a tiny village where craftspeople do woodworking.

Sleeping & Eating

The *minbak* village (*minbakchon*) opposite the Juwangsan bus terminal has 50-plus properties of varying quality, so shop around before paying. Room rates can double on weekends and

in July, August and October. The **campground** (☎ 873 0014; sites adult/youth/child W1600/1200/800), on the other side of the stream, has basic facilities and rents tents (W5000 to W8000).

Bangalo Minbak/Restaurant (방갈로 민박; ☎ 874 5200; r weekdays/weekends W25,000/50,000) About 500m from the park entrance, this place has a log-cabin exterior with central courtyard. Rooms have *ondol* or beds.

Hyangchon Sikdang-Minbak (향촌 식당 민박; ☎ 873 0202; www.juwangsanfood.co.kr; r from W30,000) With the largest sign near the park entrance, this *minbak* and restaurant is hard to miss. It also has some of the area's nicest rooms. If comfort is important, try the computer room: it's got a bed, private bathroom, desk and office chair. Downstairs in the restaurant, the *jeongsik* meal (W10,000) comes with soup and a colourful array of leafy side dishes from the local mountains, some of which are picked by the owner.

Getting There & Away

Virtually all buses to Juwangsan stop in Cheongsong (W1300, 20 minutes, every 30 minutes). Check the timetable inside the Juwangsan bus terminal for detailed schedules.

GYEONGSANGBUK-DO

Destination	Price (W)	Duration
Andong	7300	1½hr
Busan	18,900	3¾hr
Cheongsong	1600	20min
Dongdaegu	15,500	3hr
Dongseoul	23,200	5hr
Yeongcheon*	12,400	2hr

* transfer to Gyeongju

ULJIN 울진

pop 51,000

There's not much to see in this sea-coast town – its claim to fame is as the home of four of Korea's nuclear power plants. However, the area attractions are definitely worth a look.

The bus terminal is in the south of town with the main shopping area 1km away, across a bridge. For cash, the Nonghyup Bank in the shopping district handles foreign exchange.

A stay near the bus terminal is convenient for quick getaways, but the atmosphere is typical bus-terminal grim.

The shopping district, a quick taxi away (W2600), is a nicer setting at similar prices. All rates climb in summer. Chic and discrete, popular **Motel S** (☎ 781 5005; r W40,000-60,000, Sat add W10,000; ☒ ☐) is beside the bus terminal but finding a room can be difficult if you arrive late-afternoon. A dozen or so choices of varying quality line the main road as you walk towards town. 200m past the bridge, **Yongkum-jang** (용금장; ☎ 783 8844; d W30,000; ☒ ☐) is a decent budget option near restaurants and shopping.

For dinner, try **Cheonnyeon Hanu** (천년 한우; ☎ 783 6818; servings from W7000; ☯ 10am-10pm, closed 4th Sun) for comparatively expensive Korean beef or the economical *moksal* (목살; lean pork). It's not far from the town's bridge.

You can catch intercity express buses from Uljin to the following:

Destination	Price (W)	Duration
Busan	20,100	4hr
Daegu	20,300	4hr
Gyeongju	15,800	2½hr
Pohang	12,900	2hr
Seoul	24,100	5hr

AROUND ULJIN
Seongnyugul 석류굴

To spot Buddha, the Virgin Mary, a Roman palace and a wild boar all in one place, head for this 470m-long **cave** (☎ 782 4006; admission W3000; ☯ 9am-6pm Mar-Oct, 9am-5pm Nov-Feb). Impressive stalactites, stalagmites and rock formations are said to re-

semble images of these icons and dozens more, alongside caverns and pools. It was Korea's first cave to be developed for tourism. Although there are walkways and bridges inside, larger visitors (height and/or girth) may find some passages a tight squeeze. Hard hats are provided; lockers are available to store bags.

Spooky legend has it that human bones have turned up here over the years, said to date from the 1592 Japanese invasion, when locals holed up inside only to be sealed in.

The easiest way here is by taxi (W5500) from Uljin. Six buses (W1000, 10 minutes) depart Uljin from the stop opposite the bus terminal.

Bulyeong-sa 불영사

It's a pretty forest- and river-lined road through the Bulyeong Valley, but you may ask, is it worth the 18km drive from Uljin? Emphatically, yes.

At the end of this canyon, another 15 minutes' walk from the car park, **Bulyeong-sa** (admission W2000; ☯ 6.30am-6.30pm) is an idyllic, secluded spot. The temple is a centre for ascetic practice for 50 Buddhist nuns, set around a pond and ringed by mountains. Arrive early morning and you may hear nuns chanting in one of the halls.

It is said that one of the boulders topping one mountainside is a natural representation of the Buddha and, in the right light, the boulder casts its image onto the pond; hence 'Bulyeong-sa' means 'Temple of the Buddha's Shadow'.

Buses connect Uljin with the temple (W1000, 35 minutes, every one to three hours) but the best way to get around is independently: either riding a bike (note that there is a rather long uphill part through the valley) or driving a car.

Deokgu Hot Springs 덕구 온천

The main attraction at this hotel and spa complex is the water at **Deokgu Spa World** (☎ 782 0677; www.duckku.co.kr; r from W90,000, spa W10,000; ☯ 10am-7pm; ☒ ☒), said to cure digestive and skin ailments. Separate men's and women's baths are large and attractive, while the outdoor Spa World is mixed bathing. There's no nudity outdoors; everyone wears a bathing suit and cap (W3000).

Deokgu has good walks further up the valley. One takes you 1.2km to **Yongso Pokpo**, the original hot spring (no bathing facilities). A more strenuous hike (14km, 7½ hours) takes in **Eungbongsan** (999m) returning via **Minssimyo**.

Buses connect Uljin and the hot spring (W2300, one hour, hourly). From Uljin, catch the bus across the street from the country office. A taxi costs W20,000.

Gyeongsangnam-do
경상남도

The best sites in Korea either awe with beauty or deepen our understanding of the culture. Gyeongsangnam-do does both. With a dazzling mix of jagged mountain ridges and sandy beaches, rural villages and urban delights, Gyeongsangnam-do offers travellers the fullest range of choices.

Looking for big-city action? Busan's neon-drenched streets and unique Asian street feel will not disappoint. On the crowded boulevards, quiet backstreets or twisting seacoast trails, there are endless opportunities waiting to be discovered. Did we mention shopping? Busan is home to the world's largest shopping and entertainment complex. With thousands of places to eat unusual food and sample traditional drinks in between beach strolls, mountain hikes and evenings at the cinema, you'll never be bored in Busan.

For a different pace, look to the provincial cities and towns. Gyeongsangnam-do's natural beauty, inspired by verdant mountains and coastal towns untouched by tourist development, is closer than you think, thanks to an efficient transport system. Hop on a bus and you'll be rewarded with outstanding hiking trails on Jirisan, glorious temples in hideaway locations and lush rice paddies in just about every rural community. For marine treasures, board a ferry and go island hopping around Tongyeong or Geoje. On land or by sea, Gyeongsangnam-do is accessible, affordable and waiting to be explored.

HIGHLIGHTS

- Shock your taste buds with Busan seafood specialities like raw fish at **Jagalchi fish market** (p244)
- Go island hopping off the coast of **Tongyeong** (p253)
- Rejuvenate your body at **Hurshimchung** (p242), one of the world's largest hot spas
- Explore **Jirisan** (p258), one of the best places to hike in Korea
- Take a stroll on the soft, white sand at **Sangju Beach** (p257)

★ Jirisan

Hurshimchung ★

Jagalchi Fish ★
Market

Tongyeong ★

Sangju Beach ★

| ▪ TELEPHONE CODE: 055 | ▪ POPULATION: 3 MILLION | ▪ AREA: 10,500 SQ KM |

GYEONGSANGNAM-DO

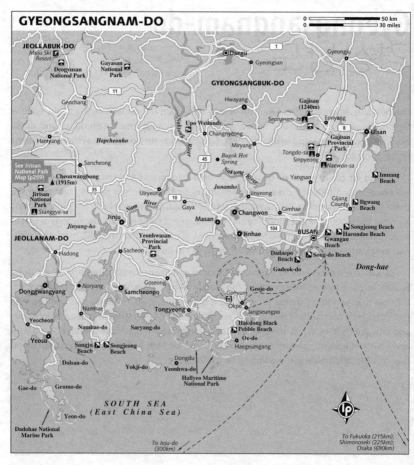

GYEONGSANGNAM-DO

SOUTH SEA (East China Sea)

Dong-hae

History

South Gyeongsang province has a long history of warfare, though it's difficult to beat the Imjin Waeran for destruction, treachery and the birth of an icon. In 1592 the Japanese were eager to secure a land route to China. The Joseon government refused assistance, so the Japanese attacked. Led by Toyotomi Hideyoshi, the Japanese landed 160,000 troops at several places including Busan, Sangju Beach and Jinju, where the Koreans made a valiant yet unsuccessful stand against a superior enemy.

The war's star was Admiral Yi Sun-sin, a brilliant tactician credited with the development of the turtle ship, an ironclad vessel instrumental in harassing Japanese supply lines. Despite his significant wartime contributions, Yi was arrested in 1597 for disobeying orders thanks to a clever ruse concocted by the Japanese, who were eager to see the good admiral removed from the war. With Yi behind bars, the Japanese launched a massive assault that destroyed all but 13 of Korea's 133 vessels. Shaken by the loss, the King released Yi and put him in charge of the tattered navy. In a classic case of size doesn't matter, the admiral destroyed or damaged 133 Japanese vessels. One year later, Yi defeated a Japanese armada near Namhae-do that cost the invaders 450 ships. It also cost Admiral Yi his life. In September of 1598, Hideyoshi died and the Japanese leadership lost its appetite for the war.

National & Provincial Parks

There are four national parks scattered across the province. On the western flank, **Jirisan National Park** is noted for serious climbs. **Hallyeo Maritime National Park** is a spectacular ocean playground encompassing coastal islands from Namhae to Geoje. Along the border separating South and North Gyeongsang provinces, **Gayasan National Park** is famous for Haein-sa, one of the country's most important temples (although Haein-sa is located in South Gyeongsang province, access is easiest from Daegu). Tucked into the northwest corner of the province, **Deogyusan National Park** is where you'll find downhill skiers and snowboarders hitting the slopes at Muju Ski Resort (p312).

There are two provincial parks: **Yeonhwasan** (40 minutes southeast of Jinju) and **Gajisan** (40 minutes north of Busan). Travellers looking for stimulating day trips from Busan should consider visiting **Gajisan Provincial Park** for beautiful temples like Seongnam-sa and a challenging hike up Mount Gaji (1240m).

Getting There & Around

International travellers with direct routes to Busan typically come through Japan by air (see p250) or by sea (see p250).

Most train travellers stop at Busan station, a glassy facility close to the city centre. Many inbound trains stop at Gupo, a handy west-end station ideal for travellers who don't need to go downtown. Train travel in the rest of the province is possible, although schedules are not always convenient. For regional trips, the bus is a superior option with departures from Seobu and Dongbu bus terminals, both close to subway stations. By air, most travellers land at Gimhae International Airport, about 30 minutes west of central Busan.

BUSAN 부산

☎ 051 / pop 3.51 million

Busan flies under the radar of most travellers to Korea. That's unfortunate because visitors often say Busan is a fun city. While it's true the built environment is a bit drab, it's the mountains criss-crossing the city and the coastline that define the urban landscape. The people can be brash and often speak in loud tones, but like any rogue there's a charming side that comes out once you scratch below the surface. Note that Busan is within the boundaries of South Gyeongsang province but is a separate administrative unit with its own telephone area code.

Orientation

Busan is a coastal city tucked into the southeastern corner of the peninsula. The city's manufacturing centre and second container port are at the western end in Gangseo-gu (off Map p238). Gimhae International Airport is 27km west of Seomyeon, Busan's city centre. Agricultural and fishing communities continue to survive in Gijang County in the city's east end, though development pressures may bring significant changes over the next decade.

A band of north–south development runs through the centre of Busan. The old container port dominates the southern coastline in and around Nampo-dong, an ageing commercial district with a mishmash of back alleys. Two passenger ferry terminals, the immigration office and a community of draggletailed buildings that serve as a living museum of 40 years past are one subway stop north at Jungang-dong. Further north, Lines 1 and 2 of the subway intersect in Seomyeon (Map p243), the city centre packed with bars, restaurants and street vendors. Continue north on Line 1 (Map p242) to find Hurshimchung spa, Beomeo-sa

---

BUSAN IN FILM

Haeundae (2009) is about a tsunami that crashes onto Busan's most famous beach. The story follows a standard disaster movie plot line: a geologist predicts a calamity by tracking seismic activity in the East Sea but nobody listens. When the inevitable tide is set to destroy Haeundae, the geologist goes to the beach to see his ex-wife.

Gritty and disturbing, *Chingu* (2001) is the story of four school-aged friends, boys whose lives move in radically different directions as men. Two friends end up in rival gangs, leading to a compelling courtroom scene. Artfully directed and skilfully acted, the semiautobiographical story based on director Kwak Kyungtaek's life is set in Busan, with local sites such as Jagalchi fish market. The DVD version has English subtitles.

BUSAN

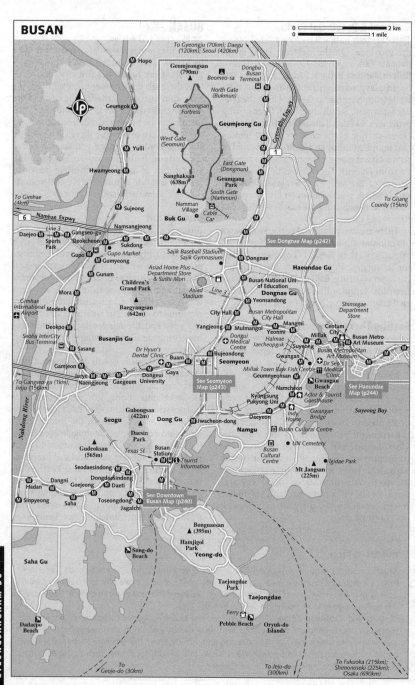

and a trail leading to Geumjeong Mountain. Beaches in Gwangan and Haeundae (Map p244) – arguably the most westernised part of the city – are easy to reach on the eastern section of Line 2.

Information
EMERGENCY
Fire & rescue ☎ 119
Police ☎ 112

INTERNET ACCESS
Is Korea a wired country? Hell yes, even the post office (below) has free internet access.

INTERNET RESOURCES
City government (http://english.busan.go.kr) For basic socioeconomic and travel data.
South Gyeongsang (http://english.gsnd.net/default.jsp) Learn about South Gyeongsang's sites and geography.

MEDICAL SERVICES
Dongui Medical Centre (Map p238; ☎ 850 8523; ⊚ Line 1 to Yangjeong, Exit 4) Marie Kim is an RN who can help travellers. Outside the exit, take local bus 8 or 8-1.
Dr Hyun (Map p238; ☎ 897 2283; ⊚ Line 2 to Gaya, Exit 2) For dental problems. His 2nd-floor office is near the exit.
Dr Seo (Map p238; ☎ 755 0920; ⊚ Line 2 to Gwangan, Exit 1) For general medical maladies. Dr Seo speaks English well. His clinic is at a major intersection beside a pharmacy in Milak-dong, 10 minutes on foot from the station. Turn right at the second corner and walk 700m.

MONEY
Most banks exchange currency, though the level of service varies; your chances of finding reasonably efficient service are greatest at the Korea Exchange Bank (KEB).
Gimhae International Airport currency exchange domestic terminal (Map p238; ⊙ 9:30am-4:30pm); international terminal (⊙ 8:30am-9pm).

POST
Central post office (Map p240; ⊙ 9am-8pm Mon-Fri, to 1pm Sat & Sun; ⊚ Line 1 to Jungangdong, Exit 9)

TOURIST INFORMATION
Busan station office (Map p238; ☎ 441 6565; ⊙ 9am-8pm) There's knowledgeable staff and a modest selection of maps.
Gimhae International Airport desk (Map p238) domestic terminal (☎ 973 4607; ⊙ 6.30am-last flight); international terminal (☎ 973 2800; ⊙ 7am-9pm) Try these when you need help finding a bus into the city.

Haeundae office (Map p244; ☎ 749 4335; ⊙ 9am-6pm) A great selection of material; beside the Busan Aquarium on Haeundae beach.
International ferry terminal (Map p240; ☎ 465 3471; ⊙ 9am-6pm) Useful information when you're coming from Japan.

TRAVEL AGENCIES
It's easy to find a travel agency. Finding one with English-speaking staff, well that's a different matter.
Kangsan Travel (Map p244; ☎ 747 0031; www.kangsantravel.com; ⊙ 9am-6pm Mon-Fri, 10am-3pm Sat; ⊚ Line 2 to Jangsan, Exit 9) provides English-language services geared towards expats. The agency is on the 4th floor, above Starbucks.

Dangers & Annoyances
It's best to avoid Texas St – a commercial district opposite Busan station that's home for hostess bars and the occasional street hold-up – late at night. Never drink tap water; don't even cook with it. Typhoon season – roughly mid-July to September – brings heavy rain, ferry cancellations, and on occasion, severe property damage. Yellow dust storms in the spring don't compare with the sheets of gunk that blanket Seoul, but there are days when it's best not to go outside.

Sights & Activities
BEOMEO-SA 범어사
This magnificent **temple** (Map p242; adult/youth/child W1000/700/500; ⊙ 7am-7pm; ⊚ Line 1 to Beomeosa, Exit 5) is perhaps Busan's best sight. Despite its city location, Beomeo-sa is a world away from the urban jungle, with beautiful architecture neatly set against an extraordinary mountain setting. It's a busy place, as the path leading to the temple is the northern starting point for trails across Geumjeongsan. Before heading back to the city, visit the restaurants near the bus stop to enjoy *pajeon* (파전; green onion pancake) for W6000. For an insight into the Beomeo-sa Temple Stay program see the boxed text, p54.

At street level from the station spin 180 degrees, turn left at the corner and walk 200m to the terminus. Catch bus 90 (W1000, 20 minutes, every 15 minutes from 8am to 8pm) or take a W3000 taxi to the temple entrance.

GEUMJEONG FORTRESS 금정산성
Travellers climbing **Geumjeongsan** (Geumjeong Mountain) expecting to see a fort will be disappointed because there isn't one. **Geumjeong**

DOWNTOWN BUSAN

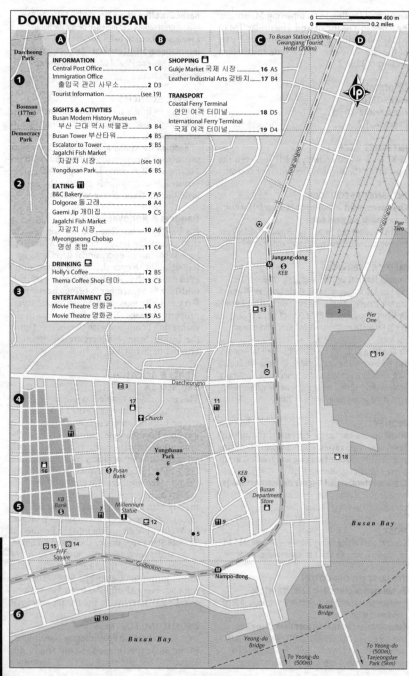

INFORMATION
Central Post Office **1** C4
Immigration Office
출입국 관리 사무소 **2** D3
Tourist Information .... (see 19)

SIGHTS & ACTIVITIES
Busan Modern History Museum
부산 근대 역사 박물관 **3** B4
Busan Tower 부산타워 **4** B5
Escalator to Tower **5** B5
Jagalchi Fish Market
자갈치 시장 .... (see 10)
Yongdusan Park **6** B5

EATING
B&C Bakery **7** A5
Dolgorae 돌고래 **8** A4
Gaemi Jip 개미집 **9** C5
Jagalchi Fish Market
자갈치 시장 **10** A6
Myeongseong Chobap
영성 초밥 **11** C4

DRINKING
Holly's Coffee **12** B5
Thema Coffee Shop 테마 **13** C3

ENTERTAINMENT
Movie Theatre 영화관 **14** A5
Movie Theatre 영화관 **15** A5

SHOPPING
Gukje Market 국제 시장 **16** A5
Leather Industrial Arts 갖바치 **17** B4

TRANSPORT
Coastal Ferry Terminal
연안 여객 터미널 **18** D5
International Ferry Terminal
국제 여객 터미널 **19** D4

fortress (Map p242) is a stone wall with four gates. Not all is lost because this is where you'll find some of the city's best hiking. Outdoor enthusiasts seeking an intimate experience with nature should avoid the mountain on holidays and weekend mornings – peak times for maddening crowds of fashionable hikers.

Most hikers start at the north end of the trail that begins with a steep climb along the left side of Beomeo-sa. This trail leads to **Bungmun** (북문; North Gate). The 8.8km hike from Beomeo-sa to **Nammun** (남문; South Gate) is a comfortable hike with a couple of steep stretches.

The least arduous route is by **cable car** (Map p242; one way/return adult W3000/6000, child W2000/3000; ⏱ 9am-6.30pm) inside **Geumgang Park** (Map p242; admission free; ⏱ 9am-6pm Mar-Oct, 9am-5pm Nov-Feb) at the southern base of the mountain. From the cable car, it's a 10-minute walk to the South Gate.

The cable car is a 15-minute walk from Oncheonjang station on Line 1, Exit 1. Walk left towards the overhead pedestrian crosswalk. Cross the street, walk down the left staircase and turn right at the first corner. Down the street, there's a sign pointing to Geumgang Park.

SEOKBUL-SA 석불사

Hard to find, difficult to reach and a wonder to behold, this **temple** (Map p242; admission free; ⏱ 7am-7pm) is a hermitage carved into rock. Two massive boulders stretching 20m in height jut out from the mountainside to form a U-shaped enclave with three rock facings, which is now a place of worship. Inside the enclave, Buddhist images have been meticulously etched into stone. Visually powerful in scale and impact, it's the kind of work that moves first-time visitors to exclaim 'wow' as they step back and arch their necks to get the full picture.

Getting to Seokbul-sa is a worthwhile challenge for anyone with a desire to explore out-of-the-way places. The most interesting – and strenuous – route is to add this stop to your Geumjeongsan hike. From **Nammum** (남문; South Gate), the path indicated by the **Mandeokchon** (만덕촌) sign leads to a collection of restaurants and a foot volleyball court in **Namman Village** (남만 마을). About 500m down the trail, look for a sign that reads 석불사 입구 (Seokbul-sa entrance) which points you down a steep, rocky trail. At the bottom, follow the cement road uphill to the temple.

On the way back, there's no need to return to Namman Village. At the top of the steep trail, turn left and pick up one of the less travelled trails meandering up to the mountaintop on your right. There are no signs so ask someone to point you to the cable car. On the other side of the mountain, ride the cable car down. Bottom line: add 4km and 1½ hours to the Geumjeongsan hike to experience one of the most unique temples in Busan.

HIKES & WALKS

If Geumjeongsan's trails seem more like work than pleasure, there are opportunities to explore Busan's natural beauty at a leisurely pace.

Igidae (이기대; Map p238; ⓜ Line 2 to Namcheon, Exit 3) is a nature park ideal for a two-hour stroll. On the way up **Mt Jangsan** (225m), you'll come to the first of three plateaus that provide panoramic views of the city. There are a myriad of trails to choose from, just be sure you eventually get over to the sea and follow the boardwalk that zigzags along the coastline. The park is a 20-minute walk down the road from the subway station. Pick up the trail behind the pier and outdoor driving range.

Taejongdae Park (태종대유원지; Map p238), on the southern tip of **Yeong-do** (영도; Yeong Island), is another chance to experience the city's rugged coastline. Walk down the stone steps and you'll come to a tiny beach. Jagged cliffs, thick pine forests, odd rock formations, a lighthouse and a kiddie tram are just some of the treats you'll experience on this two-hour walk. From Nampo-dong station, catch bus 30 (W1000) on the Jagalchi side of the street or take a taxi (W3000).

The path in **Children's Grand Park** (어린이대공원; Map p238) cuts through a forest and circles around a small lake, eventually leading to a kids' amusement park. For a more strenuous four-hour outing, pick up a trail leading to the peak of **Baegyangsan** (백양산; Baegyang Mountain, 642m). A taxi (W4500 from Seomyeon) to the park's main gate is the most practical way to start your journey.

PUBLIC BATHS

You can't really experience Busan unless you've been to a public bath.

Spa Land (Map p238; http://centumcity.shinsegae.com/main/main.asp; Shinsegae department store; adult/youth weekdays W12,000/9000, weekends W14,000/11,000; ⏱ 6am-midnight; ⓜ Line 2 to Centum City, Exit 3) is the largest public bath in Asia, perhaps the world. It's a beautiful facility with immaculate bathing

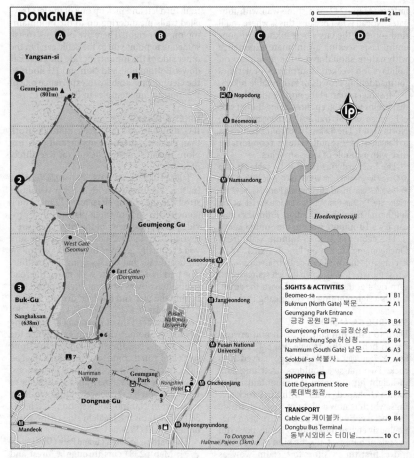

DONGNAE

0 _____ 2 km
0 _____ 1 mile

SIGHTS & ACTIVITIES
Beomeo-sa **1** B1
Bukmun (North Gate) 북문 **2** A1
Geumgang Park Entrance
 금강 공원 입구 **3** B4
Geumjeong Fortress 금정산성 **4** A2
Hurshimchung Spa 허심청 **5** B4
Nammum (South Gate) 남문 **6** A3
Seokbul-sa 석불사 **7** A4

SHOPPING
Lotte Department Store
 롯데백화점 **8** B4

TRANSPORT
Cable Car 케이블카 **9** B4
Dongbu Bus Terminal
 동부시외버스 터미널 **10** C1

tubs and two floors of hot and cold *jjimjilbang*
(sauna) rooms. Drinks and light snacks are
available with costs charged to your locker
key. Before leaving, go to the checkout desk;
a scanner reads your key to determine time in
the facility (there is a four-hour limit) and the
final bill. Kid under 13 years are not permitted; last entry is 10.30pm.

With 4300 sq metres of floor space,
Hurshimchung (허심청; Map p242; adult/youth/
child W7900/5000/3000; 5.30am-10pm; Line 1 to
Oncheonjang, Exit 1) is the second-largest place to
take the plunge. The domed roof and ornate
features make this a great place to relax, wash
and exfoliate. Last entry is 9pm. Located opposite the Nongshim Hotel, it's a 15-minute
walk from the station.

BEACHES

Haeundae (Map p244) is the country's most
famous beach. During the peak travel season
in the month of August, umbrellas mushroom across the 2km beach while frolickers
fill the water with inner tubes rented from
booths behind the beach. It's a fun family
outing with 500,000 friends, though the
marketing bumph portraying Haeundae as
a world-class resort is bunk. Take Line 2 to
Haeundae station, Exit 3 or 5, and walk to
the beach.

Among the city's seven other beaches,
Gwangan (Map p238) is the best option for
access and quality (the other beaches are
Dadaepo, Song-do, Songjeong, Ilgwang,
Imnang and Pebble Beach). Although the

GYEONGSANGNAM-DO

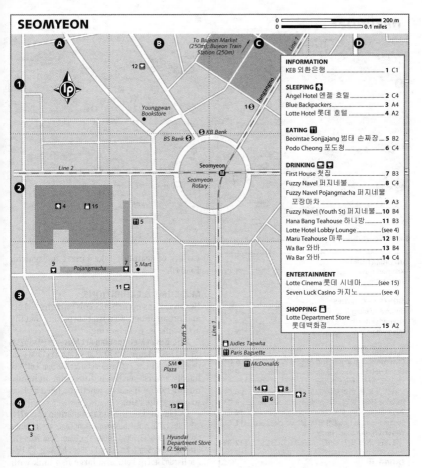

SEOMYEON

0 — 200 m
0 — 0.1 miles

INFORMATION
KEB 외환은행 1 C1

SLEEPING 🏠
Angel Hotel 엔젤 호텔 2 C4
Blue Backpackers 3 A4
Lotte Hotel 롯데 호텔 4 A2

EATING 🍴
Beomtae Sonjjajang 범태 손짜장 ... 5 B2
Podo Cheong 포도청 6 C4

DRINKING 🍷
First House 첫집 7 B3
Fuzzy Navel 퍼지네불 8 C4
Fuzzy Navel Pojangmacha 퍼지네불
포장마차 9 A3
Fuzzy Navel (Youth St) 퍼지네불 10 B4
Hana Bang Teahouse 하나방 11 B3
Lotte Hotel Lobby Lounge .... (see 4)
Maru Teahouse 마루 12 B1
Wa Bar 와바 13 B4
Wa Bar 와바 14 C4

ENTERTAINMENT
Lotte Cinema 롯데 시네마 .... (see 15)
Seven Luck Casino 카지노 .... (see 4)

SHOPPING 🛍
Lotte Department Store
롯데백화점 15 A2

wall of commercial development behind the beach diminishes the daytime experience, Gwangan really shines at night. The multicoloured light show illuminating the bridge is grand. The shortest route to Gwangan is Line 2 to Geumnyeonsan station, Exit 3. Rotate 180 degrees at street level and turn right at the corner; the beach is five minutes down the road. Or take Line 2 to Gwangan station, Exit 5.

On the other side of Dalmaji Hill in Haeundae, **Songjeong** beach (Map p236) is generally less congested than the city's two more famous beaches. A popular destination for dating, it has heaps of restaurants, cafes, singing rooms, bars and motels to fill a day and night of fun. A taxi (W5000) from Jangsan

station, the last stop on Line 2, is the best way to get here.

Largely undeveloped and rather scenic, **Dadaepo** beach is frequented by photographers with an eye for dramatic sunsets. You'll need plenty of patience to get here though, as transport requires a subway ride to Sinpyeong station, Exit 4, and a bus connection (2, 11 or 338).

YONGDUSAN PARK 용두산 공원
In the centre of this humble park stands the 118m **Busan Tower** (Map p240; adult/youth/child W3500/3000/2500; ⏰ 8.30am-10pm Apr-Oct, 9am-10pm Nov-Mar). If the haze is not too thick, daytime views of container-ship traffic in the harbour give a sense of the port's vast scale of operations.

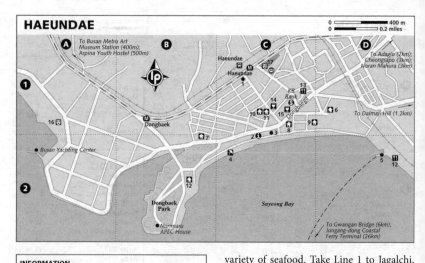

HAEUNDAE

JAGALCHI FISH MARKET 자갈치 시장

Anyone with a love of seafood and a tolerance for powerful odours could easily spend a couple of hours exploring the country's largest **fish market** (Map p240). Waterfront warehouses, tiny shops and elderly women perched on street corners sell an incredible variety of seafood. Take Line 1 to Jagalchi, Exit 10.

MUSEUMS & EXHIBITIONS

Busan frowns upon bourgeois pursuits like art and urban design, so it isn't surprising that the arts scene is, well, lacking.

The **Busan Metropolitan Art Museum** (Map p238; ☎ 744 2602; adult/youth W700/300, Sat free; ⏲ 10am-6pm, closed Mon; ⑨ Line 2 to Busan Metro Art Museum, Exit 5) is hardly a must-see but it does come in handy during typhoon season when you need a place to escape the rain.

In Haeundae, the **Busan Aquarium** (Map p244; ☎ 740 1700; www.busanaquarium.com; adult/youth/child W16,000/13,500/11,000; ⏲ 10am-9pm Mon-Fri; 9am-9pm Sat, Sun & holidays, to 10pm Jul-Aug; ⑨ Line 2 to Haeundae, Exit 3 or 5) is a large fish tank with 35,000 creatures. The aquarium also hosts a shark diving class open to nondivers (see p81 for details).

The **Busan Modern History Museum** (Map p240; ☎ 253 3845; admission free; ⏲ 9am-6pm; Tue-Sun; ⑨ Line 1, Jungang-dong, Exit 3 or 5) is a modest effort with information about Busan's development. It's located north of Yongdusan Park, 300m west of the Jungang-dong central post office.

The **UN Cemetery** (Map p238; www.unmck.or.kr; ☎ 625 1608; admission free; ⏲ 9am-6pm Jun to Sep, to 5pm Oct-May; ⑨ Line 2 to Daeyeon, Exit 5) appeals to history enthusiasts, though the photo exhibition is a modest tribute. At street level turn 180 degrees; look for the sign pointing to the UN Cemetery.

Tours

Mipo Wharf (Map p244), the small pier at the eastern end of Haeundae beach, is home for ocean tours.

Return trips run to nearby islands like Oryukdo (round trip adult/child W14,900/7500, start at 9am, schedule varies) and one-way trips to the coastal ferry terminal in Jungang-dong (adult/child W15,000/9000, start at 9am, schedule varies).

From Taejeongdae, a noisy two-hour cruise runs along the coast with views of Igidae (round-trip adult/child W8000/5000; 9am to 5pm).

City Tour Busan (www.citytourbusan.com; 1hr 40min tours adult/child W10,000/5000; ☯ every 40min) runs two daytime bus tours that whisk you to the sights. The Haeundae route includes two beaches and the UN Cemetery. The Taejeongdae bus heads south with stops at Yongdusan Park and Gukje market. One evening bus tour (7pm departure) drives towards Haeundae for a night view of Gwangan bridge. All buses start at Busan station. Ticket purchases are on the bus.

Festivals & Events

In August special events are held on the city's beaches as part of the **Busan Sea Festival**, including the **Busan International Rock Festival** (www.rockfestival.co.kr; Dadaepo beach).

The **Pusan International Film Festival** (www.piff.org) is the city's most significant festival. First launched in 1996, almost 200,000 people attended the 2008 version, which screened 315 films from 60 countries. The festival is held sometime between September and October.

Sleeping

BUDGET

Indy House (Map p238; ☎ 070 8615 6442; http://indybusan.com; Sewon Villa Bldg, Suite 201; dm W20,000; ☒ ▣ ; ⊖ Line 2 to Kyungsung-Pukyong, Exit 1) Near the Kyungsung-Pukyong party zone, it gets positive reviews for cleanliness and friendliness, two features not always available in Busan's budget accommodation market. Call from the station pay phone to arrange a pickup.

Cheonyeonjang Motel (천연장 모텔; Map p244; ☎ 743 2311; r W35,000; ⊖ Line 2 to Haeundae, Exit 3 or 5; ☒) Design inspired by neglect. Dated furnishings and faded wall coverings give this place a unique character. Opposite the Paradise Hotel, it might be the cheapest sleep option in Haeundae.

Also try the following:

Arpina Youth Hostel (아르피나; off Map p244; ☎ 731 9800; www.arpina.co.kr; dm W28,600; ⊖ Line 2 to Busan Metro Art Museum, Exit 3; ☒ ▣ ⊠) Hostel and sports in a nonsmoking facility.

Blue Backpackers (Map p243; ☎ 019 272 3962; www.bluebackpackers.com; dm W20,000; ⊖ Line 1 or 2 to Seomyeon, Exit 7; ☒ ▣) The owners have moved uptown with a bigger hostel in a central location. Budget rooms are a 10-minute walk behind the Lotte Hotel in Seomyeon. Check the web for details.

Actor & Tourist Guesthouse (Map p238; 배우와 여행자 게스트하우스; ☎ 010 3388 3184; www.actourist.com; 69-9 4F Namcheondong Suyeong-Gu; dm W15,000; ⊖ Line 2 to Namcheon, Exit 2; ▣) Simple, sometimes scruffy and minutes from Gwangan beach. Walk 25m from the station. Follow the fish sign.

MIDRANGE

Sugar Motel (슈가 모텔; Map p244; ☎ 747 8620; standard/special/VIP W50,000/70,000/90,000; ⊖ Line 2 to Haeundae, Exit 3; ☒ ▣) If your idea of a romantic getaway includes battery-operated devices, this motel is worth inspecting. Haeundae beach is just around the corner, but with so much stuff in the room you may not get that far. Walk towards the beach.

Gwangjang Tourist Hotel (광장 광광 호텔; off Map p240; ☎ 464 3141; s/d/tw/special W40,000/45,000/50,000/80,000; ⊖ Line 1 to Busan station, Exit 8; ☒ ▣) A proper tourist-class hotel for travellers who require only a proper place to lie down after a busy day of sightseeing. Walk across the plaza.

Angel Hotel (엔젤 호텔; Map p243; ☎ 802 8223; d/tw W44,000/60,000; ⊖ Line 1 or 2 to Seomyeon, follow underground signs to Judies Taewha Exit; ☒) Location is the best feature of this unpretentious property with few amenities and rooms bordering on small. Stay here for the price and central Seomyeon location, which means speedy access to the subway and many nightlife options.

Sunset Business Hotel (선셋 호텔; Map p244; ☎ 730 9900; d/tw W99,000/145,000, add W20,000/30,000 Fri & Sat; ⊖ Line 2 to Haeundae, Exit 3 or 5; ☒) Minutes from Haeundae beach, this no-frills property is an attractive compromise between the nearby beachfront international hotels and love motels.

TOP END

Westin Chosun Beach Hotel (웨스틴 조선 비치 호텔; Map p244; ☎ 749 7201; r W193,000; ⊖ Line 2 to Haeundae, Exit 3 or 5; ☒ ▣ ⊠) Busan's oldest

BUSAN'S SPECIALITY FOOD

Busan is a coastal city, so it's not surprising that seafood flavours much of the local cuisine. Raw fish, called *hoe* (회; sounds like 'when' without the 'n'), a popular dish enjoyed with a group of friends, is widely available and affordably priced (compared to prices in most cities). Busan is one of the country's favourite raw-fish destinations.

A typical *hoe* dinner starts with appetisers like raw baby octopus still wiggling on the plate. A platter of sliced raw fish is the main course. Fish is dipped into a saucer of *chogochujang* (초고 추장), a watery red-pepper sauce, or soy sauce (간장) mixed with wasabi (와사비). The meal is customarily finished with rice and a boiling pot of *maeuntang* (매운탕; spicy fish soup).

Most Koreans say *hoe* has delicate taste and smooth texture. Western travellers may find the taste bland with a slightly tough texture. A small platter starting at W40,000 is rarely sufficient for a pair of raw-fish aficionados. Japanese sushi is popular, called *chobap* (초밥). Raw fish is best accompanied with *soju* (local vodka).

The **Jagalchi fish market** (자갈치 시장; Map p240; ⊙ Line 1, Jagalchi, Exit 10) opposite Nampo-dong is the city's sprawling wholesale and retail centre for all things fishy. Head to the newly constructed market and pick your favourite live sea creature from any of the 1st-floor vendors. Expect to pay a minimum of W15,000 and for a modest fee (W3000 per person) they'll prepare your dinner and serve it upstairs in the restaurant.

Millak Town Raw Fish Centre (민락타운 외 센터; Map p238; ⊙ Line 2, Gwangan, Exit 5) is located at the northeast end of Gwangan beach. Purchase a fish for W15,000 to W30,000 and walk upstairs to eat; the woman selling you the fish will indicate which floor. Inside the seating area, your fish will be prepared and served for W10,000 per person.

Myeongseong Chobap (명성 초밥; Map p240; sushi sets from W12,000, raw fish W30,000-60,000; ⊙ Line 1, Jungang-dong, Exit 3 or 5) is a popular Japanese-style restaurant serving *chobap* and *sushi* courses (생선회 코스; raw fish set menu). Located in Jungang-dong, it's 100m north of the Tower Hotel with 'sushi' written on the signboard.

international hotel gets better with age. A hint of retro shaken, not stirred, with modern touches, creates a James Bond – a la Sean Connery – dashing cool. Inside and out, the best hotel on Haeundae beach.

Other recommendations:

Lotte Hotel (롯데 호텔; Map p243; ☎ 810 1000; d W340,000; ⊙ Line 1 or 2 to Seomyeon, Exit 5 or 7; ✗ 🖳 🖂) The top business-class hotel in Seomyeon.

Novotel Ambassador Busan (노보텔 앰버서더 호텔; Map p244; ☎ 743 1234; d W190,000; ⊙ Line 2 to Haeundae, Exit 3 or 5; ✗ 🖳 🖂) Staff could benefit from a customer-relations training seminar.

Grand Hotel (그랜드 호텔; Map p244; ☎ 740 0114; d W200,000; ⊙ Line 2 to Haeundae, Exit 3 or 5; ✗ 🖳 🖂) Better-than-average facilities (like a 50m pool) across the street from Haeundae beach.

Paradise Hotel (파라다이스 호텔; Map p244; ☎ 749 2111; tw W240,000; ⊙ Line 2 to Haeundae, Exit 3 or 5; ✗ 🖳 🖂) Busan's first casino is here.

Eating

The food in Busan is salty, spicy and raw, just like the people of this fair metropolis. Seafood in various shapes and forms – like eel, octopus, and swellfish – is popular and plentiful.

BUDGET

Dolgorae (돌고래; Map p240; meals from W3000; ⊙ Line 1, Nampo-dong, Exit 1) The interior looks like a penitentiary but the stern women who run this shop serve great *doenjang jjigae* (된장 찌개; spicy soy-bean stew). The soup bowls are small but with prices this low, order another set. Located at the end of a narrow lane one block west of the KB bank near B&C Bakery.

B&C Bakery (Map p240; meals from W3000; ☼ 8.30am-10.30pm; ⊙ Line 1, Nampo-dong, Exit 1) Stock up on tasty carbohydrates before exploring Nampo-dong's back alleys.

Beomtae Sonjjajang (범태 손짜장; Map p243; meals from W3000; ☼ 11.30am-10pm; ⊙ Line 1 or 2 to Seomyeon, Exit 5 or 7) A sterling example of a successful restaurant owner who won't update the interior. According to superstition, the good fortune a successful shop enjoys could be lost if the interior were changed. Consequently, some shoddy-looking restaurants, like this one, serve great food. The *jjambbong* (짬뽕; spicy seafood soup) and *tangsuyuk* (탕수육; sweet-and-sour fried pork) are excellent.

Podo Cheong (포도청; Map p243; ☎ 806 9797; per serving W6000; ❤ noon-midnight; ❂ Line 1 or 2 to Seomyeon, follow underground signs to Judies Taewha Exit.) It's not the best *sutbul galbi* (숯불갈비; charcoal-fired barbecue) restaurant but it is good. The main draw at this busy place is the backyard barbecue feel in the outdoor patio. Lean *moksal* (목살; pork chop) tastes great, though most Koreans choose *samgyeopsal* (삼겹살; fatty pork).

Seafood

Sushi Mori (수시 모리; Map p238; sushi plates from W1500; ❂ Line 3 to Sports Complex station, Exit 11) The environs are not especially attractive but this restaurant in the Asiad Home Plus department store food court has sushi on a conveyor belt.

Halmae Jaecheopguk (할매 재첩국; Map p238; per serving W6000; ❤ 24hr; ❂ Line 2 to Gwangan, Exit 5) Hungover in Gwangan beach? Do what many Koreans do and stumble over to this restaurant respected for hangover remedies disguised as food. *Jaecheopguk* (재첩국; marsh clam soup) is a clear shellfish broth. Located on Gwangan's one-way street, one block behind the beach road.

MIDRANGE & TOP END

Dongnae Halmae Pajeon (동래 할매 파전; off Map p242; ☎ 552 0791; http://english.dongraepajun.co.kr; meals from W18,000; ❤ noon-10pm; ❂ Line 1 to Dongnae, Exit 2) Dongnae is famous for *pajeon* (파전; green onion pancake) and this is one of the most attractive places to experience a classic Busan dish. Large wooden tables and rich earthy colours blend traditional design with modern touches. From the station, walk to the first light. Cross the street, walk right and turn left at the first road beside KT Plaza. Turn right past the motels. The restaurant is on the left. Or it's a short taxi ride from the subway.

Seafood

Gaemi Jip (개미집; Map p240; meals from W7000; ❤ 9am-11pm; ❂ Line 1 to Nampo-dong, Exit 1) The speciality is *nakji bokkeum* (낙지볶음; octopus stew), a fiery dish that can cause customers to sweat profusely, so keep a supply of beverages close at hand. Located on a small lane in Nampo-dong near the steps to Yongdusan Park.

Geumsu Bokguk (금수 복국; Map p244; meals W9000-40,000; ❤ 24hr; ❂ Line 2 to Haeundae, Exit 3 or 5) Remember *The Simpsons* episode when Homer ate blowfish and was told he had 24 hours to live? This restaurant serves that fish. A worthwhile restaurant for anyone who

wants to experience a seafood delicacy and earn bragging rights: 'I ate poisonous fish and survived'. Located on a lane opposite the Paradise Hotel.

Drinking

There are thousands of places to drink, ranging from sophisticated hotel bars to *pojangmacha*, Korean late-night drinking establishments fashioned out of tarpaulin and plastic chairs. Most of the happening bars attracting a mix of expats and locals are in Gwangan, Haeundae, the Kyungsung-Pukyong area and Seomyeon.

GWANGAN BEACH

Gwangan's interesting bars are located on the busy beachfront road (Map p238).

Thursday Party (drinks W2500; ❤ 7pm-5am weekends) This Western-style bar on the beach road is a regular meeting place for expats and locals. Cheap draught beer, curry-flavoured popcorn and bartenders who take musical requests make this a fun place. Gwangan was the original location; new outlets are in Haeundae, Seomyeon, and Kyungsung-Pukyoung.

Fuzzy Navel (drinks W4000; ❤ 7pm-6am) The recipe is simple: take one shack and decorate liberally with beach-bum graffiti. Add Plexiglas windows and presto, one of the city's most interesting concoctions. Fuzzy Navel is growing across the city with locations in Haeundae and Seomyeon.

HAEUNDAE BEACH

Drinks in Haeundae can put a serious dent in your wallet. Beachfront hotel bars are popular with the corporate crowd with expense accounts; travellers with a refined sense of budget head elsewhere. For a low-cost option, grab some beverages from a nearby convenience store and plop down on the beach.

Noran Mahura (노란 마후라; off Map p244; drinks W4000; ❤ 2pm-sunrise) It's a tent restaurant on Cheongsapo (청사포), an out-of-the-way harbour where people come for a drink to watch the sunset and unexpectedly stay for the sunrise. Snacks include *garibi* (가리비), barbecued shellfish with a salsalike sauce that tastes great. It tastes even better with *soju* at sunrise. Catch a W3000 taxi from Haeundae beach.

Adagio (off Map p244; drinks W3000; ❤ 11am-10pm Mon-Sat, noon-7pm Sun; ❂ Line 2 to Jangsan, Exit 4) Haeundae might seem like a long way to travel for coffee, but the superb espresso makes it a worthwhile trip for java lovers. Walk straight from the exit; turn left at the first street and then a quick right turn.

U2 (Map p244; drinks W3000; ◷ 7pm-3am, to 5am Fri & Sat) Finding a bar that plays George Thorogood isn't easy. Luckily, Busan has one and this is it: a rock-and-roll bar with bourbon, scotch and beer. It's opposite the Novotel Hotel.

KYUNGSUNG-PUKYONG UNIVERSITIES

The commercial district in front of Kyungsung and Pukyong universities (Map p238) is an electric party district with eating and drinking options catering to 40,000 hungry, thirsty and frugal students. Take Line 2 to Kyungsung and Pukyong station, Exit 3; turn right at the first street.

Gol Mok (골목; ☎ 625 0730; drinks W4000; ◷ 5pm-1am; ◉ Line 2 to Kyungsung-Pukyong, Exit 3) Architectural flair in Busan? It's rare, but here's one of the city's funkiest buildings with a jazz bar, restaurant, small gallery and stage theatre. From the station, turn right at the first street and left at the second lane.

Ol' 55 (drinks W4000; ◷ 7pm-2am Tue-Thu, to 5am Fri & Sat, closed Sun) A testosterone-charged tavern with everything a beer-chugging man needs: ale to match budget and taste, a prohibition on hip-hop music, and women who play billiards in high-heel shoes and cut-offs.

Vinyl Underground (drinks W4000; ◷ 7pm-5am) Bring your A-game to this hip-hopping dance club that's wall-to-wall flesh late Fridays and Saturdays. Mingle with locals sporting the latest music video–inspired club wear and the baddest home boyz to come out of Saskatchewan. It's near Ol' 55.

SEOMYEON

Maru Teahouse (마루; Map p243; drinks W5000; ◷ 10am-11pm) Savour Korean, Japanese or Chinese teas surrounded by calligraphy in the floor seating area or in one of the private rooms enclosed by paper doors. From the Younggwan bookstore, walk left around the first corner, and then left at the first street. It's 100m up the road.

Hana Bang Teahouse (하나방; Map p243; drinks W4500; ◷ 10am-11pm) Like *Maru*, this shop has a good selection of teas though the interior is modern, spacious and, for people who don't like floor seating, more relaxing. This 2nd-floor shop is hard to see from street level. On the road running behind Lotte department store; look for a sign with the phone number 806 0011.

Lotte Hotel Lobby Lounge (Map p243; drinks W4000) Here's the upscale lizard lounge you've been looking for. Palm trees, comfy chairs and live muzak created by the duo with a piano and iMac. Throw in a decent Irish coffee and you've got the perfect place to impress a date.

Other recommendations:

First House (첫집; Map p243; drinks W3000; ◷ 6pm-5am, closed 2nd and 4th Mon) On the corner behind the Lotte Department store, this *pojangmacha* is usually open an hour or two before the other nearby tent bars.

Fuzzy Navel (퍼지네불; Map p243; drinks W5000; ◷ 6.30pm-6am) A party for the 20-something crowd on Seomyeon's Youth St. It's on the 4th floor. The latest Fuzzy Navel is near the Podo Cheong meat restaurant and Angel Hotel.

Fuzzy Navel Pojangmacha (퍼지네불; Map p243; drinks W5000; ◷ 8pm-5am) There's a long line of orange *pojangmacha* tents behind Lotte Hotel. This is the black one.

Wa Bar (와바; Map p243; drinks W4000; ◷ 5pm-6am) A big ice bar with tasty microbrew draught. On Seomyeon's Youth St half a block from Fuzzy Navel. There's another one on the other side of the main street near Podo Cheong.

NAMPO-DONG

Most of the drinking establishments in Nampo-dong cater to Japanese and Korean business travellers. But there are a number of shops where you can sip espresso.

Holly's Coffee (Map p240; drinks W2000; ◷ 8am-11pm) Where else in the world can you drink great espresso and get free high-speed internet access? Well, lots of places in Nampo-dong, actually, and this is one of them.

Thema Coffee Shop (테마; Map p240; drinks W2500; ◷ 7.30am-11pm Mon-Fri, 9am-7pm Sat & Sun; ◉ Line 1 to Jungangdong, Exit 13) Fine espresso with light snacks like bagels and cheese. Turn left at the first street.

Entertainment
LIVE MUSIC

Monk (drinks W4000; ◷ 6pm-2am; ◉ Line 2 to Kyungsung-Pukyong station, Exit 3) Before and after jazz sets (often starting at 7.30pm, Wednesday to Saturday), Monk can be an empty sound stage with a few offbeat characters. When live music hits the stage, the place is full of offbeat characters. From the subway station, turn right at the first street. It's down the road and around the corner from Ol'55 in the Kyungsung-Pukyong area (Map p238).

Busan Cultural Centre (Map p238; http://bsculture. busan.kr; ◉ Line 2 to Daeyeon, Exit 3 or 5) With three

INSIDE THE COVERED WAGON

Spend time walking at night on a busy Busan street and you're likely to come across a *pojang-macha*, an orange piece of Korean street culture. Literally meaning 'covered wagon', these food-and-drink carts draped in tarpaulin are more than a convenient late-night street pub. They're an institution that delivers a unique social and sensory experience.

According to Mrs Ahn, the woman who runs First House (opposite), a *pojangmacha* in Seomyeon, 'people who love drinking come to the covered wagon because they feel comfortable.' Comfort, in this case, does not mean physical amenities, as most *pojangmacha* are equipped with bench seating, dim lighting and off-site washrooms that require a short stumble to a nearby parking lot. Comfort instead means a respite from the outside world.

Inside the *pojangmacha*, traditional barriers that prevent Koreans from socialising easily give way to conviviality. While interviewing Mrs Ahn for this book, a free-spirited discussion broke out with the other patrons. The man next to me suggested that *pojangmacha* are brilliant orange because the colour is easy to see at night. One woman said she enjoys coming to a *pojangmacha* on a rainy night because the sound of raindrops falling on tarpaulin reminds her of happy times during her childhood. As the dialogue rambles on between shots of *soju* and whiffs of cigarette smoke, Mrs Ahn sits behind the counter watching over a charcoal grill. Plumes of smoke rise to the top of the tent. The aroma of grilled chicken anus (닭똥집) and eel (곰장어구이) and mackerel (고동어) commingled with the plasticky smell of decades-old tarpaulin induce childhood memories of an overnight camping trip.

While preparing a bowl of mussel soup for a new customer, Mrs Ahn reminisces about her 24 years' working inside a *pojangmacha* and wonders about the future. There's speculation that city officials may require *pojangmacha* owners to spend W5 million to upgrade facilities and improve the streetscape. It's not clear what changes are expected but here's hoping the orange tent stays because the real magic of a *pojangmacha* takes place inside the covered wagon.

halls and a fairly active schedule, it's possible to attend a Busan Philharmonic Orchestra concert, or a show by any of the other musical and dance companies that perform here. The English website provides little useful information. Check the Busan City website calendar page (http://english.busan.go.kr/01_about/06.jsp) for a listing of current events at the centre and across the city.

SPORTS

Professional sports provide a day of fun with ticket prices in the W5000 to W15,000 range. The Lotte Giants play baseball at Sajik Stadium. From November to April, the KTF Magicwings play basketball at the next-door Sajik Gymnasium. Busan I'Park of the Korean soccer league plays in Asiad Stadium, located behind the Asiad Home Plus department store a 10-minute walk from Sajik baseball stadium.

All facilities (Map p238) can be reached by subway and a short walk; take Line 3 to Sports Complex station, Exit 11.

CINEMA

There's no shortage of theatres showing first-run English-language movies (with Korean subtitles) including multiscreen cinemas in Nampo-dong next to PIFF Sq (Map p240).

Cinematheque Pusan (Map p244; http://cinema.piff.org; ☺ 742-5377; ⊙ Line 2 to Dongbaek, Exit 3) Screens an eclectic range of movies, which in the past has included a Woody Allen retrospective. The mostly Korean website lists the current schedule. Or, check the Busan City calendar page (http://english.busan.go.kr/01_about/06.jsp). Walk 10 minutes from the station.

CGV (Map p238; Asiad Home Plus; ⊙ Line 3 to Sports Complex, Exit 11)

CGV Multiplex (Map p238; Shinsegae department store; ⊙ Line 2 to Centum City, Exit 3)

Lotte Cinema (Map p243; 10th fl, Lotte department store, Seomyeon)

Megabox (Map p244; Sfunz building, Haeundae; ⊙ Line 2 to Haeundae, Exit 1) A 10-screen facility, 100m from the station.

GAMBLING

Paradise Casino (Map p244; ☎ 742 2110; Haeundae; ☺ 24hr) Anyone who understands the science of gambling can test his or her skill.

Seven Luck Casino (Map p243; ☎ 665 6000; Lotte Hotel, Seomyeon; ☺ 24hr) Downtown travellers with an itch could try here.

Shopping

Busan's traditional markets offer a unique and occasionally shocking experience.

Bujeon Market (off Map p243; ◉ Line 1 to Bujeon-dong, Exit 5) The city's largest downtown market and best place to buy in-season fruit and vegetables.

Gukje Market (Map p240; ◉ Line 1, Nampo-dong, Exit 1) West of Nampo-dong; has hundreds of small booths with a staggering selection of items, from leather goods to Korean drums.

Experience the country's department-store culture of saturating the floor with sales assistants and free food samples. All stores have ready-to-eat food and some Western goods.

Lotte department store Seomyeon (Map p243; ◉ Line 2 to Seomyeon, Exit 5 or 7); Dongnae (Map p242; outside Myeongnyun-dong station; ◉ Line 1 to Myeong-nyun-dong, Exit 1) Upmarket retailer with the newest store in Haeundae, beside Shinsegae (Map p238).

Home Plus department store (Map p238) All across the city. The one beside Asiad stadium (Line 3 to Sports Complex, Exit 11) has a multiscreen movie theatre, 10-pin bowling lanes, a health club (W10,000 day rate; you only need to bring running shoes) and a big supermarket.

Hyundai department store (off Map p243; ◉ Line 1 to Beomildong, Exit 7) Slightly downmarket compared to Lotte, which usually means lower prices.

Shinsegae Centum City (Map p238; http://centumcity. shinsegae.com/main/main.asp; ◉ Line 2 to Centum City, Exit 3) With 5.5 million sq ft of space, it's the world's largest shopping and entertainment behemoth, out-muscling Macy's in New York for the Guinness record. After shopping, pick your favourite method of relaxation: see a movie, go ice skating, clean up in the spa (see p241), eat sushi in the food park or work on your golf swing at the driving range.

Getting There & Away

Domestic travellers often come to Busan via a KTX train service (see opposite) though there are good bus connections (see right) from most major destinations.

International travellers, especially those arriving from Japan, can fly directly to **Gimhae International Airport** (☎ 974 3114; www.gimhaeairport. co.kr); see below. There are also frequent ferry connections with Japan (see right).

AIR

International flights are mostly to Japan (Tokyo, Osaka, Nagoya and Fukuoka), with departures to Beijing, Shanghai, Hong Kong, Bangkok, Manila and Vladivostok.

On domestic routes, the Busan–Seoul run on Korean Air, Asiana or AirBusan (one hour, every 30 minutes from 7am to 9pm) usually requires reservations for weekend and holiday travel. Most flights from Busan to Seoul land at Gimpo Airport, which has few international connections. If you're flying out of the country, you'll need to catch the rail link from Gimpo to Incheon International (see p146) or book early for a seat on one of the four to six daily flights to Incheon via Korean Air or Asiana. Flights also connect Busan and Jeju-do (one hour, every 30 to 90 minutes from 7am to 8pm).

BUS

There are buses from the airport to regional cities including Gyeongju (W9000), Masan (W5700) and Ulsan (W7400).

Departures from Dongbu

Intercity (☎ 508 9966) and **express** (☎ 508 9955) buses run out the Dongbu terminal (Map p242) at Nopo-dong station on Line 1. Out-of-town buses travelling to Dongbu allow passengers to get off at Dusil station, a great time-saver if you don't need to go to the terminal.

Destination	Price (W)	Duration	Frequency
Eonyang	3000	40min	every 20min
Gyeongju	4000	50min	every 10min
Pohang	7300	80min	every 10min
Seoul	31,100	4½ hr	every 30min
Tongdosa	2000	25min	every 20min
Ulsan	4000	1hr	every 10min

Westbound departures from Seobu

Seobu intercity bus terminal (Map p238; ☎ 322 8301) is located outside Sasang station on Line 2 with street-level access through a no-name department store: walk past the underwear and head towards the large doors.

Destination	Price (W)	Duration	Frequency
Hadong	10,000	2½hr	every 20min
Jinju	7000	1½ hr	10 daily
Namhae	10,700	2½hr	20 daily
Ssanggyae-sa	12,700	2¾hr	every 1¾ hr
Tongyeong	10,100	2hr	20 daily

FERRY

There are two ferry terminals located near the immigration office (Map p240). From Jungang-dong station, take Exit 12 and walk towards the containers visible down the road and cross the major street. To find the **International Ferry Terminal** (☎ 63 3068) continue straight and turn right past the immigration office; the terminal is about 150m down the path. To find the **Coastal Ferry Terminal** (☎ 660 0117), do not walk towards the immigration office. Instead, turn right and walk 200m along the waterfront to the large building on the left.

First-floor booths in the International Ferry Terminal sell tickets to four Japanese cities (one-way fares): Fukuoka (☎ 466 7799, W90,000, departs 10.30pm, 7½ hours); Shimonoseki (☎ 462 3161, W95,000, departs 8pm, 12½ hours); Osaka (☎ 462 5482, W125,000, departs 2.40pm Sunday, Tuesday, Thursday, 18 hours) and Tsushima (☎ 465 1114, W75,000, schedules vary, 1¾ to 2¾ hours, departures every day except Tuesday).

For a quick trip to Fukuoka on the Kobee or Beetle (☎ 441 8200) hydrofoils, go to the 2nd floor. There are 10 to 13 daily departures (one way/return W115,000/190,000, three hours) depending on the season.

The Coastal Ferry Terminal handles domestic departures to Goeje Island (one-way fares): Gohyun (W21,500, 75 minutes, seven daily); Okpo (W19,200, 45 minutes, five daily); and Jangseungpo (W19,200, 45 minutes, seven daily). There is one departure daily (except Sundays) for Jeju Island (W32,000 to W150,000, 11 hours, departs 7pm).

TRAIN
Most trains depart from and arrive at Busan's downtown station (Map p238). There are departures from Gupo (Map p238), a western station with easy subway access to Line 3 that saves the hassle of going downtown. Between Busan and Seoul, KTX is the quickest service with most trips taking three hours or less (adult/child W47,900/23,900; every 30 to 60 minutes). First-class tickets are more expensive, but the wide seats have ample legroom.

The *Saemaul* used to be known as the express service. Today, the 4½-hour ride to Seoul seems like an eternity (adult/child W39,300/19,600, five daily departures). Travellers desperate to save a buck – or wanting to read an entire book on the train – could try the *Mugunghwa* service, which wheezes to Seoul in 5½ hours – or longer (adult/child W26,500/13,200, eight daily departures).

Tiny Bujeon station (Map p243) has *Saemaul* and *Mugunghwa* regional connections to places like Mokpo (adult/child

W23,100/11,650, twice daily) and Gyeongju (adult/child W9600/4800, 11 times daily). The **Korea Rail** (www.korail.go.kr) website has detailed schedules.

If you're heading to Japan, a Korea–Japan Through Ticket provides discounted travel between the two countries. It covers travel by train to Busan, the ferry crossing between Busan and Fukuoka or Shimonoseki and a train to your destination in Japan. Contact Korea Rail at Busan train station for details.

Getting Around
TO/FROM THE AIRPORT
An airport limousine from Gimhae International Airport runs to the major hotels in Haeundae (adult/child W6000/3500, one hour, every 20 minutes).

A taxi from the airport to Seomyeon takes 30 minutes and costs W25,000, depending on traffic. A 10-minute taxi from Deokcheon station costs W7000.

The most economical link between the airport and city is a W1400 bus: the 307 from Deokcheon or Gupo stations or 201 from Seomyeon station (opposite Lotte department store).

A light rail transit system, scheduled to open in 2010, will connect Sasang station and the airport.

BUS
Adult cash fares are W1000/1500 for regular/express buses. Slight discounts are available when paying with a Hanaro or Mibi card.

SUBWAY
Busan's three-line subway uses a two-zone fare system: W1100 for one zone and W1300 for longer trips. Purchasing a Hanaro or Mibi card (W4000 plus travel credits, available at ticket booths) is handy for long stays: you get a small discount on fares and avoid the hassle of buying a ticket for each trip. A one-day subway pass costs W3500. See p252 for a subway map. Subway trains run between 5.10am and 12.45am.

TAXI
Basic taxi fares start at W2200 (with a 20% premium at night). A standard taxi from Haeundae to Seomyeon at night will cost W15,000 to W20,000 depending traffic. Avoid deluxe taxis if possible, because the fares can run high.

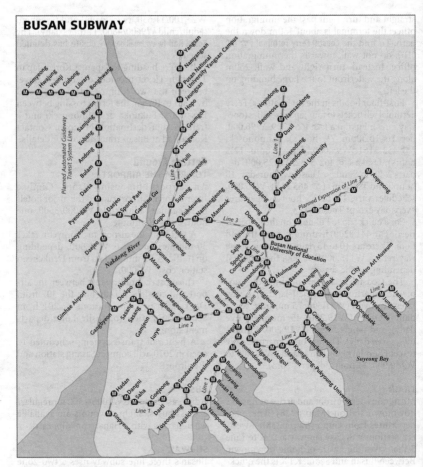

BUSAN SUBWAY

GAJISAN PROVINCIAL PARK
가지산 도립공원

This park has three sections (Map p236). The northernmost section, not far from Gyeongju, is known for rocky terrain. This is where you'll find **Gajisan** (Mt Gaji; 1240m), the park's highest peak. **Tongdo-sa**, one of the country's most commercialised Buddhist temples, is in the smallest of the three sections.

SEONGNAM-SA 석남사
An easy day trip from Busan, this **temple** (Map p236; adult/youth W1700/1000; ⏰ 3am-8pm), home to female monks training in Zen meditation, is a visual masterpiece. The 800m walk from the park entrance cuts through a heavily wooded forest where patches of sunlight struggle to

break through the thick canopy of foliage. Just before the temple, the path forks right over a bridge to a Korean-only map and starting point for a 6.4km hike to Gajisan.

Local buses depart **Eonyang** (언양; W1200, 20 minutes, every 20 minutes) and **Ulsan** (울산; W1500, 40 minutes, every one to two hours). From Busan's Dongbu terminal, take an express bus to Eonyang (W3000, 40 minutes, every 20 minutes) and transfer to a bus to Seongnamsa.

TONGDO-SA 통도사
One of the country's most important Buddhist temples, **Tongdo-sa** (Map p236; adult/youth/child W2000/1500/1000; ⏰ 3.30am-8pm) is noted for a *sari*, a crystalline substance thought to develop in-

side the body of a monk who leads a pure life. The *sari* is enshrined in a fenced area outside the main hall and cannot be seen. It is a focal point of devotion, which is why Tongdo-sa does not have a Buddha statue in the main hall, a rarity in Korea.

The **Tongdo-sa Museum** (adult/youth W2000/1000; ☯ 9am-5pm Nov-Feb, to 6pm Mar-Oct, closed Tue) houses a collection of Buddhist paintings with limited viewing hours (9am to 11.30am and 1pm to 5pm) to minimise light exposure. There are 30,000 artefacts with full-day access including gongs, roof tiles and wooden printing blocks. Before entering, place your shoes in a bag at the front door.

From Busan's Dongbu terminal, buses run to Sinpyeong (신평; W2000, 25 minutes, every 20 to 30 minutes). There are also frequent bus connections from Ulsan (W1500, one hour, every 90 minutes). Facing Sinpyeong's modest bus terminal, walk left and turn right at the first corner; the temple is past the parade of shops, restaurants and motels.

TONGYEONG 통영
pop 134,000

On the southern tip of Goseong Peninsula, **Tongyeong** (Map p236) is a coastal city wedged between Namhae-do and Geoje-do. Most of the picturesque sights are in and around **Gangguan** (강구안), a pretty harbour just made for sunset strolls. Visiting Tongyeong's truly spectacular sights – any one of the 190 or so islands dotting the coastline – usually requires an overnight stay and early-morning ferry departure to some of the most pristine territory in the province.

There are three tourist information booths (open 9am to 6pm). Outside the express bus terminal and on Gangguan harbour, there's a decent selection of material though you'll need to rely on body language because no one speaks English. You'll usually find English-speaking staff in the booth outside the Excursion Terminal.

Sights & Activities

GANGGUAN 강구안

It's not the only harbour in the city, but Gangguan is the prettiest. It's also a busy pier anchored by a promenade that serves multiple civic functions including dock, basketball court and picnic ground for package-tour travellers who aren't squeamish about a midmorning *soju* pick-me-up. Towards the

north end of the promenade, there's a **turtle ship replica** (admission free; ☯ 10am-5pm) and the **Jungang Live Fish Market** (중앙활어시장), an open-air building with grannies selling produce and seafood out of plastic tubs.

The harbour is a good starting point for two strolls. Set aside at least one hour to walk along **Seoho Bay** (서호만) in the early evening to get a brilliant neon show. Walking past the **Passenger Ferry Terminal** (여객선 터미널) towards the **Chungmu** and **Tongyeong Grand** bridges, you could pass through the **Undersea Tunnel** (해저 터널). It's a dull site but a worthwhile stop to take in the panoramic view from the other side of the bay. The second walk takes you up **Namsan**, the small mountain opposite the Gangguan pier. Up top, a pavilion provides a panoramic view of the harbour.

EXCURSIONS

On the south side of the bay, the **Excursion Terminal** (유람선 터미널) runs ferry trips to nearby islands including **Maemul-do** (매물도; 3hr trip adult/child W20,000/12,000, ☎ hrly departures 11am-2pm) and **Jeseungdang** (제승당; 1½ hr trip adult/child W9000/5000; ☎ hrly departures 11am-4pm). Often boisterous, guided tours provide an up-close look at stunning rock formations, historical insights (all in Korean) and a chance for adults to cut loose.

YEONHWA-DO 연화도

Anyone with the vaguest interest in independent exploration should take a ferry to one of the nearby islands. There are heaps of options departing the Passenger Ferry Terminal, which together could easily involve a fortnight of island hopping. If time is limited, the day trip to **Yeonhwa-do** (연환도) is such a pleasurable experience it's hard to imagine how even the crustiest of souls wouldn't be stirred by the beauty of this unspoiled island. The trip begins with a one-hour ferry ride through islands silhouetted by the early-morning sun.

Once on land, there are a couple of trail options. Travellers looking for a stimulating yet mildly challenging walk will probably be satisfied by following the cement road past garden plots of lettuce, a school and a brown cow. At the top of the hill near a pagoda, turn left and follow the narrow trail for outstanding views of the ocean and **Yongmeori** (용머리; Dragon's Head), a string of rocks cascading into the sea which islanders say resembles a dragon's head. The trail eventually leads back to a road that terminates at a fishing outpost called **Dongdu** (동두). On the road to Dongdu, there are several dirt trails that might appeal to hikers eager to get above the treeline. Travellers unable to rappel boulders stay on the road.

In Dongdu, the path behind the second *minbak* (a home that rents rooms to travellers) crosses the back end of a mountain and passes a herd of black goats not far from a rocky oceanfront.

At a leisurely pace this walk takes about three hours excluding breaks. Back at the terminal, there's a convenience store plus half a dozen raw-fish restaurants and *minbak*. Raw fish and *soju* – staples of any seaside trip – cost W30,000 per person.

HALLYEOSU-DO CABLE CAR
한려 수도 조망 케이블카

Stretching out 1975m, it's Korea's longest **cable-car ride** (www.ttdc.co.kr; one way/return adult W9000/5000, child W5500/3000; 9.30am-5pm, to 6pm Jul & Aug). Near the top of **Mireuksan** (461m) the view of **Hallyeo Maritime National Park** is dramatic. If you're up for a hike, buy a one-way ticket, walk down the back end of the mountain and head towards the Undersea Tunnel. Allow one to two hours from the mountaintop to Gangguan. Pick up a map and travel tips from the info booth near the ticket window. Note: if you're coming here on the weekend, arrive early because wait times can be long.

Eating & Drinking

Gangguan's promenade is the place for *chungmu gimbap* (충무 김밥), a spicy squid-and-radish dish, while the Seoho Bay road is known for raw fish.

Ddongbo Halmae Gimbap (똥보 할매 김밥; per serving W4000; 7am-2am) Hungry travellers with limited Korean skills come here because there's no need to speak or read: this place only serves *chungmu gimbap*. The waitress will ask how many servings you want and if necessary she'll use her fingers to count. One serving of this spicy dish, which will test the red-pepper tolerance of the hardiest Korean food lover, should be enough for a single person.

Seoul Samgyupsal (서울 삼겹살; servings from W7000; noon-11pm) The rough interior of this meat restaurant might scare away travellers with refined dining sensibilities. Pity, because the barbecued pork is excellent and, when accompanied by a bottle or two of *soju*, it's a thoroughly satisfying experience.

Prowstar Espresso Coffee (drinks W3300; 11am-10.30pm) Travelling without good coffee isn't just painful – it's pointless. That's why java lovers flock to this haven of joe, a remarkably uncommon sight in the province where coffee usually means a W300 cup of vending-machine swill. It's near the Gangguan harbour beside an entrance to the Jungang Live Fish Market.

Sleeping

Near Gangguan, there is a handful of motels on or near the lane next to the KB bank, which is where Tongyeong's seedy side comes to life at night.

Nex (넥스; 643 6568; d W50,000;) A modern design, chic baths and spacious rooms make this one of the nicer properties near the Passenger Ferry Terminal. Although one of the tallest buildings in the area, it's hard to find because it's surrounded by a cluster of similar motels.

Saejongjang (세종장; 645 5711; d W20,000;) It's not going to win any awards for interior design – unless they start handing out prizes for nouveau grunge – but the price and location are right for travellers catching an early departure from the nearby Passenger Ferry Terminal. From the southern end of the Gangguan promenade, turn right at the corner sandwich shop. The motel is down a lane near a Lotteria restaurant.

Getting There & Around

The express bus terminal is on the city's northern fringe. Local buses 10, 20, 30 and 40 (W1000) run to Gangguan. Buses 60 to 66 go to the cable car. A taxi from the bus terminal to Gangguan costs W7000. From Gangguan, buses 10 to 15 drive by the Excursion Terminal. Ask the driver for the cable-car stop. From there, it's a 15-minute uphill walk. A taxi to either location from Gangguan costs about W6000.

Express buses connect Tongyeong with Jinju (W6600, 1½ hours, every 10 to 20 minutes), Busan (W10,100, 2½ hours, every 30 minutes) and Gohyeon on Geoje-do (W2900, 30 minutes, every six minutes).

Ferries depart Tongyeong's **Passenger Ferry Terminal** (055-641 6181) daily for Yeonhwa Island (W8900, 6.50am, between 9am and 9.30am, 11am, 1pm, 3pm) with five daily return trips (W8900, 8.30am, 11.40am, 1.20pm, 3.30pm, 4.50pm).

JINJU 진주

pop 341,000

Famous for silk, bullfighting and *bibimbap*, Jinju (Map p236) is also known as 'the education city'. Students driven to succeed leave Jinju and the best way to escape is to study hard and enter a university in Seoul. Migration of the youth pool gives this easy-to-like city a laid-back feel and, with excellent bus connections, it's a refreshing day trip from Busan.

Orientation & Information

Jinju's interesting sights are located north of the Nam River. East of the Jinju Fortress, Jungangno separates two worlds: a traditional market to the east and modern trappings like coffee shops, bars and cinemas to the west. Jinju is the largest city in the area and a convenient transport hub from which to explore the province's western region.

The two gates in front of the Jinju Fortress have a good supply of English maps and brochures. If you need to get online, some downtown coffee shops have free internet access (and tasty sweet potato lattes) though better download speeds can be had in a PC *bang*.

Sights & Activities

Jinju Fortress (adult/youth/child W1000/500/300; 🕑 9am-6pm Sun-Fri, to 7pm Sat) is the city's most interesting and historically important site. Local street signs call it a castle, but it's actually a well-preserved fortress partially destroyed during the Japanese invasion of 1592. It was here that one of the major battles of the campaign was fought, in which 70,000 Koreans lost their lives. Inside the fortress walls, traditional gates and shrines dot the grassy knolls of this heavily wooded park. Enter the fortress from the North Gate, not far from a large E-Mart department store, or the East Gate. Information booths (open 9am to 6pm) have a decent selection of material though the staff can't speak English.

Inside the fortress, the **Jinju National Museum** (☎ 742 5951; admission free; 🕑 9am-6pm Tue-Fri, to 7pm Sat, Sun & holidays, closed Mon) specialises in artefacts

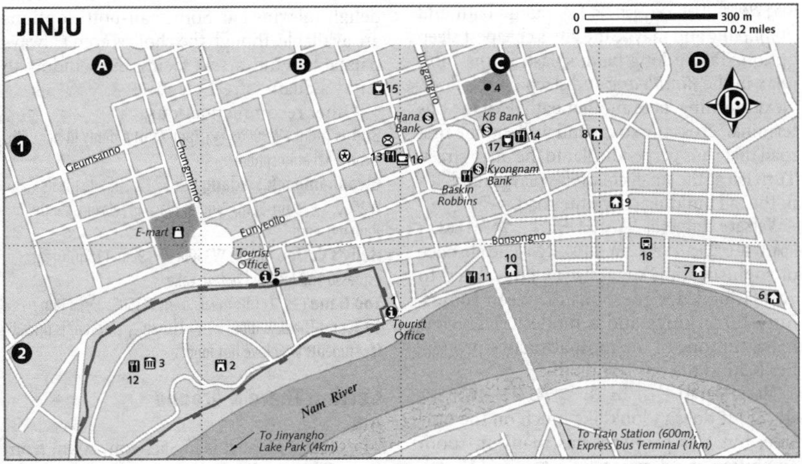

SIGHTS & ACTIVITIES
East Gate 동문 1 B2
Jinju Fortress 진주성 2 B2
Jinju National Museum 진주 국립박물관 3 A2
Jungang Live Fish Market 중앙시장 4 C1
North Gate 북문 5 B2

SLEEPING
Dong Bang Tourist Hotel 동방 호텔 6 D2
Hyundai Motel 현대 모텔 7 D2
Jageum Seong 자금성 8 C1
Movie Motel 무비 모텔 9 D1
Versace Motel 베르사체 모텔 10 C2

EATING
Eel Restaurants 장어구이 11 C2
Gwannamgaek Sikdang 관람객 식당 12 A2
Jeil Sikdang 제일식당 .... (see 4)
Yoo Gane 유가네 13 B1
Zio Ricco 14 C1

DRINKING
Bobos 15 B1
Holly's Coffee 16 C1
La Vigne 17 C1

TRANSPORT
North Bus Terminal 시외버스 터미널 18 D2

from the Imjin Waeran War (임진왜란), a seven-year bloody tussle between Joseon and Japan's Toyotomi Hideyoshi Shogunate that began with the latter invading the former in 1592.

Festivals & Events

In October several important festivals take place, including the **Nam River Lantern Festival** and **Jinju Bull Fighting Contest**.

Weekly **bullfights** are held every Saturday at **Jinyangho Lake Park** (진양호 공원; admission free; fights 1.30-6pm Mar-Nov). Catch bus 16 (W1000) opposite the express bus terminal.

Sleeping

With the exception of October, finding a room to match your budget won't be a problem. The river road behind the north-end bus terminal is lined with motels ranging from dingy to delightful. There is a good selection of low-cost *yeoinsuk* (family-run motels with small rooms) two blocks from the fortress's East Gate.

Jageum Seong (자금성; ☎ 743 8841; sauna/jjimjil-bang W4000/7000; 24hr;) A public bath and *jjimjilbang* and maybe the city's cheapest sleep option. Take a long bath, splash in the tubs, relax in the *jjimjilbang* and sleep on the floor. Next morning, take another bath. Exit the bus terminal, cross the street and walk up the first road that runs perpendicular to the main street. Turn left at the small children's playground. It's in the tall building down the road.

Versace Motel (베르사체 모텔; ☎ 741 8080; r from W40,000, Fri & Sat plus W10,000;) The absence of sophistication suggests it's not related to any fashion designer, but the clean rooms, nifty furnishings and a modest river view make this one of the most attractive properties behind the bus terminal.

Movie Motel (무비 모텔; ☎ 743 4114; d W50,000;) It doesn't look like much on the outside, but this property has many in-room amenities you'd expect in a top-end motel, like wide-screen TVs, whirlpool tubs and free internet. Exit the bus terminal, cross the street and walk up the first road that runs perpendicular to the main street. Up a couple of blocks, turn left at the lane next to the tool store.

Other recommendations:

Dong Bang Tourist Hotel (동방호텔; ☎ 743 0131; d & tw W115,000, ste from W200,000;) Jinju's only business-class hotel has satisfying though underwhelming rooms.

Hyundai Motel (현대 모텔; ☎ 743 9791; d W45,000;) Small, simple rooms behind the bus terminal.

Eating & Drinking

For something different, try one of the eel restaurants along the waterfront near the fortress. They're all about the same quality and price (W14,000 to W16,000 per person).

Zio Ricco (meals W8000; noon-midnight) With low chairs and cool music, it's a popular eatery with the locals and expats. Pasta and pizza are the specialities. Live music Saturday night from 6pm.

Jaeil Sikdang (제일식당; meals from W5000; 4am-9pm) This famous eatery inside the traditional market serves only two dishes. Until 9.30am, it's *haejangguk* (해장국), a vegetable soup thought to cure hangovers. Thereafter, it's *bibimbap* (비빔밥), a scrumptious rice and vegetable dish served with a rich, flavourful broth and, if you so desire, a helping of raw beef as well. Jaeil Sikdang is buried inside the market but the locals know where it is.

La Vigne (bottles from W28,000; 10am-2am, closed Sun) With over 400 bottles, you'll likely find a vintage to match your budget and taste in this delightful wine bar. Some half-bottle options are available, though the choices aren't always palatable. Find a seat facing the window to enjoy a quaint street view.

Other recommendations:

Bobos (drinks W5000; 7pm-7am) A dimly lit bar with a convivial atmosphere.

Gwannamgaek Sikdang (관람객 식당; meals W2500; 9am-5pm) A quiet place to relax inside the Jinju museum.

Holly's Coffee (drinks W2500; 9am-11pm) Great espresso and inspired potato cake.

Yoo Gane (유가네; meals from W3500; 11am-10.30pm) The *dakgalbi* (닭갈비; spicy chicken) is priced for students who love hot food.

Getting There & Around

AIR

The closest airport is in Sacheon, 20km from Jinju. Three daily flights connect with Gimpo Airport in Seoul via Korean Air and Asiana. Korean Air also has two flights per week to Jeju Island. Local buses connect Jinju's north-end bus terminal to Sacheon airport (W1600, 30 minutes).

BUS

There's an express bus terminal south of the river. Most travellers use the terminal north of the river. Departures from the north terminal include the following:

Destination	Price (W)	Duration	Frequency
Busan	8500	1½hr	every 10-20min
Hadong	4500	1hr	every 30min
Namhae	5100	1½hr	every 15-30min
Ssanggyae-sa	6700	1½hr	every 1-3hr
Tongyeong	6600	1½hr	every 40min

TRAIN

The train station is south of the Nam River. *Mugunghwa* connections include Dongdaegu (adult/child W10,000/5000, three hours, one daily), Daejeon (adult/child W19,600/9800, five hours, one daily) and Seoul (adult/child W29,600/14,800, seven hours, one daily).

NAMHAE-DO 남해도
pop 67,000

It's the country's third-largest island (Map p236), famous for garlic and a slower pace of life so clearly evident in the countryside where some farmers continue to use oxen to plough fields. Rugged ocean views, tiny fishing ports untouched by tourist development and charming roadside diversions are best appreciated by travellers with their own transport and an unhurried sense of exploration.

Sights & Activities

Some of Korea's nicest **beaches** are located on the southern coast, including **Sangju** (상주 해수욕장) and **Songjeong** (송정 해수욕장). Sangju is an especially attractive beach thanks to its soft white sand and a stand of trees that create an illusion of isolation.

Between Namhae City and Sangju beach, **Boriam** (보리암) is a Buddhist hermitage on Geumsan famous for spectacular sunrises. About 16km from Sangju, there's an architectural oddity: the **German Village** (독일마을) is a hillside hamlet of homes designed with a German motif. Behind the village, spend 30 minutes walking through the **Horticultural Art Village** (원예 예술촌), a public garden with outdoor art. On the way to the German Village from Sangju, **Mijo** (미조) is a rustic fishing port with superb countryside food.

Sleeping & Eating

If you need to sleep in Namhae City, the **Byzantine Motel** (비잔틴 모텔; ☎ 864 5120; standard/internet/special W40,000/45,000/50,000; 🌐 🖵) is opposite the bus terminal. From here, the city centre is a 10-minute walk. If lost, ask anyone to point the way to the Baskin Robbins ice-cream shop. One block from Baskin Robbins,

Midam (미담; servings from W10,000; 🕑 noon-9pm) is a 50-year-old *hanjeongsik* (한정식) restaurant offering a splendid cross-section of Korean food. Minimum three servings.

There are heaps of sleep options in Sangju, which tend to be full of families and partying students in July and August. Budget travellers requiring nothing more than a floor to sleep on could try any of the dozens of *minbak* opposite the beach's parking lot, which typically cost W30,000. For more space and comfort, try the **Oasis Pension** (오아시스펜션; ☎ 010 3101 5957; standard/ocean view W50,000/70,000; 🌐). Located down the road past the parking lot; most rooms come with a double bed and a basic kitchen.

In Mijo, **Daejeong Sikdang** (다정식당; meals from W5000; 🕑 7am-7pm) is a simple restaurant with outstanding *twenjang jjigae* (된장찌개; soybean stew). The soft tofu, superb balance of vegetables and seafood is a welcome treat for travellers who need a break from spicy food. Facing the police station, walk left, turn left at the lane opposite the post office and then right at the first lane.

Getting There & Around

There are frequent bus connections to Namhae from Seobu terminal in Busan and Jinju. Leaving the island, four daily buses run to Hadong (W4000, one hour, 6am, 7.10am, 10:05am and 4pm), Jinju (W5100, 1½ hours, every 15 to 60 minutes) and Busan (W10,700, 2¼ hours, every 30 to 60 minutes).

Local buses to Sangju (W2200, 40 minutes, every 30 to 50 minutes) and Mijo (W3000, 60 minutes, every 30 to 50 minutes) from Namhae are available but the return trip can involve long roadside waits. Private transport is the only practical way to Boriam. Follow the road signs up to the parking lot (W4000). Driving close to the hermitage is possible though traffic is restricted, so expect delays during the summer and on weekends. Alternatively, park the car and enjoy a two-hour hike or catch a shuttle bus (adult/infant W1000/free, 30 minutes, every 30 minutes).

GEOJE-DO 거제도
pop 230,000

Korea's second-largest island (Map p236) is famous for a massive shipbuilding industry and natural beauty. The coastal scenery varies between nice and awe-inspiring with the best views in and around **Haegeumgang** (해금강).

Outside Gohyun, the island's biggest city, public transport is not well developed. Personal transport on the island is recommended. Finding a tourist info centre is not easy. Your best bet is to stop by a travel agency and ask for a map.

Sights & Activities

The island's busiest tourist attraction is **Oe-do** (외도; ☎ 031 717 2200; www.oedobotania.com; adult/youth/child W8000/6000/4000; 8am-5pm), a tiny island cum botanical garden 4km off the coast. It's popular with Korean travellers, but unless you absolutely adore manicured gardens, long waits (if ferries are cancelled or delayed) and pushy lines, consider avoiding this place.

In Gohyun, the **Historic Park of Geoje POW Camp** (거제도 포로수용소유적공원; ☎ 055 639 8125; adult/youth/child W3000/2000/100; 9.30am-5pm Mar-Oct, to 5pm Nov-Feb) is a modest but worthwhile museum because it provides hard-to-find information about this unique aspect of the Korean War.

About halfway between Jangseungpo and Haegeumgang, the **black-pebble beach** in Hak-dong is a cosy destination for family outings and romantic getaways. Summer crowds flock to the 1.2km beach to laze and fish off the pier. During the rest of the year, you'll have the place to yourself.

About 30 minutes by car from Hak-dong, **Haegeumgang** is a collection of breathtaking rocky islets and a jagged coastline, part of the **Hallyeo Maritime National Park**, which is famous for stirring sunrises and sunsets.

Sleeping & Eating

There's a collection of motels a few blocks from the Gohyun intercity bus terminal. **Venus Motel** (비너스 모텔; ☎ 055-637 9586; r from W30,000;) has small rooms with a private bathroom and a LAN line for notebooks. If full, there are four motels nearby.

Hak-dong has an impressive selection of motels of varying quality, some closer to the beach than others. **Geoje Tiffany Rejotel** (거제 티파니 리조텔; ☎ 055-636 8866; http://geojetiffany.co.kr; r from W50,000;) is beside the beach. Nothing fancy, just nice, clean rooms with bathroom and a short walk to nearby restaurants.

Beautiful and private, the **Palm Tree Pension** (☎ 055-636 2241; www.palm-tree.co.kr; standard/deluxe W800,000/150,000;) is a gorgeous three-storey building with balconies overlooking the sea. It's located in a secluded area and a couple

of kilometres from the pebble beach and restaurants.

You'll have no problem finding a place to eat in Hak-dong, if you like raw fish. For barbecued meat, try **Ori Gung Daeng-e** (오리궁 뎅이; ☎ 055 636 6612; servings from W9000; 8am-10pm) a floor-seating restaurant with tender *samgyeopsal* (삼겹살; fatty pork). It's about 100m from the Tiffany motel.

Getting There & Around

At the time of writing, all roads to Geoje-do crossed a bridge in Tongyeong. By the time you read this, a fixed link between Busan and Geoje should be complete, consisting of a 4km tunnel and two bridges. The drive time from Busan to Geoje is expected to be one hour.

Two companies (☎ 055-636 3535 and 055-637 7080) run ferries between Gohyun to Busan (W21,500, 70 minutes, first departure 8.30am, six daily) though these and other transport schedules may change once the fixed link is complete. Ferries (☎ 055-682 0116) also connect Jangseungpo with Busan (W19,200, 45 minutes, first departure 7am, seven daily) and Okpo (W19,200, 45 minutes, first departure 9am, five daily).

Ferries depart for Oe-do from several cities including: Jangseungpo (adult/child W17,000/11,000), Hak-dong (adult/child W16,000/8000) and Haegeumgang (adult/child W18,000/8000). Schedules vary according to the weather and number of passengers. A typical return trip to Oe-do takes about three hours.

From the Gohyun intercity bus terminal there are frequent connections to Busan (W13,100, 2½ hours, 13 daily), Tongyeong (W2900, 20 minutes, every 20 minutes) and Jangseungpo (W2300, 20 minutes, every 30 minutes).

JIRISAN NATIONAL PARK – EAST
지리산 국립공원

This **park** (Map p259; admission free; 2hr before sunrise-2hr after sunset) offers some of Korea's best hiking opportunities with 12 peaks over 1000m forming a 40km ridge. Many peaks are over 1500m high, including **Cheonwangbong** (1915m), the country's second-highest mountain. There are three principal park entrances, each with a temple. Two of the three temples, Ssanggye-sa and Daewon-sa, are in South Gyeongsang province. From the west, Hwaeom-sa is accessible via Gurye in Jeollanam province (see p270).

JIRISAN NATIONAL PARK

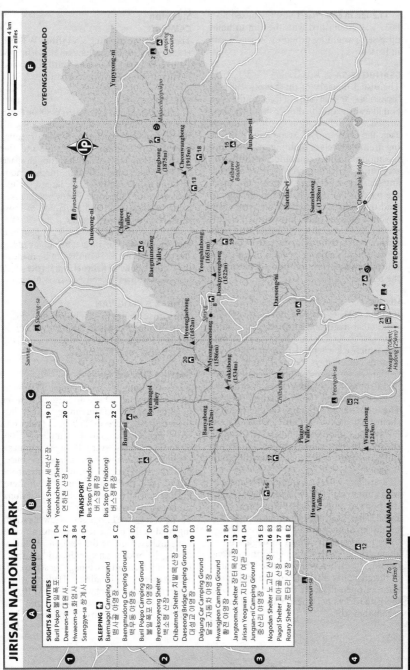

SIGHTS & ACTIVITIES

Buril Pokpo 불일폭포	1 D4
Daewon-sa 대원사	2 F2
Hwaeom-sa 화엄사	3 B4
Ssanggye-sa 쌍계사	4 D4

SLEEPING

Baemsagol Camping Ground 뱀사골 야영장	5 C2
Baengmudong Camping Ground 백무동 야영장	6 D2
Buril Pokpo Camping Ground 불일폭포 야영장	7 D4
Byeoksoryeong Shelter 벽소령 산장	8 D3
Chibatmok Shelter 치밭목 산장	9 E2
Daeseong Bridge Camping Ground 대성교 야영장	10 D3
Dalgung Car Camping Ground 달궁 자동차 야영장	11 B2
Hwangjeon Camping Ground 황전 야영장	12 B4
Jangteomok Shelter 장터목 산장	13 E2
Jirisan Yeogwan 지리산 여관	14 D4
Jungsan-ni Camping Ground 중산리 야영장	15 E3
Nogodan Shelter 노고단 산장	16 B3
Piagol Shelter 피아골 산장	17 B3
Rotary Shelter 로타리 산장	18 E2
Seseok Shelter 세석산장	19 D3
Yeonhacheon Shelter 연하천 산장	20 C2

TRANSPORT

Bus Stop (To Hadong) 버스정류장	21 D4
Bus Stop (To Hadong) 버스정류장	22 C4

The **Jirisan Bear Project** (see the boxed text, p63) was established with the aim to build up a self-sustaining group of 50 wild bears in Jirisan.

SSANGGYE-SA 쌍계사

The visual imagery of this **temple** (Map p236; admission free; ☎ dawn-dusk) is a feast for the eyes, and like any exquisite dinner should be consumed with deliberation in order to enjoy each and every morsel. Stone walls supporting multiple levels of buildings notched into the mountainside, combined with mature trees and a trickling creek, create a pleasant sensory experience. Three gates mark the path to the main hall; take the time to read the signs to appreciate the symbolism of your visit. One of the most attractive temples in the province, it's a long day trip from Busan. For a more relaxing pace, consider an overnight stopover in Jinju, Namhae or Hadong and an early-morning departure to the temple.

HIKING

It's impossible to describe the myriad of trails within this great park. The traditional course runs east to west (Daewon-sa to Hwaeom-sa), which experienced Korean hikers say requires three days. Some Lonely Planet readers have suggested an alternate three-night route that puts hikers in position for a sunrise view on top of Cheonwangbong. The route starts with a night at the Nogodan shelter. The next two nights are spent at the Baemsagol camping ground and Jangteomok shelter. On the final day, follow the trail to Jungsan-ni and then catch a bus to Jinju or Busan.

Travellers with less ambitious plans, but who want to experience Jirisan's beauty, hike the popular trail to **Buril Pokpo** (불일폭포; Buril Falls). Starting from Ssanggye-sa, the mildly challenging trail (2.4km each way, three hours return) winds through a forest along a rippling creek. About two-thirds along the way, just when you've noticed the sound of the creek has disappeared, the trail bursts onto an open field. At the foot of the falls, there's a rocky pool where hikers meditate to regain their chi.

Sleeping

CAMPING

There are nine camping sites (from W3000): Hwangjeon, Daewon-sa, Jungsan-ni, Baemsagol 1 and 2, Dalgung, Daeseong, Buril Pokpo and Baengmu-dong. Facilities are basic.

SHELTERS

There are 10 shelters (W5000 to W8000). From west to east, they are: Nogodan 1 and 2, Piagol, Baemsagol, Yeonhacheon, Byeoksoryeong, Seseok, Jangteomok, Chibatmok and the Rotary shelter. Jangteomok has enough space for 135 bodies, and sells film, torches, noodles and drinks. Seseok is the largest shelter, with space for 190 people. For overnight hikes bring bedding, food and tea/coffee, as most shelters have limited supplies.

Multiday treks require a hiking plan and bookings if you plan on staying at any of the shelters. Online reservations can be made at the website of **Korea National Park Service** (http://english.knps.or.kr/knps_eng/parks/reservation_01.asp).

MINBAK & YEOGWAN

The path to Ssanggye-sa is lined with a dozen sleep options like **Jirisan Yeogwan** (지리산 여관; ☎ 883 1668; ondol W30,000) or *minbak* offering comparably priced rooms.

Getting There & Away

Buses to Ssanggye-sa often pass through Hadong, a small village and useful transfer point in the region. If you can't get a direct bus to Ssanggye-sa, travel to Hadong and catch one of the frequent buses to the temple (W2500, 30 to 60 minutes, every 45 to 90 minutes). En route to Ssanggye-sa from Hadong, buses pass a large bridge and shortly thereafter make a quick stop in Hwagae; don't get off there. Further down the road (usually the next stop), the bus stops beside a concrete bridge. Do get out here, cross the bridge and follow the winding road to the park entrance. Return tickets are purchased inside the seafood restaurant beside the bridge. The signboard lists times for several destinations, though most travellers are best served by heading to Hadong, where frequent buses connect with Busan (W10,000, 2½ hours, every 30 to 60 minutes) and Jinju (W4500, 1½ hours, every 30 minutes).

Jeollanam-do
전라남도

This beautiful southwest province is one of Korea's least developed and greenest. The heartland of Jeollanam-do (http://english.jeonnam.go.kr) has rolling hills, the towering Sobaek Mountains to the east and 6100km of coastline to the south and west, with over 2000 islands offshore – less than 300 of which are inhabited.

With a warmer and rainier climate than its provincial mainland neighbours, bountiful Jeollanam-do is all about agriculture – the province is famous for its food and green tea, celebrated in several festivals. For all of its rural atmosphere, Jeollanam-do has urban elements that are common to the rest of Korea, such as expressways, high-speed rail lines and expanding cities filling up with anonymous apartment blocks, chief of which is Gwangju, Korea's sixth-largest metropolis with its own separate government and telephone code.

Despite all this the province retains a rebel edge, and is proud of its ceramic and artistic traditions, its exiled poets and pro-democracy martyrs. It's a place where you can admire nature in Suncheon Bay's wetlands or learn about Zen Buddhism at Songgwang-sa, ranked one of the three most important Buddhist temples in Korea. And the 2012 World Expo will be held in Yeosu.

The region's two heroes are Admiral Yi Sun-sin who defeated the Japanese navy in the 1590s and Kim Dae-jung, a 20th-century democracy warrior who became president in 1997 and finally ended the stranglehold on political power and patronage held by politicians from the eastern provinces.

HIGHLIGHTS

- Visit the university metropolis of **Gwangju** (p262) for its vibrant arts and nightlife scene, urban hiking opportunities, solemn memorials and nearby **Damyang Bamboo Crafts Museum** (p269)

- Savour the scenic location and flavours of the photogenic **Daehan Dawon Tea Plantation** (p273) in Boseong

- Voyage to the scattered, unspoilt islands of **Heuksan-do** (p281) and fabled **Hong-do** (p281)

- Marvel at the thatched-roofed houses of **Nagan Folk Village** (p270), one of the best-preserved fortress towns in Korea

- Explore the museums, restaurants, bars and nightclubs in the youthful, hip port town of **Mokpo** (p277)

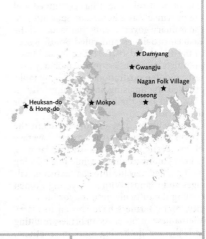

★ Damyang
★ Gwangju
Nagan Folk Village ★
Boseong ★
Heuksan-do ★ ★ Mokpo
& Hong-do

■ TELEPHONE CODE: 061/062   ■ POPULATION: 3.37 MILLION   ■ AREA: 12,553 SQ KM

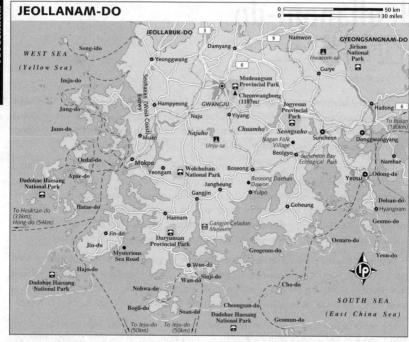

History

Far from the centre of power in Seoul during the long Joseon era, Jeollanam-do was a place of exile, often used as a dumping ground for political and religious dissidents. The tradition of political dissent has continued and the province was a hotbed of opposition to the military governments that favoured the eastern provinces and ruled South Korea in the 1960s and 1970s. Students and trade unionists led countless pro-democracy protests and demonstrations, until army tanks crushed an uprising in Gwangju city in May 1980 (see the boxed text on p265 for details).

Today about 25% of households in the province are farms, versus a national average of 7%. Pesticide-free and organic farming is being pioneered here, while fish farming has breathed new life into coastal fishing villages and islands. With local young women trading the difficult rural life for life in the city, many farmers have chosen to marry Vietnamese or other Asian brides, resulting in Jeollanam-do having more international marriages than Seoul.

National & Provincial Parks

Cruise around thousands of islands in **Dadohae Haesang National Park** (p281) and take a cable-car ride in **Duryunsan Provincial Park** (p274). You could bump into a bear in **Jirisan National Park** (p270), which spreads over three provinces, while two Zen Buddhist temples attract pilgrims to **Jogyesan Provincial Park** (p269). At weekends hikers stand in queues at **Mudeungsan Provincial Park** (p265) in urban Gwangju, while remote **Wolchulsan National Park** (p277) can be traversed in under five hours.

Getting There & Around

Most travellers arrive by train or bus and then use buses and ferries to travel around. Gwangju is the major transport hub and thus an excellent base for exploring the province.

GWANGJU 광주

☎ 062 / pop 1.4 million

Gwangju (http://eng.gjcity.net) may look like any other city with its shop-filled central area, an attractive riverside, busy restaurants, pubs and bars – all encircled by apartment blocks – but within this everyday exterior resides the heart of an artist and the soul of a revolutionary. Civic Gwangju emphasises the arts and the city has an important place in the history of Korea's democracy and human-rights movement.

Information

Central post office (Chungjangno) Free internet.
Citibank (Jukbongno; ◷ 9-4pm Mon-Fri) Global ATM with high W700,000 daily withdrawal limit.
Global ATM (Bus Terminal) Near the ticket booths.
Gwangju Bank (Shinsegae Department Store) Foreign exchange.
Gwangju International Centre (☎ 226 2733; www.gic.or.kr; KEB Bldg; ◷ 10am-1pm & 2-6pm Mon-Sat) This expat organisation offers guidebooks, tourist information, Korean-language classes, tours and social events. Located

in the KEB building directly across from the main tourist information centre.
KEB (Geumnamno) Global ATM.
Standard Chartered Bank (Geumnamno) Global ATM and foreign exchange.
Tourist information centres Bus Terminal (☎ 360 8733); Geumnamno (☎ 062 1330; ◷ 9am-9pm); Gwangju Airport (☎ 942 6160); Train Station (☎ 522 5147) The main centre (Geumnamno) in the YMCA building has free internet.

Sights & Activities

GWANGJU NATIONAL MUSEUM & VICINITY 광주국립박물관

The highlight of **Gwangju National Museum** (☎ 570 7014; adult/child W1000/500; ◷ 9am-6pm Tue-Sun) is its collection of perfectly preserved Chinese

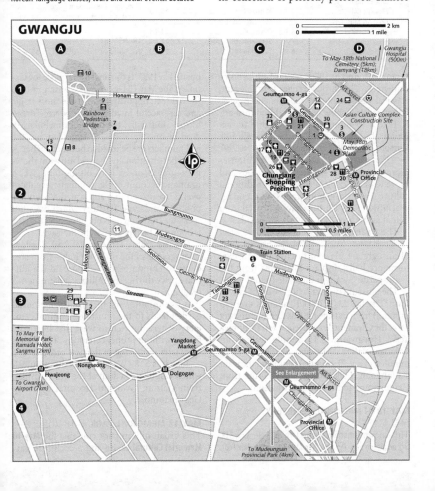

ceramics, found in 1975 inside a 14th-century shipwreck. The display ranges from elegant, classical vases to homey mortars and pestles. Other galleries show Joseon and Buddhist art.

Take a 15-minute walk through a tunnel under the expressway to the **Gwangju Folk Museum** (☎ 525 8633; adult/youth/child W600/400/200; 🕑 9.30am-5pm, closed day after national holidays). It uses dioramas, models, sound effects, videos and more to show off Jeollanam-do's traditional culture. Historical photographs at the end reveal how quickly Koreans have morphed from feudal farmers to 21st-century whiz kids.

The **Gwangju Art Museum** (☎ 529 7126; adult/youth/child W460/300/250; 🕑 9am-5pm Tue-Sun), part of an ugly art plaza with concert and performance halls, displays highlights from the avant-garde Gwangju Biennale (p266).

The museum district is northwest of downtown. Take bus 23 (W1000, 10 minutes, every 15 minutes) from outside the bus terminal and get off at the Gwangju Art Museum stop (Munhwa Yesul Hoegwan), a 15-minute walk from Gwangju National Museum. Bus 50 (W900, 20 minutes, every 30 minutes) runs from the train station to the Folk Museum; bus 55 runs from Geumnamno to the National Museum.

MAY 18TH NATIONAL CEMETERY
국립 5.18 민주묘지
This sombre **memorial park** (☎ 266 5187; www.518.org; admission free; 🕑 8am-7pm Mar-Oct, to 5pm Nov-Feb),

opened in 1997, is the final burial place for victims of the May 18 Democratic Uprising of 1980 (boxed text, opposite), one of the most tragic and disgraceful incidents in modern Korean history. Officially, the casualties include 228 dead or missing and 4141 wounded, but the real numbers are believed to be much higher. A small but emotionally charged museum shows photographs, and a hard-hitting film gives a dramatic account of the traumatic events of over 25 years ago that still scar the country's political landscape. 'History which does not speak the truth and does not remember the past is bound to be repeated' is the message.

On the right, a memorial hall displays photographs of the ordinary folk – from students to grandmothers – who paid the ultimate price during the military government's crackdown.

A five-minute walk through the memorial garden leads to the reinstated original cemetery, where the victims were first hurriedly buried without proper ceremony. The bodies were later reinterred in the new cemetery.

Take bus 518 (W1000, every 30 minutes), which can be picked up at the bus terminal, train station, Gwangju Hospital or along Geumnamno.

MAY 18 MEMORIAL PARK 5.18 기념공원
This urban hilltop park contains the **May 18 Memorial Cultural Centre** and a sculpture gar-

den with a large **monument** to the May 18 Democratic Uprising; walk below ground to see the moving Pieta-like sculpture of a mother cradling the body of her son. The surrounding park contains a number of walking trails that lead to attractions such as the **Mugak-sa Temple** and **Owolru Tower**. The park is located near City Hall in Sangmu, 10 minutes north of the Honam University subway station.

MUDEUNGSAN PROVINCIAL PARK
무등산도립공원

Overlooking Gwangju, **Mudeungsan Provincial Park** (☎ 265 0761; admission free) is a gorgeous green mountain range with a spider's web of well-signed trails leading to the peak, **Cheonwang-bong** (1187m), and up to the towering rocky outcrops called **Ipseokdae** and **Seoseokdae** that are visible from miles away.

There are three major Buddhist temples in the park, most which were rebuilt after being destroyed in the Korean War. The easiest to reach is **Wonhyo-sa**, located a short walk from the bus stop. The small but ornate temple has a sculpture garden with several bronze figures standing sentry and a fabulous bronze bell dating to 1710. Further south is **Jeungsim-sa**, the park's largest temple with a Shilla-era iron Buddha backed by red-and-gold artwork, housed in an insignificant-looking shrine behind the main hall. The tiny shrine perched on a rock next to it is dedicated to the Shamanist Mountain God. Further up is the smaller temple of **Yaksaam**.

Near Jeungsim-sa, **Uijae Misulgwan** (☎ 222 3040; admission W1000; ⏰ 9.30am-5.30pm Tue-Sun) is a chic art gallery that displays landscape, flower and bird paintings by Heo Baek-ryeon (1891–1977), whose pen name was Uijae. His rebuilt house is a short walk away. About halfway between Uijae and Jeungsim-sa is the famous **Chunseolheon tea plantation** that Uijae established, now cultivated by Jeungsim-sa monks.

The most popular route is to begin at Wonhyo-sa, climb up to Seoseokdae and Ipseokdae, down past Jeungsim-sa and Uijae, and then down into town to the Hakdong–Jeungsim-sa subway station; the hike takes about six hours. On weekends, the park is alive with Gwangjuites. Restaurant shacks that cling to the hillsides or overlook cascading streams sell pork, chicken and mountain-vegetable meals.

Take the cleverly named bus 1187 (the height in metres of Cheonwang-bong) which terminates near Wonhyo-sa; you can catch the bus (W1000, every 20 minutes) from the bus terminal or outside the Geumnamno tourist information centre.

BASEBALL 야구
Catch the Kia Tigers professional baseball team in action at **Mudeung Stadium** (www.tigers.co.kr; Mudeung; tickets from W6000) and check out the

---

MAY 18TH MASSACRE

The 1980 Gwangju Massacre was a mass demonstration and protest against an authoritarian regime that ended with deadly consequences. The incident now known as the May 18 Democratic Uprising began on the morning of 18 May 1980 with large-scale student protests against the military dictatorship of Chun Doo-Hwan, first at Chonnam National University and then downtown along Geumnamno. The army was ordered to move in, on the pretext of quelling a communist uprising. The soldiers had no bullets, but used bayonets to murder dozens of unarmed protesters and passers-by. Outraged residents broke into armouries and police stations and used seized weapons and ammunition to drive the troops out of their city.

For over a week pro-democracy citizen groups were in control, but the brutal military response came nine days later on 27 May, when soldiers armed with loaded rifles, supported by helicopters and tanks, retook the city. Most of the protest leaders were labelled 'communists' and summarily shot. At least 154 civilians were killed, with another 74 missing and presumed dead. An additional 4141 were wounded and more than 3000 were arrested, many of whom were tortured. For eyewitness accounts of the still-controversial event, read *Memories of May 1980* by Chung Sang-yong (2003) or view www.518.org.

In memory of the pro-democracy martyrs, the Gwangju Prize for Human Rights has been awarded since 2000; recipients have included Aung San Suu Kyi, the pro-democracy leader of Burma (Myanmar).

JEOLLANAM-DO

differences between the Korean and American games. You won't find peanuts or Cracker Jack, but vendors do sell dried squid, sushi, fried chicken and Korean beer. Stock up on snacks from the street vendors outside the stadium, where prices are cheaper. You're permitted to bring in food, beer, coolers and cameras. Many buses, including buses 1 and 23, can drop you there. You can also take the subway to Nongseong station and walk 30 minutes north to the stadium. Games usually start at 5pm or 6:30pm.

ASIAN CULTURE COMPLEX
아시아문화중심도시홍보관

This massive US$680 million arts complex in the old Provincial Hall and May 18th Democratic Plaza is currently under construction. Set to open in 2012, it will house galleries, performance spaces, a library and plazas. A temporary gallery with models of the project and Asian arts exhibits is located next door to the main tourist information centre (p263).

Festivals & Events

The **Gwangju Biennale** (www.gb.or.kr) is a two-month contemporary art festival that takes place every two years (due to be held in autumn 2010). Based at the Biennale Exhibition Hall, near the Gwangju Folk Museum, it features more than 500 artists and foreign curators from 60 countries.

Sleeping
BUDGET

The usual mixture of cheap *yeogwan* and love motels stuck in a 1980s time warp can be found around the train station; smart new motels surround the bus terminal and the downtown Chungjang nightlife district. New luxury hotels are located in the Sangmu District near City Hall.

Koreana Tourist Hotel (코리아나관광호텔, ☎ 526 8600; ksc7812@hanmail.net; r W30,000; 🖳) A stuffed tiger guards the lobby and chandeliers light the large coffee shop of this well-priced and well-maintained hotel set amid a bevy of love motels near Gwangju train station. Rooms are spacious with ornate furniture and a computer.

Bando Motel (반도 모텔; ☎ 227 0238; Chungjang District; r W30,000; 🕷) This basic but clean new motel is hidden in an alley between Art St and Geumnamno, behind the NH Bank

building and just steps from the action of Chungjang.

our pick Windmill Motel (윈드밀 모텔, ☎ 223 5333; Chungjang District; r W35000; 🕷 🖳) Perfectly situated on the west end of the Chungjang nightlife district, Windmill has a slight love motel feel with dark corridors, but the rooms are clean, tidy and spacious with flat-screen TVs, fridges and water coolers.

MIDRANGE
Palace Hotel (파레스 관광 호텔; ☎ 222 2525; www.hotelpalace.co.kr; r W50,000; 🕷 🖳) In the heart of the city, amid the shopping frenzy of Chungjangno, are these quiet, quality rooms which have been recently renovated and are all stocked with smart computers. There's even a nightclub in the basement.

Gwangju Prince Hotel (광주프린스호텔; ☎ 524 0025; r W60,000; 🕷 🖳) You might meet some Korean baseball stars staying at this modest, reasonably priced hotel near the museums. This is a real hotel with a lobby, sauna, restaurants, coffee shop and bar, and yet the price is not much more than a smart motel. Rooms have computers.

Hotel Hiddink Continental (호텔히딩크콘티넨탈; ☎ 227 8500; www.hotel-continental.co.kr; r from W87,000; 🕷 🖳) The discounted price makes this hotel – named after Korea's revered 2002 World Cup soccer coach – a reasonable option. The sky-lounge bar (beer W5000) is its best feature, with armchairs, great city views, an outdoor terrace and a mixed bag of live music nightly at 8pm.

Eating
Hyundai Department Store (현대백화점; ⏰ 10am-8pm) Near Gwangju train station, it has a bright and clean food court (meals W3500 to W5000) in the basement.

Olive Cafe (☎ 228 9979; Geumnamno, near cnr Jungangno; meals W8000-11,000; ⏰ 10.30am-11.30pm) In the mood for Italian? This cute little cafe has all your Italian favourites including pasta, pizza and seafood specialties. The outdoor seating facing a green park is a prime people-watching spot.

our pick Minsokchon (민속촌; ☎ 224 4577; meals W8000-13,000; 11.30am-midnight) A popular barnlike but attractive and cheery restaurant that echoes to *so galbi* (소갈비; beef) and *dwaeji galbi* (돼지갈비; pork) sizzling on table barbecues. The *galbitang* (갈비탕) is excellent with chunky, lean meat and 'wellbeing' additions.

If this Chungjang restaurant has a long queue outside, try the branch in Gwangsan-gil.

Yeongmi (영미; meals W20,000-32,000) One of the many duck restaurants in Duck St alongside Hyundai department store, it has starred on TV. The speciality is *oritang* (오리탕), which is meant for sharing, and bubbles and thickens away at your table together with a pile of vegetables.

Songjukheon (송죽헌; meals from W40,000; noon-2pm & 6-10pm) An atmospheric *hanok* (traditional mansion) where *hanbok*-clad staff serve a full-on *yangban hanjeongsik* (banquet) in your own antique-decorated room, with *gayageum* (12-stringed zither) music in the background. The restaurant is expensive but special.

Drinking

Chungjang, Gwangju's buzzing, semi-pedestrian shopping district, is also the city's prime nightlife spot with hundreds of bars, nightclubs, restaurants and cafes, particularly in the narrow alleys south of Hwanggeumgil street.

Chasaengwon (차생원; Art St; 9am-5pm) A traditional Korean teahouse offering a variety of teas, cakes and a large selection of tea sets and other supplies.

Coffee Story (Chungjang District; 11.30am-2am) You'll feel right at home at Coffee Story, a two-storey building where seating areas are divided into private, mini living rooms with comfy couches, tables, lamps and curtains. There are several locations around town but this is the best.

Soul Train (소울트레인; Hwanggeumgil; 6pm-5am) A large basement pub patronised by both

Koreans and foreigners, with a huge square bar, a pool table, sports on TV, cool music and friendly staff.

Mike & Dave's Speakeasy (drinks W4000-8000; 7pm-3am Thu-Sun) Set up by two enterprising Canadians, this bar hidden down an alley is a favourite with foreigners and has a nice selection of imported beer. A live band rocks the house every Friday at 10pm.

Ethnic Cafe (☎ 234 0901; drinks W5000-9000; Chungjang District; 2pm-2am) This unique, Middle Eastern–themed pub is set in a cave-like, candle-lit basement with a reflecting pool in the centre of the room. Remove your shoes and sit on pillows on the floor and enjoy a conversation while chill-out music plays quietly in the background. It's directly across from Coffee Story.

Shopping

Chungjang is bursting with clothing and accessory stores along the street and below ground in the Chunggeum underground shopping arcade. More trendy department stores are located downtown near the train station.

Migliore (11.30am-11pm) It has stacks of fashion outlets, a multi-screen cinema, a 24-hour *jjimjilbang* (luxury sauna; admission W5000) and regular live performances on the outdoor stage.

OKoutdoor (Jungangno; 10.30am-8.30pm) Planning a hike? This large outdoor store sells name-brand hiking and camping gear.

Art Street (Yesurui Geori) This cobblestoned road is famous for its art galleries, studios, workshops, teashops and stores selling *hanbok* (traditional Korean clothing), *hanji* (handmade paper), art books, ethnic jewellery, calligraphy brushes, tea sets and dolls.

Shinsegae Department Store (10am-8pm) Brand-name outlets rub shoulders in this department store in a gleaming, luxury ambience. There's also a Starbucks, the favourite haunt of local *doenjangnyeo*, as some Koreans might say (*doenjangnyeo* is a derogatory term for young women who only care about style and fashion).

E-Mart (10am-10pm, to midnight Fri & Sat) Stock up on cheap food and supplies at this hypermarket, next door to Shinsegae.

Entertainment

At the end of the day it's just a bus station, but **U-Square** and the adjoining **U-Square**

Cultural Center may be the coolest bus terminal you've ever seen. Opened in 2009, this glitzy complex houses an IMAX theatre and multi-screen cinema, performance halls, stores, video arcade, pool hall, art gallery, cafes, restaurants and a massive food court with Korean and Western options. U-Square is a short walk north of Nongseong subway station.

Getting There & Away

AIR

A dozen Gwangju–Seoul and nine Gwangju–Jeju flights run daily, and international flights operate to Shanghai and Macau.

BUS

Express and intercity buses to more than 100 destinations depart from the gleaming, airport-like U-Square complex, 1km north of the Nongseong subway station.

Express bus destinations:

Destination	Price (W)	Duration	Frequency
Busan	14,400	4hr	every 20min
Daegu	11,400	3hr	every 40min
Daejeon	9300	2½hr	every 30min
Jeonju	5800	1¼hr	every 30min
Seoul	17,900	4hr	every 10min

Intercity buses departing Gwangju include the following services:

Destination	Price (W)	Duration	Frequency
Boseong	5800	1½hr	every 30min
Gangjin	7600	1½hr	every 30min
Haenam	9000	2hr	every 30min
Jindo	12,900	3hr	hrly
Mokpo	6800	1¼hr	every 30min
Songgwang-sa	6300	1½hr	8 daily
Suncheon	6400	2hr	every 30min
Wan-do	12,700	2½hr	hrly
Yeongam	5500	1½hr	every 20min
Yeosu	9400	2hr	every 30min

TRAIN

KTX trains (W36,000, 2¾ hours, 11 daily) run between Gwangju and Yongsan station in Seoul.

Saemaul (W33,200, 3¼ hours, two daily) and *Mugunghwa* (W21,500, four hours, four daily) trains also run along the route. A *Tonggeun* (commuter) train (W2200, one hour) runs once a day at 6.55am from Gwangju train station to Mokpo or three times a day from Songjeong-ni train station (W1900), west of Gwangju past the airport.

Getting Around

TO/FROM THE AIRPORT

Bus 1000 (W1000, 30 minutes, every 15 minutes) runs from the airport to the bus terminals and Geumnamno. A taxi costs around W7500. Soon the new subway will provide an alternative.

BUS

Gwangju has over 80 city bus routes, and most run past the bus terminal that has bus stops on all sides. Bus 17 (W900, 20 minutes, every 15 minutes) runs between the bus terminal and Gwangju train station.

SUBWAY

Gwangju's subway is a work in progress. Currently there is one line that will eventually stretch west to the airport and beyond. A single ride is W1000; trains run from 5.30am until midnight.

AROUND GWANGJU

☎ 061

Unju-sa 운주사

This intriguing **temple** (☎ 374 0660; www.unjusa. org; adult/youth/child W2500/2000/1000; ☷ 7am-7pm Mar-Oct, 8am-5pm Nov-Feb) occupies a river valley and its hillsides in Hwasun-gun, 40km south of Gwangju. Legend has it that the site originally housed 1000 Buddhas and 1000 pagodas, built because according to traditional geomancy, the southwest of the country lacked hills and needed the pagodas to 'balance' the peninsula. The remaining 23 pagodas and some 100 Buddhas still make up the greatest numbers of any Korean temple. According to another legend they were all built in one night by stonemasons sent down from heaven, but another theory is that Unju-sa was the site of a school for stonemasons.

Whatever their origins, many works are unique and some are national treasures. Back-to-back twin Buddhas face their own pagodas, while another pair of Buddhas lying on their backs are said to have been the last works sculpted one evening; the masons returned back to heaven before the Buddhas could be stood upright.

To reach Unju-sa, catch bus 218 or 318 from Gwangju bus terminal (W3000, 1½ hours, hourly). Check with the driver as only some of the buses go all the way to Unju-sa. The last bus back to Gwangju leaves around 6.20pm.

Damyang Bamboo Crafts Museum
담양대나무박물관

This **museum** (☎ 381 4111; adult/youth/child W1000/700/500; ☯ 9am-5.30pm) in Damyang, north of Gwangju, has an amazing range of bamboo products, both ancient and modern. Furniture, exquisitely woven baskets – even a bamboo teapot and bamboo jewellery – are more interesting than you'd expect. Next door is a free display of exquisite bamboo wonders from around the world. Bamboo has 101 uses and the shops in front of the museum prove it. A few of the 46 kinds of bamboo grow behind the museum.

A two-minute walk down the road is the busy but superb **Bakmulgwan Apjip** (박물관앞집; meals W10,000-20,000; ☯ 24hr) The *daetongbap* (대통밥) is excellent – rice and nuts cooked inside a bamboo stem, bamboo-shoot *doenjang*, and a dozen dazzling side dishes are served up with free bamboo-leaf tea. The side rooms have glorious views over the rice fields.

Try and visit Damyang on the 2nd, 7th, 12th, 17th, 22nd or 27th of each month as the bamboo market is held on these days. A **bamboo crafts festival** is held in May.

Bus 311 (W1500, 40 minutes, every 15 minutes) runs between Gwangju bus terminal and Damyang, dropping off at the museum. Bus 303 runs from Gwangju train station to Damyang. If you end up in the Damyang bus terminal it's a 15-minute walk to the museum.

JOGYESAN PROVINCIAL PARK
조계산도립공원

☎ 061

This **park** (☎ 755 0107; adult/youth/child W2500/1500/ free; ☯ 8am-7pm Mar-Oct, 8am-5pm Nov-Feb) revolves around two noteworthy temples, their beauty complemented by the attractive surrounding forest.

To the west, 80km from Gwangju, **Songgwang-sa** (www.songgwangsa.org) is considered one of the three jewels of Korean Buddhism (along with Tongdo-sa and Haein-sa, in Gyeongsangnam-do). Featured in the *Little Monk* movie, it is a regional head temple of the Jogye sect, by far the largest in Korean Buddhism. It is also one of the oldest Zen temples in Korea, founded in AD 867 although most of the buildings date from the 17th century. Songgwang-sa is known for having produced many prominent Zen masters over the years, and today the temple is home to a community of monks.

On the eastern side of the mountain is **Seonam-sa**, a quieter hermitage dating back to AD 529, where the monks study and try to preserve the old ways. Below Seonam-sa is **Seunseongyo**, one of Korea's most exquisite ancient granite bridges, with a dragon's head hanging from the top of the arch.

A spectacular hike over the peak of **Janggunbong** (884m) connects the two temples.

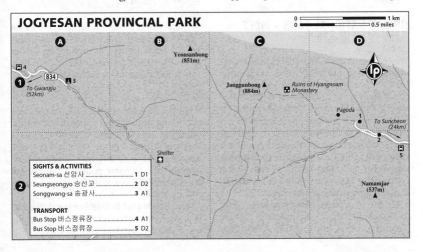

JOGYESAN PROVINCIAL PARK

SIGHTS & ACTIVITIES		
Seonam-sa 선암사	1	D1
Seungseongyo 승선교	2	D2
Songgwang-sa 송광사	3	A1

TRANSPORT		
Bus Stop 버스정류장	4	A1
Bus Stop 버스정류장	5	D2

Yeonsanbong (851m)

Janggunbong (884m)

Ruins of Hyangnoam Monastery

Pagoda

To Gwangju (52km)

To Suncheon (24km)

Shelter

Namamjae (537m)

SUNCHEON-MAN

If you're staying at or near Songgwang-sa one place you might want to consider making time to see is Suncheon-man (순천만). In 2006 this bay became the first coastal estuary in Korea to be inscribed on the Ramsar list of protected wetlands. Apart from admiring the view of the beautiful reed-studded river estuary and surrounding beaches, birdwatchers can spot the hooded crane, black-faced spoonbills and swans, all of which stop by during their migrations. There's an **eco museum** (☎ 749 3006) and walkways through the reeds that are the location for a festival held every October and November. For more information about this area and to arrange guided tours contact call ☎ 061-749 3328 or go to www.suncheonbay.go.kr.

The walk takes six hours if you go over the peak, or four hours if you go around it. Either route is fantastic.

A weekend temple stay (see p388) is available at Songgwang-sa. Accommodation and restaurants are also available by the car park at Songgwang-sa. Lodgings here range from W20,000 to W25,000. There's also a tourist village near Seonam-sa.

From Gwangju buses (W5600, 1½ hours, every 1½ hours) run to Songgwang-sa, but only one bus a day (W6000, 1¼ hours) runs from Gwangju to Seonam-sa, leaving at 7.45am.

JIRISAN NATIONAL PARK – WEST
지리산국립공원
☎ 061

While the bulk of this national park lies in the neighbouring province of Gyeongsangnam-do (p258) it is best approached from this direction if you plan to visit **Hwaeom-sa** (☎ 783 9105; www.hwaeomsa.org; adult/youth/child W3800/1800/1300; ⏰ 6am-7pm). Founded by priest Yeongi in AD 544 after his return from India, this ancient temple dedicated to the Birojana Buddha is enveloped by the beautiful natural surroundings of the park. Last rebuilt in 1636, it has endured five major devastations in its history, including the Japanese invasion of 1592.

On the main plaza is **Gakgwang-jeon**, a huge two-storey hall. Inside are paintings that are national treasures, nearly 12m long and 7.75m wide, featuring Buddhas, disciples and assorted holies. These are displayed outdoors only on special occasions. Korea's oldest and largest stone lantern fronts Gakgwang-jeon, which was once surrounded by stone tablets of the Tripitaka Sutra (made during the Shilla era). These were ruined during the Japanese invasion. Many pieces are now preserved in the temple's **museum**.

Up many further flights of stairs is Hwaeom-sa's most famous structure, a unique three-storey **pagoda** supported by four stone lions. The female figure beneath the pagoda is said to be Yongi's mother; her dutiful son offers her tea from another lantern facing her.

The temple is about 15 minutes' walk from the ticket office. It is possible to continue from the temple and along Hwaeom-sa valley. After about 2½ to three hours the trail begins to ascend to a shelter, **Nogodan Sanjang** (a strenuous four-hour hike). From the shelter the trail continues to rise until you are finally on the long spine of the Jirisan ridge. For hiking details and a map see the section starting on p258.

Temple stays (see p388) are possible at Hwaeom-sa. A large tourist village is located at the park entrance with a number of restaurants and affordable accommodation, but prices rise on weekends.

Buses (W6400, 1½ hours, every 90 minutes) run from Gwangju bus terminal to Jirisan National Park and Hwaeom-sa.

NAGAN FOLK VILLAGE
낙안읍성민속마을
☎ 061

Among Korea's many folk villages, **Nagan** (☎ 749 3893; adult/child W2000/1500; ⏰ 9am-6pm) is unique for its setting, surrounded by 1410m of Joseon-period fortress walls, built to protect the inhabitants from marauding Japanese pirates. It's Korea's best-preserved fortress town, crammed with narrow, dry-stone alleyways leading to vegetable allotments, and adobe and stone homes thatched with reeds. Some are private homes while others house working artisans or are *minbak* (private homes with rooms for rent), restaurants or souvenir shops. Some points of interest are labelled in English and there's the inevitable folk museum.

The **Namdo Food Festival** (www.namdofood.or.kr/www/page/), which receives 200,000-plus attendees, is usually held here early in October – it features 300 Korean dishes, eating contests and traditional cultural events.

Catch a bus (W1000, 15 minutes, every 30 minutes) from Beolgyo. Less-frequent buses run from Suncheon (W1000, 40 minutes, hourly).

YEOSU 여수
☎ 061 / pop 300,000

The molar-shaped, port city of Yeosu is halfway along Korea's steep, island-pocked and deeply indented south coast. Its bustling city centre is nothing special, but its shoreline, peppered with cliffs, islands and peninsulas, is spectacular. Yeosu will host the **2012 World's Fair International Exposition** (www.expo2012.or.kr); as a result Yeosu is currently one massive construction project.

Information

Gyodong post office (Chungmuro) Free internet access.
Korea Exchange Bank (near Jangang-dong Rotary) Exchanges foreign currency.
Nice Bank Global ATM located inside train station.
Tourist information centre (☎ 664 8978; www.yeosu.go.kr) At the entrance to Odong-do pedestrian causeway.
Wooribank (☻ 8am-11.30pm Mon-Fri) Exchanges foreign currency.
Yeosu post office (Gosoro)

Sights
ODONG-DO 오동도
This small, craggy **island** (☎ 690 7301; admission free; ☻ 9am-5.30pm), a favourite destination for locals, is joined to the mainland by a 750m

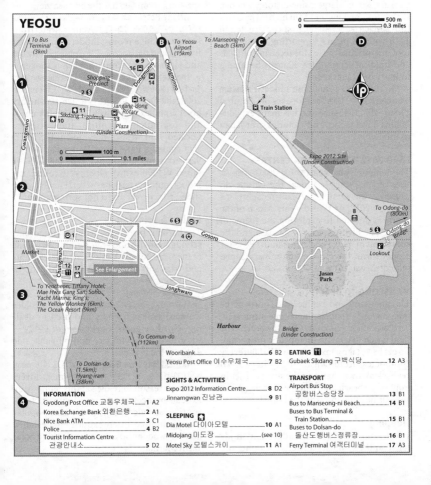

causeway that can be traversed by a **road train** (adult/youth/child W500/400/300). The island is one large botanical garden with bamboo groves and camellia trees, which are full of birdsong and can be walked round in 20 minutes. Take the lift up the **lighthouse observatory** (admission free; 🕐 9.30am-5.30pm) for the best harbour views.

Shops, restaurants, a dancing musical water fountain, a turtle-ship replica and boat trips around the harbour or around Dolsan-do are also available.

City buses 2, 8, 9, 10, 13, 15, 17 and 107 all stop at the causeway entrance. Otherwise it's a 30-minute walk from Jangang-dong Rotary.

JINNAMGWAN 진남관

In the centre of town stands this national treasure, Korea's largest single-storey wooden structure (75m long and 14m high). The beautiful **pavilion** (admission free), first constructed in 1716 with 68 pillars supporting its massive roof, was originally used for receiving officials and holding ceremonies. Later it became a military headquarters.

On the right, a small but modern **museum** (admission free; 🕐 10am-5pm) focuses on Admiral Yi Sun-sin (1545–98) and has maps explaining his naval tactics or victories over Japan in the 1590s.

EXPO 2012 INFORMATION CENTRE

This temporary **museum** (☎ 690 8290; Chungminno; admission free, 🕐 9am-6pm) near the Odong-do causeway was set up to explain Yeosu's plans for Expo 2012, or World's Fair. Much of the centre is devoted to exploring the theme of Expo, 'The Living Ocean and Coast' and the ecosystem of Yeosu and her islands. Pose for a photo with the Expo's cute molar-shaped mascot, Yeosu-rang.

MANSEONG-NI BEACH

This grey-sand-and-pebble beach north of the train station is a popular lunchtime picnic spot. Several seafood restaurants line the beach. The sand is said to contain therapeutic properties. To get here, take a taxi or bus 6 (W1000, every 20 minutes) from Jangang-dong Rotary. To get back to town, stand on the street corner in front of the beach police station and flag down any bus heading towards the tunnel.

Sleeping

There's no shortage of budget and mid-range motels, most clustered around the harbour. New luxury hotels can be found in Yeocheon.

Midojang (미도장; ☎ 663 2226; Sikdang 1-golmuk; r W25,000; 🖥) Cramped but light rooms and bathrooms are kept very clean at the area's best budget option.

Motel Sky (모텔스카이; ☎ 662 7780; Sikdang 1-golmuk; r W35,000; 🖥 🖳) A friendly welcome awaits you at this dated but well-maintained motel. The 6th floor has the best views, and some rooms have round beds or computers (W5000 extra).

Dia Motel (다이아모텔; ☎ 663 3347; Sikdang 1-golmuk; r W40,000-50,000; 🖥 🖳) This new motel with a kindly owner has some stylish features with big TVs and new computers, although bathrooms are small. The more expensive rooms are very spacious; room 606 has the best sea view.

Tiffany Hotel (☎ 685 2200; Yeocheon; r W50,000-80,000, ste 130,000; 🖥 🖳) A new waterfront hotel with huge rooms, modern furnishings, fixtures and flat-screen TVs, plus a lobby bar and Japanese restaurant. English is spoken.

The Ocean Resort (☎ 689 0000; theoceanresort.co.kr; Yeocheon; r from W286,000; 🖥 🖳 🛁 🖳) Opened in 2008, the Ocean Resort is a five-star luxury hotel complex with sleek, minimalist decor and top-notch amenities and facilities. Located 9km west of downtown, the resort also contains ParaOcean Water Park (open 9am to 8pm; adult/child W37,000/25,000, sauna W4000 extra). Open year-round, the indoor/outdoor park has several pools, water slides, a lazy river and a hot spring sauna.

Eating & Drinking

The harbour front is loaded with restaurants serving fresh fish and seafood, although none of them are cheap. A row of new restaurants and bars surround Soho Yacht Marina in Yeocheon.

Gubaek Sikdang (구백식당; ☎ 662 0900; meals W10,000; 🕐 7am-8pm) The *ajumma* (older women) staff is friendly and used to dealing with foreigners. *Saengseongui* (생선구이; grilled fish) with rice and refillable side dishes is the best deal.

ourpick Mae Hwa Gang San (☎ 692 1616; meals W10,000-25,000; 🕐 10am-10pm) Red-meat lovers will have reason to rejoice at this family-run, Korean barbecue restaurant with such favourites as *bulgogi* and *galbi*. This popular place is housed in an exquisitely designed modern wooden structure overlooking Soho Yacht Marina.

King's (☎ 685 0003; drinks W2500; ⏱ 10am-midnight) If you're just looking for a cheap place to drink, you can't beat this local haunt facing Soho Yacht Marina with friendly staff, a pleasant outdoor patio and, oh yeah, dirt-cheap beer.

The Yellow Monkey (☎ 653 6633; Jungleo 2-gil; drinks W4000-8000; ⏱ 8am-2am) A swanky cocktail bar popular with Koreans and expats alike, this posh place has plush couches, clubby decor and a full bar serving beer, spirits, cocktails, coffees, juices and milkshakes.

Getting There & Away
AIR
Yeosu airport, 17km north of the city, has flights to Seoul and Jeju-do.

BOAT
The ferry pier for island ferries is at the western end of the harbour.

BUS
The express and intercity bus terminals are together, 4km north of the port area. Buses include the following:

Destination	Price (W)	Duration	Frequency
Busan	12,200	4hr	hrly
Gangjin	13,200	3hr	every 30min
Gwangju	9400	2¼hr	every 30min
Mokpo	17,000	3½hr	hrly
Seoul	20,800	5hr	hrly

TRAIN
Trains from Yongsan in Seoul to Yeosu are provided by *Saemaul* (W35,900, 5½ hours, three daily) and *Mugunghwa* (W24,200, six hours, 12 daily) services. KTX high-speed trains will reach Yeosu by 2011.

Getting Around
BUS
The express and intercity bus terminals are 4km north of the port. Cross the pedestrian overpass to Pizza Hut and from the bus stop, almost any bus (W1000, 15 minutes) goes to Jangang-dong Rotary. From the train station the same situation applies. From the airport, buses (W2500, 40 minutes, every 30 minutes) run to Jangang-dong Rotary. Taxis are cheap and plentiful.

DOLSAN-DO 돌산도
☎ 061
This large scenic island is connected to Yeosu by a beautiful bridge that is dramatically lit at night. Perched halfway up on a cliff on its southern tip is a popular temple and small monastery called **Hyangiram** (☎ 644 3650; adult/youth/child W2000/1500/1000; ⏱ 8am-6pm), which has superb coastal views over clear blue seas when the mist disperses.

It's a steep 10-minute walk from the bus stop through the tourist village up to the temple, passing through narrow clefts in the rock. Outside one shrine are 75 stone turtles, each with a W10 coin on its back.

Walk to the right and down the access road for 50m for the signposted walk up **Geumosan** (323m). Climbing up the 350 steps takes about 30 minutes, and your reward is a fantastic vista of distant islands and a 360-degree view from the rocky summit. Carry on and the loop track brings you back down to Hyangiram (25 minutes).

Every restaurant in the tourist village sells locally made *gatkimchi* (갓김치; pickled mustard leaves), which has a mustard taste; even if you don't usually like *kimchi* you might like the mildish ones here.

By the ticket office is **Geumohoegwan** (meals W4000-12,000), which offers *saengseongui* (생선구이; spicy crab soup) or seafood *kalguksu* (칼국수; noodles). If the weather's fine, sit outside in one of the thatched shelters with a sea view.

Buses 101 and 111 (both W100, one hour, six daily) run from outside Jinnamgwan to Hyangiram. Check the times as the timetable has gaps.

BOSEONG 보성
☎ 061
This town is the gateway to the famous **Boseong Daehan Dawon Tea Plantation** (☎ 853 2595; adult/child W1600/1000; ⏱ 9am-6pm), spectacularly set on a hillside covered with curvy row after row of manicured green tea bushes. Photo opportunities abound as you walk around the tea plantation.

Dine in the **restaurant** (meals W4000-6000), overlooking the tea bushes, on *jajangmyeon* made with green-tea noodles, *bibimbap* with green tea-rice, or other green-tea themed favourites. Downstairs you can buy green-tea shakes or green-tea yogurt. Nearby is a green-tea ice-cream stall, or enjoy a simple cup of green tea. A shop sells green tea in leaf, teabag or powder form plus green-tea soap. This place is seeping with green-tea products...

Local buses to the tea plantation continue to Yulpo Beach, where **Yulpo Haesu Nokchatang**

GREEN TEA

The 'wellbeing wave', the name given to the trend towards healthy food and drinks, has boosted sales of *nokcha*, green tea, which was introduced in the 7th century. Like ginseng it is used as a flavouring for a wide variety of products from ice cream, chocolates, cakes and milk shakes to noodles, pasta and *hotteok* (sweet pita bread). Some spas even offer green-tea baths.

Korean Buddhist monks have always regarded green tea as an ideal relaxant and an aid to meditation, especially when prepared, served and drunk in the correct ceremonial way known as *dado*. They usually settle any disputes over a cup of green tea.

Korean green tea is only grown in the southern provinces and has a subtle flavour, but experts can tell when and where the tea was picked. Green tea, like wine, is a blend of flavours, a mix of aroma and taste, with its own special vocabulary and rituals.

(☎ 853 4566; adult/child W5000/3000; ☺ 6am-8pm, last entry 7pm) offers you the chance to bathe in green-tea water or seawater.

Buses pass through Boseong every 30 minutes along the Mokpo–Suncheon route. From Boseong bus terminal take any Yulpo Beach–bound bus (W1000, 10 minutes, every 30 minutes) to reach the plantation.

GANGJIN 강진
☎ 061

One of the most important ceramic centres in Korea, Gangjin has been associated with celadon (glazed green ceramic) for over 1000 years. Across the district are the remains of nearly 200 kilns. Gangjin is specifically known for etched celadon, in which shallow patterns are cut out of the piece while it's still wet and filled in with special glazes through an inlay process.

The **Gangjin Celadon Museum** (강진청자박물관; ☎ 430 3524; adult/youth/child W1000/500/400; ☺ 9am-5pm) is 18km south of Gangjin and 300m from the road. There is little English explanation but the exquisite examples of Goryeo-dynasty celadon speak with their own voices. On the left is a **pottery workshop**, where visitors can purchase new ceramic pieces. On the right is an excavated kiln site, discovered in 1968, that dates back to the 12th century.

The museum and shops outside sell reproduction Goryeo celadon. The **Gangjin Ceramic Festival** is held here during midsummer.

To get here, take a local bus from Gangjin bus terminal (platform 13) for Maryang and get off at the museum (W1600, 25 minutes, every 30 minutes), which is called *Cheongja Doyoji* in Korean.

Gangjin is a major transport hub for southern Jeollanam-do.

Buses to Gangjin include:

Destination	Price (W)	Duration	Frequency
Boseong	3600	45min	every 30min
Gwangju	7700	1½hr	every 20min
Mokpo	4500	1hr	hourly
Wan-do	5700	1hr	every 30min
Yeosu	13,200	2hr	every 30min

DURYUNSAN PROVINCIAL PARK
두륜산도립공원
☎ 061

Sights & Activities

One highlight of this park, southeast of Haenam, is **Daedun-sa** (☎ 534 5502; adult/youth/child W2500/1500/1000; ☺ sunrise-sunset), a major Zen temple complex. The temple is thought to date back to the mid-10th century, but it remained relatively unknown until it became associated with Seosan, a warrior monk who led a group against Japanese invaders in 1592–98. Since then it's been very popular with Koreans, yet it maintains an atmosphere of rusticity. A museum houses a Goryeo-dynasty bell, other Buddhist treasures and a tea-ceremony display (Seosan was also a tea master). The temple is a 40-minute walk from the bus stop.

The park's highest peak, **Duryunbong** (700m), provides a dramatic backdrop. To climb it, turn left after the temple museum. It takes 1½ hours to reach the top, and you are rewarded with a very picturesque view of Korea's southern coastline. Head back via the other trail and turn right at the first junction (20 minutes); it's another hour back down to Daedun-sa, via Jinburam.

For an easier ascent, walk back down the access road from the bus stop and turn right up the road for 800m to the **cable car** (☎ 534-8992; return W8000; ☺ 7am-7pm). It takes you 1.6km up **Gogye-bong** (638m) but does not operate on windy days. On the way is **Duryusan Oncheonland**

(☎ 534 0900; admission W6000; ☻ 5am-11pm), a smart new sauna and spa.

Sleeping & Eating

Haenam Youth Hostel (☎ 533 0170; dm/r W7000/25,000; ☒ ▣) A three-minute walk beyond the cable car is the best budget option, with clean modern rooms. All have *yo* (padded quilt mattresses on the floor); rooms have en-suite facilities.

Yuseonggwan (유성관; ☎ 534 2959; d W30,000) This idyllic traditional inn, built around a courtyard and filled with art, is inside the park about two-thirds of the way between the car park and Daedun-sa. It offers breakfast (W7000) and dinner (W10,000).

Jeonju Restaurant (meals from W10,000; ☻ 9am-10pm) It's famous for mushrooms – choose *pyogojeongol* (mushroom casserole) or *pyogosanjeok* (minced beef, seafood, mushrooms and vegetables). Look for the English sign halfway along the line of restaurants leading to the ticket office.

Getting There & Around

Access to the park is by bus (W1000, 15 minutes, every 30 minutes) from Haenam bus terminal. A minibus runs from the parking lot to Daedun-sa (W500).

Bus connections from Haenam:

Destination	Price (W)	Duration	Frequency
Busan	22,000	6hr	hourly
Gwangju	9000	1¾hr	every 30min
Jindo	4500	1hr	hourly
Mokpo	4500	1hr	every 30min
Wan-do	5000	1hr	hourly

WAN-DO 완도

☎ 061 / pop 70,000

Another island now connected by a bridge to the mainland, Wan-do is scenic with ever-changing views of scattered offshore islands. This quiet fishing village is not the most exciting city on the south coast, the main reason to visit is to catch a ferry to Jeju-do or the nearby picturesque islands.

Sights & Activities

The best and most convenient swimming beach is **Myeongsasim-ni** on neighbouring Sinji-do, an island now joined to Wan-do by an impressive bridge that is lit up at night. Take a bus (W1500, 15 minutes, hourly) from the bus terminal to this sandy beach lined with pine trees.

Wan-do's newest attraction is the futuristic **Wan-do Tower** (☎ 550 5484; admission W2000; ☻ 9am-9pm, to 10pm summer), a silver UFO-like observation platform where, on clear spring days, you can spot Jeju-do. It's 448 very steep steps up from the park entrance to the tower.

On Wan-do's south coast is **Gugyedeung Park** (☎ 554 1769; adult/youth/child W1600/600/300; ☻ 9am-5pm), a tiny park that offers views of distant cliffs and offshore islands, a pebbly beach and a 1km nature trail that runs through a thin slither of coastal woodland to the Sanho Motel (p276). Swimming is dangerous. The Seobu (western side) bus (W100, five minutes, hourly) runs from Wan-do bus terminal. Get off at Sajeong and walk 600m down to the park entrance.

Sleeping

Smart new motels topped by neon signs run all the way along the western side of Wan-do-eup harbour. Listed rates often drop during slow periods.

Naju Yeoinsuk (나주여인숙; ☎ 554 3884; r W15,000) Rock-bottom prices are charged at this pink, basic pad that couldn't be closer to the

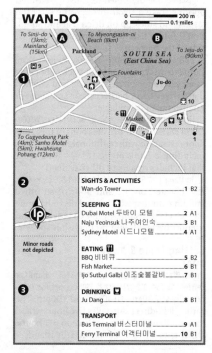

WAN-DO

0 _____ 200 m
0 _____ 0.1 miles

To Sinji-do (3km); Mainland (15km)

To Myeongsasim-ni Beach (8km)

SOUTH SEA (East China Sea)

To Jeju-do (90km)

Parkland

Fountains

Ju-do

Market

To Gugyedeung Park (4km); Sanho Motel (5km); Hwaheung Pohang (12km)

Minor roads not depicted

SIGHTS & ACTIVITIES	
Wan-do Tower	1 B2

SLEEPING	
Dubai Motel 두바이 모텔	2 A1
Naju Yeoinsuk 나주여인숙	3 B1
Sydney Motel 시드니모텔	4 A1

EATING	
BBQ 비비큐	5 B2
Fish Market	6 B1
Ijo Sutbul Galbi 이조숯불갈비	7 B1

DRINKING	
Ju Dang	8 B1

TRANSPORT	
Bus Terminal 버스터미널	9 A1
Ferry Terminal 여객터미널	10 B1

ferry terminal. Some rooms are bare, but most have beds and en suite bathrooms, although with bowls rather than hand basins.

Sanho Motel (☎ 552 4004; d from W30,000; ▓) In a remote location at the far end of Gugyedeung beach is this hilltop motel with wonderful views, a coffee shop and artworks on the wall. It's a special place with a guesthouse atmosphere in a get-away-from-it-all spot that's popular with arty types.

Sydney Motel (시드니모텔; ☎ 554 1075; r W35,000; ▓) Tired of small rooms and bathrooms? Stay at this modern motel located halfway between the bus and ferry terminals. Great sea views, too. Opened in 2003, it's still one of the spiffiest in town. All rooms have shower stalls (hooray!); *ondol* rooms are larger.

Dubai Motel (두바이 모텔; ☎ 553 0688; s/d W40,000/50,000; ▓ ▢) Probably the nicest and newest accommodation in town, this green waterfront hotel has smart, modern rooms, most with harbour views.

Eating & Drinking

Wan-do's speciality is raw seafood, but *saengseongui* (생선구이; grilled fish) and *jangeogui* (장어구이; grilled eel) are cooked-food options. Take a stroll through the busy **fish market** and stock up on dried fish and squid. You'll find a handful of bars along the east side of the harbour.

BBQ (비비큐; meals W4000-9000; ⏰ noon-11pm) Come to this casual and laid-back cubbyhole of an eatery for pizzas, burgers and chicken that arrives fried, barbecued or smoked. An English menu is available.

Ijo Sutbul Galbi (이조숯불갈비; meals W5000-12,000) Dine in your private room in this 2nd-floor restaurant with traditional Korean food, including a *hanjeongsik* (한정식) banquet that includes oysters or other seafood.

Ju Dang (☎ 555 5631; drinks W3000-8000; ⏰ 6pm-2am) Located on the 2nd floor of an office building, this bar with brothel decor has purple velvet furnishings, pink chandeliers and friendly barmaids, but no English is spoken.

Getting There & Away

BOAT
From **Wan-do Ferry Terminal** (☎ 555 0655), **Hanil Car Ferries** (☎ 554 8000; W24,000-29,050) depart for Jejudo daily at 7.30am, 10.40am and 3.30pm. The earlier, less-direct ship takes five hours; travel time on the other ships is three to 3½ hours. Other ferries run to a dozen nearby islands.

BUS
Buses depart from Wan-do for the following destinations:

Destination	Price (W)	Duration	Frequency
Busan	27,000	6hr	6 daily
Gwangju	13,400	2¾hr	every 30min
Haenam	5000	1hr	hrly
Mokpo	10,500	2hr	every 1½hr
Seoul	21,500	6hr	6 daily
Yeongam	7000	1½hr	every 30min

Getting Around

From Wan-do bus terminal, one local bus heads west (Seobu bus) while another heads east (Dongbu bus). Both go to the bridge to the mainland before heading back to Wan-do. The ferry terminal is a 25-minute walk from the bus terminal or a short taxi ride.

BOGIL-DO 보길도
☎ 061

This island southwest of Wan-do is popular in summer for its sandy beaches at **Jung-ni** and **Tong-ni**, 2.3km from Cheongbyeo port. Walk or take a bus or taxi to reach them.

The island's most famous resident was poet Yun Seondo (1587–1617), who wrote his 40-verse masterpiece of *sijo* poetry, *The Fisherman's Calendar* while living in seclusion on Bogil-do. While there he planted a Korean garden, **Seyeonjeong** (세연정; adult/youth/child W1000/700/500; ⏰ 9am-5pm), featuring big boulders, lily ponds and tree plantings surrounding a viewing pavilion. Walk on for another 10 minutes and on the right is **Munhakcheheom** (문학체험), a small park that has Yun's poems (in *hangeul*) hanging from the trees. Cross the stream to climb up the rocky hillside (15 minutes). The garden is a pleasant 20-minute walk from the ferry terminal (follow the English signs) or else take a bus or taxi.

Car ferries (☎ 555 1010; adult/child W7000/3500) ply between Bogil-do and Wan-do's Hwaheung Pohang port (70 minutes, 10 daily), 12km to the west of downtown. From Wan-do bus terminal, take the free hourly shuttle bus to Hwaheung Pohang port.

JIN-DO 진도
☎ 061 / pop 43,000

Korea's third-largest **island** (http://jindo.go.kr), south of Mokpo and connected to the mainland by a bridge, boasts some of the world's largest tides. The island is famous for an unusual natural phenomenon: for a few days each year (usually in spring), the tide drops extremely low, exposing a 2.8km-long, 40m-wide causeway that connects Jin-do to the tiny island of Modo-ri. Some 300,000 people make the crossing each year – in long rubber boots (available for rent, naturally).

The experience is known as the *Ganjuyuk Gyedo* (Mysterious Sea Road) and has long been celebrated among Koreans in legend (see the boxed text on right). With the spread of Christianity in Korea, the similarity to the Israelites' crossing of the Red Sea has only brought more enthusiasts. The **Jin-do Sea Parting Festival**, or *Jin-do Yeongdeung*, is held every spring to coincide with the crossing and includes folk music and dances, a Jin-do dog show and fireworks.

The **Jin-do Dog Research Centre** (진돗개시험 연구소; ☎ 540 3396; admission free; ⏰ 9am-6pm) is dedicated to the study and training of this unique breed of Korean canine (see p64). If you want to see a training session, telephone first (no English spoken). Otherwise, the dogs can be viewed in their pens. The centre is a 20-minute walk from the bus terminal – walk back along the main road from the terminal into Jin-do-eup for 1km and at the blue sign (in English) turn right.

Getting There & Around

Buses connect Jin-do-eup (Jin-do's main town) with many places:

Destination	Price (W)	Duration	Frequency
Busan	24,800	6hr	2 daily
Gwangju	11,300	2¾hr	every 30min
Mokpo	4700	1¼hr	hrly
Seoul	18,900/28,100	6hr	4 daily

YEONGAM 영암
☎ 061

The Yeongam district was a centre of Korea's famed ceramic industry in the 7th to 9th centuries, and the **Pottery Culture Centre** (☎ 470 2566; admission free; ⏰ 9am-5pm) has modern and traditional wood-fired kilns, some dark-glazed pots on display, and potters in a workshop delicately smoothing their pots. It's also the gateway to Wolchulsan National Forest.

Some buses from Mokpo (W3200, 20 minutes, hourly) stop outside the pottery centre, but otherwise you must take a bus from Yeongam to Gurim (W850, 10 minutes, hourly) and walk

---

GRANDMA BBONG & THE PARTING OF THE SEA

Grandma Bbong is a folk hero on Jin-do, a sort of Korean version of Moses. According to legend, a family of tigers was causing so many problems on Jin-do that all the islanders moved to nearby Mo-do, but somehow Grandma Bbong was left behind. She was broken-hearted and prayed to the Sea God to be reunited with her family. In answer to her fervent prayers, the Sea God parted the sea, enabling her to cross over to Mo-do and meet her family again. Sadly, she died of exhaustion shortly afterward. Statues, shrines and paintings of her can be seen throughout Jin-do.

1.2km (20 minutes) to the pottery centre and the folksy tiled houses around it.

WOLCHULSAN NATIONAL PARK
월출산국립공원
☎ 061

East of Yeongam, 42-sq-km **Wolchulsan** (☎ 473 5210; adult/youth/child W1600/600/300; ⏰ 5am-7pm Mar-Oct, 8am-6pm Nov-Feb), Korea's smallest national park, invites a day of hiking. There are crags, spires and unusual shaped rocks around every corner as well as an 8m Buddha rock carving, steel stairways and a 52m steel bridge spanning two ridges. Beautiful and rugged rock formations include **Cheonwangbong** (809m), the park's highest peak.

The popular route is the 8km, six-hour hike from Dogap-sa in the west to Cheonhwang-sa in the east or vice versa – the bus service to both ends is frequent. *Minbak* and restaurants can be found at both ends. Tracks are well signposted, but steep and strenuous in places due to the rocky terrain.

The gateway to the park is Yeongam, from where buses run the 11km to Dogap-sa (W1000, 20 minutes, every 20 minutes) in the west and the 4km to Cheonhwang-sa (W850, 10 minutes, every 15 minutes).

MOKPO 목포
☎ 061 / pop 250,000

The sprawling port city of Mokpo, set on a small peninsula jutting out into the West Sea, is the end of the line for trains and expressway traffic, and a starting point for sea voyages to Jeju-do and the western islands

MOKPO

0 — 500 m
0 — 0.3 miles

To Garten Bier (3km);
Hadang Bars (3km);
New York (3km);
Motel Bobos (3.5km);
Bus Terminal (4km)

Pedestrian Zone

Shopping Precinct

Mokpo Maritime University

bong-gil

Yudalsan Park

Ildeung

Madangbawi

Jung-angno

Yudal Beach

Sea Wall

To Night Street Vendors (50m)

To Badatga (3km);
National Maritime Museum
& Other Museums (3km);
Peace Park (3km);
Eulnamsam (3.5km);
Gatbawi Rocks (3.5km);
Airport (22km);

To Jeju-do (140km)

To Heuksan-do (131km);
Jeju-do (140km);
Hong-do (153km);

INFORMATION	
Global ATM	(see 3)
KB Bank 국민은행	**1** D1
Post Office 우체국	**2** C2
Tourist Information Centre 관광 안내소	**3** D1

SIGHTS & ACTIVITIES	
Botanical Garden 특정자생식물원	**4** B1
Nakjodae 낙조대	**5** A2
Sculpture Park 조각공원	**6** B1
Sightseeing Boat Tours 관광선선착장	**7** A2
Soyojeong 소요정	**8** B1
Yudalsan Park Entrance 유달산공원입구	**9** C2

SLEEPING	
Baek Je Hotel 백제관광호텔	**10** D2
Good Day Motel 굿데이모텔	**11** C3
Kumho Beach Motel 금호비치모텔	**12** D2
Shinan Beach Hotel 신안비치호텔	**13** A2

EATING	
Nam Haz 남옥	**14** D3
Namupo 나무포	**15** C1

DRINKING	
Beach Gallery 까페비치갤러리	**16** A2
Jazz Café	**17** A2

TRANSPORT	
Coastal Ferry Terminal 연안여객선터미널	**18** D3
International Ferry Terminal 국제 여객선 터미널	**19** C3
Train Station 목포역	**20** D1

of Dadohae Haesang National Park. Korea's National Maritime Museum is appropriately located here, and the craggy peaks of Yudal Park rear up in the city centre and offer splendid sea, city and sunset views. Mokpo is the hometown of late South Korean president and Nobel Peace Prize recipient Kim Dae-jung.

It's a surprisingly vibrant, hip, youthful city with a large population of expats working as English teachers or in the shipping industry. Just south of town, an ambitious Formula 1 racetrack and entertainment complex is under construction, set to open in late 2010.

Orientation

Most of the city is located on the south side of the peninsula at the mouth of the Yeongsan River. The old city centre is on the southwest side of the peninsula, between the train station and ferry terminal. Moving east, museums and other tourist attractions are clustered in the Gatbawi Culture District. On the eastern edge of town before the bridge to the mainland is Hadang, a newer neighbourhood of smart hotels, restaurants, bars, shops and the waterfront Peace Park.

Information

Global ATM At the train station.

KB Bank (Jung-angno) Foreign exchange and global ATM.

Post office (Jung-angno) Free internet access; behind it is a historical Japanese colonial building.

Tourist information centre (☎ 270 8599) At the train station.

Sights

GATBAWI CULTURE DISTRICT MUSEUMS
갓바위공원
This complex of museums and art galleries, situated between rocky hillsides and a wide river, is 4km northeast of downtown Mokpo. All museums are closed on Mondays.

The **National Maritime Museum** (국립해양유물전시관; ☎ 270 2000; adult/child W600/300; ☉ 9am-6pm Tue-Sun) is the only museum in Korea dedicated to the country's maritime history. If you have time to visit only one museum, make it this one. The highlights are two shipwrecks, one dating from the 11th century and the other from the early 14th century. Thousands of priceless items of Korean and Chinese celadon, coins and other trade items were salvaged from them. Fascinating film footage shows the treasures being salvaged, and part of the actual boats have been preserved. It has excellent English signage. Next door is Badatga restaurant (p280).

The **Culture & Arts Center** (☎ 274 3655; admission free; ☉ 9am-6pm) is a grand four-floor atrium building that displays the work of local artists who work in all genres – from traditional ink to colourful modern splodges, from photographs to the Asian art of bonsai trees. The centre also houses a 700-seat performance hall.

The **Local History Museum** (문여역사관; admission free; ☉ 9am-6pm Tue-Sun) has a natural rock collection – a popular Joseon-era hobby was collecting and displaying unusual-shaped rocks. Also on display are coins, furniture, coral and paintings by the Huh family.

Namnong Memorial Hall (남농기념관; adult/child W1000/500; ☉ 9am-6pm Tue-Sun) contains a collection of paintings by five generations of the Huh family, including work by Huh Gun, a master of Namjonghwa, a Korean art style associated with the Southern School of China.

The **Mokpo Natural History Museum** (목포자연사박물관; ☎ 276 6331; adult/child W3000/2000/1000; ☉ 9am-6pm Tue-Sun; ☷) is aimed at children, with large dinosaur skeletons, live lizards and fish, and colourful but dead butterflies.

The **Mokpo Ceramic Livingware Museum** (☎ 276 8480; adult/youth W3000/2000; ☉ 9am-6pm Tue-Fri, to 7pm Sat & Sun) traces the history and uses of Korean ceramics, from ancient pottery to biotechnology.

Mokpo Museum of Literature (adult/youth/child W2000/1500/1000; ☉ 9am-6pm Tue-Sun) explores the life and work of three Mokpo authors, Whasung Park, Bumsuk Cha and Woojin Kim. Unfortunately there is no English signage.

The oddly-named **Important Intangible Cultural Asset Training Center** (admission free; ☉ 9am-6pm) contains a small **Jade Museum** with tea kettles, Buddha statues, flatware and sculpture, all made from the green gemstone.

The riverside **Gatbawi Rocks** have been heavily eroded into shapes that are supposed to look like two monks wearing reed hats. A pier extends into the river so you can get a good look at this city icon.

Carry on from Gatbawi Rocks to hike up the rock-strewn hills behind the museums. East of Gatbawi Rocks is **Peace Park**, a lovely waterfront promenade that's popular with walkers and young couples. On weekends it's packed with street vendors and bike rental stands.

Catch bus 15 (W850, 15 minutes, every 30 minutes) from outside the train station (across the overbridge). A taxi costs W4000 from the train station.

YUDALSAN PARK 유달산
This attractive **park** (☎ 242 2344; adult/youth/child W700/500/300; ☉ 8am-6pm) filled with rocky cliffs and pavilions offers splendid views across the island-scattered sea. The park entrance, guarded by a statue of Admiral Yi, is just 20 minutes' walk from the train station or ferry terminal. Turn right to reach the glass **botanical garden** (adult/youth/child W700/500/300) to see orchids and rare Korean plants, while nearby is the **sculpture park** (adult/youth/child W1000/600/400).

If you continue on the main path for 30 minutes you'll reach **Madangbawi** (great views and two rock carvings), followed by **Ildeung** (228m). Turn left just before the white **Soyojeong** (소요정) pavilion to head down to **Yudal Beach**. Turn left at the sign to Arirang Gogae (아리랑고개) and then follow the sign to **Nakjodae** (낙조대) pavilion. From there it's a 10-minute walk down the steps to the beach.

The beach is just a tiny patch of sand, rocks and seaweed, so the main attractions are the island views (partially spoiled by a bridge under construction) and the few bars and restaurants. Sightseeing trips (adult/child W12,000/6000) cruise around the nearby islands.

Bus 1 and most of the other buses that pass by can take you back to downtown.

Sleeping
There are countless love motels and *yeogwan* around the bus terminal and between the train station and ferry terminal. More modern hotels are in Hadang.

Kumho Beach Motel (금호비치모텔; ☎ 242 5700; r W30,000;) The best accommodation between the train station and the ferry terminal is this white high-rise motel. The modern and clean rooms have a dash of style thrown in.

Good Day Motel (굿데이모텔; ☎ 243 6633; Haeanno; r W40,000-50,000;) Probably the best of the half-dozen newish motels near the ferry terminals, with wide corridors leading to smart rooms that have water views.

Baek Je Hotel (백제관광호텔; Namillo; ☎ 245 0080; fax 242 9550; s/d/ste W30,000/40,000/70,000;) A five-minute walk from the train station and the ferries, the light and natural wood decor is appealing, and it has a bar.

Motel Bobos (☎ 283 2210; r W40,000;) This sleek black and silver tower is clean, modern and stumbling distance to the Hadang nightlife area. Look for the rooftop yellow English sign.

Shinan Beach Hotel (신안비치호텔; ☎ 243 3399; www.shinanbeachhotel.com; r from W99,500;) Traditionally seen as Mokpo's top hotel, it towers over Yudal Beach and is old-fashioned classy. Welcoming rooms (mainly *ondol* or twin) have large windows; the sky lounge is disappointing. Ask for discounts during low season.

Eating

You'll find many seafood restaurants in front of the ferry terminal along Haeanno. Smart new restaurants and chains are in Hadang. For some great street food, head towards Yudal Beach, where every evening around dusk vendors set little seaside stalls along Jeonghoro.

Namupo (나무포; meals W6000-14,000; 10am-midnight) Not in a seafood mood? Try the *galbi* (갈비) grills at this thrillingly clean local favourite in the city centre. The meat of the *namupo galbi* (나무포갈비) is beautifully seasoned.

Badatga (meals W6000-20,000; 9am-9pm) This glass box with comfy armchairs next to the National Maritime Museum is perfect for lunch or just to rest your feet and have coffee while enjoying the river views. The wide-ranging menu covers Western, Korean and fusion food.

ourpick Eulnamsam (☎ 287-2080; cnr Mihangno & Umigongwon-gil, meals W7000-20,000; noon-10pm) Hidden in a residential neighbourhood a few blocks northwest of Gatbawi Rocks, this awesome Vietnamese place is a real gem. You'll find Viet trademarks like *pho* and *bun*. For some group fun, make your own spring rolls from plate-fulls of sizzling beef, duck, veg and other delights. Wash it down with green tea and Vietnamese beer. Yum!

Nam Haz (남옥; ☎ 242 9998; Haeanno; meals W10,000-45,000; 10am-10pm) Of the many seafood restaurants near the ferry port, this popular place stands out. Specialties include octopus, spicy noodle soup, crabs and sashimi. Dishes are for sharing. Look for the black and gold building.

Drinking

Mokpo's prime nightlife district is the pedestrian zone along Rose St in Hadang, crammed wall-to-wall with bars, restaurants, cafes, discos and karaoke clubs.

Beach Gallery (까페비치갤러리; Yudal Beach; noon-4am) A cafe with nightly live music in summer, outside or inside. Next door is **Jazz Cafe** (11.30am-late), where you can watch the sun set from the top deck.

New York (☎ 733 8658; Rose St; 6pm-5am) A proper American bar, New York is a favourite expat haunt with a wide selection of imported beer and whisky.

ourpick Garten Bier (☎ 283 5542; Hadang; 6pm-4am) Beer never gets warm at this German-themed bar, thanks to iced cup holders at every seat. Draught beer comes in single, double or triple sized vases. There's also a large selection of liqueur, *soju* and Korean and Western pub grub. One block north and east of New York.

Getting There & Away

AIR

Flights to and from Seoul Gimpo operate once daily from the new **Muan International Airport** (☎ 455 2114; muan.airport.co.kr), 25km north of the city.

BOAT

Mokpo's new Coastal Ferry Terminal (연안여객선터미널) handles boats to smaller islands west and southwest of Mokpo.

The International Ferry Terminal (국제 여객선 터미널) has four sailings a day to Jeju-do. Slower car ferries leave at 9am and 2.30pm and take 4½ hours. The faster, pricier Pink Dolphin leaves at 2pm, taking three hours. Fares start at W13,650 and vary based on class; under 12s' fares are half-price. Contrary to its name, there are no international routes from this terminal.

BUS

Mokpo's bus terminal is some distance from the centre of town. Turn left outside the bus terminal, then left at the end of the road and walk down to the main road where bus 1 (W1000, 10 minutes, every 20 minutes) stops on the left. It runs to the train station, the ferry terminals and then on to Yudal Beach.

Departures include the following:

Destination	Price (W)	Duration	Frequency
Busan	23,400	5hr	hrly
Gwangju	6800	1¼hr	every 30 min
Haenam	5100	1hr	every 30 min
Jin-do	5200	2hr	hrly
Seoul	20,000	4½hr	every 20min
Wan-do	10,500	2hr	7 daily
Yeongam	3200	30min	every 30min
Yeosu	16,500	3½hr	hrly

TRAIN

KTX provides a fast service to Seoul's Yongsan station (W43,300, 3¼ hours, 11 daily), as well as *Saemaul* (W38,300, 4½ hours, two daily) and *Mugunghwa* (W25,700, 5½ hours, five daily) services. Less frequent but cheap trains also serve Gwangju, Boseong and Yeosu.

Getting Around

It's a 15-minute walk from the train station to the ferry terminals or to the entrance to Yudalsan Park.

Airport buses (W2500, 30 minutes) depart from near the train station and are timed to meet flights. They also stop by the bus terminal.

Local bus 1 (W1000, 10 minutes, every 20 minutes) serves the bus terminal, train station and Yudal Beach. Bus 15 (W1000, 15 minutes, every 30 minutes) runs to the Gatbawi Park museums. Taxis are cheap and plentiful.

OEDAL-DO 외달도
☎ 061

Just 1km by 1km, tiny butterfly-shaped Oedal-do is known as 'love island' because young couples and families frequent it. The island has several B&Bs, a beach, hiking trails and a popular swimming pool, but the pool is only open July and August. Ferries (W7000 return, one hour, five daily) run there from the Coastal Ferry Terminal in Mokpo.

DADOHAE HAESANG NATIONAL PARK
다도해해상국립공원
☎ 061

Consisting of over 1700 islands and islets and divided into eight sections, Dadohae Haesang (Marine Archipelago) National Park occupies much of the coast and coastal waters of Jeollanam-do. Some of the isles support small communities with fishing and tourism income; others are little more than tree-covered rocks.

Mokpo is the gateway to the western sector, including Hong-do and Heuksan-do, the most visited and scenic of the islands. In July and August the boats there get full so book ahead.

Hong-do 홍도

The most popular and beautiful of the islands west of Mokpo is **Hong-do** (Red Island; visitor fee W2500). Some 6km long and 2.5km wide, it rises precipitously from the sea and is bounded by sheer cliffs, bizarre rock formations and wooded hillsides cut by ravines. The island is ringed by islets and sunsets can be spectacular, but the only way you can see most of it is by boat, because with the exception of the villages, Hong-do is a protected nature reserve; entry is prohibited.

Ferries to Hong-do arrive at Ilgu village, which like the smaller, northerly village of Igu has a tiny cove that provides shelter to the fishing boats. A boat connects the two villages.

Boat tours (W15,000, two hours, twice daily) around the island are the way to appreciate the island and its rocky islets and arches. Ilgu has several *minbak* and *yeogwan*, all charging about W30,000 to W50,000 per night.

Heuksan-do 흑산도

Heuksan-do, on the way to Hong-do, is the larger, more populated and more accessible of the two islands. Views from its peaks show why Dadohae Haesang means 'marine archipelago'. Fishing villages are linked by trails, but walking around the island would take around nine hours. Fortunately, local buses circle most of the island – a recommended trip is up the **Bonghwadae** peak, on the north coast hill, Sangnasan.

The largest village, **Yeri**, formerly a whaling centre, is where ferries dock and is home to several basic accommodation options of *minbak* and *yeogwan*. Seafood restaurants are plentiful but prices, ranging from W10,000 to W25,000, are significantly higher than the mainland.

GETTING THERE & AWAY

The same ferries serve Heuksan-do, 90km west of Mokpo, and Hong-do, another 20km further away. Leaving from Mokpo's Coastal Ferry Terminal, ferries run to Heuksan-do (adult/child one way W26,700/5750, 1½ hours, three daily) and continue on to Hong-do (adult/child one way W32,600/5750, 2¼ hours).

There are three ferries per day between Hong-do and Heuksan-do (W8000), with additional boats during summer months.

Jeju-do 제주도

Set against a tropical backdrop of swaying palm trees, sandy beaches and towering volcanic features, Jeju-do (http://english.jeju.go.kr) is South Korea's top holiday and honeymoon destination. Foreign travellers, too, are quickly discovering this island paradise and the warm hospitality of its native population. With beautiful beaches, waterfalls, gardens, museums, folk villages, golf courses, casinos, scuba diving, hiking and countless festivals, there is plenty to see and do.

Most spectacular are the volcanic landscapes. Smack in the middle of the island is South Korea's highest mountain, Hallasan (1950m), a national park with varied ecological zones, cute little roe deer and wonderful azalea blooms. On the east is the incredible volcanic crater, Ilchulbong, and its black sand beaches. Nearby, on the island of U-do, black-lava cliffs contrast against a white coral-sand beach. In the northeast is Manjanggul, the world's longest lava tube.

On the south coast, eroded sheer cliffs plunge dramatically into the turquoise waters of the South China Sea. The sea temperature is the warmest in Korea and the coral near Seogwipo is as colourful as the sunsets. Whether you take the 200km challenge of hiking the Jeju Olle footpaths across the island, partake in the unique local cuisine or lie back and toast on the sand, Jeju-do is one part of Korea that you don't want to miss.

HIGHLIGHTS

- Hike to the crater lake atop volcanic **Hallasan** (p303), South Korea's highest mountain, with its spectacular views and four distinct ecological zones

- Take an underground stroll through the world's largest lava-tube cave system, **Manjanggul** (p292)

- Climb to the top of the forested volcanic crater atop **Seongsan Ilchulbong** (p293), cool off with a dip at the **Ilchulbong black sand beach**, followed by a lunch of freshly caught seafood

- Explore the colourful coral and sea life with a **scuba dive** (p298) off the coast of **Seogwipo** (p296), a wonderfully laid-back town housing two amazing waterfalls

- Visit the beaches, waterfalls, museums, luxury spas and hotels of Korea's top honeymoon destination, **Jungmun Resort** (p300)

- Experience the island's best bits in a day at **Hallim Park** (p303), home to lava tubes, gardens and nearby beaches

| ▪ TELEPHONE CODE: 064 | ▪ POPULATION: 560,000 | ▪ AREA: 1847 SQ KM |

History

Despite being just 85km from the mainland, Jeju-do was little visited for centuries. As a result it acquired its own history, traditions, dress, architecture and dialect.

According to legend, Jeju-do was founded by three brothers (p288) who came out of holes in the ground and established the independent Tamna kingdom. Early in the 12th century the Goryeo dynasty took over, but in 1273 Mongol invaders conquered the island, contributing a tradition of horsemanship, a special horse (*jorangmal*; p302) and quirks in the local dialect.

In 1653 a Dutch trading ship was wrecked on the island (p301). A kindly Jeju-do governor looked after the 36 survivors, but when a few tried to escape they were severely beaten. After 10 months they were taken to Seoul and were forced to stay in Korea for 13 years, until some of them escaped in a boat to Japan. One of the escapees, Hendrick Hamel, published his experiences, the first detailed account of the 'hermit kingdom' by a European.

During the later Joseon period, the island became home to over 200 exiles: intellectuals, Catholic converts and political undesirables who spent their time teaching the islanders and composing wistful poems.

Through it all, the locals carried on earning their living by fishing and farming. The island is famous for tangerines, which are grown on the southern coastal lowlands and are for sale throughout the year. Inland, pastures support horses and cattle.

Like the rest of the country, the past few decades have seen the island change radically – most of the coastline is now built up and many farms have been turned into golf courses. The catalyst has been a flood of tourists from the mainland and abroad, which peaks from mid-July to mid-August. The numbers of *haenyeo* (traditional female divers; see the boxed text, p295) are in steep decline.

In 2006 the island was made into a special autonomous province, giving it a level of self-government that is hoped will encourage further economic development.

Climate

The island's climate is less extreme than that of the Korean peninsula, and the mild winters

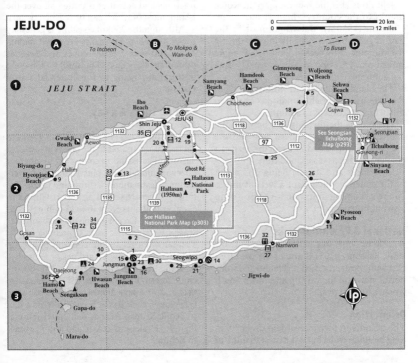

mean palm trees, cacti, tangerine orchards and even pineapple plants thrive. Despite this, don't expect tropical temperatures, but rather a moderate but fickle, four-seasons-in-a-day climate.

Jeju-do is also the rainiest place in Korea thanks to the country's highest mountain, Hallasan (1950m). But while most of the nation gets up to 60% of its rainfall during the summer rainy season, Jeju-do's is more spread out. Downpours are least likely during autumn.

The island is noted for its strong winds, but they are usually brief. Conditions are often misty or hazy, except in autumn.

Hallasan is the dividing line between the subtropical oceanic southern side and the temperate north. Conditions on the peak can change rapidly, as it's a cloud trap.

Swimmers and divers: being 33° north of the equator, you'll want a wetsuit unless you're swimming in July and August – or in a swimming pool.

National & Provincial Parks

Jeju-do has only one national park, but volcanic **Hallasan** (p303) is one of the country's best with roe deer, varied vegetation and wonderful views on the way up and down South Korea's highest peak.

Orientation

The island and province of Jeju-do is 70km long by 30km wide, but it is easiest to think of it in four quadrants: north (the island's capital, Jeju-si, and environs), south (Seogwipo, Jungmun Beach and environs), west and east, with Hallasan National Park in the centre. A mixed bag of historical and recreational attractions and activities is dotted all over the island, most of which can be reached by bus.

Although the 250km coastline is generally rocky, the black-lava cliffs are often picturesque and over a dozen coves and beaches punctuate the coast. The midlands have a pastoral air, rising to the crater lake atop Hallasan.

Getting There & Away
AIR

Flying is the fastest and usually cheapest way to get to Jeju-do, thanks to the boom in low-cost airlines. The island is connected by air to a dozen mainland cities, plus a handful of international destinations in China and Japan. The most frequently served airport is Gimpo in Seoul, with flights every 10 to 15 minutes from dawn to dusk. Except during the busy summer season, it's rarely necessary to prebook flights. You can often get discounts simply by asking, or by bartering between airlines.

Mainstream airlines serving Jeju-do include **Korean Air** (Map p286; ☎ 1558 2001; www.korean air.co.kr) and **Asiana Airlines** (☎ 1588 8000; www. flyasiana.com); each has at least 20 flights a day to Seoul. Korean Air has daily international flights to Osaka and Tokyo, and four per week to Beijing.

Of the half-dozen low-cost airlines, **Jeju Air** (☎ 1599 1500; www.jejuair.net) is the largest and usually the cheapest; turboprop planes fly between Jeju-do and Gimpo 13 times a day; discounted fares start at W49,100 – about W20,000 lower than its mainstream rivals. Other no-frills airlines include **JinAir** (☎ 713 9422; www.jinair.com), **Air Busan** (☎ 1588 8009; www.flyairbusan.com), **Eastar Jet** (☎ 1544 0080; www.eastarjet.com) and **Hansung Airlines** (☎ 1599 9090; www.gohansung.com). All charge about the same; sample fares include Busan (W45,000) and Cheongju (W51,500).

BOAT

Inexpensive, comfortable ferries sail between Jeju-si and four cities on the peninsula. Most ships have three classes: 3rd-class passengers sit on the floor in big *ondol*-style rooms; 2nd class gets you an airline-style seat; 1st class gets you a private cabin with bed and en suite bathroom. Ask about discounts for students and seniors.

Getting Around

TO/FROM THE AIRPORT

Jeju International Airport (Map p283; ☎ 742 3011; www.airport.co.kr/doc/jeju_eng/) is only 4km from downtown Jeju-si. The limousine airport bus 600 (every 20 minutes) drops off and picks up passengers at major hotels and resorts all round the island. Buses 300 and 100 (W1000, 15 minutes, every 20 minutes) shuttle between the airport and Jeju-si.

BICYCLE

If you're a dedicated and fit cyclist, you can hire a bicycle (p289) and pedal around the island (250km) in four or five days. The designated cycleway is relatively flat, much of it parallel to the beautiful coast. Don't forget rain gear.

BUS

Buses radiate from the terminals in Jeju-si (Map p286) and Seogwipo (Map p296) and cover most of the island, with services running round the coast every 20 minutes. Some cross-island buses also run every 20 minutes. Carry an ample supply of W1000 notes as changing a higher note can be difficult. Some buses don't always go all the way to the beach or tourist site, so check with the driver. Pick up an English bus timetable from the airport tourist office.

CAR

Since the sights and activities are scattered around the island, it makes sense to rent a car. Many road signs are in English and the hire cost is reasonable. The problem is that, despite speed traps and road humps, driving habits on the island are only slightly less mad than on the mainland. Still, if you're brave enough to give it a go, there are four car-hire companies at Jeju airport. Don't pay the official rates as they are invariably discounted 60% or more, except during the summer peak. Expect to pay about W44,000 per day for a compact car plus W12,000 per day for insurance.

To rent a car in Korea, you must be 21 years old and have an international driving licence. Car-rental agencies include the following:

Avis (☎ 1544 1600; www.avis.co.kr)
Jeju Rent (☎ 747 3301; jrent@jejurentcar.co.kr)
Kumho/Hertz (☎ 751 8000; www.kumhorent.com)

FERRIES FROM JEJU-SI

All ferries use the Jeju Ferry Terminal (Map p286) except the *Queen Mary* and *Hanil Car Ferry I*, which use the International Ferry Terminal, 2km further east. City bus 92 (W1000, every 20 minutes) runs to and from both ferry terminals, but a taxi is more convenient. Contrary to the latter terminal's name, there are currently no international routes.

Destination	Ship's name	Telephone	Price (W)	Duration	Frequency
Busan	Cozy Island	751 1901	32,000-170,000	11hr	Mon, Wed, Fri
	Seoul Bong Ho	751 1901	43,000-170,000	11hr	Tue, Thu, Sat
Incheon	Ohamana	725 2500	65,000-364,000	13hr	Tue, Thu, Sat
Mokpo	Car Ferry Rainbow	758 4234	26,500-56,500	4hr 40min	daily Mon-Sat
	Queen Mary	758 4234	26,500-274,500	4hr 20min	daily Tue-Sun
	Pink Dolphin	758 4234	49,650	3hr 10min	daily
Wando	Hanil Car Ferry I	751 5050	24,000-59,600	2hr 50min	daily Mon-Sat
	Hanil Car Ferry II	751 5050	24,000	3hr 10min	daily Sun-Fri
	Hanil Car Ferry III	751 5050	24,000-33,300	5hr	daily

JEJU-DO

SCOOTER

It's not the 'greenest' transport method, but the coolest way to see Jeju-do is on a scooter, which can be hired in Jeju-si and Seogwipo. Expect to pay about W20,000 to W25,000 per day.

TAXI

Taxis charge W2000 for the first 2km, while a 15km journey costs about W10,000. You can hire a taxi driver for around W100,000 a day (plus meals and lodging), but this goes up to W150,000 for an English-speaking driver. Agree on the route and price beforehand.

WALKING & HIKING

Since 2007, **Jeju Olle** (☎ 739 0815; www.jejuolle. org) has created more than 200km of marked walking and hiking trails to showcase the hidden beauty of Jeju-do. There are currently 12 interlinked *olle* (narrow paths) routes on the southern half of the island, marked by blue arrows or ribbons. Jeju Olle, launched by former Korean journalist and Jeju native Suh Myungsook, is always on the lookout for volunteers. Information and detailed route maps are posted on the website.

JEJU-SI 제주시
pop 294,000

Jeju-si (Jeju City), the island's capital, sits at the middle of the north coast. The city centre, a mere 4km east of Jeju airport, is hardly glam but it does have a few historic structures, a large market, the Chiseongno shopping precinct and

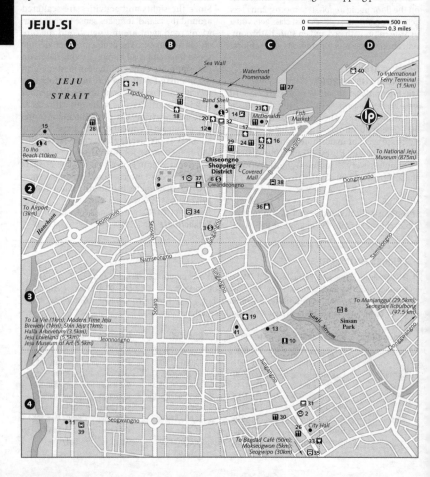

lively student bars and restaurants opposite the old City Hall. The seafront has no beach but still manages a seaside atmosphere in summer with a funfair and pool. The nearby sterile suburb of Shin Jeju (New Jeju) is a mix of midrange and luxury hotels, office buildings, restaurants and bars, but no real tourist attractions.

Information

Central post office (Gwandeongno; ⊙ 9am-6pm Mon-Fri, 1-6pm Sat) Has a global ATM, armchairs, toilets and free internet access.

City Hall post office (Jungangno)

KB Bank (Jungangno) Money exchange and global ATM.

KEB Bank (3rd fl, airport terminal) Global ATM.

KTO tourist information office (☎ 742 0032; 1st fl airport terminal) Free internet.

Ramada Plaza Jeju (Tapdongno) Global ATM.

Shinhan Bank (1st fl, airport terminal) Global ATM.

Tourist information centres Jeju-si ferry terminal (☎ 758 7181; ⊙ 6.30am-8pm); Jeju airport (☎ 742 8866; ⊙ 6.30am-8pm); Yongduam Rock car park (☎ 750 7768; ⊙ 9am-8pm) Free internet access at the airport and Yongduam Rock centres. There is a seasonal tourist kiosk downtown by the band shell.

Woori Bank (Gwandeongno) Money exchange.

Sights & Activities

JEJU-SI SEAFRONT 제주시해안

Though there's no beach in Jeju-si, the seafront is a lively promenade, especially in the evenings at the eastern end where you can hire skates and rollerblade along the sea wall or shoot some hoops on the outdoor basketball courts. The small amusement park **Fantasia** (rides W1000-3000) produces more screams than a rock concert. The outdoor **Water Park** (adult/child W8000/6000; ⊙ 10am-6pm Jul & Aug) makes a good beach substitute. The outdoor **band shell** hosts summer music and dance performances.

JEJU-MOK GWANA & GWANDEOK-JEONG 목관, 관덕정

The island's administrative centre under the Joseon dynasty, the **Jeju-Mok Gwana** (☎ 702 3081; Seomunno; adult/youth/child W1500/800/400; ⊙ 7am-7pm) has been reconstructed. The cluster of historical buildings built in 1448 has an austere style that is designed to promote virtue. Next door is the 15th-century **Gwandeok-jeong** (admission free; ⊙ 24hr), an impressive and recently renovated pavilion that was used for receiving official guests and hosting banquets.

YONGDUAM ROCK 용두암

On the seashore to the west of city, Yongduam Rock (Dragon's Head Rock) attracts coachloads of Korean tourists, but foreign visitors usually wonder why these oddly shaped volcanic lava rocks attract such large crowds. A rocking suspension bridge connects Yongduam to the downtown promenade. Besides rock-watching,

DOLHARUBANG

Giant stone statues known as *dolharubang* ('grandfather' statues carved from lava rock) are the symbol of Jeju-do. The original *dolharubang* were carved around 1750 and placed outside the island's fortresses, and 45 of these still exist – two can be seen outside Samseonghyeol Shrine (below).

No one knows their original purpose; they may have been good-luck totems, border markers or fertility symbols. They are nearly life-sized with a helmet-style hat, bulging eyes, a squashed nose, and hands on their stomach, one slightly higher than the other. They look stern yet friendly.

Nowadays you can see *dolharubang* images all over the island, including bright blue *dolharubang*-shaped telephone kiosks, and of course you can buy your own portable-sized *dolharubang* at the many souvenir shops.

plane-spotting is another popular activity; aeroplanes fly just a few hundred meters overhead on their final approach to the island. Jeju-si's main **tourist information centre** is located nearby in the car park here.

SAMSEONGHYEOL SHRINE 삼성혈

The main feature of this unusual **shrine** (☎ 722 3315; Samseongno; adult/youth/child W2500/1700/1000; 🕙 8am-7pm Mar-Oct, to 6pm Nov-Feb) is three holes in the ground. Legends say that three brothers, Go, Bu and Yang, came out of the holes and founded the Tamna kingdom with help from three princesses who arrived by boat together with cattle and horses. The brothers divided the island kingdom into three sections by each shooting an arrow and taking the third where his arrow landed.

The shrine was originally built in 1526 and the spirit tablets of the island's first ancestors are honoured with food and music in a ceremony held three times a year: on 10 April, October and December. At the entrance are two of the 45 remaining original *dolharubang*, which are over 250 years old.

Ask to see the English version of a 15-minute film about the legend; it's shown in the exhibition hall.

FOLKLORE & NATURAL HISTORY MUSEUM 민속자연사박물관

This wide-ranging **eco-museum** (☎ 722 2465; Samseongno; adult/youth/child W1100/500/free; 🕙 8.30am-6.30pm) in Sinsan Park has well-labelled exhibits on Jeju-do's varied volcanic features including volcanic bombs, lava tubes and trace fossils. Fortunately the volcanoes have all been dormant for the last thousand years, although earthquakes were felt in the 16th century. Other highlights to look out for are excellent wildlife films, the bizarre oar fish, and panoramas of the island's six ecological zones.

NATIONAL JEJU MUSEUM 국립제주박물관

This **museum** (☎ 720 8000; adult/youth/child W1000/500/free; 🕙 9am-6pm Tue-Sun) is housed in a large, inconveniently located building. It's a clone of the many other local museums dotted around the country but antiques addicts can get their fix here. Many city buses stop outside, including bus 26 (W1000, every 15 minutes).

HALLA ARBORETUM 한라 수목원

A short drive north of the hustle and bustle of Shin Jeju lies the tranquil oasis of **Halla Arboretum** (☎ 710 7575; Hwy 1100; admission free; 🕙 9am-6pm). This 15-hectare arboretum, also known as Halla Botanical Garden, is a collection of 100,000 individual plants, trees and shrubs comprising 1100 species. The arboretum is divided into 11 separate gardens including evergreens, tropicals, herbs, a bamboo forest and a four-season flowering garden. Meandering footpaths wind through the beautifully landscaped gardens, ponds and greenhouses. It's a great place to get lost for a few hours. Most buses will drop you off at the intersection of Hwy 1100 and the arboretum access road, then you can walk 6km to the entrance.

JEJU MUSEUM OF ART 제주도립ㅇㅣ술관

Opened in 2009, the **Jeju Museum of Art** (JMOA; ☎ 710 4300; http://jmoa.jeju.go.kr; Hwy 1100; 🕙 9am-6pm Tue-Sun, to 8pm Jul-Sep) brings some highbrow culture to Jeju-do with a collection of permanent and temporary exhibits of contemporary visual art. There's also a children's gallery for little visitors. The beautifully designed building appears to float on a pool of water. It's located 2km north of the Halla Arboretum near the Mysterious Road (see the boxed text, opposite). At the time of our visit, admission was free; a future fee is pending.

JEJU LOVELAND 제주러브랜드

Feeling frisky? Then head over to this **erotic theme park** (☎ 712 6988; www.jejuloveland.com; Hwy 1100; admission W7000; ☼ 9am-midnight) featuring 140 sexy sculptures, soft-core art galleries and adult toy stores. Most of the artworks are more comical than erotic. The park was started in 2002 by art students and graduates of Seoul's Hongkik University. It's quite popular with South Korean honeymooners looking for inspiration (or education). It's located next door to the more mainstream Jeju Museum of Art. A taxi from Jeju-si to Loveland will set you back about W9500. Leave the kids at home.

MOKSEOGWON 목석원

About 6km south of Jeju-si, **Mokseogwon** (☎ 702 0203; adult/youth/child W2000/1500/1000; ☼ 8am-6.30pm Feb-Nov, to 5.30pm Dec & Jan) is both a garden and art park with 1500 oddly shaped rocks and gnarled roots. It's a labour of love, put together over many years by a local resident, and if your switch is flipped 'on', you could find it a wondrous place. Installations are creations of wood and stone (Mokseogwon translates as 'Wood-stone garden'). To reach Mokseogwon, take city bus 500 (W1000, 30 minutes, every 15 minutes) bound for Jeju National University – pick it up along Jungangno.

IHO BEACH 이호해수욕장

The nearest beach to Jeju-si along the west coast is blessed with an unusual mixture of yellow and grey sand, which means that you can build two-tone sandcastles. The beach is a decent size with shallow water that makes for safe swimming, and changing-room facilities are open in July and August. Further out to sea you can pit your free-diving skills against *haenyeo* divers searching around the rocks for seafood and edible seaweed. A small fishing port is on one side, and terns dive for fish too.

Buses (W1000, 20 minutes, every 20 minutes) leave Jeju-si bus terminal for Iho Beach – get off at Heon-sa Village stop and it's a 150m walk to the beach.

CYCLE, SCOOTER & SKATE HIRE

Pedal west along the coast road (lunching in one of the many restaurants) or even all the way round the island on bicycles rented from **Smart Bicycle** (스마트자전거; ☎ 755 1134; Seogwangno; per day W6000; ☼ 8am-7pm) or **Tabalo Bicycle** (타발로하이킹; ☎ 751 2000; per day W8000; ☼ 8am-8pm), which has new bikes. Around the corner from the Water Park, **Jeju Pro Shop** (☎ 702 8243; ☼ 10am-9pm) rents bicycles (per day W10,000) and in-line skates (per hour W2000); staff speak basic English.

Sleeping

There are dozens of hotels along the seafront; most budget and moderate lodging options are located just south of Tapdongno. Newer and pricier hotels can be found in Shin Jeju. Discounts are often available, except during high season (July and August).

BUDGET & MIDRANGE

Usu Yeogwon (우수여관; ☎ 756 1746; r W20,000; ✕) The cheapest option in town, this barebones *yeogwan* (motel with small en suite) is located directly behind the Jeju Palace Hotel. It's nothing special but it's a good, clean option if you're on a tight budget.

HK Hostel (숭광민박; ☎ 703 6775; Tapdongno; r W30,000; ✕) With its great location, friendly staff and amenities normally only found in more expensive hotels, this new hostel is the best budget deal in town. Clean and tidy rooms have real beds (no bunks!), private bathroom and TV. You'll also enjoy shared kitchen and laundry facilities and a nice rooftop deck.

Global Motel (글로벌모텔; ☎ 756 5943; r W30,000-40,000; ✕) Down by the seafront, and run by friendly *ajumma* (older women), the

---

MYSTERIOUS & GHOST ROADS
신비의 도로, 도깨비도로

For a 'Twilight Zone' moment, drive on to one of these stretches of road, turn off the engine, shift to neutral, and your car will appear to roll uphill. If you pour water or roll a ball on the pavement, there's a similar effect. It's really an optical illusion due to the angle of the road relative to sight lines, but it certainly looks convincing. If you decide to test it, watch out for other vehicles trying the same thing!

The first stretch to be discovered (allegedly by a taxi driver taking a break) is **Sinbiui Doro** (Mysterious Road), in the hills about 7km south of the airport. **Dokkaebi Doro** (Ghost Road) is to the east.

cheaper rooms are smallish but blissfully modern, smart and clean.

ourpick Tapdong Hotel (탑동호텔; ☎ 723 3600; Haejingno; r W40,000, ste W50,000; ✂ 🖵) One of the best high-rise motels near the seafront with spacious, stylish rooms and bathrooms. Rooms are fully equipped with a computer as well as unusual extras like electric kettle and claw-footed tubs. The staff are friendly and speak basic English.

Bobos Motel (모텔보보스; ☎ 727 7200; Haejingno; r W40,000; ✂ 🖵) A classy motel, opposite Tapdong Hotel, where the staff are welcoming and most rooms have ornate furniture as well as modern fittings. Rooms with computers are W5000 extra.

Jeju Palace Hotel (제주팔레스호텔; ☎ 753 8811; www.cjpalace.co.kr; Tapdongno; r W60,000; ✂ 🖵) On the seafront, the rooms are fine if you turn a blind eye to the small bathrooms with dated fittings. Other retro features like chandeliers have some charm and the restaurant has a sea view when the mist lifts. You can email from the lobby and male guests can steam in the sauna.

White Beach Hotel (화이트비치호텔; ☎ 753 8400; r W80,000; ✂) The seafront location is the reason for staying here as long as you don't mind a small bathroom. Rooms with a sea view are W20,000 extra. City-view rooms face the amusement park so it can be a bit noisy. The ground-floor restaurant serves Jeju-do specialities (W12,000 to W15,000), while the rooftop bar (opposite) is a hidden gem.

TOP END

Jeju KAL Hotel (제주KAL호텔; ☎ 724 2001; www.kalhotel.co.kr; Jungangno; s/d W170,000/202,000; 🖵 ✂ 🍴) This plush Korean Airlines high-rise in the heart of downtown has the best city views and all the top-end bells and whistles including a casino, a lap pool, aerobics and yoga classes, and a 19th-floor sky bar (beer W8000) with a live band.

Ramada Plaza Jeju (☎ 729 8100; www.ramadajeju.co.kr; Tapdongno; r W200,000; ✂ 🖵 🍴) This newish hotel with a casino and conference centre makes the most of its seafront location and nautical design that gives guests the illusion they're at sea on a luxury liner. The atrium lobby has 'wow' factor. Rooms have floor-to-ceiling windows, staff go the extra mile, and the only negative is the small toilet cubicles. Prices rise at weekends and rooms with sea views cost more, but breakfast is included.

Eating

E-Mart Food Court (이마트; Tapdongno; meals W2500-6000; ⏱ 10am-9pm) The food court on the 5th floor has sea views and a smorgasbord of cheap eats but is on the tatty side. Hidden away at the far end of the basement supermarket is a great takeaway section – sushi, kebabs, spare ribs, chicken and raw-fish platters (*hungeo*, raw ray) are W12,000.

Nikko Nikko (☎ 721 5288; sushi W3000-4000, rolls 6000-14,000; ⏱ noon-9pm) In the mood for sushi? Look no further than this branch of a popular Southern California chain featuring good sushi and even better rolls. The weekday set-meal lunch specials (W6000) are excellent value.

Zapata's (☎ 722 3369; meals W3000-9000; ⏱ noon-10pm; 🖵) Jeju's newest and best Mexican restaurant serves up nearly authentic tacos, burritos, fajitas and quesadillas, plus excellent lemon margaritas (W6000) and a large selection of tequilas and Mexican beer.

JEJU-DO CUISINE

The island is well known for certain foods that are difficult or impossible to find elsewhere in Korea. *Okdomgui* is ubiquitous and tasty, a local fish that is semi-dried before being grilled and has a gourmet taste that appealed to Joseon monarchs. *Heukdwaeji* (pork from the local black-skinned pig) is also common – look for a picture of a black pig on restaurant signs. *Jeonbok juk* (abalone rice porridge) is another island favourite, but abalone is so expensive these days that the amount of abalone in the porridge is declining. A few restaurants serve up *kkwong* (Jeju-do pheasant), including Gombawi in Seongsan Ilchulbong (p294). If you love raw fish, you won't want to leave Jeju-do as every kind of *hoe* (raw fish) and seafood is available from restaurants and direct from *haenyeo*, the island's traditional female divers (see the boxed text, p295).

For gifts, tangerines (especially the knobbly *hallabong*) are number one, but there is also prickly-pear jam, black *omija* tea, honey and the less appealing local chocolates. Hallasan *soju* (local vodka) is smoother than some.

** our pick Bagdad Café** (☎ 757 8182; meals W9000-15,000; ⊙ 11am-2am; ⌨) This wonderful Indian restaurant-cafe-bar, named after the film not the city, has music, stylish English-speaking staff and a lovely outside terrace. It has more character and atmosphere than all the city's other restaurants put together. An Indian chef cooks up authentic curries, *naan* bread and mango lassis. Weekends can be busy with a mixed crowd of Koreans and homesick Brits. Look for the pink building two blocks west of Jungangno, just off Sinseongno.

Dompekon (동버 ㅣ ㅍ ㅊ; ☎ 753 0008; mains W9000-30,000; ⊙ noon-2am) This hip, award-winning Korean barbecue restaurant serves up the island's tastiest speciality, black-pig pork. Dishes are huge and meant for sharing.

Haejin Seafood Restaurant (해진횟집; ☎ 722 4584; Sashimi Street; W10,000-60,000; ⊙ noon-10pm) Of the many restaurants overlooking the harbour on Sashimi Street, Haejin is the largest and most popular place to try Jeju-do's raw seafood specialities like cuttlefish, eel, squid, octopus, sea cucumber and abalone. The set meal (W30,000) is the best deal and feeds two people. Ask for the English menu.

Other recommendations:

Jeongdaun (정 다 운; meals W7000-25,000; ⊙ 24hr) With views over the sea, this 2nd-floor restaurant serves up fresh fish and *hoedeopbap* (회 덮 밥; vegetables, rice and raw fish).

El Paso (엘파소; meals W9000-20,000; off Jungangno; ⊙ noon-11pm) The city's original Mexican restaurant has overly-spicy Tex-Mex favourites.

Drinking

Jeju-si's prime nightlife spot is Shi-Cheong, the semi-pedestrian student pub area west of City Hall. More bars and nightclubs are scattered around Shin Jeju.

Jeju Chocoart (☎ 721 3337; www.jejuchocoart.com; cnr Jungangno & Seogwagno; ⊙ 10am-11pm) Equal parts cafe, confectionery and patisserie, this is a magnet for coffee lovers and chocoholics. The milkshakes are especially tasty.

White Beach Hotel Bar (beers/cocktails W3000/6000; ⊙ 2pm-2am) Enjoy a wonderful sea view from a modernist glass box atop this seafront hotel. On a fine day the outside terrace is the perfect spot for a date or a sundowner.

Sand & Food (☎ 752 7013; cnr Tapdongno & Jungangno; items W4000-6000; ⊙ 8.30am-11pm; ⌨) Facing the sea, this friendly cafe has a good selection of coffee drinks, bagels, sandwiches and free internet.

The Factory (Sicheongnam-2-ro; beer/cocktails from W4000/6000; ⊙ 7pm-4am) Like Andy Warhol's studio for which it's named, the Factory is a dark and moody bar that attracts artists, musicians and other hipsters. It's a favourite haunt for Jeju's expat community. There's occasional live music, or request a song from the resident DJ.

** our pick La Vie** (☎ 747 8303; Shin Jeju; ⊙ 6pm-late) With cool artwork, comfy furnishings, great music and a library, you'll feel right at home at this tiny neighbourhood pub that's popular with locals and expats alike. The menu features comfort food like grilled cheese sandwiches, hamburgers, vegie options and milkshakes. The pub is hidden on the small road behind the Milano Crown Hotel. Owner Youngsook speaks English; tell her we said 'hello!'.

Modern Time Jeju Brewery (☎ 748 4180; 263-6 Yeon-dong, Shin Jeju; beer W3000-6000; mains W8000-30,000; ⊙ 11am-3am) Jeju's first and only brewery is a welcome change from the usual Korean beer offerings. There are seven types of beer; our favourite is the crisp, copper, slightly floral Pale Ale. An extensive menu features Western pub grub. It's around the corner from Jeju Grand Hotel.

Entertainment

Juliana (줄리아나 나이트클럽; Haksasaero; admission W35,000; ⊙ 7pm-late) This nightspot in the student entertainment zone opposite City Hall operates on the Korean system and the high admission price buys three beers and *anju* (snacks). The music is mixed but mainly hip-hop. Extra beers are W4000.

Academy Cinema (아카데미극장; admission W7000) Like all Korean cinemas, Academy screens foreign films in their original language, subtitled in *hangeul*.

Shopping

The city's three prime shopping zones are Dongmun market, which spreads bustling and cheerful retail therapy over a large area in the city's heartland; nearby Jungang underground shopping centre; and the Chiseongno shopping precinct with its youthful fashion stores and brand-name boutiques stocked with clothes, accessories and cosmetics.

E-Mart (이마트; Tapdongno) has a souvenir section near the lift exit on the 4th floor, which stocks gift boxes of oranges and *dolharubang*-shaped jars of *omija* (berry) tea, soaps, chocolate and cactus honey tea.

Getting Around

There are streams of city buses, most of which can be picked up outside the bus terminal or along Jungangno, and taxis are cheap and convenient.

EASTERN JEJU-DO

Samyang Beach 삼양해수욕장

The first beach along the coast road east of Jeju-si is Samyang, which has the darkest sand on the island and is jet-black when wet. In the summer, join the locals and bury yourself in the iron-rich sand for a therapeutic sand bath, said to relieve dermatitis, arthritis and athlete's foot.

Take the Seongsan Ilchulbong bus (W1000, 25 minutes, every 20 minutes); several local buses, such as bus 26, go there too.

Gimnyeong Beach & Sailing Club
김녕해수욕장, 김녕세일링클럽

The white sand of small Gimnyeong beach contrasts with the black-lava rocks. **Emerald Pension Castle** (에메랄드펜션개슬; ☎ 782 1110; r W50,000-80,000), five steps from the beach, has super sea views; Emerald room is lovely and worth every won.

West of the beach is a small harbour and the **Gimnyeong Sailing Club** (☎ 011-639 5379), where English-speaking Mr Kim can sort you out some sailing in a dinghy or cruiser. Just take the boat out, or lessons can be arranged. The harbour is a perfect spot for novices to learn and Jeju is famous for its wind – you can see wind turbines spinning round nearby.

Take the Seongsan Ilchulbong bus from Jeju-si bus terminal to Gimnyeong (W1000, 50 minutes, every 20 minutes) or else a number of local buses go there.

Sangumburi 산굼부리

Halfway between Jeju-si and Seongeup Folk Village, this impressive green **volcanic crater** (☎ 783 9900; adult/youth & child W3000/1000; ⏱ 9am-6pm) is the second largest on the island, 350m in diameter and 100m deep. It's just one of the 360 'parasitic cones' (secondary volcanoes) found on Jeju-do, but has the easiest access, a five-minute walk. Another five-minute walk goes a short way around the crater rim. That's all that's allowed so it's a short stop. The crater is lush and forested with over 420 varieties of plants. In the distance, across the plains, are more of Jeju-do's volcanic humps. Some buses (W1800, 30 minutes, hourly) that run be-tween Jeju-si bus terminal and Seongeup and Pyoseon stop at the entrance to the crater – look out for ivy-covered walls.

Manjanggul 만장굴

East of Jeju-si and about 2.5km off the coast road is the world's longest system of **lava-tube caves** (☎ 783 4818; adult/youth & child W2000/1000; ⏱ 9am-6pm Mar-Oct, to 5pm Nov-Feb). The caves are 13.4km long, with a height varying from 2m to 30m and a width of 2m to 23m. If you've never been inside a lava tube before, don't miss this chance. As you venture inside the immense black tunnel with its swirling walls and pitted floor, it looks like the lair of a giant serpent and it's hard to imagine the titanic geological forces that created it aeons ago, moulding rock as if it was Play-Doh.

Take a jacket, as the cave ceiling drips and the temperature inside is a chilly 10°C. The lighting is dim so a torch (flashlight) is a good idea. You can walk for 1km along the black tube to a 7m lava pillar, the cave's outstanding feature. The walk takes 40 minutes as the floor is pitted and full of puddles.

A 20-minute walk back down the access road is **Gimnyeongsagul** (김녕사굴, Snake Cave), which is officially closed, but just fol-low the sign to walk through the first double-decker lava-tube cave and on to the even larger second lava cave, which you can venture down if you have a torch. On the other side of the road, right of the shop just past a fence, is an **unnamed lava-tube cave**. It has two levels and runs underneath the road.

GETTING THERE & AWAY

Take the Seongsan Ilchulbong bus (W1900, one hour, every 20 minutes) from Jeju-si bus terminal. It drops you on the main road, 2.5km from Manjanggul, but the 35-minute walk down the access road is lined with ole-ander trees and goes past fields bordered by dry-stone walls, woodland inhabited by pheasants, lava-tube caves and an excellent maze (see below). A bus (W850, five minutes, 11 daily) runs along the road but the service is usually irregular.

Gimnyeong Maze 김녕미로공원

A 10-minute walk from Manjanggul is this popular **hedge maze** (☎ 782 9266; adult/youth/child W3300/1650/880; ⏱ 8.30am-7pm Mar-Oct, to 6pm Nov-Feb), which is as much fun for adults as for children. Created from 2232 Leyland cypress trees, it's fiendishly clever and a real challenge. Owner/American expat Fred Dunstin is often around to share a good yarn.

Woljeong Beach 월정해수욕장

This small, white, sandy beach is so little known that it's not on most maps. Stay here for an off-the-beaten-track experience where you can even spot dotterels on the beach. **Miworld Pension** (미월드펜션; ☎ 784 7447; r W60,000-120,000) has smart rooms with kitchens and balconies, though bathrooms are cramped. Take the Seongsan Ilchulbong bus from Jeju-si bus terminal, get off at the Manjanggul stop, continue walking east along Hwy 1132 for 500m then turn left down the access road to the beach.

Seongsan Ilchulbong 성산 일출봉

Seongsan-ri (Fortress Mountain Village) is at the extreme eastern tip of Jeju-do, at the foot of the spectacular extinct volcano **Ilchulbong** (Sunrise Peak; ☎ 784 0959; adult/youth & child W2000/1000; ☺ before sunrise-sunset). The summit (182m) is shaped like a punchbowl, though there's no crater lake here because the volcanic rock is porous. The crater is a forested Lost World ringed by jagged rocks and the sides of the mountain plunge vertically into the surf. It is one of Jeju-do's most impressive sights.

Climbing the steep stairs to the crater rim only takes 20 minutes. Doing it in time to catch the sunrise is a life-affirming journey for many Koreans – expect plenty of company. To do the sunrise expedition, you'll have to spend the night in Seongsan-ri. The path is clear, but if you're concerned bring a torch. Not an early riser? It's also a popular daytime hike. The Seongsan Sunrise Festival, an all-night New Year's Eve party, is held here every December 31.

To the right of the Ilchulbong ticket office is the small temple of **Dong Am Sa** that you're free to peruse.

At the eastern base of the volcano, a staircase leads down to the lovely little **black sand beach**, tucked in a crescent-shaped cove backed by weather-beaten lava cliff walls and boulders. On the left side of the cove you'll find **Haenyeo House** (☎ 783 1145; mains W10,000-20,000; ☺ 9am-6pm), a small restaurant run by Jeju-do's famous female divers (see the boxed text, p295) who

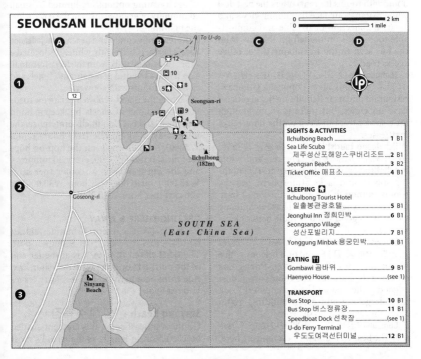

SEONGSAN ILCHULBONG

SIGHTS & ACTIVITIES	
Ilchulbong Beach	**1** B1
Sea Life Scuba	
제주성산포해양스쿠버리조트	...**2** B1
Seongsan Beach	**3** B2
Ticket Office 매표소	**4** B1

SLEEPING 🏠	
Ilchulbong Tourist Hotel	
일출봉관광호텔	**5** B1
Jeonghui Inn 정희민박	**6** B1
Seongsanpo Village	
성산포빌리지	**7** B1
Yonggung Minbak 용궁민박	**8** B1

EATING 🍴	
Gombawi 곰바위	**9** B1
Haenyeo House	(see 1)

TRANSPORT	
Bus Stop	**10** B1
Bus Stop 버스정류장	**11** B1
Speedboat Dock 선착장	(see 1)
U-do Ferry Terminal	
우도도여객센터미널	**12** B1

Map labels: To U-do; Seongsan-ri; Ilchulbong (182m); Goseong-ri; SOUTH SEA (East China Sea); Sinyang Beach; 0 — 2 km; 0 — 1 mile

serve fresh raw octopus, conch, abalone and other delicacies. The *haenyeo* put on a free performance of their skills every day at 1.30pm and 3pm. Next to the restaurant, small **speedboats** (선착장; per trip W10,000) can whisk you out to sea for another perspective on Ilchulbong.

There is another longer and narrower **black sand beach** along the isthmus connecting Seongsan to Goseong-ri, fronted by several modern hotels and restaurants. Nearby, Mr Park at **Sea Life Scuba** (제주성산포해양스쿠버리조트; ☎ 782 1150; Seongsanpo; ♡ 7am-6pm) speaks some English and can take you diving inside underwater caves and around coral reefs. A day trip with two dives costs W150,000, including guide and all equipment.

SLEEPING & EATING

Accommodation usually includes fully equipped kitchenettes and varies from W15,000 for a *yo* (padded quilt) mattress in a tiny cell with shared facilities to stylish and spacious rooms with superb views for up to W40,000.

Yonggung Minbak (용궁민박; ☎ 782 2379; r W25,000; ✻) This red-brick *minbak* (private home with rooms for rent) offers the best deal with great in-your-face Ilchulbong views and a varied collection of sizeable and comfortable rooms. It's on the left on the way from the bus stop to the Ilchulbong ticket office access road.

Jeonghui Inn (정희민박; ☎ 782 2169; r W30,000; ✻) Large rooms here – opposite Gombawi restaurant and near Ilchulbong ticket office – have no views, but there is room enough for a soccer team to sleep on the floor on *yo* mattresses.

Ilchulbong Tourist Hotel (일출봉관광호텔; ☎ 782 8801; r W39,000; ✻) The red-and-white hotel at the entrance to Seongsan-ri is nothing special and lacks atmosphere, but the rooms (although not the bathrooms) have been recently renovated and have Ilchulbong views. It's a good standby if the better places are full.

Seongsanpo Village (성산포빌리지; ☎ 782 2373; r W40,000; ✻ ▢) Sit out on a balcony with a wonderful view of the sea and anything going on along the harbour. The rooms are almost as good as the view and have computers. Look for a large red-and-green building, 100m along the Seongsanpo seafront.

Gombawi (곰바위; meals W5000-25,000; ♡ 7am-4pm) The best view and the best food are here,

on the 2nd floor above LG 45 convenience store on the access road to Ilchulbong. Try the local speciality, pheasant and buckwheat noodle hotpot (W10,000) or the tofu casserole (W5000). Ask for an English menu.

GETTING THERE & AWAY

Buses (W3800, 1½ hours, every 20 minutes) run to Seongsan-ri from Jeju-si and Seogwipo bus terminals. Make sure that the bus goes right into Seongsan-ri as a few stick to the main road and drop you 2.5km from town. The ferry terminal (우도도여객선터미널) to U-do is on the north end of Seongsan peninsula.

U-do 우도

Northeast of Seongsan-ri, 3.5km off the coast, is U-do (Cow Island), which has 1750 inhabitants yet still manages to be rural and relaxing despite throngs of tourists and tour buses, particularly at weekends. The highlights are the black-lava cliffs at Tolkani and the lighthouse that you can walk up to (15 minutes) for panoramic views of patchwork fields and brightly painted roofs. Take a picnic to the island as eating options are limited. A small community of *haenyeo* dives in the cove below the lighthouse.

Korea's only coral-sand beach, **Hongjodangoe Haebin Beach**, is brilliantly white. It's located a short 15-minute walk from the ferry terminal. You'll find a handful of restaurants, hotels and changing rooms with showers.

To tour the island's cobweb of narrow roads you have a choice of wheels, but keep in mind that the island is 17km in circumference: the tough way is by bicycle (two hours rental W5000), the soft way is on the hop-on hopoff tourist buses (W5000, every 30 minutes), and the fun way is on a scooter (per hour W15,000), quad bike (per hour W30,000) or golf cart (per hour W30,000).

GETTING THERE & AWAY

Car ferries (W4500 return, 10 minutes, at least hourly) cross to U-do from Seongsan port. The **ticket office** (☎ 782 5671) is at the far end of the port, a 15-minute walk or a short taxi ride from Seongsan-ri. The last ferry leaves U-do at 6pm.

Sinyang Beach 신양해수욕장

On the southeast coast, this crescent-shaped beach, 1.5km in length, is the island's most

HAENYEO

At 9am on Seongsan-ri harbour, 30 or so wrinkled grandmas are pulling on wetsuits, diving masks, weight belts and gloves, prior to a boat ride out to sea where they will use their low-tech gear – polystyrene floats, flippers, nets, knives and spears – to gather seaweed, shellfish, sea cucumbers, spiky black sea urchins, octopus and anything else edible that they can catch. Great physical stamina is a prerequisite. They use no oxygen tanks, but are able to hold their breath underwater for up to two minutes and reach a depth of 20m.

The women divers look so old and bent that it's amazing that they continue to dive for long hours in all weather. They work as a cooperative and share their catch. They shout at each other because most wear earplugs and are probably a bit deaf as well.

Haenyeo have been free-diving for generations around the waters of Jeju-do and off the coasts of Japan and China. Sadly these will be the last generation of divers because their daughters have not followed in their mothers' flippers – instead choosing easier jobs in shops, offices or the tourism industry. At their peak in the 1950s there were almost 30,000 *haenyeo* on Jeju-do but now they number fewer than 3000.

The new **Haenyeo Museum** (해녀 박물관; ☎ 782 9898; adult/youth W1100/500; ☼ 9am-6pm) does an excellent job explaining the history and culture of these amazing women. It's 15km north of Seongsan in Sehwa; any bus plying the Jeju-si to Seongsan route will drop you off near the museum entrance. For another perspective, check out the 2004 Korean film *My Mother the Mermaid*.

sheltered. Many consider it Korea's best beach for windsurfing; in summer you can rent sailboats and windsurfers and take lessons on how to use them. A 1km walk away is the rocky outcrop Seopjikoji, which has provided a backdrop to Korean movie scenes. The adjacent small town has *minbak* and restaurants.

Buses (W3800, 1¾ hours, every 20 minutes) from Jeju-si bus terminal drop you at the main road, 2km from the beach. An hourly bus runs to the beach or you can walk, thumb a lift or take a taxi.

Seongeup Folk Village 성읍민속마을

A 10-minute bus ride north of Pyoseon Beach lies Jeju-do's former provincial capital of Seongeup, where government assistance has encouraged the preservation and renovation of the traditional rock-walled, thatched-roofed houses. Modern intrusions include souvenir shops, restaurants and car parks, but parts still look fantastically feudal.

The village of 480 households is worth taking the time to explore. Some inhabitants offer free guided tours of their compound, but afterwards they want you to buy local products such as black *omija* tea (W25,000 per kilogram) or paper-thin dried fish called *myeongtae*, both of which are delicious.

Just ramble down the narrow lanes and discover the place for yourself. Remember the houses are still occupied, but if the gate poles

are down (see the boxed text, p297) you are welcome to enter.

Buses leave from Jeju-si bus terminal (W2700, 45 minutes, every 20 minutes) and from Pyoseon or Jeju Folk Village (W1100, 10 minutes, every hour).

Jeju Folk Village 제주민속촌

Just outside Pyoseon and close to the town's extensive beach, **Jeju Folk Village** (☎ 787 4501; www.jejufolk.com; adult/youth/child W6000/4000/2000; ☼ 8.30am-6pm) is more re-creation than preservation, but in its way this living history museum is more educational than Seongeup Folk Village. Various sections cover Jeju-do's culture from shamans to *yangban* (aristocrats), and the differences between mountain, hill-country and fishing villages. Some of the buildings are *hanok* (traditional Korean houses) brought intact from other parts of the island and are 200 to 300 years old; the modern construction has been done in authentically traditional style.

The folk village has its own flora and fauna, country-style restaurants and traditional song and dance performances. The English-language audio guide (W2000) is worth the investment.

Direct buses run to the entrance gate from Jeju-si bus terminal (W3600, one hour, every 20 minutes) and Seogwipo (W1900, 30 minutes, every 20 minutes). Or walk 1km from the bus stop in Pyoseon-ri.

Pyoseon Beach 표선해수욕장

At low tide a huge expanse of white sandy beach appears that stretches as far as the eye can see, and in the middle a lagoon forms. If you like plenty of space, this is the beach to visit. Behind is a small town with all facilities.

Buses run here from Jeju-si via the 97 road cross-island route (W3400, one hour, every 20 minutes) or via the east-coast road (W5100, two hours, every 20 minutes).

Namwon 남원

A favourite Korean pastime is visiting the filming locations of popular Korean movies, many of which were shot in Jeju-do. For a brief history of Korean cinema, visit the **Shinyoung Cinema Museum** (신영 영화박물관; ☎ 764 7778; admission W6000; ⏰ 9am-6.30pm, to 7.30pm summer). Unfortunately, few signs are in English, and unless you're a real Korean film buff, you may wonder what all the hoopla is about.

Just 100m along the coast road west of the Cinema Museum, turn right at the hamburger sign, then left at another sign to reach the two-storey wood cabin that is **Red Pond Herb Farm** (붉은못허브팜; hamburgers W15,000; ⏰ 10am-9pm;

). The English-speaking staff sell unique hamburgers the size of Frisbees – enough for three people or you can take away what you cannot eat. In a giant herbal bun packed with salad and even apple is a thin patty made from Jeju black-pig pork or else soy bean for a vegetarian option. Free herbal tea is included.

SOUTHERN JEJU-DO
Seogwipo 서귀포
pop 84,300

Amid the tangerine groves on the lower slopes of Hallasan sits Seogwipo, Jeju-do's second-largest city. It's much smaller and more laid-back than Jeju-si, and sports the warmest climate in the country. Seogwipo is beautifully situated on a rocky volcanic coastline and dotted with lush parks, a deep gorge and two of the country's most famous waterfalls. The clear blue waters and mild water temperatures make Seogwipo the best scuba-diving destination in Korea. The town centre (up a steep slope from the harbour) is chock-full of motels and hotels. The main bus terminal and other attractions are clustered around the World Cup Stadium, west of town in Shin Seogwipo.

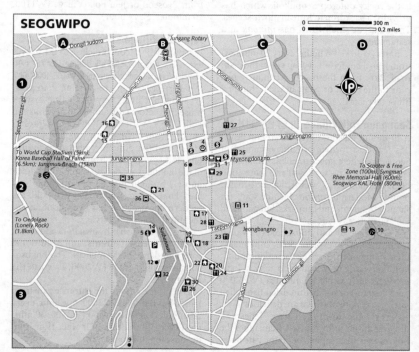

INFORMATION	Jeongbang Pokpo 정방폭포 **10** D2	EATING 🍴
Family Mart **1** C2	Lee Jung-Seop	Ankori Pakori 안거리 박거리 **23** C2
Jeju Bank **2** C2	Art Gallery & Park...........**11** C2	Chungmun Sikdang 중문식당 ..**24** C3
Jeju Bank ....(see 5)	Outdoor Theatre **12** B3	Meokbo Bunsik 먹보분식 **25** C2
KB Star Bank 국민은행 **3** B2	Seobok Exhibition Hall...........**13** D2	Saesom Galbi 새솜 갈비 **26** B3
Post Office 우체국 **4** B2	Ticket Office 매표소 **14** B2	Seogwipo Covered Market
Tourist Information Centre		서귀포시장 **27** C1
관광 안내소 **5** B2	SLEEPING 🛏	Tok Sung Won 덕성원 **28** B2
Tourist Information Kiosk...........(see 10)	Galaxy Hotel 은하호텔 **15** A2	
	Hotel Daeguk Isle Inn	DRINKING 🍷🍸
SIGHTS & ACTIVITIES	대국아일린호텔 **16** A1	G Bar **29** C2
Baseball Hitting Practice	Hotel Little France **17** B2	Milano 밀라노 **30** B3
야구연습장 **6** B2	Jeju Hiking Inn 제주하이킹인...**18** B3	New York 뉴욕 **31** C2
Big Blue 33 빅블루 **7** C2	Napoli Hotel 나포리호텔 **19** B2	Pyeonuijeom 편의점 **32** B3
Cheonjiyeon Pokpo	Shinsung Hotel 신성호텔 **20** C3	Vetro Coffee 베트로커피 **33** B2
천지연폭포 **8** A2	Sun Beach Hotel 호텔 썬비치.....**21** B2	
Daekuk Subsea Company	Wooseong Motel 우성모텔 **22** B3	TRANSPORT
대국해저관광 **9** B3		Bus Terminal 버스터미널 **34** B1
		Limousine Bus Stop.......................**35** B2
		Limousine Bus Stop.......................**36** B2

INFORMATION

Family Mart (Myeongdongno) Global ATM.

Jeju Bank (Jungjeongno) The far-right machine is a global ATM with a high W1,000,000 withdraw limit.

KB Star Bank (Jungangno) Foreign exchange only.

Post office (Jungjeongno) Free internet access.

Tourist information centre (관광 안내소; ☎ 064 1330 or 760 3544; ⏰ 10am-6pm) Located at the Cheonjiyeon Pokpo waterfall ticket office. Free internet access and global ATM. A smaller tourist kiosk is located at Jeongbang Pokpo waterfall.

SIGHTS & ACTIVITIES
Waterfalls

The 22m-high **Cheonjiyeon Pokpo** (천지연폭포; ☎ 733 1528; adult/youth/child W2000/1000/600; ⏰ 7am-10pm), west of downtown, is a 15-minute walk via a path through a beautifully forested, steep gorge. After heavy rain the waterfall can be impressive, but at other times it's more noisy than wide.

Jeongbang Pokpo (정방폭포; ☎ 733 1530; adult/youth/child W2000/1000/600; ⏰ 7.30am-6.30pm Mar-Oct, 7.30am-5.30pm Nov-Feb) is 23m high and up to 8m wide, depending on the levels of recent rainfall. It's said to be the only waterfall in Asia that falls directly into the sea. Jeongbang Pokpo is a 15-minute walk east of the town centre. Also included with your ticket is entrance to the nearby **Seobok Exhibition Hall** and adjoining Chinese garden, which were closed for renovation during our visit.

Museums

The **Lee Jung-Seop Art Gallery & Park** (☎ 733 3555; adult/youth/child W1000/500/300; ⏰ 10am-6pm, to 8pm Jul-Sep) features the works of beloved Korean artist Lee Jung-Seop. Outside, a lovely manicured lawn with fragrant trees has a mock-up of a traditional Jeju house and other interactive displays.

The small, private **Syngman Rhee Memorial Hall** (☎ 763 2100; adult/youth/child W2000/1500/1000; ⏰ 10am-7pm May-Oct, 10am-6pm Nov-Apr) has English descriptions and is dedicated to South Korea's first president, Syngman Rhee (1875–1965).

Oedolgae (Lonely Rock) 외돌개

About 2km west of Seogwipo, the 20m-tall volcanic basalt pillar called Oedolgae juts out of the ocean. Like other unusual-shaped rocks there's a legend associated with it – a Korean general is said to have scared away Mongolian invaders by dressing the rock up to look like a giant soldier. Oedolgae is a pleasant walk through pine forests to a

---

GATE POLE MESSAGES

Jeju-do has traditionally described itself as having lots of rocks and wind, but no beggars or thieves. In Jeju-do's folk villages, instead of locked fences in front of homes you'll often see a *jeongnang* gate, two stone pillars that support three wooden poles between them. Three poles straight across means 'We're not home, please keep out'. Two down and one across means 'We're not home, but we are within shouting distance'. If all the poles are on the ground, it means 'We're home, please come in'.

beautiful cliffside lookout at Sammae-bong Park.

Bus 8 (W850, five minutes) runs to Oedolgae, or you can take a pleasant 30-minute walk from town.

Scuba Diving 스쿠버다이빙

Diving off Seogwipo is surprisingly good with walls of very colourful soft coral, 18m-high kelp forests (March to May), schools of fish and the occasional inquisitive dolphin. Diving here always surprises first-timers because it's a mixture of the tropical and temperate – rather like diving in Norway and the Red Sea at the same time! Visibility is best from September to November but is around 10m at other times, and water temperature varies from 15°C to 28°C.

A recommended dive operator is **Big Blue 33** (☎ 733 1733; www.bigblue33.co.kr; Chilispri 4-Ro; ◷ 9am-7pm), run by German expat Ralf Deutsch, a genuine diving enthusiast who speaks English, German and Korean (see p81). A two-tank dive trip costs W105,000 with all equipment and guide. A five-day NAUI certification course costs W500,000.

World Cup Stadium 제주 월드컵 경기장

Six kilometres west of downtown in Shin (New) Seogwipo, the graceful soccer stadium built for the 2002 World Cup is the centrepiece of an entertainment complex that includes a multiplex cinema, E-Mart discount store, **Water World** (admission W25,000; ◷ 11am-11pm) water park, **Dak Paper Doll Museum** (adult/youth W6000/5000; ◷ 9am-7pm), **World Eros Museum** (adults only, admission W7000; ◷ 9am-9pm) and **Seri World** (www.seriworld.co.kr; tickets W15,000-25,000; ◷ 9am-9pm), a small amusement park with go-kart racing and tethered hot-air balloon rides. Seogwipo's new bus terminal (버스터미널) is located just outside the stadium.

Submarine & Sightseeing Boat Tours 잠수함, 유람

Daekuk Subsea Company (대국해저관광; ☎ 732 6060; submarine tours adult/youth/child W51,000/40,600/30,200, sightseeing boat tours adult/child W16,500/11,000) operates well-established and popular 30-minute submarine tours down to a depth of 30m around Munseom island, which has coral and fish dressed up in carnival colours. Tours run at least hourly; reservations recommended.

Baseball 야구

At **Baseball Hitting Practice** (야구연습장; Jungangno; per 10 pitches W500) pick up a baseball

bat, put a coin in the box and the robot pitches 18 balls in quick succession.

The small **Korea Baseball Hall of Fame** (한국야구명여ㅣ전당; ☎ 760 3437; adult/youth W1000/700; ◷ 9am-6pm) traces the evolution of baseball from its American roots to its role today as Korea's national pastime. Unfortunately there is no English signage. It's a short taxi ride north of the World Cup Stadium.

SLEEPING
Budget

Jeju Hiking Inn (제주하이킹인; ☎ 763 2380; www.hikinginn.com; r W20,000; 🖳) Despite its old and tattered appearance, this is still Seogwipo's most popular backpacker hotel. Amenities include free internet, shared kitchen and laundry facilities and bicycle rentals. The owner speaks English. On our recent visit we were disappointed to discover our 'confirmed' room had been given away. You must back up your reservation with a deposit; the complicated instructions are on the hotel website.

Woosoeng Motel (우성모텔; ☎ 732 5700; r W25,000; 🞱) Simple but well-kept rooms are cheerful and welcoming. Rooms on the 4th floor (no lift), such as room 405, have sea views. The elderly owners don't speak English, but are friendly and will even help with your laundry.

Galaxy Hotel (은하호텔; ☎ 733 6678; r W25,000; 🞱) This motel is well kept, has friendly staff and the upper rooms are light and airy.

Napoli Hotel (나포리호텔; ☎ 733 4701; fax 733 4802; r W40,000; 🞱) There's nothing Italian here, but the standard motel rooms are pleasant enough and some have sea views.

Midrange

Hotel Little France (☎ 732 4552; www.littlefrancehotel.co.kr; r W60,000-90,000; 🞱 🖳) This modern, stylish hotel is located in the heart of downtown. Guests have a choice of four room styles: modern, oriental, antique and royal classic. Rooms with harbour views cost more. There's also an adjoining restaurant and pleasant bar.

Shinsung Hotel (신성호텔; ☎ 732 1415; fax 732 1417; r W70,000; 🞱 🖳) A classy new midcity motel with a hard-to-miss metal-and-chequerboard exterior. Rooms have a computer and jacuzzi, but don't try to use both at the same time. A room with a sea view costs W10,000 extra, even if it's too misty to see the sea.

Hotel Daeguk Isle Inn (대국아일린호텔; ☎ 763 0002; www.isleinnhotel.co.kr; r W80,000; 🞱 🖳)

The bright (fake) balcony flowers add a touch of class to this hotel's continental European look and feel. Although the rooms are nothing special, it is a real hotel with no hint of a love motel, and the lobby has email access.

Sun Beach Hotel (호텔 썬비치; ☎ 732 5678; www.hotelsunbeach.co.kr; Taepyeongno; r incl breakfast W80,000; ⊠) A reasonable option if you're into retro and hanker for these midrange tourist hotels that resemble a grand dame somewhat past her prime but still retaining an air of faded gentility.

Top End
Seogwipo KAL Hotel (☎ 733 2001; www.kalhotel.co.kr; r from W200,000; ⊠ ⊡ ⊠) An overall design of muted colours and pastels pervades this calm and soothing luxury hotel that has a trout farm in the garden. Add W50,000 for ocean views and another 20% at weekends.

EATING
Fish restaurants cluster round the harbour, but food is not Seogwipo's strong point. Seogwipo Covered Market (서귀포시장; Jungjeongno) has wonderful fruit and live seafood direct from local orchardists and fishermen.

Tok Sung Won (덕성원; ☎ 762 2402; noodle dishes W4000-6000, mains W15,000-50,000; ⊠ 11am-8.30pm) Having outgrown its old location, this popular Chinese restaurant is now in a sleek, big black building with an outdoor patio. You'll find all your favourite Chinese dishes plus exotic specialities like fried pheasant and sea slug. Ask for an English menu. The portions are absolutely huge and perfect for sharing.

Ankori Pakori (안거리 박거리; ☎ 763 2552; mains W5000-6000; ⊠ 10am-9pm) This simple, family-run restaurant offers up cheap and filling Korean set meals like *bibimbap* (rice, egg, meat and vegies with chilli sauce) and other comfort foods. It can get very busy during lunch.

our pick Saesom Galbi (새솜 갈비; ☎ 763 2552; mains W12,000-30,000; ⊠ 10am-11pm) You haven't visited Jeju-do until you've sampled the island's famous black-pig pork, and there's no better place to pig out than at this unbeatable Korean barbecue joint. Perched on a cliff overlooking the harbour, visitors can sit Korean-style on the floor or at real tables; the latter offer the best views. Don't miss it!

Other recommendations:

Meokbo Bunsik (먹보분식; meals W1000-4000; ⊠ 24hr) Just down the road opposite the covered market is this

cheap diner with homemade *mandu* (만두; dumplings) steaming in big pots outside.

Chungmun Sikdang (중문식당; meals W4000-10,000) A simple, clean restaurant with a good-deal *jeongsik* (정식; meal with lots of side dishes) or *sundubu* (순두부; soft tofu) for W4000.

DRINKING
Vetro Coffee (Jungjeongno; drinks W2000-5000; ⊠ 10am-11pm) Buy a cake from the bakery opposite and eat it with one of Vetro's special home-roasted coffees. Iced latte is popular.

our pick Pyeonuijeom (편의점; Rose Marina; drinks W2000-5000; ⊠ 10.30am-4am) This tumbledown, waterfront shack is as quirky and informal a bar as you'll find anywhere on Planet Korea. Sit outside by the harbour or on the deck decorated with snowboards, kayaks and giant trees growing through the floorboards. Top it off with cheap drinks and a great music selection, and you've got yourself a favourite new local pub.

Milano (밀라노; beers/cocktails W3000/5000; ⊠ 7pm-4am) Sit inside on the red seats or outside near the barbecue (meals W8000 to W25,000) under the trees with harbour views.

New York (뉴욕; ☎ 733 8658; Myeongdongno; local beer/cocktails W4000/8000; ⊠ 7pm-6am) This dark, classy bar has a long list of imported beers and attracts expats and their friends at the weekends. Meals are W10,000 to W13,000.

G Bar (beer & cocktails W5000-12,000; ⊠ 7pm-5.30am) You might burn a few G's at this overpriced but super-chic, jet-black cocktail lounge that caters to young professionals. Most staff speak English.

GETTING THERE & AROUND
From Jeju-si, buses (W7500, two hours 40 minutes, every 20 minutes) run along the east or west coast to Seogwipo, while buses on cross-island routes take half the time and cost half as much. The Seogwipo bus terminal is being moved 6km west to the World Cup Stadium, but frequent buses (W850, 10 minutes) will link the town with the new bus terminal.

Seogwipo is small enough to walk around its wooden pavements, but taxis are plentiful and cheap. Local buses can be picked up at Jungang Rotary.

Fancy the freedom of your own wheels? **Scooter & Free Zone** (스쿠터 앤 프리존; ☎ 762 5296; 315-8 Cheonji-dong; 50cc/125cc per 24hr W20,000/25,000; ⊠ 8.30am-9pm) is a funky new

JEJU-DO

HONEYMOON ISLAND

Jungmun, with its three luxury resort hotels, is a favourite haunt for Korean honeymooners, particularly in the summer months. If you spot couples wearing matching outfits, riding tandem bicycles, or stuffing food into each other's mouths, they're likely honeymooners. Jungmun Resort is also becoming popular with Japanese and Chinese honeymooners. Horse riding, regarded as an exotic and romantic activity, is popular with honeymooners, as is the Teddy Bear Museum.

The island also attracts business and professional conferences, so your hotel might be swarming with Asian dentists or telecom execs. In spring, waves of South Korean high-school students spread over the island on school trips, excited to be in what is almost a foreign country.

---

coffee shop that rents new scooters. Owner Hong Seung Jo speaks English and she's a wealth of local information. It's 100m north of the Seobok Exhibition Hall, just up the hill from the Kosa Mart.

Jungmun Resort & Vicinity
중문 휴양지

Tourist brochures often tout Jejo-do as the Hawaii of Korea, but this is the only place on the island where the analogy fits. Located a 25-minute bus ride west of Seogwipo, Jungmun Resort is South Korea's primary tourist resort, a complex of unspoilt, white sandy beaches, swaying palm trees, black volcanic cliffs, waterfalls, luxury hotels, casinos, restaurants and museums.

At the entrance to the resort, the **Jungmun tourist information centre** (☎ 064 1330; ☼ 9am-6pm, to 7pm summer) has maps, brochures and free internet.

SIGHTS & ACTIVITIES
Jungmun's most popular natural attraction is the legendary waterfall **Cheonjeyeon Pokpo** (천제연폭포; ☎ 738 1529; adult/youth/child W2500/1370/850; ☼ sunrise-sunset), a three-tier cascade tucked deep inside a forested gorge. Above soars a footbridge with sculptures of the seven nymphs who served the Emperor of Heaven and who, it is said, used to slide down moonbeams to bathe here every night.

At the start of the access road to the resorts and beach is the huge, glass-enclosed **Yeomiji Botanical Garden** (여미지; ☎ 735 1000; www.yeomiji.or.kr; adult/youth/child W7000/4500/3500; ☼ 9am-6pm). Indoor sections mimic rainforests, deserts and other landscapes, while outdoor plantings and designs include Italian, Japanese, palm and herb gardens.

The **Teddy Bear Museum** (☎ 738 7600; adult/youth/child W7000/6000/5000; ☼ 10am-7pm, to 8pm summer) is a cheesy attraction that claims to be the world's biggest such museum. Next door, the **Sound Island Museum** (☎ 739 7782; adult/youth/child W6500/5000/4000; ☼ 9am-8pm) is a more interesting and interactive tribute to sound and music. On the far eastern end of Jungmun, the impressive **Museum of Africa** (☎ 738 6565; adult/youth/child W6500/5000/4000; ☼ 9am-7pm, to 10pm summer) is modelled after the Grand Mosque of Djenné. It's worth a visit for its fine collection of African art and occasional live music and dance performances.

Overlooking Jungmun Beach is **Pacific Land** (퍼시픽랜드; ☎ 738 2888; adult/youth/child W12,000/10,000/8000; ☼ shows 11.30am, 1.30pm, 3pm & 4.30pm), an ageing complex that puts on animal shows featuring dolphins, sea lions and monkeys doing all sorts of tricks. The same company runs **catamaran cruises** (W30,000 to W60,000).

Just south of the International Convention Centre is **Jusangjeolli Rocks** (주상절리), a dramatic 2km stretch of coastline, known for hexagonal rock columns that look as if they were stamped out with a cookie cutter. The formations are the result of the rapid cooling and contraction of lava (just what you'd expect to happen when molten lava pours into the sea).

Although the Buddhist temple **Yakcheon-sa** (약천사; ☎ 738 5000; admission free; ☼ sunrise-sunset) was only constructed between 1987 and 1997, it is one of Jeju-do's most impressive buildings. The ornate hall is filled with vibrant murals of scenes from Buddha's life and illustrations of his teachings. Upstairs are cases containing some 18,000 tiny Buddhist figurines. Overnight temple stays are possible. The temple is less than 1km east of the Convention Centre.

Outdoor Activities
Jungmun Beach (중문해수욕장), a 560m stretch of golden sand with its jungly backdrop, only becomes crowded in summer, when it's patrolled by lifeguards. Walk along the beach, up the steps to the Hyatt Regency Hotel,

continue along the boardwalk and down the steps to reach an even more scenic and secluded beach: aquamarine water and golden sand backed by sheer black cliffs eroded into cylindrical shapes.

Parasailing (☎ 739 3939), **jet-skiing** and **water-skiing** (☎ 738 5111; W20,000-40,000) operators are based between Pacific Land and the International Convention Centre. **Jetboats** (☎ 739 3939; W25,000) operate from an inlet east of the Convention Centre. **Kayaks** and **boogie boards** (per 2hr W15,000/5000) can be hired on Jungmun Beach.

Ever fired a gun? Now's your chance at **Daeyoo Land** (대유랜드; ☎ 738 0500; www.daeyoo land.net; activities W25,000-165,000), a private retreat several kilometres north of Jungmun offering **pheasant hunting** and **target shooting**. Less-deadly activities include **ATV tours** and **horseback riding**.

Of the many golf courses on the island, **Jungmun Beach Golf Club** (☎ 738 4359; green fees W90,000-130,000), perched on a seaside cliff, is easily the most scenic.

SLEEPING

Minbak, pension (upmarket accommodation) and restaurants are strung out along Hwy 12 near the 1km-long access road to Jungmun Beach, while luxury hotel resorts are down towards the beach.

Lu Chantay House (여행동화; ☎ 739 4778; dm/r W10,000/30,000; 🛜) This blue-and-white guesthouse is above a fish restaurant, set back from the main road and overlooking Yeomiji botanical glasshouse. The dorms are big and the accommodation is new with a youthful vibe. Upstairs, wood-panelled rooms are very attractive and some have kitchenettes.

Gold Beach Minbak (골드비치민박; ☎ 738 7511; r W50,000; 🛜) Smart wood-panelled rooms with balconies and kitchenettes can be found here. Room 305 is one of the best. Look for a peach-and-green building above a restaurant, 200m east of the Jungmun Beach access road.

ourpick **Hyatt Regency Jeju** (☎ 733 1234; www. hyattcheju.com; r from W170,000; 🛜 🖥 🛜) This white, beehive-shaped edifice is the closest hotel to the beach with the best sea views. Though it's the oldest resort in Jungmun, it's still the best and classiest hotel in the area. The stylish rooms feature minimalist decor and all the amenities of a five-star hotel. The wonderful outdoor swimming pool features a swim-up bar hidden behind a waterfall, though it's only open in July and August.

Lotte Hotel Jeju (☎ 738 7301; r from W300,000; 🛜 🖥 🛜) This palatial resort brings Las Vegas to Jeju-do with an over-the-top fantasy garden containing windmills, a boating lake and a swimming pool. A nightly outdoor show involves music, lights, fountains, volcanoes and dragons. It's the most glitzy hotel and has a foreigner-only casino.

Shilla Jeju (☎ 738 4466; www.shilla.net; r from W300,000; 🛜 🖥 🛜) Classier than Lotte, Shilla drips designer cool with muted colours, modernist artworks and an understated Zen decor beneath a Spanish-style, red-tile roof.

EATING

Gallery Challa (☎ 738 1061; admission free; mains W7000-14,000; 🕙 10am-9pm Tue-Sun) East of the Sound Island Museum, this lovely little art gallery houses a tranquil cafe and restaurant with an all-vegetarian menu including vegie burgers, dumplings and barbecue.

Island Gecko's (☎ 739 0845; www.geckosterrace.com; mains W10,000-15,000, drinks W3000-8000; 🕙 10am-2am) South Jeju-do's most popular expat hangout features Western comfort foods like Philly cheesesteaks, burgers, pizza, quesadillas, curry and more. Staff speak English and there's even a bus pick-up service. It really gets cranking after 9pm. It's about 2km inland from Jungmun; just ask any taxi driver.

Ha Young (☎ 738 6011; mains W25,000-50,000; 🕙 10am-10pm) Just east of the Gold Beach Minbak is Jungmun's most popular Korean barbecue restaurant specialising in Jeju-do's famous black pig. Look for the tall grey building with a patio and blue fairy lights.

GETTING THERE & AWAY

Buses (W1100, 20 minutes, every 20 minutes) leave Seogwipo bus terminal for Jungmun, dropping you at the Jungmun Beach access road, 1km from the beach. Local buses such as bus 100 also run to Jungmun.

Sanbanggul-sa & Yongmeori Coast
산방굴사, 용머리해안

A steep, 10-minute walk up the south-facing side of the dramatic, craggy **Sanbangsan** (395m) is a stone Buddha in an atmospheric cave called **Sanbanggul-sa** (☎ 794 2940; adult/youth/child W2500/1500/free; 🕙 8.30am-7pm). It's been a sacred site since Goryeo times, and the water flowing from the ceiling is said to be magically curative. Lower down, by the ticket office, are other shrines and statues of more recent origin.

Across the road, a footpath leads downhill to the spectacular **Yongmeori coast**, an oceanside promenade of soaring cliffs, pockmarked by erosion into catacombs, narrow clefts and natural archways. It's a *National Geographic* opportunity for photographers. Note the walk along the cliffs closes during very high seas.

At the promenade exit is a replica of the **Sperwer**, a Dutch merchant ship that was wrecked here long ago in August 1653. A sailor on board, Hendrick Hamel (1630–92), survived the shipwreck but was forced to stay in Korea for 13 years before managing to escape in a boat to Japan; he wrote the first book on Korea by a Westerner.

The entry ticket to Sanbanggul-sa includes entry to the Yongmeori coast and Hamel's ship. **Hwasun Beach** is only 1km away but is marred by a power station at one end.

Buses (W2300, 45 minutes, every 40 minutes) leave from Seogwipo bus terminal for Sanbangsan.

Jeju Art Park 제주조각공원

For a bit of culture, get off at the stop before Sanbangsan at **Jeju Art Park** (☎ 794 9680; adult/youth/child W4500/3500/2500; ☀ 8.30am-8pm Apr-Oct, to 5.30pm Nov-Mar). It claims to be the largest outdoor sculpture garden in Asia, with over 180 modern sculptures.

Mara-do & Gapa-do 마라도, 가파도

These two islets, both flat as pizzas with black rocky crusts, lie off Jeju-do's southwest tip. Mara-do is Land's End, the most southerly point of Korea, and is so windswept that there are virtually no trees. Around 20 families live there. It has an isolated, wild mood despite the tourists and only takes 30 minutes to walk around. Gapa-do, the nearer and larger of the two, is more ordinary and attracts fewer visitors.

Frequent buses (W2700, one hour, every 20 minutes) run between Seogwipo and Moseulpo. From Moseulpo pier, **ferries** (☎ 794 5490) depart 12 times daily to Mara-do (adult/child return W15,500/10,000, 30 minutes). Ferries to Gapado (adult/child return W8000/4000, 15 minutes) depart at 8.30am and 2pm.

O'Sulloc Tea Museum 오설록차박물관

On the rolling, 52-hectare plantation of Sulloc, one of Korea's largest growers of *nokcha* (green tea), the teacup-shaped **museum** (☎ 794 5312; admission free; ☀ 10am-5pm) has swell views of tea

fields and a rather on-the-nose video about tea. There is a great collection of ancient tea implements, some of which date back to the 3rd century. Visitors are welcome to stroll the fields, and in the shop you can enjoy green tea, a slice of green-tea cake and green-tea ice cream. Unfortunately no buses pass by.

WESTERN JEJU-DO

Spirited Garden 생각하는 정원

Bunjae (bonsai) trees may seem esoteric, but this **bonsai park** (☎ 772 3701; www.spiritedgarden.com; adult/youth/child W9000/6000/5000; ☀ 8am-6.30pm, to 10pm late Jul–mid-Aug) has some excellent examples. It's the life's work of Mr Sung Bumyoung, who opened the park in 1992 and has never looked back. The park has hosted dignitaries from all over the world.

Mr Sung has filled the park with 700 dwarf trees – the oldest is some 500 years old. Signs translated into English espouse his personal philosophy. Infrequent buses between Hallim and Gosan stop here; your best bet is a taxi from Hallim.

Jeju Racetrack 제주경마장

Enjoy a weekend afternoon at the races at the popular **Jeju Racetrack** (☎ 741 9412; admission W800; ☀ 12.30-5pm Sat & Sun, to 9pm Sat & Sun Jul & Aug), 15km from Jeju-si. The facilities are first class and foreigners have their own lounge. What is unique is that all the horses are *jorangmal*, Jeju descendants of horses brought to the island by invading Mongols centuries ago.

Cross-island buses (W1300, 30 minutes, every 20 minutes) between Seogwipo and Jeju-si stop outside the racetrack. A taxi from Jeju-si costs W10,000.

Acrobat Shows

Running away with the circus? There are three shows along Road 1135 worth checking out. **Green Resort** (제주그린리조트; ☎ 792 6102; admission W12,000; ☀ shows 10.30am, 2.30pm, 4.30pm & 5.40pm) combines Chinese and Mongolian acrobats. Smarter and more high-tech is **Happy Town** (해피타운; ☎ 794 4444; adult/child W15,000/8000; ☀ shows 10.30am, 2pm, 3.30pm & 5pm), starring contortionists, motorbike stunt riders and acrobats. Stunning aerial acrobatics and motorbike tricks are highlights of **Jeju Magic World** (제주매직월드; ☎ 746 9005; www.jejumw.co.kr; adult/youth/child W15,000/10,000/7000; ☀ shows 10am, 2pm, 4pm, 6pm Mar-Sep, 10am, 2pm, 3.30pm & 5.20pm Oct-Feb).

Cross-island buses pass by all three venues every 20 minutes from Seogwipo and Jeju-si.

Hallim Park 한림공원

No time to explore Jeju-do? Just visit **Hallim Park** (☎ 796 0001; adult/youth/child W7000/4500/3500; ⏱ 8.30am-6pm, to 7.30pm summer), which has everything – a botanical and bonsai garden, a mini folk village, and two walks through a lava-tube cave – all in one place. The park is filled with such beautiful plantings, most notably in a botanical garden full of local plants, that it's hard to believe that the area was originally barren rocks. The caves, **Hyeopjae** and **Ssangyong**, are a part of a larger, 17km-long lava-tube system and are said to be the only such caves in the world to contain both stalagmites and stalactites. Across the street, lovely **Geumneung Beach** and nearby **Hyeopjae Beach** have white sand and crystal-clear waters perfect for snorkelling.

Westbound circular buses (from Jeju-si W3000, 50 minutes; from Seogwipo W4500, 80 minutes) stop directly at the park entrance.

Glass Castle 유리성

Opened in 2009, the **Glass Castle** (☎ 772 7777; adult/child W9000/8000; ⏱ 9am-6pm) is a fascinating but overpriced theme park featuring more than 250 glass sculptures created by worldwide artists, including the world's largest glass ball and the world's largest glass diamond. Highlights include an all-glass labyrinth, a mirror room covered in more than 5000 mirrors, glass *dolharubang* statues and a two-storey-tall glass beanstalk from *Jack and the Beanstalk*.

Unfortunately there is no public transportation here. Your best bet is to take a bus to Hallim, then taxi (W7000) to Glass Castle.

Hallasan National Park
한라산국립공원

Hiking up **Hallasan** (☎ 713 9950; www.hallasan.go.kr; admission free) is a highlight of any trip to Jejudo. At 1950m, it is the tallest mountain in the country. It is a shield volcano, though luckily has not erupted since 1007.

The best plan is to hike up the **Eorimok trail** (어리목탐방로), which starts after a 15-minute walk from the Eorimok bus stop. It's 4.7km, starting with a steep climb up

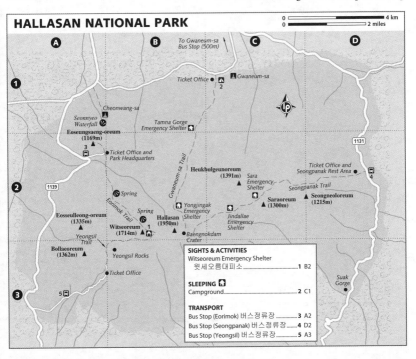

HALLASAN NATIONAL PARK

0 —— 4 km
0 —— 2 miles

To Gwaneum-sa
Bus Stop (500m)

Ticket Office • 🅰 Gwaneum-sa
2

Cheonwang-sa

Seonnyeo
Waterfall
Tamna Gorge
Emergency Shelter 🔺
Eoseungsaeng-oreum
(1169m)
3 🔺
🔺 Ticket Office and
Park Headquarters

Heukbulgeunoreum
(1391m)
Sara
Emergency
Shelter 🔺

Ticket Office and
Seongpanak Rest Area •
4

1131

Seongpanak Trail

1139

🔺 Spring

Spring

Yongjingak
Emergency
Shelter 🔺
Saraoreum
(1300m)
🔺 Seongneoloreum
(1215m)

Eosseulleong-oreum
(1335m)
Witseoreum
(1714m) 🔺 🅰
Hallasan
(1950m)
🔺
🔺 Baengnokdam
Crater
Jindallae
Emergency
Shelter 🔺

Eorimok Trail

Gwaneum-sa Trail

Yeongsil
Trail
Bollaeoreum
(1362m) 🔺
Yeongsil Rocks
Ticket Office
5 🔺

Suak
Gorge

SIGHTS & ACTIVITIES
Witseoreum Emergency Shelter
윗세오름대피소 **1** B2

SLEEPING 🔺
Campground **2** C1

TRANSPORT
Bus Stop (Eorimok) 버스정류장 **3** A2
Bus Stop (Seongpanak) 버스정류장 **4** D2
Bus Stop (Yeongsil) 버스정류장 **5** A3

through a deciduous forest (gorgeous coloured leaves in autumn). Halfway up, the dense trees give way to an open, subalpine moorland of bamboo, grass, dwarf fir trees and hillsides of azaleas that flower in April and May. If you're lucky, you might spot small roe deer. After 2¼ hours you should reach **Witseoreum shelter** (1700m), which has no accommodation but sells instant noodles to hungry hikers. Ahead are the craggy cliffs of Hallasan's peak, but the path to the crater is closed for the foreseeable future to allow for plant regeneration.

After lunch, head down the 3.7km **Yeongsil trail** (영실탐방로), which is wetter but has grand scenery – panoramas of green *oreum* (craters) and pinnacle rocks atop sheer cliffs as you hike through a dwarf-fir forest, before reaching the mixed deciduous and evergreen forest lower down. It's a 1½-hour hike down to the road and then a 30-minute walk along a roadside footpath to the bus stop.

The other two routes are longer and more difficult, but reach the peak (1950m) with outstanding views of the crater lake. The **Gwaneum-sa trail** (관음사탐방로) is 8.7km, takes five hours and is the most scenic of the four trails. There is a basic **campground** (관음사캠프장; per tent W3000) near the entrance. Note there is no direct bus to this trail. The **Seongpanak trail** (성판악탐방로) is 9.6km, takes five hours and offers the most gradual ascent of Hallasan.

Set out early; all shelters are for emergency use only and cannot be booked for overnight stays. Be prepared for bad weather that can arrive in the blink of an eye.

Buses to Eorimok run from Jeju-si bus terminal (W2300, 35 minutes, nine daily) and Jungmun (W3200, 50 minutes, nine daily) along the West Cross-Island Hwy (Road 1139). The same buses stop at Yeongsil.

To get to Gwaneum-sa from Jeju-si or Seogwipo bus terminals, take an East Cross-Island Hwy (Road 1131) bus to the Gwaneum-sa turnoff (Road 1117) and walk 4km to the trailhead, past Gwaneum-sa Temple. The same buses stop directly at Seongpanak.

Jeollabuk-do
전라북도

The southwestern province of Jeollabuk-do (www.jeonbuk.go.kr) is Korea's rice bowl. The image of white egrets standing in terraced rice fields is a provincial icon. As Korea's agricultural heartland, this fertile, green area has influenced Korean cuisine more than any other part of the country.

For foodies, no trip to Korea is complete without eating your way through Jeollabuk-do. The provincial capital city of Jeonju is a must-stop for any fan of Korean food, especially for its most well-known export, *bibimbap*, a dish of rice, meat and vegetables served up by countless restaurants nationwide and abroad.

Rural Jeollabuk-do is an outdoor-lover's paradise. Much of this province is parkland. With unspoilt national and provincial parks covering its beautiful mountains, this rural province offers some of Korea's finest get-away-from-it-all hikes and scenery. In summer, sun worshippers head out to the white sandy beaches of the West Sea islands like Seonyu-do. In the winter, thrill-seekers descend on the slopes of Muju Ski Resort, offering the highest and most picturesque slopes in Korea.

Jeollabuk-do is deeply tied to its traditional culture and roots. Buddhist temples and folk villages abound. Modern Jeonju bumps up against its historic urban village of *hanok* (traditional houses) containing craft workshops, museums and rustic teashops. The province is the birthplace of *pansori,* a traditional musical drama performed by a singer and drummer.

JEOLLABUK-DO

HIGHLIGHTS

- Get lost exploring the back alleys of the fascinating **Jeonju Hanok Maeul** village (p307)
- Retrace Korea's most famous love story, *Chunhyang-jeon,* at the romantic **Gwanghallu-won Garden** in Namwon (p313)
- Ski or snowboard the slopes at **Muju Ski Resort** (p312)
- Zip round **Seonyu-do** (p317) on a nippy quad bike before relaxing on the beach
- Amble through pretty **Seonunsan Provincial Park** (p315) to a giant Buddha carving on a cliff
- Be amazed by the unique rock-pinnacle temple garden in **Maisan Provincial Park** (p311) in the shadow of 'Horse Ears Mountain'

| ■ TELEPHONE CODE: 063 | ■ POPULATION: 2 MILLION | ■ AREA: 8050 SQ KM |

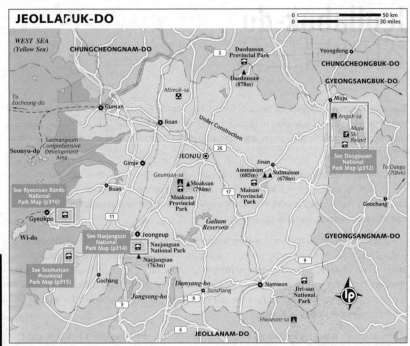

JEOLLABUK-DO

History

The Donghak rebellion, led by Chon Pong-jun, took place mainly in Jeollabuk-do in 1893 when a ragtag force of peasants and slaves, armed with various homemade weapons, seized Jeonju fortress and defeated King Gojong's army, before being destroyed by Japanese forces. Their demands included the freeing of slaves, better treatment of the *chonmin* or low-born, the redistribution of land, the abolition of taxes on fish and salt, and the punishment of corrupt government officials. Jeollabuk-do and Jeollanam-do were one joint province until 1896; Jeonju was the capital of this combined province. Tourism has become an important source of income in recent years, thanks mainly to its numerous national parks.

National & Provincial Parks

An atmospheric temple, coastal views and a waterfall are features of **Byeonsan Bando National Park** (p316). **Daedunsan Provincial Park** (p311) is a year-round, outdoor-lovers' paradise with hiking and skiing. **Maisan Provincial Park** (p311) is famous for its 'Horse Ears' mountains and mystical stone towers.

Moaksan Provincial Park (p311) has a superb temple. **Naejangsan National Park** (p314) has a great ridge hike. Pretty **Seonunsan Provincial Park** (p315) is famous for its giant Buddha cliff carving.

Getting There & Around

If you arrive by train or bus, base yourself in Jeonju, where buses radiate to every nook and corner of the province.

JEONJU 전주

pop 622,000

Jeonju (www.jeonju.go.kr), the provincial capital, is famous for being the birthplace of both the Joseon dynasty and Korea's most well-known culinary delight, *bibimbap* (rice, meat, egg and vegetables with a hot sauce). Centrally located, the city is the perfect base from which to explore Jeollabuk-do as it's the regional hub for buses and trains. The downtown historical folk village has many outstanding *hanok* buildings housing museums, cute teahouses and workshops offering handmade souvenirs like paper products, fans, dolls, boxes and more.

Information

Citibank (Daedong-gil) Global ATM and foreign currency.
IBK 365 The blue machine under the pedestrian bridge is a global ATM.
KB Bank (Girin-ro) Global ATM and foreign currency exchange.
Main post office (9am-8pm Mon-Fri, 9am-6pm Sat) Free internet access.
Main tourist information centre (☎ 282 1338; Taejo-ro) Free internet access.
Post office (China St)
Shinhan Bank (Girin-ro) Global ATM and foreign-currency exchange.
Tourist information centre bus terminal (☎ 281 2739; outside Express bus terminal); Taejo-ro (☎ 232 6293; outside Gyeonggijeon)

Sights & Activities

JEONJU HANOK MAEUL 전주한옥마을

Just southeast of Jeonju's modern downtown is **Hanok Maeul** (http://hanok.jeonju.go.kr), a wonderful historical urban neighbourhood untouched by time. This *maeul* (village) has more than 800 *hanok* (traditional Korean houses), which is one of the largest such concentrations in the country. Residents retain their old ways and traditions. Many of the buildings contain museums, workshops, restaurants, teahouses and boutiques. You could spend all day exploring the narrow maze of alleys and architecture. Pick up a free English map at any tourist information centre.

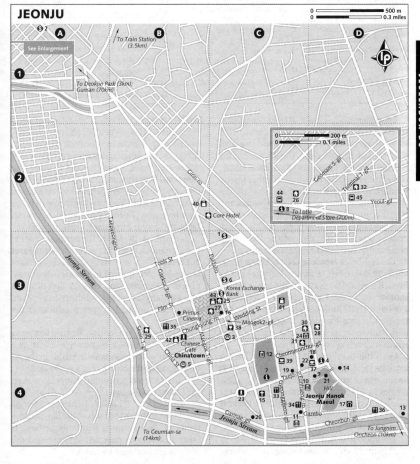

JEOLLABUK-DO

Gyeonggijeon (경기전; ☎ 281 2790; Taejo-ro; admission free; ◷ 9am-6pm) was originally constructed in 1410, reconstructed in 1614 and contains a portrait of Yi Seong-gye, the founder of the Joseon dynasty (1392–1910), whose family came from Jeonju. Portraits of six other Joseon monarchs, and palanquins, are also on display. On the left are shrines, storehouses and guardrooms relating to the Confucian rituals once held here. Treating ancestors with utmost respect was a cornerstone of the Confucian philosophy that ruled Korea for centuries.

The red-brick **Jeondong Catholic Church** (전동 성당; ☎ 284 322; Taejo-ro; admission free) was built by French missionary Xavier Baudounet on the spot where Korean Catholics were executed in 1781 and 1801. Built between 1908 and 1914, the architecture is a fusion of Asian, Byzantine and Romanesque styles. The stained-glass windows portray early martyrs.

On a hill overlooking the entire village is **Omokdae** (오목대), a pavilion where General Yi Seong-gye celebrated a victory over Japanese pirates in 1380, prior to his overthrow of the Goryeo dynasty. Cross the bridge to **Imokdae** (이목대), a monument to one of Yi Seong-gye's ancestors written by King Gojong.

The **Oriental Medicine Culture Centre** (전주한방 문화센터; ☎ 232 2500; www.hanbangcenter.com; admis-sion free; ◷ 10am-6pm) offers medical tests and diagnosis (W1000 to W4000) and recommends herbal, acupuncture, moxibustion and massage therapies, but language can be a problem.

Housed in a beautiful old *hanok*, the **Traditional Wine Museum** (전통술박물관; ☎ 287 6305; admission free; ◷ 9am-6pm Tue-Sun) has a *gosori* (traditional still). You can learn how to make your own *soju* (Korean vodka) and, of course, taste and buy traditional Korean liquors.

See sheets of *hanji* (handmade paper) being manufactured in the **Jeonju Korean Paper Institute** (전주전통한지원; ☎ 232 6591; admission free; ◷ 9am-5pm), housed in a gloriously atmospheric *hanok* down an alley. A slop of fibres in a big tank magically solidifies into paper. Purchase handmade paper products at the giftshop.

The tiny but fascinating **Kkotsuki Gongbang** (꽃숙이공방; Taejo-ro; ◷ 10am-9pm Mon-Sat) is a workshop where lessons are available in the art of making traditional Korean paper dolls.

Run by a third-generation Jeonju fan maker, the **Folding Fan Museum** (전통 부채 전시관(죽 전 선자방); ☎ 232 2008; 67 Eunhaeng-ro; admission free; ◷ 9am-9pm) has the tools of the fan-maker's father on display along with antique fans. It takes 12 hours to complete one fan and the designs are burnt on by hand.

Housing the artwork and art collection of a well-known 20th-century calligrapher, Song Sung-yong (pen name, Gangam), is **Gangam Calligraphy Museum** (강암서예관; ☎ 285 7442; admission free; ⏰ 10am-5pm Tue-Sun).

Stroll around **Jeonju Hyanggyo** (전주향교; ☎ 288 4548; admission free; ⏰ 10am-7pm), a well-preserved and very atmospheric Confucian shrine, school and dormitory complex dating to 1603 (see right).

The **Craft Treasures Centre** (공예품전시관; ☎ 285 4403; Taejo-ro; admission free; ⏰ 10am-7pm) is a large complex of shops selling lanterns, boxes, ties, clothing and paper products. The courtyard is pleasant for a rest.

Just past the Traditional Culture Centre, go under the bridge to **Hanbyeokdang Pavilion** (한 벽당) on rocks overlooking the river, where herons, egrets and swallows can be seen in summer.

PUNGNAM-MUN 풍남문
An impressive stone-and-wood gateway is all that remains of Jeonju's fortress wall and four gateways. First built in 1398 but renovated many times since, it marks the beginning of the sprawling **Nambu Market** (남부시장), where farmers' wives sell fresh produce.

JEONJU GAEKSA 전주 객사
This rebuilt former government office is a downtown landmark that lends its name to the surrounding Gaeksa District, Jeonju's primary shopping and nightlife area.

DEOKJIN PARK 덕진공원
Join Korean couples who hire paddleboats in this charming **park** (☎ 281 2436; admission free; ⏰ 5am-11pm), in the north of the city, to view the lotus lilies in July.

JUNGNIM ONCHEON 죽림온천
Soak and steam all night and day in Jeonju's best **hot-spring spa** (☎ 232 8832; admission W5000-7000; ⏰ 24hr). A free shuttle bus (9.35am, 11.35am, 2.35pm and 4.35pm) leaves from outside the Jeonju Core Riviera Hotel (p310).

Festivals & Events
The **Jeonju International Film Festival** (www.jiff.or.kr) is a nine-day event every April/May that focuses mainly on indie, digital and experimental movies. Around 200 films from 40 countries are shown in the Primus cinema multiplex and others nearby, many in English or subtitled.

Sleeping
Budget and midrange hotels are located in the Gaeksa District; cheaper love motels surround the bus and train stations. For a truly unique experience, stay in a traditional *hanok*.

BUDGET
Good Morning Motel (굿모닝모텔; ☎ 251 9948; r W30,000; ✗ ▣) This big, blue, no-fuss motel has helpful staff and spacious rooms with modern, clean bathrooms. Rooms vary so look at more than one – some have round, heated waterbeds; rooms with computers are W5000 extra.

Sydney Motel (시드니 모텔; ☎ 255 3311; r W30,000; ✗ ▣) Located directly behind the inter-city bus terminal, this salmon-pink, clean love motel is nicer and less sleazy than its neighbours.

MIDRANGE
Hotel Hansung (한성 호텔; ☎ 288 0014; Gaeksa; s/d W40,000/50,000; ✗ ▣) This recently renovated hotel in the heart of the Gaeksa District offers Western and *ondol*-style rooms with TV, fridge and comfy robes. It's sparkling clean, modern and staff speak English. Rooms facing the main drag can be noisy on weekends.

Art Hotel (아트모텔; ☎ 231 3807; Gaeksa; r W40,000-50,000; ✗ ▣) Just east of the main pedestrian road in Gaeksa, this modern boutique-style hotel is newer and posher than Hotel Hansung, but not quite as warm or foreigner-friendly.

HYANGGYO & SEOWON

Hyanggyo were neighbourhood schools established by *yangban* (aristocrats) in the 1500s to prepare their sons for the *seowon* (Confucian academies), where the students took the all-important government service exams. The pupils studied Chinese characters and key Confucian texts. Over 600 *seowon* were spread across the country, making Korea more Confucian than China. In the 1860s Regent Heungseon Daewongun forced most of them to close as he reasserted the king's authority, but the buildings remain as symbols of Koreans' unwavering passion for education.

our pick **Seunggwangje** (승광제; ☎ 288 4566; r from W60,000) Live like a king at Jeonju's best *hanok*. The small rooms have TV, fridge, *yo* (padded quilt or mattress on the floor) and tiny, modern en-suite bathroom. Seunggwangje is owned by English-speaking Lee Seok, a grandson of King Gojong, who lives in the adjoining *hanok*. It's a special place down an alley with royal photographs on display. Breakfast is W5000.

Jeonju Traditional Life Experience Park (전주 한옥생활체험관; ☎ 287 6300; www.jjhanok.com; r W60,000-120,000) Stay in tiny bare rooms and sleep on a *yo* in this newly built but traditional-style *hanok*. Prices include a Korean-style breakfast and free loan of a bicycle.

Jeonju Tourist Hotel (전주관광호텔; ☎ 280 7700; r/ste W60,000/80,000; ☐) This reasonably priced tourist hotel has a retro feel and the central location is close to Jeonju's main entertainment and shopping area.

TOP END

Jeonju Core Riviera Hotel (전주코아리베라호텔; ☎ 232 7000; core-riviera.co.kr; r/ste from W140,000/280,000; ☒ ☐) Ask for a room overlooking the *hanok* district in Jeonju's best hotel, which has spacious rooms and suites that feature natural wood decor, glass showers and a computer. Live music livens up the Windsor Bar (beers/cocktails W5000/6600; open 6pm to 2am) at 10pm. There are also restaurants, a fitness club and a sauna.

Eating & Drinking

For traditional fare, head to the restaurants and teahouses of Hanok Maeul. Modern restaurants, bars and Western fast-food chains are located in the Gaeksa District, Jeonju's prime nightlife spot.

Gimbap Maeul (김밥마을; meals W2000-4000; ☻ 10am-9pm) A small, clean eatery that offers budget meals such as *gimbap* (김밥; sesame-oil flavoured rice wrapped in seaweed) that includes cheese, tuna and salad.

The Star (83 Gyeonggijeon-gil; drinks W2300-3500; ☻ 8am-late) Need a caffeine jolt? This lovely little coffeehouse offers coffees, espresso drinks and tea.

Sambaekjip (삼백집; meals W3500; ☻ 24hr) This restaurant specialises in *kongnamul gukbap* (콩나물국밥), a local Jeonju dish of rice, egg, bean sprout and seasoning cooked in a stone pot. It's said to be a hangover cure and comes with side dishes.

Daho Teahouse (다호찻집; teas W4000; ☻ 11am-midnight) The best of the *hanok* teahouses is down an alleyway and has rustic, goblin-sized rooms overlooking an attractive garden where birds flit around. Listen to ethereal music as you sip the excellent teas such as *daechucha* (대추차; red date) and pink *omijacha* (오미자차; dried five-flavour berries).

Jeonju-hyang (전주향; ☎ 284 2588; mains W12,000-20,000; ☻ 11am-10pm) Located in an old *hanok*, the popular Jeonju-hyang is regularly rated as one of the city's best traditional restaurants, offering huge set meals that can feed a small army.

Traditional Culture Centre (전통문화센터; ☎ 280 7000; meals W9000-30,000; ☻ 10am-9pm) A stylish, upmarket restaurant in a modernist building offers Jeonju *bibimbap*, *galbi jeongsik* (갈비정식; ribs and side dishes) or a full-on *hanjeongsik* (한정식; banquet). Next door is a teashop and a hall that hosts traditional music and dance shows.

our pick **Deepin** (☎ 231 9695; Gaeksa; ☻ 7pm-4am) A foreigner-friendly watering hole, this tiny, dark and smoky bar is the local expat hang-out with comfy red couches, Polaroids and chalk messages on the walls, cool music and cheap beer. From the Jeonju Gaeksa, cross the main road, turn right, make an immediate left and go to the end of the street; Deepin is on the left, just passed the bricked Wedding St.

Shopping

Hanbok shops are at the far end of Jungangno, while the bustling Dongbu and Nambu Markets sell everything under the sun. **Ntepia** (엔테피아; ☻ 11am-11pm) is a large fashion store in the youthful Gaeksa District, surrounded by beauty shops and Western restaurants such as Outback Steakhouse and Pizza Hut. **Lotte** (☻ 10.30am-8pm) and **Core** (☻ 10.30am-8pm) department stores are modern shopping malls.

Getting There & Away

BUS

Destinations from the express bus terminal include the following:

Destination	Price (W)	Duration	Frequency
Daegu	11,000	3½hr	hrly
Daejeon	4600	1½hr	hrly
Gwangju	5800	1¼hr	every 30min
Seoul	11,000	3hr	every 10min

Departures from the intercity bus terminal include the following:

Destination	Price (W)	Duration	Frequency
Buan	4000	1hr	5 daily
Daedunsan	5000	1¼hr	8 daily
Gochang	5400	1½hr	hrly
Gunsan	4200	1hr	every 15min
Gurye (Jirisan)	7700	2hr	hrly
Gyeokpo	6600	2hr	hrly
Jeongeup	3200	1hr	every 15min
Jinan	3600	50min	every 30min
Muju	7500	1½hr	hrly
Naesosa	6200	2hr	1 daily

TRAIN

There are KTX (Korea Train Express; W29,600, 2¼ hours, 19 daily), *Saemaul* (express; W25,400, three hours, four daily) and *Mugunghwa* (semi-express; W17,000, 3½ hours, 14 daily) trains to/from Yongsan station in Seoul; KTX trains involve a change at Iksan. Trains also run south to Jeollanam-do.

Getting Around

Numerous buses (W850) run from near the bus terminals to downtown, while buses 105, 509 and others run to the train station. Taxis are plentiful and cheap.

GEUMSAN-SA & MOAKSAN PROVINCIAL PARK
금산사, 모악산도립공원

This **park** (☎ 548 1734; adult/youth/child W2600/1700/1000; ☯ 8am-7pm), which contains Moaksan mountain (794m), is only 40 minutes from Jeonju and is a popular destination for hikers at weekends. The main attraction is **Geumsan-sa**, a temple that dates back to AD 599. To stay in the temple (W40,000 including meals), contact the **information office** (☎ 548 1330; ☯ 9am-6pm, closed 2 weekdays a week). The **Maitreya Hall** is a three-storey wooden structure built in 1635 that retains an air of antiquity. Inside is an impressive Mireuk-sa Buddha, the Buddha of the Future.

On the left is a museum and a hall with carvings of 500 unique Buddha helpers. Near the entrance, sip soothing tea in the serene, Zen-style atmosphere of **Sanjang Dawon** (teas W6000). Between 10 and 20 monks live here.

The usual climbing route up Moaksan goes past the temple, up Janggundae and along the ridge up to the peak. The hike is relatively easy and you can be up and down in three hours.

Overlooking the car park on the left is **Hwarim Hoegwan** (화림회관; meals W5000-20,000), a restaurant where you can sit inside or outside under the wisteria. Choose between local black pig, *tokkitang* (토끼탕; spicy rabbit soup) or roast *ori* (오리; duck).

Geumsan-sa and Moaksan are easily reached by bus from Jeonju. Local bus 79 (W1500, 45 minutes, every 15 minutes) can be picked up along Girin-ro, Jeonju's main street. Don't get on buses that go to the other end of Moaksan park; ask for Geumsan-sa.

DAEDUNSAN PROVINCIAL PARK
대둔산도립공원

Yet another of Korea's beautiful parks, **Daedunsan** (☎ 263 9949; adult/youth/child W1300/850/450; ☯ 8am-6pm) offers craggy peaks with spectacular views over the surrounding countryside. Although relatively small, it's one of Korea's most scenic mountain areas.

Aside from the superb views, the climb to the summit of Daedunsan (878m) along steep, stony tracks is an adventure in itself, as you cross over a 50m-long cable bridge stretched precariously between two rock pinnacles and then climb up a steep and long steel-cable stairway. Vertigo sufferers are advised to take the alternative route! Otherwise, a five-minute **cable-car ride** (one way/return W3000/6000) saves you an hour of up-hill hiking.

Daedun-san Tourist Hotel (☎ 263 1260; fax 263 8069; r W65,000; ✗ 💻) has an *oncheon* (hot spring bath) and a sauna (W3000), perfect for soaking aching hiking muscles. Relax further, playing pool or four-ball in the bar (open 1pm to midnight) or sitting in an armchair with a view.

Many restaurants serve *sanchae bibimbap* (산채비빔밥; rice, egg, meat and mountain vegies) and the usual country-style food.

Daedunsan can be reached by bus from Jeonju (W5000, 70 minutes, six daily) or from Seodaejeon bus terminal in Daejeon (W2500, 40 minutes, six daily).

MAISAN PROVINCIAL PARK
마이산도립공원

This is a must-see **park** (☎ 433 3313; adult/youth/child W2000/1500/900; ☯ sunrise-sunset). Maisan means 'Horse Ears Mountain', which refers to two extraordinary rocky peaks as they appear from the access town of Jinan. The east peak, **Sutmaisan** (Male Maisan), is 678m while

JEOLLABUK-DO

the west peak, **Ammaisan** (Female Maisan), is slightly taller at 685m. Both ears are made of conglomerate rock, which is rare in Korea. Only Ammaisan can be scaled. It's a steep half-hour climb, but grinning grandmas make it to the top without any problem.

Tap-sa (Pagoda Temple), at the base of the female ear, has a unique sculptural garden of 80 stone towers or pinnacles that were piled up by a Buddhist mystic, Yi Kapmyong (1860–1957). Up to 15m in height, they represent religious ideas about the universe and miraculously never seem to crumble, although no cement has been used. The diverse stone towers are an intriguing sight, evoking the atmosphere of a lost world.

Nearby is **Unsu-sa**, a temple with a Dangun shrine, a centuries-old pear tree and attractive gardens, and you can even bang the big drum.

An easy 1½-hour, 1.7km hike with a splendid view at the top and ever-changing views of Ammaisan starts by Tap-sa and takes you back to the car park at the entrance. In April the cherry trees around the nearby lake burst into blossom.

Frequent buses (W3600, 50 minutes, every 30 minutes) run along the scenic route from Jeonju to the small town of Jinan. From Jinan, buses (W1000, five minutes, every 40 minutes) run to the park entrance.

DEOGYUSAN NATIONAL PARK & MUJU SKI RESORT
덕유산국립공원, 무주리조트

A fabulous mountain resort in the northeast corner of Jeollabuk-do, **Deogyusan National Park** (☎ 322 3174; http://deogyu.knps.or.kr/eng; adult/youth/child W3200/1200/600; ☼ sunrise-sunset) is a year-round playground offering skiing, hiking, biking and golf.

The park is best known as the home of **Muju Ski Resort** (☎ 322 9000; www.mujuresort.com). Opened in 1990, Muju is the only Korean ski resort located in a national park, with 30 runs including the highest altitude and longest slope (6.1km) in the country. Snowboarding, sledding, night and mogul skiing and lessons in English are on offer. The ski season runs mid-December to April.

When the snow melts, lace up your hiking boots and explore the park on foot. The

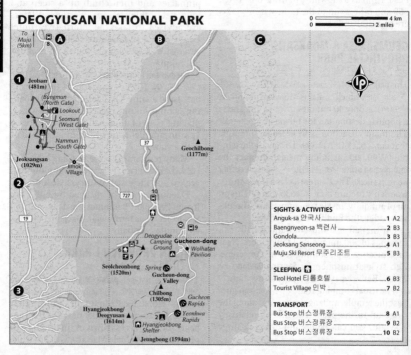

DEOGYUSAN NATIONAL PARK

0 —— 4 km
0 —— 2 miles

tourist village at **Gucheon-dong** is the start of the park's best hike (1¾ hours, 6km) that follows the river and valley past 20 beauty spots to a small temple, **Baengnyeon-sa** (백련사). Fairies are said to slide down rainbows to bathe in the pools. The enchanting trail continues to a strenuous, steep, 1½-hour ascent of **Hyangjeokbong** (1614m). Yew trees, azaleas and alpine flowers adorn the summit.

In the northwest of the park is **Jeoksang Sanseong**, a fortress rebuilt in the 17th century. Encircled by the 8km wall are the ruins of a Joseon-dynasty archive, a reservoir and **Anguk-sa** (안국사), a temple built in the 1860s. Buses only run along the main road to Gucheon-dong, so you must get off at the access road and walk (4km) or hitchhike.

Although winter is the high season, a few shops, restaurants, bars and attractions are open year-round, including the **gondola** (adult/child return W10,000/7000; ☯ 10am-4pm) to the peak of **Seolcheonbong** (1520m). **Mountain bikes** (adult/child per hr W10,000/8000; ☯ 9am-7pm) can be hired to ride round a special track.

Muju is home to the **Muju Firefly Festival** (http://firefly.or.kr), an environmental awareness event held in mid-June. **Taekwondo Park** (www.worldtaekwondopia.org/eng/park/park01.asp), a theme park devoted to Korea's national sport, is set to open in 2013.

Sleeping & Eating

The resort has top-notch dining, drinking and sleeping options in all price ranges; the best place to stay in the park is **Tirol Hotel** (티롤호텔; ☎ 320 7617; www.mujuresort.com; winter/summer r from W380,000/115,000; ☒ ▢), a wonderful Austrian-styled chalet. Cheaper *minbak* accommodation (private homes with rooms for rent) is located in the tourist village near the park entrance. For the best deals here, buy a package that includes accommodation, ski and equipment hire, transport and lift tickets.

Getting There & Away

The nondescript town of Muju is the gateway to Deogyusan National Park and Muju Ski Resort. Muju is connected by bus to Daejeon (W6500, one hour, every 40 minutes), Geumsan (W2800, one hour, hourly), Jeonju (W11,000, 1½ hours, hourly), Seoul (W13,700, three hours, six daily) and other cities.

From Muju, take the Gucheon-dong bus (W3300, 30 minutes, 10 daily), which drops

you off near the tourist village. Alternatively from Muju, take the Muju Resort Shuttle Bus (free, one hour, six daily, more frequently during ski season).

NAMWON 남원

Nicknamed the City of Love, Namwon is famous throughout Korea as the setting of *Chunhyang-jeon*, a *pansori* folk tale akin to Romeo and Juliet. The story follows the forbidden courtship and marriage between a young commoner girl named Chunhyang (Spring Fragrance) and a nobleman's son, Yi Mongryong. Yi must later save his love from the clutches of an evil politician, and they live happily ever after.

The city's crown jewel is **Gwanghallu-won Garden** (adult/child W2000/1100; ☯ 8am-8pm), one of the most beautiful gardens in southwest Korea and a shrine to the Chunhyang-jeon story.

At the heart of the garden is **Gwanghallu Pavilion** (Palace of the Moon), originally built in 1419 and the legendary spot where Yi courted his beloved Chunhyang. The pavilion is fronted by a lovely reflecting pond with three tiny islands and criss-crossed by the stone **Ojak-gyo** (Magpie Bridge); it is said that couples who cross the bridge once a year will have a happy marriage.

West of the pavilion, the Chunhyang Memorial Hall visually retells the story through paintings. The Chunyang Shrine contains a portrait of the beautiful heroine; another legend claims singles will find love if they pray here.

Across the road from the park entrance, take the ornate footbridge over the Yocheon River to reach the **Namwon Tourist Complex** of restaurants, shops, hotels, **Namwon Land** amusement park, the **Chunhyuang Theme Park and Folk Museum** (☎ 620 6836; adult/child W3000/2000; ☯ 9am-10pm) and the **National Centre for Korean Folk Traditional Performing Arts** (☎ 620 2331; admission free; ☯ 9am-5pm) with its fine collection of musical instruments and regular live performances.

Trains serve Jeonju (W5000, 35 minutes, 16 daily), Seoul (W20,400 to W30,300; three hours, 40 minutes; 16 daily) and Yeosu (W6700 to W9800, 100 minutes, 17 daily). Buses serve Jeonju (W6000, 45 minutes, every 15 minutes), Gwangju (W4800, one hour, every 30 minutes), Banseon (W4400, one hour, 18 daily) and Seoul (W14,000, four hours, 17 daily).

NAEJANGSAN NATIONAL PARK
내장산국립공원

The mountainous ridge in this **park** (☎ 538 7875; http://naejang.knps.or.kr/eng; adult/youth/child W3200/1300/700; ☺ sunrise-sunset) is shaped like an amphitheatre. A spider's web of trails leads up to the ridge, but the fastest way up is by **cable car** (adult/child one way W4000/2000, return W5500/3000). The hike around the rim is strenuous, but with splendid views on a fine day. The trail is a roller-coaster ride, going up and down six main peaks and numerous small ones before you reach Seoraebong, from where you head back down to the access road.

There are metal ladders, bridges and railings to help you scramble over the rocky parts. Give yourself four hours to hike around the amphitheatre, with an hour for breaks and a picnic. If you find the hike too difficult, turn right at any time and follow one of the many trails back down to Naejang-sa.

An easy and picturesque 2km walk from Naejang-sa goes through Geumsong valley, which becomes a steep ravine before leading to a cave, a natural rock arch and a waterfall.

A tourist village clusters around the entrance, but it's not usually busy except in October. **Camping** (small/large tent W3000/6000) is available before the tourist village. A shuttle bus (W1000; 9am to 6pm) runs between the ticket office and the cable-car terminal, saving a 2km, 20-minute walk.

The **tourist information centre** (☎ 537 1330) has free internet access. Across the road is a **bicycle**

NAEJANGSAN NATIONAL PARK

hire stall (☎ 011-9449 4383; per hr W3000; ☻ 9am-6pm). Cycle up to the temple or around the nearby farms and villages.

Buses (W3000, one hour, every 15 minutes) run from Jeonju to Jeongeup. From just outside the bus terminal on the left, local bus 171 (W1000, 30 minutes, every 20 minutes) runs to Naejangsan.

GOCHANG 고창

Perched on a hill overlooking the small village of Gochang, **Moyang Fortress** (고창읍성, ☎ 560 2710; admission W1000; ☻ 9am-7pm Mar-Oct, 9am-5pm Nov-Feb) is an impressive structure built in 1453 during the Joseon dynasty. The ivy-covered, 1.6km-long fortress wall with three gates surrounds a complex of reconstructed buildings including a prison and pavilion. A local legend says if a woman walks three times around the wall with a stone on her head in a leap year, she will never become ill and will enter paradise. To the right of the fortress is the **Pansori Museum** (☎ 560 2761; adult/youth/child W800/500/free; ☻ 9am-6pm Tue-Sun), with memorabilia on this unique solo opera musical form. The hills surrounding Gochang are filled with thousands of dolmen, prehistoric tombs from the Bronze and Iron Ages.

Buses serve Gochang from Jeonju (W5400, 80 minutes, every 30 minutes) and Gwanju (W4300, one hour, every 30 minutes).

SEONUNSAN PROVINCIAL PARK 선운산도립공원

This pretty **park** (☎ 563 3450; adult/youth/child W2500/1800/1300; ☻ sunrise-sunset) has always been popular with monks and poets alike. A 20-minute walk along a rocky, tree-lined river brings you to **Seonun-sa**. Just behind the temple is a 500-year-old **camellia forest** that flowers around the end of April, although a few blooms linger into summer.

Another 35 minutes further on is **Dosol-am hermitage** and just beyond is a giant **Buddha rock carving** dating to the Goryeo dynasty; the amazing image is carved into the cliff face and is 13m high. Despite centuries of erosion the Buddha is still an impressive sight, a testament to the faith of ancient times. On the right is a very narrow grotto, and next to it stairs lead up to a tiny shrine and a great view. From the Buddha, you can climb **Nakjodae** and carry on to **Gaeippalsan** and **Seonunsan**, with views of the West Sea, before heading back down to Seonun-sa.

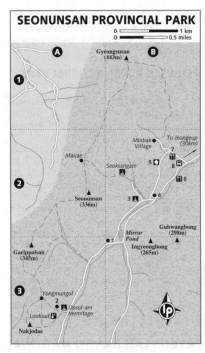

SEONUNSAN PROVINCIAL PARK

SIGHTS & ACTIVITIES	
Garden 공원	1 B3
Giant Buddha Rock Carving 마애불상	2 A3
Seonun-sa 선운사	3 B2
Ticket Office 매표소	4 B2

SLEEPING 🏠	
Seonunsan Tourist Hotel 선운사 관광 호텔	(see 5)
Seonunsan Youth Hostel 선운산유스호스텔	5 B2

EATING 🍴	
Food Stalls 분식포장마차	6 B2
Restaurants 식당가	7 B2

TRANSPORT	
Bus Stop 버스정류장	8 B2

The small tourist village near the park entrance has a handful of lodgings, restaurants and shops. The clean but dated **Seonunsan Tourist Hotel** (선운산관광호텔; ☎ 561 3377; r W60,000-100,000) has Western and *ondol*-style rooms. The basic **Seonunsan Youth Hostel** (선운산유스호스텔; ☎ 561 3333; fax 561 3448; r W60,000) is cheaper but does fill up fast on weekends.

JEOLLABUK-DO

Buses (W4000, 1½ hours, every 30 minutes) run from Jeonju to Gochang, from where buses (W2000, 20 minutes, hourly) run to Seonunsan.

BYEONSAN BANDO NATIONAL PARK
변산반도국립공원

This coastal **park** (☎ 582 7808; http://byeonsan.knps. or.kr/eng; adult/youth/child W3200/1300/700; ☼ sunrise-sunset) contains the large temple of **Naeso-sa** (내소사), originally built in 633 and last renovated in the 19th century. It certainly looks old, with lots of unpainted wood. Take a close look at the main hall, especially the lattice doors, the painting behind the Buddha statues, and the intricately carved and painted ceiling with musical instruments, flowers and dragons among the motifs.

Hike up the unpaved road to **Cheongnyeonam** (청련암; 20 minutes) for sea views; another 15 minutes brings you to the ridge where you turn left for Gwaneumbong. From the peak follow the path, which goes up and down and over rocks for an hour until you reach **Jikso Pokpo** (직소폭포), a 30m-high waterfall with a large pool. Another pretty

spot is **Seonyeotang** (선녀탕, Angel Pool). From there walk along the unpaved access road past the ruins of **Silsang-sa** (실상사지), destroyed during the Korean War. You may need to hitch a lift as buses are infrequent. For a more challenging hike head up **Nakjodae**, which is famous for its sunset views.

Beaches along the coast attract crowds in summer. **Byeonsan Beach** is a wide beach of fine sand, clear water and backed by pine trees. Further south, **Gyeokpo Beach** has dramatic stratified cliffs and caves as well as seafood restaurants. The beach is safe for swimming but the sea disappears at low tide. Gyeokpo is also the starting point for ferries to the island of **Wi-do**, which has a sandy beach; every house in the little fishing village of Jinli is a *minbak*-cum-restaurant.

Only one direct bus (W6000, two hours) runs from Jeonju to Naeso-sa. Otherwise take a bus from Jeonju to Buan (W4000, one hour, five daily) and then a local bus to Naeso-sa (W2000, one hour, every 30 minutes). Buses (W6400, two hours, hourly) also run from Jeonju to Gyeokpo.

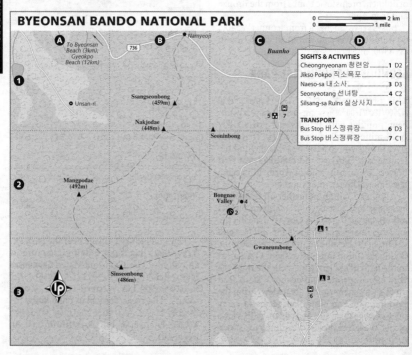

BYEONSAN BANDO NATIONAL PARK

SIGHTS & ACTIVITIES	
Cheongnyeonam 청련암	**1** D2
Jikso Pokpo 직소폭포	**2** C2
Naeso-sa 내소사	**3** D3
Seonyeotang 선녀탕	**4** C2
Silsang-sa Ruins 실상사지	**5** C1

TRANSPORT	
Bus Stop 버스정류장	**6** D3
Bus Stop 버스정류장	**7** C1

Ferries (☎ 581 0023) go from Gyeokpo to Wi-do (W6500 one way, 40 minutes, three daily September to June, six daily July and August).

SEONYU-DO 선유도

A 43km ferry trip from the industrial port city of Gunsan brings you to the relaxing tropical island of Seonyu-do, situated amid 60 mostly uninhabited small islands. When the tide is in and the sun is out, the views from here are unbelievably beautiful. These days there are more bicycle-hire stalls than fishing boats; you can hire bicycles (W3000 per hour) or a quad bike (W20,000 per hour) to pedal or zip around the laid-back fishing villages on Seonyu-do and the three islands that are linked to it by bridges. Six-person *bungbungka* (auto rickshaws; per hour W30,000) take pensioner parties on fun tours.

The main attraction is the 1.6km **beach**, a 10-minute walk from the ferry pier, on a spit of soft, golden sand with great island views on both sides. At the far end the adventurous should climb up rocky **Mangjubong**. Take the right turn towards Saeteo village and on your left are tracks leading through the grass up to some ropes that are fixed to the rock, which you can use to haul yourself up to a wooded gully. The view from the top is a wonderful panorama of islands.

You'll find plenty of inexpensive restaurants and *minbak* in the main fishing village, a 10-minute walk from the jetty near the beach.

Buses (W4500, one hour, every 15 minutes) leave from Jeonju for Gunsan. Ferries (adult/child one way W12,800/6400, 1½ hours, five daily) leave from the new **Yeonan Yeogaek** (Gunsan Coastal Ferry Terminal; 연안여객터미널; ☎ 467 6000), a 15-minute, W7500 taxi ride from Gunsan bus terminal.

Chungcheongnam-do
충청남도

It's close to Seoul and home to the fifth largest city in South Korea, Daejeon, but Chungnam – as it's more commonly known – is not the most scintillating of provinces. Its attractions are largely very old (5th-century Baekje capitals) or utterly recreational (a bevy of beaches). Much of the buzz in recent years has focused on a new administrative national capital Sejong City, to be built near Gongju, but whether it materialises depends on the political winds in Seoul.

For now, it's Daejeon that's the capital manqué, with flashy KTX services, all the trappings of modern Korean life and all its lack of urban charms as well. More interesting are the small towns left in its wake: little Geumsan is the hub of the ginseng industry, while Gongju and tiny Buyeo were once capitals of the ancient Baekje dynasty. The latter towns have retained a surprising number of old fortresses, tombs and relics, chief among them the tomb of King Muryeong in Gongju – like King Tut's tomb, it was uncovered in modern times with all its burial artefacts miraculously intact.

The province's other main draw is its beaches. Daecheon Beach in the south is widely considered to be the best on the western coast, while travellers preferring some solitude can hop on a ferry to one of the nearby islands. To the north is Taean Haean National Park, dotted with more islands, beaches and the promise of wind-whipped fresh air – just what most day-trippers from Seoul are looking for.

CHUNGCHEONGNAM-DO

HIGHLIGHTS

- Marvel at the 1500-year-old treasures from **King Muryeong's tomb** (p325) in Gongju
- Climb up the fortress in **Buyeo** (p328) where the Baekje army made its last stand
- Chill out at **Daecheon Beach** (p331) and indulge in some mud spa treatments
- Hike from one end of **Gyeryongsan National Park** (p323) to the other, taking in pagodas and *pokpo* (waterfalls) along the way

★ Daecheon Beach ★ Gongju
★ Gyeryongsan National Park
★ Buyeo

■ TELEPHONE CODE: 041 (DAEJEON: 042)   ■ POPULATION: 2 MILLION   ■ AREA: 8586 SQ KM

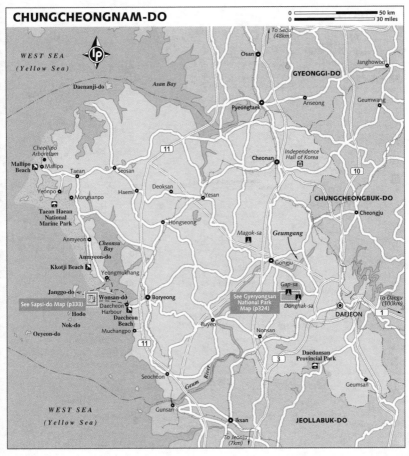

CHUNGCHEONGNAM-DO

History

When the Baekje dynasty (57 BC–AD 668) was pushed south by an aggressive Goguryeo kingdom in AD 475, this is where the Baekje ended up, establishing their capital first in Ungjin (modern-day Gongju), then moving further south to Sabi (modern-day Buyeo). Its culture was fairly sophisticated, but after Sabi fell to the joint army of Shilla and China in AD 660, the region passed into obscurity. It remains to be seen whether plans for a new capital, Sejong City, will rejuvenate the province.

National Parks

Chungnam has two national parks: the mountains of **Gyeryongsan** (p323) and the marine swathe of **Taean Haean** (p333). Gyeryongsan has relatively low peaks (for Korea) and is crisscrossed with hiking trails. Taean Haean consists of numerous islands and beaches, some of which can be reached only by boat.

Getting There & Around

High-speed KTX trains connect Cheonan and Daejeon to Seoul and Busan, while *Saemaul* (express) and *Mugunghwa* (semi-express) trains run from Seoul to Daecheon station in Boryeong. Other towns are served only by buses.

DAEJEON 대전

☎ 042 / pop 1.5 million

The fifth-largest city in South Korea, **Daejeon** (www.daejeon.go.kr/language/english) is the locus of

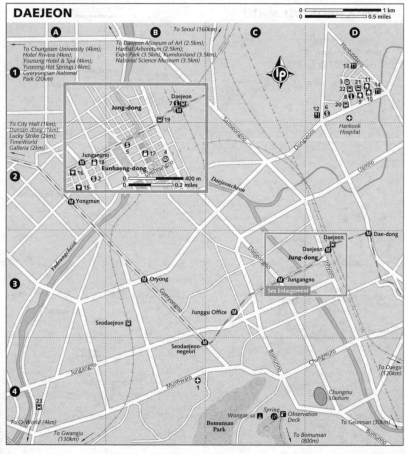

science and technology and government administration, spread across a cookie-cutter landscape of looming apartment buildings, squat research establishments and traffic-snarled streets. It's large enough to merit its own telephone code, subway and KTX trains, but possesses few attractions for travellers other than Yuseong Hot Springs and nearby Gyeryongsan National Park (p323) and Daedunsan Provincial Park in Jeollabuk-do (p311).

Daejeon's transformation from small town into overgrown suburb-of-Seoul began in the 1970s, when science institutes began to set up shop (including KAIST aka the 'MIT of South Korea'). In the decades since, it's shown no signs of slowing down or acquiring any graces.

Though it's less abrasive than Seoul can be, there's little reason to stop here or linger, unless you're simply starved of city life.

Orientation

Daejeon is a sprawling city with three major bus terminals and two train stations. The Dongdaejeon (East Daejeon) and express bus terminals are close together, with motels, restaurants and a Home Plus department store. Seodaejeon (West Daejeon) bus terminal and Seodaejeon train station are in a more run-down area with fewer amenities. The 'old downtown' area of Eunhaeng-dong is near Daejeon train station and Jungang Market, while the 'new downtown' of Dunsan-dong is home to City Hall, the unimaginatively-

INFORMATION		SLEEPING		SHOPPING	
Chungnam National University		Cosmos Tourist Hotel		Jungang Market 중앙로시장	**17** B2
Hospital 충남대병원	**1** B4	코스모스관광호텔	**9** D1	Milano 21 밀라노 21	**18** A2
KB Bank 국민은행	**2** A2	Jinju Park 진주파크	**10** D1		
Post Office 우체국	**3** D1	Limousine Motel 리무진모텔	**11** D1	TRANSPORT	
Post Office 우체국	**4** B2			Bus Stop 버스정류장	**19** B1
SC 진주파크	**5** B2	EATING		Bus Stop 버스정류장	**20** D1
Shinhan Bank 신한은행	**6** D1	Pungnyeon Samgyetang		Dongdaejeon Intercity	
Tourist Information Centre		풍년삼계탕	**12** D1	Bus Terminal	
관광안내소	**7** B1	Subuk Sikdang 수북식당	(see 20)	동대전시외버스터미널	**21** D1
Tourist Information Centre		Tesco Home Plus Food Court		Express Bus Terminal	
관광안내소	**8** D1	테스코홈플러스푸드코트	**13** D1	고속버스터미널	**22** D1
		Yeongsuni 영순이	**14** D1	Seodaejeon Intercity Bus Terminal	
		DRINKING		서대전시외전버스터미널	**23** A4
		Brickhouse	**15** A2		
		Club J-Rock	**16** A2		

named Government Complex, and new shopping and entertainment areas.

North of this is a recreational area with some museums, Expo Park and Hanbat Arboretum on either side of the river Gapcheon. To the west lie Chungnam University and Yuseong, the latter area dotted with hot-spring spas and hotels. South of the city centre is Bomunsan (457m), a pleasantly wooded hill with a park.

Information

Chungnam National University Hospital (☎ 220 7114; www.cnuh.co.kr; Munhwaro)

KB Bank (Daejeongno) Exchanges foreign currency and has a global ATM.

Post offices On Inhyoro and opposite Dongdaejeon bus terminal.

SC (Jungangno) Exchanges foreign currency and has a global ATM.

Shinhan Bank (Dongseoro) Exchanges foreign currency.

Tourist information centre Outside express bus terminal (☎ 632 1338) Inside Daejeon train station (☎ 221 1905) At Seodaejeon train station (☎ 523 1338)

Sights & Activities

Except for the hot springs at Yuseong, Daejeon's attractions, such as they are, belong strictly in the 'if you have time to kill or kids to amuse' category. The **National Science Museum** (국립중앙과학관; ☎ 601 7894; www.science.go.kr; adult/child W1000/500; planetarium show W1000/500; ☻ 9.30am-5.50pm Tue-Sun; ♿) has three levels of exhibits and interactive displays about science and technology, all targeted at children (minimal English captions only). Pick up bus 104 (W1000, 15 minutes, every 15 minutes) from the bus stop opposite City Hall and get off just after the bus crosses the river.

The city has two amusement parks. The older **Kumdoriland** (꿈돌이랜드; ☎ 863 2633; day pass adult/youth/child W22,000/18,000/15,000; ☻ 10am-5pm, later in summer) is beside Expo Park, across the pedestrian bridge from the National Science Museum. The more elaborate **O-World** (오월드; ☎ 580 4820; www.oworld.kr; adult/youth/child W25,000/20,000/18,000; ☻ 9.30am-6pm Mon-Fri, to 10pm Sat & Sun) comprises a zoo with a safari, landscaped gardens and amusement park. Take bus 311 or 314 (W1000, 45 minutes, every 15 minutes) from Daejeon train station.

YUSEONG HOT SPRINGS 유성 온천

The western neighbourhood of Yuseong has many hotels and *oncheon* (hot-spring spas) that draw their water from sources 350m underground. One of the most established is **Yousung Spa** (☎ 820 0100; W5000; ☻ 5am-10pm) at the eponymous hotel (유성호텔), which has indoor and outdoor pools, with small waterfalls. Across the road is the spiffier **Hotel Riviera** (호텔 리베라; ☎ 824 4050; W6000; ☻ 6am-10pm), with a Finnish-style dry sauna and a wet sauna with Asian herbal treatments.

Take bus 102 or 106 (W1000, 25 minutes, every 15 minutes) from outside the express bus terminal. After the bus passes Chungnam University, look out for Hotel Hongin on the left side of the road and get off at the stop for Yuseong Spa Station Exit 6. Walk backwards to the intersection and turn left, following Oncheonmunhwa-gil to the hotels.

Sleeping

The motel clump around the Dongdaejeon bus terminal has some seedy corners, but new motels were coming up at the time of research.

Jinju Park (진주파크; ☎ 624 4776; Yongjeon Gosok 1-gil; r W20,000; ❄) This *yeogwan* (motel with small en suite) in a pink three-storey building has the cheapest rooms around. They're small and nothing fancy but pass muster, and the place is run by friendly folks.

Limousine Motel (리무진모텔; ☎ 621 1004; Youngtap 3-gil; r W35,000; ❄ ▢) A love motel with all the trimmings: spacious rooms, huge flat-screen TVs, contemporary furnishings and windows that can be shuttered for complete privacy. Look for the motel with Korean movie posters decorating the exterior walls.

Cosmos Tourist Hotel (코스모스 관광호텔; ☎ 628 3400; www.hotelcosmos.co.kr; r W45,000, ste W150,000; ❄ ▢) Just about the nicest rooms around the bus terminals, although the decor can be a little overwrought, from the reflective gold on the exterior facade to the glitzy wallpaper in the rooms. Prices rise by W10,000 on weekends.

Hotel Riviera (호텔 리베라; ☎ 824 4050; www.shinan.co.kr/yusong/eng/index_yuseong.asp; r W180,000, ste W300,000; ❄ ▢) One of the plusher options at Yuseong, with smart rooms that offer views of the area. Every room is internet-ready and guests get a 50% discount for the sauna (p321).

Eating

For cheap bites near Dondaejeon bus terminal, there are some eateries across the road and a food court in Home Plus.

Yeongsuni (영순이; ☎ 633 4520; meals W4000-15,000) Choose from a range of hearty set menus with *shabu kalguksu* (샤부칼국수), where you cook your own meat and noodles in a spicy mushroom and vegetable soup. More elaborate sets come with seafood (해물), *ssam* (상추쌈; grilled meats wrapped in vegetable leaves) or *bossam* (세트 메뉴; steamed pork and *kimchi* eaten *ssam*-style; served with the set menu).

Subuk Sikdang (수북식당; Yongjeongosok 4-gil; meals W5000-8000) Right next to the express bus terminal, this restaurant has plenty of Korean comfort food, such as *kimchi jjigae* (*kimchi* stew), *galbitang* (beef-rib soup) and *bibimbap* (rice with vegetables, meat and egg).

Pungnyeon Samgyetang (풍년삼계탕; ☎ 632 5757; meals W9000-10,000) The signature dish at this unpretentious restaurant comes with a whole small chicken, with a salt-and-pepper dip on the side. If that's not enough, order some *pajeon* (green-onion pancake) or *mukmuchim* (묵무침; acorn jelly) to fill up.

Drinking

There are two lively clubbing areas: in the 'old downtown' of Eunhaeng-dong (은행동) and in the 'new downtown' of Dunsan-dong (둔산동) near the shopping mall TimeWorld Galleria.

Club J-Rock (☎ 320 8523; www.facebook.com/home.php#/group.php?gid=8396716919) On weekends it's standing room only at this boisterous expat watering hole. It's got a pool table and a foosball table, plush-looking red couches, a menu of Tex-Mex fare and regular poker nights.

Brickhouse (☎ 223 6515; www.facebook.com/home.php#/group.php?gid=21016380541) A rollicking sports bar, big-screen TVs and all. Even when there aren't any games on, regulars come by for darts and pool, or just some good pub grub, including a lovingly made Irish stew.

The snug wooden bar **Lucky Strike** plays lots of classic rock and the bartenders make some fine cocktails (try the mojitos). To find it, walk backwards about 50m from the bus stop at TimeWorld Galleria and go up the lane across the road. Lucky Strike is at the corner two lanes ahead.

Shopping

Bargain buys can be found at the sprawling Jungang market, while young people clog the pedestrianised streets of Eunhaeng-dong. The more upscale shopping area is in Dunsan-dong around TimeWorld Galleria.

Getting There & Away

AIR

The nearest airport is at Cheongju (p338), 40km north. Buses run from Dongdaejeon bus terminal to the airport (W3300, 45 minutes, six daily).

BUS

Daejeon has three bus terminals: Seodaejeon (west) intercity bus terminal, Dongdaejeon (east) intercity bus terminal and the express bus terminal. The latter two are across the road from each other.

Buses depart the express bus terminal for the following destinations:

Destination	Price (W)	Duration	Frequency
Busan	14,400	3¼hr	every 2 hours
Daegu	78400	2hr	hrly
Gwangju	10,100	3hr	every 30min
Seoul	8700	2hr	every 15min

From Dongdaejeon intercity bus terminal, destinations include the following:

Destination	Price (W)	Duration	Frequency
Cheongju	3400	50min	every 10min
Gongju	3800	1hr	every 40min

Departures from the Seodaejeon intercity bus terminal:

Destination	Price (W)	Duration	Frequency
Boryeong	10,500	3hr	hrly
Buyeo	6100	1¼hr	every 30min
Daedunsan	3000	40min	3 daily
Jeonju	5100	1½hr	9 daily

TRAIN

Daejeon train station serves the main line between Seoul and Busan. KTX trains run from Seoul (W21,400, one hour, every 20 minutes) in the early mornings and evenings, and from Busan (W26,700, two hours, every 30 minutes) all day. From Seoul, there are also hourly *Saemaul* (14,900, 1¾ hours) and *Mugunghwa* (W10,000, two hours) services to Daejeon.

Seodaejeon station, in the west of the city, serves the lines to Mokpo and Yeosu. There are *Saemaul* (W14,700, 1¾ hours, 13 daily) and *Mugunghwa* (W9800, two hours, hourly) trains from Yongsan station in Seoul to Seodaejeon.

Getting Around
BUS

City buses are very regular and bus stops have GPS-enabled signs with arrival information. From outside the express bus terminal, useful buses (W1000, every 10 to 15 minutes) include the following:

Bus 2, 201, 501 or 701 (15 minutes) To Daejeon train station and Eunhaeng-dong. The bus stop for the latter is along Jungangno after Daejeon train station, opposite the huge Milano 21 store.

Bus 102 or 106 (25 minutes) To Yuseong.

Bus 106 (20 minutes) To City Hall and Dunsan-dong. The bus stop for the latter is just after TimeWorld Galleria.

Bus 701 (35 minutes) To Seodaejeon bus terminal.

SUBWAY

Daejeon's subway line (per trip W1000 to W1100) has 22 stations. Useful stops for travellers are Daejeon station, Jungangno (near Eunhaeng-dong), City Hall and Yuseong Spa.

GYERYONGSAN NATIONAL PARK
계룡산국립공원

This **park** (☎ 825 3003; http://gyeryong.knps.or.kr/ Gyeryongsan_eng/; adult/youth/child W2000/700/400; ⏱ 6am-7pm) is one of the smallest in the South and it's possible to hike from one end to the other in less than a day. The name is just as unassuming – Gyeryongsan means 'Rooster Dragon Mountain', because locals thought the mountain resembled a dragon with a rooster's head. There are two park entrances: the eastern one closer to Daejeon, the western one closer to Gongju.

Eastern Entrance

A gentle 15-minute climb from the entrance is the nunnery Donghak-sa, said to have been founded during the Shilla era, although the buildings date only from the early 19th century. From here, you can hike up to the pagodas at Nammaetap, then on to Sambulbong (775m) and the highest peak **Gwaneumbong** (816m), before returning to Donghak-sa via the waterfall Eunseon Pokpo. The route is about 6.5km; allow four hours in all. Alternatively, from Gwaneumbong you can push on west to **Yeoncheongbong** (738m) and descend to the western park entrance via the temple Gap-sa (3.5km, 2½ hours).

The tourist village has restaurants, accommodation and a **tourist information centre**; the latter provides handy schedules (Korean only) for buses to Daejeon, Gongju and other towns. For accommodation, head up the lane beside the park entrance to **Gyeurintel** (그린텔; ☎ 825 821; r W35,000; 🅿), which has better rooms than its drab exterior suggests. **Camping** (☎ 824 6005; W3000-6000) is also available.

The mushroom-shaped restaurant **Mushroom** (머쉬룸; meals W6000-20,000) looks like an escapee from a Disney film set and serves its namesake ingredient in *beoseot jeongol* (버섯전골) or with *ssambap* (머쉬룸쌈밥; rice and lettuce wraps). Single diners can try the *beoseot deopbap* (버섯덮밥; mushrooms with sauce on rice) or *sanchae bibimbap* (*bibimbap* made with mountain vegetables). Mushroom meals may include meat.

From outside Daejeon's express bus terminal, take bus 102 or 106 and get off at the bus stop for Yuseong Spa Station Exit 6. Walk up to the street corner and turn right, heading for the bus stop for Yuseong Spa Station Exit 5. Bus 107 (W1000, 25 minutes, every 20 minutes) goes to the eastern end of the park.

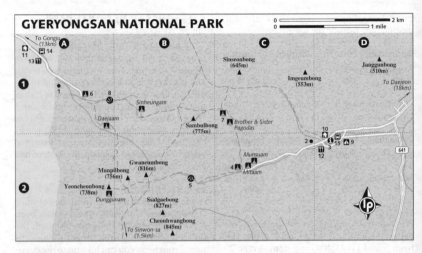

GYERYONGSAN NATIONAL PARK

Western Entrance

The temple **Gap-sa** is an easy 15-minute walk from the entrance. The main hall contains three gleaming Buddha statues, while a smaller shrine houses three shamanist deities – Chilseong, Sansin and Dokseong. The temple is also known for its bronze bell, crafted in 1584, with both Shilla and Joseon characteristics. From Gap-sa you can ascend Sambulbong directly; en route are the small waterfall Yongmun Pokpo and the small hermitage Sinheungam (3km, 2¾ hours).

The tourist village is very small, consisting only of a few restaurants, shops and **Kyeryongsan Gapsa Youth Hostel** (계룡산갑사 유스호스텔; ☎ 856 4666; www.kapsayouthhostel. com; dm/f W60,000/106,000; 🔲), where guests sleep on a *yo* (padded quilt). Restaurants serve vegetable-laden meals, such as *sannamul jjigae baekban* (산나물 찌개백반; wild vegetable stew with rice and side dishes) and *pyogo beoseot deopbap* (표고버섯 덮밥; shiitake mushroom with sauce on rice). One of the standard *banchan* (side dishes) here is *dotori bindaetteok* (도토리 빈대떡; acorn pancake).

From Gongju's local bus terminal, take a bus for Gap-sa (W1100, 30 minutes, hourly), the western park entrance, or Donghak-sa (W1100, 30 minutes, three daily), the eastern one.

GONGJU 공주
pop 127,400

Once the capital of Korea's oldest dynasty Baekje, dusty **Gongju** (www.gongju.go.kr/html/en) came to national attention in 1971 with the discovery of the Baekje king Muryeong's tomb. These days it's more often mentioned in the same breath as its native son, Major League baseball player Park Chan Ho, or the new national capital coming up nearby, Sejong City. The town is divided by the river Geumgang: the old part in the south, where all the Baekje monuments are, seems to be drifting along at its own pace, while the new part in the north looks much like any Korean town, with modern high-rises and love motels.

There's a **tourist information centre** (☎ 856 7700) beside the car park at the Gongsanseong entrance and a smaller booth near the path to King Muryeong's tomb. Enquire at the former about the bus tours in English, held every Sunday and second and fourth Saturday from April to November. The tour is free, but museum and fortress admission charges apply.

Gongju hosts an extravagant **Baekje Cultural Festival** (www.baekje.org/ctnt/engl) in October every odd-numbered year, with a huge parade, games, traditional music and dancing, and a memorial ceremony for its erstwhile kings. The festival is held in Buyeo in even-numbered years.

Sights

TOMB OF KING MURYEONG 백제 무령왕릉
On a hillside lie seven ancient Baekje **tombs** (Muryeongwangneung; ☎ 856 0331; adult/youth/child W1500/1000/700; ⏰ 9am-6pm), including that of King Muryeong. No grand mausoleums here – the tombs are modest and grass-covered, looking like gentle hillocks. They're sealed for protection, but the aptly named **Replica Museum** contains full-size replicas of the tombs that you can enter. Look for the intricate tomb murals in Tomb No 6, the only such example known around Baekje sites.

The museum also has replicas of some artefacts from King Muryeong's tomb, which was discovered, miraculously intact, in 1971 (see the boxed text, p328). There's detailed information in English and it's best to visit the museum first, then take a gander about the tombs. To see the actual artefacts, visit the Gongju National Museum (right).

Catch bus 1 or 25 (W1100, five minutes, every 15 minutes) from Gongsanseong to the tombs, or walk the distance in about 20 minutes. A taxi costs W2000.

GONGSANSEONG 공산성
This commanding hilltop **fortress** (adult/youth/child W1200/800/600; ⏰ 9am-6pm Mar-Oct, 9am-5pm Nov-Feb) is a reminder of a time when Gongju (then called Ungjin) was Baekje's capital. Successive dynasties continued to use the fortress: its name dates from the Goryeo period and it was during the Joseon dynasty that the original mud structure was rebuilt into today's stone fortress. It's possible to walk the entire 2.6km length all around.

Within the walls lie numerous pavilions and building sites – many of them have been reconstructed. The best views are in the northwest overlooking the river, from an observation platform or **Manharu Pavilion** near the temple Yeongeun-sa, whose warrior monks fought valiantly against the Japanese in the 1590s. The small plateau to the southwest near Ssangsujeong – the pavilion where King Injo rested during his 10-day refuge from an insurrection – may have been the site of a Baekje palace.

The place has the feel of a spacious park, albeit one where some inevitable climbing is involved. At the main entrance gate of **Geumseoru**, a 10-minute Baekje changing of the guard ceremony takes place hourly between 11am and 4pm on Saturday and Sunday in April, May, June, September and October. A good time to visit is in the late afternoon, to catch the sunset glow upon Geumseoru; linger for dinner at Gomanaru (see p326) and you'll also enjoy a stunning floodlit view of the fortress.

GONGJU NATIONAL MUSEUM
공주국립박물관
This **museum** (☎ 850 6300; http://gongju.museum.go.kr; admission free; ⏰ 9am-6pm Tue-Fri, 9am-7pm Sat & Sun) exhibits the treasures discovered in the tomb of King Muryeong. Only a few hundred of the 2906 tomb artefacts are on display here, but together with some videos (with English subtitles), they paint a vivid picture of Baekje culture. The museum's exhibits include the intricate and distinctive gold diadem ornaments that you'll see images of all over Gongju, as well as many small decorative objects, jewellery and Chinese ceramics.

The museum is a 15-minute walk from the royal tombs or a W2500 taxi ride from the fortress entrance.

Sleeping
Minarijang (미나리장; ☎ 853 1130; Bldg 7, Minari 2-gil; r W30,000; 🚻 🖵) One of a dozen *yeogwan* clustered opposite the fortress, this one has a homely feel with clean, smart rooms. All rooms have computers and the place is run by a friendly older couple.

Ganseojang (강서장; ☎ 853 8323; Pungmul Geori; r without/with computer W30,000/35,000; 🚻 🖵) Another good *yeogwan*, where at the entrance you swap your shoes for floral household slippers. Rooms are bright and spotless, and some have bathtubs. Look for the red building with a blue-tiled roof.

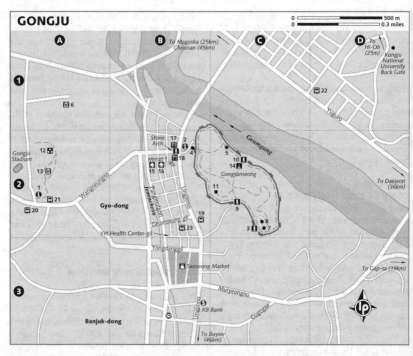

GONGJU

Eating & Drinking

There's a cluster of *naengmyeon* eateries (serving buckwheat noodles in cold broth) around the stone arch in front of Gongsanseong, offering meals from W3500 to W6000. Both restaurants below have menus with English.

Gomanaru (고마나루; Ungjinno; meals W6000-20,000) Get a table by the window with a fortress view at this charming restaurant. Locals come for the *ssambap* (assorted ingredients with rice and lettuce wraps) and *dolsotbap* (hotpot rice), and the smoked duck specialities are good too.

Sura (수라; ☎ 855 1385; meals W8000-20,000) It's all meat, all the time at this barbecue restaurant, set back from the main road. Order your favourite cuts of *galbi* (beef ribs) or *samgyeopsal* (streaky pork belly), or lighter meals of *galbitang*, *naengmyeon* and *bibimbap*. Some come with *yukhoe* (육회; raw beef), which might appeal to fans of steak tartare.

If you're itching for a drink, head to the back gate of Kongju National University (Gongjudae humun; 공주대 후문), which has scads of bars, cheap eateries and cafes servicing the university crowd. **Hi-Ob** has a playlist that veers towards Korean chart-toppers, and draws a lively college crowd and some expats. It's in the building adjoining Office Depot, about 50m downhill from the university back gate.

Getting There & Away

The intercity and express bus terminals are together north of the river, although most buses from Daejeon will drop passengers off in the city centre. Departures from the terminals include the following:

Destination	Price (W)	Duration	Frequency
Boryeong	6700	1¾hr	every 30min
Buyeo	3400	45min	every 30min
Cheonan	4700	1hr	every 20min
Daejeon	3800	1hr	every 40min
Seoul	7300	1¾hr	every 30min

AROUND GONGJU
Magok-sa 마곡사

A pleasant half-day trip from Gongju, this utterly serene **temple** (☎ 841 6221; www.magoksa. or.kr; adult/youth/child W2000/1500/1000; ⏰ 6am-6.30pm) enjoys a pastoral setting beside a river. It was founded near the end of the Baekje dynasty in the 7th century and, like most Korean temples, has had its buildings restored and reconstructed through the years. Unlike most temples, however, its extant buildings are being allowed to age gracefully, and there are quite a few atmospheric halls and pavilions.

The elaborate entry gates Cheonwangmun and Haetalmun feature colourful statues of various deities and bodhisattvas. Cross the 'mind-washing bridge' to reach the main hall, behind which stands a rare two-storey prayer hall, Daeungbojeon. Other buildings include a dormitory for monks and Yeongsanjeon, a hall decked out with over a thousand gleaming miniature Buddha statues.

From Magok-sa, three hiking trails head up the nearby hills (there's a signboard with a map, in Korean only), passing small hermitages. The longest trail (6.5km, 3½ hours) hits the two peaks, **Nabalbong** (나발봉; 417m) and **Hwarinbong** (활인봉; 423m).

GAGA OVER GINSENG

It's stumpish and a woody colour, with wispy roots trailing from its ends. Use your imagination and you might see the shape of a body, complete with limbs, perhaps even a head-shaped tip with thinning 'hair'. No wonder the Chinese call it ginseng (literally, 'man root'). To the Koreans it's *insam* (인삼), and they have been cultivating it for over 1500 years. It's credited with myriad health benefits, from relieving pain and fatigue, to curing cancer and improving sexual stamina.

Most foreigners encounter ginseng in *samgyetang* (ginseng chicken soup), but it's an ingredient in many dishes and also ingested in tea, liquor, capsules or by the slice. The centre of the Korean ginseng business is **Geumsan** (금산; www.geumsan.go.kr), which despite its size (population 22,000) handles 80% of the ginseng trade. There are hundreds of stores, from mom-and-pop operations to wholesalers, and you'll find ginseng sold raw (*susam*), as an extract, in shampoo and soap, and in tea, candy, biscuits and chocolate. The street vendors make fresh *insam twigim* (인삼튀김; fried ginseng in batter; W1000), which you can wash down with *insam makgeolli* (인삼막걸리; rice wine made with ginseng; W1000).

If you're buying ginseng, the most prized variety is *hongsam* or red ginseng (홍삼), which is four to six years old and has been steamed and dried to concentrate its medicinal properties. More common is *baeksam* or white ginseng (백삼), a less processed four-year-old version. One *chae* (750g) of ginseng costs W10,000 to W50,000, depending on its quality and grade.

The best days to visit Geumsan are on market days every 2nd, 7th, 12th, 17th, 22nd and 27th days of the month. In September the town hosts a 10-day Insam Festival, with tours and activities to show how ginseng is grown, harvested, processed and served.

To get to Geumsan, take an intercity bus from Daejeon's Dongdaejeon bus terminal (W3600, one hour, every 10 minutes) or Seoul's express bus terminal (W10,700, 2¾ hours, every two hours). After you exit the Geumsan bus terminal, turn left and follow the canal for about 10 minutes. When you see SAE-Kumsan Hospital, turn right onto the road Bihoro. You'll pass the restaurant Matkkalbokjip (맛깔복집; meals W15,000 to W20,000) on your left; it serves ginseng-infused dishes such as *insam tangsuyuk* (인삼탕수육; fried beef in sauce) or *insam bokjjim* (인삼복찜; braised puffer fish). The market lies ahead, after you cross the wide road Insamno.

CHUNGCHEONGNAM-DO

THE GLORY OF BAEKJE

The dynasty ceased over 1300 years ago, but in its heyday in the 4th century, the Baekje kingdom controlled much of western Korea up to Pyongyang and, if you believe certain controversial records, coastal regions of northeastern China too. By the time it moved its capital to Chungnam, however, its influence was under siege. Its centre of power Hanseong (in the modern-day Seoul region) had fallen to Goguryeo from the north, and in AD 475 Baekje had to relocate its capital to Gongju (then known as Ungjin), where the mountains offered some protection.

The dynasty thrived anew, nurturing relations with Japan and China, and in AD 538 King Seong moved the capital farther south to Buyeo (then known as Sabi). Unfortunately his Shilla allies betrayed him, killing him in battle. Baekje fell into decline and was finally vanquished in AD 660 by a combined army from Shilla and China's Tang dynasty, though pockets of resistance lingered for some years.

In 1971 interest in Baekje got a much-needed shot in the arm when workers at an old tomb in Gongju stumbled across another one, hitherto undiscovered. Inside lay a wealth of funerary objects that had not seen the light of day in 1500 years: the remains of the king and queen's wooden coffins, golden diadem ornaments that would have been set upon their heads, gold jewellery and clothing accessories, the king's sword and much more – all contained in a space about 4m long, 3m wide and 3m high. A stone tablet confirmed that the tomb belonged to King Muryeong, the longest-ruling Baekje king at Gongju, and the royal treasures have taken pride of place in the town ever since.

If the idyllic, hassle-free setting is appealing, there are two surprisingly sharp motels nearby. **Cello Motel** (첼로 모텔; ☎ 841 7977; ⚹) and **Magok Motel** (마곡모텔; ☎ 841 0042; www. magokmotel.com; ⚹) are along the access road to the temple, with good rooms at W30,000 (add W10,000 on weekends and W20,000 during the summer). It's also possible to arrange a temple stay at Magok-sa.

The tourist village is small, with a few restaurants and shops. The restaurants serve typical country fare (W10,000 to W25,000): *sanchae bibimbap, pyogo jjigae jeongsik* (표고찌개정식; shiitake mushroom stew with side dishes) and *tokkitang* (토끼탕; spicy rabbit soup).

Magok-sa is 25km from Gongju. Buses (W1100, 45 minutes, hourly) run from Gongju's local bus terminal and the temple is a 20-minute walk from the tourist village.

BUYEO 부여
pop 24,000

It's smaller and more of a backwater than Gongju, yet **Buyeo** (www.buyeo.go.kr) has just as many historical Baekje sites and relics. King Seong, a statue of whom presides over the roundabout in the town centre, moved the capital here in AD 538, when it was known as Sabi. It lasted till AD 660, when the combined Shilla–Tang army destroyed it.

Today Buyeo is a compact, walkable town, saddled with fewer Korean chain stores than most. New buildings cannot be taller than five storeys and this is the kind of place where you'll stumble across children playing in the streets after school. A couple of hours drifting about town or atop Busosanseong, and you could detach yourself quite easily from the mania of modern Korea.

There is a **tourist information centre** (☎ 830 2523) with English-speaking staff beside the entrance to Busosanseong. Tourist information kiosks are at Buyeo National Museum and Jeongnimsaji.

Sights
BUSOSANSEONG 부소산성

This **mountain fortress** (adult/youth/child W2000/1100/1000; ⏱ 7am-7pm Mar-Oct, 8am-5pm Nov-Feb) covers the forested hill of Busosan (106m) and shielded the Baekje capital of Sabi within its walls. A number of pavilions, shrines and temples have been reconstructed in a park-like setting, with some like Banwollu Tower offering lovely views of the surrounding countryside. The fortress is best approached from the southern entrance off Wangungno.

One shrine, **Samchung-sa**, is dedicated to three loyal Baekje court officials, including General Gyebaek. Despite being outnumbered 10 to one, he led his army of 5000 in a last stand against the final Shilla and Chinese onslaught in AD 660. The Baekje army dauntlessly repulsed four enemy attacks but were defeated in the fifth – the *coup de grâce* for the kingdom.

In response, it is said, on the northern side of the fortress 3000 court ladies threw themselves off a cliff into the river Baengmagang, rather than submit to the conquering armies. The rock where they jumped is now called **Nakhwa-am**, 'falling flowers rock', in their honour; it also offers the best view of the area.

From Nakhwa-am there's a rocky and somewhat steep path down to the tiny temple at the bottom of the cliff, **Goran-sa**. Behind it is a spring that provided the favourite drinking water of Baekje kings. Slaves collecting the water had to present it along with a leaf from a nearby plant that only grows near here, to show that the water came from this spring.

At Goran-sa, **ferries** (adult/child one way W3500/2200, return W5500/2800, ☉ sunrise-sunset) head to **Gudurae sculpture park** (구두래공원). The 1.5km trip takes 10 minutes. From Gudurae it's a 15-minute walk to the town centre.

BUYEO NATIONAL MUSEUM
부여국립박물관

This **museum** (☎ 833 8562; http://buyeo.museum.go.kr; admission free; ☉ 9am-6pm Tue-Sun) houses one of the best collections of Baekje artefacts. It has extensive English captions, making it a good place to get a primer on pre-Baekje and Baekje culture.

The highlight of the collection is a glittering Baekje-era incense burner. Weighing 12kg, the burner and its pedestal are covered with

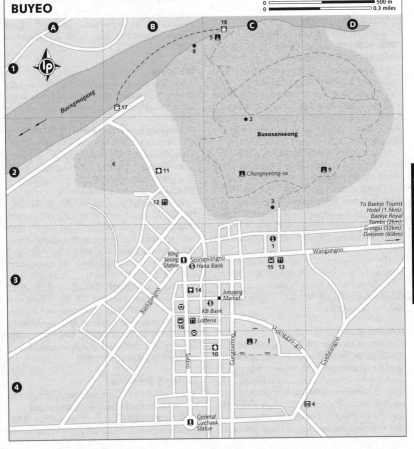

incredibly intricate and well-preserved metal-work, crested with the legendary *bonghwang* bird. There's also an eclectic outdoor display of artefacts from temples and archaeological sites.

BAEKJE ROYAL TOMBS 백제왕릉

Dating from AD 538 to 660, these seven royal **tombs** (adult/youth/child W1000/600/400; 🕑 8am-6pm Mar-Oct, 8am-5pm Nov-Feb) are less impressive than those in Gongju (p325), but you can peer into Tomb No 1, where paintings on the walls and ceiling have been restored. This is the only tomb here with a painted interior and it depicts the four celestial creatures that guard the compass points (dragon, tiger, tortoise and phoenix).

Most of these tombs had been robbed before they were properly surveyed, so there aren't many artefacts in the site **museum**. It does have a small-scale model of the oldest tomb, believed to be that of King Seong (who installed the Baekje capital at Buyeo). Outside is the now-empty temple site, where the famous Baekje incense burner was unearthed in 1993.

The tombs are on a hillside 3km east of Buyeo. Take a bus (W1000, five minutes, every 30 minutes) from Wangungno, opposite Busosanseong. It heads to Nonsan (논산) and has no number.

JEONGNIMSAJI 정림사지

This **temple complex** (☎ 830 2532; adult/youth/child W1500/900/700; 🕑 9am-7pm Mar-Oct, 10am-5pm Nov-Feb, closed Mon) comprises both ancient relics and a sleek modern museum about Buddhism. The latter is mostly in Korean, but outside there are informative signs in English about the relics: a five-storey Baekje-era stone pagoda that survived the sacking of the town in AD

660, and a lumpy-looking Goryeo-era Buddha statue, so damaged by fire and worn by age that it's hardly recognisable.

At the time of research the Buddha statue was housed in an austere building with bare interiors. However, construction was getting under way for an elaborate temple complex with a two-storey hall, to be completed in 2012.

Sleeping

There are plenty of motels clustered around the bus terminal in the centre of town. Many look run-down, but aren't as seedy as they appear.

Samjeong Buyeo Youth Hostel (삼정부여유스호스텔; ☎ 835 3791; dm/f W16,000/44,000; 🅥 🖥️) This airy hostel has better rooms than most of its ilk. Dorm rooms have two double bunks and good bathrooms. Family rooms are of motel standard and have twin beds.

Arirang Motel (아리랑 모텔; ☎ 832 5656; r W40,000; 🅥 🖥️) It looks as generic as its neighbours, but this motel has sleek, large rooms with modern decor and auto-locking doors. It's run by a cheerful *ajumma* (middle-aged woman) and staff will clean the room every day if you stay for more than one night.

Baekje Tourist Hotel (백제 관광 호텔; ☎ 835 0870; www.bchotel.co.kr; r W68,000; 🅥) The nicest hotel in Buyeo is also the most out-of-the-way, right beside Busosan and overlooking the river. Despite the dated look, the rooms are very large and comfortable. Breakfast costs an extra W8000 to W11,000.

Eating & Drinking

The road between Gudurae sculpture park and the town centre is lined with restaurants.

House of Baekje (백제의 집; meals W6000-18,000) This busy restaurant serves generous banquet-style meals. The house specialties are *seodong mabap* (서동마밥; rice cooked in a stone pot with *bulgogi*) and *ori mabap* (오리마밥; the same dish with duck); hungry diners can order the *jeongsik* version of these dishes (ie with an abundant spread of side dishes).

Gudurae Dolssambap (meals W7000-17,000) This quirky, cosy establishment is decorated with classic movie posters (in Korean) for *Ben Hur* and *Spartacus*. The menu here features *dol-sotbap* and *ssambap,* or get the best of both worlds with *dolssambap* (hotpot rice and let-tuce wraps), served with succulent fried pork. English menus are available.

Bubble Castle (Sabiro; ☻ 4pm-2am) Popular with the locals, this brightly lit bar has comfy booths, a K-pop soundtrack and small TVs showing the latest sports events.

Getting There & Away
Many intercity buses depart from the Buyeo bus terminal:

Destination	Price (W)	Duration	Frequency
Boryeong	4500	1hr	hrly
Daejeon	6100	1hr	every 20min
Gongju	3400	45min	every 30min
Seoul	12,800	2¾hr	every 30min

BORYEONG 보령
pop 108,000

Boryeong is the gateway to Daecheon Beach (10km away) and Daecheon Harbour (a fur-ther 2km), from which ferries sail to a dozen rural islands. The buses that connect Boryeong bus terminal and train station with Daecheon Beach continue to the harbour.

The **tourist information centre** (☎ 932 2023; www.boryeong.chungnam.kr) is inside Daecheon train station (despite the name it's in Boryeong, not Daecheon Beach). Interpretation services for **English** (☎ 011-438 3865), **Chinese** (☎ 010-6545 4848) and **Japanese** (☎ 016-477 0930) are available.

Getting There & Away
BUS
Departures from Boryeong include the following:

Destination	Price (W)	Duration	Frequency
Buyeo	4500	1hr	hrly
Daejeon	10,500	2½hr	hrly
Jeonju	8400	2½hr	3 daily
Seoul	9900	2½hr	hrly

TRAIN
Saemaul (W16,900, 2¾ hours, seven daily) and *Mugunghwa* (W11,400, 2¾ hours, nine daily) trains run between Daecheon station and Yongsan station in Seoul.

DAECHEON BEACH 대천해수욕장
The best beach on the west coast, this strip of almost golden-hued sand runs 3.5km long and is about 100m wide during low tide. The main hub of activity is at its southern end, near the **Civil Tower Plaza** (시민탑 광장), but in the summer the entire stretch gets over-run with beachgoers, especially during the increasingly bacchanalian Boryeong Mud Festival (see the boxed text, p332).

Though it's well-supplied with motels, res-taurants, bars, cafes and *noraebang* (karaoke rooms), Daecheon Beach is less a proper town than a resort outpost, surrounded by rice pad-dies and the sea. Developed only in the 1990s, it has all the aesthetic finesse of a tawdry Las Vegas – think neon nightscapes and plastic palm trees, with more hotels and amenities in the works. If it gets too touristy, head to the harbour **Daecheonhang** (대천항), which has more rustic seafood restaurants.

There are no banks in Daecheon Beach. The **tourist information centre** (☎ 931 4022; ☻ 8am-8pm) is in the Boryeong Mud Skincare Center. For interpretation services, call the numbers given for Boryeong (left).

Activities
Boryeong Mud Skincare Center (보령 머드체험관; ☎ 931 4022; adult/child W5000/3000; ☻ 8.30am-6pm) is a modern facility with a sauna, mud bath and aroma spa. Massages and mud packs cost extra, and you can buy mud soaps, shampoos and other cosmetics from the shop. All the mud products are made from local mud, said to be full of health-giving minerals. The Center is on the beach-front near the Civil Tower Plaza; if you're approaching from Boryeong, it's to the left of the access road.

In the summer there's lots to do at the beach: waterskiing, canoeing, windsurfing, horse-and-carriage rides, and speedboat, ba-nana boat and jet-ski rides.

The **waterpark** (adult/child W30,000/20,000; ☻ 10am-5pm) at Legrand Fun Beach Hotel (p332) has numerous rides, including the only flowrider in Korea, and a full sauna. Admission costs W10,000 to W20,000 more in summer.

MUD, GLORIOUS MUD

Every July, Daecheon Beach is the principal venue for the nine-day **Boryeong Mud Festival** (www.mudfestival.or.kr), which since its debut in 1997 has grown to attract over 1.5 million attendees. What began as a way of promoting the health benefits of the mud, which is rich in germanium and other minerals, has since developed a reputation for the unabashed, alcohol-fuelled frolics of expats, US GIs and international travellers, who make up about half the festival crowd.

After being baptised in a vat of the oozing grey stuff, participants can enter the 'mud prison' and get doused with buckets of warmed mud. There's a mud super-slide, a mud rain tunnel and a very muddy game of soccer played on the mudflats. Every evening there's a concert or rave on the beach and the festival is book-ended by parades and fireworks.

Many English-speaking volunteers are on hand and there are free lockers, a campsite and basic clean-up facilities, making this one of the most foreigner-friendly events held in Korea. Accommodation gets booked up months in advance, even in Boryeong, so many come for the day or on tours run by outfits such as **Adventure Korea** (www.adventurekorea.com) or **Work n Play** (www.worknplay.co.kr).

Sleeping

There are plenty of large, modern motels and a handful of *minbak* (private homes with rooms for rent) which charge about the same rates. The older establishments are near Civil Tower Plaza, while Fountain Plaza (분수광장) to the north has newer outfits. Prices double on weekends and easily triple in summer.

Motel Coconuts (모텔코코넛츠; ☎ 934 6595; r W30,000; 🈁) Decorated in bright solid colours and with funky bed linen prints, this motel has a contemporary zing lacking in most of its competitors. Rooms on the upper level might have a snatch of sea view. It's beside the Lotteria to the left of the access road from Boryeong, with green plastic coconut trees out front.

Singung Motel (신궁 모텔; ☎ 931 0900; r W40,000; 🈁 🖥) No sea views here, but this motel is quiet yet close to the main strip. Rooms are small, clean and comfortable. It's to the right of the access road, behind Opera Motel.

Legrand Fun Beach Hotel (레그랜드 펀비치; ☎ 939 9000; www.fun-beach.com; r W70,000; ste W161,000; 🈁 🖥 💦) The swankiest option in Daecheon Beach has plush, carpeted rooms with contemporary decor and cables for internet access. Its waterpark (p331) has numerous rides and a full sauna.

Eating

You'll be hard-pressed to find a meal that doesn't involve seafood. Restaurants lining the beachfront have aquariums of fish, eels, crabs and shellfish outside, and you can get a platter of *modeumhoe* (모둠회; assorted raw fish) or *jogae modeumgui* (조개 모듬구

이; mixed shellfish), to be barbecued at your table, for W30,000 to W40,000. Try the local specialty *kkotgejjim* (꽃게찜; steamed blue crab), or round off your meal with some spicy *haemultang* (assorted seafood soup). Go early for dinner and grab a seat on the upper floor to enjoy the sea view.

Getting There & Away

Buses (W1100, every 30 minutes) run from Boryeong terminal and Daecheon train station in Boryeong, to Daecheon Beach and on to Daecheonhang. All the places mentioned above are at the Civil Tower Plaza; get off at the first stop in Daecheon Beach, opposite Legrand Fun Beach Hotel.

SAPSI-DO 삽시도

If you like undeveloped beaches, farmhouse villages and roads with more pedestrians and cyclists than four-wheeled vehicles, skip out to this small island, just 13km from Daecheonhang. There isn't much to do here except hit the beach or wander the main village near Sulttung marina (술뚱선착장). You'll see locals mending fishing nets, collecting shellfish at low tide or working in the rice paddies – and that's about it.

The pace speeds up in summer, with three beaches and about 50 *minbak* drawing visitors from the mainland. The nearest beach to Sulttung is **Geomeolneomeo** (거멀너머 해수욕장), a 15-minute walk past the primary school. Curving between two rocky headlands, this flat, wide beach is backed by sand dunes and fir trees. Orange-roofed beachside cottages were coming up at the time of research.

Except at high tide, you can clamber over the rocks on the left to the smaller **Jinneomeo beach** (진너머 해수욕장).

Along the southern coast is the sweeping **Bamseom beach** (밤섬 해수욕장), the largest of the three. Follow the road to the left of the *minbak* village at Bamseom marina (밤섬 선착장). All the beaches have no restrooms or showers.

There are plenty of *minbak* but prices spike in summer. A good option is the centrally located **Haedotneun** (해돋는민박; ☎ 935 1617; r W30,000), a cheery red-brick *minbak* with rooms that are of motel standard, equipped with a fridge and kitchenette.

Most visitors bring a picnic or eat at their *minbak*. **Haedotneun** (meals W5000-25,000) has a homely dining area in the front room and the menu depends on the catch of the day. On the Sulttung waterfront, **Badahoe Sikdang** (바다회 식당; ☎ 936 1133; meals W5000-7000) serves *naengmyeon* and a range of spicy soups such as *yuk-gaejang* (with beef and vegetables), *jogaetang* (with clams) and *chueotang* (with loach).

Getting There & Around

Ferries (☎ 934 8896; one way adult/child W9550/4800) run from Daecheon Ferry Terminal to Sapsi-do at 7.30am, 1pm and 4pm. The trip takes 40 minutes, longer if the ferry is rerouted to other islands first. At low tide the ferry goes to Bamseom marina in the south; at high tide it goes to Sulttung marina in the north. The island has no public transport (and indeed, hardly any cars), but locals sometimes offer visitors a lift. It's a 40-minute walk from one end of the island to the other.

The last ferry returns directly to Daecheon at 5.30pm (check which marina it leaves from). If you take an earlier one at 8.10am or 1.45pm, the return trip takes 1½ to two hours as the ferry stops at other islands – Janggo-do, Godae-do and Anmyeon-do (below) – en route.

The Daecheon Ferry Terminal (대천 연 안 여객선 터미널) is at Daecheon Harbour. Buses for Daecheon Beach all continue to the harbour. Other ferries from Daecheon (adult W4500 to W15,700, child W2300 to W7900) run to even more remote islands – Hoja-do, Wonsan-do, Ho-do, Nok-do and Oeyeon-do – where few foreigners have ventured.

TAEAN HAEAN NATIONAL PARK
태안해안국립공원

This beautiful **marine park** (☎ 672 9737; http://taean.knps.or.kr/Taeanhaean_eng; admission free; ☻ sunrise-sunset) covers 327 sq km of land and sea, with 130 islands and islets, and over 30 beaches. It was badly hit by South Korea's worst-ever oil spill in December 2007, but the coast has been cleaned up and fishing and tourism have resumed with aplomb.

The largest island is **Anmyeon-do** (안면도; www.anmyondo.com) and of its many beaches, one of the best is **Kkotji Beach** (꽃지해수욕장), a gentle 3.2km-long stretch that's a glorious 300m wide at low tide. You can get there by bus (W1000, 15 minutes, hourly) from the bus terminal in the island's main town **Anmyeon** (안면).

You can get to Anmyeon by bus from Seoul (W10,000, 2¾ hours, hourly), Daejeon (W11,600, three daily) and Taean (W2500, every 30 minutes). But the most picturesque journey is to take a ferry from Daecheon Ferry Terminal (W7350, six daily) or Sapsi-do (W76000, three

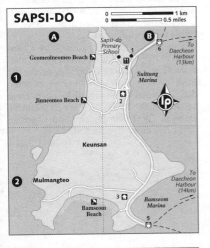

SAPSI-DO

0 —————— 1 km
0 —————— 0.5 miles

HE CAME, HE SAW, HE PLANTED

Cheollipo Arboretum outside Taean has gained international recognition as an outstanding botanical institution, yet it was founded and built by a man without formal training in that field. American Carl Ferris Miller was a banker in Seoul when he bought his first plot of farmland in Cheollipo in the 1970s, intending it as a weekend retreat. He began planting trees and studying botany on his own – then gradually acquired more land and more plant specimens. By the time he died in 2002 at the age of 81, Cheollipo Arboretum had become an exquisite showcase of over 7000 botanical species from over 60 countries, laid out with diligent care across 64 hectares of lush coastal property.

Miller had settled in South Korea after the Korean War and became a naturalised Korean citizen in 1979, renaming himself Min Byung Gal. He had a corresponding interest in Korea's native plants and spent time studying them and sharing information with academics and horticulturists. He also relocated several Korean *hanok* (traditional houses) to the arboretum in order to preserve them. By many accounts he was almost completely Koreanised, and after his death, he was buried, fittingly, in his beloved gardens.

---

daily) bound for Yeongmukhang (영묵항). The journey takes 45 minutes to two hours depending on the ferry route. Once you disembark at Yeongmukhang, turn right and then fork left for the two-minute uphill walk to the bus stop. The bus for Anmyeon (W1700, one hour, hourly) takes a rugged, circuitous route along backcountry roads between rice paddies and rustic farmhouses.

Closer to the town of **Taean** (태안; www.taean.go.kr) is **Mallipo Beach** (만리포), not quite as stunning as Kkotji but still an attractive getaway, fringed by pine trees. Development is ramping up around the beachfront restaurants, *minbak* and motels, so it's unlikely to remain peaceful for long. Avid gardeners or photographers may want to head another 2.5km up the road to the privately owned **Cheollipo Arboretum** (천리포수목원; ☎ 672 9310; www.chollipo.org; admission weekdays/weekend W7000/8000; ◷ 9am-4.30pm, closed Nov-Mar), an impressive garden that grew out of an American-turned-Korean-citizen's dedication to plants (see the boxed text, above).

You can get to Mallipo Beach by a local bus (W1700, 30 minutes, hourly) from platform 11 at Taean's bus terminal, or directly from from Seoul (W9600, three hours, seven daily). Taean is well served by buses from Seoul (W8200, 2¼ hours, every 20 minutes), Daejeon (W11,000, hourly) and Cheonan (W11,100, every 10 minutes).

Chungcheongbuk-do
충청북도

The only land-locked province in the South, Chungbuk (as it's known informally) is largely mountainous and agricultural, with a few scenic man-made lakes for reprieve. The province is a sleepy sort of place and its major cities are not particularly compelling, though bibliophiles may be inclined to make a pilgrimage to Cheongju, where in 1377 Buddhist monks printed the world's oldest extant book with moveable metal type.

The province's charms can better be appreciated in its smaller towns and three national parks, which are also home to an assortment of intriguing Buddhist sites. In Songnisan National Park lies a sprawling ancient temple Beopju-sa, with statues both old (a Shilla-era bodhisattva) and new (a tall gold-plated Buddha looming over the compound). Woraksan National Park has mysterious Goryeo-era relics, their origins shrouded in legend. Hot-spring town Suanbo is also close by.

The darling of the region is Danyang, a small and friendly resort town snuggled amid mountains beside a placid river. There's plenty to see and do here: climb the azalea-covered peaks of Sobaeksan, descend into the otherworldly caverns of Gosu Donggul, or simply savour the views along the river and at nearby Chungju Lake. Not far away is Guin-sa, a Buddhist temple ensconced in a tight valley, as imposing as the mountain slopes on either side of it. If you have a few days to while away, this is the place to do it.

HIGHLIGHTS

- Wake up to glorious mountain views in **Danyang** (p344) and hike up nearby **Sobaeksan** (p346)

- Meditate on ancient Buddhist carvings and the evocative ruins of Mireuksaji at **Woraksan National Park** (p343)

- Soothe your stresses at an *oncheon* (hot-spring spa) in **Suanbo** (p342), then feast on a smorgasbord of pheasant dishes

- Admire the gold-plated Buddha at Beopju-sa in **Songnisan National Park** (p340), then overnight at a charming *yeogwan* (motel) beside a burbling river

| ■ TELEPHONE CODE: 043 | ■ POPULATION: 1.5 MILLION | ■ AREA: 7432 SQ KM |

CHUNGCHEONGBUK-DO

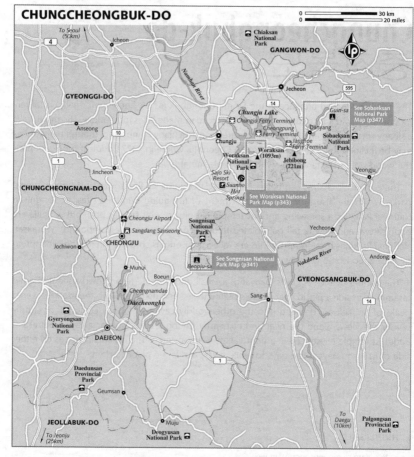

CHUNGCHEONGBUK-DO

History
This province was the southern boundary of the Goguryeo kingdom and the hot springs at Suanbo have supplied *oncheon* (spas) for a thousand years. More recently, Chungcheongbuk-do has become known as the place where monks printed books before Gutenberg did, and as the birthplace and childhood home of UN Secretary-General Ban Ki-Moon.

National Parks
The largest national park in the province is **Sobaeksan National Park** (p346), famous for the royal azaleas that blossom in May, as well as the unusual temple of Guin-sa. **Songnisan National Park** (p340) has a temple dating back

over 1500 years, as well as an attractive riverside *yeogwan* (motel with small en suite). **Woraksan National Park** (p343) has the ruins of ancient temples and other religious sites, and some fairly challenging climbs.

Getting There & Around
The province is served by rail, but the most convenient way to get there and around is by bus. The lake cruise across Chungjuho is a pleasant way to get to the eastern end of the province.

CHEONGJU 청주
pop 644,000
Like most provincial capitals, **Cheongju** (http://english.cjcity.net) – not to be confused with nearby

Chungju – is not terribly captivating. Its primary claim to fame is as the place where the world's oldest book was printed using moveable metal type.

As a modern city it's somewhat redeemed by a youthful vibe, thanks to its universities, but if not for its proximity to Songnisan National Park and presidential villa Cheongnamdae, there'd be little reason to stop here. Every September it hosts a **Jikji Festival** (www.jikjifestival. com), with a demonstration of ancient printing techniques, exhibitions of old printed books, and traditional music and drama performances.

The **tourist information centre** (☎ 233 8431; ✤ 8.30am-6pm) is outside the intercity bus terminal in a two-storey blue-green building. There's free internet access and tourist information for the entire province. Volunteer guides, organised along the same lines as Goodwill Guides (p395), can be arranged through the city website (http://english.cjcity. net/community/03-Volunteering.asp).

Sights

EARLY PRINTING MUSEUM 고인쇄박물관
This small **museum** (☎ 269 0556; adult/youth/child W800/600/400; ✤ 9am-6pm Tue-Sun) tells you everything about the Jikji, the oldest book in the world printed with moveable metal type (see the boxed text, p340). Unfortunately the book is not here but in the National Library of France. The museum stands beside the site of Heungdeok-sa, where the Jikji was printed. The temple's main hall and pagoda were being rebuilt at the time of research.

The museum has extensive information in English and exhibits many early books of Korea, including handwritten sutras and books printed using woodblocks. Look out for Korea's oldest printed document, the Dharani Sutra, dating back to at least AD 751.

To get there, catch bus 831 or 831-1 (W1100, 15 minutes) from outside the express bus terminal. Get off at the bus stop beside the pedestrian bridge with green and yellow arches. The museum is about 150m ahead.

SANGDANG SANSEONG 상당 산성
This large **fortress** (admission free) is 4km northeast of Cheongju, on the slopes of the mountain Uamsan. Originally built in the 1590s and renovated in the 18th century, the walls stretch 4.2km around wooded hillsides, offering great views of farms, mountains and the city.

A hike around the top of the wall takes about 1½ hours. The route is completely exposed and can be steep-going. The easier direction is counter-clockwise. From where the bus drops you, walk back along the road and look on the left for a paved path that ascends to the top of the wall. Along the walk, there are hardly any signs or resting places, and no maps, food stalls, vending machines or toilets – so bring your own water and a good hat. There are restaurants (below) and shops near the bus stop.

Bus 862 (W1000, 30 minutes, hourly) leaves from the Cheongju Stadium bus stop and goes up to the fortress. Buses 863 and 864 go up Uamsan, but drop you 1km from the fortress. To get to the stadium, hop on any bus heading downtown to Sajingno (사직 로) from outside the intercity bus terminal. The stadium bus stop is just after a five-storey golden pavilion.

Sleeping

There are numerous love motels around the bus terminals. **Plaza Motel** (프라자모텔; ☎ 234 1400; r without/with computer W30,000/35,000; ✗ 💻) is run by a genial older couple who will offer to clean your room *(cheong so)* every day and ask to keep the room key when you go out. The newer **Motel Olive** (올리브 모텔; ☎ 231 0207; r without/with computer W35,000/40,000; ✗ 💻) has faux castle exteriors *and* interiors; the spacious rooms have large beds and ultramodern bathrooms. **Baekje Tourist Hotel** (백제관광호텔; ☎ 236 7979; r/tw W90,000/130,000; ✗ 💻) has snazzy decor, though it's sometimes thwarted by gloriously iridescent fabrics; prices include breakfast.

Eating & Drinking

You can scrounge up cheap eats in the downtown shopping area around Seongan-gil or with the students near Chungbuk National University (Chungdae jungmun; 충대 중 문). To get to the latter, take any bus headed downtown from outside the intercity bus terminal and get off at the stop for Sachang Intersection, which is after the Cheongju High School stop.

Golden Pine (황금소나무; ☎ 231 0588; meals W4000-8000) Meat-lovers can check out the range of *galbi* (beef ribs), *samgyeopsal* (streaky pork belly) and *yangnyeom bulgogi* (양념불고기; spicy marinated beef) here. For something

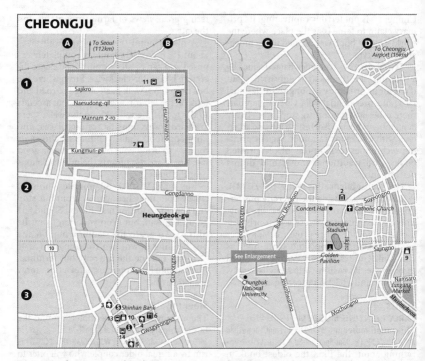

easier on the arteries, there's *naengmyeon* (buckwheat noodles in cold broth), *galbitang* (beef-rib soup) and *ttukbaegi bulgogi* (뚝배 기불고기; beef simmered in an earthenware dish).

Sangdangjip (상당집; meals W5000-13,000) Opposite the bus stop at Sangdang Sanseong, this restaurant makes its own tofu in a giant cauldron beside the entrance. A light starter is *dubujjim* (두부찜; steamed tofu); for a fuller meal, try the *jeongol* (hotpot) or *duruchigi* (두루치기; spicy stew). Although the chief ingredient is tofu, dishes may include meat. The last bus (p337) to town leaves at 9.50pm.

Pearl Jam (펄잼; 6pm-late) A stalwart on the local bar scene, this comfortable rock-music den often has live music on weekends. There's Guinness on tap, lots of imported beer, and bar bites like burgers and Tex-Mex food (W8000 to W12,000). The friendly owner speaks good English.

Shopping

The express bus terminal is right beside Lotte Mart and Dream Plus; the latter has a 24-hour

jjimjibang, a sad-looking food court, cinemas and shops.

Downtown, the pedestrianised streets around Seongan-gil are chock-a-block with shops, restaurants and cafes, with **Home Plus** (10am-10pm) and **Lotte Young Plaza** (10.30am-8pm) a stone's throw away. From outside the intercity bus terminal, many buses run to Sajingno (사직 로) and Daeseongno (대성로).

Getting There & Away

AIR

Cheongju Airport (210 6110) has flights to Jeju-do and China. It's 18km from the city. Take bus 747 from outside the intercity bus terminal (W1000, one hour). A taxi costs W20,000.

BUS

Departures from the express bus terminal include the following:

Destination	Price (W)	Duration	Frequency
Busan	15,800	3½hr	9 daily
Daegu	10,300	2½hr	hrly
Dong-Seoul	6000	1¾hr	every 30min
Seoul	6000	1¾hr	every 10min

Departures from the intercity terminal include the following:

Destination	Price (W)	Duration	Frequency
Chuncheon	15,400	3½hr	hrly
Chungju	7700	1½hr	every 20min
Daejeon	3400	50min	every 10min
Danyang	13,800	3½hr	6 daily
Gyeongju	15,900	3¼hr	9 daily

TRAIN

Cheongju station (청주역; ☎ 232 7788) connects primarily with Daejeon (W2900, 40 minutes, eight daily), while Jochiwon station (조치원역) connects to Seoul (W7700, 1½ hours, every 30 minutes). From the intercity bus terminal, take bus 502 or 511 to Cheongju station, or 616, 617 or 911 to Jochiwon.

AROUND CHEONGJU
Cheongnamdae 청남대

Once the holiday home of South Korean presidents, this **villa** (☎ 220 5677; http://chnam.cb21.net/; adult/youth/child W5000/4000/3000; ⏰ 9am-6pm Tue-Sun) is no Camp David, but it makes a beautiful lakeside park, with 185 hectares of well-manicured grounds and 2.3km of paths along the lakefront and across the gently rolling hills. You can linger in the Chogajeong Pavilion where President Kim Dae-jung liked to sit and think, or look over the golf course that President Roh Tae-woo favoured but President Kim Young-sam disapproved of (too many associations with corruption).

Cheongnamdae was built in 1983 by President Chun Doo-hwan (he whose takeover of power sparked the Gwangju Uprising in 1980). Twenty years later, the much-loved President Roh Moo-Hyun opened it to the public. While Korean visitors are simply curious about where their presidents used to vacation, for foreign visitors it's probably the parkland that's more attractive than the surprisingly modest villa. There's a hagiographic exhibition (mostly Korean) on all the presidents in the main hall.

Take local bus 311 (W1450, 50 minutes, 15km, hourly) from outside Cheongju's intercity bus terminal to Munui. Walk out

---

THE PRINTED WORD, MADE BY MONKS

While the Gutenberg Bible needs no introduction, the Jikji languished for many years in obscurity, even though it is the oldest book in the world printed with moveable metal type. It was printed in 1377 (78 years before the Gutenberg) at the temple of Heungdeok-sa in modern-day Cheongju. In the mid-19th century it was acquired by a French official in Korea, who took it to France. After it was put on display at the 1900 World's Fair in Paris, it disappeared without fanfare from the public eye, and it was only in 1972 that Korean historian Park Byeng-Sen rediscovered it at the National Library of France.

The Jikji itself is a small book: 38 sheets of thin mulberry paper, each one measuring just 24.6cm x 17cm. Its full title is *Baegun hwasang chorok buljo jikji simche yojeol* – that is, an anthology of the monk Baegun Gyeonghan's teachings on Seon Buddhism (more commonly known in the West as Zen Buddhism). It's the second and only extant volume of a two-volume collection of these teachings, delivered at Heungdeok-sa in the 1370s. The last page of the book indicates that it was printed by two of Baegun's disciples, Seokchan and Daldam, with funding from a nun named Myodeok.

The Jikji has been exhibited at international book fairs since 1972 and South Korea lobbied till it was admitted to Unesco's Memory of the World Register in 2001. However, the book still resides within the National Library of France, along with other cultural relics from Korea's early dynasties. Understandably South Korea would like to see the book returned, but there's no indication if that's likely to happen.

---

of Munui's small bus depot and turn left. In a couple of minutes you'll reach the parking lot and ticket office for the **shuttle bus** (return W2400, 15 minutes, every 30 minutes) to Cheongnamdae, which operates 9am to 4.30pm February to November, 9am to 3.30pm December and January.

SONGNISAN NATIONAL PARK
속리산국립공원

With forested mountains and rocky granite outcrops, this **park** (☎ 542 5267; http://songni.knps. or.kr/eng; adult/youth/child W3000/1400/1000; ☻ 5am-8pm) covers one of central Korea's finest scenic areas. Though it often goes by the touristy catchword Chungbuk Alps, its name has a more solemn meaning – 'Remote from the Ordinary World Mountain', referring to the temple **Beopju-sa**, which dates back to AD 553. The temple lies about 1km from the park entrance and has a 33m-high gold-plated Maitreya Buddha statue, a unique five-storey wooden pagoda, a weathern-worn Shilla-era bodhisattva statue and an enormous iron cauldron, once used for cooking for up to 3000 monks.

Beyond the temple, hiking trails run up to a series of 1000m-high peaks. A popular hike is the relatively easy 6km climb up **Munjangdae** (1033m). Back in 1464 King Sejo was carried up in a palanquin; using your own feet, it's three hours up and two hours down. You can also return via Sinseondae, further south via Birobong or, for the truly gung-ho, push on to the highest peak Cheonhwangbong (1058m).

There is a **tourist information centre** (☎ 542 5267) diagonally across the road from the bus terminal.

Sleeping & Eating

Two camping grounds (W2000) are open in July and August. There are plenty of motels in the lanes to the left of the main road (looking towards the park entrance).

Eorae Motel (어래모텔; ☎ 5433882; r W30,000; ☒) This is the closest budget option to the park entrance. Rooms are clean and adequate.

ourpick **Birosanjang** (비로산장; ☎ 011-456 4782; r W40,000; weekends W50,000, summer W60,000) If only every national park had this – a homely, delightful *yeogwan* right beside a gurgling river in the middle of the park. Nothing fancy here, just nine *ondol* (heated-floor) rooms (reservations recommended) and meals such as *bibimbap* (rice with vegetables, meat and egg; W7000) and *sanchae jeongsik* (banquet of mountain vegetables; W10,000) whipped up by the friendly owner, who speaks a little English. It's on the trail between Beopju-sa and Sinseondae.

Lake Hills Hotel Songnisan (레이크힐스호텔 속리산; ☎ 542 5281; www.lakehills.co.kr; W150,000; ☒) The nicest digs, right by the park entrance.

Rates may be discounted up to 40% during low season.

Lining the main road to the park entrance are many restaurants, offering the usual tourist-village fare: *sanchae jeongsik* (산채 정식), *beoseot jeongsik* (버섯 정식; mushroom set menu) and *sanchae bibimbap* (*bibimbap* with mountain vegetables).

Getting There & Away

Buses leave Cheongju's intercity bus terminal (W7500, 1¾ hours, every 40 minutes) for Songnisan National Park. There are also direct buses to the park from Dong-Seoul (W15,100, 3¾ hours), Seoul Gangnam (W14,500, 3½ hours) and Daejeon (W6900, 1¾ hours).

CHUNGJU 충주
pop 209,000

Chungju (www.cj100.net/english) might be the town where UN Secretary-General Ban Ki-Moon grew up, but there are really only three reasons to come to here: to get the bus to the Chungju Lake ferries or Woraksan National Park, to attend the World Martial Arts Festival (see the boxed text, p342), or because you really,

really like apples (there's an Apple Festival every October).

A **tourist information centre** (☎ 850 7329) is located inside the bus terminal.

Sleeping & Eating

Unlike most towns, there are no motels around the bus terminal. There's a clump of love motels opposite the train station, in an area otherwise populated by car workshops. From the bus terminal (turn right as you exit) it's a 15-minute walk or five-minute taxi ride (W2200) across a treeless wasteland. **Lexy Hotel** (렉시; ☎ 847 8874; r W30,000-40,000; ✉ ☐) has a dull grey exterior with purple and yellow streaks, but inside everything's new and spiffy; prices increase by W20,000 to W30,000 on weekends. Across the road is the castle-inspired **Titanic Motel** (타이타닉모텔; ☎ 842 5858; r without/with computer W30,000/35,000; ✉ ☐), which has decent rooms with all the usual love-motel trimmings.

Good eats aren't easy to scare up in Chungju, but there are some good options along the road to the left as you exit from the bus terminal. **Gamjatang** (감자탕; meals W5000-8000) serves a

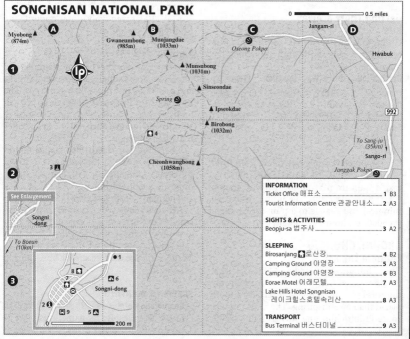

SONGNISAN NATIONAL PARK

0 ——————— 0.5 miles

MARTIAL ARTS FIESTA

Every September/October, Chungju hosts a week-long **World Martial Arts Festival** (☎ 850 6740; www.martialarts.or.kr), alongside a cultural festival with food stalls, music and dance. Over 2000 martial arts exponents from 30 countries come to demonstrate their amazing and varied skills. It's a chance to see both traditional Korean martial arts, such as *hapkido* and *takkyeon*, and a slew of snappy moves such as Chinese *wushu*, Malaysian *silat*, Brazilian *capoeira*, Indian *kalan* and Uzbekistan *kurash*. See also p83.

very hearty version of its namesake dish (a rich, spicy peasant soup with meaty bones and potatoes), while **Bohae Galbi** (보해갈비; ☎ 848 2595; meals W5000-10,000) specialises in barbecue and also has *bulgogi* (barbecued beef slices, served with rice) and *seolleongtang* (beef and rice soup). In the skeevy motel area on the road to the train station is **Pongaksan** (폰각산; meals W5000-15,000; ⏰ 24hr), a pleasant oasis that serves just about everything.

Getting There & Away
BUS

Chungju's bus terminal adjoins a Lotte Mart. Buses running from here include the following:

Destination	Price (W)	Duration	Frequency
Cheongju	7700	1½hr	every 20min
Daejeon	9000	2¼hr	hrly
Danyang	7500	1½hr	11 daily
Seoul	6200	2hr	every 15min

TRAIN

Chungju receives only one direct train from Seoul (W12,500, 2¾ hours). Alternatively, take a train from Seoul to Jochiwon station (조치원역; W7700, 1½ hours, every 30 minutes) and change to a train for Chungju (W5000, 1¼ hours, eight daily).

AROUND CHUNGJU
Chungju Lake 충주호

The Chungju Lake **cruise** (☎ 851 5771; www.chungjuho.com) is a scenic way to make your way towards Danyang, though the scenery is more placid than awe-inspiring. The most popular route (adult/child one way W15,000/7500,

return W22,000/15,000; fast boat 1½ hours, ferry 2¼ hours) is from Chungju Dam to Cheongpung, then Janghoe (and in reverse); the rocky cliffs are most dramatic between the latter stops. Another cruise is from Chungju Dam to Worak and back (adult/child W10,000/5000, return only, one hour). The cruises get very busy on weekends and there's a pre-recorded sightseeing commentary (Korean only), so it may not be the most relaxing experience.

Near the Janghoe ferry terminal is an entrance to **Woraksan National Park** (admission free; ⏰ sunrise-sunset). A 2.5km hike up Jebibong (721m) takes three hours return. To find the trail, exit the ferry terminal and turn right, following the road for 100m. On your left, across the road, you'll see the ranger hut at the trail entrance.

From Janghoe you can continue to Danyang by bus (p346). The ferry used to run to Danyang but doesn't anymore because of low water levels.

The ferry schedule is subject to weather conditions and passenger volume, so enquire at the tourist information centre in **Chungju** (☎ 850 7329) or **Danyang** (☎ 422 1146) before you head to the terminal. To get to the Chungju Dam ferry terminal (충주댐 선착장) take bus 301 (W1100, seven daily) from opposite the Chungju bus terminal.

Suanbo 수안보

This tiny spa resort has baths, restaurants and motels clustered snugly across several streets, and a small ski resort less than 2km away. The town looks as if it's seen better days, but can be lively, even touristy. If you're headed to Woraksan National Park, this makes a better base than Chungju.

There are two **tourist information centres** (☎ 845 7829) – one at the entrance to town, the other at the other end of the main street, opposite the bus terminal.

The modest **Sajo Ski Resort** (사조스키리조트; ☎ 846 0750; www.sajoresort.co.kr; lift pass W45,000, ski rental W15,000) has seven slopes and three lifts, and offers night skiing. Near the slopes are a hotel and a youth hostel, but you can stay in Suanbo and use the free shuttle buses during ski season.

SLEEPING & EATING

Sinheungjang Hotel (신흥장 호텔; ☎ 846 3711; r W25,000; ✷) Despite its name, this place is more of a *yeogwan,* with well-worn, passable rooms. There's a small *oncheon* downstairs (nonguests/guests W4000/free, open 6am to 7pm). Room prices increase W10,000 on Saturdays. Look on the main street for the three-storey building with a stone exterior.

Suanbo Royal Hotel (수안보로얄호텔; ☎ 846 0190; r W55,000; ⊠ ▯) This blockish concrete-and-glass hotel looks sterner but newer than the others on the main road. Rooms are cosy and warm, and there's an *oncheon* (nonguests/guests W6000/3500).

Suanbo Sangnok Hotel (수안보상록호텔; www. sangnokhotel.co.kr; ☎ 845 3500; r W120,000, ste W220,000; ⊠ ▯ ▣) To the right of the entrance to Suanbo stands this upmarket hotel, with a restaurant, tennis court and nightclub. Rooms are smart and modern, even carpeted. The main attraction is the *oncheon* (guests only, W7000).

Restaurants specialise in rabbit (*tokki*; 토끼), duck (*ori*; 오리) and pheasant (*kkwong*; 꿩) meals, such as *toki doritang* (토끼도리탕; rabbit stew) and *kkwong jeongsik,* meant for at least two diners. Also popular is *sanchae deodeok jeongsik* (산채더덕정식), a set meal with mountain vegetables and a herbal root similar to ginseng. **Satgatchon** (삿갓촌; meals W5000-30,000) has *kkwong shabu shabu* (꿩샤브샤브) with pheasant served in seven different ways: kebabs, dumplings, meatballs, barbecued, *shabu shabu*–style, raw and in soup. To find it, walk down the side road by Suanbo Sangnok Hotel to the three green signs and look left – it's the restaurant with black tiles on the roof.

GETTING THERE & AWAY
From outside Chungju's bus terminal, catch bus 240 or 246 (W1150, 35 minutes, 21km, every 40 minutes) to Suanbo's main street. To return to Chungju, pick up bus 610 on the main street (W1150) or get a more comfortable intercity bus (W2200, 25 minutes). Tickets for the latter are sold at the grocery store beside the bus 'terminal', which consists of a yellow and blue sign planted beside some orange seats. Other intercity buses go to Daegu (W13,500, three hours, six daily) and Dong-Seoul (W11,300, 2½ hours, hourly).

WORAKSAN NATIONAL PARK
월악산국립공원
Spread across two serene valleys, this **park** (☎ 653 3250; http://worak.knps.or.kr; admission free; ☼ sunrise-sunset) offers fine hiking through picturesque forests,

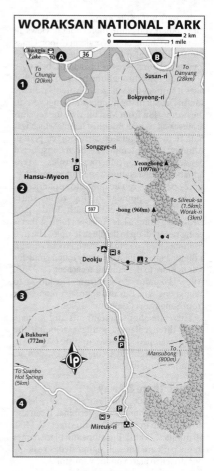

WORAKSAN NATIONAL PARK

with pretty waterfalls, ancient Buddhist structures and, if you climb high enough, views all the way to Chungjuho. Woraksan (Moon Crags Mountain) is also home to the endangered long-tailed goral (see the boxed text, below).

A road runs through the park; the bus that plies it stops at the villages of Mireuk-ri in the south, Deokju in the middle and Songgye-ri in the north. 1km from Mireuk-ri lie the remains of **Mireuksaji**, a small Buddhist temple which was built in the late Shilla or early Goryeo period. Although a new temple has been constructed beside it, the stark, weatherbeaten ruins – an enigmatic Buddha statue, stone lantern and five-storey pagoda – can be quite atmospheric.

The most popular hiking route starts from Deokju. A gentle path leads past Deokjusanseong, a late Shilla-era fortress that is being restored, up to **Deokju-sa** temple. The trail continues for 1.5km to **Ma-aebul**, a rock face with a Buddha image, then it's pretty tough going for 3.4km more to the summit **Yeongbong** (1097m). Allow 3½ hours to get from Deokju-sa to Yeongbong. You can also approach Yeongbong from Songgye-ri (2½ hours, 4.3km).

There are shops, restaurants and *minbak* at all three villages, Songgye-ri being the most developed. There's camping (W3000 to W6000 per night) at Deokju and Datdonjae, but no mountain shelters.

Getting There & Away

Bus 246 (W4000, one hour, six daily) leaves from outside Chungju's bus terminal. It can also be picked up in Suanbo's main street (W1100, 10 minutes, 11km). Bus stops and place names in the park are not well signposted, so ask the bus driver to alert you for your stop.

DANYANG 단양
pop 32,000

A little gem of a resort town, Danyang (http://english.dy21.net) is cosied right up to the mountains of Sobaeksan National Park, at a bend in the river Namhangang. This is small-town Korea at its most charming: you can stay at a riverfront motel and explore limestone caves, hiking trails and a one-of-a-kind Buddhist temple, basking in mountain views wherever you go. It's a great place to dawdle for a couple of days.

The annual highlight is the 10-day Royal Azalea Festival in May. Hikers come to see the flowers bloom on Sobaeksan, while the riverside comes alive with concerts, fireworks, food stalls and a funfair.

The **tourist information centre** (☎ 422 1146) is located across the bridge and has English-speaking staff.

Sights

GOSU DONGGUL 고수동굴

This stunning **limestone cave** (☎ 422 3072; adult/youth/child W5000/3000/2000; ☑ 9am-5pm) is a rabbit's warren of metal catwalks and spiral staircases running through 1.7km of dense, narrow grottoes. It's quite an intimate experience where you get up close with the rock formations, but the downside is that many are discoloured from years of human contact. Unlike garishly lit caves, Gosu Donggul feels old and drippy – perhaps not as old as its 150,000 years, but certainly less cleaned-up and comfortable (some might say more authentic).

There are few explanatory signs, except for a few earnest exhortations to, 'for a moment, look back please!'. Walkways are often wide enough for one person to pass through, so on a busy day it might get a little jammed up and noisy – definitely not for the claustrophobic.

The cave is about a 10-minute walk from Danyang. Cross the bridge to the tourist information centre and follow the road to the right. The cave entrance is tucked away up a stone staircase behind the tourist village. At the latter, you can refresh yourself with a cup (or jar) of

---

THE GENTLE GORAL

Don't let the grinning cartoon on signs in Woraksan National Park fool you. The long-tailed goral, part of the goat-antelope family, is a remarkably shy creature and you're unlikely to come across one. That also makes the elusive animal – which is brownish-grey, has short horns and resembles a goat – difficult for scientists to track. It's been a protected species in South Korea since 1967, and the current estimated population is 700.

Most wild gorals can be found in Seoraksan National Park or the DMZ, but Woraksan is also an important habitat. Fifteen to 20 gorals live in the park and there are plans to release more. If you happen to see one, don't startle or feed it – just let it go about its way.

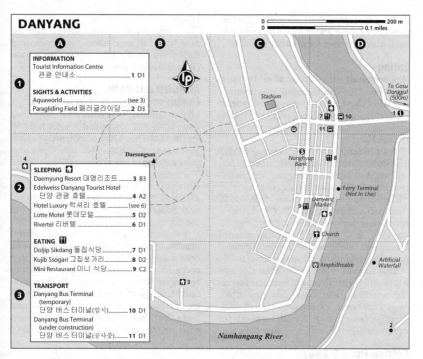

DANYANG

local flavours like *omija*, (five-flavour berry), honey (*kkul*; 꿀) or yam (*ma*; 마) drinks.

Activities

Dansim Mugung (단심무궁 패러글라이딩; ☎ 011-361 4882; http://cafe.daum.net/dypara) offers paragliding (W70,000) from Yangbaeksan, the peak overlooking the town that's topped by an astronomical observatory. For whitewater rafting along the Namhangang, contact **DYL** (☎ 423 5600; www.dy8.co.kr; W25,000-40,000).

Tamer options are to go swimming at the indoor water park **Aquaworld** (아쿠아월드; ☎ 420 8385; adult/child W20,000/14,000; ☯ 10am-8.30pm) or drop by its **sauna** (adult/child W8000/6000; ☯ 7am-8pm), which has mineral baths and jade, charcoal or amethyst saunas.

Sleeping

Most of the riverside motels are dated and faded, but can't be beat for location.

Rivertel (리버텔; ☎ 422 2619; www.erivertel.com; r W30,000; ☯ 💻) Despite the shabby exterior and worn red carpet, this place has the cheapest rooms-with-a-view – pleasant though none too large. The owner speaks some English

and plenty of travel information is available at the reception desk.

Lotte Motel (롯데모텔; ☎ 423 0765; r 30,000; ☯ 💻) No relation to the conglomerate, this humble riverfront motel has wood-laminate floors and modern furniture that makes it feel much nicer than its neighbours. The only pity is there isn't much of a view.

Hotel Luxury (럭셔리 호텔; ☎ 421 9911; www. hotel-luxury.co.kr; r W50,000, ste W70,000; ☯ 💻) This spanking new outfit brings love-motel chic to Danyang, with stylish rooms decorated in bold colours. The VIP suite sleeps three (W90,000) and comes with a whirlpool bath.

Edelweiss Danyang Tourist Hotel (단양 관광 호텔; ☎ 423 7070; www.danyanghotel.com; r W50,000, ste W100,000; ☯ 💻) It's out of town but with a stepped-terrace design, many rooms enjoy lovely views. Rooms are nice, if sometimes alarmingly ornate, and rates increase about W10,000 on weekends.

Daemyung Resort (대명리조트; ☎ 420 8385; www.daemyungresort.com; r W210,000, ste W310,000; ☯ 💻) This condominium is equipped with full facilities such as Aquaworld (see left), *noraebang* (karaoke room) and billiard rooms, and a restaurant. Rooms can sleep up to four persons. Enquire about its off-season packages, which come at significant discounts.

Eating

Mini Restaurant (미니 식당; ☎ 423 1914; meals W2000-4000) Dirt-cheap eats in a surprisingly cosy cafe. There's a range of *ramyeon* (instant noodles in soup) and *udong* (thick white noodle broth), served with *kimchi*, egg or *yubu* (유부; fried beancurd).

Doljip Sikdang (돌집식당; meals W6000-15,000) This busy restaurant has private dining rooms and serves elaborate *jeongsik*, with main-course options such as *suyuk* (더마나 곤드레; boiled beef slices) and *maneul* (마늘쌈정식; garlic), or *beoseot jjigae* (버섯찌개; mushroom stew). Lighter options are *doenjang sotbap* (된장솥밥; claypot rice with fermented bean paste, jujube and vegetables) or *dolsot bibimbap* (*bibimbap* in a stone hotpot).

Kujib Ssogari (그집쏘가리; ☎ 423 2111; meals W10,000-20,000) This riverfront restaurant serves the mandarin fish *ssogari* raw (쏘가리회; *ssogari hoe*) or as a spicy soup (쏘가리매운탕; *ssogari maeuntang*). A milder option is the catfish *bulgogi* (메기불고기; *megi bulgogi*).

Getting There & Away

BOAT

The closest ferry terminal for the Chungjuho ferry (p342) is at Janghoe. After you exit the terminal, turn right at the main road and walk down for about 100m. Beside the trail entrance to Woraksan National Park is the waiting point for the bus to Danyang (W1850, 30 minutes, 21km, every 2½ hours). It's marked with a circular red sign that reads '단양버스정류소'.

BUS

A new bus terminal was being built at the time of research and is scheduled to open in 2012. Meanwhile, buses are operating from a temporary **office** (☎ 421 8800) right beside the bridge. Destinations include:

Destination	Price (W)	Duration	Frequency
Chungju	7500	1½hr	11 daily
Daejeon	16,500	3hr	4 daily
Guin-sa	3100	30min	hrly
Seoul	12,100	3½hr	every 30min

Local buses don't have numbers, but signs (Korean only) indicate the destination at the front of the bus.

TRAIN

The train station is in old Danyang, about 3km from the main town. Eight trains run daily from Seoul's Cheongnyangni station (W11,000, three hours).

AROUND DANYANG

Cheondong Donggul 천동동굴

Like a children's adventure activity, this **cave** (☎ 422 2972; adult/youth/child W3000/3000/2000; 🕙 9am-5.30pm) has 470m of extremely narrow passageways that necessitate tight squeezing, some bending over and the occasional waddle. The signs may say 'Stalactite no touch', but you can't help brushing up against them. It's a passable diversion if you have time to kill near Sobaeksan National Park, but pales in comparison to Gosu Donggul (p344).

The bus (W1050, 10 minutes, hourly) heading to Darian (opposite) stops here. The cave is a 10-minute walk from the bus stop and a 15-minute walk from the entrance to Sobaeksan National Park. Look for the restaurant Myeongseong Sikdang (명성식당) with the red signboard and follow the path behind up to the ticket office. At the cave entrance, enter on the right-hand side (marked '들어가는곳').

SOBAEKSAN NATIONAL PARK 소백산국립공원

This **park** (☎ 423 0708; admission free; http://sobaek.knps.or.kr/Sobaeksan_eng; 🕙 2hr before sunrise-2hr after sunset) is the third largest in South Korea and the daintily named Sobaeksan (Little White Mountain) is one of the highest mountains in the country. While the climbs are not particularly steep, they can be demanding, wending through dense forests and picturesque valleys.

The main trail (6km, 2½ hours) heads from the park entrance at Darian to the highest peak **Birobong** (1439m), famous for royal azaleas which bloom in late May. Views are incredible from the grassy mountaintop. It can also be approached from the campground at Samga (5.7km, 2½ hours). From Birobong, you can push on to the three peaks of **Yeonhwabong** (2.5km to 6.8km); the National Astronomical Observatory is here but not open to visitors.

Guin-sa 구인사

This stately **complex** (☎ 420 7315; www.cheontae.org; admission free) truly looks like a mountain

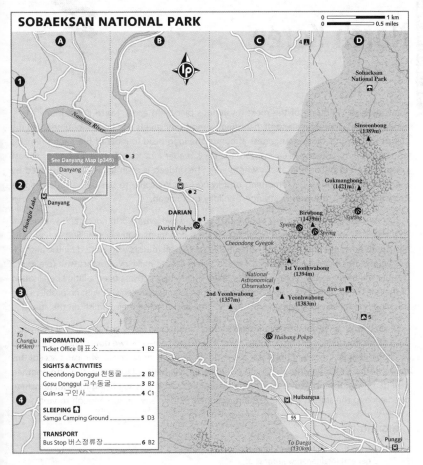

SOBAEKSAN NATIONAL PARK

INFORMATION	
Ticket Office 매표소	**1** B2
SIGHTS & ACTIVITIES	
Cheondong Donggul 천동굴	**2** B2
Gosu Donggul 고수동굴	**3** B2
Guin-sa 구인사	**4** C1
SLEEPING	
Samga Camping Ground	**5** D3
TRANSPORT	
Bus Stop 버스정류장	**6** B2

temple – its 30-odd buildings are wedged into a valley, with steep, forested slopes on either side. The gold-roofed buildings are as elaborate as you'd expect, juxtaposed very closely together and connected with elevated walkways. The communal kitchen serves free vegetarian meals (6am to 7.30am, 11.30am to 1.30pm and 6.30pm to 9.30pm) and it's also possible to do a temple stay here.

The temple is the headquarters of the Cheontae sect of Korean Buddhism, which was re-established by Sangwol Wongak in 1945. The most opulent structure is the three-storey hall dedicated to him (대조사전) at the rear of the complex. From there, it's a steep climb of 30 minutes to his tomb atop the hill.

Sleeping & Eating

There is a delightful *minbak* village at Darian, many also have restaurants. They are also fairly spread out so it doesn't feel too crowded or noisy. Rooms cost from W25,000 and you can wake up right next to the mountains.

Camping (W2000) is available at Samga. Take the bus (W1050, every 30 minutes) heading to Yeongju (영주).

Getting There & Away

Buses (W1050, 10 minutes, hourly) leave from outside Danyang's temporary bus terminal for Darian (다리안). Direct buses (W3100, 30 minutes, hourly) head from Danyang's bus terminal to Guin-sa.

North Korea

Asia's dark star and one of the most mysterious places on earth, North Korea immediately evokes images of nuclear standoff, hauntingly empty city streets and huge monuments to the cult of Kim Il-sung. More strangeness abounds: the long-dead founder of the nation remains its 'eternal' president and his ailing son, the Dear Leader Kim Jong-il, a man who has almost never spoken in public and about whom very little indeed is even known, is considered by the local population to be something of a living god. Welcome to the Democratic People's Republic of Korea, the world's strangest holiday destination.

It comes as a surprise to many people that you can even visit North Korea, and yet tourism to the world's most isolated and totalitarian state is booming, relatively speaking. A few years ago South Koreans and Americans were unable to visit, all tourists were vetted by the authorities before visas were issued and locals would barely dare to make eye contact with foreigners. Despite still being a very repressive police state, there's nevertheless been a little liberalisation of the rules governing visits – now South Koreans and Americans can visit with no problem and the more gregarious locals are even happy to chat and practise their English on the street.

A trip here is strictly on the government's terms though, and it's essential to accept that you'll have no independence during your trip – you'll be accompanied by two government-appointed local guides at all times and only hear a one-sided view of history. Those who can't accept this might be better off staying away – those who can will have a fascinating trip into another, unsettling world. Simply to see a country where the Cold War is still being fought and where obedience to the state is universally unquestioned is, for many, reason enough to visit.

HIGHLIGHTS

- Marvel at the architecture, monuments and general totalitarian weirdness of **Pyongyang** (p361)

- Feel the full force of Cold War tensions during a visit to **Panmunjom** (p373) in the Demilitarized Zone (DMZ), where an uneasy armistice holds

- Visit Pyongyang between August and October to see the incredible **Mass Games** (p359), a gymnastic spectacle featuring thousands of athletes and dancers in perfect formation

- Explore the remote far north and Korea's highest peak and holy mountain **Paekdusan** (p376)

- Enjoy pristine mountain walks and some lovely beaches along the coast in and around **Mt Chilbo** (p378)

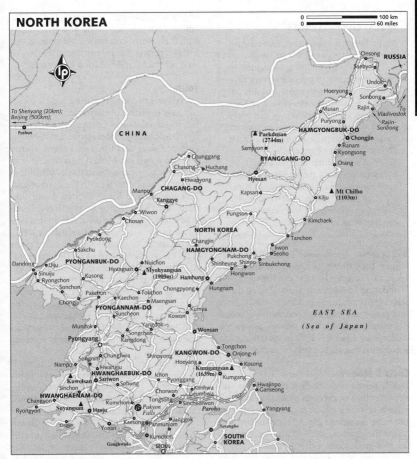

Getting Started

You need do nothing special to get a visa save pay through the nose for a guided tour. North Korea is not dangerous and for travellers it's very comfortable. By law though, two guides must accompany you everywhere you go outside your hotel and they will control what you see and the spiel you hear while seeing it. Itineraries are always provisional and some things are usually cancelled at the last moment for no discernable reason, although something else will always be substituted in its place.

No matter where you're from or what you want to see, you'll need to book via a travel agency (see p350). Consider your itinerary and the amount of time you'd like to spend in North Korea carefully, as itineraries can be hard (if not always impossible) to change once there. Days are long in North Korean tourism – you'll see a surprising amount in just a four-day tour, and possibly be burned out on a full-week of resolutely revolutionary sightseeing.

When to Go

The best time to plan a trip is during the Mass Games (mid-August until mid-October most years) or during a national holiday when you'll see mass dances or even big parades, which make for a uniquely North Korean experience. In general, the most pleasant months for a visit are April, May, June, September and October. July and August are often unpleasantly humid

RESEARCH CHALLENGES

North Korea presents challenges for all tourists, but for Lonely Planet researchers it is a particularly difficult destination to cover. Even more so than normal we have to remain deeply undercover and it is impossible for us to go everywhere and see everything. For this edition we personally visited Pyongyang, Kaesong, Panmunjom, Paekdusan, Samjiyon, Chongjin and Mt Chilbo; accounts of other places and reviews of some hotels and restaurants are based on accounts from trusted second-hand sources. No hotel or restaurant prices are given in this chapter as all travellers will pay for an all-inclusive tour, covering accommodation and all meals.

and overcast. Tours don't usually run in the winter: they finish in November then start again in February in time for Kim Jong-il's birthday on 16 February. Those finding themselves in North Korea in winter will discover that power shortages are common (although not usually in hotels) and that it's generally a cold, rather miserable time to visit, though in sunshine it can still be very beautiful.

Costs & Money

North Korea is no budget destination and opportunities to cut costs by staying in youth hostels or using public transport simply do not exist. As well as paying for your bed and board in advance, you will also have to pay for two guides and a driver, making travelling as part of a group one of the few ways to save money.

As a rough guide, solo travellers should bank on paying about €250 per day for guides, hotels and full board. This can be reduced to around €150 per day if you go as part of a group. Note that the euro and Chinese yuan are the accepted currencies for visitors to use (local currency cannot legally be spent by foreigners) and that small change in both currencies (euro coins and yuan in denominations under 10) is a huge advantage as most places can't change big notes.

Once in North Korea, the only major expenses will be souvenirs and other gifts that are on sale at every tourist attraction. Apart from evening drinks and telephone costs, there is little opportunity to spend your money elsewhere. It's customary to tip the guides at the end of each tour assuming you were happy with their work. Recommended amounts are €10 per person for a short tour (five days or less) per guide, and €20 for a longer tour.

Tours

Every foreign tourist visiting North Korea will have to go through Ryohaengsa, or Korea International Travel Company (KITC), the North Korean equivalent to Intourist. Nearly everyone does this through a travel agency that has a well-established relationship with Ryohaengsa, though it is in theory possible to organise a visit directly with the Ryohaengsa. You may save a bit of money doing this, though it's unlikely to be worth the headache of dealing with an organisation that is so unused to dealing with individuals. Another advantage of dealing through a third party is that travel agents are IATA (International Air Transport Association) bonded and will return your money if your trip is cancelled, whereas Ryohaengsa will not. If you're determined to deal with them in person, the Beijing representative of **Ryohaengsa** (☎ +86-10-8576 9465; fax 8576 9984; kitcbri@gmail.com) is your best hope, though note that there is no office you can visit.

The number of North Korean specialists is very limited, and Beijing-based Koryo Tours are by far the most popular choice and the only company exclusively dealing with DPRK tours. Leading operators are listed here:

Koryo Tours (☎ 10-6416 7544; www.koryogroup.com; 27 Beisanlitun Nan (East Courtyard), Chaoyang District, 100027 Beijing) are the unrivalled experts on tourism to the DPRK, having operated tours for two decades and knowing the country inside out. The website is a great place to start for anyone interested in travelling to North Korea, packed as it is with lots of information and photographs. The friendly team here offers specialist itineraries including those aimed at American groups, special Mass Games trips and one of the cheapest North Korea tours available (€990 for its 'March Madness' five-day trip). Itineraries for individuals and groups can also be tailor-made.

Specialists in obscure destinations, UK-based **Regent Holidays** (☎ 0845 277 3317; www.regent-holidays.co.uk; Mezzanine Ste, Froomsgate House, Rupert St, Bristol BS1 2QJ) have been taking groups into North Korea since the late 1980s. A weekend trip to Pyongyang starts at £850, while a mammoth

16-day tour taking in almost everything there is to see in the country starts at £1995 (both beginning and ending in Beijing, not London). Individual itineraries are also available.

VNC Travel (☎ 030-231 1500; www.vnc.nl; Catharijnesingel 70, Postbus 79, 3500 AB Utrecht) is a Dutch company that specialises in travel to Asia, and includes both group and individual tours to North Korea. A variety of tours are offered including the standard seven-day tour taking in Pyongyang, Kaesong, the DMZ and Mt Myohyang. Longer tours are also available.

Other operators that offer tours to North Korea include:

Asia Pacific Travel (☎ 1-847-251-6400; www.northkorea 1on1.com; PO Box 350, Kenilworth, IL 60043-0350, USA)

Bestway Tours & Safaris (☎ 1-604 2647378; www. bestway.com; Suite 206, 8678 Greenall Avenue, Burnaby, British Columbia, V5J 3M6, Canada)

Explore (☎ 44-(0)845 013 1537; www.explore.co.uk; Nelson House, 55 Victoria Rd, Farnborough, Hampshire, GU14 7PA, UK)

Geographic Expeditions (☎ 1-415-922-0448; www. geoex.com; 1008 General Kennedy Avenue, PO Box 29902, San Francisco, CA 94129-0902, USA)

Korea Konsult (☎ 46-(0)73 981 0372; www.koreakon sult.com; Rödklövervägen 79, 165 73 Hässelby, Sweden)

Lupine Travel (☎ 44-(0)1942 704525; www.lupine travel.co.uk; 12, Warnford St, Wigan, Lancs, WN1 2EQ, UK)

North Korea Travel (☎ 852 3175 0904; www.north -korea-travel.com; 5/F, Tower 1, Silvercord, 30 Canton Rd, Kowloon, Hong Kong)

Tin Bo Travel Services (☎ 1-613 238 7093; www. tinboholidays.com; 2nd fl, 725 Somerset St W, Ottawa, Ontario K1R 6P7, Canada)

See (p382) for information about travelling on your own.

Travel Literature

The single best book to read if you're curious to know what a trip to the DPRK is like is Guy Delisle's graphic novel *Pyongyang: A Journey in North Korea*. A French-Canadian cartoonist 'on the margins of the globalised world', Delisle was seconded to Pyongyang to work on cartoons, and his methodical documentation of all aspects of his trip is priceless. Highly recommended, even more so for any recent visitors who will find themselves laughing out loud in recognition.

North Korea Through the Looking Glass (Kong Dan Oh, Ralph C Hassig, Kongdan Oh) has established itself as a classic overview of DPRK politics and society, although it has the usual limitations of any work concerning one of the most secretive governments on earth: much is conjecture and cannot be adequately supported by documented evidence. For all that, it's still a fascinating introduction to the country.

Bruce Cumings has written over a dozen books about Korea, the division of the peninsula and its future. Highly recommended is *War and Television*, which recounts his experiences recording interviews in North Korea for a documentary on the Korean War. His other authoritative histories of the peninsula include *Korea's Place in the Sun*, one chapter of which gives an impressive analysis of the DPRK's political culture.

For a very readable, yet still substantial account of North-South relations since 1948, Don Oberdorfer's *The Two Koreas* is excellent. Oberdorfer puts the politics of both countries squarely in the context of constant efforts by both governments to reunify the peninsula, by peaceful means or otherwise.

Perhaps the closest North Korea has come to its own *Gulag Archipelago* is the horrific *The Aquariums of Pyongyang: Ten Years in the North Korean Gulag* by Kang Chol-hwan. This book describes the hell on earth that is life as a political prisoner here. Not for the

---

DON'T LEAVE HOME WITHOUT...

Anything medical or electrical that you will need during your stay; this includes simple everyday products such as painkillers, tampons, condoms, memory cards and batteries. Such basic items are sometimes available, but their price and quality can be quite different from elsewhere. Bringing a bag of fruit from China is a great idea for snacking between sights. Small change in euros and yuan (€1 and 1 yuan notes are especially useful) are a huge help, as there's rarely hard currency change in shops. Small token gifts for your guides will be appreciated, though they are not essential (and a cash tip will be expected whatever else you give them). Popular gifts include cigarettes (for male guides only), chocolates and quality beauty products. Most of all, bring a sense of humour and an open mind – you'll need both to make North Korea enjoyable and rewarding.

SHOULD YOU VISIT?

North Korea is a police state with a human-rights record among the worst on earth. Concentration camps, executions, state-orchestrated terror and mass-control by a vast propaganda machine are a daily reality for millions here. All the revenue from your trip will go directly to the government, and given the cost of just one traveller's tour this totals a sizeable amount. So should you visit, and is it morally acceptable to do so?

The case against visiting, as outlined above, is strong. On the other hand, those who argue that you *should* visit point out that tourism is one of the few ways of encouraging openness in the DPRK, of letting people see that the West is interested and, more importantly, friendly – not an insignificant fact for a population brought up on a relentless diet of anti-US propaganda.

Part of the fascination of travelling in North Korea is trying to divine the real from the fake and attempting to see past the ideology. While you may be horrified, amazed or awestruck by what you see in North Korea, you won't be able to help yourself seeing the world from a different perspective once you've been here.

If you do decide to come, the one thing you should never do is visit with the intent of stirring up trouble or making any kind of protest – your guides and any North Koreans having contact with your group will suffer very serious consequences and you'll achieve nothing more than a speedy deportation. If you do come, listen to the version of history given to you by the guides, accept that this is their version (however untrue) and leave serious criticism until you are back at your hotel.

faint-hearted, but definitely recommended for anyone seeking the whole picture.

Pyongyang: The Hidden History of the Hidden Capital, by Chris Springer, is a city guide that tells the stories behind the mysterious buildings, monuments and ministries of the capital, and is by far the most detailed guide to Pyongyang available.

North Korea by Robert Willoughby is the most comprehensive guidebook to the country, although much of it is irrelevant for travellers as most of the towns included are off limits to non-NGO workers and diplomats.

Internet Resources

The scarcity of information from North Korea has created a large web community of DPRK-watchers, and although every subject from annual grain production to Kim Jong-il jokes is covered, very few websites give entirely objective North Korea coverage. The following sites offer the best coverage of events.

www.chosunjournal.com This self-styled 'Gulag Archipelago meets the Drudge Report' is a non-profit website devoted to documenting human-rights abuses in North Korea, mobilising people to protest and supporting North Korean refugees. Essential reading.

www.koryogroup.com The Beijing-based North Korean travel specialists offer the best introduction to travelling around the DPRK on their excellent website. Here you'll find everything from travel tips to itineraries and photos.

www.nautilus.org The website of a very highbrow US research fund called the Nautilus Institute for Security and Sustainability. Its stated mission is to 'solve interrelated critical global problems', putting North Korea at the top of the agenda.

www.nkeconwatch Curtis Melvin's excellent site provides a huge amount of authoritatively sourced background information on the DPRK and is a great resource for academics, researchers and anyone interested in the North Korean economy.

www.northkoreanrefugees.com An important website for the excellent Japanese charity of the same name that offers support and lobbies for the rights of North Koreans who have escaped into China.

HISTORY

For an overview of Korean history before the division of the peninsula, see p25.

Division of the Peninsula

The Japanese occupation of the Korean peninsula between 1910 and 1945 was one of the darkest periods in Korean history; the occupation forces press-ganged many Korean citizens into slave labour teams to construct factories, mines and heavy industry – particularly in the north. Moreover, the use of Korean girls as 'comfort women' for Japanese soldiers – a euphemism for enforced prostitution – remains a huge cause of resentment and controversy today in both Koreas (p40).

Most of the guerrilla warfare conducted against the Japanese police and army took place in the northern provinces of Korea and neighbouring Manchuria; northerners are still proud of having carried a disproportionate burden in the anti-Japan struggle. In fact, some modern history books would have you believe that Kim Il-sung defeated the Japanese nearly single-handedly (with a bit of help from loyal comrades and his infant son).

While his feats have certainly been exaggerated, Kim Il-sung was a strong resistance leader, although not a strong enough force to rid Korea of the Japanese. This task was left to the Red Army, who, in the closing days of WWII, entered Manchuria and Northern Korea as the Japanese forces retreated. The USA, realising that the strategic importance of the peninsula was too great for it to be left in Soviet hands similarly began to move its troops to the country's south. Despite an agreement at Yalta to give joint custodianship of Korea to the USSR, the USA and China, no concrete plans had been made to this end, and the US State Department assigned the division of the country to two young officers, who, working from a *National Geographic* map, divided Korea across the 38th parallel.

American forces quickly took possession of the southern half of the country while the Soviets established themselves in the north, both sides stopping at the largely arbitrary dividing line. The intention to have democratic elections across the whole peninsula soon became hostage to Cold War tensions, and after the North refused to allow UN inspectors to cross the 38th parallel, the Republic of Korea was proclaimed in the South on 15 August 1948, while the North proclaimed the Democratic People's Republic just three weeks later on 9 September 1948.

The Korean War

Stalin, it is rumoured, personally chose the 33-year-old Kim Il-sung to lead the new republic. The ambitious and fiercely nationalistic Kim was an unknown quantity, although Stalin is said to have favoured him due to his youth. He would have had no idea that Kim would outlive not only him and Mao Zedong, but communism itself, to become the one of the world's longest serving heads of state. As soon as Kim had assumed the leadership of North Korea, he applied to Stalin to sanction an invasion of the South. The man of steel refused Kim twice in 1949, but perhaps bolstered by Mao's victory over the nationalists in China the same year and the USSR's own A-bomb project, he gave Kim the green light a year later.

The brutal and pointless Korean War of 1950–53 saw a stunning North Korean advance into the South, where it almost drove US forces into the sea, followed by an equally

---

TOP FIVE DPRK DOCUMENTARIES

The following documentaries are all highly recommended for a glimpse into the DPRK, and are a great way for prospective visitors to get an idea of what to expect.

- *A State of Mind* (www.astateofmind.co.uk) Unprecedented access to the lives of normal North Koreans is the hallmark of this beautiful documentary about two young Korean girls preparing for the Mass Games in Pyongyang.

- *Friends of Kim* (www.friendsofkim.com) A wry look at the pro-regime Korea Friendship Association's annual pilgrimage to North Korea and a wonderful portrait of the eccentrics who truly believe that the country is paradise on earth.

- *Seoul Train* (www.seoultrain.com) This superb documentary looks at the huge problems facing North Korean refugees, how they escape the North, survive in China and – if they're lucky – make it to South Korea.

- *Crossing the Line* Telling the incredible story of an American soldier who defected to the DPRK in the 1960s and continues to live there today, this bittersweet film provides haunting insight into life in the North.

- *A High Level Delegation* A Belgian parliamentary delegation comes off looking very helpless and buffoonish during a visit to the DPRK, when faced with official intransigence and endless propaganda.

impressive counter-attack by the US and the UN, which managed to occupy most of North Korea. As the situation began to look bleak for the North, Kim advocated retreating to the hills and waging guerrilla warfare against the South, unaware that China's Mao Zedong had decided to covertly help the North by sending in the People's Liberation Army in the guise of 'volunteers'. Once the PLA moved in the North pushed the front down to the original 38th parallel, and with two million dead, the original stalemate was more or less retained. The armistice agreement obliged both sides to withdraw 2000m from the ceasefire line, thus creating the Demilitarized Zone (DMZ), still in existence today.

Rebuilding the Country

Despite the Chinese having alienated Kim by taking control of the war – Chinese commander Peng Dehuai apparently treated Kim as a subordinate, much to the thin-skinned future Great Leader's anger – the Chinese remained in North Korea and helped with the massive task of rebuilding a nation all but razed to the ground by bombing.

Simultaneously, following his ill-fated attempt to reunite the nation, Kim Il-sung began a process of political consolidation and brutal repression. He executed his foreign minister and those he believed threatened him in an attempt to take overall control of the Korean Workers' Party. Following Khrushchev's 1956 denunciation of Stalin's personality cult, Central Committee member Yun Kong-hum stood up at one of its meetings and denounced Kim for similar crimes. Yun was never heard from again, and it was the death knell for North Korean democracy.

Unlike many communist leaders, Kim's outlandish personality cult was generated almost immediately – the sobriquet *suryong* or 'Great Leader' was employed in everyday conversation in the North by the 1960s – and the initial lip service paid to democracy and multiparty elections was soon forgotten.

The first decade under Kim Il-sung saw vast material improvements in the lives of workers and peasants. Literacy and full health care were soon followed by access to higher education and the full militarisation of the state. However, by the 1970s, North Korea slipped into recession, one from which it has never recovered. During this time, in which Kim Il-sung had been raised to a divine figure

in North Korean society, an *éminence grise* referred to only as the 'party centre' in official-speak began to emerge from the nebulous mass of Kim's entourage.

At the 1980 party congress this enigmatic figure, to which all kinds of wondrous deeds had been attributed, was revealed to be none other than the Great Leader's son, Kim Jong-il. He was awarded several important public posts, including a seat in the politburo, and even given the honorific title 'Dear Leader'. Kim Jong-il was designated hereditary successor to the Great Leader and in 1991 made supreme commander of the Korean Army, despite never having served a day in it. From 1989 until 1994, Kim father and son were almost always pictured together, praised in tandem and generally shown to be working in close proximity, preparing the North Korean people for a hereditary dynasty far more in keeping with Confucianism than communism.

Beyond Perestroika

It was during the late 1980s, as communism shattered throughout Eastern Europe, that North Korea's development began to differ strongly from that of other socialist nations. Its greatest sponsor, the Soviet Union, disintegrated in 1991, leaving the North at a loss for the subsidies it ironically needed to maintain its facade of self-sufficiency.

North Korea, having always played China and the USSR off against one another, turned to the Chinese, who have played godfather to the DPRK ever since. Quite why the People's Republic has done so has never been explicit. Chinese 'communism' has produced the fastest expanding economy in the world and any ideological ties with Maoism remain purely superficial, while China's increasingly close relationship to both the South and Japan also makes its reluctant support for the Kim regime all the more incongruous. Yet China remains the North's one trusted ally, although several times since the early '90s Beijing has laid down the law to Pyongyang, even withholding oil deliveries to underscore its unhappiness at the North's continuous brinkmanship.

The regime's strategy did pay off in 1994, however, when North Korea negotiated an agreement with the Clinton administration in which it agreed to cancel its controversial nuclear program in return for US energy supplies in the short term. This was to be followed by an international consortium constructing two light-water reactors for North Korean energy needs in the long term.

Midway through negotiations, Kim Il-sung suffered a massive heart attack and died. He had spent the day personally inspecting the accommodation being prepared for the planned visit of South Korean president Kim Young-sam. This summit between the two leaders would have been the first ever meeting between the heads of state of the two nations, and Kim Il-sung's stance towards the South had noticeably changed in the last year of his life.

Kim's death rendered the North weaker and even less predictable than before. Optimistic Korea-watchers, including many within South Korea's government, expected the collapse of the regime to be imminent without its charismatic leader. In a move that was to further derail the reunification process, Kim Young-sam's government in Seoul did not therefore send condolences for Kim's death to the North – something even President Clinton felt obliged to do. This slight to a man considered (officially, at least) to be a living god was a miscalculation that set back any progress another five years.

While the expected collapse did not occur, neither did any visible sign of succession by the Dear Leader. North Korea was more mysterious than ever, and in the three years following Kim Il-sung's death, speculation was rampant that a military faction had taken control in Pyongyang, and that continuing power struggles between them and Kim Jong-il meant that there was no overall leader.

Kim Jong-il finally assumed the mantle of power in October 1997 after a three-year mourning period. Surprisingly, the presidency rested with the late Kim Il-sung, who was declared North Korea's 'eternal' president, making him the world's only dead head of state. However, the backdrop to Kim Jong-il's succession was horrific. While the North Korean economy had been contracting since the collapse of vital Soviet supplies and subsidies to the DPRK's ailing industrial infrastructure in the early 1990s, the terrible floods of 1995 led quickly to disaster. Breaking with a strict tradition of self-reliance (of course, one that had never reflected reality – aid had long been received secretly from both communist allies and even the South two months previously), the North

appealed to the UN and the world community for urgent food aid.

So desperate was the Kim regime that it even acceded to unprecedented UN demands for access to the whole country for their own field workers, something that would have previously been unthinkable in North Korea's staunchly secretive military climate. Aid workers were horrified by what they saw – malnutrition everywhere, and the beginnings of starvation, which led over the next few years to the death of up to three million people.

Axis of Evil

Kim Jong-il's pragmatism and relative openness to change came to the fore in the years following the devastation of the famine, and a series of initiatives to promote reconciliation with both the South and the US were implemented. These reached their height with a swiftly convened Pyongyang summit between the South's Kim Dae-jung and the Dear Leader in June 2000; the first ever meeting on such a level between the two countries. The two leaders, their countries ready at any second to launch Armageddon against one another, held hands in the limousine from the airport to the guesthouse in an unprecedented gesture of solidarity. The summit paved the way for US Secretary of State Madeleine Albright's visit to Pyongyang later the same year. Kim Jong-il's aim was to have his country legitimised through a visit from the American president himself. However, as Clinton's second term ended and George W Bush assumed power in 2001 the international climate swiftly changed.

In his 2002 State of the Union address, President Bush labelled the North (along with Iran and Iraq) part of an 'Axis of Evil', a phrase that has since passed into everyday language and haunted the DPRK leadership ever since. This speech launched a new era of acrimonious relations between the two countries, exemplified the following year by North Korea resuming its nuclear program, claiming it had no choice due to American oil supplies being stopped and the two promised light-water reactors remaining incomplete. Frustrated at being ignored by the US throughout the Bush presidency, North Korea test launched several missiles in July 2006, followed by the detonation of a nuclear device on its own soil three months later.

An Uncertain Future

When two US journalists who had been caught illegally entering North Korea were sentenced to 12 years' 'reform through hard labour' in March 2009, the world was shocked at the incredibly harsh sentences handed down. Five months later Laura Ling and Euna Lee were lucky enough to have Bill Clinton fly in and rescue them (providing for the North Koreans a much-gloated over meeting between the former US President and Kim Jong-il), but this rare display of leniency on Pyongyang's part is definitely not the norm for one of the most repressive nations on earth.

Far more common is for North Korean hostages and kidnap victims to remain forever captive – see p361. An even more unpleasant tale of the North's uncompromising nature is the lesser known case of a 53-year-old South Korean female tourist shot dead by North Korean soldiers in 2008 after allegedly wandering into a military zone from the holiday resort in Kumgangsan. This incident caused the South Koreans to suspend tourism in the North for a year in protest.

The Six Party talks (between the North, the South, China, Japan, Russia and the US), which were designed to bring the North in from the cold by tackling their nuclear program, ground to a halt in 2009 after six years of negotiations. The breakdown in dialogue followed North Korea's launch of what it claimed was a satellite in April 2009, but that many believe to have been a test launch of a Taepodong-2 intercontinental ballistic mis-sile, one that if successful could potentially reach the US. International condemnation of North Korea followed, including strong censure from the UN Security Council and tougher sanctions from a number of countries, to which North Korea defiantly reacted a month later by detonating a nuclear device underground.

At the same time the endless speculation about the successor to Kim Jong-il (who is believed to have suffered a serious stroke in 2008) has apparently been somewhat resolved, with newspapers in South Korea reporting in 2009 that Kim Jong-il's third son, Kim Jong-un, will succeed his father. Very little is known about Kim Jong-un – there's only one photograph available of him (aged 11) outside of North Korea and it's not even certain whether he was born in 1983 or 1984. The 'brilliant comrade' appears to be Kim Jong-un's epithet, and the heir apparent is believed to have been given various government roles, in an eerie echo of how Kim Jong-il was groomed for power by his own father in the 1980s.

Domestically change remains glacial, but there have been some significant developments in openness in recent years, including the admission of both US and South Korean tourists previously banned from the country, the introduction of a mobile phone network in Pyongyang (albeit for the privileged) and the gradual loosening of tight controls on private enterprise.

Outside Pyongyang rural poverty remains grinding, however. Cautious economic re-

---

TIME LINE

1392 The start of the Joseon dynasty, unsympathetic to northerners

1866 The *General Sherman* goes aground on the Taedong River; all on board are killed

1910 Japanese occupation begins

1948 Declaration of the Democratic People's Republic of Korea

1950 North Korean invasion of South Korea

1953 Korean War ends in stalemate

1980 Kim Jong-il anointed 'Dear Leader' and successor to his father

1983 North Korean bomb kills many South Korean cabinet members in Rangoon

1994 Kim Il-sung dies

1995 Floods devastate North Korea

2000 Kim Dae-jung and Kim Jong-il meet in an unprecedented summit in Pyongyang

2002 President George W Bush labels North Korea part of his 'Axis of Evil'

2006 North Korea test fires seven missiles and carries out a nuclear detonation leading to international condemnation and UN sanctions

2009 Bill Clinton visits Pyongyang to secure the release of two American journalists caught illegally entering North Korea

A COUNTRY UNDER ARMS

With an estimated 1.21 million of its citizens in uniform, North Korea is one of the most highly militarised societies on earth, something that is immediately apparent as soon as you step foot in the country. In comparison, South Korea has an army of around 680,000. Both sexes are obliged to devote at least three years of military service to the state, with up to 20% of men aged between 17 and 54 in the regular armed forces according to US State Department sources.

The army is the subject of most films, songs, books and art. It's hard to overstate the importance of the military in North Korean culture, as witnessed by the Military First campaign, which sees priorities in all fields going to the army. North Korea has the world's fifth-largest standing army and the social status of anyone in uniform is very high – rations increase in proportion to the individual's importance to the regime's survival.

forms over the past decade have allowed a degree of free trade including private markets (off limits to tourists, sadly), where most North Koreans now shop, but there's still no sign of any real attempt to reform the country's lumbering, fuel-crippled economy, and incredibly you'll often see lorries chugging down the streets fuelled by charcoal, a backwards technology not seen in most countries since WWII. More often than not though, people will just walk wherever they need to go, as even having a bicycle is something of a privilege for your average citizen.

Against all odds though, the country has survived almost two decades since the end of the Cold War, and the Kim regime still has an iron grip on the country – once more going against the predictions of many Korea-watchers. Most chillingly of all, after 50 years of total repression of all opposition, it appears there are simply no surviving networks of dissent. How long the status quo can go on remains a mystery, but the fact that Kim Jong-il has seen the country through its most devastating famine on record, complete international isolation and recurring energy crises suggests that the quick dissolution of the 'hermit kingdom' is far from certain.

THE CULTURE
The National Psyche

To say that the North Korean national psyche is different to that of their southern cousins is an understatement. While North Korean individuals are generally exceptionally friendly, curious and polite people, if rather shy at first, their psyche as a nation is one defined by a state-promulgated obsession with the country's victimisation by the forces of American and Japanese imperialism and one most notable for its refusal to move on in any way

from the Korean War. Of course the Korean War was horrific and its legacy of a divided nation is rightly the source of great sorrow for people on both sides of the DMZ, but the North's constant propaganda about how the war was everyone's fault but North Korea's is quite extraordinary, especially given the true history of the conflict. One of the key ingredients to a pleasant trip here is understanding that this persecution complex is inculcated from birth and that it's borne of ignorance rather than wilful rewriting of history on the part of individuals.

The North Koreans are also a fiercely nationalistic and proud people, again largely due to endless nationalist propaganda fed to the population since birth. Even more significant is the cult of Kim Il-sung (the Great Leader) and Kim Jong-il (the Dear Leader), which pervades everyday life to a degree that most people will find hard to believe. There are no Kim Il-sung jokes, there is no questioning of the cult and almost no resistance to it (all adult members of the population must wear a loyalty badge to Kim Il-sung – submitting to that alone is a psychological step most foreigners would find inconceivable).

While North Koreans will always be polite to foreigners, there remains a large amount of antipathy towards both the USA and Japan. Both due to propaganda and the very real international isolation they feel, North Koreans have a sense of being hemmed in on all sides – threatened particularly by the South and the USA, but also by Japan. The changes over the past decade in both China and Russia have also been cause for concern. These two big brothers who guaranteed survival and independence have both sought rapprochement with the South.

On a personal level, Koreans are very good humoured and hospitable, yet remain extremely socially conservative, the combination of centuries of Confucianism and decades of communism. By all means smile and say 'hello' to people you see on the street, as North Koreans have been instructed to give foreigners a warm welcome, but don't take photos of people without their permission, and it may be far more relaxing for both of you to simply leave the camera in its bag. Similarly, giving gifts to ordinary people could result in unpleasant consequences for them, so ask your guide at any point what is appropriate and they will advise.

Kids are remarkably forthcoming and will wave back and smile ecstatically when they see a foreign tour group. Personal relationships with North Koreans who are not your tour guides or business colleagues will be impossible. Men should bear in mind that any physical contact with a Korean woman will be seen as unusual, so while shaking hands is perfectly acceptable, do not greet a Korean female with a kiss in the European manner. Korea is still a very patriarchal society and despite the equality of women on an ideological level, this is not the case in day-to-day life.

Lifestyle

Trying to give a sense of day-to-day North Korean life is a challenge indeed. It's difficult to overstate the ramifications of half a century of Stalinism – and it is no overstatement to say that North Korea is the most closed and secretive nation on earth. Facts meld with rumour about the real situation in the country, but certain things are doubtless true; power cuts are regular, and food shortages remain facts of everyday life. Outside Pyongyang (and even in the capital after 10pm) you'll notice how few lights there are, with most windows lit only by candlelight, if at all. While at the time of writing starvation was no longer a problem in North Korea, most North Koreans will eat meat only a few times a year, the rest of the time living off a diet of rice and gruel that is usually limited to one or two meals a day.

The system of political apartheid that exists in North Korea has effectively created a three-strata society. All people are divided up by taedo – a curious post-feudalist caste system – into loyal, neutral or hostile categories in relation to the regime. The hostile are deprived of everything and often end up in forced labour camps in entire family groups, maybe for nothing more than having South Korean relatives or for one family member having been caught crossing into China. The neutral have little or nothing but are not persecuted, while the loyal enjoy everything from Pyongyang residency and desk jobs (at the lower levels) to Party membership and the privileges of the upper classes. At the top of the tree, the Kim dynasty and its vast array of courtiers, security guards, staff and other flunkies are rumoured to enjoy great wealth and luxury, although evidence of this is hard to produce – the North Korean elite is also obsessed with secrecy.

North Korea is predictably austere. The six-day week (which even for office workers includes regular stints of backbreaking labour in the rice fields at planting and harvest time) makes for an exhausted populace, but this makes Sundays a real event and Koreans visibly beam as they relax, go on picnics, sing songs and drink in small groups all over the country. A glance at the showcase shops and department stores in Pyongyang confirms that there is only a small number of imported goods available to the general population, highly priced and of variable quality. Testimonies taken from North Korean refugees in China give a particularly grim picture of daily life in the north of the country: malnourishment is a common fact of life for much of the rural population and standards of living are particularly low (see also the boxed text on p374).

While in the 20 years following the Korean War it could genuinely be claimed that Kim Il-sung's government increased the standard of living in the North, bringing literacy and health care to every part of the country, the regression since the collapse of communism throughout the world has been just as spectacular, and most people are now just as materially poor as their grandparents were in the early 1950s. Outside Pyongyang the standard of living is far worse, and this is visible on the streets, although your carefully planned bus journeys will never fully expose the poverty of the nation to the casual tourist. Still, glimpses of life in rural villages from the bus can be chilling.

Population

A 2008 UN-sponsored census was the first in 15 years and pronounced the population of the country at just over 24 million people, which surprised many DPRK-watchers who expected the population to have declined following a series of famines in the late 1990s during which millions of people starved to death.

North Korea is conspicuous for its ethnic homogeneity, a result of the country's long history of isolation and even xenophobia, dating back to the 'hermit kingdom' days. The number of foreigners living in North Korea is very small, all of them either diplomats or temporary residents working in the aid or construction industries. All of the three million inhabitants of Pyongyang are from backgrounds deemed to be loyal to the Kim regime. With a complete lack of free movement in the country (all citizens need special permission to leave their town of residence), no visitor is likely to see those termed 'hostile' – anyway, most people in this unfortunate category are in hard-labour camps miles from anywhere. All North Korean adults have been obliged to wear a 'loyalty' badge since 1970 featuring Kim Il-sung's portrait. You can be pretty certain that anyone without one is a foreigner.

Sport

Soccer is the national sport, and seeing an international match in Pyongyang is sometimes a possibility (local fixtures are off limits to foreigners). Volleyball is the game you're most likely to see locals playing though, as both sexes can play together.

The North's greatest sporting moment came at the 1966 World Cup in England, when they thrashed favourites Italy and stunned the world. They subsequently went out to Portugal in the quarterfinals. The story of the team is told in a strangely touching documentary – one of the few ever to be made by Western crews in the DPRK – called *The Game of Their Lives*. North Korea have qualified for the 2010 World Cup, the first time they've been in the competition since 1966.

Weightlifting and martial arts are the other sporting fields in which North Korea has created an international impact, although its bronze and silver-medal winning shooter Kim Jong-su was disqualified from the Beijing Olympics in 2008 when he failed a drugs test.

One homegrown sporting phenomenon (for want of a more accurate term) that visitors should try to see is the Mass Games, held annually at the May Day Stadium in Pyongyang. These mass gymnastic displays involve over 100,000 soldiers, children and students holding up coloured placards to form enormous murals in praise of North Korea's achievements – truly an amazing sight. See p371.

Religion

In North Korea, all traditional religion is regarded, in accordance with Marxist theory, as an expression of a 'feudal mentality' and has been effectively banned since the 1950s. However, as the Kim regime became more and more deified in the 1990s, official propaganda against organised religion accordingly stopped. Indeed, one guide on a recent visit told us that Juche (see the boxed text, p366) was a religion and that one could not follow both it and Buddhism. A number of Buddhist temples are on show to tourists, although they're always showpieces – you won't see locals or any real Buddhist community. However, in recent years three churches have been built in Pyongyang, catering to the capital's diplomatic community.

TRADITIONAL RELIGIONS

The northern version of Korean shamanism was individualistic and ecstatic, while the southern style was hereditary and based on regularly scheduled community rituals. As far as is known, no shamanist activity is now practised in North Korea. Many northern shamans were transplanted to the South, chased out along with their enemies the Christians, and the popularity of the services they offer (fortune-telling, for instance) has endured there. Together with the near-destruction of southern shamanism by South Korea's relentless modernisation, we have the curious situation where the actual practice of northern Korean shamanism can only be witnessed in South Korea.

Northern Korea held many important centres of Korean Buddhism from the 3rd century through the Japanese occupation period. The Kumgangsan and Myohyangsan mountain areas, in particular, hosted large Zen-oriented (Jogye) temple-complexes left over from the Goryeo dynasty. Under the communists, Buddhism in the North (along with Confucianism and shamanism) suffered a fate identical to that of Christianity.

Some historically important Buddhist temples and shrines still exist, mostly in rural or mountainous areas. The most prominent among them are Pyohon Temple at Kumgangsan, Pyohon Temple at Myohyangsan, and the Confucian Shrine in the Songgyungwan Neo-Confucian College just outside of Kaesong.

Arts

North Korean film enjoys something of a cult following with movie buffs, mainly as cinema has been a lifelong interest of Kim Jong-il's and the industry has been well financed for decades. Perhaps the most famous North Korean film is Shin Sang-ok's *Pulgasari,* a curious socialist version of *Godzilla* made by the kidnapped South Korean director, who escaped back to the South in 1986 (see opposite), though his involvement in the film is denied by the North Koreans.

Separating truth from myth is particularly hard with the film industry in North Korea; despite claims that scores of films are produced annually, the reality is probably far less impressive. Cinema visits are sometimes included on tours, when local films are shown with English subtitles, and are a fascinating experience. You can also request a visit to the Pyongyang Film Studios (p368) when booking your tour – and you may even be lucky enough to see a political-propaganda piece in production.

North Korean literature has not profited from the Kim dynasty, which has done nothing to encourage original writing. Despite an initial artistic debate in the 1950s, all non-party-controlled forms of expression were quickly repressed. Bookshops stock an unimaginably restrictive selection of works, focusing heavily on the works of Kim Il-sung and Kim Jong-il.

Tourists with an interest in traditional arts can request visits to performances of traditional Korean music, singing and dance, though these are rarely available. More feasible is a visit to a (revolutionary) opera or a classical music concert in Pyongyang; see p371).

ENVIRONMENT

North Korea is spookily litter free, with streets cleaned daily and litter very rarely dropped. Indeed, the only graffiti you're likely to see has been scratched onto the windowpanes of the Pyongyang Metro, explained by the fact that they were sold from East Berlin after German reunification. However the country's cities are polluted and there is little or no environmental consciousness.

The varying climatic regions on the northern half of the Korean peninsula have created environments that are home to subarctic, alpine and subtropical plant and tree species. Most of the country's fauna is contained within the limited nature reserves around the mountainous regions, as most of the lower plains have been converted to arable agricultural land. An energetic reforestation program was carried out after the Korean War to replace many of the forests that were destroyed by the incessant bombing campaigns, a notable exception being the area to the north of the DMZ, where defoliants are used to remove vegetation for security purposes. The comparatively low population has resulted in the preservation of most mountainous regions.

Areas of particular biodiversity are the DMZ, the wetlands of the Tumen River and the Paekdusan and Chilbo mountains in the far north. For those interested in tours with a greater emphasis on nature, it is possible to organise an itinerary with your Korean tour company, though any hopes of a truly nature-focused tour are likely to be dashed by the ubiquitous revolutionary sights that always take priority over hikes.

Two particular flora species have attracted enormous attention from the North Koreans, and neither of them are native. In 1965 Indonesia's then President Sukarno named a newly developed orchid after Kim Il-sung – *kimilsungia* – popular acclaim overcoming Kim's modest reluctance to accept such an honour. Kim Jong-il was presented with his namesake, *kimjongilia,* a begonia developed by a Japanese horticulturist, on his 46th birthday. The blooming of either flower is announced annually as a tribute to the two Great Leaders and visitors will notice their omnipresence throughout official tourist sites.

Environmental Issues

The main challenges to the environment in North Korea are from problems that are harder to see. The devastating floods and economic slowdown during the 1990s wreaked havoc not only on property and agricultural land, but also on the environment. Fields were stripped of their topsoil, which, combined with fertiliser shortages,

---

KIDNAP VICTIMS

Nobody could accuse the North Korean government of lacking pragmatism. Need to teach spies Japanese? The obvious solution is to kidnap Japanese civilians and employ them to do the job. By their own sheepish admission in 2002, the DPRK government kidnapped 13 Japanese nationals between 1977 and 1983, including couples enjoying romantic walks on desolate beaches and even tourists who were visiting Europe.

The Japanese government is unlikely to normalise relations with North Korea and pay billions of dollars in compensation for its colonial rule of the peninsula until the DPRK gives a fuller and more truthful account of the fate of its kidnap victims. As well as Japanese citizens, more than 400 South Koreans, mainly fishermen, have been abducted by the North and their fates remain unknown.

The most sensational kidnap of all was orchestrated by Kim Jong-il himself, according to reports from the BBC and the *Guardian*. The keen cineaste, appalled by the state of film production in the North, ordered that South Korean director Shin Sang-ok and his movie-star wife Choi Eun-hee be kidnapped and brought north to make films. After surviving four years in the Gulag for attempting to escape, Shin and Choi were brought before Kim Jong-il who greeted them like old friends, explaining how much he needed them. Given unlimited funds and the elite lifestyle exclusive to the inner circle of Kim Jong-il, Shin made seven films before managing to escape with Choi during a visit to Vienna. His autobiography *Kingdom of Kim* makes for some chilling reading about life in North Korea's heart of darkness.

---

forced authorities to expand the arable land under cultivation. Unsustainable and unstable hillside areas, river banks and road edges were brought under cultivation, further exacerbating erosion, deforestation, fertiliser contamination of the land and rivers and the vulnerability of crops. The countryside is slowly recovering from the devastation of the 1990s, though the threat of floods and famine remain.

FOOD & DRINK
Staples & Specialities

While tour groups eat sumptuously by North Korean standards, the standard fare is usually fairly mediocre. There is no danger of tourists going hungry though, and you'll find you get by very well on a diet of *kimchi,* rice, soups, noodles and fried meat. Vegetarians will be catered for without a problem, but their meals will usually be fairly bland and heavy on the rice, egg and cucumber. One culinary highlight is the good barbecues of both duck and squid often given to tourists.

Drinks

Taedonggang, a pleasant locally produced lager, is the most commonly found beverage, although imported beers such as Heineken are also common.

Other drinks on offer include a range of North Korean fruit juices and sodas, and Coke and Fanta are also available in some Pyongyang hotels and restaurants.

Soju (the local firewater) is also popular; it's rather strong stuff. Visitors might prefer Korean blueberry wine; the best is apparently made from Mt Paekdu blueberries. Blueberry wine comes in two forms: the gently alcoholic, which tastes like a soft drink, and the reinforced version, which could stun an elephant.

PYONGYANG

☎ 02 / pop 3.3 million

It's no exaggeration to say that Pyongyang ('flat land') is unlike any other capital city on earth. An ideological statement forged in concrete, bronze and marble, Pyongyang is the ultimate totalitarian metropolis, built almost entirely from scratch following its destruction in the Korean War.

Every visit focuses heavily on Pyongyang – this is after all a city built to impress with a population of approved, privileged citizens and a slew of awe-inspiring sights your guides visibly beam with pride to show you. It's worth trying to get to know the city during your trip, as this is one of the few places you'll have more than just a fleeting glimpse of from your tour bus.

The guides will be falling over themselves to show you a succession of monuments, towers,

NORTH KOREA

PYONGYANG

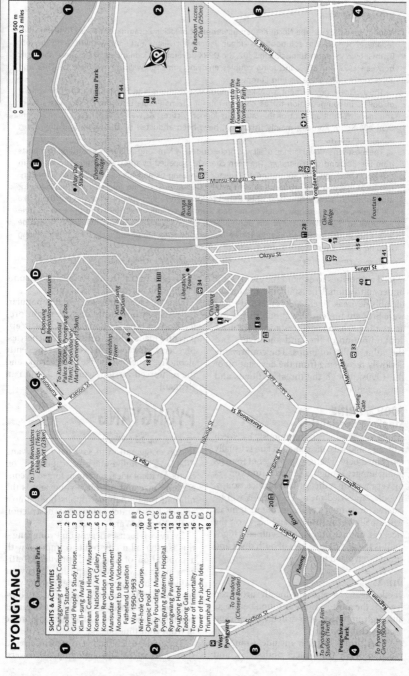

A Changgan Park

F Munsu Park

E May Day Stadium

Chongnyu Bridge

D Chonsung Revolutionary Museum

To Kumsusan Memorial Palace (500m); Pyongyang Zoo (1km); Revolutionary Martyrs' Cemetery (1.5km)

Moran Hill

Kim Il-sung Stadium

Friendship Tower

Liberation Tower 34

Chilsong Gate

Runga Bridge

Okryu St

Munsu-Kangan St

Monument to the Foundation of the Workers' Party

Ton'gdaewon St

Okryu Bridge

Fountain

Sungri St

Ponghwa Gate

Mansudae St

Kaeson St

Kumsong St

C To Three Revolutions Exhibition (1km); Airport (23km)

Pipa St

Moranbong St

An-Sang Taek St

B West Pyongyang

To Dandong (Chinese Border)

Hoan St

Potong River

To Pyongyang Film Studios (1km)

Pungwhasan Park

To Pyongyang Circus (500m)

Sochon St

Hyoksin St

Ponghwa St

Raewon St

Sosong St

To Random Access Club (250m)

Taehak St

SIGHTS & ACTIVITIES
Changgwang Health Complex..........1	B5
Chollima Statue..........2	D3
Grand People's Study House..........3	D5
Kim Il-sung Mural..........4	C2
Korean Central History Museum..........5	D5
Korean National Art Gallery..........6	D5
Korean Revolution Museum..........7	C3
Mansudae Grand Monument..........8	D3
Monument to the Victorious Fatherland Liberation War 1950–1953..........9	B3
Nine-hole Golf Course..........10	D7
Olympic Pool..........11	C6
Party Founding Museum..........(see 1)	
Pyongyang Maternity Hospital..........12	E3
Ryongwang Pavilion..........13	D4
Ryugyong Hotel..........14	B4
Taedong Gate..........15	D4
Tower of Immortality..........16	C1
Tower of the Juche Idea..........17	E5
Triumphal Arch..........18	C2

0 — 500 m
0 — 0.3 miles

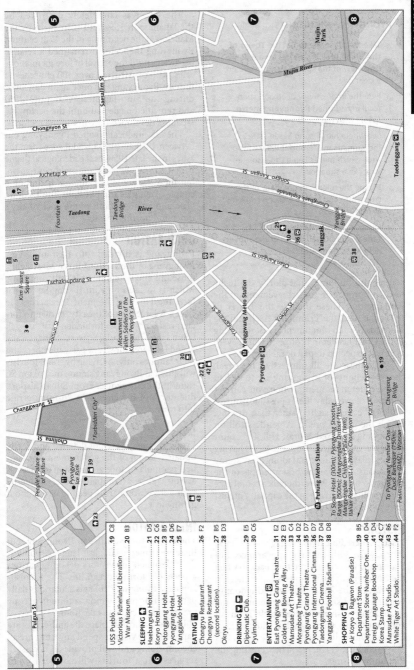

USS Pueblo	**19**	C8
Victorious Fatherland Liberation		
War Museum	**20**	B3
SLEEPING 🏠		
Haebangsan Hotel	**21**	D5
Koryo Hotel	**22**	C6
Potonggang Hotel	**23**	B5
Pyongyang Hotel	**24**	D6
Yanggakdo Hotel	**25**	E7
EATING 🍴		
Chongryu Restaurant	**26**	F2
Chongryu Restaurant		
(second location)	**27**	B5
Okryu	**28**	D3
DRINKING 🍷 🍸		
Diplomatic Club	**29**	E5
Pyulmori	**30**	C6
ENTERTAINMENT 🎭		
East Pyongyang Grand Theatre	**31**	E2
Golden Lane Bowling Alley	**32**	E3
Mansudae Art Theatre	**33**	C4
Moranbong Theatre	**34**	D2
Pyongyang Grand Theatre	**35**	D7
Pyongyang International Cinema	**36**	D7
Taedongmun Cinema	**37**	D4
Yanggakdo Football Stadium	**38**	D8
SHOPPING 🛍		
Air Koryo & Ragwon (Paradise)		
Department Store	**39**	B5
Department Store Number One	**40**	D4
Foreign Language Bookshop	**41**	D4
Korea Stamp	**42**	C7
Mansudae Art Studio	**43**	B6
White Tiger Art Studio	**44**	F2

PYONGYANG HIGHLIGHTS

- Take the lift to the top of the **Tower of the Juche Idea** (opposite) for a magnificent view of the sprawling cityscape on a clear day

- Ride the impressively deep and spectacularly adorned **Pyongyang metro** (p367) with the locals

- See where Kim Il-sung lies in state at the **Kumsusan Memorial Palace** (opposite), which makes Lenin's mausoleum look like a shoebox

- Escape the relentless grandeur of the city centre and have a walk on relaxed **Moran Hill** (p367)

- Enjoy an unforgettable night of bizarrely coordinated dance at the stunning **Mass Games** (p371)

---

statues and buildings that glorify the Juche idea and propagate the achievements of the Kim regime. These include the Tower of the Juche Idea, the Triumphal Arch and the Mansudae Grand Monument, a vast rendering of the Great Leader in bronze, to which every visitor is expected to pay floral homage.

While these are all impressive, if surreal, the real delights of Pyongyang are to be had in the quieter moments when you can get glimpses of everyday life. If possible, suggest walking between sights rather than driving, which the guides prefer. A gentle stroll on Pyongyang's relaxed Moran Hill, for example, is a great chance to join the locals having picnics, playing music and idling away sunny afternoons. Despite the best attempts of the Korean Workers' Party, there is a semblance of normality surviving in the capital. You just have to look hard for it.

HISTORY

It seems incredible to think it, given its stark, thoroughly 20th-century appearance, but Pyongyang is ancient, stretching back to when the Goguryeo dynasty built its capital here in AD 427. By the 7th century the kingdom of Goguryeo had started to collapse under the strain of successive, massive attacks from Sui and Tang China. Cutting a deal with the Tang Chinese, the Shilla kingdom in the South was able to conquer Goguryeo in 668, creating the first unified Korea.

The city was completely destroyed by the Japanese in 1592 and then again by the Manchus at the beginning of the 17th century. Pyongyang thenceforth remained a relative backwater until the arrival of foreign missionaries, who constructed over 100 churches in the city. Pyongyang was once again destroyed during the Sino-Japanese War (1894–95) and remained neglected until the occupying Japanese developed industry in the region.

The US practically wiped Pyongyang out between 1950 and 1953, and it rose from the ashes in the late 1950s as the ideological theme park it is today. Few historic buildings remain, but there are some in evidence, including a couple of temples and pavilions, the Taedong Gate and a few sections of the ancient city's inner and northern walls.

ORIENTATION

Pyongyang is divided into East and West Pyongyang by the Taedong River. Most sights, museums and hotels are in West Pyongyang, which is focused on Kim Il-sung Sq (which faces the Tower of the Juche Idea across the river). A large area of the city, known to foreign residents as 'the forbidden city', is back behind the Kim Il-sung Sq west of Changwang St and is an area for senior party members and their families only. Arriving by train, tourists will alight at Pyongyang station on Yokjon St, right in the city centre. From Sunan airport, due north of the city, it's a 20-minute ride into town.

Maps

Pyongyang maps are not detailed and rarely updated, a sign of the government's continued paranoia about foreign invasion. However, as you will be accompanied everywhere by your guides, you hardly need to worry about getting lost.

INFORMATION

There is no tourist office in Pyongyang, but there are numerous English-language publications designed for visitors detailing various aspects of North Korean life. The English-language *Pyongyang Times* is a hilarious daily paper full of propaganda, although a copy makes a great curio to take home.

Hotels, as the only place the authorities are happy to have visitors spend any time, are all encompassing and will provide all necessary services. Most tourists will not need to do laundry, as trips are rarely longer than a week, although the facilities exist in all Pyongyang hotels. Most hotels also have a 24-hour doctor on call.

SIGHTS

The city's points of interest divide neatly into two categories: the profoundly impressive yet ultimately pointless proliferation of statues, monuments and other monoliths to the Kims, the Juche Idea and the North Korean military; and the less obviously impressive – but far more interesting – slices of daily North Korean life to be found in excursions to funfairs, cinemas, public transport and parks. You don't have to be a genius to work out which your guides will prefer to show you, or to guess which most tour groups will enjoy the most.

Mansudae Grand Monument

Every itinerary features this larger-than-life bronze statue of the Great Leader. You can't help but baulk at Kim Il-sung's shamelessness – this is no memorial, but rather was unveiled in 1972 to celebrate Kim's 60th birthday. It was originally covered in gold leaf, but apparently at the objection of the Chinese who were effectively funding the North Korean economy, this was later removed in favour of the scrubbed bronze on display today.

As the epicentre of the Kim cult, visitors need to be aware of the seriousness with which North Koreans – officially at least – consider this monument and the respect they believe foreigners should accord it. Your tour leader will usually buy flowers and elect one member of the group to place them at the statue's feet. As this is done, the whole group will be expected to bow. Photographers will be instructed never to photograph one part of the monument – all pictures should be of the entire statue to avoid causing offence.

Chollima Statue

Just north of the Mansudae Grand Monument is the Chollima Statue – a bronze statue of the Korean Pegasus, the steed Chollima. It's an interesting example of how the Kim regime has sought to incorporate traditional Korean myths into its socialist cult. According to legend, Chollima could carry hundreds of kilometres a day and was untameable. Kim Il-sung appropriated the myth in the period of reconstruction following the Korean War

so that the zeal of the North Korean workers to rebuild their shattered nation and construct monuments to the leadership became known as 'Chollima Speed' (see the boxed text, p366). Indeed, when North Korea broke through to the quarterfinals of the World Cup in 1966, it was apparently because Kim senior had urged them to play 'Chollima football'.

Kumsusan Memorial Palace

Kim Il-sung's residence during his lifetime, the Kumsusan Palace remains so in death. The palace is eerie, with bricked-in windows and a vast square before it. The embalmed corpse of the Great Leader (a baseball-sized calcium growth on the back of his neck well hidden) lies in state here on the top floor for you to pay your respects to, but just getting here is adventure enough. First of all you'll need to be dressed smartly (shirts, ties and trousers for men, modest dress for women), then you'll go through airport-style security, allowed to take only your wallet and camera with you, pass along miles of mind-numbingly slow red travelators where walking is frowned upon and then be dusted off by both automatic shoe cleaners and a giant dusting machine. Then the real fun begins, when you enter the unbearably sombre Hall of Lamentations, the highlight of which is a rather hysterical English-language handset narrating the Korean people's grief at Kim Il-sung's death. This completed, you'll finally ascend to the viewing chamber itself, where you'll proceed to the glass bier and bow three times (once on each side, but not bowing when you're standing behind the Great Leader's head). This completed, it's back on the travelators in sombre silence, after which you're released into the square outside to take pictures of the bizarre place. If you had any doubt that your trip to North Korea would keep you in dinner party anecdotes for decades to come, the Kumsusan Memorial Palace will quash them.

Just as eerie is the **Tower of Immortality**, under which the traffic to the palace must pass from central Pyongyang. This tower, one of hundreds throughout the country, bears the legend 'The Great Leader Comrade Kim Il-sung will always be with us'.

Tower of the Juche Idea

On the other side of the Taedong River from Kim Il-sung Sq, this tower honours Kim Il-sung's

NORTH KOREA SPEAK

It's a good idea to familiarise yourself with some of the linguistic and idiomatic quirks peculiar to the North, although your ever-zealous tour guide will be delighted to fill in any ideological gaps that become apparent.

Chollima Speed Nothing it seems, in North Korea, is capable of moving with anything other than Chollima Speed. Not simply a grand way of saying 'fast', Chollima Speed dazzles and amazes. Whether you feel like it or not, you too will be dazzled and amazed when various buildings, factories or monuments are described to you in terms of their amazingly brief construction periods. Chollima is an ancient Korean myth, a Pegasus who was capable of travelling 1000 *ri*, or 400km, in one day, and could not be tamed by any rider. The Chollima movement, launched in the shadow of China's equally disastrous Great Leap Forward, engaged the population in trying to over-fulfil already ridiculously ambitious production targets. While its results were impressive on paper, the reality was, of course, somewhat different. However, the myths, both ancient and modern, remain, and if you really want to please your guide, say *jongmal Chollima soktoimnida* ('that really is Chollima Speed').

Juche Pronounced 'joo-chay', this is the cornerstone of North Korean philosophy, as witnessed by the Tower of the Juche Idea, the vast Pyongyang phallus designed by the Dear Leader himself. Juche encompasses many things but essentially stresses self-reliance and the individual's role in forging his destiny, the latter probably getting a cool reception at the concentration camps. Likewise, your guide will be delighted at your ideological progress if you say *Igosun Juchejog-imnida* ('It is Juche oriented').

The Great Leader This universally employed phrase describes Kim Il-sung (1912–94) who founded the DPRK and, over five decades in power, sought to apotheosise himself and his son.

The Dear Leader This reverential title refers to Kim Jong-il, the first person to lead a communist country by primogeniture. To confuse matters, since his father's death he has also been referred to as the 'Great Leader'. To make your guide's day, try to throw the phrase *widaehan ryongdoja* Kim Jong-il *tongji-ui mansumugang-ul samga chugwon hamnida* into the conversation ('I wish the Great Leader Comrade Kim Jong-il a long life in good health').

philosophy Juche (see the boxed text, above), and was unveiled to mark the president's 70th birthday in 1982. Indeed, the tower is made up of 25,550 granite blocks – one for every day of Kim's life until his 70th birthday. The tower stands at 170m and a trip to the top by lift (€5) is well worth it, providing a great view over the capital on a clear day. For the best views go in the morning, as the sun is still in the east, lighting up the western, more interesting side of the city. The pavilions surrounding the tower feature a trio of workers holding aloft the emblem of the DPRK and in the river immediately in front are two water jets that reach 150m on the occasions they are working.

Triumphal Arch

Your guides will tell you with barely concealed glee that the Triumphal Arch is 3m higher than its cousin in Paris, making it the largest in the world.

The arch marks the site where Kim Il-sung first addressed the liberated Koreans after the end of Japanese occupation in 1945. The gloss you hear will omit the fact that the Soviets liberated Pyongyang, not Kim Il-sung's partisans, who themselves gave full credit to the Soviets at the time. A vast **mural** a short walk away details the event and pictures a young Kim addressing a wildly enthusiastic local population. Set back from the arch is the Kim Il-sung Stadium.

Kim Il-sung Square

Pyongyang's central square and marching ground is strange in its emptiness, the open spaces seemingly cowed by the massive buildings surrounding it. Most impressive of these is the **Grand People's Study House**, the country's largest library and national centre of Juche studies. This is one of Pyongyang's most striking buildings, a socialist realist structure melded with traditional Korean architecture.

With over 30 million books, finding what you want is inevitably quite a challenge – and you will be proudly shown the incredible system of conveyor belts that can deliver books in seconds. Our request for a copy of *Nineteen Eighty-Four* didn't go down very well here.

Other structures on the square include the **Korean National Art Gallery**, sometimes included on tours, though it's frankly fairly dull, and the **Korean Central History Museum**, which is rarely visited. There's a great view from the riverside bank across the Taedong to the Tower of the Juche Idea, where groups usually go to take photos.

Historic Pyongyang

To see something of Pyongyang's prewar history is a challenge. The **Taedong Gate** was the eastern gate to the original walled city of Pyongyang, and was built in the 6th century. The current gate was rebuilt in 1635, but is one of the oldest remaining structures in the city – a reminder that Pyongyang was once a traditional Asian city rather than the thoroughly modern creation you see today.

Nearby are the other major historical sites: the **Pyongyang Bell**, a bronze early-warning system for fire and invasion dating from 1726, and the beautiful **Ryongwang Pavilion**, originally built in 1111 and rebuilt in 1670.

Mangyongdae Children's Palace

This centre for extra-curricular activity – from martial arts to the playing of traditional instruments – makes for a great visit. Note the model of a 'North Korean' space shuttle at the entrance, a replica of the Soviet *Buran*. The palace visit will include displays of incredibly talented martial artists, gymnasts and musicians, all beaming at you with terrified smiles as they perform. The tour usually culminates in the huge main auditorium with a stellar display by fantastically regimented youth. The grand finale is usually a loyalty song to Kim Jong-il.

Moran Hill

This is Pyongyang's top recreation ground for the masses. Couples wander, families picnic and there are people playing guitars and sometimes even dancing in an incongruously relaxed area of the capital. It's particularly busy on a Sunday and a lovely place to stroll and absorb something of daily life. Even the guides seem to relax more here and will usually allow you some freedom to wander about unaccompanied.

Pyongyang Metro

The Pyongyang metro is definitely a highlight of the capital. The network, which is made up of two lines, has a simultaneous function as a nuclear bunker in the event of the long-awaited American invasion. Stations are deep below ground, and you can even see blast doors that will close if Pyongyang ever comes under nuclear bombardment (see the boxed text, p368).

Museums

Pyongyang's museums unsurprisingly offer the regime's version of history. While one or two can be interesting for a totally new perspective on events, the novelty can soon wear thin.

The **Victorious Fatherland Liberation War Museum** is one of the best on offer. The key battles of the Korean War are depicted vividly in dioramas, and there's some fascinating military hardware ranging from war-damaged tanks and aircraft to torpedo boats used by both sides. These were all placed in the basement and the museum was then built around them. Nearby, opposite the little Potong tributary of the Taedong, there's the impressive **Monument to the Victorious Fatherland Liberation War 1950–1953**, unveiled in 1993 to mark the 40th anniversary of the war's end. The sculptures reflect the different battles of the war; the Victory Sculpture is the centrepiece.

A visit to the **Korean Revolution Museum** behind the Mansudae Grand Monument is sometimes included on itineraries. Despite the museum's rather misleading name, its main function is to document the death of Kim Il-sung (including a film of the extraordinary public reaction to it) and the succession of Kim Jong-il during the turbulent 1990s. One of the more bizarre items on display is a tin of Nivea handcream that the Dear Leader thoughtfully gifted to factory workers with sore hands.

The **Party Founding Museum** is located on the southern slope of Haebang Hill where it originally housed the Central Committee of the Korean Workers' Party, as well as Kim Il-sung's office from where he 'led the building of a new democratic Korea'. Next door is the Great Leader's conspicuously modest residence, used after coming to power and presumably before the masses demanded he build himself numerous palaces.

THE MYSTERY UNDERGROUND

As tourists, visiting the Pyongyang metro will involve a one-stop trip between Puhung (Rehabilitation) and Yonggwang (Glory) stations. All state visitors, from US Secretary of State Madeleine Albright to former South Korean President Kim Dae-jung, were given the same show trip, giving rise to a rumour that power cuts and lack of repair have meant that the rest of the system no longer functions on a day-to-day basis. In fact the whole system is used, although it's possible that during the years of austerity in the late 1990s much of it was closed to make energy savings.

The entire system's construction was overseen by the Great Leader, who offered his 'on-the-spot guidance'. A guidebook to the Metro describes his wise words on opening the new network in 1973:

'The Great Leader President said to officials in a thoughtful tone "I think it is difficult to build the metro, but it is not to cut the tape." Hearing his words, which considered the trouble of builders first, the participants in the opening ceremony felt a lump in their throats and gave enthusiastic cheers, waving bundles of flowers.'

One of the deepest metros in the world, it is also one of the most elaborately decorated – including marble platforms, glittering chandeliers and impressive murals extolling the virtues of Juche and detailing yet more of the heroic activities of guess who...

Korean Central History Museum is all rather tedious and predictable – a large number of exhibits about the North's struggle against imperialism and oppression.

A rarely visited museum is the surreal **Three Revolutions Exhibition**, North Korea's answer to Florida's Epcot Centre. The sprawling complex details the 'three revolutions' Kim Il-sung brought about in post-war Korea: ideological, technical and cultural. The six halls detail advances across the board in electronics, heavy industry, agriculture and technology (advances appear to be fairly slim though, with all the technical exhibits looking more like a display of antiques). The world's weirdest planetarium can be found within the electronics industry hall, which looks like a silver replica of Saturn. There's also an interesting outdoor display of vehicles produced in North Korea.

Pyongyang Film Studios

Several films a year are still churned out by the country's main film studios in the suburbs of Pyongyang. Kim Il-sung visited the complex around 20 times during his lifetime to provide invaluable on-the-spot guidance, while Kim Jr has apparently been more than 600 times, such is his passionate interest in films.

Like all things North Korean, the two main focuses are the anti-Japanese struggle and the anti-American war. The main complex is a huge, propaganda-filled suite of office buildings where apparently post-production goes on, even though it feels eerily empty. A short uphill drive takes you to the large sets, however, which are far more fun. Here you'll find a generic ancient Korean town for historic films (you can even dress up as a king or queen and be photographed sitting on a 'throne' carpeted in leopard skin), a 1930s Chinese street, a Japanese street, a South Korean street (look for the massage signs that illustrate their compatriots' moral laxity) and a fairly bizarre range of structures from a collection of 'European' buildings. Some groups have been lucky and seen films being made during their visit, although you're more likely to find it empty.

Pyongyang Zoo

Rarely offered on standard tours, Pyongyang Zoo is nevertheless worth a visit for the chance it provides to see locals enjoying themselves in an informal setting. It has a good aquarium and reptile house and a large array of animals, most of whom look pretty forlorn. Worst off are the big cats, nearly all gifts of long-dead communist big wigs around the world – the wonderful lions, tigers and leopards are kept in woefully inadequate compounds and many have lost the plot as a result. The zoo's two elephants and its hippo all look exceptionally lacklustre as well.

There's more fun to be had with the baboons and a collection of lemurs, while perhaps the oddest thing is the huge cage of domestic cats. It's very relaxed here; you'll find North Korean families on outings and this is one of the few environments where you can communicate with locals in a relatively carefree way.

Mangyongdae

Located 1km from the centre of Pyongyang, Mangyongdae has long been a destination for day trippers from the capital, due to its idyllic setting amid the gentle hills where the Sunhwa River flows into the Taedong. The suburb also houses the place of Kim Il-sung's birth – interesting to visit, as much to see the pretty setting, the funfair and the relaxing Pyongyangites, as for the flourishing Kim cult.

Kim Il-sung's birthplace is a collection of traditional huts: a typical Korean peasant house with a thatched roof and a block of living rooms, as well as a small barn, most of which looks as if it were built in the past few decades. The emphasis is very much on the president's humble origins, and indeed, it's an open question as to whether Kim Il-sung was really born here at all.

The **Mangyongdae Revolutionary Museum**, located nearby, continues the theme of the Great Leader's childhood and makes the point that all his family members were Korean patriot revolutionaries of the humblest possible order.

You may also be lucky enough to visit the **Mangyongdae Revolutionary School**, where Pyongyang's elite sons are trained for the next generation of leadership. This is a fun tour through the various classrooms and gymnasiums, where children look at you with wonder.

To relax after the relentless propaganda, the **Mangyongdae Funfair** is a pleasant oasis built around the base of Song Hill, where you can relax with some day-trippers from the capital. You can throw a ball at American Imperialists at the coconut shy, take a ride on a North Korean roller coaster (we survived, though it's probably the most dangerous ride on earth) and nauseate yourself on the Mad Mouse (a harmless looking mini-roller coaster that nearly cost us our lunch).

Pyongyang Maternity Hospital

This smart hospital, designed apparently to look like a mother's outstretched arms about to embrace her child, is sometimes available for group tours. Here all Pyongyang women give birth for the first time (whether they like it or not); after that it's the preserve of the privileged or the vulnerable. It's an impressive place, with relatively modern equipment and spotless floors. The tour typically includes patient rooms, treatment rooms and the incubators where you can see Pyongyang's newborns.

It's interesting that North Korean fathers have no contact with their children for five days after their birth for health reasons. In the meantime, the camera phone booths on the ground floor are where interaction is restricted to, although such technology simply underscores how much of a showpiece this place really is.

SLEEPING

Pyongyang's hotels are, like much of the city's architecture, built to impress, and while their facades are often striking, their interiors tend to be less so. The city's skyline is dominated by the incredible pyramid of the Ryugyong Hotel – designed to be the world's largest luxury hotel in the 1980s, abandoned half-way through construction during the economic collapse in the 1990s and finally being finished at the time of writing and due to open in 2012.

Yanggakdo Hotel (☎ 381 2134; fax 381 2930/1; ✖ ❷) This is where most tour groups stay, a massive mid-'90s tower on its own island right in the middle of Pyongyang. The rooms are already showing their age, but they are at least spacious and comfortable, with great views over the city. As well as a pool and sauna, there are numerous restaurants, a bowling alley, a golf course, three pool tables, a karaoke lounge, several shops, a casino and a foreigners-only disco. The advantage of the Yanggakdo is that you can wander around outside without your guides (although don't even think of crossing the bridge into the city), something you can't really do in other hotels in Pyongyang.

Koryo Hotel (☎ 381 4397; fax 318 4422; ✖ ❷) The city's other premier hotel, this 1985 orange-bronze structure is the preferred place to lodge UN functionaries and business people as well as some tour groups. Each of its twin towers has a revolving restaurant on top, though only one of them is open as, in a spectacular failure of forethought, the other overlooks the highly secretive 'forbidden city'. The relative bustle of Changgwang St, a short walk from Pyongyang

---

THE GENERAL SHERMAN & USS PUEBLO

During the 'hermit kingdom' phase of the Joseon dynasty, one of Korea's first encounters with Westerners was the ill-fated attempt of the American ship, the *General Sherman*, to sail up the Taedong River to Pyongyang in 1866. It arrogantly ignored warnings to turn around and leave, and insisted on trade. When it ran aground on a sand bar just below Pyongyang, locals burnt it and killed all those on board including a Welsh missionary and the Chinese and Malay crew. An American military expedition later pressed the Seoul government for reparations for the loss, otherwise the incident was virtually forgotten in the South. However, northerners have always regarded it with great pride as being their first of many battles with, and victories over, the hated Yankee imperialist enemy.

Also of great pride to the North Koreans is the 'fact' that none other than the Great Leader's great-grandfather had participated in burning the ship. Today, all that is left of the *General Sherman* is a plaque. The site is overshadowed by the nearby ship the USS *Pueblo*, a US surveillance vessel that was seized by the North Koreans off the east coast of Korea in January 1968 during a heightening of tensions between the North and South. You can step aboard and hear another lecture on the violations of the ceasefire agreement by the US, and on the embankment look out for the recent addition of an alleged US submersible captured by the North Koreans in 2006.

---

train station, makes this a popular choice for visiting business people.

Potonggang Hotel (☎ 381 2229; fax 381 4428; ☒ ☒) Famously the only hotel in North Korea to get CNN, the Potonggang is owned by Unification Church leader Reverend Moon, and has the best rooms in the city, though it's rare for groups to stay here. The hotel is situated by the small Potong River, about 4km from the city centre, and offers some good restaurants, a bar, pool, karaoke and indoor golf.

Haebangsan Hotel (Sungri St) Centrally located, this hotel has decent enough rooms, a good shop, pool tables and an office for booking international train tickets.

Pyongyang Hotel (Sungri St) Popular with foreign residents in the capital mainly for its excellent Arirang restaurant (supposedly the best in the city), the Pyongyang Hotel is pretty basic, though one floor has recently been redone to a good standard.

Chongnyon Hotel (Chongchun St; ☒) The 'Youth' Hotel is located in the bizarre sports district around Chongchun St, and while its rooms are damp and depressing the hotel boasts an outdoor pool and a lurid karaoke room.

Sosan Hotel (Chongchun St) Also in the sports district of Chongchun St, the Sosan Hotel is run by Golden Cup, the North Korean sports tourism company. Facilities include a driving range.

EATING & DRINKING

Pyongyang has by far the best restaurants in North Korea, though that's not always say-

ing a huge amount. Almost all tour groups will eat out at least once a day, usually twice. Any restaurant outside your hotel that you are taken to is likely to be the exclusive preserve of foreigners and the elite – there are popular local restaurants, such as those on Changgwang St, but foreign tour groups will not usually be taken there.

On tours all eating out will be included in your price, although there are extra charges for additional beers or specialties such as the local favourite, cold noodles.

Pyongyang Number One Duck Barbeque is one of the best places in town, and will often be where groups go on their last evening. Here you'll be served up delicious strips of duck meat you cook at your table.

The **Chongryu Restaurant** opposite the Romanian Embassy is nearly always on the itinerary. It's a pleasant place where you make your own hotpot dish on little individual gas stoves, although it's equally notable for its ropey Swiss rolls served as a dessert. There's a second branch of this restaurant housed in a boat-shaped restaurant overlooking the Potong River by the ice rink. Tourists are charged extra if they eat here though, as it's one of Pyongyang's best eateries.

Okryu is one of the city's best-known restaurants, a recently renovated faux-traditional structure on the riverside that's famed for its cold noodles and very popular with locals. For this reason it's not usually on the schedule for groups, but you may be lucky.

Pyongyang's first pizza joint, imaginatively called **Italian Restaurant** (Kwangbok St), caused a sensation when it opened in 2009 after Kim Jong-il reportedly sent a team of chefs to Italy to learn how to make the perfect pizza. The results are apparently very good indeed, though at the time of writing Italian Restaurant was not on the 'tourist list' – the KITC list of eateries where tourists can go.

Pyulmori is a refreshingly well-run joint venture restaurant, coffee shop and bar near the Koryo Hotel. You can get decent food, coffee and excellent cake here, and in the evenings it's a popular bar and expat hangout.

Nightlife in Pyongyang is almost nonexistent, although hotel bars can be rowdy, especially at weekends. The large diplomatic and NGO presence in town means that there are some private clubs where foreigners can relax away from the strictures of everyday Pyongyang life, though these are usually inaccessible to foreign tourists.

The **Diplomatic Club** ('the diplo' to any self-respecting foreign resident) by the Juche Tower and the **Random Access Club** (RAC) in the diplomatic quarter of Munsudong are popular. 'The diplo' can be visited by tourists, though the RAC is for foreign residents only.

ENTERTAINMENT

The nature of visiting North Korea is that the most mundane, everyday things become instantly fascinating. Given that contact with locals is kept to a minimum, while in Pyongyang you should take advantage of the relatively wide choice of evening entertainment to see how the capital's residents like to relax. Of course, what you will and won't be able to do depends on your guides, so put in any requests as early on as possible. There will often be a nominal charge of €5 to €20 for extra activities in the evening.

The ultimate Pyongyang night out is the unforgettable **Mass Games**, a truly unique show that takes place nightly between August and October at the **May Day Stadium**. The show currently being performed is *Arirang*, the story of Korea's history told in an incredible combination of dance, acrobatics, music and mass coordination involving over 100,000 performers. However, a new show is currently in the works for the 2012 centenary of Kim Il-sung's birth. Tickets are steeply priced, starting at €75 for a 'third class' ticket and rising to €250 for VIP tickets – but the experience is worth every cent.

The **Pyongyang Circus** is a popular afternoon or evening out, though it's housed in a palatial building a million miles away from the traditional big top and sawdust floor. Here you'll see a stellar display of acrobatics, some very funny clowns and some deeply sad looking bears who skip rope while dressed in outlandish costumes.

One suitably military pastime is a trip to the **Pyongyang shooting range** off Chongchun St, where all Pyongyang's sporting facilities are concentrated. It costs €1 for three bullets using a 2.2mm rifle or pistol.

The huge **Golden Lane Bowling Alley** on Munsu-Kangan St is a good chance to mix with locals and watch some stellar displays of local bowling talent.

Cinema, theatre and opera trips are also possible (although rare), and while performances aren't likely to be of a particularly gripping order, again, it's the experience that is interesting. The two cinemas on offer are the newly refurbished **Taedongmun Cinema** on Sungri St and the **Pyongyang International Cinema**, a six-screen complex on Yanggak Island, near the Yanggakdo Hotel. The biennial **Pyongyang Film Festival** is held here in September of even-numbered years. Screenings that foreigners are allowed to attend are usually subtitled in English.

The main theatres are the **Pyongyang Grand Theatre**, the **East Pyongyang Grand Theatre,** the **Moranbong Theatre** and the **Mansudae Art Theatre**, although spectacles vary little from one to the other. Drama is not usually shown, and instead you'll usually see orchestras performing classical and traditional Korean music, or one of the five North Korean revolutionary operas such as *The Flower Girl* and *A Daughter of the Party*. Jump at the chance to see these, as they are sumptuous productions with very high production values.

Soccer, a very popular local spectator sport, is a good way to spend an evening with ordinary Koreans. Sadly though, foreigners are only allowed to attend international fixtures, though it's worth asking the guides if there are any on during your stay. Matches are played at Yanggakdo Football Stadium.

For anyone interested in the surreal, a round at the nine-hole **Golf Course** at the Yanggakdo Hotel will make a great anecdote for years to come – how many people can say they've played golf in North Korea? Other sports are possible by prior arrangement, especially if you're travelling with a sports group. The **Olympic Pool** and the **Changgwang Health Complex** are both open to foreigners on Saturday.

If you're stuck in your hotel for the evening then **karaoke**, **pool** and a visit to the **sauna** are the main entertainment options, though the Yanggakdo Hotel, the most common residence of tourists in Pyongyang, also boasts a **casino**, **ten-pin bowling**, **pool tables** and a **microbrewery** serving up delicious beer. Note that the Chinese sauna at the Yanggakdo is a 'special service' sauna for tired businessmen, so it's best to stick to the normal sauna, unless you are looking for more risqué activities.

SHOPPING

Every Pyongyang sight has a small stand selling books, postcards and other trinkets. There are good book shops at both the Yanggakdo and Koryo Hotels and the **Foreign Language Bookshop** is the best in the city.

Next door to the Koryo Hotel is **Korea Stamp**, and it's definitely worth your time to stop in, as North Korean stamps are spectacular propaganda pieces. T-shirts and postcards are also on sale here.

Department stores can often be visited if the guides agree, and they can be a fascinating insight into what's available. The one most regularly visited is the **Ragwon (Paradise) Department Store. Department Store Number One**, the city's busiest, is currently off limits to foreigners.

Art is another popular purchase in Pyongyang. Of the big art studios in the city, the best choice is available at the **White Tiger Art Studio** in East Pyongyang, where the selection runs from traditional painting to socialist realism via dogs playing poker. Another good selection can be bought at the **Mansudae Art Studio** (Saemaul St), where wood-block prints of Pyongyang start at around €15.

Insam (ginseng) is for sale in hotels, but prices are high, especially for the prized Paekdusan *insam*. You may be able to pick up some more cheaply in Kaesong; ask your guide for advice. However, you can buy all grades of *insam* much more cheaply in South Korea.

GETTING AROUND

All tourists will be driven around Pyongyang either by car, minibus or coach. Using public transport is not possible, save for the metro ride between the two stations foreigners are permitted to visit on a tour (see the boxed text, p368). Foreign residents in the city may have more freedom to use the extensive bus, tram, trolleybus and metro network, however.

Taxis are available outside all hotels for you to travel in with your guide, should the need arise. Reception can also book taxis for you if there are none outside the hotel.

AROUND NORTH KOREA

All tours begin and end in Pyongyang, but most also include a trip to other parts of the country. Almost everyone visits the DMZ at Panmunjom and the nearby city of Kaesong. Visits to mountain resorts elsewhere on the peninsula and even the far-flung mountains in the country's northeast are also sometimes included.

KAESONG
pop 330,000

Though just a few miles from the DMZ and the world's most concentrated build-up of military forces, Kaesong is a fairly relaxed place just off the Reunification Hwy from Pyongyang. The city itself is dominated by a massive statue of Kim Il-sung atop a large hill, while the city's main street runs from the hill to the highway. In recent years Kaesong's economy has been given a much needed boost by the Kaesong Industrial Park, a special administrative area nearby run in conjunction with South Korea to encourage mutual economic collaboration. The city's main railway station, built with money from the South, is incongruously modern as a result.

Once the capital of the Goryeo dynasty, Kaesong has an interesting old quarter as well as the country's most atmospheric hotel, but KITC are not inclined to spend much time here, and you are usually just billeted at the hotel for the night before returning to Pyongyang having seen the DMZ.

Despite Kaesong's history you won't see many relics of antiquity here due to three major wars, each leaving little but rubble. At least there is the **Songgyungwan Neo-Confucian College**, originally built in AD 992 and rebuilt after being destroyed in the 1592 Japanese invasion. Today it is host to the **Koryo Museum** of celadon pottery and other Buddhist relics. The buildings surround a wide courtyard dotted with ancient trees, and the surrounding grounds are very pleasant to walk around. There are also two good souvenir shops outside as well, one selling ginseng and another selling commemorative stamps and souvenirs. It's a short drive northeast of town.

Kaesong may be your only chance while in the DPRK to see an authentic Korean royal tomb. The best one by far is the **Tomb of King Kongmin** (the 31st Goryeo king, who reigned between 1352 and 1374) and his queen. It is richly decorated with traditional granite facing and statuary. It's a very secluded site about 13km west of the city centre; there are splendid views over the surrounding tree-covered hills from a number of vantage points.

The third great tourist site is the 37m-high **Pakyon Falls**, one of the three most famous in North Korea. It's found in a beautiful natural setting some 24km north of town. Theoretically at least, some great hiking can be done around here: from the falls to the **Taehungsan Fortress**, to the mid-Goryeo **Kwanum Temple** (with cave) and the **Taehung Temple**, though again, tourists aren't usually given the chance to do this.

Kaesong itself is a modern city with wide streets. It's of scant interest, though it does have an interesting older section consisting of traditional tile-roofed houses sandwiched between the river and the main street. Within the town are a number of lesser tourist sights: the **Sonjuk Bridge**, a tiny clapper bridge built in 1216 and opposite, the **Songin Monument**, which honours Neo-Confucian hero Chong Mong-ju; the **Nammun** (South Gate), which dates from the 14th century and houses an old Buddhist bell; the **Sungyang Seowon** (Confucian academy); and **Chanamsan**, the hill from which Kim Il-sung's statue stares down at the city (and from where there are good views over the old town).

If you stay over here, you'll be based at the **Kaesong Folk Hotel**, a wonderful place consisting of 20 traditional Korean *yeogwan* (small, well-equipped en-suite rooms) all off a courtyard, and featuring a charming stream running through it. Power cuts are common here, but some light in the evening and half an hour's hot water can usually be rustled up. It's basic (the rice husk pillows are distinctly hard!) but fascinating.

PANMUNJOM

The sad sight of a pointlessly divided nation remains one of the most memorable parts of any trip to North Korea. While military history buffs will really be in their element, you don't have to be an expert to appreciate the weirdness of the site where the bloody Korean War ended in an unhappy truce more than half a century ago. Seeing the situation from the North, facing off against US troops to the south is a unique chance to witness things from a new perspective.

The eerily quiet drive down the six-lane Reunification Hwy – the road is deserted save for military checkpoints – gives you a sense of what to expect. Just before you exit to the DMZ, the sign saying 'Seoul 70km' is a reminder of just how close and yet how far normality is.

There are several aspects to the DMZ visit. Your first stop will be at a **KPA post** just outside the DMZ. Here a soldier will show you a model of the entire site, pointing out South Korean as well as North Korean HQ and watchtowers. Then you'll be marched (single file!) through an anti-tank barrier to rejoin your bus, and you'll drive down a long concrete corridor. Look out for the tank traps either side – huge slabs of concrete ready to be dropped into the road at any minute in the event of a land invasion.

The next stop is the **Armistice Talks Hall**, about 1km into the DMZ. Here negotiations were held between the two sides from 1951 until the final armistice, which was signed here on 27 July 1953. You'll see two copies of the agreement on display in glass cases, along with the original North Korean and UN flags. Next door there's an exhibition of photos from the war. Outside, a plaque in red script best sums up the North Korean version of the ceasefire. It reads:

> It was here on July 27, 1953 that the American imperialists got down on their knees before the heroic Chosun people to sign the ceasefire for the war they had provoked June 25, 1950.

From here you'll reboard the bus and drive to the demarcation line itself, and are reminded in more than usually severe language about sticking together 'for your own safety'. The site consists of two sinister-looking headquarters staring at each other across the line (the North Korean is built to be the bigger of the two) and several huts built over the line for meetings. Amazingly, you can cross into South Korea a

NORTH KOREAN REFUGEES IN CHINA

Since the early 1990s, there has been an increasing number of North Korean refugees making it across the heavily guarded border with China. The reasons are mainly economic: working for a few months in China can earn enough money to support a North Korean family through the winters by buying food from the private markets, and often refugees return to North Korea once they've saved some money there.

In 2000, under pressure from the DPRK government, the Chinese authorities launched their harsh 'Strike Hard' campaign. The aim is to forcibly repatriate any North Koreans found in Northern China and send already malnourished individuals back to a country where at the very least they will be imprisoned, and perhaps executed for illegally leaving. Even those lucky enough not to get caught often fall victim to people traffickers who force women into prostitution or marriage.

Those lucky enough to survive and make the journey through a complex underground network via Bangkok to South Korea are forming refugee support networks, such as **Life Funds for North Korean Refugees** (www.northkoreanrefugees.com). These vital networks provide financial and emotional support for those who have managed to escape the DPRK. For a disturbing and upsetting first-hand account, read Soon Ok-Lee's incredible testimony to the US Senate at http://judiciary.senate.gov/hearings/testimony.cfm?id=292&wit_id=665.

few metres within the huts, but the doors out to the south are closed and guarded by two soldiers. See p152 for an account of the South Korean tour to the same place.

Being at the very centre of the biggest military face-off on earth is rather like being in the eye of a storm – tension is in the air, but it is so peaceful as to make the very idea of imminent combat seem ridiculous. South Korean and American soldiers eyeball their northern counterparts as they have done every day since 1953. Do not be fooled by the prevailing air of calm, though; any attempt to even approach the border proper will result in you being shot on the spot, possibly from both sides. In the 1980s, however, a Soviet tourist found a unique way to flee the communist bloc, and defected amid gunfire from both sides. Unless you are really short of time, this is not an advisable way to get to Seoul.

Throughout the 1970s and 1980s, the North Koreans tunnelled under the DMZ into South Korean territory (see p153). The largest tunnel was discovered in 1975, and US military experts estimated that 10,000 men per hour could pass through the tunnel into the South. The last tunnel was discovered in 1990 – this persistent phenomenon gave the Pentagon such headaches that they allegedly hired psychics to help them find the tunnels.

The other interesting sight at the DMZ is the **Korean Wall**, a US-constructed anti-tank barrier that runs the length of the entire 248km border. It has been hijacked as an emotive propaganda weapon by the North, who

since 1989 have been comparing it with the Berlin Wall. Indeed, the issue has proven an emotive one in the South as well, where students have demanded it be dismantled. You will inspect the wall with binoculars and be shown a particularly hilarious North Korean propaganda video.

MYOHYANGSAN

A trip to this pretty resort area just 150km north of Pyongyang provides an easy chance to experience the pristine North Korean countryside, along with an inevitable slice of personality cult. Mt Myohyang and the surrounding area of hills, mountain trails and waterfalls make for a charming trip, and if you begin to miss the relentless pomp and propaganda of Pyongyang, the **International Friendship Exhibition** (IFE) will remind you that you are still very much in North Korea.

Myohyangsan means 'mountain of mysterious fragrance' and it's certainly no misnomer. The scenery is quite wonderful, and in summer the area is awash with flowers. The focus of all trips are, however, the two vast shrines that make up the IFE. The first one contains all the gifts presented to the eternal president Kim Il-sung. Before entering the vast traditional building, you will be asked to put on shoe covers in keeping with the reverential attitude shown by one and all. A member of your group may be honoured with the task of opening the vast doors that lead into the exhibit – after putting on ceremonial gloves to protect the polished door knob.

Kim Il-sung's gifts are very impressive. Particularly noteworthy is the beautiful armoured train carriage presented to him by Mao Zedong and a limousine sent to Kim by that great man of the people, Josef Stalin. The exhibits are arranged geographically, although you will thankfully only be shown the highlights of over 100,000 gifts spread over 120 rooms. Gifts from heads of state are displayed on red cloth, those from other officials on blue and gifts from individuals on brown. The undeniable highlight is a stuffed crocodile holding a tray of wooden glasses, presented to the Great Leader by the Sandinistas.

The tone of the visit is very strict and sombre, so avoid the very real temptation to ice-skate across the ridiculously over-polished floor in your foot covers. The most reverential and surreal part of the exhibit is the final room, in which there is a grinning life-sized waxwork of the Great Leader, to which you will be expected to bow your head before leaving respectfully. The waxwork itself was apparently a gift from the Chinese and Kim Il-sung is depicted standing against a 3D landscape of bucolic idyll, replete with birdsong, gentle breeze and elevator music. The tone is so remarkably odd that you'll have to concentrate not to get the giggles, especially when your guide insists on how serious it all is.

Next is Kim Jong-il's similarly spectacular warehouse where gifts given to him are housed in a vault built into the cave wall, recalling the secret lair of one of the Bond villains. There is a noticeable shift away from the grand fraternal gifts of fellow communist dictators that characterise Kim Il-sung's exhibit. Instead, Kim Jong-il's collection smacks of corporate and political gesture – characterising much of his reign since 1994. For example, where Kim Snr received gifts from Ceausescu and Honecker, Kim Jnr has gifts from Hyundai and CNN, as well as a good luck note from Jimmy Carter and a basketball from Madeleine Albright. Indeed, some parts of the exhibit look like any upmarket electronics showroom – row after row of wide-screen televisions and stereo equipment donated by industrialists.

Like his father's, Kim Jong-il's warehouse ends with a rare statue of the Dear Leader, depicting the Marshall seated benevolently, back-lit with pink soft-tone lighting.

Having completed a tour of both exhibits, the perfect way to unwind from the seriousness is with some walking on the beautiful mountain trails. Sangwon Valley is the most common place for a hike and is directly northeast of the IFE.

Don't miss **Pyohon Temple**, the most historically important Buddhist temple in western North Korea. The temple complex dates back to 1044, with numerous renovations over the centuries. It's just a short walk from the IFE, at the entrance to Sangwon Valley. It features several small pagodas and a large hall housing images of the Buddha, as well as a museum that sports a collection of wood blocks from the Buddhist scriptures the Tripitaka Koreana.

It is common for tours to visit the **Ryongmun Big Cave** either prior to or after a visit to Myohyangsan. This 6km-long limestone cave has some enormous caverns and a large number of stalactites. Enjoy sights like the Pool of Anti-Imperialist People's Struggle, the Juche Cavern and the Mountain Peak of the Great Leader.

Sleeping

Tourists are usually put up at the **Hyangsan Hotel**, a 15-storey pyramidal building with a fake waterfall attended by plastic deer in its lobby. The hotel itself is now in a rather poor state of repair, but totally fine. In keeping with North Korean hotel tradition, there is a revolving restaurant on the top floor, complete with net curtains, from which absolutely nothing is visible in the evenings due to the hotel's isolated mountain location.

KUMGANGSAN

South of the port city of Wonsan on the east of the Korean peninsula, the most dramatic scenery in the entire country begins to rise. Kumgangsan (Diamond Mountains) have exerted a strange hold over people for centuries, including the notoriously insular Chinese who deigned to include Kumgangsan among the five most beautiful mountain ranges in the known world (the other four ranges were in China). Located just north of the 38th parallel, the area has also been annexed for very heavily controlled South Korean tourism organised by Hyundai Asan (www.hyundai-asan.com). This was briefly suspended in 2008 following a shocking incident when a South Korean tourist was shot dead (p356), though tourism began again in late 2009.

Kumgang is divided into the Inner, Outer and Sea Kumgang regions. The main tourist activities are hiking, mountaineering, boating and sightseeing. The area is peppered with former Buddhist temples and hermitages, waterfalls, mineral springs, a pretty lagoon and a small museum. Maps of the area are provided by park officials to help you decide where you want to go among the dozens of excellent sites.

If your time here is limited, the best places to visit in the Outer Kumgang Region are the **Samil Lagoon** (try hiring a boat, then rest at Tanpung Restaurant); the **Manmulsang Area** (fantastically shaped crags); and the **Kuryong** and **Pibong Falls** (a 4.5km hike from the Mongnan Restaurant).

In the Inner Kumgang Region, it's worth visiting the impressively reconstructed **Pyohon Temple**, founded in AD 670 and one of old Korea's most important Zen monasteries. Hiking in the valleys around Pyohon Temple or, really, anywhere in the park is rewarding and memorable. **Pirobong** (1639m) is the highest peak out of at least a hundred.

The usual route to Kumgangsan is by car from Pyongyang to Onjong-ri via Wonsan along the highway (around 315km, a four-hour drive). Along the way to Wonsan, your car or bus will usually stop off at a teahouse by **Sinpyeong Lake**. From Wonsan, the road more or less follows the coastline south, and you'll get glimpses of the double-wired electric fence that runs the entire length of the east coast. There may also be a stop for tea at **Shijung Lake**.

Your final destination is the village of **Onjong-ri** and the **Kumgangsan Hotel**. The hotel is quite a rambling affair consisting of a main building and several outer buildings that include chalets, a shop, a dance hall and bathhouse (fed by a hot spring). The food served here is good, especially the wild mountain vegetable dishes.

PAEKDUSAN

One of the most stunning sights on the Korean peninsula, Paekdusan (Mt Paekdu) straddles the Chinese–Korean border in the very far northeastern tip of the DPRK. Apart from it being the highest mountain in the country at 2744m, and an amazing geological phenomenon (it's an extinct volcano now containing a vast crater lake at its centre), it is also of huge mythical importance to the Korean people.

Paekdusan is not included on most tours, as it involves chartering an internal flight

to Samjiyon and then travelling an hour and a half into the mountains from there. However, if you have the time and money to include a visit on your trip, you will not be disappointed. It's also possible to approach Paekdusan from the Chinese side of the border on a ferry and bus tour from Sokcho in South Korea (p179).

The natural beauty of the extinct volcano now containing one of the world's deepest lakes is made all the more magical by the mythology that surrounds the lake, both ancient and modern. The legend runs that Hwanung, the Lord of Heaven, descended onto the mountain in 2333 BC, and from here formed the nation of Choson – 'The Land of Morning Calm', or ancient Korea. It therefore only seems right and proper that four millennia later Kim Jong-il was born nearby 'and flying white horses were seen in the sky' according to official sources. In all likelihood, Kim Jong-il was born in Khabarovsk, Russia, where his father was in exile at the time, but the all-important Kim myth supersedes such niggling facts.

Trips here are strictly organised as this is a sensitive border region and thus a military zone. Having arrived at the military station at the bottom of the mountain, you'll be checked in and will take the funicular railway up the side of the mountain. From here it's a 10-minute hike up to the mountain's highest point, past some superb views down into the crater lake. You can either walk down to the shore of Lake Chon (an easy hike down, but somewhat tougher coming back up!) or take the cable car (€7 per person return) for the easy option. Ensure you bring warm clothes for this trip – it can be freezing at any time of year, with snow on the ground year round.

Much like Myohyangsan, an area of great natural beauty is further enhanced by revolutionary 'sights' such as **Jong-il peak** and the **Secret Camp**, the official birthplace of Kim Jong-il and from where Kim Il-sung supposedly directed some of the key battles during the anti-Japanese campaigns of WWII, despite the fact that no historians outside the DPRK have ever claimed that the area was a battle scene.

North Korea's current history books also claim that he established his guerrilla headquarters at Paekdusan in the 1920s, from where he defeated the Japanese. To prove this, you'll be shown declarations that the Great

Leader and his comrades carved on the trees – some so well preserved you might think that they were carved yesterday. The North Korean book *Kim Jong-il in His Young Days* describes the Dear Leader's difficult childhood during those days of ceaseless warfare at Paekdusan:

> His childhood was replete with ordeals. The secret camp of the Korean People's Revolutionary Army in the primeval forest was his home, and ammunition belts and magazines were his playthings. The raging blizzards and ceaseless gunshots were the first sounds to which he became accustomed. Day in and day out fierce battles went on and, during the breaks, there were military and political trainings. On the battlefield, there was no quilt to warmly wrap the new-born child. So women guerrillas gallantly tore cotton out of their own uniforms and each contributed pieces of cloth to make a patchwork quilt for the infant.

The Dear Leader's birthplace is a nondescript log cabin that you aren't allowed to enter (though you can peer in through the windows), and it's a bit of a let down after a long drive. But with the revolutionary sites out the way you can enjoy the real reason to come here; the glories of nature: vast tracts of virgin forest, abundant wildlife, lonely granite crags, fresh springs, gushing streams and dramatic waterfalls.

Samjiyon, the slightly sinister new resort town where most travellers stay overnight on the visit to Paekdusan, also boasts a couple of attractions – most notably the **Samjiyon Grand Monument**, which must be the most impressive paean to the leadership in the country outside Pyongyang. Set in a huge clearing in the woods with views to Mt Paekdu and overlooking a large lake, the monument commemorates the battle of Pochombo, where the anti-Japanese forces first moved from guerrilla tactics to conventional warfare and took the town of the same name. The centrepiece of the monument is a 15m-high statue of a 27-year-old Kim Il-sung, as well as a smaller version of Pyongyang's Juche Tower and several large sculptures of various revolutionary scenes. Elsewhere in Samjiyon there's the **Paekdu Museum**, a very ho-hum recreation of

all the sights of the region and a small **Children's Palace**, where groups will sometimes be shown a performance.

Sleeping

Hotels in this area include the **Pegaebong Hotel** just outside the resort town of Samjiyon, a decent option with modern rooms and hot running water in its newest wing. Further away, you can also stay in the town of Hyesan, at the second-class **Hyesan Hotel**.

Getting There & Away

Paekdusan is only accessible from around late June to mid-September; at all other times it is forbiddingly cold and stormy. Access to the mountain is by air only, followed by car or bus. These charter flights can hold up to 40 people, for around €4600 per plane per round-trip flight. In a decent-sized group it isn't unreasonable, but it's a bit much for a solo trip.

WONSAN
pop 300,000

The port city of Wonsan on the East Sea is not a big tourist draw, but makes for an interesting stop en route to the Kumgangsan mountains from Pyongyang. As it's not usually a destination, it reflects real North Korean life to a good extent. The city is an important port, a centre of learning with 10 universities and a popular holiday resort for Koreans, with beaches at nearby Lake Sijung and Lake Tongjong.

The city, 200km east of Pyongyang, is surrounded by verdant mountains and is full of modern high-rise buildings. Wonsan is also pleasantly attractive, especially during the summer months. The two main tourist hotels are the **Songdowon Tourist Hotel** and the **Tomgmyong Hotel**, both second class.

The nicest part of Wonsan is the suburb of **Songdowon** on the northwestern shore. There is a clean sandy beach here set among pines where the Jokchon Stream runs into the East Sea, and a small zoo and botanical garden, both pleasant enough to walk in.

NAMPO
pop 730,000

On the Taedong delta, 55km southwest of Pyongyang is Nampo, North Korea's most important port and centre of industry. Nampo has made its name for being the 'birthplace of the Chollima movement', after the workers at the local steel plant supposedly 'took the lead in bringing about an upswing in socialist construction' according to local tourist pamphlets. Sadly there's nothing much to see in the town itself.

The reason tourists come here (usually on an overnight stop en route to Kaesong) is to see the **West Sea Barrage**, built across an 8km estuary of the Taedong, which solved the irrigation and drinking-water problems in the area. The impressive structure, built during the early 1980s and opened in 1986, is nevertheless rather a dull visit – in every way a classic piece of socialist tourism. You'll drive across it, then up to a hill at the far end from where you'll get good views and enjoy a quick (hilarious) video at the visitor centre. You'll then (if all is running to plan) drive down to the sluice gates and watch them open – the purported highlight of the trip.

It's now common to include Nampo in an overnight trip from Pyongyang, where your group will sleep some way outside the city at the **Ryonggang Hot Spring House**, a former government guesthouse now open to tourists. It's a fairly unique place – some 20 well-appointed villas with several bedrooms each are spread out in the sprawling grounds, each room containing its own spa bath where you can take the waters in your room for a maximum of 15 minutes a time – it's not clear what will happen if you stay in for longer than 15 minutes, but the guides make it clear that it would be bad.

On the other side of the West Sea Barrage, there are nice **beaches** about 20km from Nampo. Here, if you are lucky enough to go, you will see the locals enjoying volleyball and swimming.

SINCHON

This small, nondescript place is often visited on trips between Nampo and Kaesong. It's interesting to stop here, as this is a small North Korean town and it's easy to get a sense of daily life from passing through.

The reason you're here, though, is to visit the **Sinchon Museum**, which details the US atrocities committed in the town against civilians during the Korean War. That US atrocities were committed here and in other places is not in question (both sides frequently violated the Geneva Convention), but the typically hyperbolic portrayal of these sad events does nothing for the victims save making them into a propaganda tool.

On arrival the museum director brings tourists into the administration building and gives a long, one-sided lecture about how Americans 'never change' and how the bloodthirsty US soldiers enjoyed carrying out the murder of some 35,000 people here.

The museum itself is a real joke with its 'historic' paintings of American brutality (which apparently was endlessly complex and ingeniously esoteric: people having their heads sawn open, a man being pulled in two by two cows attached to either arm, people being burned at the stake) – the entire display makes Pyongyang's more sober museums look like objective places.

Following the museum, the standard tour includes laying a wreath at a memorial next door and then travelling to the site of two barns where mothers and children were allegedly burned alive by the US Army. Sinchon is sadly emblematic of North Korea's lack of will to move on from the horror of the Korean War, and its determination to memorialise its dead as a propaganda tool. There is no hotel in Sinchon, but from here it's a three-hour drive to Kaesong.

CHILBO

The area around Mt Chilbo is one of the most beautiful places in North Korea. It's also incredibly remote – the only way to get here is to charter a flight from Pyongyang to Orang Airport (approximately €4,500 return per plane), from where Mt Chilbo is a three-hour drive down a rather Mediterranean-looking coastline of high jagged cliffs, small fishing villages and sandy beaches. Tours here are normally done with bigger groups to offset the expense of the charter flight. The World Tourism Organization has pioneered a **homestay program** here, though it's some way from what you might imagine from the term 'homestay' – a Potemkin Village of large traditional-style houses (as well as some 'European' style ones) where one family lives in part of the house, and guests in the other. While it does feel rather contrived, it's still one of the best opportunities in the country to meet and talk with North Koreans, though the main problem is communicating, unless you speak some Korean or Chinese. There's a restaurant and a shop in the homestay and another restaurant on the nearby beach where squid barbecues are often laid on. Elsewhere in Chilbo there's the **Waechilbo Hotel**, though it's rare to stay there these days.

TONY DOES THE DPRK *Tony Wheeler*

I have a fascination with cities and countries that seem to exist at a 90-degree angle to reality. In the world today North Korea is undoubtedly the best example of this phenomenon, and when George W Bush – himself a denizen of a strange parallel universe – decided to skewer North Korea on his axis of evil, I simply had to go.

Unfortunately a solo visit to the 'hermit kingdom' is really impossible – you can go by yourself, but it's still on an organised tour. But one glance at the group that assembled under tour guide Nicholas Bonner's watchful eye at the Beijing railway station was enough to confirm this would be no ordinary group tour.

Day 1 Our overnight train from Beijing arrived at the Chinese border town of Dandong in the early morning. Remarkably there's a giant Mao statue still standing in the square outside the railway station. That evening (the train is very slow) we arrived in Pyongyang and immediately went to pay homage to the Great Leader's Mansudae statue.

Day 2 Apart from our little group, Pyongyang International Airport was deserted. We flew up to the northwest corner of the country then took a bus along the beautiful coastline and in to the forested mountains of Outer Chilbo.

Day 3 Another flight took us to the Paekdu region where Lake Chon's icy surface crosses the border into China. It was here that Kim Jong-il was *said* to be born.

Day 4 Back in Pyongyang we go to the Arirang Mass Games in the 150,000-seat May Day Stadium, the world's biggest stadium. In the stands opposite 20,000 kids flip open card books with synchronised precision to make a steady stream of pictures, while tens of thousands more children, women, men and soldiers dance across the stadium floor. If wars are ever decided by whose army dances best, the North Koreans have it wrapped up.

Day 5 A day's solid sightseeing covers everything from the Victorious Fatherland Liberation War Museum (p367; see how North Korea almost single-handedly defeated the Japanese in WWII) to the Great People's Study Hall and the spy ship USS *Pueblo*, before we end the evening in the Egypt Palace Karaoke Bar in the hotel basement. For me the day's highlight was a chance to wander unescorted for 45 minutes in the shopping delights of Department Store No 1.

Day 6 A bus takes us across the peninsula to the port town of Wonsan. At our hotel, the restaurant staff have moved some dividers between our table and a tour group of well-lubricated Chinese who are singing loudly. Nick leaps from his seat and pulls the dividers aside, yelling in Chinese, 'We will have no divisions here!' A roar goes up and at their invitation we render our own drinking songs.

Day 7 After a visit to a collective farm and a park temple, we cross back over the peninsula to Pyongyang. We were all so knocked out by our visit to the Mass Games that we organise a second showing.

Day 8 We barrel down the six-lane (but extremely empty) highway to the somewhat inaccurately named DMZ – there's nothing very demilitarised about it. On the way back to Pyongyang we make an all-too-brief stop in the provincial town of Kaesong and at the beautiful hillside Kongmin mausoleums just outside the town.

Day 9 The airport is rather busier today when we fly out to Shinnying in China. Remarkably an Air Korea flight from Seoul taxis in right behind us; the bags from North and South are jumbled together on the luggage carousel.

There's very little to do here save enjoy the spectacular scenery, and you'll usually be driven around the attractive valleys, peaks and viewpoints of Mt Chilbo, including a stop at the **Kaesim Buddhist Temple**, which dates from the 9th century.

CHONGJIN

Jump at the chance to visit Chongjin (tours rarely go there), North Korea's third largest city and a great way to see how many North Koreans really live. This vast industrial port is a world away from gleaming Pyongyang, and despite a few attempts to ape the capital's socialist grandeur around the city centre, it's a poor, ugly, polluted and depressing place. Coming here is definitely fascinating though –

most locals have never even seen foreigners and this is about as 'real' an experience of the country as you'll ever get. As such, the rules about photography are very strict here, your guides will become far more stern and you'll see very little of the city save what you glimpse out of the bus as it speeds through the city's deserted avenues at high speed.

The only two sights currently on offer are the **Kim Il-sung Statue** on the town's main square, where you'll be expected to bow after presenting flowers, and the adjacent **Revolutionary Museum**, where you'll hear the strange story of how locals were burned alive protecting trees with revolutionary slogans on them during a forest fire (their charred paraphernalia as well as the trees they were so ideologically committed to saving are both to be found here under glass).

It's usually just possible to visit Chongjin on an overnight stop here after visiting Mt Chilbo. Accommodation is at the imaginatively named **Chongjin Hotel**, which has a very friendly manager and a team of frustrated singers working as waitresses in the restaurant who love to perform songs and dance for the guests after dinner. There's usually no hot water in the rooms, but there's a communal sauna for a wash. Chongjin is an hour's drive north of Orang Airport, and while trains run here from Pyongyang, foreigners aren't able to travel on them.

RAJIN-SONBONG

This eccentric corner of North Korea, right on the border with China and Russia has been designated a 'free trade zone' since 1991, but the name seems to be something of a joke as there's very, very little going on. The two towns of Rajin and Sonbong (sometimes referred to collectively as Rason) are both unremarkable industrial ports surrounded by attractive hills, wetlands and forest.

There's very little to see or do. The Chinese-owned five-star **Emperor Hotel** is here (possibly the country's best, as the only five-star hotel in North Korea), although its casino (the main attraction for many Chinese) has closed so it's even quieter than usual. Rajin-Sonbong also boasts what must be the world's worst **zoo**: on our last visit it contained three ducks, an exceptionally large turkey, some foxes we couldn't see, a picture of a monkey, three bears – one of which was missing an arm – and a cow tied to a fence (we couldn't decide whether the cow was part of the display or just passing through).

Despite the lack of things to do, Rajin-Sonbong is uniquely beautiful, with its rocky cliffs, lakes and sandy coastline, but it feels like the end of the universe, and it's very unusual to come here these days. There are two guesthouses for tourists who don't stay at the Emperor.

NORTH KOREA DIRECTORY

ACCOMMODATION

All accommodation in North Korea is in state-run hotels, which are all of a perfectly decent standard – particularly those in Pyongyang.

You won't usually have much control over where you stay, but you can always make requests. All hotels have the basics of life: a restaurant, a shop (although bring everything you need outside Pyongyang) and usually some form of entertainment, from the ubiquitous karaoke to pool tables and a bar.

A new homestay scheme in Chilbo opened in 2006, although it's about as far from a homestay as you can imagine, being set in something of a showcase village (see p378). Elsewhere homestays are not possible.

While many hotels may indeed be bugged, there's only a very small chance that anyone's listening, so there's no need to worry about what you say in your room.

CHILDREN

While North Koreans love children, a DPRK tour is not suitable for kids. The long, exhausting days and endless sightseeing may tire out even diehard Kimophiles, and they are likely to bore a child to tears. Equally, the lack of creature comforts and facilities for foreign children may make prospective foreign residents think twice before bringing their families.

CUSTOMS

North Korean customs procedures vary in severity from general polite inquiries to thorough goings over. This book and other North Korea guides are fine to bring in, although any other books about the country and its politics or history should be left at home. Cameras of almost any size and nonprofessional video recorders are fine, though huge zoom lenses and tripods are not allowed. Mobile phones are also forbidden, though you can bring them to North Korea with you and leave them at customs (they are very used to this and it's perfectly safe). Even if you are flying in and taking the train out, your phone will be returned through your guides. Laptops, once not allowed, are now fine to bring with you. Religious materials for personal use are also fine.

DANGERS & ANNOYANCES

As a foreigner you will be conspicuous in North Korea, but this is no annoyance – the stares and smiles of a curious population are never threatening. Crime against foreigners is almost totally unknown, though, that said, keep your money safely in an inside pocket or money belt and don't assume that crime doesn't exist at all.

The major annoyance in North Korea is the obligation to be with your guides at all times outside the hotel. This means that individual exploration is totally impossible and usually leads to some frustration for seasoned travellers unused to the confines of a group.

North Korea isn't a dangerous destination, but you'd be foolhardy to openly criticise the regime in general, or either of the Kims in particular. Spare a thought for your guides – despite being official representatives of the regime, it's they who are vulnerable to persecution should you decide to speak your mind, make any form of protest or insult the leadership. Likewise, escaping the group, disobeying photography instructions or otherwise stirring up trouble will be far more dangerous for them than for you.

When meeting North Koreans in the street, take your lead from the guides. Ask before you take photographs, keep conversations non-political and accept that at present you're unable to freely mix with locals – exchanging a few brief pleasantries is normally the furthest you can get with anyone before the guides get nervous.

EMBASSIES & CONSULATES

North Korea now enjoys diplomatic relations with most EU countries, although few maintain embassies in Pyongyang. In theory, North Korean embassies can all process visa applications abroad, but in practice the Beijing embassy remains the most useful:

China (☎ 10-6532 1186/1189, visa section ☎ 6532 4148/6639; fax 6532 6056; Ritan Beilu, Chaoyang District, Beijing) The entrance to the consular section is on the east side of the building at the northern end of the fruit-and-vegetable stalls.

Embassies & Consulates in North Korea

The few embassies that might be of help to travellers are listed here.

The UK Embassy represents the interests of Australians, Canadians, New Zealanders and citizens of the Republic of Ireland, while the Swedish legation looks after US citizens and EU citizens whose own country does not have representation in Pyongyang. Most embassies are located in the Munsudong diplomatic compound.

China (☎ 381 3133, 381 3116; fax 381 3425)
Germany (☎ 381 7385; fax 381 7397)
India (☎ 381 7215, 381 7274; fax 381 7619)
Russia (☎ 381 3101/2; fax 381 3427)
Sweden (☎ 381 7485; fax 381 7663)
UK (☎ 382 7980, 381 7980; fax 381 7985)

HOLIDAYS

New Year's Day 1 January
Kim Jong-il's birthday 16 February
Kim Il-sung's birthday 15 April
Armed Forces Day 25 April
May Day 1 May
The Death of Kim Il-sung 8 July
Victory in the Fatherland Liberation War 27 July
National Liberation (from Japan) Day 15 August
National Foundation Day 9 September
Korean Workers' Party Foundation Day 10 October
Constitution Day 27 December

Note that North Korea does not celebrate Christmas or the Lunar New Year, nor many of South Korea's major traditional holidays. National holidays are a good time to visit North Korea – try to be in Pyongyang during May Day or Liberation Day as both are celebrated with huge extravaganzas featuring military-style parades that rank among North Korea's most memorable sights.

INTERNET ACCESS

There is no internet access to be had in the DPRK for tourists. You can apparently send an email (though not receive a reply) via the communication centre at the Yanggakdo Hotel in Pyongyang, though we've never actually heard of anyone doing this.

Intranet (ie a closed internet with no connections to the wider web) is being developed in quite a few places in the country, but obviously this remains entirely government controlled.

LEGAL MATTERS

It is extremely unlikely that a tourist will experience legal problems with the North Korean authorities, but if this does occur, stay calm and ask to speak to your country's diplomatic representative in North Korea. Usually, tourists who break the law in North Korea are deported immediately.

MAPS

You do not need a map of anywhere in North Korea, due to the unique hand-holding arrangement with the guides. However, Pyongyang maps are available at most hotels and shops in the capital and can be helpful for getting to grips with the capital's layout. There are few good-quality maps of North Korea available outside the country; the best on offer from travel specialists is the general map of Korea published by Nelles Maps.

MONEY

The unit of currency is the North Korean won (KPW). Bank notes come in denominations of one, five, 10, 50, 100, 500, 1000 and 5000. However, visitors do not usually deal with local currency: everything can be paid for with euro or Chinese yuan (but bring small change of both; big notes can be impossible to change). While you are unlikely to use the won, it may be possible to get some from your guides as a souvenir (it's officially illegal to take it out of the country, so hide it deep in your luggage).

Credit cards are completely useless everywhere in the country, so bring as much cash as you'll need with some leeway for any unexpected expenses. Bring your cash in euros or yuan, though US dollars and Japanese yen can also be exchanged at poor rates. Travellers cheques are not usable in North Korea, and there are no ATMs anywhere in the country.

PHOTOGRAPHY & VIDEO
Restrictions

Always ask first before taking photos and obey the reply. North Koreans are especially sensitive about foreigners taking photos of them without their permission, acutely aware of the political power of an image in the Western press. Your guides are familiar with the issue of tourists taking photos that end up in a newspaper article that contains anti-DPRK content, and it's not unusual for them to ask to see your photos. Taking photographs from the bus is officially banned as well, though in practice it's not a big deal as long as you are discreet and are not photographing sensitive objects. Avoid taking photos of soldiers or any military facilities, although you're encouraged to do so at the DMZ.

Equipment

Memory cards are not easily available in North Korea, so bring as many as you'll need to store pictures on. Visitors nearly always take huge numbers of shots, so come prepared! Having a laptop to download your pictures to gives you double protection if your camera is checked on the way out of the country (which is pretty common). Any pictures of soldiers or anything customs officials deem unflattering to the country will be deleted.

Video

Restrictions are similar to those with a camera. But, as a number of journalists have made video documentaries about the country in the guise of simply filming tourist sights, the guides and customs officers have become far stricter about their use. Note that filming the Mass Games in full is not possible – you will be closely monitored and expected to film only relatively short pieces of the show.

POST

Like all other means of communication, the post is monitored. It is, however, generally reliable and the colourful North Korean stamps, featuring everything from tributes to the Great Leader to Princess Diana commemoratives, make great souvenirs. Some people have suggested that postcards arrive more quickly, as they do not need to be opened by censors. In either medium, keep any negative thoughts about the country to yourself to ensure your letter gets through.

SOLO TRAVELLERS

The concept of 'solo traveller' in North Korea is somewhat redundant, as even when 'alone' you are with two official guides, which can be intense. With the fairly constant deification of the Great and Dear Leaders, solo travellers can find long trips in North Korea trying without a group of fellow-foreigners to raise eyebrows at. However, if you want your own itinerary or need to travel when there are no tours, travelling solo is your only option. Most travel agencies offering group tours to the DPRK, such as those listed on p350, will also be happy to negotiate tailor-made itineraries for individuals with Ryohaengsa.

TELEPHONE & FAX

North Korean telephone numbers are divided into 381 numbers (international) and 382 (local). It is not possible to call a 381 number from a 382 number or vice versa. International calls start at €3 per minute to China and €8 to Europe. To dial North Korea, the country code is 850. Nearly all numbers you dial from abroad will be Pyongyang numbers, so dial +850-2-381 and then the local number.

Mobile phones are not used by the vast majority of people, but a network has been established in Pyongyang for the well-connected and boasted 50,000 users in 2009. You are not allowed to bring mobile phones into the country (and they wouldn't work even if you did), but it's fine to declare your handset and it will be taken away from you and returned when you leave the country.

Faxing can still be useful in a land without email, assuming anyone you know has a fax machine. From Pyongyang hotels it's not exactly cheap – one page to China will cost you €4.50, while a page to Europe will set you back €13! Following pages are slightly less expensive.

TIME
The time in Korea is GMT plus nine hours. When it is noon in Korea it is 1pm in Sydney or Melbourne, 3am in London, 10pm the previous day in New York and 7pm the previous day in Los Angeles or San Francisco.

You will also see years such as Juche 8 (1919) or Juche 99 (2010). Three years after the death of Kim Il-sung, the government adopted a new system of recording years, starting from Juche 1 (1912) when Kim No 1 was born. Despite the wide use of these dates internally, they are always clarified with 'normal' years.

TOILETS
In Pyongyang and around frequently visited tourist sites, toilet facilities are basic and smelly, usually with squat toilets. There are regular cuts in the water supply outside Pyongyang, and often a bucket of water will be left in your hotel room or a public toilet for this eventuality. A straw poll of tour operators reveals the worst toilet in North Korea to be at the rest stop on the Pyongyang–Wonsan highway. Toilet paper is supplied in hotels, but it's always a good idea to carry tissues for emergencies, especially as diarrhoea is a common problem for visitors.

TRAVELLERS WITH DISABILITIES
North Korean culture places great emphasis on caring for the disabled, especially as the Korean War left such a brutal legacy among young recruits. Despite this, seeing disabled people on the streets is actually relatively rare. Facilities are basic, but manageable, and even in situations where disabled access is a problem, the guides are likely to find some locals to help out. Most hotels have lifts due to their large size and many floors.

VISAS
People of all nationalities need a visa to visit North Korea. Traditionally visas have not been issued to US, South Korean or Israeli travellers, but nationals of these countries can now visit under restricted conditions (normally only between August and October and for a maximum of five days).

Restrictions have relaxed somewhat across the board. It used to be necessary to provide a full CV listing all your previous employment as well as a letter from your employer detailing the duties of your current job. As this still didn't prevent journalists entering the country in the guise of tourists, this practice seems to have stopped, and now you just have to supply the name of your employer and your job. If you work in the media, human rights or any other potentially controversial professions, then be sure not to put this on the application form.

Each visa needs approval from Pyongyang, so apply at least one month before you travel. Your travel agency will handle the application for you, and in most cases the visa is a formality if you travel with a well-known agency.

Tour groups usually have visas issued in Beijing the day before travel, so don't worry about leaving home without one in your passport. It does mean that you need to spend 24 hours in Beijing before going on to Pyongyang, though, but you won't have to go to the embassy yourself in most cases. Individual visas can usually be issued at any North Korean embassy.

The embassy visa charges (€30 in Beijing) are included in some, but not all, packages. North Korean visas are not put into passports, but are separate documents taken from you when you exit the country. If you want a souvenir, make a photocopy. No stamp of any kind will be made in your passport.

WOMEN TRAVELLERS
While communist ideology dictates equality of the sexes, this is still far from everyday reality in a traditionally patriarchal society. However, women travellers will have no problems at all in the country, as no North Korean would be foolhardy enough to get themselves in trouble for harassing a foreigner. There are an increasing number of female guides being employed by Ryohaengsa and it is possible to request them for individual travel.

NORTH KOREA TRANSPORT

GETTING THERE & AWAY
Beijing is the only real transport hub for people entering North Korea, offering both regular trains and flights to Pyongyang. Air traffic entering from Vladivostok in Russia has fallen

off to a trickle. This situation is exacerbated by the fact that tourists are often obliged to pick up their visas in Beijing, thus making the use of other routes impossible.

Entering the Country

Once you've got your visa you can breeze into North Korea, even if the welcome at immigration is rather frosty. Your guides will take your passport for the duration of your stay in North Korea. This is totally routine, so do not worry about it being lost.

AIR

The national airline, Air Koryo, runs a fleet of old Soviet Tupolevs and Ilyushins that fly to Beijing, Shenyang and Vladivostok. By far the most commonly used route is the flight from Beijing, operated every day except Wednesday on Air Koryo or Air China. On Wednesdays there's a flight between Pyongyang and Shenyang in both directions, and on Thursdays there's a return flight between Pyongyang and Vladivostok, both operated by Air Koryo. Pyongyang's airport code is FNJ.

The **Air Koryo** (☎ 10-6501 1557/1559; fax 6501 2591; Swissôtel Bldg, Hong Kong-Macau Center, Dongsi Shitau Lijiao, Beijing 100027) building adjoins the Swissôtel, but the entrance is around the back. You must have a visa before you can pick up your ticket, though if you're travelling in a group your travel agency will have the ticket.

TRAIN

There are four weekly overnight trains in either direction between Beijing and Pyongyang, the journey takes about 23 hours, though delays are not uncommon. Trains run on Monday, Wednesday, Thursday and Saturday. On each day, train No 27 leaves Beijing at 5.30pm and arrives at Pyongyang the next day at 6pm. Going the other way, train No 26 departs from Pyongyang at 10.10am arriving in Beijing at 8.34am the next morning. In contrast to the plane, it's possible to pick up your train tickets to Pyongyang without a DPRK visa.

The North Korean train is actually just two carriages attached to the main Beijing–Dandong train, which are detached at Dandong (Chinese side) and then taken across the Yalu River Bridge to Sinuiju (Korean side), where more carriages are added for local people. You'll remain in the same carriage for the entire journey however, and can mingle with locals in the dining car on both legs of the trip. Accommodation is in four-berth compartments, though sometimes two-berth compartments are available.

The trains usually spend about four hours at the border for customs and immigration – two hours at Dandong and two hours at Sinuiju. At Sinuiju you can sometimes wander around the station.

If Sinuiju station is your introduction to North Korea, the contrasts with China will be quite marked. Everything is squeaky-clean and there are no vendors plying their goods. A portrait of the Great Leader looks down from the top of the station, as it does at all train stations in North Korea.

Food is available from the restaurant car on both legs of the journey. Make sure you have some small denomination euro or yuan notes to pay for meals (€6) from the North Korean buffet car, as this is not usually included in tours. There are no facilities for changing money at Sinuiju or on the train.

Your guide will meet you on arrival at Pyongyang train station and accompany you to your hotel. Be very careful taking pictures from the train in North Korea. While you'll get some great opportunities to snap everyday DPRK scenes, do not take pictures in stations as these are considered to be military objects.

As well as the service to Beijing there's a weekly train in both directions between Moscow and Pyongyang, which travels via Dandong and through Northern China along the route of the Trans-Manchurian Railway. The trip takes seven days.

Leaving the Country

If you are departing by air, your guides will accompany you to the airport and see you off there. A €10 departure tax on flights is included in the cost of your air ticket. Similarly your guides will leave you at Pyongyang station if you are taking the train out and you'll then travel to China unaccompanied. There is no departure tax for the train.

GETTING AROUND

All accommodation, guides and transport must be booked through the government-run Ryohaengsa, or via a travel agency (see p350) who will deal with Ryohaengsa themselves.

The main office of **Ryohaengsa** (☎ +86-10-8576 9465; fax 8576 9984; kitcbri@gmail.com) is in Beijing, but it's not open to the public, you can only call or email. There are also branches in Dandong, Liaoning Province and in Yanji in Jilin.

Directory

CONTENTS

ACCOMMODATION

In general you don't need to worry about where to stay in Korea – motels (p387) are so numerous that there is usually no need to book ahead. Outside of the big cities and towns – where you'll find regular hotels and hostels – the most common type of accommodation will be *minbak* – private homes with rooms for rent.

Expect to pay W15,000 to W20,000 for a dorm bed in a hostel; W30,000 for a *yeogwan* (motel with small en suite) or basic countryside *minbak;* W30,000 to W40,000 for a motel; W50,000 for a *pension* (upmarket rural retreat) or smart *minbak;* at least

W90,000 for an upper midrange hotel; and upwards of W200,000 for top-end luxury. Upper midrange and top-end hotels usually add 21% tax and service to the bill, but this has been included in all the prices quoted in this guidebook. See the boxed text (p387) for more information.

Accommodation is normally charged per room, so solo travellers receive little or no discount. Still it's always worth asking. If you're staying a few days or if it's off season (outside July and August on the coast or outside July, August, October and November in national parks), you can always try for discounts.

Only staff in Seoul guesthouses and upper midrange and top-end hotels are likely to speak any English. An extra bed or *yo* (mattress or futon on the floor) is usually available. Check-out time is generally noon. Prices can rise on Friday and Saturday and at peak times (July and August near beaches or national parks, and October and November near national parks).

Although some motels and many hostels offer use of a washing machine (and sometimes a dryer) laundry can be a problem – out of Seoul you may find yourself having to wash your clothes in the bathroom and hanging them up in your room to dry, or laying them on the *ondol*-heated floor.

In general, booking accommodation is unnecessary and is difficult in the case of motels as staff very rarely speak any English.

Budget accommodation is defined as double rooms with en-suite facilities that cost less than W40,000 (less than W50,000 in Seoul), midrange is rooms from W40,000 to W150,000 (W50,000 to W200,000 in Seoul), and top end is anything over W150,000 (over W200,000 in Seoul).

Backpacker Guesthouses & Hostels

Although the backpacker scene is well established in Seoul, which sports dozens of small guesthouses, it's less common elsewhere in Korea. When you find them, these internationally minded hostels are ideal for budget-oriented tourists, with staff who are friendly and speak English. They offer dormitories (from W15,000 per night) and double rooms (from W40,000), some of which are en suite. Communal facilities include toilets, showers, satellite TV, a kitchen and washing machine. Free internet and breakfast is also typically provided.

Camping & Mountain & Forest Huts

Camping at beaches and at the entrances to some national and provincial parks is possible. The cost is only W3000, but facilities are very basic and they are usually only open in July and August. Mountain and forest huts cost the same although the better, newer ones cost W5000.

In general, *yeogwan,* motel and *minbak* accommodation at the national-park entrances are reasonably priced, and only a few major hikes in Seoraksan and Jirisan National Parks require overnighting in a mountain hut. Huts and camping grounds can be fully booked at weekends and peak times – log on to www.knps.or.kr to make a reservation.

Hanok

Staying in a *hanok* – a traditional wooden house (see the boxed text on p59) – is a unique experience, particular because so few have survived the Korean War and the postwar bulldozers. Rooms tend to be very small and grouped around a courtyard, guests usually sleep on a *yo* (thin mattress) on an *ondol*-heated floor, and bathrooms are usually shared. Seoul (p119), Jeonju (p309) and Hahoe (p231) are among the handful of places to experience a *hanok* stay.

Homestays

View www.homestaykorea.com to contact Korean families and individuals willing to offer rooms in their homes to foreigners. Guests often receive royal hospitality, and the cost starts at US$40 (single) or US$60 (double) for bed and breakfast. Rates are greatly reduced for long stays. It's your best opportunity to experience the local lifestyle at first hand. Book online at least two weeks before you arrive.

Another option is www.couchsurfing.org, a non-profit organisation hooking up people around the world who are willing to offer a free bed to travellers in their home, in the expectation that participants in the program will offer the same hospitality to them.

Hotels

Luxury hotels are relatively scarce outside of major cities and Jeju-do. The lobbies, fitness centres, restaurants and other services are often their strong points – when it comes to room design and facilities, motels tend to offer a better deal. We list rack rates (including service and taxes) in this guide, but discounts or packages are nearly always available.

Websites that offer discounted prices and special deals include www.koreahotels.net and www.khrc.com. Always check if discounted prices include the 21% service and tax. The discounts look good but may be less than you could obtain direct on a hotel's own website.

BOOK ACCOMMODATION ONLINE

For more accommodation reviews and recommendations by Lonely Planet authors, check out the online booking service at www.lonelyplanet.com. You'll find the true, insider lowdown on the best places to stay. Reviews are thorough and independent. Best of all, you can book online.

Minbak & Pension

Most *minbak* provide simple accommodation (and usually meals) on islands, near ski resorts, in rural areas and near beaches and national parks. Expect to pay W30,000 for a room but double that in peak seasons. You sleep on a *yo* on an *ondol*-heated floor usually with a TV and a heater or fan in the room. Facilities may not be en suite. Lots of people can squeeze into one room – an extra person usually costs W10,000. Nowadays there are more upmarket *minbak,* which are similar to *pension* and cost W50,000 or more, and provide smart, stylish rooms with beds and kitchenettes. *Pension* are more luxurious than most *minbak* and cost from W50,000 upwards with spacious rooms, often with stylish furniture, balconies and kitchens.

Motels

They started out as love hotels (places couples rent by the hour), and they still function like this, but nowadays motels also provide the best-deal accommodation for touring Korea. Generally priced at W40,000 (but up to W100,000 extra for special facilities like a waterbed, jacuzzi or a computer), the newest ones provide a midrange style of room at a budget price. Most motel rooms are just regular rooms, although you might find large mirrors, mood lighting and maybe round beds or a free packet of condoms. It's unusual to come across erotic art, but erotic videos (and regular ones) are generally available for viewing.

In modern motels, rooms and bathrooms are reasonably sized, with a high standard of fittings, furnishing and decor, a comfortable double bed, a large TV, video player (free videos available), air-con, a fridge with free soft drinks, a water dispenser, small towels, a hairdryer, shampoo, lotions and even hair brushes and toothbrushes. TVs have satellite or cable links. Windows are double (or triple) glazed for quietness. Modern high-rise motels have 30 or so rooms and an elevator, but usually no English is spoken, no staff are employed to help with bags, and there is no coffee shop, laundry, restaurant, bar or communal facility. You just get a clean, facility-filled room.

Every city, town and tourist area has batches of motels, usually surrounding the bus terminal or train station. Some look like Disneyland castles, while others are metal clad or have big neon signs on the roof. Staff rarely understand

> **ACCOMMODATION TAX MORATORIUM**
>
> During 2009 the government allowed hotels to waive the 10% tax (thus lowering the amount added to bills to the 10% service charge). Some, but not all, of the upper-end hotels charging tax and service passed this discount on to customers. It was unclear at the time of research if the tax moratorium would continue into 2010 and beyond.

any English so write '방을 좀 볼 수 있을까요?' (Can I see a room please?) on a piece of paper and hand it over to the receptionist, who is usually hidden away behind a small glass window. At some in the lobby there are wall panels showing illuminated photos of the rooms available and their prices.

As with *yeogwan,* twin beds are not usually available, but you can ask for an *ondol* room (sleeping on padded quilts on the floor), or ask for a *yo* to be put in a room with a double bed. Any extra person usually costs W10,000. Don't be mislead by the name 'motel' – some *yeogwan* call themselves a motel, but the exterior usually gives it away.

Rental Accommodation

Many expat workers live in accommodation supplied by their employers, but a few live in a guesthouse, homestay or *yeogwan* on a monthly basis and negotiate a reduced daily cost. Serviced apartments and apartment sharing are other options in Seoul and other large cities, although spare rooms are difficult to find. The following link from Korea4Expats.com is useful: www.korea4expats.com/article-housing-seoul-korea.html.

Renting an apartment is tricky because of the traditional payment system. *Jeonsei* is when you loan from W50 million to W200 million (or more) to the landlord and get it all back at the end of the rental period. *Wolse* is when you pay a smaller returnable deposit of W3 million to W10 million plus a monthly rental fee. Very little accommodation is available to foreigners on the Western system, with a small refundable deposit and a monthly rent.

If you are looking to rent, take note that real estate is still often measured in *pyeong* (1 *pyeong* is 3.3 sq metres), even though the law now states it should be measured in square

DIRECTORY

metres. A large apartment is 50 *pyeong* and medium-sized is about 30 *pyeong,* though smaller budget ones of 15 *pyeong* to 20 *pyeong* do exist.

Sauna Dormitories

Saunas and *jjimjilbang* (luxury saunas) nearly all have a dormitory or napping room. They are not really meant for overnight sleepovers, but they can be used for that purpose. Pay the entry fee (usually under W10,000), use the facilities and then head for the dormitory. Don't expect much in the way of bedding, and the pillow may be a block of wood.

Serviced Apartments

Seoul has several serviced apartment complexes, such as Fraser Suites (p129), and **Co-Op Residences** (http://rent.co-op.co.kr) which are an alternative to small hotel rooms and the hassle of finding and renting an apartment. Known locally as residences or suites, prices start at W90,000 a day for a studio apartment, with big discounts for month-long stays.

Temple Stays

Some 80 odd temples across the country provide overnight accommodation in the form of a **temple stay program** (http://eng.temple stay.com). Those in the Jogye Order of Korean Buddhism are geared to accepting foreign guests, but other temples will also happily let you stay if you bring someone along who can speak Korean to help translate. For around W30,000 per night simple, usually shared accommodation is offered including all meals. You'll also get to participate in the life of monks. See the boxed text on p54 for more information about this unique and recommended experience.

Yeogwan

Yeogwan provide old-fashioned budget rooms, but are only W5000 to W10,000 cheaper than the much better modern motels. Rooms (and bathrooms) are smallish but are fully equipped with satellite or cable TV, a fan, air-con, heating, a fridge, bed and sometimes a table and chairs. Furnishings and fixtures will be dated, rooms and corridors are usually gloomy, and bedding is often quilts rather than sheets. Quilts are usually aired rather than washed so you may want to bring a pair of sheets with you. 'Adequate but shabby' sums up most *yeogwan.*

Youth Hostels

Hostelling International Korea (www.kyha.or.kr) runs 70 large youth hostels around the country. Modern and clean, the dormitories offer a good deal for solo travellers on a budget at around W15,000 a night. Private and family rooms cost as much as motel rooms and are unlikely to be as good. Not many foreigners stay in these hostels, perhaps because they are rather institutional, can be inconveniently located and are sometimes full of noisy children on a school trip. Annual membership costs W25,000 for adults, W18,000 for youths.

ACTIVITIES

See the Active Korea chapter (p80) for information on hiking, cycling and mountain biking, diving, winter sports, martial arts and hot-spring spas.

BUSINESS HOURS

For most government and private offices, business hours are from 9am to 6pm Monday to Friday. Tourist information centres are usually open from 9am to 6pm daily while national parks are open daily from sunrise to sunset. Keep in mind that many (but not all) government-run museums and tourist sites close on Mondays.

Banking hours are from 9am to 4pm Monday to Friday. The hours that ATMs are available vary and are written on the machine, but they are not generally open 24 hours. Post offices are generally open from 9am to 6pm Monday to Friday, but some are open longer hours.

Shops are generally open from 10am to around 8pm daily, but the trend towards more days off means that some do now close on Sunday. Department stores traditionally open from 10.30am to 7.30pm daily and a few open until even later in the evening. Bigger shopping malls tend to stay open until 10pm. Small general stores often stay open until midnight, even in suburban areas, and many convenience stores are open 24 hours. Travel agents may take Saturday afternoon off as well as Sunday.

Restaurants usually open from 11am to 10pm every day. Pubs and bars open daily from 6pm to 1am but they close later on Friday and Saturday. Those serving food may open at noon.

There is plenty for night owls to do in Korean cities as some saunas, restaurants, PC *bang* (internet rooms), DVD *bang* (room for watching DVDs), *noraebang* (karaoke rooms), convenience stores, bars and nightclubs stay open all night.

CHILDREN

Koreans adore children and make them the centre of attention so travelling with your offspring here is highly recommended. Expect the locals to be particularly helpful and intrigued. Check out www.travelwithyourkids.com for general advice and a first-hand report on Seoul for kids, which gives the city a thumbs up.

Only luxury hotels are likely to be able to organise a cot, but you could always ask for a *yo*. Few restaurants have high chairs. Nappy-changing facilities are more common in Seoul toilets than in the provinces. Babysitting services are almost nonexistent.

Zoos, funfairs and parks can be found in most cities along with cinemas, DVD rooms, internet rooms, video-game arcades, ten-pin bowling alleys, *noraebang,* pool tables and board-game cafes. Children will rarely be more than 100m away from an ice-cream, cake or fast-food outlet. In winter hit the ski slopes, and in summer head for the water parks or beaches. To keep kids happy in Seoul, see p118. For general advice also pick up a copy of Lonely Planet's *Travel with Children.*

CLIMATE CHARTS

Korea has four very distinct seasons: spring from mid-March to the end of May; summer from June to August; autumn from September to November; and winter from December to mid-March. Of course the actual weather doesn't always fit these neat categories.

Temperatures vary hugely between mid-summer and midwinter, with August being very hot and sticky, while December and January are literally freezing. Winters in the north are colder than in the more southerly Busan or Jeju-do. Heavy rainfall always arrives with the summer monsoon season (late June to late July). See p14 for advice about the best times to visit.

COURSES

Bullish for *bulgogi* or keen on *kimchi*? Seoul offers a couple of Korean cooking classes in English (p117).

Untangle *hangeul* at Korean-language classes in Seoul (p117).

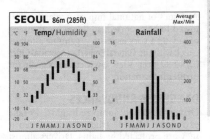

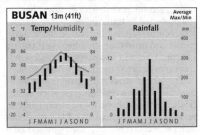

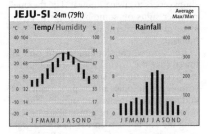

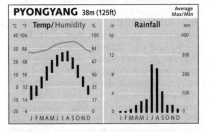

CUSTOMS

All plants, fresh fruit and vegetables that you bring into Korea must be declared. You are not allowed to bring in meat. If you have more than US$10,000 in cash and travellers cheques, this should be declared and you have to fill in a form.

Entering the country, the duty-free allowance is not generous: 1 litre of alcohol, 200 cigarettes and 59ml (2oz) of perfume.

Antiques of national importance are not allowed to be exported, so if you are thinking of buying a very expensive, genuine antique, check with the **Cultural Properties Appraisal Office** (☎ 02-662 0106). View www.customs.go.kr for further information.

DANGERS & ANNOYANCES

Drivers routinely jump red lights, so take extra care on pedestrian crossings even if they are protected by lights. Drivers almost never stop for pedestrian crossings that are not protected by traffic lights, so they are useless. Motorcyclists often drive along pavements and pedestrian crossings, particularly in Seoul. Cars also find pavements and pedestrian crossings a convenient place to park.

The lack of street names, signs and numbers can make navigation around cities difficult. This guidebook lists a street name in reviews where one exists and is signed, but don't expect taxi drivers, passers-by and even shopkeepers to always know it. Tip: the small number signs on some buildings have the street name underneath, although only in *hangeul*.

Rules on where smoking is and isn't allowed (like the driving rules) are not always enforced. In theory smoking is banned in schools and hospitals and on public transport, and restricted to designated smoking areas in other public places. The nonsmokers are winning the war but hardcore smokers still light up in restaurants, cafes, bars and PC *bang*.

DISCOUNT CARDS

Bring your student or pensioner card to Korea if you have one, although benefits are fairly limited. A youth-hostel membership card provides a few discounts. Trains and subways are discounted for seniors, and other transport operators and government-run tourist attractions often offer discounts or free entry to anyone aged over 65 years old. Other organisations may restrict discounts to local residents, but it is always worth a try so just ask.

EMBASSIES & CONSULATES

For details of overseas South Korean diplomatic missions see www.mofat.go.kr. Foreign embassies in Seoul include the following:
Australia (Map pp96-7; ☎ 02-2003 0100; www.south korea.embassy.gov.au; 11th fl, Kyobo Bldg, Jongno 1-ga, Jongno-gu; ⊕ Line 5 to Gwanghwamun, Exit 4)

Canada (Map pp100-1; ☎ 02-3455 6000; www. canadainternational.gc.ca/korea-coree; 16-1, Jeong-dong, Jung-gu; ⊕ Line 1 or 2 to City Hall, Exit 2)
China (Map pp96-7; ☎ 02-738 1038; www.chinaemb. or.kr; 54 Hyoja-dong, Jongno-gu; ⊕ Line 3 to Gyeong-bokgung, Exit 3)
France (Map pp94-5; ☎ 02-3149 4300; www.amba france-kr.org/france_coree; 30 Hap-dong, Seodaemun-gu; ⊕ Line 6 to Chungjeongno, Exit 9)
Germany (Map pp102-3; ☎ 02-748 4114; www.seoul. diplo.de; 308-5 Dongbinggo-dong, Yongsan-gu; ⊕ Line 6 to Itaewon, Exit 4)
Ireland (Map pp96-7; ☎ 02-774 6455; www.ireland house-korea.com; 13th fl, Leema Bldg, 146-1 Sosong-dong, Jongno-gu; ⊕ Line 5 to Gwanghwamun, Exit 2)
Japan (Map pp96-7; ☎ 02-2170 5200; www.kr.emb -japan.go.jp; 18-11 Junghak-dong, Jongno-gu; ⊕ Line 3 to Anguk, Exit 6)
Netherlands (Map pp96-7; ☎ 02-737 9514; http:// southkorea.nlembassy.org; 14th fl, Kyobo Bldg, Jongno 1-ga, Jongno-gu; ⊕ Line 5 to Gwanghwamun, Exit 4)
New Zealand (Map pp96-7; ☎ 02-730 7794; www. nzembassy.com/korea; 15th fl, Kyobo Bldg, Jongno 1-ga, Jongno-gu; ⊕ Line 5 to Gwanghwamun, Exit 4)
Russia (Map pp100-1; ☎ 02-318-2116; http://seoul. rusembassy.org; 34-16 Jeong-dong, Jung-gu; ⊕ Line 1 or 2 to City Hall, Exit 2)
Singapore (Map pp96-7; ☎ 02-774 2464; www.mfa. gov.sg/seoul; 28th fl, Seoul Finance Center, 84 Taepyeongno 1-ga, Jung-gu; ⊕ Line 5 to Gwanghwamun, Exit 5)
UK (Map pp100-1; ☎ 3210 5500; http://ukinkorea.fco. gov.uk; Taepyeongno 40, 4 Jeong-dong, Jung-gu; ⊕ Line 1 or 2 to City Hall, Exit 2)
USA (Map pp96-7; ☎ 02-397 4114; http://seoul. usembassy.gov; 32 Sejongno, Jongno-gu; ⊕ Line 5 to Gwanghwamun, Exit 2)

FESTIVALS & EVENTS

Festival and event dates alter – for up-to-date information check the website of the **Korean Tourism Organisation** (http://english.visitkorea.or.kr) or pick up their free *Korea Festival Guidebook*, which lists 57 different festivities. Also see p17, p119, p164, and p245 for more recommendations.

Snow Festivals (January) Held in Taebaeksan (p196) and other mountain areas. Expect giant ice sculptures, sledding fun and igloo restaurants.
Cherry Blossoms (April) Every region has streets and parks where people go to enjoy the blossoms.
World Ceramics Biennale (April to May; www.wocef. com) Korea's top bash for people potty about pottery is held in odd-numbered years in Icheon (p160).

Buddha's Birthday Parade (May) Held in Seoul starting at 7pm on the Sunday evening before Buddha's birthday. It's the country's biggest and most joyful street parade.

Chuncheon International Mime Festival (May; www.mimefestival.com) The lakeside city (p174) hosts street performers, magicians, acrobats and quirky shows such as a soap-bubble opera.

Dano Festival (May or June; www.gntour.go.kr/eng/sub. jsp?Mcode=404) Held according to the lunar calendar, this traditional festival (see the boxed text, p189) features shamanist rituals, mask dances and market stalls.

Boryeong Mud Festival (July; www.mudfestival.or.kr) Held on Daecheon Beach (see the boxed text, p332) with stacks of muddy fun and games.

Gwangju Biennale (September to November; www. gwangju-biennale.org) Held in even-numbered years, Korea's leading international art show (p266) is a two-month carnival of the avant-garde.

Pusan International Film Festival (September/October; www.piff.org) Korea's top international film festival is held in Busan (p245).

Mask Dance Festival (late September/early October; www.maskdance.com) A well-established 10-day festival that brings together more than 20 traditional dance troupes in Andong (p229).

Chungju World Martial Arts Festival (October; www. martialarts.or.kr) See all sorts of unusual martial arts (see the boxed text, p342).

Baekje Cultural Festival (October; www.baekje.org/ ctnt/engl) This major festival (p325), packed with events, is held in Buyeo in even-numbered years and in Gongju in odd-numbered years.

Gwangju Kimchi Festival (October; www.kimchi. gwangju.kr/index.jsp) Join the celebrations for Korea's most famous contribution to the culinary arts (see the boxed text, p267).

FOOD

Becoming acquainted with Korea's unique and diverse cuisine is one of the pleasures of any visit – see p68. Western, Japanese, Chinese and fast food is also widely available. Price categories for the eating listings in this book are:

Budget Most meals under W7000.

Midrange Most meals in the W7000 to W18,000 range.

Top end Most meals cost more than W18,000.

GAY & LESBIAN TRAVELLERS

It isn't unusual to see warm physical contact between two male or two female friends, including holding hands in the street. This does not mean there is general tolerance of same-sex relationships, however. Beneath a mask of modernity lurk conservative Confucian and fundamental Christian ideas.

The good news is that attitudes in urban centres such as Seoul are becoming more tolerant, even if they remain light years behind most of the West. Hong Suk-chun, a popular TV personality who came out publicly in 2000, saw his career rapidly vanish amid intense public criticism. Two years after Hong's firing, the very network that gave him the axe aired a documentary on his story – the highest-rated program that night – and Hong's acting work has picked up once again.

Seoul hosts semiregular gay film festivals and the Korean Queer Cultural Festival (see the boxed text, p140), with its parade attracting greater numbers each year. Several popular TV dramas have featured gay themes, and 2005 and 2006 saw the first mainstream movies to do so (*The King and the Clown; No Regrets*). Though still facing harassment, gay student

---

UNUSUAL FESTIVALS

Some of the more offbeat Korean festivals include the following:

■ **Jumunjin Cuttlefish Festival** (www.gntour.go.kr/eng/sub.jsp?Mcode=405) – held over the summer and includes not only squid tastings but a squid tug-of-war contest!

■ **Ganggyeong Fermented Seafood Festival** (www.ggfestival.net) – in October, learn how to salt fish and make *kimchi*.

■ **Jinju Bullfighting Festival** – there's no matador involved in this tournament, held during October's Gaecheon Arts Festival in Jinju (p255); instead it's about bulls locking horns and pushing and shoving.

■ **Muju Firefly Festival** (www.firefly.or.kr) – at this environmentally friendly fest witness flickering insects and a 'Bridge of Love' illuminated by 110,000 bulbs.

■ **Gimje Horizon Festival** (http://festival.gimje.go.kr/english) – a celebration of rice-farming and agriculture, including a men vs women tug-of-war, in September/October.

organisations have cropped up in greater frequency on the nation's campuses. The English phrase 'coming out' has been hybridised into a commonly used Korean verb with the same meaning, and in recent years there's been a flourish of Korean-language information and chat rooms online for gays and lesbians.

These are huge strides, to be sure – but for most young Koreans, revealing their personal lives to their coworkers or parents is still risky, both financially and emotionally. If you want to find out more contact **Chungusai** (Between Friends; chingusai.net) – while primarily a gay men's human rights group, the site features links to several Korean lesbian groups. **Sappho Korea** (sappho_korea@googlegroups.com) is a mostly expat lesbian group that runs meetings, trips and parties; they have a Facebook page.

HOLIDAYS
Public Holidays
Eight Korean public holidays are set according to the solar calendar and three according to the lunar calendar, meaning that they fall on different days each year. Restaurants, shops and tourist sights stay open during most holidays, but may close over the three-day Lunar New Year and Chuseok (Thanksgiving) holidays. School holidays means that beaches and resort areas are busy in August.

New Year's Day (1 January) Bells ring out at midnight.

Lunar New Year (3 February 2011, 23 January 2012, 10 February 2013) Korea grinds to a halt during this three-day holiday when everybody returns to their hometown, visits relatives, bows to their elders and eats rice cakes. Trains and planes are booked up months ahead and expressways are one long traffic jam.

Independence Movement Day (1 March) The anniversary of the day in 1919 when nationwide protests against Japanese colonial rule began.

Children's Day (5 May) Take the darlings out for the day and load them up with gifts.

Buddha's Birthday (21 May 2010, 10 May 2011, 28 May 2012, 17 May 2013) Baby Buddha is ceremoniously washed, and colourful lanterns decorate all the Buddhist temples and overflow into the streets.

Memorial Day (6 June) Honours those who died fighting for their country.

Constitution Day (17 July) Commemorates the founding of the Republic of South Korea in 1948.

Liberation Day (15 August) Celebrates the day the Japanese surrendered to Allied forces in 1945, marking the end of their 35-year rule of Korea.

Chuseok (Thanksgiving; 22 September 2010, 12 September 2011, 30 September 2012, 19 September 2013) The Harvest Moon Festival is a three-day holiday when families get together, eat crescent-shaped rice cakes and visit their ancestors' graves. Avoid travelling at this time.

National Foundation Day (3 October) Dangun, the legendary founder of the Korean nation, was supposedly born on this day in 2333 BC.

Christmas Day (25 December) It's Santa's turn to hand out presents.

INSURANCE
A policy covering theft, loss, medical expenses and compensation for cancellation or delays in your travel arrangements is highly recommended. If items are lost or stolen, make sure you obtain a police report straightaway – otherwise your insurer might not pay up. There is a wide variety of policies available, but always check the small print. See p406 for health insurance and p403 for car insurance.

Insurance is available online at www.lonely planet.com/bookings/index.do.

INTERNET ACCESS
With one the highest rates of internet usage in the world, you'll find ubiquitous internet rooms (or PC 방) right across the country, mainly serving youthful computer game addicts playing StarCraft or Lineage. They charge W1000 to W2000 per hour. Many post offices and some tourist information centres, cafes and other establishments provide free internet access, as do guesthouses in Seoul. Some motels and nearly all hotels provide computers with broadband access. Internet Service Providers (ISPs), such as **Korean Telecom** (www.kt.com), **Dreamline** (ww.dreamline.co.kr) and **SK Broadband** (ww.skbroadband.com), offer an English-language home page and continuous broadband access for around W25,000 a month.

LEGAL MATTERS
Most tourists' legal problems involve visa violations or illegal drugs. In the case of visa transgressions, the penalty is normally a fine and possible expulsion from the country. As for using or selling narcotics, don't even think about it: you could spend a few years researching the living conditions in a South Korean prison.

MAPS
The Korean Tourism Organisation (KTO) and tourist information centres in every province and city hand out free tourist maps

in English, which are good enough for most purposes. Ask at the ticket booths at national and provincial parks for good-quality hiking maps which usually contain some English.

Chungang Atlas (Map pp96-7; ☎ 02-730 9191; Sambong-gil, Insadong; ☷ 9am-6.30pm Mon-Sat; ☷ Line 1 to Jonggak, Exit 2) specialises in maps of Seoul and Korea, but most are in *hangeul*.

MONEY

The South Korean unit of currency is the won (W), which comes in W10, W50, W100 and W500 coins. Notes come in denominations of W1000, W5000, W10,000 and W50,000. ATMS don't typically provide the new W50,000 note so be prepared to carry around a thick wad of notes.

See p15 for the cost of everyday items, and the inside front cover for exchange rates at the time of printing.

ATMS

If you're using a foreign credit or cash card, you need to find an ATM with a 'Global' sign or the logo of your credit-card company to get money. Most Global ATMs have basic instructions in English and operate in units of W10,000. ATMs can be found outside banks and post offices and inside deluxe hotels, subway stations and department stores. Restrictions on the amount of money you can withdraw vary from machine to machine; it can be below W300,000 per day, but many ATMs have a W700,000 limit. Another problem is that many ATMs have time restrictions and most only operate between 9am and 10pm, although a few are open 24 hours.

Changing Money

Banks in most high streets offer foreign-exchange services (look for a 'Foreign Exchange' or currency sign), although changing money can take some time. Tourist shops and hotels exchange money, but compare their rates and commissions with the banks before using their services. US dollars are the easiest to exchange but any major currency is accepted. Travellers cheques have a slightly better exchange rate than cash.

Don't forget to reconvert any surplus won into another currency before you leave the country. If you reconvert more than US$2000 worth of won at Incheon airport, you will have to show bank receipts to prove that you exchanged the money legally.

Credit Cards

More and more motels, hotels, shops and restaurants in cities and tourist areas accept foreign credit cards, but there are still plenty of *yeogwan*, restaurants and small businesses that don't. Be prepared to carry around plenty of cash, especially if you are touring around outside the main cities.

PHOTOGRAPHY & VIDEO

Korea is more than up to date with all the latest digital equipment and services. Due to the arrival of the Digital Age, photographic shops are not as numerous as they once were, but they can burn your memory-stick photos onto a CD (W3000). All the major camera and video brands are available including the local ones, such as Samsung, which are challenging the Japanese manufacturers. Yongsan Electronics Market and Techno Mart in Seoul (p144) are the best places to buy the latest camera and video equipment.

Some Koreans are shy, reluctant or even hostile about being photographed, so always ask first. Never take photographs inside Buddhist shrines or of shamanist ceremonies without asking permission first, and don't expect Seoul's riot police to be too happy to be snapped either. In and around the Demilitarized Zone (DMZ; p152) there are very strict rules about what can and can't be photographed. For professional hints on how to improve your pictures, purchase Lonely Planet's *Travel Photography*.

POST

Korean **postal services** (www.koreapost.go.kr) are reliable and reasonably cheap, and post offices often have free internet access. Domestic postal rates start at W250 for a 25g letter, which might take three or four days, or W1840 for overnight express. A 2kg parcel costs W5000. Airmail letters (10g) cost W580 for Zone 3, which includes North America, Europe, Australia and New Zealand. A 2kg parcel costs W27,700 to the US or W22,500 to Australia.

Don't seal your package if you want to take advantage of the lower rate that applies to sending printed papers only. Larger post offices have a packing service that costs from W2000 to W5500.

SHOPPING

Korea has a justified reputation as a shopper's paradise. Bustling traditional markets that sell everything under the sun can still be found in most cities and towns, while modern malls and ritzy departments stores provide anything else. Korean craft shops abound and souvenir shops are mixed in with restaurants in the tourist villages that have grown up at the entrances to national and provincial parks. In Seoul, specialist markets cover everything from fashion, fish and flowers to electronics, embroidery and eel-skin bags.

Good buys include clothing, eye glasses (prescription lenses and frames can be a bargain), ginseng, cosmetics, traditional craft products such as *hanji* (handmade paper), electronics and traditional, unusual liquors such as *bokbunjaju* (raspberry wine) or *maisilju* (plum wine).

Global Refund (☎ 02-776 2170; www.globalrefund. com) offers a partial refund (between 5% and 7%) of the 10% value added tax (VAT) on some items. Spend more than W30,000 in any participating shop and the retailer gives you a special receipt, which you must show to a customs officer at Incheon International Airport. Go to a Customs Declaration Desk (near the check-in counters) *before* checking in your luggage, as the customs officer will want to see the items before stamping your receipt. After you go through immigration, show your stamped receipt at the refund desk to receive your won refund in cash or by cheque.

SOLO TRAVELLERS

Solo travellers are sometimes at a disadvantage in Korea. Few motels and hotels have single rooms, and singles pay the same or almost the same as a couple. Some traditional Korean meals are for sharing and are not available in single portions, so find a companion if you want to enjoy *hanjeongsik* (Korean-style banquet), *jjimdak* (steamed chicken in a hot sauce) or a barbecue meal.

On the plus side, lone travellers in particular can expect locals to go out of their way to help or act as a tourist guide.

TELEPHONE & FAX
Fax

If you want to send a fax, first ask at your guesthouse, motel or hotel. If they can't help you, try the nearest stationery store or photocopy shop.

International Calling Cards

Much cheaper international call rates are offered by international calling cards on sale in places such as Itaewon and Dongdaemun in Seoul. Some cards are discounted on their face value and they all have different tariff structures so shop around for one that works out best for the country you wish to call.

Mobile Phones

Korean mobile phones operate on the CDMA system, which few countries other than Japan and Korea use, but you can rent mobile phones at Incheon International Airport from **KT** (www.kt.com), **LG Telecom** (www.lgtelecom.com), **SK Telecom** (www.sk.com) or **S'Roaming** (http://skyperoaming.com). They offer similar but not identical schemes. With online discounts phone rental is usually W1500 a day. Incoming calls are free and outgoing domestic calls cost around W600 a minute, while calls to the US, for example, cost W900 a minute. Check that prices quoted include the 10% VAT, and since the industry is in constant flux, don't be surprised if things have changed.

Korean mobile phone numbers have three-digit area codes, always beginning with 01, eg ☎ 011-1234 5678. Note that when you make a call from your cell phone you always input the area code, even if you're in the city you're trying to reach. For example, in Seoul when calling a local Seoul number you would dial '02-123 4567'.

Phone Codes

Korea's nine provinces and seven largest cities have their own area codes. It's easy to forget that the major cities have their own codes – thus Gwangju City's code (☎ 062) is one digit different to the surrounding province of Jeollanam-do (☎ 061). South Korea's country code is ☎ 82. Do not dial the first zero of the area codes if you are calling from outside Korea. Phone numbers that begin with a four-figure number starting with 15 do not have an area code. The international access code is ☎ 001.

Public Phones & Phonecards

With practically everyone having a mobile phone it's increasingly rare to find public pay phones. Ones accepting coins (W50 or W100) are even rarer. Public phone telephone cards (W2000 to W10,000) usually give you a 10% bonus in value and can be bought at convenience stores and many small shops. There are two types of cards so if your card does not fit in one type of pay phone, try a different-looking one. The more squat pay phones accept the thin cards. A few public phones accept credit cards. Local calls cost W40 for three minutes.

TIME

South Korea has one time zone, Greenwich Mean Time (GMT) plus nine hours. When it is noon in Seoul it is 1pm in Sydney, 3am in London, 10pm the previous day in New York and 7pm the previous day in San Francisco. Korea does not have a daylight-saving period, but was considering implementing one at the time of research.

TOILETS

Korea's *hwajangsil* (public toilets) have greatly improved and there are more and more clean, modern and well-signposted ones. Virtually all toilets are free of charge, some are decorated with flowers and pictures, and cleaning staff generally do an excellent job. But always carry paper tissue around with you as not all restrooms supply toilet paper. If there is toilet paper it's usually somewhere outside the cubicles.

All tourist attractions, parks, subway stations, train stations and bus terminals have public toilets. It's quite OK to use toilets in office blocks or anywhere else if the need arises. Even when you go hiking in the mountains there are lots of toilets although some are very basic. Asian-style squat toilets are losing their battle with European-style ones with seats, but there are still a few around. Face the hooded end when you squat.

TOURIST INFORMATION

In Seoul the excellent **KTO tourist information centre** (KTO; Map pp96-7; ☎ 1330; www.visitkorea.or.kr; Gwanghwamun; ◷ 9am-8pm; ◉ Line 1 to Jonggak, Exit 5) has stacks of brochures on every region as well as helpful and well-informed staff. They can book hotels for you and advise you about almost anything. Chat to them also about the nationwide system of **Goodwill Guides** (http://english. visitkorea.or. kr/enu/GK/GK_EN_2_7_3_1.jsp).

A very useful **tourist phone number** (☎ 1330; ◷ 24hr) connects you with English-speaking tourist information staff. They can also act as interpreters if someone can't understand you and you have a mobile phone. Dial ☎ 02-1330 if you're on a mobile phone. If you want to contact a tourist information centre outside

Seoul, dial the provincial or metropolitan code first – so for information on Gangwon-do, dial 033-1330.

Many tourist areas throughout the country have their own tourist information centres, so it's not a problem to find one – you'll find details in each of the destination chapters.

KTO offices abroad include:

Australia (☎ 02-9252 4147; Level 18, Australia Square Tower, 264 George St, Sydney, NSW 2000)

Canada (☎ 416-348 9056; Suite 1903, 700 Bay St, Toronto, Ontario, M5G 1Z6)

UK (☎ 020-7321 2535; 3rd fl, New Zealand House, Haymarket, London SW1Y 4TE)

USA Chicago (☎ 312-981 1717; Suite 910, 737 N Michigan Ave, Chicago, IL 6061); Los Angeles (☎ 323-634 0280; 5509 Wilshire Blvd, Los Angeles, CA 90036) New York (☎ 201-585 0909; Suite 750, 2 Executive Dr, Fort Lee, New Jersey 07024)

TRAVELLERS WITH DISABILITIES

Facilities for disabled travellers in Seoul and some other cities are far from perfect but are improving. Most subway stations in Seoul now have stair lifts, elevators and toilets with wheelchair access and handrails, while buses have ramps to aid wheelchair access. Tourist attractions, especially government-run ones, offer generous discounts or even free entry for disabled people and a helper. There are also some hotels with rooms adapted for disabled use.

For the inspiring story about Lee Sang-mook, a geophysicist paralysed from the neck down who has battled against local prejudices against the disabled, see www. nytimes.com/2008/04/19/world/asia/19lee. html and www.pbs.org/wgbh/nova/science now/0408/03.html.

Before setting off get in touch with your national support organisation (preferably with the travel officer, if there is one). For general travel advice in Australia contact **Nican** (☎ 02-6241 1220; www.nican.com.au); in the UK contact **Tourism For All** (☎ 0845-124 9971; www.tourismforall. org.uk); in the USA try **Accessible Journeys** (☎ 800-846 4537; www.disabilitytravel.com), an agency specialising in travel for the disabled, or **Mobility International USA** (☎ 541-343 1284; www.miusa.org).

VISAS

With a confirmed onward ticket, visitors from nearly all West European countries, New Zealand, Australia and around 30 other countries receive 90-day permits on arrival.

DIRECTORY

Visitors from the USA and a handful of countries receive 30-day permits, citizens of Italy and Portugal receive 60-day permits, and Canadians receive a six-month permit.

Around 20 countries, including the Russian Federation, China, India, the Philippines and Nigeria, do not qualify for visa exemptions. Citizens from these countries must apply for a tourist visa, which allows a stay of 90 days. You cannot extend your stay beyond 90 days except in rare cases such as a medical emergency; if you overstay the fine starts at W100,000. Log on to www.moj.go.kr or www.mofat.go.kr to find out more.

Applications for a work visa can be made inside Korea, but you must leave the country to pick up the visa. Most applicants fly (or take the Busan ferry) to Fukuoka in Japan, where it usually takes two days to process the visa. You can also apply for a one-year work visa before entering Korea but it can take a few weeks to process. Note that the visa authorities will want to see originals (not photocopies) of your educational qualifications. This a safeguard against fake degree certificates.

You don't need to leave Korea to renew a work visa as long as you carry on working for the same employer. But if you change employers you must normally apply for a new visa and pick it up outside Korea.

If you don't want to forfeit your work or study visa, you must apply at your local immigration office for a re-entry permit before making any trips outside South Korea. The fee is W30,000 for a single re-entry or W50,000 for multiple re-entry, but permits are free for some nationalities and foreign investors.

If you are working or studying in Korea on a long-term visa, it is necessary to apply for an alien registration card (ARC) within 90 days of arrival, which costs W10,000. This is done at your local immigration office.

VOLUNTEERING

Volunteers are always needed to teach English and entertain children who live in orphanages. Koreans are very reluctant to adopt children, partly because of the huge educational costs and partly because of the traditional emphasis on blood lines. Charities working in this area include US-based **Korean Kids & Orphanage Outreach Mission** (www.kkoom.org), which works with several orphanages in South Korea,

and **HOPE** (Helping Others Prosper through English; www.alwayshope.or.kr), a Korean-based non-profit run by foreign English teachers that helps out at orphanages, assists low-income and disadvantaged children with free English lessons and serves food to the homeless.

In Seoul, the Seoul Global Center (p105) is a good place to start looking for other volunteer possibilities. More charities and organisations with volunteer opportunities include:

American Women's Club of Korea (www.awcseoul.org/joomla/) Help out at their Second Hand Rose Thrift Shop in Seoul.

Amnesty International (www.amnesty.or.kr/index.htm) Works mainly on raising awareness in Korea about international human rights issues.

Animal Rescue Korea (www.animalrescuekorea.org) Help out at an animal shelter in Asan near Daejeon.

Cross-Cultural Awareness Program (CCAP; http://ccap.unesco.or.kr/) Volunteer activities for this Unesco-run program include presenting a class about your own culture to Korean young people, in a Korean public school, or on a weekend trip to a remote area.

Korea Women's Associations United (KWAU; ☎ 02-2273 9535; kwau21@women21.or.kr) Represents the progressive women's movement in Korea.

Korea Women's Hot Line (KWHL; ☎ 02-2269 2962; http://eng.hotline.or.kr) Nationwide organisation with 25 branches that also runs a shelter for abused women.

Korean Federation for Environmental Movement (KFEM; ☎ 02-735 7000; http://english.kfem.or.kr) Volunteer to help out on various environmental projects and campaigns.

Seoul International Women's Association (www.siwapage.com) Organises fund-raising events to help charities across Korea.

Seoul Volunteer Center (http://volunteer.seoul.go.kr) Get involved in language and culture teaching, environmental clean ups and helping out at social welfare centres.

Willing Workers on Organic Farms (WWOOF; ☎ 02 723 4458; www.wwoofkorea.co.kr) Welcomes volunteer workers to farms across Korea who work five to seven hours a day, five to six days a week in return for free board and lodging. For a W50,000 joining fee (W60,000 for two) you'll receive a booklet with contact details.

WOMEN TRAVELLERS

Korea is a relatively crime-free country for all tourists including women, but the usual precautions should be taken. Korea is a very male-dominated society, although it is becoming less so. See Volunteering (left) for some contact details of women's organisations, including the very active **Seoul International Women's Association** (www.siwapage.com).

WORK

Although a few other opportunities are available for work (particularly for those with Korean language skills), the biggest demand is for English teachers. Koreans have an insatiable appetite for studying English and the country is a deservedly popular place for English-language teachers to find work.

Native English teachers on a one-year contract can expect to earn around W2.5 million or more a month, with a furnished apartment, return flights, 50% of medical insurance, 10 days paid holiday and a one-month completion bonus all included in the package. Income tax is very low (around 4%), although a 4.5% pension contribution (reclaimable by some nationalities) is compulsory. Careful spenders can save heaps.

Most English teachers work in a *hagwon* (private language school) but some are employed by universities or government schools. Company classes, English camps and teaching via the telephone are also possible, as is private tutoring although this is technically illegal. Teaching hours in a *hagwon* are usually around 30 hours a week and are likely to involve split shifts, and evening and Saturday classes.

A degree in any subject is sufficient as long as English is your native language. However, it's a good idea to obtain some kind of English-teaching qualification before you arrive, as this increases your options and you should be able to find (and do) a better job.

Some *hagwon* owners are less than ideal employers and don't pay all that they promise, so check out the warnings on the websites at the end of this section before committing yourself. Ask any prospective employer for the email addresses of foreign English teachers working at the *hagwon*, and contact them for their opinion and advice. One important point to keep in mind is that if you change employers, you will usually need to obtain a new work visa, which requires you to leave the country to pick up your new visa. Your new employer may pick up all or at least part of the tab for this.

The best starting point for finding out more about the English-teaching scene is the **Association for Teachers of English in Korea** (ATEK; www.atek.or.kr). The English-language newspapers have very few job advertisements, but vacancies are advertised on the following websites:

http://koreabridge.net Has jobs in Busan and elsewhere.

www.englishspectrum.com Has stacks of job offers (job seekers can advertise too) and a bulletin board with accommodation options.

www.eslcafe.com New job postings daily and useful forums on working and living in Korea.

www.planetesl.com Not only job listings but also lesson plans and a whole lot of other info about living and working in Korea.

Also, for a reality TV–style glimpse of living and teaching in Seoul, tune into the third series of the web video show **Jet Set Zero** (www.jetsetzero.tv).

Transport

CONTENTS

GETTING THERE & AWAY

ENTERING THE COUNTRY

Disembarkation in Korea is a straightforward affair, but you have an extra form to fill in if you are carrying more than US$10,000 in cash and travellers cheques. Most visitors don't need a visa, but if your country is not on the visa-free list, you will need one (see p395).

AIR
Airports & Airlines

Most international flights leave from Incheon International Airport (p145), connected to Seoul by road (80 minutes) and train (60 minutes). There are also some international flights (mainly to China and Japan) from Gimpo International Airport (p146), Gimhae International Airport (p250) for Busan, and Jeju-do International Airport (p284) on Korea's southern holiday island. View www.airport.co.kr for information on all the airports.

Many airlines serve Korea:

Aeroflot (airline code SU; ☎ 02-551 0321, Incheon airport 032-744 8672; www.aeroflot.com)
Air Canada (airline code AC; ☎ 02-3788 0100, Incheon airport 032-744 0898; www.aircanada.ca)
Air China (airline code CA; ☎ 02-774 6886, Incheon airport 032-744 3256; www.airchina.com)
Air France (airline code AF; ☎ 02-3483 1033, Incheon airport 032-744 4900; www.airfrance.com)

All Nippon Airways (airline code NH; ☎ 02-752 5500, Incheon airport 032-744 3200; www.fly-ana.com)
Asiana Airlines (airline code OZ; ☎ 1588 8000, Incheon airport 032-744 2132; http://flyasiana.com)
Cathay Pacific Airways (airline code CX; ☎ 02-311 2800, Incheon airport 032-744 6777; www.cathaypacific.com)
China Airlines (airline code C1; ☎ 02-317 8888, Incheon airport 032-743 1513; www.china-airlines.com)
China Eastern Airlines (airline code MU; ☎ 02-518 0330, Incheon airport 032-744 3780; www.ce-air.com)
China Southern Airlines (airline code CZ; ☎ 02-775 9070, Incheon airport 032-744 3270; www.cs-air.com)
Emirates (airline code EK; ☎ 02-2022 8400; www.emirates.com)
Garuda Indonesia Airways (airline code GA; ☎ 02-773 2092, Incheon airport 032-744 1990; www.garuda-indonesia.com)
Japan Airlines (airline code JL; ☎ 02-757 1711, Incheon airport 032-744 3601; www.jal.com)
KLM Royal Dutch Airlines (airline code KL; ☎ 02-2011 5500, Incheon airport 032-744 6700; www.klm.com)
Korean Air (airline code KE; ☎ 1588 2001, Incheon airport 032-742 7654; www.koreanair.com)
Lufthansa Airlines (airline code LH; ☎ 02-3420 0400, Incheon airport 032-744 3400; www.lufthansa.com)
Malaysia Airlines (airline code MH; ☎ 02-777 7761, Incheon airport 032-744 3501; www.malaysiaairlines.com)
Northwest Airlines (airline code NW; ☎ 02-732 1700, Incheon airport 032-744 6300; www.nwa.com)
Philippine Airlines (airline code PR; ☎ 02-1544 1717, Incheon airport 032-744 3720; www.philippineair.com)
Qantas Airways (airline code QF; ☎ 02-777 6871, Incheon airport 032-744 3283; www.qantas.com.au)
Singapore Airlines (airline code SQ; ☎ 02-755 1226, Incheon airport 032-744 6500; www.singaporeairlines.com)

THINGS CHANGE...

The information in this chapter is particularly vulnerable to change. Check directly with the airline or a travel agent to make sure you understand how a fare (and ticket you may buy) works and be aware of the security requirements for international travel. Shop carefully. The details given in this chapter should be regarded as pointers and are not a substitute for your own careful, up-to-date research.

Thai Airways International (airline code TG; ☎ 02-3707 0011, Incheon airport 032-744 3571; www.thaiair.com)
United Airlines (airline code UA; ☎ 02-757 1691, Incheon airport 032-744 6666; www.united.com)

Tickets

Be sure you research all the options carefully to make sure you get the deal that best suits your circumstances and requirements. The internet is a useful resource for researching airline prices.

Automated online ticket sales work well if you're doing a simple one-way or return trip on specified dates, but are no substitute for a travel agent with the low-down on special deals, strategies for avoiding layovers and other useful advice.

Paying by credit card offers some protection if you unwittingly end up dealing with a rogue fly-by-night travel agency, as most card issuers provide refunds if you can prove you didn't receive what you paid for. Alternatively, buy a ticket from a bonded agent, such as one covered by the **Air Travel Organisers' Licensing** (ATOL; www.caa.co.uk) scheme in the UK. If you have doubts about the service provider, at the very least call the airline and confirm that your booking has been made.

The following websites can search for air fares to Korea when booking online or researching prices prior to visiting your travel agent:

www.cheapflights.com Really does post some of the cheapest flights, but get in early to get the bargains.
www.dialaflight.com Offers worldwide flights out of Europe and the UK.
www.expedia.com A good site for checking worldwide flight prices.
www.kayak.com Great search engine for flight deals with links through to its selections.
www.lastminute.com Start here and choose sites specifically for Australia, the UK and the US as well as a variety of other European countries.
www.statravel.com STA Travel's US website. There are also UK and Australian sites (www.statravel.co.uk and www.statravel.com.au).
www.travel.com.au A good site for Australians to find cheap flights.

Korean airport departure taxes are included in the ticket price.

Ticket prices have not been listed in this section as they vary so much depending on a range of factors including the season, the amount of competition, the level of demand and so on. Ever-increasing security, fuel and other surcharges add another element of uncertainty. Prices of flights from Korea can increase 50% in July and August, and special offers are less common during holiday periods. The peak of the peak for outbound flights is early August, when it can be difficult to find a seat.

INTERCONTINENTAL TICKETS & AIR PASSES

These round-the-world tickets can provide a good deal if you want to visit other countries besides Korea. A typical ticket could include India, Southeast Asia, Europe and America as well as Korea.

Australia

For flights from Sydney, Melbourne or Brisbane to Incheon airport, try Cathay Pacific or Malaysia Airlines, which may have special deals. Qantas has direct services between Sydney and Seoul.

Two well-known agencies for cheap fares, with offices throughout Australia, are **Flight Centre** (☎ 133 133; www.flightcentre.com.au) and **STA Travel** (☎ 1300 733 035; www.statravel.com.au).

Canada

Look out for special offers on return flights from Toronto or Vancouver to Incheon airport – try Air Canada or Asiana for a start. Prices to destinations like Winnipeg are expensive even in the low season.

Travel CUTS (☎ 866 246 9762; www.travelcuts.com) is Canada's national student travel agency.

China & Hong Kong

Keep an eye out for specials deals between Beijing and Incheon airport – try www.ease travels.com or www.statravel.com.cn. These days Incheon airport is linked to more than 20 Chinese cities as tourism and trade between the two countries booms. Regional Korean airports, such as Gimhae (for Busan), Daegu, Gwangju and Jeju-do, also have flights to Chinese cities.

There are also direct flights to Hong Kong. The Tsim Sha Tsui area is Hong Kong's budget travel-agency centre. Try **Hong Kong Student Travel** (☎ 2730 2800; www.hkst.com) or **Traveller Service** (☎ 2375 2222; www.taketraveller.com). In 2009 the budget airline **Jin Air** (☎ 1600 6200; www.jinair. com), owned by Korean Air, started to offer flights between Incheon and Macau.

Continental Europe

The cheapest return flights from different cities in Continental Europe to Incheon airport are usually similar, although ultra specials are sometimes available – for starters try Aeroflot, KLM or Lufthansa.

Specialising in youth and student fares **Nouvelles Frontières** (☎ 0825-000 747; www.nouvelles -frontieres.fr) has branches across France. Also try **Anyway.com** (☎ 0892-302 301; http://voyages.anyway. com) and **Lastminute** (☎ 0892-705 000; www.fr.last minute.com).

Recommended agencies in Germany include **STA Travel** (☎ 069-7430 3292; www.statravel.de) and **Travel Overland** (☎ 01805-276 370; www.travel -overland.de).

In Italy try **CTS Viaggi** (☎ 06-441 1166; www.cts.it), in the Netherlands **Airfair** (☎ 0900-771 7717; www. airfair.nl) and in Spain **Bacelo Viajes** (☎ 902-200 400; www.barceloviajes.com).

Japan

With Japanese tourists making up the majority of foreign visitors to Korea, and increasing numbers of Koreans flying to Japan (sometimes just for the weekend), competition is keen on routes between the neighbours.

There are direct nonstop flights from over 20 Japanese airports to Incheon and seven from Gimpo, but flights from Tokyo (either Haneda or Narita) are usually the cheapest. Fares go up and down with the seasons, with those for Japan's Golden Week holidays (around late April, early May) and August costing up to twice the price of low-season fares. Flights are also available from Japan to airports in Busan, Daegu and Jeju-do, with budget airline **Jeju Air** (☎ 1588 5301; www.jejuair. com) offering good rates to Jeju-do.

Reliable discount agencies in Japan with English-speaking staff include **No 1 Travel** (☎ 03-3205 6073; www.no1-travel.com), **Across Travellers Bureau** (☎ 03-5467 0077; www.across-travel.com) and **STA Travel** (☎ 03-5391 2922; www.statravel.co.jp). Also check classified advertisements in the *Japan Times* or on its website (www.japantimes. co.jp), which operates an online travel service, as well as the weekly listings magazine *Metropolis* (http://metropolis.co.jp).

New Zealand

Airlines seem to take it in turns to offer the lowest fare, but try Malaysia Airlines as a starting point. Korean Air may have a reasonable fare if you are continuing on to Europe. Return flights from Incheon airport to New Zealand are rarely discounted (due to plenty of Koreans visiting, studying and even emigrating to NZ).

Flight Centre (☎ 0800 243 544; www.flightcentre. co.nz) and **STA Travel** (☎ 0800 474 400; www.statravel.

co.nz) have branches in Auckland and elsewhere in the country; check the websites for complete listings.

Singapore & Thailand

Cut-price youth fares can slash the cost of return flights from Singapore to Incheon airport. **STA Travel** (☎ 65-6737 7188; www.statravel.com. sg) and other travel agents sometimes have special offers.

Bangkok has a number of excellent travel agencies but there are also some suspect ones; you should ask the advice of other travellers before handing over your cash. **STA Travel** (☎ 662-236 0262; www.statravel.co.th) is a reliable place to start. Also check out flights on Korean-based budget airline **Jin Air** (☎ 1600 6200; www.jinair.com) between Incheon and Bangkok.

UK

The UK has an endless number of worldwide discount flights, so it's always worthwhile to do a thorough check before buying a ticket. From Heathrow or Gatwick airports (both near London) try Emirates via Dubai or direct flights on Korean Air. Off-season specials are always likely.

Reputable UK-based agencies:

ebookers (☎ 0871-223 5000; www.ebookers.co.uk)
Flight Centre (☎ 0870-499 0040; www.flightcentre.co.uk)
STA Travel (☎ 0871-230 0040; www.statravel.co.uk)
Trailfinders (☎ 0845-058 5858; www.trailfinders.com)

From Korea, buy tickets as early as you can or go via Southeast Asia to reduce the cost of flights.

USA

From New York, Los Angeles, and San Francisco there are usually return-flight specials to Incheon airport – try Asiana, United, Northwest or Malaysia Airlines. Taxes, fuel, security surcharges and all the rest of it can add substantially to the fare.

Check out **STA Travel** (☎ 1-800-781 4040; www.statravel.com) for discounted fares.

LAND

Having North Korea as a hostile neighbour for over 50 years has turned South Korea into a virtual island. However, if North Korea does ever relax its isolationist policies, the South could quickly be linked by road and rail through North Korea to China, Russia and beyond. It's an exciting prospect but unlikely to happen any time soon.

SEA

International ferries are worth considering if you're travelling around North Asia.

China

Ferries link 10 Chinese ports with Incheon (p165). A ferry-and-train package is available from cities in Korea to Beijing, Shanghai, Hangzhou or Shenyang in China via the Incheon–Tianjin ferry – see www.korail.com for details.

There are also direct ferry connections between Gunsan in Jeollabuk-do and Qindao.

Japan

Regular ferries shuttle between Busan and four Japanese cities: Fukuoka, Shimonoseki, Osaka and Tsushima. Faster services are available on **hydrofoils** (www.mirejet.co.kr) from Busan to Fukuoka – see p250 for full details.

Korail (www.korail.com) offers the Korea–Japan Joint Railroad Ticket which lasts a week and offers discounts of up to 30% on rail fares in Korea and Japan and on ferry tickets between the two countries from Busan.

There's also a ferry from Sokcho to Niigata; see p179 for details.

Russia

Ferries run between Sokcho in Gangwon-do and Zarubino and Vladivostok in Russia; it's possible to transit by bus to Hunchun in China via Zarubino and onwards to Paekdusan on the North Korea–China border – see p179 for details.

GETTING AROUND

South Korea is a public-transport dream come true. Planes, trains and express buses link major cities, intercity buses link cities and towns large and small, while local buses provide a surprisingly good service to national and provincial parks and villages in outlying rural areas. Car ferries ply numerous routes to offshore islands. Local urban buses, subways and taxis make getting around cities and towns easy. All transport works on the Korean *ppalli ppalli* (hurry hurry) system, so buses and trains leave on time, and buses and taxis tend to be driven fast with little regard to road rules.

TRANSPORT

SEOUL–BUSAN: A TIME/COST COMPARISON

With President Lee Myung-bak's plan of a 'grand canal' linking Seoul and Busan set aside amid a hail of public criticism, travellers are left pondering whether to connect between Korea's two main cities via air, rail or road. The following comparison may help you decide.

Seoul to Busan (384km) by bus costs between W21,000 and W34,200 depending on the class of bus and takes 4½ hours with services departing at least every 30 minutes. The train options are KTX (high-speed; W44,800, two hours 40 minutes, every 30 minutes), *Saemaul* (express; W39,300, 4½ hours, five daily) and *Mugunghwa* (semi-express; W26,500, 5½ hours, eight daily) – all of which tend to be more comfortable than buses.

Flying costs from around W42,000 one way with **Air Busan** (http://flyairbusan.com) and only takes an hour, but add on at least another two hours for travelling to and from the airports and for check-in and security clearance.

AIR
Airlines in Korea

South Korea's domestic carriers:

Air Busan (☎ 1588 8009; http://flyairbusan.com) Partly owned by Asiana Airlines.

Asiana Airlines (☎ 1588 8000; www.flyasiana.com)

Eastar Jet (☎ 1544 0080; www.eastarjet.com)

Hansung Airlines (☎ 1599 9090; www.gohansung.com)

Jeju Air (☎ 1588 5301; www.jejuair.com)

Korean Air (☎ 1588 2001; www.koreanair.com)

Korean Air and Asiana, the two major domestic airlines, provide flights to and from a dozen local airports, and charge virtually identical but very reasonable fares – competition is being supplied by budget newcomers such as Eastar Jet, which has services between Seoul, Gunsan and Cheongju to Jeju-do. Gimpo International Airport handles nearly all of Seoul's domestic flights, but Incheon International Airport handles a handful of domestic flights to Busan, Daegu and Jeju-do. The longest flight time is just over an hour between Seoul Gimpo and Jeju-do.

Fares are 15% cheaper from Monday to Thursday when seats are easier to obtain. Flights on public holidays have a surcharge and are often booked out. Students and children receive discounts, and foreigners should always carry their passports on domestic flights for ID purposes.

BICYCLE

As part of his plan for tackling Korea's rising carbon emissions, President Lee Myung-bak plans to boost Korea's bicycle industry so it becomes the third largest in the world. Seoul's metropolitan government is supporting the plan by expanding cycling infrastructure in the city, creating 207km of dedicated cycle lanes, centres at four major subway stations where bikes can be stored and hired, and showers and lockers for cycle commuters at 16 subway stations.

Something will have to be done about poor local driving habits though, because currently these make cycling in Korea a less than pleasurable experience, especially in urban areas. This said, hiring a bike for short trips in areas with bike paths or little traffic is a good idea – see p80 and individual destination chapters for recommended cycling trips. Bicycle hire is usually W3000 an hour, but try for a discount for a day's hire. You'll have to leave your passport or negotiate some other ID or deposit. Helmets are typically not available and you may need your own padlock.

Jan Boonstra's website **Bicycling in Korea** (http://user.chollian.net/~boonstra/korea/cycle.htm) has some useful information.

BOAT

Korea has an extensive network of ferries that connects hundreds of offshore islands to each other and to the mainland. The large southern island of Jeju-do can be reached by ferry from Mokpo or Wan-do in Jeollanam-do or on longer boat trips from Busan and Incheon, although most people fly these days.

On the west coast, ferries from Incheon's Yeonan Pier service a dozen nearby and more distant islands, while other west-coast islands further south can be reached from Daecheon harbour and Gunsan. Mokpo, Wan-do, Yeosu and Busan provide access to countless islands strung along the south coast.

Remote Ulleung-do off the east coast can be reached by ferry from Pohang or Donghae. Inland ferries run along a couple of large scenic lakes – Soyang Lake in Gangwon-do and

Chungju Lake in Chungcheongbuk-do. See the provincial chapters for details on all these floating excursions.

BUS

Thousands of long-distance buses whiz to every nook and cranny of the country, every 15 minutes between major cities and towns, and at least hourly to small towns, villages, temples and national and provincial parks. Only a selection of bus destinations are given in the transport sections of each city, town or tourist site covered. All the bus frequencies given are approximate, as buses don't usually run on a regular timetable and times vary throughout the day. Bus terminals have staff on hand to ensure that everyone boards the right bus, so help is always available. Most buses don't have toilets on board, but on long journeys drivers take a 10-minute rest every few hours.

Express buses link major cities, while intercity buses stop more often and serve smaller cities and towns. The buses are similar, but they use separate (often neighbouring) terminals. Expressways have a special bus lane that operates at weekends and reduces delays due to heavy traffic. Buses always leave on time (or even early!) and go to far more places than trains, but are not as comfortable or smooth, so for travelling long distances trains can be the better option.

Udeung (superior-class express buses) have three seats per row instead of four, but cost 50% more than *ilban* (standard buses). Buses that travel after 10pm have a 10% surcharge and are generally superior class.

Expect to pay around W4000 for an hour-long journey on a standard bus.

Buses are so frequent that it's not necessary to buy a ticket in advance except on weekends and during holiday periods. Buy tickets at the bus terminals. You can check schedules on www.kobus.co.kr and www.easyticket.co.kr.

CAR & MOTORCYCLE
Bring Your Own Vehicle

Contact **customs** (http://english.customs.go.kr/) for information on regulations concerning importing your own car. The vast majority of cars running in the country are Korean-made, although a few luxury cars are imported. Repairs and spare parts are not generally available for most imported cars, but finding petrol is no problem.

Driving Licence

Drivers must have an international driving licence, which should be obtained before arrival as they're not available in Korea. After one year, a Korean driving licence must be obtained. For more info see the website of the **Driver's License Agency** (www.dla.go.kr/english/index.jsp).

Hire

Driving in Korea is not recommended for first-time visitors, but travellers who wish to hire a car must be 21 years or over and must by law have an international driving licence (a driving licence from your own country is not acceptable). Rates start at around W63,000 per day for a compact car but can be discounted by up to 50%. Insurance costs around W10,000 a day, but depends on the level of the excess you choose. Chauffeur service is also an option.

There are a few car-hire desks at Incheon International Airport. Check the website of **Kumho-Hertz** (www.kumhorent.com) to see what it has to offer.

Insurance

Insurance is compulsory for all drivers. Since the chance of having an accident is higher than in nearly all other developed countries obtain as much cover as you can, with a low excess.

Road Conditions

Korea has an appalling road-accident record, and foreign drivers in large cities are likely to spend most of their time lost, stuck in traffic jams, looking for a parking space or taking evasive action. Impatient and careless drivers are a major hazard and traffic rules are frequently ignored. Driving in rural areas or on Jeju-do is more feasible, but public transport is so good that few visitors feel the urge to sit down behind a steering wheel.

Speed cameras are ubiquitous, and your credit card may be debited for a speeding fine even after you've handed your hire-car back.

Road Rules

Vehicles drive on the right side of the road. The driver and front-seat passengers must wear seatbelts, drunk drivers receive heavy fines, and victims of road accidents are often paid a big sum by drivers wanting to avoid a court case.

HITCHING

Accepting a lift anywhere always has an element of risk so we don't recommend it. Also

TRANSPORT

hitching is not a local custom and there is no particular signal for it. However Korea is relatively crime-free, so if you get stuck in a rural area, stick out your thumb and the chances are that some kind person will give you a lift. Drivers often go out of their way to help foreigners. Normally bus services are frequent and cheap enough, even in the countryside, to make hitching unnecessary.

LOCAL TRANSPORT
Bus

Local city buses provide a frequent and inexpensive service (around W1000 a trip, irrespective of how far you travel), and although rural buses provide a less-frequent service, many run on an hourly or half-hourly basis, so you don't usually have to wait long. Put the fare in the glass box next to the driver – make sure you have plenty of W1000 notes because the machines only give coins in change.

The main problem with local buses is finding and getting on the right bus – bus timetables, bus-stop names and destination signs on buses are rarely in English, and bus drivers don't speak English. Writing your destination in big *hangeul* (Korean phonetic alphabet) letters on a piece of paper will be helpful. Local tourist information centres usually have English-speaking staff, and are the best places to find out which local bus number goes where, and where to pick it up.

Subway

Six cities have a subway system: Seoul, Busan, Daejeon, Daegu, Gwangju and Incheon. The subway is a cheap and convenient way of getting around these major cities, and since signs and station names are in English as well as Korean, the systems are foreigner-friendly and easy to use.

Taxi

Taxis are numerous almost everywhere and are so cheap that even high-school students use them. Fares vary only slightly in different areas. Every taxi has a meter that works on a distance basis but switches to a time basis when the vehicle is stuck in a traffic jam. Tipping is not a local custom and is not expected or necessary.

Ilban (regular taxis) cost around W2400 for the first 2km, while the *mobeom* (deluxe taxis) that exist in some cities cost around W4500 for the first 3km.

Any expressway tolls are added to the fare. In the countryside check the fare first as there are local quirks, such as surcharges or a fixed rate to out-of-the-way places with little prospect of a return fare.

Since very few taxi drivers speak any English, plan beforehand how to communicate your destination to the driver; if you have a mobile phone you can also use the ☎ 1330 tourist advice line to help with interpretation. Ask to be dropped off at a nearby landmark if the driver doesn't understand what you're saying or doesn't know where it is. It can be useful to write down your destination or a nearby landmark in *hangeul* on a piece of paper.

TRAIN

South Korea has an excellent but not comprehensive train network operated by **Korail** (☎ 1544 7788; www.korail.com), connecting most major cities and the towns along the way. Trains are clean, comfortable and punctual, and just about every station has a sign in Korean and English. Trains are the best option for long-distance travel. Go to the website to access all the train schedules and fares and to make online bookings.

Classes

There are four classes of trains. High-speed KTX trains can travel at over 300km/h. The high-speed track extends from Seoul to Busan on the east coast. The next fastest and most luxurious are *Saemaul* trains, which also stop only in major cities. *Mugunghwa* trains stop more often and are almost as comfortable and fast as *Saemaul* trains. *Tonggeun* (commuter) trains are the cheapest and stop at every station, but only run infrequently on certain routes and are a dying breed.

Many trains have a train cafe where you not only buy drinks and snack foods but also surf the internet, play computer games, even sing karaoke. If a train is standing-room only, hanging out in the train cafe for the journey is the best way to go.

Costs

The full range of discounts is complicated and confusing. For fares and schedules see the Korail website. KTX trains are 40% more expensive than *Saemaul* trains (and KTX 1st class is another 40%). *Saemaul* 1st class is 22% more than the standard *Saemaul* fare.

Saemaul standard fares are 50% more than *Mugunghwa* class, which is 80% more expensive than *tonggeun* (commuter) class. KTX tickets are discounted 7% to 20% if you buy them seven to 60 days before departure. Tickets are discounted 15% from Tuesday to Thursday, and *ipseokpyo* (standing tickets) are discounted 15% to 30% depending on the length of the journey; with a standing ticket, you are allowed to sit on any unoccupied seats. Children travel for half price and seniors receive a 25% discount.

Reservations

The railway ticketing system is computerised and you can buy tickets up to two months in advance online, at railway stations and some travel agents. There are far fewer trains than buses, so seat reservations are sensible and necessary on weekends, holidays and other busy times.

Train Passes

Foreigners can buy a KR Pass at overseas travel agents or online (www.korail.com/kr_pass.jsp). The KR Pass offers unlimited rail travel (including KTX services) for three/five/seven/10 consecutive days at a cost of US$76/114/144/166. Children (four to 12 years) receive a 50% discount, and youths (13 to 25 years old) receive a 20% discount.

Are they worth it? The problem is that distances in Korea are not great, trains don't go everywhere, and the pass is unlikely to save you much, if any, money unless you plan to shuttle even more frequently than a Lonely Planet researcher back and forth across the country.

TRANSPORT

Health

CONTENTS

Health issues and the quality of medical care vary significantly depending on whether you stay in cities or venture further out into rural areas.

Travellers tend to worry about contracting infectious diseases while abroad, but infections are a rare cause of serious illness or death while overseas. Accidental injury (especially traffic accidents) and pre-existing medical conditions such as heart disease account for most life-threatening problems. Becoming ill in some way, however, is relatively common. Fortunately most common illnesses can either be prevented with some common-sense behaviour or be treated easily with a well-stocked traveller's medical kit.

The following advice is a general guide only and does not replace the advice of a doctor trained in travel medicine.

BEFORE YOU GO

Pack medications in their original, clearly labelled containers. A signed and dated letter from your physician describing your medical conditions and regular medications (use generic names) is also a good idea. If carrying syringes or needles, be sure to have a physician's letter documenting their medical necessity.

If you have a heart condition bring a copy of your ECG taken just prior to travelling.

If you take any regular medication, bring double your needs in case of loss. In Korea you need a local doctor's prescription to buy medication, and it may be difficult to obtain particular branded medications available in Western countries.

INSURANCE

Even if you are fit and healthy, don't travel without health insurance – accidents do happen. Declare any existing medical conditions you have; the insurance company will check if your problem is pre-existing and will not cover you if it is undeclared. You may require extra cover for adventure activities. If your health insurance doesn't cover you for medical expenses abroad, consider getting extra insurance. If you're uninsured, emergency evacuation is expensive; bills of over US$100,000 are not uncommon.

Find out in advance if your insurance plan will make payments directly to providers or reimburse you later for overseas health expenses; in many countries doctors expect cash payment. Some policies offer lower and higher medical-expense options; the higher ones are mainly for countries with very high medical costs, such as the USA. You may prefer a policy that pays doctors or hospitals directly, rather than you having to pay on the spot and claim later. If you have to claim later, be sure to keep all documents. Some policies ask you to call back (reverse charges) to a centre in your own country where an immediate assessment of your problem is made.

HEALTH ADVISORIES

It's usually a good idea to consult your government's travel-health website before departure, if one is available:
Australia www.smartraveller.gov.au
Canada www.phac-aspc.gc.ca/tmp-pmv/index-eng.php
New Zealand www.safetravel.govt.nz
UK www.dh.gov.uk
USA www.cdc.gov/travel/

RECOMMENDED VACCINATIONS

No special vaccinations are required or recommended for South Korea, but check the latest situation with your tour company before visiting the North.

MEDICAL CHECKLIST

Recommended items for a personal medical kit:

- For diarrhoea consider an oral rehydration solution (eg Gastrolyte), diarrhoea 'stopper' (eg Loperamide) and antinausea medication (eg Prochlorperazine)
- Antibiotics for diarrhoea – Norfloxacin or Ciprofloxacin or Azithromycin for bacterial diarrhoea; Tinidazole for giardiasis or amoebic dysentery
- Laxative, eg Coloxyl
- Antispasmodic for stomach cramps, eg Buscopan
- Indigestion tablets, for example Quick-Eze, Mylanta
- Throat lozenges
- Antihistamine – there are many options, eg Cetrizine for daytime and Promethazine for night
- Decongestant, eg pseudoephedrine
- Paracetamol
- Ibuprofen or another anti-inflammatory
- Your personal medicine if you are a migraine sufferer
- Sunscreen and hat
- Antiseptic, eg Betadine
- Antibacterial cream, eg Muciprocin
- Steroid cream for allergic/itchy rashes, eg 1% to 2% hydrocortisone
- Antifungal cream, eg Clotrimazole
- For skin infections, antibiotics such as Amoxicillin/Clavulanate or Cephalexin
- Contraceptive method
- Thrush (vaginal yeast infection) treatment, eg Clotrimazole pessaries or Diflucan tablet
- Ural, or equivalent, if prone to urinary-tract infections
- DEET-based insect repellent
- Mosquito net impregnated with a substance like permethrin
- Permethrin to impregnate clothing
- Iodine tablets (unless you are pregnant or have a thyroid problem) to purify water
- Basic first-aid items such as scissors, sticking plasters, bandages, gauze, thermometer (but not mercury), sterile needles and syringes, safety pins, tweezers

INTERNET RESOURCES

There's a wealth of travel-health advice on the internet. For further information:

Centers for Disease Control and Prevention (CDC; www.cdc.gov) Has good general information.

MD Travel Health (www.mdtravelhealth.com) Provides complete travel-health recommendations for every country and is updated daily.

World Health Organization (www.who.int/ith/en/) Publishes the annually revised *International Travel and Health,* available online at no cost.

FURTHER READING

Lonely Planet's pocket-sized *Healthy Travel Asia & India* is packed with useful information including pretrip planning, emergency first aid, immunisation and disease information and what to do if you get sick on the road. *Travel with Children* from Lonely Planet includes advice on travel health for young kids. Other recommended references include *Traveller's Health* by Dr Richard Dawood (Oxford University Press), and *Travelling Well* by Dr Deborah Mills, available at www.travellingwell.com.au.

IN TRANSIT

DEEP VEIN THROMBOSIS (DVT)

Deep vein thrombosis occurs when blood clots form in the legs during plane flights, chiefly because of prolonged immobility. The longer the flight, the greater the risk. Though most blood clots are reabsorbed uneventfully, some may break off and travel through the blood vessels to the lungs, where they may cause life-threatening complications.

The chief symptom of DVT is swelling or pain of the foot, ankle, or calf, usually but not always on just one side. When a blood clot travels to the lungs, it may cause chest pain and difficulty in breathing. Travellers who find that they have any of these symptoms should immediately seek medical attention.

To prevent the development of DVT on long flights, you should walk about the cabin, perform isometric compressions of the leg muscles (ie contract the leg muscles while sitting), drink plenty of fluids, and avoid alcohol and tobacco.

JET LAG & MOTION SICKNESS

Jet lag is common when crossing more than five time zones; it results in insomnia, fatigue, malaise or nausea. To avoid jet lag,

HEALTH

try drinking plenty of fluids (nonalcoholic) and eating light meals. Upon arrival, seek exposure to natural sunlight and readjust your schedule (for meals, sleep etc) as soon as possible.

Antihistamines such as dimenhydrinate (Dramamine), prochlorperazine (Phenergan) and meclizine (Antivert, Bonine) are generally the first choice for the treatment of motion sickness. Their major side effect is drowsiness. A herbal alternative is ginger, which works like a charm for some people.

IN KOREA

AVAILABILITY & COST OF HEALTH CARE

South Korea is a well-developed country, and the quality of medical care reflects this. Standards of medical care are higher in Seoul and other cities than in rural areas, although making yourself understood can be a problem anywhere.

North Korea is poverty-stricken and medical care is completely inadequate throughout the country including Pyongyang. Shortages of routine medications and supplies are a common problem.

INFECTIOUS DISEASES
Filariasis

A mosquito-borne disease that is very rare in travellers; mosquito-avoidance measures are the best way to prevent this disease. It's widespread in rice-growing areas in southwest Korea.

Hepatitis A

A problem throughout the country, this food-and water-borne virus infects the liver, causing jaundice (yellow skin and eyes), nausea and lethargy. There is no specific treatment for hepatitis A; you just need to allow time for the liver to heal. All travellers to Korea should be vaccinated against hepatitis A.

Hepatitis B

The only sexually transmitted disease that can be prevented by vaccination, hepatitis B is spread by body fluids, including sexual contact. Up to 10% of the population are carriers of hepatitis B, and usually are unaware of this. The long-term consequences can include liver cancer and cirrhosis.

HIV

HIV is also spread by body fluids. Avoid unsafe sex, sharing needles, invasive cosmetic procedures such as tattooing, and needles that have not been sterilised in a medical setting.

Influenza

Influenza (flu) symptoms include high fever, muscle aches, runny nose, cough and sore throat. It can be very severe in people over the age of 65 or in those with underlying medical conditions such as heart disease or diabetes – vaccination is recommended for these individuals. There is no specific treatment, just rest and paracetamol.

Japanese B Encephalitis

This viral disease is transmitted by mosquitoes, but is very rare in travellers. Most cases occur in rural areas, and vaccination is recommended for travellers spending more than one month outside cities. There is no treatment, and a third of infected people will die, while another third will suffer permanent brain damage. The highest risk is in the southwest rice-growing areas.

Leptospirosis

Leptospirosis is contracted after exposure to contaminated fresh water (eg rivers). Early symptoms are similar to the 'flu' and include headache and fever. It can vary from a very mild to a fatal disease. Diagnosis is through blood tests, and it is easily treated with Doxycycline.

Lyme Disease

This tick-borne disease occurs in the summer months. Symptoms include an early rash and general viral symptoms, followed weeks to months later by joint, heart or neurological problems. Prevention is by using general insect-avoidance measures and checking yourself for ticks after walking in forest areas. Treatment is with Doxycycline.

Rabies

This sometimes fatal disease is spread by the bite or lick of an infected animal – most commonly a dog. You should seek medical advice immediately after any animal bite and commence post-exposure treatment. If an animal bites you, gently wash the wound with soap and water, and apply iodine-based antiseptic. If you are not pre-vaccinated, you will need to receive rabies immunoglobulin as soon as possible.

STDs

Sexually transmitted diseases are common throughout the world and the most common include herpes, warts, syphilis, gonorrhoea and chlamydia. People carrying these diseases often have no signs of infection. Condoms prevent gonorrhoea and chlamydia but not warts or herpes. If after a sexual encounter you develop any rash, lumps, discharge or pain when passing urine, seek immediate medical attention. If you have been sexually active during your travels, have an STD check on your return home.

Tuberculosis

Only North Korea has significant risk. While tuberculosis is rare, travellers, medical and aid workers, and long-term travellers with significant contact with the local population, should take precautions. Vaccination is usually only given to children under five, but adults at risk are recommended to undertake pre- and post-travel TB testing. Symptoms are fever, cough, weight loss, night sweats and tiredness.

Typhoid

This serious bacterial infection is spread via food and water. It gives a high and slowly worsening fever and headache, and may be accompanied by a dry cough and stomach pain. It's diagnosed by blood tests and treated with antibiotics. Vaccination is recommended, but note that vaccination isn't 100% effective – you must still be careful with what you eat and drink.

Typhus

Scrub typhus is present in Korea's scrub areas. This is spread by a mite and is very rare in travellers. Symptoms include fever, muscle pains and a rash. Following general insect-avoidance measures when walking in the scrub will help you avoid this disease. Doxycycline works as a prevention and treatment for typhus.

TRAVELLERS' DIARRHOEA

Travellers' diarrhoea is the most common problem which affects travellers – between 10% and 20% of people visiting South Korea will suffer from it. The risk in North Korea is more like 40% to 60%. In the majority of cases, travellers' diarrhoea is triggered by a bacteria (there are numerous potential culprits), and therefore responds promptly to treatment with antibiotics, which will depend on your circumstances: how sick you are, how quickly you need to get better, where you are etc.

Travellers' diarrhoea is defined as the passage of more than three watery bowel actions within 24 hours, plus at least one other symptom such as fever, cramps, nausea, vomiting or feeling generally unwell. Treatment consists of staying well hydrated; rehydration solutions like Gastrolyte are the best for this. Antibiotics such as Norfloxacin, Ciprofloxacin or Azithromycin will kill the bacteria quickly.

Loperamide is just a 'stopper' and doesn't get to the cause of the problem. It can be helpful, for example, if you have to go on a long bus ride. Don't take Loperamide if you have a fever, or blood in your stools. Seek medical attention quickly if you do not respond to an appropriate antibiotic.

Giardiasis

Giardia is a parasite relatively common in travellers. Symptoms include nausea, bloating, excess gas, fatigue and intermittent diarrhoea. 'Eggy' burps are often attributed solely to Giardia, but work in Nepal has shown that they are not specific to Giardia. The parasite will eventually go away if left untreated but this can take months. The treatment of choice is Tinidazole, with Metronidazole being a second-line option. Giardia isn't common in South Korea.

ENVIRONMENTAL HAZARDS
Air Pollution

Air pollution, particularly from vehicles, is a problem in Seoul. If you have severe respiratory problems, speak with your doctor before travelling to any heavily polluted urban centres. This pollution also causes minor respiratory problems such as sinusitis, dry throat and irritated eyes. If troubled by the pollution, leave the city for a few days and get some fresh air.

Food

Eating in restaurants is the biggest risk factor for contracting travellers' diarrhoea. Ways to avoid it include eating only freshly cooked food and avoiding shellfish and food that has been sitting around in buffets. Peel all fruit and cook vegetables. Eat in busy restaurants with a high turnover of customers.

Insect Bites & Stings

Insects are not a major issue in Korea; however, there are some insect-borne diseases present.

Ticks are contracted after walking in rural areas, and are commonly found behind the ears,

HEALTH

HEALTH

DRINKING WATER

The **Water Environment Partnership in Asia** (WEPA; www.wepa-db.net) has found that water quality in Korea is improving and Seoul's mayor Oh Se-hoon has launched a personal campaign to convince his fellow citizens that it's safe to drink the capital's tap water. However, if you want to play safe:

■ drink bottled rather than tap water – check the seal is intact at purchase

■ check ice has not been made with tap water

■ boiling water is the most efficient method of purifying it

■ the best chemical purifier is iodine, but it should not be used by pregnant women or those with thyroid problems

■ water filters should also filter out viruses; ensure your filter has a chemical barrier such as iodine and a small pore size (eg less than 4 microns)

---

on the belly and in armpits. If you've had a tick bite and experience symptoms such as a rash at the site of the bite or elsewhere, fever or muscle aches, you should see a doctor. Doxycycline prevents and treats tick-borne diseases.

Bee and wasp stings are mainly problems for people who are allergic to them. Anyone with a serious bee or wasp allergy should carry an adrenaline injection (eg Epipen) for emergency treatment. For others pain is the main problem – apply ice to the sting and take painkillers.

Parasites

The most common parasite in Korea is Clonorchis. Infection occurs after eating infected fresh-water fish – these may be raw, pickled, smoked or dried. Light infections usually cause no symptoms; however, heavy infections can cause liver problems. In some areas up to 20% of the local population are infected.

WOMEN'S HEALTH

Sanitary products are readily available. Birth-control options may be limited, so bring adequate supplies of your own contraception. Heat, humidity and antibiotics can all contribute to thrush. Treatment is with antifungal creams and pessaries such as Clotrimazole. A practical alternative is a single tablet of Fluconazole (Diflucan). Urinary tract infections can be precipitated by dehydration or long bus journeys without toilet stops; bring suitable antibiotics.

Pregnant women should receive specialised advice before travelling. The ideal time to travel is in the second trimester (between 16 and 28 weeks), when the risk of pregnancy-related problems are at their lowest and pregnant women generally feel their best. During the first trimester there is a risk of miscarriage and in the third trimester complications such as premature labour and high blood pressure are possible. It's wise to travel with a companion. Always carry a list of quality medical facilities available at your destination and ensure you continue your standard antenatal care at these facilities. Avoid rural travel in areas with poor transportation and medical facilities. Most of all, ensure travel insurance covers all pregnancy-related possibilities, including premature labour.

Travellers' diarrhoea can quickly lead to dehydration and result in inadequate blood flow to the placenta. Many of the drugs used to treat various diarrhoea bugs are not recommended in pregnancy. Azithromycin is considered safe.

TRADITIONAL & FOLK MEDICINE

Traditional medicine in Korea is known as Oriental medicine and is based on traditional Chinese medicine (TCM). Although Korean traditional medicine is heavily influenced by TCM, it has developed its own unique methods of diagnosis and treatment. Acupuncture techniques and herbal medicines are widely used.

Unique to Korean traditional medicine is Sasang Constitutional Medicine; it classifies people into four types (Taeyangin, Taeumin, Soyangin and Soeumin) based on body type, and treats each differently according to their constitution. In Korea 'fusion medicine', which combines traditional and Western medical systems, is increasingly popular. The World Health Organization has more than one research facility looking into traditional medicine in Seoul.

Note that 'natural' doesn't always mean 'safe', and there can be drug interactions between herbal and Western medicines. If you are utilising both systems, ensure you inform both practitioners what the other has prescribed.

Language

CONTENTS

Korean is a knotty problem for linguists. Various theories have been proposed to explain its origins, but the most widely accepted is that it is a member of the Ural-Altaic family of languages. Other members of the same linguistic branch are Turkish and Mongolian. In reality Korean grammar shares much more with Japanese than it does with either Turkish or Mongolian. Furthermore, the Koreans have borrowed nearly 70% of their vocabulary from neighbouring China, and now many English words have penetrated their language.

Chinese characters (*hanja*) are usually restricted to use in maps, government documents, the written names of businesses and in newspapers. For the most part Korean is written in *hangeul*, the alphabet developed under King Sejong's reign in the 15th century (see the boxed text, p34). Many linguists argue that the Korean script is one of the most intelligently designed and phonetically consistent alphabets used today.

Hangeul consists of only 24 characters and isn't that difficult to learn. However, the formation of words using *hangeul* is very different from the way that Western alphabets are used to form words. The em-phasis is on the formation of a syllable, and the end result bears some resemblance to a Chinese character. For example, the first syllable of the word *hangeul* (한) is formed by an 'h' (ㅎ) in the top left corner, an 'a' (ㅏ) in the top right corner and an 'n' (ㄴ) at the bottom, the whole syllabic grouping forming a syllabic 'box'. These syllabic 'boxes' are strung together to form words.

ROMANISATION

In 2000, the Korean government adopted a new method of romanising the Korean language. Most of the old romanisation system was retained, but a few changes were introduced to ensure a more consistent spelling. The new system has been energetically pushed throughout the government and tourist bureaus, but some corporations, individuals, academics and news outlets are reluctant to adopt it.

We use the new romanisation style throughout this book, but you'll come across many spelling variations. To avoid confusion it's always best to go back to the original Korean script. It's well worth spending a few hours to learn the Korean alphabet, even though we've provided Korean script throughout this book for place names and points of interest.

PRONUNCIATION

In the words and phrases in this chapter, the use of the variants **ga/i**, **reul/eul** and **ro/euro** depends on whether the preceding letter is a vowel or a consonant respectively.

Vowels & Vowel Combinations

ㅏ	**a**	as in 'are'
ㅑ	**ya**	as in 'yard'
ㅓ	**eo**	as the 'o' in 'of'
ㅕ	**yeo**	as the 'you' in 'young'
ㅗ	**o**	as in 'go'
ㅛ	**yo**	as in 'yoke'
ㅜ	**u**	as in 'flute'
ㅠ	**yu**	as the word 'you'
ㅡ	**eu**	as the 'oo' in 'look'
ㅣ	**i**	as the 'ee' in 'beet'
ㅐ	**ae**	as the 'a' in 'hat'
ㅒ	**yae**	as the 'ya' in 'yam'
ㅔ	**e**	as in 'ten'

ㅖ	ye	as in 'yes'
ㅘ	wa	as in 'waffle'
ㅙ	wae	as the 'wa' in 'wax'
ㅚ	oe	as the 'wa' in 'way'
ㅝ	wo	as in 'won'
ㅞ	we	as in 'wet'
ㅟ	wi	as the word 'we'
ㅢ	ui	as 'u' plus 'i'

Consonants

Unaspirated consonants can be difficult for English speakers to render. To those unfamiliar with Korean, an unaspirated **k** will sound like 'g', an unaspirated **t** like 'd', and an unaspirated **p** like 'b'.

Whether consonants in Korean are voiced or unvoiced depends on where they fall within a word. The rules governing this are too complex to cover here – the following tables show the various alternative pronunciations you may hear.

Single Consonants

The letter ㅅ is pronounced 'sh' if followed by the vowel ㅣ, even though it is transliterated as **si**.

In the middle of a word, ㄹ is pronounced 'n' if it follows ㅁ (**m**) or ㅇ (**ng**), but when it follows ㄴ (**n**) it becomes a double 'l' sound (**ll**); when a single ㄹ is followed by a vowel it is transliterated as **r**.

ㄱ	g/k
ㄴ	n
ㄷ	d/t
ㄹ	r/l/n
ㅁ	m
ㅂ	b/p
ㅅ	s/t
ㅇ	–/ng
ㅈ	j/t
ㅊ	ch/t
ㅋ	k
ㅌ	t
ㅍ	p
ㅎ	h/ng

Double Consonants

Double consonants are pronounced with more stress than their single consonants counterparts.

ㄲ	kk
ㄸ	tt
ㅃ	pp

| ㅆ | ss/t |
| ㅉ | jj |

Complex Consonants

These occur only in the middle or at the end of a word.

ㄱㅅ	–/ksk/–
ㄴㅈ	–/nj/n
ㄴㅎ	–/nh/n
ㄹㄱ	–/lg/k
ㄹㅁ	–/lm/m
ㄹㅂ	–/lb/p
ㄹㅅ	–/ls/l
ㄹㅌ	–/lt/l
ㄹㅍ	–/lp/p
ㄹㅎ	–/lh/l
ㅂㅅ	–/ps/p

POLITE KOREAN

Korea's pervasive social hierarchy means that varying degrees of politeness are codified into the grammar. Young Koreans tend to use the very polite forms a lot less than the older generation, but it's always best to use the polite form if you're unsure. The sentences in this section use polite forms.

ACCOMMODATION

I'm looking for a ...	... reul/eul chatgo isseoyo	...를/을 찾고 있어요.
guesthouse	yeogwan/ minbak jip	여관/ 민박집
hotel	hotel	호텔
youth hostel	yuseu hoseutel	유스호스텔

I'd like (a) ...	... ro/euro juseyo	...로/으로 주세요.
bed	chimdae	침대
single bed	singgeul chimdae	싱글 침대
double bed	deobeul chimdae	더블 침대
twin beds	chimdae dugae	침대 두개
room with a bathroom	yoksil inneun bang	욕실있는 방
to share a room	gachi sseuneun bang	같이 쓰는 방
Western-style room	chimdae bang	침대 방
a room with sleeping mats	ondol bang	온돌 방

Where is a cheap hotel?

ssan hoteri eodi isseoyo   싼 호텔이 어디
                                있어요?

제3조 **(회원의 철회권)** 회원은 할부매출일로부터 7일 이내에 가맹점에 서면으로 거래의 철회를 요청할 수 있으며, 가맹점으로 철회요청을 한 경우에 가맹점의 요청 사실을 소멸하여 서면을 신용제공자에게 제출(발송)함으로써 할부거래에 관한 의 철회를 요청할 수 있다. 단, 상품의 성질 또는 계약체결의 형태에 비추어 철회를 인정 할 수 없는 경우와 회원의 귀책사유에 의하여 상품의 멸실, 훼손 되었을 경우 또는 20만원 이하의 상품인 경우에 철회할 수 없다.

제4조 **(회원의 항변권)** 할부구매에 대한 분쟁에 있어 할부거래에 관한법률 제12조 제1항 에서 정한 요건에 해당하는 경우 회원은 신용제공자에게 분쟁의 해결을 요청하고 대금지급을 거절할 수 있다. 단, 상행위 목적의 거래나 신용카드 본 래의 용도 이외의 거래로 판단되는 경우 또는 20만원 미만인 경우는 제외된다.

제5조 **(회원의 기한이익 상실)** 회원은 할부금액을 2회이상 연속 연체하고, 연체 금액이 할부잔금의 1/10을 초과하는 경우등에는 할부금 지급에 대한 기한의 이익을 주장하지 못한다.

제6조 **(회원의 소유권 유보)** 회원은 할부계약이 종료되기 전까지 목적물의 소유권이 유보될 수 있다.

제7조 **(가맹점의 할부계약 해제)** 가맹점이 회원의 할부금 지급의무 불이행을 이유로 할부계약을 해제하고자 하는 경우에는 14일이상의 기간을 정하여 그 이행을 서면으로 회원에게 최고하여야 하며, 각 당사자는 그 상대방에 대하여 원상회복의 의무를 진다. 또한, 소유권이 가맹점에 유보된 경우에 가맹점은 계약을 해제하지 않고는 그 반환을 청구할 수 없다.

제8조 **(특약사항)** 신용카드업자 상호간의 업무제휴 계약에 따라 매출표 전면에 표시된 카드 발급사가 하단의 신용제공자와 다른 경우에는 카드 발급사를 신용제공자로 본다.

[표1] 신용제공자의 주소 및 할부수수료율

카드사	주 소	할부수수료율
롯데카드	서울 중구 남창동 51-1 롯데손해보험빌딩	년 14.9 ~ 18.9%
비씨카드	서울 서초구 서초동 1587	년 11.5 ~ 22.9%
삼성카드	서울 중구 태평로2가 250	년 10.0 ~ 21.8%
신한카드	서울 중구 충무로1가 21 포스트타워	년 11.3 ~ 21.8%
현대카드	서울 영등포구 여의도동 15-21	년 14.7 ~ 22.8%
KB국민카드	서울 중구 내수동 167	년 13.5 ~ 21.4%
우리은행	서울 중구 회현동1가 203	년 14.5 ~ 19.5%
하나SK카드	서울 중구 다동 140번지	년 14.9 ~ 22.7%
외환은행	서울 중구 을지로2가 181 외환은행본점	년 9.9 ~ 20.9%
NH농협은행	서울 중구 충정로1가 75	년 14.25 ~ 20.5%

※ 상기 할부수수료율은 카드사 사정에 따라 변경될 수 있습니다. (SK M&C_C)

철회 · 항변요청서

상품구매일	구매장소	구매품목	금액
철회·항변 요청사유 (구체적으로 기재)			
회원번호	회원성명	전화번호	철회·항변요청일
	(인)		

※ 철회·항변 요청시에는 상기사항을 빠짐없이 기재하시어 해당카드사에 제출하여 주십시오.

할부거래계약서

제1조 **(할부수수료율)** 할부수수료율의 실제 년간요율은 [표1]과 같다.

제2조 **(목적물의 인도등)** 목적물의 인도는 할부거래 계약서를 교부받은 날을 인도일로 한다.

제3조 **(회원의 철회권)** 회원은 할부매출일로부터 7일 이내에 가맹점에 서면으로 할부 거래의 철회를 요청할 수 있으며, 가맹점으로 철회요청을 한 경우에 가맹점앞 철회 요청 사실을 할부한 서면을 신용제공자에게 제출(발송)함으로써 할부거래에 관한 계약 의 철회를 요청할 수 있다. 단, 상품의 성질 또는 계약체결의 형태에 비추어 철회를 인정 할 수 없는 경우와 회원의 귀책사유에 의하여 상품의 멸실, 훼손 되었을 경우 또는 20만원 이하의 상품인 경우에 철회할 수 없다.

제4조 **(회원의 항변권)** 할부구매에 대한 분쟁에 있어 할부거래에 관한법률 제12조 제1항 에서 정한 요건에 해당하는 경우 회원은 신용제공자에게 분쟁의 해결을 요청하고 대금지급을 거절할 수 있다. 단, 상행위 목적의 거래나 신용카드 본 래의 용도 이외의 거래로 판단되는 경우 또는 20만원 미만인 경우는 제외된다.

What is the address?
jusoga eotteoke dwaeyo   주소가 어떻게 돼요?

Do you have any rooms available?
bang isseoyo   방 있어요?

May I see it?
bang jom bolsu isseoyo   방 좀 볼수 있어요?

How much	*e ... eolma*	에...얼마에
is it ...?	*eyo*	요?
per night	*harutbam*	하룻밤
per person	*han saram*	한사람

Where is the bathroom?
yoksiri eodi-e isseoyo   욕실이 어디에 있어요?

I'm/We're leaving now.
jigeum tteonayo   지금 떠나요.

CONVERSATION & ESSENTIALS

Hello. (polite)
annyeong hasimnikka   안녕 하십니까.

Hello. (informal)
annyeong haseyo   안녕 하세요.

Goodbye. (to person leaving)
annyeong-hi gaseyo   안녕히 가세요.

Goodbye. (to person staying)
annyeong-hi gyeseyo   안녕히 계세요.

Yes.
ye/ne   예./네.

No.
aniyo   아니요.

Please.
juseyo   주세요.

Thank you.
gamsa hamnida   감사 합니다.

That's fine./You're welcome.
gwaenchan seumnida   괜찮습니다.

Excuse me.
sillye hamnida   실례 합니다.

Sorry (forgive me).
mian hamnida   미안 합니다.

See you soon.
tto mannayo/najung-e buteobwayo   또 만나요/나중에 봐요.

How are you?
annyeong haseyo   안녕 하세요?

I'm fine, thanks.
ne, jo-ayo   네 좋아요.

May I ask your name?
ireumeul yeojjwobwado doelkkayo   이름을 여쭤봐도 될까요?

My name is ...
je ireumeun ... imnida   제 이름은...입니다.

SIGNS		
입구	*ipgu*	**Entrance**
출구	*chulgu*	**Exit**
안내	*annae*	**Information**
영업중	*yeong eop jung*	**Open**
휴업중	*hyu eop jung*	**Closed**
금지	*gumji*	**Prohibited**
방있음	*bang isseum*	**Rooms Available**
방없음	*bang eopseum*	**No Vacancies**
경찰서	*gyeongchalseo*	**Police Station**
화장실	*hwajangsil*	**Toilets**
신사용	*sinsayong*	**Men**
숙녀용	*sungnyeoyong*	**Women**

Where are you from?
eodiseo oseosseoyo   어디서 오셨어요?

I'm from ...
jeoneun ... e-seo wasseumnida   저는...에서 왔습니다.

Just a minute.
jamkkan manyo   잠깐만요.

DIRECTIONS

behind ...	*... dwi-e*	...뒤에
in front of ...	*... ap-e*	...앞에
far	*meolli*	멀리
near	*gakka-i*	가까이
opposite	*bandae pyeon-e*	반대편에
beach	*haesu yokjang*	해수욕장
	haebyeon	해변
bridge	*dari*	다리
castle	*seong*	성
island	*do*	도
	(when used in place names)	
	seom	섬
	(when used as a generic noun)	
market	*sijang*	시장
palace	*gung*	궁
ruins	*yetteo*	옛터
tower	*ta-wo/tap*	타워/탑

Where is ...?
... i/ga eodi isseoyo   ...이/가 어디 있어요?

Can you show me (on the map)?
boyeo jusillaeyo   보여 주실래요?

Go straight ahead.
ttokbaro gaseyo   똑바로 가세요.

Turn left.
oenjjogeuro gaseyo   왼쪽으로 가세요.

Turn right.
oreunjjogeuro gaseyo   오른쪽으로 가세요.

LANGUAGE

at the next corner
da eum motungi e-seo 다음 모퉁이에서
at the traffic lights
sinhodeung e-seo 신호등에서

EATING OUT

We'd like nonsmoking/smoking, please.

geumyeon seogeuro/	금연석으로/
heupyeon seogeuro	흡연석으로
juseyo	주세요.

Do you have an English menu?

| *yeong-eoro doen menyu* | 영어로 된 메뉴 |
| *isseoyo* | 있어요? |

Do you have seating with tables and chairs?

| *teibeul isseoyo* | 테이블 있어요? |

Is this dish spicy?

| *i eumsik maewoyo* | 이 음식 매워요? |

Could you recommend something?

| *mwo chucheonhae* | 뭐 추천해 |
| *jusillaeyo* | 주실래요? |

Excuse me. (please come here)

| *yeogiyo* | 여기요. |

Water, please.

| *mul juseyo* | 물 주세요. |

The bill/check, please.

| *gyesanseo juseyo* | 계산서 주세요. |

Bon appetit.

| *masitge deuseyo* | 맛있게 드세요. |

It was delicious.

| *masisseosseoyo* | 맛있었어요. |

I don't eat meat.

| *jeon gogireul* | 전 고기를 |
| *anmeogeoyo* | 안 먹어요. |

I can't eat dairy products.

| *jeon yujepumeul* | 전 유제품을 |
| *anmeogeoyo* | 안 먹어요. |

Do you have any vegetarian dishes?

| *gogi andeureogan* | 고기 안 들어간 |
| *eumsik isseoyo* | 음식 있어요? |

Does it contain eggs?

| *gyerani deureogayo* | 계란이 들어가요? |

I'm allergic to (peanuts).

| *jeon (ttangkong)e* | 전 (땅콩)에 |
| *allereugiga isseoyo* | 알레르기가 있어요. |

HEALTH

I'm ill.

| *jeon apayo* | 저 아파요. |

It hurts here.

| *yeogiga apayo* | 여기가 아파요. |

I'm ...	*... isseoyo*	...있어요
asthmatic	*cheonsik*	천식
diabetic	*dangnyo byeong-i*	당뇨병이
epileptic	*ganjil byeong-i*	간질병이

EMERGENCIES

Help!

| *saram sallyeo* | 사람살려! |

There's been an accident.

| *sago nasseoyo* | 사고 났어요. |

I'm lost.

| *gireul ireosseoyo* | 길을 잃었어요. |

Go away!

| *jeori ga* | 저리가! |

Call ...!	*... bulleo*	...불러
	juseyo	주세요!
a doctor	*ui-sareul*	의사를
the police	*gyeongchareul*	경찰을
an ambulance	*gugeupcha*	구급차
	jom	좀

I'm allergic	*... allereugiga*	...알레르기가
to ...	*isseoyo*	있어요
antibiotics	*hangsaengje*	항생제
aspirin	*aseupirin*	아스피린
penicillin	*penisillin*	페니실린
bees	*beol*	벌

antiseptic	*sodong yak*	소독약
condoms	*kondom*	콘돔
contraceptive	*pi imyak*	피임약
diarrhoea	*seolsa*	설사
hospital	*byeongwon*	병원
medicine	*yak*	약
sunblock cream	*seon keurim*	선크림
tampons	*tampon*	탐폰

LANGUAGE DIFFICULTIES

Do you speak English?

| *yeong-eo haseyo* | 영어 하세요? |

Does anyone here speak English?

| *yeong-eo hasineunbun* | 영어 하시는 |
| *gyeseyo* | 분계세요? |

How do you say ... in Korean?

| *... eul/reul hangug-euro* | ...을 한국어로 |
| *eotteoke malhaeyo* | 어떻게 말해요? |

What does ... mean?

| *... ga/i museun* | ...가/이무슨 |
| *tteusieyo* | 뜻 이에요? |

I understand.

| *algeseoyo* | 알겠어요. |

I don't understand.

| *jalmoreugenneun deyo* | 잘 모르겠는데요. |

Please write it down.

| *jeogeo jusillaeyo* | 적어 주실래요. |

NUMBERS

Korean has two counting systems. One is of Chinese origin, with Korean pronunciation, and the other is a native Korean system – the latter only goes up to 99 and is used for counting objects, expressing your age and for the hours when telling the time. They're always written in *hangeul* or digits, but never in Chinese characters. Sino-Korean numbers are used to express minutes when telling the time, as well as dates, months, kilometres, money, floors of buildings, and numbers above 99. Either Chinese or Korean numbers can be used to count days.

	Sino-Korean		Korean	
1	il	일	hana	하나
2	i	이	dul	둘
3	sam	삼	set	셋
4	sa	사	net	넷
5	o	오	daseot	다섯
6	yuk	육	yeoseot	여섯
7	chil	칠	ilgop	일곱
8	pal	팔	yeodeol	여덟
9	gu	구	ahop	아홉
10	sip	십	yeol	열

	Combination	
11	sibil	십일
12	sibi	십이
13	sipsam	십삼
14	sipsa	십사
15	sibo	십오
16	simnyuk	십육
17	sipchil	십칠
18	sippal	십팔
19	sipgu	십구
20	isip	이십
21	isibil	이십일
22	isibi	이십이
30	samsip	삼십
40	sasip	사십
50	osip	오십
60	yuksip	육십
70	chilsip	칠십
80	palsip	팔십
90	gusip	구십
100	baek	백
1000	cheon	천

PAPERWORK

name	ireum/	이름/
	seongmyeong	성명
nationality	guk jeok	국적
date of birth	saengnyeon woril/	생년월일/
	saeng-il	생일
place of birth	chulsaengji	출생지
sex (gender)	seongbyeol	성별
passport	yeogwon	여권
visa	bija	비자

QUESTION WORDS

Who? (as subject)	nugu	누구
What? (as subject)	mu-eot	무엇
When?	eonje	언제
Where?	eodi	어디
How?	eotteoke	어떻게

SHOPPING & SERVICES

I'm looking for ...	... reul/eul chatgo isseoyo	...를/을 찾고 있어요.
a bank	eunhaeng	은행
a church	gyohoe	교회
the city centre	sinae jung simga	시내 중심가
the embassy	dae sigwan	대사관
the market	sijang	시장
the museum	bangmulgwan	박물관
the post office	uche-guk	우체국
a public toilet	hwajangsil	화장실
the telephone centre	jeonhwa guk	전화국
the tourist office	gwan gwang annaeso	관광 안내소

I'd like to buy ...	... reul/eul sago sipeoyo	...를/을 사고 싶어요.
How much is it?	eolma yeyo	얼마예요?
I don't like it.	byeollo mam-e andeuneyo	별로 맘에 안드네요.
May I look at it?	boyeo jusillaeyo	보여 주실래요?
I'm just looking.	geunyang gugyeong haneungeo-eyo	그냥 구경 하는 거에요.
It's cheap.	ssa-neyo	싸네요.
It's too expensive.	neomu bissayo	너무 비싸요.
I'll take it.	igeoro haraeyo	이걸로 할래요.

more	deo	더
less	deol	덜
smaller	deo jageun	더작은
bigger	deo keun	더큰

I want to	... reul/eul	...를/을
change ...	bakku ryeogo	바꾸려고
	haneun deyo	하는데요.
money	don	돈
travellers	yeohaengja	여행자
cheques	supyo	수표

I'd like a ...	... hanjang	...한장
ticket.	juseyo	주세요
one-way	pyeondo pyo	편도표
return	wangbok pyo	왕복표
1st-class	il-deung seok	일등석
2nd-class	i-deung seok	이등석

TIME & DATES

What time is it?

jigeum myeot si-eyo   지금 몇시 에요?

It's (10 o'clock).

(yeol) siyo   (열)시요.

in the morning	achim-e	아침에
in the afternoon	ohu-e	오후에
in the evening	jeonyeok-e	저녁에
When?	eonje	언제
today	o-neul	오늘
tomorrow	nae-il	내일
yesterday	eo-je	어제

Monday	woryoil	월요일
Tuesday	hwayoil	화요일
Wednesday	suyoil	수요일
Thursday	mogyoil	목요일
Friday	geumyoil	금요일
Saturday	toyoil	토요일
Sunday	iryoil	일요일

January	irwol	일월
February	iwol	이월
March	samwol	삼월
April	sawol	사월
May	owol	오월
June	yu-gwol	육월
July	chirwol	칠월
August	parwol	팔월
September	guwol	구월
October	siwol	시월
November	sibirwol	십일월
December	sibiwol	십이월

TRANSPORT

Public Transport

What time does the ... leave/arrive?

... i/ga (eonje tteonayo/eonje dochak-haeyo)

...이/가 언제 떠나요/언제 도착해요?

airport bus	gonghang beoseu	공항버스
boat (ferry)	yeogaekseon	여객선
bus	beoseu	버스
city bus	sinae beoseu	시내버스
intercity bus	si-oe beoseu	시외버스
plane	bihaerg-gi	비행기
train	gicha	기차

I want to go to ...

... e gago   ...에 가고

sipseumnida   싶습니다.

The train has been (delayed).

gichaga (yeonchak)   기차가 (연착)

doe-eosseumnida   되었습니다.

The train has been (cancelled).

gichaga (chwiso)   기차가 (취소)

doe-eosseumnida   되었습니다.

the first

cheot   첫

the last

maji mak   마지막

bus station

beoseu jeongnyu jang   버스정류장

platform number

peuraetpom beonho   플랫폼번호

subway station

jihacheol yeok   지하철역

ticket office

pyo paneun got   표 파는곳

ticket vending machine

pyo japangi   표 자판기

timetable

sigan pyo   시간표

train station

gicha yeok   기차역

Private Transport

I'd like to	... reul/eul	...를/을
hire a/an ...	billi-go	빌리고
	sipeoyo	싶어요.
4WD	jipeu cha	지프차
bicycle	jajeongeo	자전거
car	jadongcha	자동차
	(or simply cha, 차)	
motorbike	otoba-i	오토바이

Is this the road to ...?

i-gil daragamyeon ...   이길 따라가면...

e galsu isseoyo   에갈수 있어요?

Where's a service station?

annae soga eodi   안내소가 어디

isseoyo   있어요?

Please fill it up.

gadeuk chaewo juseyo   가득 채워 주세요.

ROAD SIGNS

우회로	uhwoe-ro	**Detour**
길없음	gil-eupseum	**No Entry**
추월금지	chuwol geumji	**No Overtaking**
주차금지	jucha geumji	**No Parking**
입구	ipgu	**Entrance**
접근금지	jeopgeun geumji	**Keep Clear**
통행료	tonghaeng-ryo	**Toll**
톨게이트	tol geiteu	**Toll Gate**
위험	wi heom	**Danger**
서행	seo haeng	**Slow Down**
일방통행	il-bang tonghaeng	**One Way**
나가는길	naganeun gil	**Freeway Exit**

diesel	dijel	디젤
petrol/gas	hwi baryu	휘발유

I'd like (30) litres.
(samsip) liteo neo-eo   (삼십)리터 넣어
juseyo   주세요.
(How long) Can I park here?
(eolmana) jucha halsu   (얼마나) 주차 할수
isseoyo   있어요?
I need a mechanic.
jeongbi gong-i biryo   정비공이 필요
haeyo   해요.
The car/motorbike has broken down at ...
... eseo chaga/   ...에서차가/
otoba-i ga   오토바이가
gojang nasseoyo   고장 났어요.
The car/motorbike won't start.
chaga/otoba-i ga   차가/오토바이가
sidong-i geolli-ji   시동이 걸리지
annayo   않아요.

I have a flat tyre.
taieo-e peongkeu   타이어에펑크
nasseoyo   났어요.
I've run out of petrol.
gireumi tteoreo   기름이 떨어
jeosseoyo   졌어요.
I've had an accident.
sago nasseoyo   사고 났어요.

TRAVEL WITH CHILDREN

Is there (a/an) ...	... isseoyo	...있어요?
I need (a/an) ...	piryo haeyo	...필요해요.
baby change room	gijeogwi galgosi	기저귀 갈 곳이
babysitter	agi bwajuneun saram	아기 봐주는 사람
car seat	yu-a jadongcha anjeon uija	유아자동차 안전의자
child-minding service	agi bwajuneun seobiseu	아기봐주는 서비스
children's menu	eorini menyu	어린이 메뉴
(disposable) diapers	ilhoeyong gijeogwi	일회용 기저귀
highchair	agi uija	아기의자
infant milk formula	bunyu	분유
potty	agi byeon-gi	아기변기
stroller/pusher	yu-mocha	유모차

Do you mind if I breastfeed here?
yeogi-seo agi jeotmeok   여기서 아기 젖먹
yeodo doenayo   여도 되나요?
Are children allowed?
eorinido doennikka   어린이도됩니까?

Also available from Lonely Planet:
Korean Phrasebook

Glossary

For more food and drink terms, see the Food Glossary (p75); for general terms see the Language chapter (p411).

ajumma – a married or older woman
~am – hermitage
anju – snacks eaten when drinking alcohol

bang – room
bawi – large rock
~bong – peak
buk~ – north
buncheong – Joseon-era pottery with simple folk designs

celadon – green-tinged pottery from the early-12th century
cha – tea
~cheon – small stream
Chuseok – Thanksgiving Day

dae~ – great, large
dancheong – ornate, multicoloured eaves that adorn Buddhist temples and other buildings
Dangun – mythical founder of Korea
DEP – Democratic Party
DMZ – the Demilitarized Zone that runs along the 38th parallel of the Korean peninsula, separating North and South
-do – province, also island
-dong – neighbourhood or village
dong~ – east
donggul – cave
DPRK – Democratic People's Republic of Korea (North Korea)
DVD bang – room for watching DVDs

-eup – town

-ga – section of a long street
~gang – river
geobukseon – 'turtle ships'; iron-clad warships of the late-16th century
gil – small street
GNP – Grand National Party
-gu – urban district
gugak – traditional Korean music
~gul – cave
-gun – county

~gung – palace
gwageo – Joseon government service exam

hae – sea
haenyeo – traditional female divers of Jeju-do
hagwon – private school where students study after school or work
hallyu – (Korean Wave) increasing interest in Korean pop culture from other parts of Asia
hanbok – traditional Korean clothing
hang – harbour
hangeul – Korean phonetic alphabet
hanja – Chinese characters
hanji – traditional Korean handmade paper
hanok – traditional Korean one-storey wooden house with a tiled or thatched roof
harubang – lava-rock statues found only on Jeju-do
~ho – lake
hof – local pub

insam – ginseng

jaebeol – huge family-run corporate conglomerate
~jeon – hall of a temple
~jeong – pavilion
jjimjilbang – upmarket spa and sauna
Juche – North Korean ideology of economic self-reliance

KTO – Korea Tourism Organisation
KTX – Korea Train Express; fast 300km/h train service

minbak – private homes with rooms for rent
mudang – female shaman
Mugunghwa – semi-express train
~mun – gate
-myeon – township
~myo – shrine

nam~ – south
~neung – tomb
~no – street
noraebang – karaoke room
~nyeong – mountain pass

oncheon – hot-spring bath
ondol – underfloor heating system

pansori – traditional Korean solo opera
PC bang – internet cafe

pension – upmarket accommodation in the countryside or near beaches
pocketball – pool
pokpo – waterfall
pyeong – a unit of real estate measurement equal to 3.3 sq metres

~reung – tomb
-ri – village
~ro – street
ROK – Republic of Korea (South Korea)
~ryeong – mountain pass

-sa – temple
Saemaul – luxury express train
samulnori – drum-and-gong dance
~san – mountain
sanjang – mountain hut
sanseong – mountain fortress
seo~ – west
Seon – Korean version of Zen Buddhism

~seong – fortress
seowon – Confucian academy
shamanism – set of traditional beliefs; communication with spirits is done through a *mudang*
~si – city
sijang – market
sijo – short poems about nature and life; popular in the Joseon period
soju – the local firewater; often likened to vodka
ssireum – Korean-style wrestling

taekwondo – Korean martial art
tap – pagoda
tonggeun – commuter-class train

yangban – aristocrat
yeogwan – motel with small en suite
yeoinsuk – small, family-run budget accommodation with shared bathroom
yo – padded quilt that serves as a mattress or futon for sleeping on the floor

The Authors

SIMON RICHMOND — Coordinating Author, Seoul, Gyeonggi-do

Long before he became a travel writer and photographer Simon spent several years living in Japan. He finally made it to Seoul in 2004 on a brief visit that left him hungering for more – especially of the deliciously spicy food. The six-week research trip for this guide allowed him to dig deeper into what makes this fascinating country tick, to sample a far wider range of its cuisine and to get excited about its high-tech future. Simon has authored many guides for Lonely Planet in the region, including *Malaysia, Singapore & Brunei* and the *Trans-Siberian Railway*. See photos and read some of the background to his research for this guide at simonrichmond.wordpress.com.

YU-MEI BALASINGAMCHOW — Food & Drink, Gangwon-do, Chungcheongnam-do, Chungcheongbuk-do

After years of lapping up Korean food and film, Yu-Mei made her first foray into South Korea for this guidebook. During her research trip, she tramped for miles along quiet stretches of coastline (and even quieter stretches of hiking trails), scrambled guiltily over limestone formations at the behest of a cave guide, and wrestled with squirming *sannakji* (raw octopus) as it tried to writhe off her chopsticks. Her only disappointment was not making it up Taebaeksan because of bad weather. Yu-Mei lives in Singapore, where she writes about travel, food, history and the arts. She worked on the latest edition of Lonely Planet's *Vietnam* guidebook and has co-authored a popular history of Singapore.

CÉSAR G SORIANO — Active Korea, Jeollanam-do, Jeju-do, Jeollabuk-do

César's first trip to South Korea was not by choice. As a young US Army soldier in 2000, he was deployed to Seoul and later to an undisclosed bunker near the North Korean border, having never seen beyond Itaewon. For this book, César made up for lost time by exploring the southwest on land and sea, eating several pigs' worth of *bulgogi* (barbecued meat slices) in Jeollabuk-do, drinking too much *soju* (local vodka) in Jeollanam-do and working it off by hiking and diving in Jeju-do. A career journalist and former USA TODAY foreign correspondent, César has authored several Lonely Planet guidebooks. You can follow his exploits on his website (www.cesarsoriano.com). César and his wife, Marsha, live in Washington, DC.

LONELY PLANET AUTHORS

Why is our travel information the best in the world? It's simple: our authors are passionate, dedicated travellers. They don't take freebies in exchange for positive coverage so you can be sure the advice you're given is impartial. They travel widely to all the popular spots, and off the beaten track. They don't research using just the internet or phone. They discover new places not included in any other guidebook. They personally visit thousands of hotels, restaurants, palaces, trails, galleries, temples and more. They speak with dozens of locals every day to make sure you get the kind of insider knowledge only a local could tell you. They take pride in getting all the details right, and in telling it how it is. Think you can do it? Find out how at **lonelyplanet.com**.

ROB WHYTE   The Culture, Gyeongsangbuk-do, Gyeongsangnam-do

For the best part of 15 years, Rob has been living in Korea. He teaches the past tense to college students and twists Malcolm Gladwell's ideas into talking points for elementary and secondary school teachers. A shocking example of someone who never bothered to formulate a life plan, his advice for anyone with hopes of becoming an English teacher in Korea is simple: don't get too comfortable, otherwise you might end up staying a lot longer than you ever imagined. Rob lives in Busan with his family, where his only regret is the lack of affordable golf.

CONTRIBUTING AUTHORS

North Korea was newly researched for this edition, but we have chosen not to identify our author so as to protect his identity and that of the North Koreans who assisted him on his travels.

Dr Trish Batchelor is a general practitioner and travel medicine specialist who works at the CIWEC Clinic in Kathmandu, Nepal, as well as being a Medical Advisor to the Travel Doctor New Zealand clinics. Trish teaches travel medicine through the University of Otago, New Zealand, and is interested in underwater and high-altitude medicine, and in the impact of tourism on host countries. She has travelled extensively through Southeast and East Asia and particularly loves high-altitude trekking in the Himalayas.

Behind the Scenes

THIS BOOK

Lonely Planet's first Korea guidebook was published in 1988. The 6th edition was written by Martin Robinson, Andrew Bender and Rob Whyte. The 7th edition was updated by Martin Robinson, Ray Bartlett and Rob Whyte. For this 8th edition Simon Richmond took over the reins with Yu-Mei Balasingamchow, César G Soriano and Rob Whyte. This guidebook was commissioned in Lonely Planet's Melbourne office, and produced by the following:

Commissioning Editor Judith Bamber, Tashi Wheeler
Coordinating Editor Nigel Chin
Coordinating Cartographers James Bird, Valeska Cañas
Coordinating Layout Designer Nicholas Colicchia
Managing Editors Sasha Baskett, Liz Heynes
Managing Cartographers Shahara Ahmed, Alison Lyall
Managing Layout Designer Sally Darmody
Assisting Editors Carolyn Bain, Monique Choy, Jackey Coyle, Andrea Dobbin
Assisting Cartographers Andras Bogdanovits, Dennis Capparelli, Xavier Di Toro, Mark Griffiths, Ross Macaw, Brendan Streager
Cover research Katy Murenu, lonelyplanetimages.com
Internal image research Jane Hart, lonelyplanet images.com

Language Content Laura Crawford
Project Manager Chris Love
Thanks to Lucy Birchley, Ross Butler, Nayoung Choi, JD Hilts, Laura Jane, Yvonne Kirk, Chris Lee Ack, Annelies Mertens, Wayne Murphy, Maryanne Netto, Haerin Park, Sookie Park, Raphael Richards, Kerrianne Southway

THANKS
SIMON RICHMOND

Many thanks to Tonny who accompanied me on my first visit to Seoul and who patiently endured my absence this time around. Cheers to Judith for choosing me to take on this challenging project and to Tashi for shepherding it along in her usual pragmatic style. Fellow author Yu-Mei deserves a special call out for her unflagging enthusiasm and dedication to the project.

In Seoul, I benefited greatly from the expertise of the many folks at the national and city tourism organisations including Han Younghee, Son Sae-hyeong, Hong Woo-seok, Joanne Jalbert, Jan Won Bok, Samuel Koo, Kim Kyung-hee, Maureen O'Crowley and Michael Spavor. A special thanks to my patient guide Kim Hee-yong and to the indefatigable Bill Swisshelm. For their insights into the city and for allowing me the time to interview them my thanks goes to Robert Koehler, Charm

---

THE LONELY PLANET STORY

Fresh from an epic journey across Europe, Asia and Australia in 1972, Tony and Maureen Wheeler sat at their kitchen table stapling together notes. The first Lonely Planet guidebook, *Across Asia on the Cheap*, was born.

Travellers snapped up the guides. Inspired by their success, the Wheelers began publishing books to Southeast Asia, India and beyond. Demand was prodigious, and the Wheelers expanded the business rapidly to keep up. Over the years, Lonely Planet extended its coverage to every country and into the virtual world via lonelyplanet.com and the Thorn Tree message board.

As Lonely Planet became a globally loved brand, Tony and Maureen received several offers for the company. But it wasn't until 2007 that they found a partner whom they trusted to remain true to the company's principles of travelling widely, treading lightly and giving sustainably. In October of that year, BBC Worldwide acquired a 75% share in the company, pledging to uphold Lonely Planet's commitment to independent travel, trustworthy advice and editorial independence.

Today, Lonely Planet has offices in Melbourne, London and Oakland, with over 500 staff members and 300 authors. Tony and Maureen are still actively involved with Lonely Planet. They're travelling more often than ever, and they're devoting their spare time to charitable projects. And the company is still driven by the philosophy of *Across Asia on the Cheap*: 'All you've got to do is decide to go and the hardest part is over. So go!'

Lee, Monica Cha, Peter Bartholomew, Kyung Won-chung, Lee Eunji, Lee Sungjo, Stephen Revere, Joe McPherson, Brian Lio, Heather Evans, Kay Green Lee, Anne Ladouceur and Olivier Mouroux of Korea 4expats. Cheers also to Kim Ki-dong at Everland, Jackie & Ingolf in Daecheon Beach, Jung Byung-gyu who sorted out my spectacles, the lovely Ms Choi Young-Ju, my guide around Hahoe, Marion Goldberg and Jason Zahorchak.

YU-MEI BALASINGAMCHOW

I would not have made it to Korea, nor made as much sense of it, without the kindness and support of many friends, strangers and strangers-who-be-came-friends. A big thank you to Wan and Gary Kam for kick-starting things over *soju* and *pajeon,* and Gary also for unfailing hospitality in Seoul. David Park, Mr Kim and Mr Ko were absolutely generous with their time and enthusiasm for hiking, and Kay Green Lee went above and beyond on so many occasions. On the road I had the advice, companionship, good humour and insight of Kim Hee Sun, Shane Sanker, Hyun Choi, Kim Dong Baik, Kim Hwa Ran, Yoon Yi Ji, Gavin Hudson, Jeon Young Min, Eric Richter, Cameron Birch, Joan Ho, Mark Barnett, Becky, Jean Chavannes and Hailie Lee. Thanks also to So Seok Ho and Kim Yeun Hee for adopting me for a day in Hwajinpo, the energetic and resource-ful Lee Ji Yeon, and to Tammy Park, Seo Hyun-Suk, Joseph Jeong, Christoph and Stefan, Brett Bou-chard, Elly Kang and Jonathan Knisely. Kudos to the many Koreans – bus drivers, fellow hikers, tourism officers, passers-by, all – who graciously stopped to lend a hand.

At home, James Koh, Tan Pin Pin, Kumiko Kaneda, Peter Yuh, Cheryl Lee, Erik Mobrand and Hyejin Kim were incredibly helpful with suggestions. Last but not least, thank you to Mom and Dad, Yu Hui, Joyce, Deanna, Suzie, Yvonne and James.

CÉSAR G SORIANO

First and foremost, thank you to my wife Marsha for your love and support during my frequent absences. To Laura Pohl, thanks for my mugshot, translation help and for your insider knowledge of South Korea. In Mokpo, thanks to Sarah Epp for your hospitality and for introducing me to the evils of *soju*. In Jeju-si, Sara Stillman for show-ing me around town. At Lonely Planet, Simon, Tashi and Yu-Mei. Thanks to Ramy and the folks at Korea Tourism Organisation in London. And thank you to the people of South Korea who helped me through the language barrier to find my way forward. *Kamsamnida.*

SEND US YOUR FEEDBACK

We love to hear from travellers – your comments keep us on our toes and help make our books better. Our well-travelled team reads every word on what you loved or loathed about this book. Although we cannot reply individually to postal submissions, we always guarantee that your feedback goes straight to the appropriate authors, in time for the next edition. Each person who sends us information is thanked in the next edition and the most useful submissions are rewarded with a free book.

To send us your updates – and find out about Lonely Planet events, newsletters and travel news – visit our award-winning website: **lonelyplanet.com/contact**.

Note: we may edit, reproduce and incorporate your comments in Lonely Planet products such as guidebooks, websites and digital products, so let us know if you don't want your comments reproduced or your name acknowledged. For a copy of our privacy policy visit lonelyplanet.com/privacy.

BEHIND THE SCENES

ROB WHYTE

Thanks first to my wife and daughter for vacating the apartment when it was time for me to sit down and write. Also to my wife for her ongoing support by repeatedly asking one nagging question, 'Are you done with that damn LP book yet?' For tips and insights, Jason Russell, Stan Jordan, Trey Coffie and Chris Stacey all provided great information. In Andong, an appreciative thanks to Mr Lee for giving me a lift when I was stuck on the side of the road. In the Yeongju bus terminal, thanks to the grandmother who was determined that I understand the bus directions even if she had to yell at me for 10 minutes.

OUR READERS

Many thanks to the travellers who used the last edition and wrote to us with helpful hints, useful advice and interesting anecdotes:

A Julien Allegrini, Debbie Amos, Kim Andren, Adele Arthur, JM Ascienzo **B** Courtney Baker, Joachim Bergmann, Ludovic Boulicaut, Michael Breshears, Antonella Broglia **C** Rene Cabos, James Chen, Johnnie Cho, Abi Cisek, Vincent Cosse, Karen Crawford **D** Patricia Dawn Davis, Janet Denning, Ann Desmond, Peter Duffy, Julie Dupuis **E** Nicole Ebert, Stephen Edwards, Mike Eggert, Chi-He Elder **F** Jindrich Fanfrlik, Richard Freeman, Deanna Fuoco **G** Gina Gage, Katie Gallagher, Bernward Gehle, Lucas Goetz,

Andrew Goldstein, Peter Goltermann, Alexia Guillois **H** Tage Haun, Charles Hayter, Morwenna Hicks, Jackie Horsewood, G Hutch **I** Kenneth Ingham **J** Da Won Jeong, Sang-Hwa Jeong, Seo Yeong Jeong, Irene Jordet, Michelle Josselyn, Sehi Jung **K** Shou Kin Kam, Albert Karsai, Ulrich Kellermann, Jessica Kemnitz, Gyeong-Pil Kim, Hyung Suk Kim, Jane Kim, Jeongjung Kim, Aaron Klein, Katie Klemsen, Kimberly Kohler, Scott Kolwitz, Morgan Krutulis, Mi Ae Kwon **L** Kyoungock Lee, Seungmin Lee, Tiffany Leonard, Elodie Lorenz, Alexi Lynch **M** John Mayston, Scott Meyer, Dirk Mohrdiek **N** Han Sang Noh **O** Gillian O'Connor **P** James Page, Jerome Penicaud, Robin Peterson, Michael Poesen, Deborah Pollak, Erin Propas, Denise Pulis **R** Nils Henry Rasmussen, Michael Raue,

Christoph Riess, Terry Robinson, Brent Robson, Matteo Romitelli, Kallon Ryan **S** Michael Salomon, Keithea Schaedler-Hildebrand, Byron Schmuland, Sherry Schwartz, Kurt Shipley, Michael Siegler, Cecilia Song, Ray Stevens, Dennis Storoshenko, Reiner Manfred Subke **T** Carol Thelen, Ron Thomas, Rhonda Tulk **V** Marcel Van Der Meer, Martina Van Eijndhoven, Lotte Van Ekert, Mary Vic **W** Chas Warren, Timothy Willish, Michael Winands **Z** Manuele Zunelli

ACKNOWLEDGMENTS
Many thanks to the following for the use of their content:

Globe on title page ©Mountain High Maps 1993 Digital Wisdom, Inc.

Index

INDEX

GreenDex

South Korea is taking steps to make itself a more environmentally friendly country (see p66). The following is an index of the local businesses, events and organisations that have been selected by Lonely Planet authors because they demonstrate a commitment to preserving or improving the natural environment, enabling greater cultural understanding and generally contributing towards sustainability. Among the listings you'll find national parks, restaurants that specialise in organic produce, and hotels and other businesses that take into account the environmental impact of their operations and seek to minimise this. The index is not exhaustive but does provide a place to start for those who like to make informed choices in how they spend their holiday time and money.

Choosing sustainable travel products, just like running a business that tries to be eco-friendly, is not an exact science and is also a continuous process. We know we haven't got it 100% right yet! We very much welcome feedback on our selections via www.lonelyplanet.com/feedback as well as recommendations for anything that we should be including in this list the next time around. For more information on travelling responsibly see p15 and www.lonelyplanet.com/responsibletravel.

440

MAP LEGEND
ROUTES

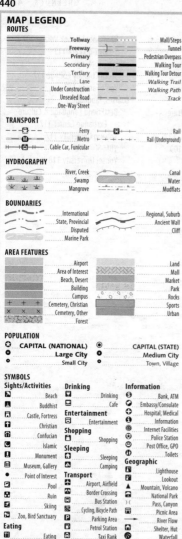

Tollway	Mall/Steps
Freeway	Tunnel
Primary	Pedestrian Overpass
Secondary	Walking Tour
Tertiary	Walking Tour Detour
Lane	Walking Trail
Under Construction	Walking Path
Unsealed Road	Track
One-Way Street	

TRANSPORT

Ferry	Rail
Metro	Rail (Underground)
Cable Car, Funicular	

HYDROGRAPHY

River, Creek	Canal
Swamp	Water
Mangrove	Mudflats

BOUNDARIES

International	Regional, Suburb
State, Provincial	Ancient Wall
Disputed	Cliff
Marine Park	

AREA FEATURES

Airport	Land
Area of Interest	Mall
Beach, Desert	Market
Building	Park
Campus	Rocks
Cemetery, Christian	Sports
Cemetery, Other	Urban
Forest	

POPULATION

CAPITAL (NATIONAL)	CAPITAL (STATE)
Large City	Medium City
Small City	Town, Village

SYMBOLS

Sights/Activities
- Beach
- Buddhist
- Castle, Fortress
- Christian
- Confucian
- Islamic
- Monument
- Museum, Gallery
- Point of Interest
- Pool
- Ruin
- Skiing
- Zoo, Bird Sanctuary

Eating
- Eating

Drinking
- Drinking
- Cafe

Entertainment
- Entertainment

Shopping
- Shopping

Sleeping
- Sleeping
- Camping

Transport
- Airport, Airfield
- Border Crossing
- Bus Station
- Cycling, Bicycle Path
- Parking Area
- Petrol Station
- Taxi Rank

Information
- Bank, ATM
- Embassy/Consulate
- Hospital, Medical
- Information
- Internet Facilities
- Post Office, GPO
- Police Station
- Toilets

Geographic
- Lighthouse
- Lookout
- Mountain, Volcano
- National Park
- Pass, Canyon
- Picnic Area
- River Flow
- Shelter, Hut
- Waterfall

LONELY PLANET OFFICES

Australia (Head Office)
Locked Bag 1, Footscray, Victoria 3011
☎ 03 8379 8000, fax 03 8379 8111
talk2us@lonelyplanet.com.au

USA
150 Linden St, Oakland, CA 94607
☎ 510 250 6400, toll free 800 275 8555
fax 510 893 8572
info@lonelyplanet.com

UK
2nd fl, 186 City Rd,
London EC1V 2NT
☎ 020 7106 2100, fax 020 7106 2101
go@lonelyplanet.co.uk

Published by Lonely Planet
ABN 36 005 607 983

© Lonely Planet 2010

© photographers as indicated 2010

Cover photograph: Geumsan-sa, Korea, Topic Photo Agency/Age Fotostock. Many of the images in this guide are available for licensing from Lonely Planet Images: lonelyplanetimages.com.

Mixed Sources
Product group from well-managed forests and other controlled sources
www.fsc.org Cert no. SGS-COC-005002
© 1996 Forest Stewardship Council
FSC